CW00656805

Irish Catholicism since 1950

The Undoing of a Culture

Irish Catholicism since 1950
The Undoing of a Culture

Louise Fuller

Gill & Macmillan

For those who have been a support
and an inspiration

Gill & Macmillan Ltd
Hume Avenue
Park West
Dublin 12
with associated companies throughout the world
www.gillmacmillan.ie

0 7171 3156 4
Index compiled by Cover To Cover
Print origination by Carole Lynch
Printed by ColourBooks Ltd, Dublin

This book is typeset in New Baskerville 10 on 12pt.

The paper used in this book comes from the wood pulp of managed forests. For every tree felled, at least one tree is planted, thereby renewing natural resources.

A catalogue record is available for this book from the British Library.

1 3 5 4 2

Contents

List of Tables

Acknowledgements

I wish to formally acknowledge and thank a number of people for their assistance in the completion of this book. My thanks are due first and foremost to Professor R.V. Comerford of the Department of Modern History, NUI Maynooth. At the outset, Professor Comerford helped me in my choice of a research topic which has proved particularly interesting and rewarding for me and which I have by no means exhausted as yet. His interest in my research and his constant encouragement and guidance helped sustain me through the more trying moments of this work. He was always there to challenge, affirm or discuss as the occasion demanded, and to the extent that a rather ambitious project has all 'come together', it is in no small measure attributable to his inspiration and dedication. I am very grateful to him for the many insights he shared with me, for his unfailing courtesy at all times and for how generously he always gave of his time.

I have experienced tremendous help from many people in the course of this research. Some deserve particular mention. I interviewed the late Fr Seán O'Riordan CSsR on a number of occasions in the course of this work. As one of the founder members of the *Furrow* and a reporter of the Second Vatican Council for that journal, he was very enlightening on many aspects of changing Catholic culture in both Ireland and continental Europe. He answered my questions most willingly at all times, was very supportive in every way and very kindly read a draft of the entire work and offered me his advice.

I am very grateful to the many people I interviewed in the course of my research, among them the following: the late Fr P.J. Brophy, former president of St Patrick's College, Carlow; Fr Martin Clarke, spokesperson for the Episcopal Conference and Director of the Catholic Communications Office; Fr Gabriel Daly OSA, theologian; Fr Ronan Drury, editor of the *Furrow*; Mgr Patrick Devine, former secretary of the Bishops' Advisory Committee on Ecumenism; Fr Austin Flannery OP, former editor of *Doctrine and Life*; Sr Goretti Griffin of the Mercy Sisters, Tralee; Fr Patrick Hannon, professor of Moral Theology, Maynooth; Fr Kevin Hegarty CC, former editor of *Intercom*; Fr Patrick McGoldrick, professor of Liturgy, St Patrick's College, Maynooth; Seán Mac Réamoinn, religious affairs broadcaster and reporter of the Second Vatican Council for RTÉ; Liam Murphy, chairman of the Catholic Headmasters' Association and chairperson of the Council of Managers of Catholic Secondary Schools, 1977–87; Bishop William Murphy of Kerry; Mgr Denis O'Callaghan PP, Mallow; Mgr Daniel O'Riordan PP, Tralee, Co. Kerry; Joe Power, former religious affairs correspondent of the *Irish Independent*; Bishop Laurence Ryan (recently retired) of Kildare and Leighlin, first president of the National

Conference of Priests of Ireland; Bishop William Walsh of Killaloe, chairman of Accord Catholic Marriage Counselling Service (formerly CMAC). They have all greatly facilitated my study.

I am grateful also to a number of people who very kindly read drafts of chapters of my work. Fr Patrick McGoldrick read drafts of the chapters concerning liturgy and liturgical changes, and offered me very helpful advice in this area. Fr Michael Hurley SJ read a draft of the chapter on ecumenism and shared his knowledge and expertise with me. Likewise Fr Tom Kiggins of the Irish Missionary Union read a draft section of the chapter relating to missionary developments in the Irish Church and again was very helpful in his comments. Liam Murphy was kind enough to read the chapters on education and share with me his intimate knowledge of educational developments in Ireland over the past forty years, for which I thank him. I wish to record my thanks also to Frank Murray, who also perused the chapters on education from the critical standpoint of somebody who has been closely involved with the events and developments documented therein. Mgr Denis O'Callaghan read a number of chapters and I am very grateful to him for sharing his reflections on the late 1960s and early 1970s and the controversy surrounding the encyclical *Humanae Vitae.* As professor of Moral Theology at Maynooth at the time, and chairman of the ITA, he was closely involved in events as they unfolded.

My sincere thanks are due also to Fr Gabriel Daly OSA, for reading and commenting on several chapters. From the standpoint of a theologian who has observed and spoken publicly on aspects of Catholic culture over the years, the reflections he shared with me were most valuable. Fr Austin Flannery OP also read a number of chapters, including those relating to the liturgy and the *Furrow.* Given his association with Canon J.G. McGarry, who founded the *Furrow,* and his involvement with him in matters liturgical over the years, his willingness to take time to recall his experiences gave me a sense of the man and the times. Likewise Fr Patrick Hannon was kind enough to read sections of the text and also to share his knowledge with me, together with his memories of Fr Peter Connolly, who played a significant role in changing Catholic culture. Needless to say, one cannot overstate the importance of the contribution of those who have lived through and, in many cases, personally experienced the events being documented. Indeed, they bring a project such as this to life. My interest in this topic goes back a long way, and the late Fr Gearóid Ó Súilleabháin of UCC and his lectures in catechetics played no small part in sowing the seeds. Likewise Jim Callan of the Education Department, NUI Maynooth, and his interest in the history of ideas and culture, provided a backdrop and perspectives from which to explore the subject matter of this book.

My thanks are also due to many others, who have communicated so much information to me with great generosity of spirit and efficiency, among them the following: Fr Paul Byrne OMI, director of the Irish Episcopal Commission for Emigrants; Jim Cantwell and Angela Place of the Catholic Press and Information Office; Fr Donal Dorr SPS of the Irish Missionary Union; Ann Hanley and Teresa Finegan of the Council for Research and Development, Maynooth; Bernadette Kinsella, administrative officer of the Association of

Management of Catholic Secondary Schools; Sr Eileen Randles IBVM, secretary of the Catholic Primary School Managers' Association; Sr Brigid Reynolds SM, of the Justice Office of the Conference of Religious of Ireland; Bishop Michael Smith of Meath; and Mgr John Wilson, financial administrator of the Dublin diocese.

The library staff in NUI Maynooth have been very helpful at all times. The librarian, Agnes Neligan, has facilitated me for many years and I am most thankful to her. I also wish to convey a particular word of thanks to Mary Kearney and Elaine Bean who have been exceedingly helpful to me in an ongoing way. I wish to thank David Sheehy, archivist, Dublin Diocesan Archives, for his generous help and guidance with my research in the archives, and Tom May, Galway Diocesan Archives, for taking the time to trace important letters for me. I am grateful also to the staff of Dublin Diocesan Library for facilitating me and for their help with my enquiries, in particular the librarian, Peter Folan. In similar vein, I wish to thank the Central Catholic Library. Seamus Haughey of the Oireachtas Library has also been very helpful with my queries. My sister, Aileen, fortunately for me, shares my love of history and has been immersed in this project from the word go. She has read and commented upon many drafts and re-drafts of chapters. She has combined interest, enthusiasm, and practical and moral support in her own inimitable way. For this, and a lot more, my debt to her can never be repaid.

I would also like to say a particular word of thanks for their interest and encouragement to David, Mary and Stephen, Billy O'Hara, Seosaimhín Ní Chuirc, and David and Eva Teskey. I was fortunate a number of years ago to have had the assistance of Catherine Heslin in the final processing of the thesis upon which this book is based. Her competence, patience and generosity of spirit at that time, I still recall with gratitude. I would also like to thank Fergal Tobin of Gill & Macmillan for his interest and enthusiasm in relation to this book from the outset. He has been most helpful and accommodating towards me at all times. Likewise Deirdre Rennison Kunz of Gill & Macmillan has been very patient and understanding at times when it counted a great deal and this has been much appreciated.

Finally, the task of writing a book has its ups and downs and could not have been completed without the ongoing patient support and encouragement of my family. For this, I cannot thank them enough. Likewise my friends – a very special word of thanks must go to my friend Mary Dillon who has rescued me on more than one occasion when technology has let me down! A number of people who played an important role in this work over many years, sadly, have not lived to see its completion. I dedicate it to them. Last but by no means least, my sister Jean has lived through the highs and lows of this project. Her generosity of spirit knows no bounds and has meant a great deal. Always forthcoming with advice, encouragement, support and even the odd lecture, as the occasion demanded, she can now rejoice that her efforts have not been in vain – the enterprise has been completed.

Louise Fuller
September 2002

Abbreviations

AAS	*Acta Apostolicae Sedis*
AMCSS	Association of Management of Catholic Secondary Schools
ASTI	Association of Secondary Teachers of Ireland
CCII	Catholic Communications Institute of Ireland
CCSS	Conference of Catholic Secondary Schools
CHA	Catholic Headmasters' Association
CMCSS	Council of Managers of Catholic Secondary Schools
CMRS	Conference of Major Religious Superiors
C of I	Church of Ireland
CTSI	Catholic Truth Society of Ireland
DDA	Dublin Diocesan Archives
EEC	European Economic Community
F.I.R.E.	*Future Involvement of Religious in Education*
GAA	Gaelic Athletic Association
ICC	Irish Council of Churches
ICD	*Irish Catholic Directory*
IER	*Irish Ecclesiastical Record*
IMA	Irish Medical Association
INTO	Irish National Teachers' Organisation
ITQ	*Irish Theological Quarterly*
IVEA	Irish Vocational Education Association
Messenger	*Irish Messenger of the Sacred Heart*
NCPI	National Conference of Priests of Ireland
NUI	National University of Ireland
OECD	Organisation for Economic Cooperation and Development
PTAA	Pioneer Total Abstinence Association
RTÉ	Radio Telifis Éireann
TBA	Teaching Brothers' Association
TUI	Teachers' Union of Ireland
UNESCO	United Nations Educational, Scientific and Cultural Organisation
VEC	Vocational Education Committee
WCC	World Council of Churches

Introduction and Overview

It is part of accepted conventional wisdom in recent times to say that Catholic culture in the Republic of Ireland has undergone significant change since the 1950s. Surprisingly, little serious work has been done in this specific area, however, and what is there is by way of journal articles or is of a journalistic or conjectural nature. A number of books have been published since 1950 exploring different aspects of Irish Catholicism — *The Irish and Catholic Power* written by Paul Blanshard (1954); *The Church in Contemporary Ireland* by Jean Blanchard (1963); *Is Ireland Dying? Culture and the Church in Modern Ireland* by Michael Sheehy (1968); *Church and State in Modern Ireland 1923–1979* by J.H. Whyte (1980); *Irish Catholics: Tradition and Transition* by John J. ó Ríordáin CSsR (1980); *Is Irish Catholicism Dying?* by Peadar Kirby (1984); *Keeping the Faith in a Changing Society* by Martin A. Convey (1994); *Moral Monopoly: The Catholic Church in Modern Irish Society* (1987, 1998) by Tom Inglis; *Ireland and the Vatican: The Politics and Diplomacy of Church–State Relations, 1922–1960* by Dermot Keogh (1995); *Goodbye to Catholic Ireland* by Mary Kenny (1997, 2000); and *Cultures Apart? The Catholic Church and Contemporary Irish Youth* by Oliver V. Brennan (2001).

A number of these are now dated and some are limited in their scope. On the other hand, Whyte has carefully sketched the contours of the area of church–state relations, and his authoritative study has proved to be a very useful reference work for the purposes of this research. The work of the following writers has also been enlightening on aspects of Irish culture: Michael Adams, *Censorship: The Irish Experience* (1968); Terence Brown, *Ireland: A Social and Cultural History, 1922–1985* (1985) and Séamas Ó Buachalla, *Education Policy in Twentieth Century Ireland* (1988). While all of the above writers deal with aspects of Irish Catholicism/culture, they do not set out to document the broad sweep of Catholic cultural change or provide an in-depth analysis of why change took place. The primary purpose of this book is to fill this gap.

This kind of research has been carried out in continental Europe and the United States. The following studies are noted: *The Evolution of Dutch Catholicism 1958–1974* by John Coleman (1978); *American Catholics: A History of the Roman Catholic Community in the United States* by James Hennessy SJ (1981); *The American Catholic Experience: A History from Colonial Times to the Present* by Jay P. Dolan(1987); *Roman Catholics in England: Studies in Social Structure since the Second World War* by Michael P. Hornsby-Smith(1987); *Privilege, Persecution and Prophecy: The Catholic Church in Spain 1875–1975* by Frances Lannon (1987); and *The Catholic Church and the French Nation 1589–1989* by Norman Ravitch (1990).

Because change can be assessed only by contrasting the new with the old, this book firstly aims to capture aspects of the ethos of Catholicism as it existed before it began changing. Secondly, it sets out to identify and document the changes that have taken place, and attempts to understand the particular context or set of circumstances that gave rise to them. Irish Catholicism has to be seen as one manifestation of a wider Catholic culture which is international. This book seeks to determine whether changes came about as a result of decisions taken at the local Irish Church level, or whether they arose from the changed thinking or 'new' theology which emerged in world-wide Catholicism after the Second Vatican Council, or whether, in fact, they were precipitated by political and socioeconomic developments in Ireland from the late 1950s. This book is as concerned with forces (internal and external) that were *changing* Catholic culture, as it is with the *changes* that actually took place.

The original doctoral thesis upon which this book is based was concerned with the period from 1950 to 1979. It examined the extent to which Catholicism was the informing 'spirit' of the whole way of life of the Irish Republic during this period, and when, and if, the position changed, and, if so, why. Two chapters have been added to the original work — a prologue which sketches the historical background to Irish Catholicism in the nineteenth century, and an epilogue which recounts some of the major developments that have taken place from the 1980s. These two chapters are in the nature of overviews. The dates 1950 to 1979 were not chosen in an arbitrary fashion. This period is marked by a number of important milestones. It began with the controversial 'mother and child affair'. The pontificate of Pope John XXIII and the Vatican Council dominated the middle years, and the period ended with the visit to Ireland of Pope John Paul II in 1979. All of these events had profound implications for the Catholic Church in Ireland.

Throughout the period examined, Catholicism was the professed religion of 92 per cent and more of the population of the Republic of Ireland by the census returns.[1] A review of the census returns from 1946 to 1991 demonstrates the numerical strength of Catholicism in the Republic of Ireland. The figures show that the state was and is remarkably homogenous in its religious affiliation (See Appendices A and K). Census figures or statistics on their own might not mean very much. But what was distinctive about Irish Catholicism was that this large majority was not just nominally Catholic but professed to be both committed and practising, unlike other traditionally Catholic countries, such as France, Spain, Italy or Portugal, where a large proportion was nominally Catholic, but where many had lost contact with the institutional church. This fact was borne out as recently as 1991 by the Mac Gréil survey, which has indicated the levels of participation at Mass, Holy Communion and confession by Irish Catholics[2] (See Appendix B). While surveys in the 1970s and 1980s did indicate a decline in religious practice, that decline was gradual. In the 1991 census, 92 per cent of the population of the Republic registered as Catholic (See Appendix K). However, surveys in the 1990s showed a more rapid and significant decline in attendance at Mass, and confession in particular. More recent trends (though not the primary subject matter of this book) will be examined briefly in the epilogue.

Ireland was a predominantly rural, agricultural economy until the 1960s. Irish society underwent profound changes as a result of the changed direction of economic and political policy from the late 1950s. T.K. Whitaker's paper, *Economic Development*, and the government's White Paper — the *Programme for Economic Expansion* (commonly referred to as the First Programme for Economic Expansion) — broke the mould in economic/political policy in Ireland.[3] The extent to which the changed directions had repercussions for the sociocultural fabric, in terms of values, attitudes, religious belief, customs, and thereby Catholic culture, is a central theme in this book. But there were also internal influences in Catholicism at this time which would threaten the status quo, the principal one being the revolution in Church thinking that took place during the papacy of Pope John XXIII and in the course of the Second Vatican Council. The centrality of this event and its far-reaching implications were even more pronounced in Ireland, because of the conservative Catholic ethos in pre-Vatican II Ireland.

The Council forms a natural division in the heart of this study. Catholics speak of the pre-Vatican and the post-Vatican II Church. Chapters 1 to 7 are concerned with portraying Irish Catholicism in the 1950s and the period leading up to the Council. Chapters 8 to 16 explore the changes that followed the Council, and highlight and analyse the issues that came to be centre-stage in Irish society and in the Church from the 1960s. Both the changes and the issues bespoke a profound change in Irish Catholic culture.

To set about an examination of Catholic culture in the Irish Republic at any time is a challenging and somewhat daunting task. For the period marked by this research, it is particularly so because the changes experienced in the culture were profound and far-reaching. This author has been keenly aware that the expansive nature of the topic, ranging over a period when so many changes took place, could lead to fragmentation or to a too general, and thus superficial treatment of many issues. In an attempt to avoid this pitfall, a selection has been made of key aspects of Catholic culture, and these aspects have been examined in an in-depth fashion within an overall context of change. This decision has meant that many other equally important features of changing Catholic culture had to be given less emphasis than they intrinsically merit. The same considerations have dictated that the examination should be confined to the Republic of Ireland.

A thematic/chronological approach has been adopted throughout this book as it was felt that this would do justice to the data and lend itself to analysis of the issues emerging. Throughout the work, for reasons of convenience and to avoid unwieldy expression, the word 'he' is sometimes used in the generic sense to denote male and/or female. Where the term 'the Church' is used, it denotes the Roman Catholic Church. This is to avoid repetition and is without prejudice to the ecclesiastical status of other denominations. The other main denominations in the Republic are the Church of Ireland, the Presbyterian Church, the Methodist Church, the Religious Society of Friends and the Jewish Congregation (See Appendices A and K). Should any of these denominations be in question, it will be specifically mentioned. The nomenclature of Catholic

Church will be inclusive and will from time to time connote the institutional or official church as represented by the pope and hierarchy, and at other times will signify the whole membership. The term universal Church will be used to differentiate between the Roman Church worldwide and the local (Irish) or continental Church. The use of such terms will in the main be self-explanatory. Likewise, for convenience, the term Irish will be used to denote the people and institutions of the Republic of Ireland, unless otherwise stated.

Review of Sources

This research is concerned with the public rather than the private face of Catholicism for the period of the 1950s–1970s. The Catholic Church in Ireland is organised into four provinces — Armagh, Dublin, Cashel and Tuam — and twenty-six dioceses. It is important to point out that this research had to be conducted (in the main) without the assistance of episcopal archives. Apart from Archbishop McQuaid's papers, some of which began to be made available in 1999, these archives are largely unavailable for the second half of the twentieth century, and they are unlikely to be available for the foreseeable future. The concerns of the bishops of the various dioceses can best be ascertained by examining their pastoral letters, statements and other public pronouncements. In the period of this research, it will be seen that the type of pastoral and its tone and content changed significantly. The official presentation of Catholicism in Ireland altered during this time. Bishops' pastorals received comprehensive coverage in the *Irish Independent* in the 1950s and 1960s, and also in provincial newspapers. This in itself, and the fact that the coverage became more sketchy in the *Irish Independent* from the late 1960s, is a key indicator of Catholic culture and how it was changing in the period of this research. What was reported as news, and how it was reported, provides a yard-stick of how people thought and felt at a particular time and what was seen as important.

Journals such as the *Irish Ecclesiastical Record* (*IER*) and the *Furrow* provided comprehensive coverage of the public statements and pronouncements of the bishops on all manner of issues pertinent to Catholic life, and they have been consulted extensively. Encyclical letters, papal decrees and instructions from Rome, also published in the *IER* and the *Furrow*, represent Catholic thinking at its nerve centre, so to speak, and are also central to this study. A sensitivity to the interaction between the local and the international level of the Church is particularly important in the period under review, because of the major watershed in Church history which took place from 1962 to 1965 — the Second Vatican Council — and the decrees promulgated by the Council also constitute crucial source material.

It is possible to chronicle the successive changes in the liturgy of the Church, with the help of official documentation, but what of their impact on people's religious practice and on how they conducted their lives? This is more nebulous, and the concept of culture aims to capture this. One of the central changes that the Council made was to de-emphasise the hierarchical model of the Church and to reconceptualise the Church as the pilgrim 'people of God'.

Bearing this in mind, this book, as well as being concerned with the mind-set of the bishops, is also concerned with how ordinary Catholics lived their everyday lives, and the texture of their piety in the pre- and post-conciliar eras. Religion as a belief system is given cultural expression in devotional activities and in people's values, customs, mores and behaviour patterns. The 'Chronicle' section of the *Irish Catholic Directory* (*ICD*) provides an invaluable insight into the religious routines and rituals so characteristic of Irish life in the 1950s, as does the 'Notes and Queries' section of the *IER*. The *ICD* provides factual information about Church personnel, and records the important newsworthy events of Catholic life, and in this way reflects the spirit of Irish Catholicism.

While official documents, like encyclical letters, decrees, instructions from Rome, pastoral letters and bishops' statements, form the backbone of the data, prominence has also been given to contemporary observers' accounts of aspects of what might be termed unofficial, or lived culture, or culture in the making. Crucial source material of this kind is also furnished by Catholic journals in existence at the time — journals like the aforementioned *Furrow*, and the *IER*, and also *Christus Rex* and *Doctrine and Life*. Articles in such journals recorded social and cultural phenomena, topical issues, events, prevailing opinions, trends and so on. Sometimes they reflected and sometimes they questioned the status quo.

Whereas the *IER* and *Christus Rex* (particularly in its early years) reinforced the Catholic ethos as it obtained, the *Furrow* and *Doctrine and Life* tended more to question it. The *Irish Theological Quarterly*, a scientific theological journal which re-appeared in 1951 after an absence of nearly thirty years, affords a glimpse into the theological discourse and the various influences coming to bear on theology in continental Europe over the years, which would in due course percolate through to affect the daily lives of Catholics everywhere.

The role of the *Furrow*, in particular, is central to this book, both as a record and as an agent of change. A monthly journal founded in 1950 by Canon J.G. McGarry, professor of Sacred Eloquence and Pastoral Theology at Maynooth, with the aim of renewing the Catholic Church in Ireland, it spans the entire period of this research. The circulation figure of the journal in the 1950s was in the region of 5,000 copies; by the late 1970s, it had reached about 7,000 copies. Whereas in the 1950s, 95 per cent, or more, of the circulation was clerical, by the late 1970s lay people accounted for about 25 per cent.[4] The journal circulated in religious houses and convents, which meant that the actual readership was considerably in excess of the circulation figure at any given time.

The *Furrow* has been selected as a central source for this research for a number of reasons. Firstly, it is the most general of the above works, in terms of its subject matter. Secondly, the changing pulse of Catholic life throughout this period is captured uniquely, both in its articles and in its documentation. While the prevailing ethos of Irish Catholicism in the 1950s was triumphalist and very wary of what were perceived as alien influences of the post-war era, the *Furrow* picked up changes happening in Europe and elsewhere, and it is fair to say that, had it not been in circulation, the Catholic population in

Ireland would have been considerably more 'disturbed' by the welter of changes which were to come about in the 1960s.

The fact of Ireland's insular position, that it remained neutral in the Second World War, and the fact that it was an agrarian rather than an industrial society, meant that social changes being felt in Europe since the nineteenth century, which gained a new momentum in the aftermath of the world wars, were not part of the Irish experience. Rapid urbanisation and its concomitant problems — dislocation of communities, alienation and exploitation of workers, secularisation — had stimulated debate among liturgists, theologians and churchmen on mainland Europe since the turn of the century and, particularly in the post-war era, produced a ferment of ideas, which would find expression in the Second Vatican Council's decrees. These were an effort to recast Catholicism — to re-define it to meet the challenges of a radically new industrial society.

The *Furrow*, clued in as it was to social changes and thinking in Europe, anticipated the changing cultural patterns for Ireland. As well as reflecting the changes going on in continental Catholicism, it precipitated and prepared the way for change in Ireland. As an intellectual journal giving expression to, and thus fertilising, new ideas, it was a creative force in changing Catholic culture in Ireland, as we shall see. It proposed its own vision of 'ideal' Catholic culture by questioning prevailing taken-for-granted assumptions and raising issues hitherto little heard of. Its role was prophetic. While the hierarchy set out in official pronouncements to define the rules and norms of ideal behaviour for Irish Catholics very specifically, the *Furrow* and the Catholic intelligentsia which began to emerge in the 1950s proposed a somewhat different, less legalistic 'ideal' of Catholic culture. This study is sensitive to both these 'ideals', at the same time bearing in mind that ideals have to be checked with reference to actual performance.

Empirical social research, statistical enquiry, opinion polls and such-like did not become routine in Ireland until the 1960s, and in the Irish Church until the 1970s. Despite the rarity of socioreligious research data in Ireland at that time, Irish culture has been so interwoven with Catholicism that such surveys as do exist, while they may not specifically relate to Catholicism, in many cases throw light on, have implications for, or are influenced in their deliberations by, Catholicism. The report of the commission set up in 1948 to examine the problem of emigration[5] and also Bishop Lucey's minority report as a member of the same commission[6] provide an insight into the major social upheaval being caused by emigration, which was slowly bringing about changes in Irish Catholic culture. Fr Alexander Humphreys' sociological research, which focused on a sample of twenty-nine first-generation Dublin Catholic families in 1949–51,[7] gives a valuable insight into the changing inter-generational attitudes which would ultimately lead to more questioning of the Catholic ethos.

The *Limerick Rural Survey* (1964)[8] and the OECD report, *Investment in Education* (1966),[9] were pioneering studies of aspects of Irish life. Given the Catholic Church's predominant influence on, and control over, the area of education, the deliberations of the latter report had fundamental significance for Irish Catholic culture. They signalled a major ideological shift in educational thinking. The contrast in thinking between the new and the old is readily seen, when this report is compared with the *Report of the Council of Education on the Curriculum of the Secondary School*, which was published in 1962, just a few years earlier.[10]

In the period after the Second Vatican Council, there was an increasing recognition by the Church authorities of the necessity to monitor the changes in religious practice and belief, and the economic, political and sociocultural developments which precipitated such changes. By the 1970s the position in relation to empirical research had altered radically following the setting up of a research and development unit by the Irish Episcopal Conference in 1970. The Council for Research and Development which it later (1973) came to be called is important on two counts. Firstly, in itself it represents an important development in Irish Catholic culture. Secondly, its considerable output of research in the course of the 1970s constitutes crucial source material for the latter period of this research.[11]

Useful information was also gleaned from interviews with key figures who have themselves lived through, observed, analysed and written about the changes in Catholic culture. Finally, a wide variety of excellent published works have served as very valuable background reading on the historical (Irish and international), theological and cultural dimensions of this topic. In relation to the Prologue, the author wishes to acknowledge her debt to the research into Irish Catholicism in the nineteenth century carried out by a number of scholars. In particular, the work of Patrick Corish, Emmet Larkin, David Miller, Donal Kerr, Sean Connolly, K.T. Hoppen, E.R. Norman, Thomas Bartlett and Oliver MacDonagh is invaluable in sketching the historical backdrop against which many developments in twentieth-century Irish Catholicism need to be understood. A list of the works consulted appears in the Bibliography. Many of the contemporary works listed proved useful in capturing the spirit of the times.

Prologue

Any attempt to understand the power and influence of Catholicism in Irish society must examine sociopolitical developments in nineteenth-century Ireland. When it is considered that the Irish bishops in the first years of the nineteenth century were prepared to concede to the British government a veto on episcopal appointments, in return for Catholic emancipation,[1] and when this is contrasted with the bishops' forceful stance in opposition to attempts by the British government to extend conscription to Ireland in 1918,[2] some insight can be gained into the bishops' confidence in their increasingly influential role, not only vis-à-vis the British government, but also in respect of the emerging state. Political, social and religious developments in the course of the nineteenth century hold the key to understanding the enormous change in the prestige of Irish Catholicism in the intervening time. Firstly, the Catholic bishops and clergy became increasingly politicised in the course of the nineteenth century. Secondly, the bishops sought to build up the Church organisation in terms of its physical plant, personnel and discipline; and, thirdly, they set about improving the level and quality of the laity's devotional practice.

When it came to light in 1808 that the Irish bishops had, in fact, accepted a veto on Episcopal appointments in 1799, Daniel O'Connell organised the massive lay opposition that it provoked. On foot of this protest, a national synod held in Dublin in September 1808 condemned, by a majority of 23 votes to 3, every form of interference by the crown in appointments or other matters of government of the Catholic Church.[3] When a bill was introduced in 1813 which offered emancipation in return for the veto, Catholics were split on the issue, and O'Connell led the opposition. The matter came to a head in the years 1814 and 1815, when the principle of the veto received formal Vatican approval in a rescript issued by Mgr Giovanni Quarantotti, secretary to the Congregation of Propaganda. In a further synod, held in 1815, the bishops responded by resolving unanimously that they should 'at all times and under all circumstances deprecate and oppose in every canonical and constitutional way any such interference', adding that 'it must essentially injure and may eventually subvert the Roman Catholic religion in this country'.[4] With that, the veto issue was effectively over.

The Irish bishops had turned a corner between 1799 and 1815. Undoubtedly the British government's failure to concede Catholic emancipation was influential in the bishops' change of heart, but an even weightier factor was the intense popular pressure they faced from the laity. The struggle was the first of many in which the bishops engaged through the nineteenth century, and it had all the elements which would typify subsequent confrontations. The British government had to be faced down, as indeed had Rome, and the laity was very much a force to be reckoned with. In fact, the influence of the laity was a crucial element in the equation, and one with which, in the course of the nineteenth century, the bishops would increasingly have to come to terms. Indeed, the bishops' success or failure in balancing the vested interests of Rome, London and their own constituency — the Irish Catholic laity — was, as time went by, to dictate their power and influence as an institution in Irish life.

The row over the veto had demonstrated that Catholic lay power, endorsed by the bishops and led by O'Connell, could prove formidable, and this led to the suppression of the Catholic Board which had been formed in 1811 to forward the cause of emancipation. It was only a matter of time before the agitation would re-emerge, and when Lord Wellesley, who was favourable to Catholic emancipation, was appointed viceroy in 1822, O'Connell seized the opportunity and founded (with Richard Lalor Sheil) the Catholic Association. What O'Connell and his organisation, however, had to contend with was that the vast bulk of the Catholic population at this time was poverty stricken and landless and identified understandably with specific local issues having to do with rents, evictions and the securing of a potato patch which would enable them to feed and maintain their families. They had little in common with the prosperous Catholic merchant class emerging in towns in the late eighteenth century, or with those Catholic landowners who had managed to survive confiscations and hold on to their land, or indeed purchase land over the years from landlords who had bankrupted themselves through mismanagement of their estates.

On the face of it, it might seem that winning the right for Catholics to sit in parliament would mean little to the mass of the people. But in the popular consciousness emancipation meant a lot more. Irish peasants saw themselves as victims of oppression and injustice in all aspects of life, at the hands of the landlord, the parson and the magistrate. They were second-class citizens in relation to their Protestant neighbours. Bartlett has pointed out that large sections of the Catholic peasantry were becoming increasingly disaffected, sectarianised, politicised and volatile in the years between 1790 and 1820.[5] But the problem for O'Connell and his organisation was that the forty-shilling freeholder, who had been granted the franchise in 1793, and thus could wield powerful electoral influence, was essentially the property of the landlord.[6] In order to transform this potential influence into an effective political machine, it was necessary to break the stranglehold of the Protestant proprietor. What O'Connell succeeded in doing was tapping into Catholics' discontent and sense of grievance[7] — a legacy of penal discrimination, which crossed social boundaries. He mobilised a mass movement by forging a common consciousness, which papered over divisions of class and wealth, to create a united Catholic front.[8] O'Connell constantly appealed to the Catholic people of Ireland as a nation[9] — denouncing the laws that deprived them of equality and emancipation was to be the panacea for all the ills and injustices endured by Catholics down the years.

By getting the backing of the Catholic bishops, he was able to incorporate the clergy, thus securing the only institutional apparatus that permeated, however imperfectly, to the grassroots.[10] The structure of the association was based on the parish network. Enrolment and collection of the 'Catholic rent' were managed by the Catholic clergy.[11] The parish structure was also used for the formation of association branches and the promotion of meetings and demonstrations, and priests were involved in bringing voters to the polls at the time of elections. The political effectiveness of the organisation was demonstrated first in Waterford in 1826, and later in the Clare by-election, in June 1828, when O'Connell opposed Vesey Fitzgerald and won by 2,057 votes to 982.[12] Fearing a mass rebellion, the government reluctantly caved in, passing the Emancipation Act of 1829, which removed the oaths offensive to Catholics, replacing them with a simple oath of allegiance.

The event was a watershed for Catholics. The Catholic laity, the clergy, the bishops and the British government's policy vis-à-vis Ireland would never be quite the same again. In the course of the agitation which led to emancipation, for the vast bulk of Catholics, the process by which they became politically conscious was as important as the outcome. They were now more aware of their grievances such as tithes, rack-rents and evictions, and became more anxious to seek redress and justice. The bishops realised the power of constitutional politics and, while they may have resolved otherwise as a body at particular times, they were never again apolitical as individuals. Priests, on the other hand, had got a taste for politics at a local level and, while from time to time bishops may have decreed that they disengage from politics, in practice this proved unenforceable. The British government came face to face for the first time with the political power of the Catholic lobby, and, for the rest of the nineteenth century, whether it was a Liberal or Conservative government that was in power in Westminster, this lobby increasingly had to be reckoned with. This led to understandable insecurity and alarm among the Protestant community, and an increased determination to support and preserve the union at all costs, which they saw as their only safeguard against the Catholic majority.

When, after the success of the emancipation campaign, O'Connell announced his intention to seek a repeal of the Act of Union, the bishops issued a joint statement in 1830, counselling clergy to keep aloof in the future from all political activity.[13] As far as the bishops were concerned, repeal was a purely political issue, and they had priorities that were infinitely more urgent at the time. A chief priority for the bishops right through the nineteenth century was the provision of Catholic schooling. In the eighteenth century, a system of parish schools existed, and, from the early nineteenth century, religious orders began to establish schools. However, these were in no way adequate to provide for the needs of a growing Catholic population. This period also saw the growth of many voluntary religious groups, such as the London Hibernian Society, the Baptist Society for Promoting the Gospel in Ireland, and the Sunday School Society which began to set up schools.[14] Such schools were proselytising in intent, and the fact that they got government grants caused disquiet to the bishops and Catholic clergy. The government in 1811 founded the Kildare Place Society to set up schools which children of all religions could freely attend. It was grant-aided, and the only religious instruction was the reading of the Bible. At first, Catholics supported those schools, but when the society began to give money to the Bible societies, Catholics began to withdraw their support.

In a curious way, the interests of the government and the Catholic Church authorities coincided at this time. Against the background of the agitation for emancipation and repeal politics, the government saw that schools could serve the purposes of socialisation, cultivating attitudes of loyalty to the crown and cultural assimilation.[15] The government abandoned the Kildare Place Society when it was perceived as having failed to maintain neutrality as between the confessions. In 1831, Lord Stanley, the Chief Secretary for Ireland, announced the institution of a 'board for the superintendence of a system of national education in Ireland'[16] which would be state-aided and multi-denominational. The Commissioners of the Board were to encourage particularly, local applications for new schools coming jointly from Protestants and Catholics.[17] Elaborate arrangements were made to separate regular instruction, which would be common to all, from religious instruction, which would be given to their own adherents by ministers of the various faiths.[18] Anglican opposition to the neutrality of the new system led to the setting up, in 1839, of the Church Education Society, to support Church of Ireland schools. Presbyterians were also unhappy with the system of neutral education. In 1840, they reached an accommodation with the Commissioners whereby they were allowed to conduct their schools along distinctly more denominational lines, and yet stay within the system. This made the national system more acceptable to Anglicans also, and from the 1850s most Church of Ireland schools were forced, because of financial pressures, to enter the system.[19]

Ironically, however, those who stood to gain most from the concessions were Catholics. By organising the local applications for schools, Catholic priests were able to become managers of national schools.[20] While the system still fell short of the denominational education sought by all church authorities, in practice it gave to the Catholic Church a great deal of the control over primary-level education, which it had been in danger of losing over the previous fifty years.[21] Demographics dictated that the bulk of national schools were attended by Catholics, thus making schools which were in theory mixed, de facto denominational by mid-century.[22] Thus, bishops and priests again provided the institutional framework whereby a political ideal could be realised — in this case an ideal which suited the British government, but one which the bishops pragmatically accepted and worked with, so that, more and more over time, it came to resemble an ideal situation from their point of view.

Access to parliamentary politics and access to education were the twin pillars on which the power and prestige of Catholicism would be built in the course of the nineteenth century. Before examining further milestones along the way, it will be instructive to look more closely at the state of the Catholic Church in Ireland in the first half of the nineteenth century. Ecclesiastically the country was divided into four provinces: Armagh, Dublin, Cashel and Tuam. The affairs of the Irish Church were dealt with by the Sacred Congregation for the Propagation of the Faith, the congregation which looked after churches in non-Catholic countries, generally referred to as Propaganda. There were twenty-seven bishops who were obliged to send to the Congregation regular reports concerning their dioceses, but apart from this a bishop was independent in the day-to-day running of his diocese.

The Irish bishops developed a sense of corporate identity by virtue of the fact that they held regular annual meetings.[23] From 1820, all the bishops met annually to discuss ecclesiastical affairs[24] and while the decisions taken were not binding on individual bishops, it did help in the development of co-ordinated policy which, on the one hand, increased their authority over the clergy and laity, and, on the other hand, strengthened their bargaining power with the government.[25] The meetings were an indication of the re-organisation which was taking place in the Church as the bishops attempted to instil greater unity of practice and bring the Irish Church into conformity with the universal Church.[26] It is important, of course, to point out that the Church, whether referring to bishops or priests, can never be seen as monolithic. Among the Irish bishops of the nineteenth century were a number of very strong personalities who differed vehemently and publicly on matters from education to politics.[27]

In 1834, a commission was set up to inquire into religious and other public instruction in Ireland, and the commission's report, the first of its kind, published in 1835, provided for the first time details of the religious affiliations of Irish people, and an insight into their level of religious practice.[28] Catholics in Ireland numbered 6,436,000 or 80.9 per cent of the Irish population. Anglicans numbered 853,160, and Dissenters 664,940 of the population. Four-fifths of Catholics lived on the land.[29] In the west of the country particularly, and to a varying degree elsewhere, most of these lived at subsistence level.[30] The subsistence sector was made up of marginal farmers, cottiers, labourers and paupers who lived in cabins on potato patches.[31] In the 1820s and 1830s, the problem was getting worse. The population was growing all the time as farmers were sub-dividing their farms to service the needs of their families. Living on tiny plots of land, totally dependent on the potatoes they could grow, this group was becoming increasingly vulnerable.

Under such circumstances, attendance at Sunday Mass had not become the measure of the practising Catholic that it was to become in the late nineteenth century and twentieth century. Based on his analysis of the statistics in the *Report of the Commissioners of Public Instruction*, Miller estimated that Mass attendance varied considerably — from nearly 100 per cent in certain towns and prosperous eastern rural areas, to 30 per cent and less in certain western districts.[32] Corish has estimated that in the four large cities — Dublin, Cork, Belfast and Limerick — and in the 'rural maritime' areas, the practice rate was 75 per cent and higher, and in the 'subsistence economy' it was at best 50 per cent, and often lower.[33] At best, practice can be described as uneven. This, however, cannot be adduced as evidence that Irish Catholics were not devout. Leaving aside restrictions placed on people by virtue of poverty and hardship, in this post-Penal Laws era a popular folk religion was very much in evidence.

Far removed from Tridentine theology and Roman orthodoxy, this peasant religion found expression in patterns, pilgrimages, holy wells, stations and wakes. In keeping with Tridentine Catholic practice everywhere, the bishops and clergy sought to suppress and, at minimum, control popular forms of piety, fearful of their superstitious and pagan overtones.[34]

A problem for the church authorities in achieving control over their flocks in the early nineteenth century was that the number of clergy was inadequate to minister to the needs of the growing population. Maynooth College had been established and funded by the government in 1795, in response to representations from the Irish bishops, when revolutionary developments in Europe had closed the continental seminaries.[35] While this increased the supply of priests, it still fell short of demand. Thus, while the number of parochial clergy rose from 1,614 in 1800 to 2,159 in 1835, the average number of Catholics in relation to each priest also rose from 2,676 in the former year to 2,991 in the latter year.[36] The situation was further exacerbated by the fact that such averages glossed over a very uneven distribution between the four ecclesiastical provinces.[37] The Church also had to cope with clerical indiscipline at this time. Larkin has noted the letters which found their way to Propaganda in Rome, from priests making all manner of accusations against each other and their bishops, ranging from simony and causing scandal to drunkenness, factiousness, and sexual irregularities.[38]

This less-than-satisfactory state of affairs is easily understood when one considers the breakdown of ecclesiastical discipline and the depletion in the ranks of the hierarchy caused by the Penal legislation against Catholics, enacted from 1695 to 1745. In 1707, there were only two or three bishops in Ireland, and it took forty years to fill all the sees. It took the bishops until the mid-nineteenth century to come to terms with the problems arising since early penal times, and their attempts to reassert episcopal control met not infrequently with clerical opposition.[39] Ironically, one of the outcomes of the disturbed state of the Church during penal times was that the links between priest and parishioner became closer than those between priest and bishop.[40] While this may indeed have been problematic for the bishops at this time, in any assessment of how Catholicism became all-pervasive in Irish life, this has to be seen as a key factor.

This closeness, which was to endure well into the twentieth century, was, to a considerable degree, attributable to the church authorities' resistance to government proposals made from time to time to give state payment to Catholic clergy, on the basis that removal of clerical dependence on their flocks would lessen the influence of the one on the other. While dues and stipends were very often a source of friction between clergy and laity, and the regulation of payments for services was one of the key disciplinary areas tackled by the church authorities in the nineteenth century, nonetheless, had the Catholic Church accepted state payment, it would not have developed into the independent formidable institution that it did, nor would the bond between people and clergy have been as close. It is important to point out the political liberalism of the Irish Church in this regard. In his 1864 *Syllabus of Errors*, Pope

Pius IX condemned outright the idea that 'the Church ought to be separated from the State, and the State from the Church'.[41]

One of the constants of Catholic socioreligious history through the nineteenth century was that the bishops and priests, when it came to political involvement, did not so much lead, as follow where the laity led. On issues like emancipation and education, it was understandable that they themselves should have a vested interest, but when it came to issues such as repeal (of the Act of Union) and the land agitation and independence later, they were a great deal more cautious. But ultimately, whether as a body or as individuals, bishops and clergy could not totally eschew involvement, because the people were their *raison d'être*, and they were paid by the people. The closeness between priests and people was much commented upon by travellers through the nineteenth century. In 1835, de Tocqueville was astonished by the 'unbelievable unity between the Irish clergy and the Catholic population'. This he attributed (partly) to the fact that 'the clergy are paid by the people'.[42]

A tangible sign of Irish Catholics' attachment to their faith was the number of churches built in the first half of the nineteenth century. The *Catholic Directory* in 1844 pointed out that 'within the last thirty years *nine hundred* Catholic churches have been built or restored in Ireland'.[43] In 1844, Kohl, a German Lutheran travelling in Ireland, observed that 'all over the country the Irish Catholics are vying with the English Protestants in the zeal with which they build new churches and repair old ones'.[44] Thackeray, also travelling in Ireland around this time, commented on 'the many handsome cathedrals for their [the Catholics'] worship which have been built of late years in this country by the noble contributions of the poor man's penny and by the untiring energies and sacrifices of the clergy'.[45] Against the background of the poverty already described, it is little wonder that travellers marvelled at such an impressive building programme. A further sign of the resurgence of Catholicism was the number of religious orders which founded congregations. Nano Nagle founded the Presentation Sisters in 1782, Edmund Rice the Christian Brothers in 1802, Mother Mary Aikenhead the Sisters of Charity in 1816, Frances Ball the Sisters of Loreto in 1822, and Catherine McAuley the Sisters of Mercy in 1827.[46] These were to be major players in the fields of education, hospital care and social welfare well into the twentieth century.

Turning now to the area of clerical discipline, a matter of crucial concern to the bishops in building up the institutional church in the first half of the nineteenth century, Larkin has pointed out that 'by 1830 the worst was over, since Irish bishops with the help of Rome finally secured the upper hand over their priests'.[47] And while the church authorities were frequently dubious in relation to certain aspects of the devotional practice of the laity in the early nineteenth century, many contemporary visitors were impressed with the religious fervour of the people. James Johnson, an English physician who was touring Ireland in 1843, observed that 'in no country have I ever observed the people more zealous and sincere in their religious devotions than the Catholics of Ireland'.[48]

Such evidence, as well as reports by parish priests to their archbishops (between 1830 and 1846) examined by Kerr, together with evidence from the

Catholic Directory of 1846 relating to Dublin and Waterford, attest to a satisfactory level of attention by parishioners to their religious duties, and also to the existence of many lay confraternities and devotions.[49] While Larkin has attributed the 'devotional revolution' — whereby Catholics were socialised into a strong religious belief, practice and moral order — primarily to the latter half of the nineteenth century, after the appointment of Paul Cullen as Archbishop of Armagh, more recently McGrath has argued that these changes would be more appropriately conceptualised as the 'Tridentine revolution' and seen as the working out of the decrees of the Council of Trent — a process which started after Trent, was obstructed by political circumstances until 1775, accelerated after the Famine, and continued until the time of the Second Vatican Council in 1962.[50]

In addition to devotions, the catechesis of the laity constituted an important priority for the bishops and, with this in mind, work was under way from the eighteenth century on, standardising the many catechisms which were in use.[51] The emergence of a wealthy Catholic middle class in the towns during the eighteenth century led to impressive developments in the publication of Catholic devotional and apologetical literature.[52] The *Catholic Directory* began in 1836.[53] All of these developments were crucial in strengthening the Irish Catholic sense of community and identity in the first half of the nineteenth century.

All in all, considering that Irish Catholicism was only recovering from the penal era, Catholic self-confidence had grown enormously by the 1840s. The clergy, in terms of their outlook and standard of living, were becoming increasingly sophisticated. That said, many of the developments described above impacted little on the more deprived areas. While the range and quality of pastoral services had certainly been improved as part of the general tightening of ecclesiastical discipline, a major stumbling block in this regard was the deterioration in the ratio of priests per head of the Catholic population. Between 1791 and 1841, the population had increased from 4.5 million to 8.1 million, further swelling the ranks of the rural poor — that sector among whom the influence of 'official' Catholicism had made least inroads.[54]

What radically changed this was the impact of the Great Famine. What had, over many years, been a grave situation turned into a tragedy of catastrophic proportions for those living on the margins of Irish society, when the potato crop failed over a number of years from 1845. As Corish has pointed out, the Famine constituted 'a great divide in the religious history of the Irish Catholic community'.[55] The Famine dealt a mortal blow to the 'subsistence economy', and thus to Gaelic Ireland. It was the poor who suffered most from death, disease and emigration — the huge reduction in the numbers of landless labourers, cottiers and marginal farmers after 1850 resulted in Irish society becoming more homogeneous and, paradoxically, more prosperous.[56]

The virtual liquidation of this class, and the passage of the Encumbered Estates Act, in 1849, gave landlords the opportunity to clear their estates, and the better-off tenant farmers were thus able to consolidate more substantial holdings. On the other hand, many landowners whose estates were heavily mortgaged now faced ruin, and their estates were bought out as freehold by wealthy Catholic farmers and merchants.[57] In the period after the Famine, from the 1850s to the 1870s, agricultural prices rose steadily, and the tenant farmers holding thirty acres or more benefited from further prosperity. This was to mark a permanent change in Irish social structure — a change which was to the advantage of the Catholic Church. Ironically, the result of these developments was that the Church, itself benefiting from renewal and reforms as described, was now ministering to a reduced but more prosperous population. This Catholic population was more orthodox in its religious outlook, thus making it closer in mentality to the clergy. The ratio of priests to each Catholic, always a problem, improved enormously, and a more affluent Catholic laity was better able to support its clergy.

It was against this historical politico-religious background that Paul Cullen arrived in Ireland in 1849.[58] Born in 1803 into a prosperous farming family in Co. Kildare, in 1820 he went to Rome to study for the priesthood. He was ordained in 1829 and became rector of the Irish College. During his years in Rome, he acted as agent for most of the Irish bishops in their dealings with the Congregation of Propaganda. He was appointed Archbishop of Armagh in 1849 by Pope Pius IX. In 1852, he was translated to Dublin, and was made cardinal in 1866.[59] When he came to Ireland, he had been given by the Pope the powers of an apostolic delegate, with the mission of convening a national synod, in order that the Irish Church be better regulated and governed.[60]

The importance of emphasising the power and authority of the papacy and centralising the power of the Church in Rome had been an issue since the reforms of Trent. The movement known as Gallicanism was a thorn in the side of the Church from the seventeenth century.[61] Gallicans were opposed to Roman centralisation and wanted to restrict the pope's power to intervene in the affairs of national churches. Enlightenment ideas, the collapse of the *ancien régime* at the time of the French Revolution, the Young Italy revolts of Garibaldi and Mazzini in 1848 and 1849, and the threat to the Papal States all served to underline the vulnerability of the papacy. As a result, the Church settled in to an increasingly defensive mould. Its response to intellectual and social challenges in the nineteenth century was to close ranks.

The siege mentality came to a climax with the publication in 1864 of the *Syllabus of Errors*, in conjunction with the encyclical, *Quanta Cura*, by Pius IX, and, a few years later, in 1870, at the first Vatican Council, with his definition of papal infallibility. Ultramontane Catholics, in contrast to Gallicans, considered that a strong centralised papacy was the only hope for the Church in an age that was becoming anti-church and anti-clerical.[62] The whiff of Gallicanism had lingered over the Irish Church for some time, because many Irish students had trained for the priesthood in France, before the foundation of the national seminary in Maynooth, and even more so after its establishment because a number of the professors were either French or had been educated in France. That the Irish Church should be seen as unquestionably ultra-montane was a top priority for Cullen from the outset.

The Synod of Thurles, convened by Cullen in 1850, was the first national assembly of the Irish Church for almost 700 years. The synod introduced a comprehensive and up-to-date code of ecclesiastical law, summarising the reforms of the previous fifty years.[63] When decisions were reached, they were submitted to Rome for ratification and, when ratified, they were binding on all. The synod concerned itself with the proper administration of the sacraments and the closer regulation of the life of the clergy. Thurles signified for priests a new regime, which reflected developments everywhere in the Catholic world — they were to be subject to stricter discipline and were expected to have a greater sense of religious commitment. From then on, the priest would be differentiated by his dark clerical garb and Roman collar, and his clerical life was to be strengthened by regular retreats and clerical conferences. From that time, the pattern of Tridentine Catholicism which had been difficult to implement in Ireland would become the norm.[64] Cullen remained suspicious of Maynooth and, for this reason, he set up a Dublin diocesan seminary in Clonliffe in 1859.

With the benefit of their increased personnel, more rigorous learning, better church facilities and a more receptive laity, the priests focused attention on the Mass, confession and the reception of Holy Communion. The laity was encouraged by missions held in parishes all over Ireland and devotional exercises designed to encourage more frequent participation in the sacraments and to instil piety. These devotions included the rosary, devotions to the Sacred Heart, the Immaculate Conception, the Forty Hours, Benediction, pilgrimages, shrines, retreats and processions. Practice was regularised by setting up sodalities, confraternities and altar societies which would be overseen by spiritual directors. This communal devotion was strengthened by means of devotional aids such as beads, medals, missals, prayer books, catechisms, holy pictures and scapulars, and promised spiritual rewards by way of indulgences which guaranteed to shorten either the devotee's or a nominee's time in purgatory. There was a strong sensuality about these devotions — music, singing, rich vestments, incense and candles all combined to make the rituals/ liturgical experience a very evocative and intense one at a time when, for many, there was little in the way of drama or colour to stimulate the imagination. Inevitably, they came to exercise a profound influence.

Attendance at church and at school became the means whereby people were socialised into the routines, rules and regulations — the ethos of the Catholic way of life. Maynooth College played a very significant role in the transition. By the second half of the nineteenth century, half of the priests of Ireland had been educated in Maynooth.[65] It is often alleged that the Maynooth-trained priest was a moral rigorist, and that the rather anxious and severe strain associated with Irish Catholicism came about as a result of the influence of Jansenism on the theological formation of students for the priesthood in the 'Gallican' atmosphere of Maynooth. Jansenism originated with Cornelius Jansen, a professor at the University of Louvain, who appealed to the authority of St Augustine in propounding his theories on human nature, grace and original sin. Jansenists emphasised the darker side of human nature. This led to a pessimistic theology, which was reflected in moral rigorism. While there seems little doubt that the Maynooth priest took a rigoristic view of morality, there has been much scholarly debate as to the origins of this, and it is very clear that the picture is considerably more complex than some analysts suggest.[66]

Ireland must be considered in the context of Britain and the rest of Western Europe in the nineteenth century. The Catholicism that evolved from that time was a peculiarly Irish hybrid of Tridentalism, folk religion and Victorian puritanism — what has sometimes been referred to derisively as '*la catholicisme du type Irlandaise*'. The strong emphasis which was undoubtedly laid on sexual restraint cannot be totally attributed to the Catholic influence. It was part of the wider civilising process in Western Europe at that time.[67] The political decision to introduce primary education was central to this process — a way of gentling the masses and, indeed, exercising social control. In Ireland, it suited the Catholic Church to assume this role, and the national school also played an important part in the catechesis of the laity.

The two issues which were of most concern to Cullen and the Irish Church right through the century were education and proselytism, very often linked. Catholic–Protestant relations, despite the Irish historical legacy, were characterised by a considerable degree of tolerance and co-operation in the first two decades of the nineteenth century.[68] This situation deteriorated rapidly after 1820. The first half of the nineteenth century had witnessed the steady growth of the Protestant evangelical movement, which led to a new interest in missionary activity, directed not only overseas, but also at the Catholic population of Ireland. The different societies trained and supported recruits who travelled around the country, distributing Bibles, and preaching often through the medium of Irish. This period was known as the 'Second Reformation'.

The influence of these societies was receding in the south west by the late 1840s, and in Connacht from the mid-1850s,[69] but the legacy of suspicion that they engendered between Catholics and Protestants endured well into the twentieth century. They tended to be more heavily concentrated in poor rural areas, and their activities in the west were one of the reasons why Archbishop MacHale of Tuam set his face against the national-school system, when the government would not accede to the bishops' demands that it should be formally denominational. MacHale was not the only bishop unhappy with the national-school system, but the majority saw it as an improvement on what already existed. This group, led by Archbishop Murray of Dublin, had its position endorsed by Rome in 1841.[70] That said, the bishops were never entirely satisfied with the situation — the issues of catechesis and teacher education were always contentious — so they persisted in their demand for a fully denominational system, but had to be content with piecemeal concessions over time.[71]

Secondary education was less contentious because it became more and more concentrated in the hands of the clergy, brothers and nuns.[72] University education was also problematic for Catholics. Until 1845, the only university available to Catholics was Trinity College, Dublin, which was founded in 1592 and had a deeply Protestant ethos. The British government, despite the persistent demands of the bishops, was opposed to state endowment of a denominational university system, and resisted their overtures. The more moderate wing of the bishops, led by Murray of Dublin, were prepared to accept mixed-religio-secular systems in education, and were more inclined to pin their hopes upon gradual concessions as a reward for inculcating respect for established authority and supporting whatever British party would concede most reform.[73] In 1845, the government provided for three non-denominational Queen's Colleges, in Belfast, Cork and Galway. In 1850, the Synod of Thurles condemned the 'godless' Queen's Colleges, and, in 1854, the bishops established the Catholic University in Dublin, under papal authority and under the rectorship of John Henry Newman. The university had no endowments and was beset by financial and other difficulties.

One of the issues which was to bring about a split between O'Connell and the Young Ireland movement — which contained some liberal Protestants — was O'Connell's willingness to repay the bishops and priests who supported him in his campaign for Repeal by pressing their demands for denominational education. The movement split in 1846 as Ireland was about to face the greatest crisis in its history. It was the same year that Pius IX became pope, and the year before O'Connell died. The depopulation of the countryside as a result of starvation, disease, emigration and the hardship suffered by those who could not afford to pay their rent all served as a catalyst which changed the political climate for the rest of the century. Political activity from then on was focused on the issue of land ownership and, in due course, political self-determination.

The Tenant League was founded by Charles Gavan Duffy in 1850 to press the demands of tenant farmers. These were known as the three Fs — fair rent, fixity of tenure and freedom of sale. During 1850 and 1851, Cullen, MacHale and seven other bishops expressed in the press their goodwill towards the League and its objectives.[74] Despite his initial sympathy with their cause, Cullen grew more wary for a number of reasons. Over the years, there had been complaints of intimidation on the part of clergy, and matters came to a head after the general election of 1852, when instances occurred of MPs being unseated on petition because of accusations of clerical intimidation.[75] In addition to this, Cullen had always been wary of Charles Gavan Duffy's background in the Young Ireland revolutionary movement of 1848. Cullen had been in Rome at that time and had lived through the contemporary revolution instigated by Young Italy, which had threatened the papacy. Despite the fact that the differences between the two movements were as important as the resemblances, Cullen persisted in equating them, seeing Duffy as an Irish Mazzini.[76] At a National Council of Bishops in 1854, legislation was passed, limiting the activities of the clergy in politics.[77]

That said, there were many in the 1850s in Ireland, and more, arguably, among the Irish in America, who felt that constitutional politics had had its day, and who began to look to the revolutionary tradition of the Young Irelanders for a remedy for their ills. The Fenian movement, or the Irish Republican Brotherhood, was founded in 1858. As a secret, oath-bound society, it was, from the outset, viewed by the church authorities as sinister. At their meeting in Dublin in 1862, the bishops condemned secret societies as dangerous to religion and society.[78] Fenianism galvanised those who had fled the countryside in the post-famine period and found their way to Irish towns or to Britain or America.[79] What was interesting about Fenianism was that it was a type of class movement, deriving much of its support from artisans, tradesmen, shop assistants and national teachers — 'a fraternity of young, unpropertied, educated, urban-dwellers'.[80]

Clerical censures did not prevent Irish Catholics from joining the Fenian movement. As far as the Fenians were concerned, they were happy to take their religion from the clergy, but in their newspaper, the *Irish People*, the message 'no priest in politics' was constantly reiterated.[81] Charles Kickham, one of the paper's chief editorial writers, repeatedly challenged the right of priests to dictate to the people in political matters. Thus, the movement presented a challenge to the social control exercised by the Church. Undoubtedly, the bishops, sensing the climate of violence spreading through the country, were aware of the potential fall-out for the Church. Writing, in May 1862, to Kirby, his successor as rector of the Irish College in Rome, Cullen saw the society as 'very dangerous'. He hoped 'that our people will be saved from the danger of adopting the wicked maxims of Mazzini and Garibaldi'.[82] Bishop Keane of Cloyne, also writing to Kirby, captured the dilemma for the church authorities when he asserted that Fenianism 'is destined to exercise an extraordinary influence on the future relations between priests and people'. 'The mass of the public', he went on, 'are either Fenians or sympathetic with the Fenians ....' 'If once the masses', he warned, 'throw off the respect they always had for their priests, then will come the real Irish difficulty for England and for all concerned.'[83]

In order to understand the church authorities' fear of Fenianism, it is necessary to look beyond the Irish situation to the historical context of mid-nineteenth-century Europe. *The Communist Manifesto* was published in 1848. In it, Marx outlined his ideas on the exploitation of the working classes by those in society who represented the establishment. Comerford has noted that charges of 'communism' and 'socialism' were frequently levelled at those who advocated the rights of tenants.[84] The fact that membership of the Fenian movement held out the prospect of land for the unpropertied and dispossessed was seen as subversive of property rights. This posed a very real threat to the social stability of that section of society comprising those who had managed to increase their holdings in post-famine Ireland. As far as the Church was concerned, popular democratic movements (especially those of a socialist hue) that threatened the status quo were a direct threat to the power and influence of the Church, which was, after all, an integral part of the establishment. The theories which derived from the French revolution, which found expression in the political programmes of Mazzini and other continental revolutionaries, did not simply aim at overthrowing government. Revolutionary socialists like Mazzini had as their goal a new pattern of society, in which Christianity had no part to play.[85] As it happened, the planned Fenian rising fizzled out in a few local skirmishes, but the republican tradition that it symbolised was a force in

Irish politics from then on. It was a tradition that could threaten the status quo if it were not contained.

Political developments in Britain played into the hands of the bishops at this point. William Gladstone and John Bright were consolidating support for the Liberal Party — wooing various nonconformists and other minority interests.[86] It did not require much political pragmatism to foresee that the formulation of policies to address Irish Catholic grievances could tip the scales in favour of the Liberals and effectively decide the next government and prime minister. Since 1863, Archbishop Leahy of Cashel had been in indirect contact with the Liberation Society of England, a body dedicated to ending state support for churches.[87] At a banquet, following the laying of the foundation stone of the O'Connell monument in Dublin, Leahy hinted strongly that the bishops were prepared to be associated once again (as in O'Connell's time) with a movement of political agitation.[88]

In as much as the bishops were prepared to align themselves with English radicals and Dissenters, who endorsed the idea of the secular state and equality as between different religious groupings, they were acting in direct opposition to the Pope's stand against nineteenth-century liberalism — against what Pope Pius IX most dreaded, namely, 'a free church in a free state'.[89] Such were the circumstances which led, in December 1864, to the inauguration of the National Association of Ireland. The inaugural meeting in the Rotunda was addressed by Cullen.[90] The organisation's demands were legislation to disendow the established church, to secure state support for denominational education, and reform of the law on landlord and tenant. The programme reflected a pragmatic compromise between clerical goals and those of the tenants.

In 1866, Gladstone became leader of the Liberals in England. In 1868, he fought and won a general election under the slogan of 'justice for Ireland'. His promise to disestablish the Church of Ireland was a major issue in this election.[91] The National Association, led by Cullen and the bishops, was active in securing the return to parliament of candidates who pledged to support their interests. The established church was a long-standing grievance with Irish Catholics. By law, it was the state church, but its congregation constituted about 10 per cent of the population. It was very wealthy. Its wealth was based on extensive landed property and also on the tithe, a tax levied irrespective of one's religious affiliation.[92] In October 1867, at their meeting, the Catholic bishops made an unequivocal demand for disestablishment, disendowment and the use of church wealth for general charitable purposes.[93] Gladstone introduced the Irish Church Bill on 1 March 1869, and it became law in July 1869. From 1 January 1871, the minority church was no longer legally recognised as the national church.[94]

While disestablishment was enormously symbolic, it was of little practical help to the vast majority of tenant farmers, who, after the passing of the Irish Franchise Act of 1850, constituted the influential class in the electorate.[95] The interests of this class were to dominate Irish politics for the rest of the century.[96] This was the group who had survived the Famine relatively unscathed, who had benefited from the increased prosperity of the post-famine era, and among whom the Church's devotional revolution was most effective. In the post-famine era, these people were aspiring to new models of respectability and social prestige. Bishops and clergy were mainly drawn from this social group, so they shared the same mores and values. They had seen destitution, poverty and misery as the price exacted by the Famine for unrestrained fertility, and were happy to adopt the Church's strict code of sexual behaviour. Indeed, as the population consistently fell over the remainder of the century, many would say that their adherence to it became obsessive.[97] Land was the priority of this group.

Cullen and the other bishops were in Rome at the Vatican Council when Gladstone introduced his Land Bill early in 1870. They were not very happy with the Act as passed,[98] but Cullen did not wish to alienate Gladstone while the education question was still at issue. While in Rome, he was successful in securing a condemnation of Fenianism, and also the excommunication of those who supported the Fenians or any other such society.[99] The establishment by Isaac Butt of the Home Government Association, in 1870, heralded a new era in Irish politics. Cullen did not favour the Home Rule movement, and he reacted by setting up, in 1872, a new organisation called the Catholic Union, the aim of which was the support and defence of Catholic interests in Ireland and abroad.[100] The dramatic turn events had taken in Rome undoubtedly influenced Cullen. The Dogmatic Constitution, *Pastor Aeternus*, which proclaimed the infallibility of the pope, was voted on and carried by 533 'placets' to 2 'non placets', on 18 July 1870, against the background of a dramatic thunder and lightning storm.[101] The drama did not end there. The outbreak of war between France and Prussia the following day brought about the withdrawal of French troops from Rome at the beginning of August, leaving the way open for Italian troops to advance on the city. On 20 September 1870, Rome fell to the Italians, bringing an end to the pope's power as a temporal ruler. A month later, the Pope suspended the Council indefinitely.[102]

The Catholic Union was to be non-political, and its first priority was the education question due to come before parliament in early 1873. The education bill introduced in the Commons on 13 February was a disappointment practically all round. It gave no endowment to the Catholic University, and neither did it yield on the principle of mixed education. The Irish Liberals (at the instigation of the bishops) voted against the bill. The bill was defeated, and the Liberal alliance with Gladstone's government was over.[103] By late 1873, Home Rule enjoyed wide support among priests, and Archbishop MacHale of Tuam and Bishop Keane of Cloyne continued to be its most prominent supporters among the bishops. Cullen was still wary, but he made no public pronouncement.[104] In 1873, Butt turned his association into a political party. The Home Rule Party had made little impact by the time Cullen died in October 1878. Pope Pius IX had died in the same year, the previous February. Things were about to change, however.

Charles Stewart Parnell had been elected Home Rule MP for Meath in April 1875. Agricultural depression set in as a result of disastrous harvests in the late 1870s. Once again, the land became the principal focus that was to galvanise all other forces. By 1879, many farmers could not pay their rents, and they faced evictions. The situation was particularly bad in the west. In 1879, Michael Davitt founded the Land League, and Parnell, realising that land rather than Home Rule was the core issue in Irish society, became leader of a combined agrarian and political movement. In the short term, rent reduction was the programme of the League, but a longer-term aim became that of enabling tenants to become owners of their land. Once again, the government was spurred into action by the power of mass agitation. In 1881, Gladstone's second land act was passed, which set up land courts to decide what a fair rent was.

Larkin has pointed out that the vast majority of the junior clergy, a smaller majority of the senior clergy, and a minority of the bishops committed themselves to the League. A majority of the bishops — eighteen or so — remained either hostile or suspicious, but they soon found this position untenable.[105] In a letter to Kirby in Rome, in December 1879, John MacEvilly, Bishop of Galway and Coadjutor to the Archbishop of Tuam, explained the dilemma they faced. He pointed out that the people would attend League meetings whether priests wished them to or not. 'If the priests attend,' he pointed out, 'they will keep the people attached to them.' He cautioned Rome against interfering, because it would render the Holy See 'very odious to seem to be influenced by the English against those who sacrificed everything for the faith', and, he added, when general evictions came, 'it would ruin us, if the [Roman] authorities could be quoted as against our people.' 'Religion in this country', he warned, 'would never get over it.'[106] When Rome did, in fact, in 1888, issue a papal decree against the Plan of Campaign, the bishops were forced to take sides. Fearing massive public rejection and loss of political power and influence, they followed the people rather than Rome.[107]

While MacEvilly, like the majority of the bishops, refused to have anything personally to do with the League, his reflections here show the delicacy of the Church's position. The bishops' caution is understandable, because the land war unleashed tensions and frustrations that often spilled over into violence, and just how dangerous and unruly these forces could be became obvious when Parnell was arrested and the League banned in 1881, and the country lapsed into chaos. Realising that he was the only hope if order was to be restored, the government released Parnell, and he founded a new organisation called the Irish National Land League, which was firmly in his control. Between 1882 and 1885, he structured and contained the political consciousness that he had already successfully focused in the Land League by creating a national and local political apparatus, and, in so doing, Larkin has argued, he gave 'substance and coherence to the ideal of a "de facto" Irish state'.[108]

In 1884, the bishops, now convinced of Parnell's commitment to constitutional methods and obviously impressed by the power he wielded, decided that it was time to make a move. At their October meeting, they resolved to 'call upon the Irish Parliamentary Party ... to urge generally upon the government the hitherto unsatisfied claims of Catholic Ireland in all branches of the education question'.[109] The clerical–nationalist alliance that evolved from this arrangement was the culmination of O'Connell's work in the first half of the century — a grand coalition, described by Boyce as 'that hybrid of Fenianism, the Church, constitutionalists and agrarian radicals'.[110] Therein lies the key to understanding Irish politico-religious history well into the twentieth century. In return for representing their interests in education, the bishops were prepared to support the party's position on Home Rule and on the land question. They, in turn, secured the right to be consulted as to the suitability of candidates for election within their ecclesiastical jurisdiction, and also the right to define their clergy's role in the approval of candidates.[111] After the 1885 election, the Irish Parliamentary Party had 85 MPs in parliament, thus enabling Parnell to play a pivotal role in British party politics. Neither Liberals nor Conservatives could now afford to ignore Irish issues. The Conservative government passed the Ashbourne Land Act of 1885, which gave generous loans on attractive terms to tenants to enable them to buy out their farms. It was the first in a series of schemes which, over a period of time, changed the pattern of land-holding from tenancy to ownership.

However, even more was on the horizon. Gladstone introduced a Home Rule Bill in April 1886. Defeated by the combined forces of the Conservative Party and the newly formed Unionist Party, and some of Gladstone's own Liberal Party, it precipitated the fall of Gladstone's government. That said, the possibility of self-government was now placed permanently on the political agenda. It formed the basis for an ongoing alliance between the Irish Parliamentary Party and the Liberals for thirty years, and the Catholic Church was at the heart of that alliance.

The Conservatives who were in power for most of the next twenty years, from 1886 to 1892 and from 1895 to 1905, directed their efforts into introducing a number of reforms in Ireland, which would redress Irish grievances, in the hope that this might divert attention from the demand for Home Rule. Further Land Acts were passed in 1891, 1896 and 1903.[112] Despite the reforms, the Conservatives did not succeed in weaning the Irish voter away from the idea of Home Rule. The Conservatives had also tried to find a solution to the university problem for Catholics. The failure of their efforts was, indeed, what enabled some kind of working relationship between the bishops and the Parliamentary Party to remain in place after the disillusionment of the Parnell–O'Shea divorce scandal in 1890, and the subsequent failure of Gladstone's second Home Rule Bill, in 1893.

The bishops' main priority through this time was the education question, but, depending on the way the political wind was blowing, Home Rule and the land question more often than not dominated the political agenda. It was not until 1905 that the bishops as a body felt that they could endorse the Parliamentary Party, now re-united under John Redmond, in the same manner as they had done in 1884. In a resolution which was to be read in the churches, the bishops' standing committee urged the 'whole country' to 'rally round our Parliamentary representatives … in their endeavour to secure ordinary civic rights for Irish Catholics in educational, and all other matters'.[113] In December of that year, the Conservative government fell, and hopes for a resolution of what now seemed like an impasse were transferred to the Liberal government. Finally, after much negotiation, a bill was introduced on 31 March 1908, which proposed that there would be two new universities, one in Dublin and one in Belfast.[114] The university in Dublin would have three constituent colleges — one in Cork and one in Galway, which would take the place of the former Queen's colleges, and one in Dublin. Religion tests would not be permitted in either university, but the senates of both universities and the governing bodies of the four colleges would be nominated at first by the crown, but with such representation of the various religious denominations as would ensure that the bodies would be acceptable to members of the predominant denomination attending each college.[115]

Finance was to be made available for the building of the new college and for extension of the existing colleges, but no portion of the grants given was to be used for providing a church or chapel or religious worship or theological chairs.[116] The general body of the bishops followed Archbishop Walsh, who had been appointed to Dublin in 1885, in accepting the plan, whilst recognising its imperfections, and the bill was signed into law on 1 August 1908.[117] A solution had at last been found to the problem which had exercised the minds and energies of the bishops for so long. The Church now effectively controlled all levels of what was essentially a system of denominational education, financed by the state. The clerical–nationalist alliance had more than rewarded the clergy and the larger tenant farmers by the first decade of the new century.[118] Both the Church and the farming sector were destined to be influential power brokers in any political arrangement that came to pass. The issue of self-government was still to be resolved.

While the clerical–nationalist alliance in support of Home Rule had remained in place, the Parliamentary Party lost momentum after the Parnell crisis, the subsequent split in the party and the failure of the second Home Rule Bill. A number of groups emerged towards the end of the century to fill the vacuum and challenge the prevailing political consensus. They were concerned that the Irish had lost their cultural identity by the nineteenth century. The plantations, the Penal Laws, the Famine and the national-school system had all contributed in their various ways to the decline of the Irish language and culture. The Catholic religion increasingly became the Irish badge of identity — Irish and Catholic had become synonymous by the end of the nineteenth century. These groups argued that the achievement of political self-determination would be meaningless, if not accompanied by a revival of the Gaelic cultural heritage. The Gaelic Athletic Association, founded in 1884, the Gaelic League (1893), the Irish Literary Revival movement (1899), Sinn Féin (1905) and many other groups all strove to make Ireland more conscious of being Irish. This was to be done by reviving the Irish language, folklore, legends, games, customs and traditions which had been lost through Anglicisation policies resulting from the English connection over the centuries. Sinn Féin, founded by Arthur Griffith, was the most overtly political, but each of the above-mentioned movements, and others as well, served as a breeding ground for a new generation of political leaders who emerged at the time of the

Easter 1916 Rising, and who subsequently took leadership in the new political order.

While many of the clergy were attracted to the cultural nationalism of what was generally described as the Irish-Ireland movement, the vast majority of the bishops in early 1917 still supported the Parliamentary Party and were wary of Sinn Féin.[119] A number of developments caused them to change their allegiance over a short few years, however. Unionist reaction to Asquith's Home Rule Bill in 1912, the outcry provoked by the executions after the 1916 rebellion, and resistance throughout the country to the British government's attempt to enforce conscription in Ireland in April 1918 — all in their different ways indicated the way the political winds were blowing. The bishops' decision to lead the popular resistance to conscription was a major turning point for the Church in Ireland. Traditional Catholic theology held that it was morally wrong to contravene the law of the existing government.[120] To understand the bishops' stance, Murray points out, 'one must take account of the capacity of the Church to accommodate itself to successful or popular revolt', and grant it 'retrospective priestly benediction'.[121] The election of December 1918 made it even clearer who now held the political mandate, and the bishops weighed in accordingly.

What made it easier for them to do so was the essential Catholicity of the new political movement and leaders, and the fact that they shared the Church's socially conservative outlook. Unlike revolutionary movements on the Continent, these revolutionaries were neither anti-religious nor anti-clerical.[122] Political independence was their goal — they were not going to bring about radical social changes, which would undermine the rights of the Church and Christian values. The Church could accommodate such 'revolutionaries' and reach a viable working relationship with them (as with O'Connell and Parnell), which would be to the benefit of both politicians and church leaders. After the election, O'Riordan of the Irish College in Rome sought the opinions of a large number of the bishops as to the soundness of the new party, and those who replied all bore testimony to what exemplary Catholics its members were. Bishop Foley of Kildare and Leighlin spoke of how the anti-conscription movement had galvanised the country. Writing of how young and old had 'displayed the most marvellous fervour in prayer, reception of the sacraments, assisting at Mass etc, that had ever occurred in the country', he added that 'no mission that was ever held so profoundly affected the lives of the whole Catholic people, and the Sinn Féiners were second to no others'.[123]

In any review of nineteenth-century Irish history, what emerges, on the one hand, is the political pragmatism of the bishops, and, on the other hand, their stubborn individualism and independent-mindedness, depending on the vested interest they were pursuing. When Sinn Féin split after the Treaty, which was signed in London by the Irish delegation in the early hours of 6 December 1921, and ratified by the Dáil on 7 January 1922 by 64 votes to 57, the bishops threw their weight behind the pro-Treaty side. The latter won the Dáil vote and the June election. Thus, they represented the democratic wishes of the Irish people. For this reason, the bishops, in a joint pastoral in October

1922, formally declared themselves against de Valera and his republican followers.[124] The Church's place in the political consensus was, by this time, guaranteed by a hundred years of history. By the beginning of the twentieth century, the bishops had become a powerful force, destined to wield extraordinary influence in the new state. In the same way as Parnell and O'Connell before him had needed, and paid in kind for, the Church's support, so also did the fledgling Free State government, as we shall see.

Part One

1

The Legitimisation of the Catholic Ethos by the Free State and Subsequent Irish Governments: The Historical Perspective

One of the most outstanding features of Irish Catholic culture in the post-independence era was the extent to which the state, by the actions, words and public appearances of its representatives, legitimated the Catholic ethos. An alliance was formed between the Catholic Church authorities and the Free State government during the Civil War years, and W.T. Cosgrave during his tenure of office looked to the Church to augment the authority of his government. The alliance was a mutually reinforcing one. The bishops were prepared to throw their weight behind the new state and endorse its political legitimacy, which was being contested by the anti-treaty Republicans, and the rulers of the new state were not disposed to question the authority of the Church in matters having to do with education, health or sexual morality, traditionally seen by the Church as its areas of competence.

The church–state consensus that evolved after independence has to be understood against a backdrop of historico-political developments in Ireland in the centuries before independence. The Irish Catholic Church had survived through the seventeenth, eighteenth and nineteenth centuries in the face of well-nigh overwhelming odds — plantation, the discrimination of the Penal Laws, persecution — and had emerged victorious. Against this background, by the end of the nineteenth century, a symbiosis of Catholic and Irish had taken shape which was to have enormous political consequences. Emmet Larkin has stated it thus: 'What really evolved ... in the making of the Irish state was a unique constitutional balance that became basic to the functioning of the Irish political system'.[1] He elaborates: 'The price Parnell paid ... for the accommodation of the church ... was to make his *de facto* Irish state essentially a confessional one ... it was left to de Valera to make that state ... formally confessional'.[2]

The stakes were high as far as the Church was concerned. In return for placing its resources and organisational ability at the disposal of Parnell and O'Connell before him, the prize was control over education, a commanding voice over the transmission of culture.[3] The Church's control of education and the state's acceptance and support of the Church's policy on education was a crucial factor influencing Irish culture in the post-independence era. Likewise, the Church's contribution to the health services in terms of the building and servicing of hospitals and its involvement in social welfare services from the nineteenth century was crucial to the power it was able to wield. The areas of education and caring were key areas of potential influence over people's lives, as far as the Church was concerned, and they were guarded jealously, as we shall see in later chapters.

On the basis that the census of 1911 revealed that the population was 89.6 per cent Catholic[4] — and that the percentage exceeded 90 per cent at every subsequent census (see Appendices A and K) — a politician did not need great powers of discernment to realise that, as Miller has so aptly put it, 'the active disapproval of his actions by the church will cost him votes — more votes than would the disapproval of any other agency'.[5] Cosgrave, and de Valera later, sought to protect what they saw as the distinctive Irish Catholic tradition by means of legislation and censorship.

When the possibility of making facilities available for divorce in the Irish Free State was raised in 1923, Cosgrave sought and complied with the advice of the hierarchy[6] that 'it would be altogether unworthy of an Irish legislative body to sanction concession of such divorce',[7] and the issue was closed never to resurface again while he was at the head of government. The Film Censorship Act of 1923 was another example of the Church's influence on government at an early stage. The Censorship of Publications Act followed in 1929, in response to agitation from the mid-1920s by the Dominican-inspired Irish Vigilance Association, the Catholic Truth Society of Ireland and the Priests' Social Guild. Cosgrave further cemented his relations with the Church when, in 1930, he established diplomatic relations with the Vatican, over the heads of the bishops, not all of whom were impressed.[8]

In the 1932 election campaign, while Cumann na nGaedheal based its election platform on religion and law and order, Fianna Fáil concentrated on economic and social policy, but not at the expense of the Catholic perspective. In a speech on work creation Seán T. O'Kelly quoted extensively from encyclicals, claiming that 'Fianna Fáil policy was the policy of Pope Pius XI'.[9] The 1932 election result installed Éamon de Valera in power for sixteen years. The timing could not have been more opportune. Dublin was the venue for the Eucharistic Congress in the summer of 1932. Whatever reservations the bishops may have had about Éamon de Valera and his anti-treaty stance in the Civil

War, their doubts were more than dispelled by the manner in which de Valera and Fianna Fáil handled the congress. It proved to be an organisational triumph for the state no less than the Church.[10]

From the beginning, de Valera pursued a policy of economic and cultural nationalism. In de Valera's vision of true Irishness, the existence of the peasant on a small farm represented a purity or integrity of life, uncontaminated by the mercenary values which were steadily overtaking the more industrial societies of Ireland's European neighbours. He placed emphasis on the distinctiveness of the Gaelic way of life — a life in which the Catholic religion, like the Irish language, was a badge of identity. This vision in which there was an almost instinctual association of Catholicism with the Irish way of life was extolled time and again in the course of his speeches. The *Irish Press*, founded by de Valera in 1931, with its unabashedly polemical style, praised Fianna Fáil's economic programme, urging the decentralisation of industry as was purportedly the case in France and Italy, which 'are Catholic nations, while Germany and Britain are not. In Catholic countries man has not yet lost his importance in the scheme of things. He remains of more concern to the rulers than the machine'.[11]

The observations recorded here echoed the kind of fears that were constantly being expressed in papal encyclicals and statements at this time, and which continued into the 1940s and 1950s.[12] The adverse consequences of industrialisation, urbanisation and mechanisation, for the dignity of the person, had been of concern to popes since Pope Leo XIII's promulgation of *Rerum Novarum* in 1891. It was a theme that de Valera returned to repeatedly. When he opened Radio Éireann's Athlone station in 1933, he asserted:

> The Irish genius has always stressed spiritual and intellectual values.... The great material progress of recent times, coming in a world where false philosophies already reigned, has distorted men's sense of proportion; the material has usurped the sovereignty that is the right of the spiritual.[13]

In a St Patrick's Day broadcast to the United States in 1935, de Valera saw Catholic Ireland and the Irish nation as synonymous:

> Since the coming of St Patrick, fifteen hundred years ago, Ireland has been a Christian and a Catholic nation. All the ruthless attempts made through the centuries to force her from this allegiance have not shaken her faith. She remains a Catholic nation.[14]

Perhaps the most famous distillation of de Valera's vision was in his much quoted 1943 St Patrick's Day broadcast to the Irish people, when he reflected:

> That Ireland which we dreamed of would be the home of a people who valued material wealth only as a basis of right living, of a people who were satisfied with frugal comfort and devoted their leisure to things of the spirit.[15]

The concern of statesmen like de Valera and Cosgrave, and others before and after them, to affirm their Catholicism was understandable in view of the necessity for the state to establish an identity after the disillusionment and acrimony of the Civil War. As Fanning has put it:

> Though the treaty remained the 'dream that went bust', though the island remained partitioned and the republic a mirage, there remained Catholic ideals to bind together a riven nation. Catholicism, always central to so much of Irish nationalist ideology, thus took on an additional significance in the search for national identity.[16]

The preservation of the Catholic faith in the face of persecution and the possession of a spiritual empire abroad as a result of Irish missionary conquests led to an understandable national pride, which provided the foundation for a much-needed consensus which served to bolster national morale, and this was sorely needed after the Civil War divisions. Against this background, it is perhaps not surprising that a certain triumphalism became the hallmark of Irish Catholicism, and an exalted sense of its resilience and merits found echo time and again in the discourse of statesmen and pastoral letters of bishops.

De Valera was equally as zealous as Cosgrave had been in ensuring that Catholic morality would be upheld by legislation and that all manner of public and state occasion — be it the opening of a new housing estate or the opening of a factory or school — would be blessed by official clerical presence. In 1933, he placed a tax on imported daily newspapers. This was in response to moralists and bishops who for years had campaigned vociferously against the English gutter press. In 1929, the Censorship Act had made it illegal to advocate the use of contraceptives. In 1935, the Criminal Law (Amendment) Act, section 17, prohibited the sale and importation of artificial contraceptives. In the same year, the government passed the Public Dance Halls Act, which likewise alleviated episcopal anxiety. By means of this and the other pieces of legislation alluded to, the Catholic moral code became enshrined in the law of the land.[17] This process continued uninterrupted, and culminated in the drawing up of a new constitution in 1937.

De Valera had always opposed the 1922 constitution, which had made Ireland a dominion of the British crown, and he wanted to replace it with a document which would be indigenously Irish, as he saw it. The 1922 constitution was a typical liberal democratic document, which would have been appropriate for any country, of whatever religious persuasion or persuasions. Article 8 contained the only reference to religion, and simply guaranteed religious liberty and equality to all under the constitution. The constitution drawn up by de Valera, and accepted by the electorate in a referendum on 1 July 1937, reflected how deeply influenced he was by Catholic teaching. In the drafting of the constitution, de Valera had engaged in extensive consultations with key Catholic Church personnel, in particular Dr John Charles McQuaid.[18] It is in articles 41 to 44 that the constitution of 1937 becomes particularly Catholic in its thrust. Article 41.1.1, 'recognises the Family as the natural primary and fundamental unit group of Society',[19] and in section 3.1 of the article, 'the State pledges itself to guard with special care the institution of Marriage, on which the Family is founded, and to protect it against attack'. On this basis, section 3.2 declares that 'no law shall be enacted providing for the grant of a dissolution of marriage'. Article 42 provides a summary of Catholic teaching on education, emphasising the parents' role as the primary educators of the child, going on to assert that 'the State shall not oblige parents in violation of their conscience ... to send their children to schools established by the State, or to any particular type of school designated by the State'.[20] Thus, the rights of the State in education are heavily circumscribed.

Article 43 reflects Catholic teaching on man's right to private property. However, it is in Article 44 that de Valera's ideas about the proper relationship between church and state are most obvious. The article guarantees 'freedom of conscience' and not to 'endow any religion',[21] and prohibits discrimination on the grounds of religious belief, as did the 1922 constitution, but in the 1937 constitution these guarantees are preceded by another section missing from the 1922 constitution, which asserts that 'the State recognises the special position of the Holy Catholic Apostolic and Roman Church as the guardian of the Faith professed by the great majority of the citizens'.[22]

Given the recognition of the Church of Ireland, the Presbyterian Church, the Methodist Church, the Religious Society of Friends, 'as well as the Jewish Congregations and the other religious denominations existing in Ireland at the date of the coming into operation of [the] Constitution', as far as de Valera was concerned, the 'special position'[23] accorded to the Catholic Church quite simply reflected what was sociological fact. In the Dáil he pointed out:

> 93% of the people in this part of Ireland and 75% of the people of Ireland as a whole ... belong to the Catholic Church ... believe in its teachings, and whose whole philosophy of life is the philosophy that comes from its teachings.... If we are going to have a democratic State, if we are going to be ruled by the representatives of the people, it is clear their whole philosophy of life is going to affect that, and that has to be borne in mind and the recognition of it is important.[24]

De Valera went on to point out that 'it might be said that this does not go, from the Catholic point of view, the distance that would be desired by a number'.[25] De Valera was convinced that his constitution would establish Ireland as giving a lead to the world 'as a Catholic nation',[26] and Seán T. O'Kelly was to proclaim that 'the constitution was worthy of a Catholic nation'.[27]

Fianna Fáil was replaced on 18 February 1948 by the Inter-Party government, which was made up of all the parties in the Dáil except Fianna Fáil. The Taoiseach, John A. Costello, not to be outdone by the preceding governments of Cumann na nGaedheal and Fianna Fáil, sent a message of homage to Pope Pius XII, as follows:

> On the occasion of our assumption of office and of the first cabinet meeting, my colleagues and myself desire to repose at the feet of Your Holiness the assurance of our filial loyalty and of devotion to your August Person, as well as our firm resolve to be guided in all our work by the teachings of Christ and to strive for the attainment of a social order in Ireland based on Christian principles.[28]

The message set the tone that would characterise the administration during Costello's tenure of office. Seán MacBride, Minister for External Affairs, represented the government at the opening of the Holy Year ceremonies in 1950 in Rome.[29] President Seán T. O'Kelly also made the Holy Year pilgrimage to Rome.[30] Ireland was officially represented at the proclamation of the Dogma of the Assumption in November 1950.[31] Whyte has pointed up the 'mood' of increasing integralism'[32] in Ireland in the late 1940s as follows:

> All sorts of forces were at work to make Ireland a more totally committed Catholic state than it had yet become: ... more totally committed to Catholic concepts of the moral law, more explicit in its recognition of the special position of the Catholic Church ... this had been the direction of thrust in Irish history ever since Independence, and it was in these years that the process reached its culmination.[33]

The judgements of Mr Justice Gavan Duffy throughout the 1940s were important in the consolidation process. He was a member of the High Court from 1936 to 1946, and president of that court until he died in 1951. When an issue appertaining to religion arose, his policy was to invoke the provisions of the constitution to create new legal precedents which would be favourable to the Catholic viewpoint.[34]

Another feature of Irish Catholic sub-culture in the late 1940s and into the 1950s was the organisation known as Maria Duce.[35] While this movement, led by Fr Denis Fahy CSSp, cannot be regarded as representative of the broader spectrum of Irish Catholicism, neither can it be wholly discounted. It was symptomatic of an extremist wing of Catholic thinking which prevailed into the 1950s. Its most distinctive feature was its complaint that the state did not go far enough in Article 44 of the constitution, when it acknowledged the 'special position' of the Catholic Church. Towards the end of 1949, it began to lobby for an amendment to this article, which would recognise the Catholic Church as the one true church.

A rather more influential group, the Knights of St Columbanus had, since their foundation in 1915, been playing their part in consolidating Catholicism on a more practical level. They were anxious to enhance the material well-being of Catholics in business and corporate life.[36] Legislation had bolstered a Catholic moral order, and there were intensive efforts now to enhance and to ensure a Catholic social order also.

The coalescence of interests and mutual regard in which the state held the Church, and vice versa, was to be seen in all sorts of ways. Archbishop McQuaid was present at the airport to see the Taoiseach off on pilgrimage to Rome on 11 January 1950,[37] and likewise he was there to welcome back President O'Kelly on 26 April 1950.[38] Archbishop D'Alton, the Archbishop of Armagh and Primate of all Ireland, was seen off on pilgrimage by Seán MacBride, Minister for External Affairs.[39] It was customary also for President O'Kelly to send a birthday telegram to Pope Pius XII. The anniversary of the pope's coronation was commemorated by solemn High Mass every year in the Pro-Cathedral. The Taoiseach, the Tánaiste, members of the diplomatic corps, representatives of the Army, the civic authorities and the Garda Síochána were normally present. The impression is gained of a very solemn Church–State occasion. The atmosphere was one of pomp and ceremony. On 13 March 1950, for this occasion, the President and Mrs O'Kelly drove to the church with a motor-cycle escort.[40]

Public representatives, from the president down, acted as role models and set the tone on these occasions. They always knelt before the bishop and kissed his ring. The fact that he was addressed as 'My Lord', and that the house he lived in was referred to as the bishop's palace, reinforced in the minds of people the sense of his powerfulness and that of the Church. John McGahern, reflecting on his own youthful impressions, in an *Irish Independent* article in 1993, wrote: 'With his crozier and rich colours and tall hat he was the image of God the Father'.[41] The bishops did, in fact, see themselves as father figures protecting their flock, as shall be seen.

A hymn which was part of the warp and woof of Catholic culture in those days was 'Faith of Our Fathers'.

Faith of our fathers living still
In spite of dungeon fire and sword
Oh, how our hearts beat high with joy
Whene'er we hear that glorious word.
Faith of our fathers, holy faith,
We will be true to thee till death.

Interestingly, this was composed in the nineteenth century by Father Faber, a well-known English hymnist, and it also evoked the spirit of English Catholicism. When Cardinal D'Alton returned from Rome on 28 January 1953 after his investiture, he was greeted by the Taoiseach, Mr de Valera, and 'packed balconies' at the airport resounding to the singing of 'Faith of our Fathers'.[42] It was sung in conjunction with 'Amhrán na bhFiann', the National Anthem, at All-Ireland football finals, thus reinforcing the dual identity of Irish and Catholic. Another tradition on such occasions was that the Archbishop of

Cashel, patron of the Gaelic Athletic Association since its foundation in 1884, would throw in the ball at the beginning of the match. Both practices ceased in 1979.

Cultural theorists point out the importance of ritual, songs, slogans, processions and ceremonies in cultivating an ethos.[43] In Ireland in the 1950s, such rituals, ceremonies and processions, which will be described in the following chapter, were the symbolic systems that gave public expression to a culture. They bespoke taken-for-granted assumptions, shared meanings and a world-view all of which were informed by the spirit of Catholicism and served to reinforce the essentially cohesive nature of the community. Durkheim has shown how religious ritual functioned to reaffirm group solidarity in traditional societies.[44] In such traditional societies as Ireland was in the 1950s, where anything more than basic education was the privilege of the few, ritual could conjure up an emotional response and a sense of the aesthetic, to which a literary formulation of ideas and values could not aspire. As such, it was a powerful way to impress and legitimate certain values, attitudes, customs and ideas.

Such rituals represented a public ceremonial language which served to define the community and endow various actions with legitimacy and meaning. Ceremony, according to Skorupski, says 'this is how things should be, this is the proper, ideal pattern of social life'.[45] The singing of 'Faith of our Fathers' in conjunction with the national anthem and the custom of the bishop throwing in the ball at All-Ireland football finals served to express and sustain a way of looking at things. On the one hand, such rituals take collective sentiments for granted, and, on the other hand, they serve to reinforce them, and in so doing reinforce the individual's social identity within their meaning parameters. Above all, they mould consciousness.

In Ireland in the 1950s, the Catholic Church exercised a type of cultural hegemony. The concept has been developed by Gramsci to capture the complex process whereby powerful institutions or groups in society can disseminate their forms of consciousness through society as a whole.[46] This moulding of consciousness had its roots in the nineteenth century when, as Larkin has pointed out, 'the Church had managed to build itself into the very vitals of the nation'.[47] The laity had been socialised into a strong religious belief, practice and moral order which provided an all-encompassing definition of reality. Thus, as discussed, a highly disciplined and institutionalised church had emerged from the nineteenth century. This continued into the twentieth century, and the Church's position was strengthened in the period after independence.

The symbolic forms of Catholicism were everywhere to be seen, in the home as well as in public — the holy pictures, particularly the picture of the Sacred Heart with the eternal lamp, the papal marriage blessing, the crucifix, the statues of the Blessed Virgin, the Infant of Prague, St Joseph and various other saints, St Martin de Porres and the 'black babies' boxes in grocery shops and in public houses alike. The fact that the state shared the Catholic Church's definition of reality and publicly legitimated its symbolic forms was, of course, crucial.

The interpenetration of Church and state has nowhere been as obvious as in the field of education. Church control over the education process in Ireland had been hard won in the nineteenth century, and was jealously guarded. Control over education was seen by the Catholic Church authorities as vital as a means of transmitting the Catholic cultural heritage. And when power was transferred to the Free State government in 1922, a ready-made school system held inestimable practical and financial advantages for the native government, seeking to establish itself.

Politicians from the time of independence were very careful not to trespass on what the Church regarded as its own domain. Ó Buachalla has shown that successive governments between 1922 and 1957, irrespective of party politics, approached educational issues with a deep caution and sensitivity.[48] Eoin MacNeill, the first Free State Minister for Education, set the tone for his successors when he deplored what he called 'statism' in education.[49] In 1956, the same lack of assertiveness was typified in Richard Mulcahy's famous reference to his role as Minister for Education as being that of a 'kind of dungaree man' or 'plumber' who would 'take the knock out of the pipes', but would refrain from 'pontificating' on the deeper philosophical issues of education.[50] This he left to the teachers, the managers and the churches. He was, however, careful to point out that teachers, syllabuses and textbooks in every branch of education should be informed by the 'spirit' underlying the Catholic conception of education.[51] A survey of *Dáil Reports* and a perusal of the laudatory speeches made by politicians and ministers of education on the occasion of the opening of new schools, as recorded in the *ICD* in the 1950s and 1960s, points to the satisfaction with which this situation was viewed until the 1960s.

Richard Mulcahy (Minister for Education during the periods of office of both inter-party governments, 1948–1951 and 1954–1957) established the Council of Education in April 1950. Very Rev. Martin Brenan, president of St Patrick's Diocesan College, Carlow, from 1949 to 1956, was appointed chairman of the Council. Prior to his Carlow appointment, Fr Brenan had been professor of education and lecturer in Catechetics in Maynooth. The membership of twenty-nine nominated by the Minister included eleven clerics of various religious denominations. The Council's remit was to examine and report on the curricula of the primary and secondary school.

The best insight into the ethos and role of education, as seen in the 1950s, is to be found in the deliberations of the Council of Education on the primary school system, published in 1954,[52] and on the secondary school curriculum, published in 1962.[53] The former report noted that:

> Our primary schools today are essentially religious and denominational in character. They are owned and managed almost exclusively by religious bodies, and their purpose is religious.[54]

The report emphasised 'the primacy of religious values in the school' and 'the importance which the state itself attaches to religious education', going on to point out that 'a religious spirit should inform and vivify the whole work of the school'.[55] The dominant purpose of schooling in the latter report on secondary education was seen as the 'inculcation of religious ideals and values' and 'the preservation and transmission' of the cultural heritage.[56]

As well as influencing the spirit of the education enterprise, the Church also legitimated certain types of knowledge. In terms of curricular emphasis, the secondary-school report team came down heavily in favour of the classical humanist tradition of education with its literary, academic bias. The team determined to retain the sharp divide between liberal or general education, considered suitable for the secondary school, and applied or technical education, to be provided in vocational schools. General education, the report pointed out, 'aimed at development of the faculties of the human person, rather than his specialised preparation for a particular skill or profession'.[57]

For this reason, those on the team were dubious in relation to the inclusion in the curriculum of so-called 'useful' subjects, as in the case of commerce or manual instruction.[58] The report expressed a particular caution in relation to science, lest interest in it 'subordinate the general education of the secondary school to specialist study and sacrifice the formation of the man in the interest of scientific progress', and thus they decided against making it a compulsory subject.[59] The Church's traditional wariness of scientific and technological progress, voiced many times by Pope Pius XII, finds echo here in the deliberations of the report team.[60] The more long-term impact of these reports will be examined in Chapter 11.

The Church also influenced how knowledge was approached. The predominant philosophy of Irish Catholic education in the 1930s, 1940s and 1950s was influenced by the encyclical *Divinii Illius Magistri*, promulgated by Pope Pius XI in 1929, in which the primary rights of the Church and family in education were endorsed, and the state's subsidiary role enunciated.[61] The encyclical did not confine itself, however, to matters of control in education, but extended its brief to treat of matters of knowledge and related pedagogy. It upheld a predominantly conservative pedagogy, condemning contemporary educational developments having to do with 'the child's so-called autonomy and unrestricted liberty'.[62] Fears were expressed that such developments 'belittle or suppress entirely the authority and activity of the teacher'.[63]

Such fears were entirely in keeping with the Church's censorial approach to knowledge, and its fear of any questioning of what were seen as accepted patterns of thought. The Church's world view was based on scholastic philosophy, and the very essence of the scholastic outlook was that it saw knowledge as fixed, unchanging. Knowledge was perceived as existing outside, independent of, and in a sense superior to, the person. People were supposed to conform to a ready-made corpus of knowledge, rather than question it. This philosophy had implications for all aspects of Catholic culture — aspects as diverse as schooling, the education and training of priests, religious and nuns, catechesis and issues of morality, justice and poverty, and they will be looked at in turn in the course of this book. The Church's structural control over education ensured that the classical liberal curricular tradition would, until the latter period of this research, be seen as more prestigious than vocational education. It became what Raymond Williams has referred to as the 'selective' culture or tradition.[64]

As far back as the turn of the century, critical voices had been raised in relation to the profound influence of Catholicism on Irish life and education. In the same year as Max Weber published his seminal study, *The Protestant Ethic and the Spirit of Capitalism*,[65] Horace Plunkett published his book, *Ireland in the New Century* (1904), in which he expressed the view that the influence of Catholicism was detrimental to Irish economic development because it shifted 'the human centre of gravity to a future existence', [66] an idea vigorously refuted the following year by Monsignor Michael O'Riordan, the head of the Irish College in Rome, in his book, *Catholicity and Progress in Ireland* (1905).[67] But criticism was not confined to the Protestant tradition. Catholics like P.D. Kenny and W.P. Ryan — who succeeded him as editor of the *Irish Peasant*, one of the most influential of the Irish-Ireland newspapers — were critical of the Church's control over education, and thus over intellectual activity, which they saw as having an adverse influence on the economic development of the country.[68] Cultural nationalists like Kenny and Ryan were concerned that priests' focus was overmuch on the spiritual dimension, to the neglect of modern, scientific methods which could bring about a more self-sufficient economy. Emanating from a cultural nationalist perspective, Kenny's ideas were further elaborated in his books, *Economics for Irishmen* (1907)[69] and *The Sorrows of Ireland* (1907),[70] as were Ryan's in his book, *The Pope's Green Island* (1912).[71]

When the state did take an initiative in education by introducing the Vocational Education Act, 1930, to provide a measure of technical education for the 14–16 age group, the power of the Church to influence the organisation, selection and distribution of knowledge was particularly in evidence. From the outset, the hierarchy was consulted, and the proposed new vocational schools were tolerated only on the basis of reassurances given by the then Minister for Education, J.M. O'Sullivan, to Bishop Keane of Limerick (representing the hierarchy), that they would not encroach in any way on the provision of general education, as operating in the secondary schools.[72] He pointed out that 'by their very nature and purpose the schools to be provided are distinctly not schools for general education' and went on to reassure the Catholic Church authorities that there would be 'no new principle of control in education'.[73] (This was despite the fact that the minister in his letter to the bishop, had pointed out that 'for the great bulk of our young people the education at present provided ... in secondary schools is neither available nor suitable'.[74])

A binary system of education evolved, which made a sharp distinction between the practical, vocational subjects of the technical school and the classical liberal curricular tradition of the secondary school. Ecclesiastical lack of esteem for the former tradition, which was simply tolerated, saw to it that applied knowledge was not perceived as high-status knowledge, and the 'tech' was regarded very much as a second-class educational establishment. The fact that advanced education was a privilege to be availed of by the very few, and that this was the way things were and taken for granted as such, could be seen from de Valera's remark in the course of a 1940 estimates speech, when he pointed out that 'for nine out of ten of our people, the primary school is their only educational experience'.[75]

The communications media — the radio and press — played a key role also in legitimating the Catholic ethos. On 15 August 1950 a new daily feature was inaugurated by Radio Éireann, at the instigation of Archbishop McQuaid, whereby the ringing of the Angelus bell at the Pro-Cathedral was broadcast over the air at six o'clock each evening.[76] The *Irish Independent*, the newspaper with the largest daily circulation, advertised itself as a Catholic paper at least until the mid-1950s.[77] It gave extensive coverage to news of Catholic interest well into the 1960s. As well as printing the texts of bishops' pastorals often running to two or three pages of newsprint, the leader writer also, on occasion, made reference to them, summarising the main points and reinforcing them.[78]

The *Irish Catholic*, which began publication in 1888, and the *Standard*, founded in 1928, were the two Catholic weekly papers. In 1947, the *Irish Catholic* was estimated to have a circulation figure of 30,000, and the *Standard* a circulation figure of 45,020.[79] In this regard, it is interesting to compare the Irish situation with that of the Netherlands, where Dutch Catholics were only one of several religious groupings, and there were two Catholic national daily papers and a network of regional newspapers.[80] Coleman has pointed out that religious pluralism in the Netherlands meant that the Dutch could not take their Catholicism for granted as an Irish person might. This led to a 'conscious' Catholicism.[81] In the Netherlands, the various religious and ideological groups organised their own political parties, trade unions and leisure clubs, and established their own press and broadcasting services.[82] Because of the homogenous nature of Irish society it was not necessary for Catholics to do this — and to a great extent many of these institutions took on a religious hue per se.

All of the evidence so far points to the fact that Catholic culture was *the* popular culture in most of the Republic of Ireland in the 1950s. One could perhaps be forgiven for deducing that there was at that time no other cultural tradition. But this was by no means the case. There was in the Republic also the Protestant tradition. Against the background of the Catholic Church–State consensus and the pursuit of a nationalist Catholic policy by successive governments in the post-Independence era, perhaps for its own pragmatic reasons, this tradition became somewhat muted. In the same way as the *Irish Independent* presented Catholic news, *The Irish Times* was seen as the organ of Irish Protestants in the 1950s. Given that Protestants formed 5 per cent or less of the total population of the Republic of Ireland throughout the period covered by this book, the capacity of Protestantism to be a viable alternative culture to that of Catholicism was negligible, and for much of this period there was little overt questioning by Protestants of the prevailing Catholic ethos. (See Appendices A and K.)

In the Republic of Ireland these two traditions co-existed peacefully, apart from a few isolated incidents, which have been documented by Whyte.[83] That said, there was limited interaction, and not a little fear and suspicion, on both sides. The origins of such attitudes were deeply embedded in four centuries of religious/political history. On the Catholic side, memories of Protestant proselytising activity in the nineteenth century were still very raw. Catholic attitudes have also to be understood in the wider church context of post-Tridentine efforts to regain lost ground and to defend Catholicism against heresy. This led to a combination of fearfulness and defensiveness, which resulted in Catholic–Protestant relations being circumscribed by very strict rules.

The principle of separate denominational schooling had been adhered to and fought for by both Catholic and Protestant church authorities in Ireland since the nineteenth century. The rigour with which this principle was applied is captured in Archbishop McQuaid's annual Lenten regulations when he reminded parents of their 'most serious duty to secure a fully Catholic upbringing for their children', going on to point out that 'only the Church is competent to declare what is a fully Catholic upbringing.' 'Accordingly', McQuaid went on to point out:

> Those schools alone, of which the Church approves, are capable of providing a fully Catholic education. Therefore the Church forbids parents and guardians to send a child to any non-Catholic school, whether primary or secondary or continuation or university.[84]

'Deliberately to disobey this law is a mortal sin,' the Archbishop warned, 'and they who persist in disobedience are unworthy to receive the sacraments'.[85] He went on to point out that the NUI was 'by its charter, a neutral educational establishment' and while 'failing to give due acknowledgement to the One, True Faith', might, because of 'the measures taken by the ecclesiastical authorities to protect Faith and Morals ... be considered to be sufficiently safe for Catholic students'.

McQuaid's concerns may be better understood against the background of the repeated warnings of the bishops in the nineteenth century in relation to non-Catholic university education, and the continuous campaign that they waged for the establishment of a university which would be acceptable to Catholics. In 1875, they had extended their decree of condemnation of the 'godless' Queen's Colleges to include Trinity College. When eventually in 1908 the British government met their demands and established the National University of Ireland, which, though theoretically non-denominational, was designed in such a way as to guarantee considerable influence for the Catholic bishops, the condemnation of Trinity College became more emphatic at the next general synod held in Dublin in 1927. This time, the bishops went one step further and one of the decrees of the synod made the position clear in no uncertain terms:

> Since there are in the Irish Free State three university colleges sufficiently safe as regards faith and morals, we strictly and under grave obligation forbid all priests and clerics to recommend by advice or otherwise parents or others having charge of young people to send these to Trinity College.[86]

The attitudes of the bishops had hardened even more by the time of the 1956 Maynooth Synod, when they imposed an outright ban on Catholics attending 'that college', declaring this prohibition to be 'under grave obligation'. From the time of the accession of McQuaid to Dublin in 1940, more stringent controls were instituted and the Maynooth Synod of 1956 further decreed:

> Only the Dublin Ordinary is competent to decide, in accordance with the instructions of the Apostolic See, in which circumstances and with what guarantees against the danger of perversion, attendance at that college can be tolerated.[87]

At both diocesan and national synod level in the second half of the nineteenth century, legislation was passed prohibiting Catholics from participating in worship with non-Catholics, under pain of mortal sin.[88] The new *Code of Canon Law* promulgated in 1917, however, distinguished between active participation, which was illicit, and participation or presence at such ceremonies as Protestant weddings or funerals for a good reason as a matter of civic duty or courtesy, provided that there be no danger to faith or scandal to others.[89] The Dublin Diocesan Synod of 1927 and the Maynooth Synod of 1956, in keeping with the new *Code of Canon Law,* omitted the relevant prohibitions.[90]

However, this relaxation of the law did not find its way into practice. The event that most graphically illustrated this was the occasion of the funeral service of Douglas Hyde, the first President of Ireland, in St Patrick's Cathedral, Dublin, on 14 July 1949, when leading political figures could not see their way in conscience to be even passively present at the funeral of the head of state. Austin Clarke has immortalised the occasion as follows:

> At the last bench
> Two Catholics, the French
> Ambassador and I, knelt down.
> The vergers waited. Outside.
> The hush of Dublin town,
> Professors of cap and gown,
> Costello, his Cabinet,
> In government cars, hiding
> Around the corner, ready

Tall hat in hand, dreading
Our Father in English. Better
Not hear that 'which' for 'who'
And risk eternal doom.[91]

The convention of the day held that attendance at a Protestant service, be it baptism, marriage or a funeral, was sinful for Catholics. The funeral of a president was no exception and, in keeping with the tenor of the times as described above, government ministers gave the lead in upholding the Catholic ethos. Catholic practice was in strict conformity to this principle until the late 1960s.

The area which caused most uneasiness in relations between Catholics and Protestants in the Republic was that of mixed marriages. The ecclesiastical legislation governing marriage in Ireland, and thereby having implications for mixed marriages, was the *Ne temere* decree promulgated in 1907[92] and implemented in Ireland from 1908, the *Code of Canon Law* of 1917,[93] and the Maynooth statutes of 1956.[94] Under the terms enforced by canon law, the Catholic Church demanded that each party of a mixed marriage give a written guarantee that all children born to the marriage be baptised and brought up in the Catholic Church. The promises they made constituted the '*cautiones*' or conditions for granting a dispensation from the 'impediment' of mixed religion. Related to this there was an obligation on the Catholic partner to strive for the conversion of the non-Catholic partner.

Another condition laid down for the conducting of any mixed marriage by a Catholic priest was that it could not take place in any consecrated building, that there could be no religious vestments or rites, and that the priest must not bless the couple. He was there solely to act as a witness, so that the canonical form of Catholic marriage could be observed. Such restrictions conveyed in no uncertain terms that there was no question of ecclesiastical approval or religious celebration of such marriages. Quite the opposite: the wedding was treated as a second-class affair and normally took place in a sacristy. Mass was strictly forbidden. These regulations were in force until after the Second Vatican Council.[95]

The seriousness with which these rules were viewed and the stringency of their application may be discerned by perusing the section that Archbishop McQuaid devoted from year to year to these prescriptions in his Lenten Regulations. In 1963, quoting the relevant canons 1060 and 1071, and statute 193 of the Plenary Council of Maynooth, 1956, he pointed out that:

> The Church, to safeguard the Faith and Morals of her children, forbids everywhere and most severely the marriage of a Catholic with a non-Catholic.[96]

'For grave reasons,' he pointed out, and 'to avoid greater evils, the Church at times grants a dispensation' but only on the following conditions:

1 — That the Catholic and non-Catholic parties promise to have all the children of the marriage baptised as Catholics and reared as Catholics.
2 — That the non-Catholic party promise not to interfere in any way with the Faith or practice of the Catholic party.
3 — That it be morally certain that these guarantees will be observed.[97]

He added that 'the Catholic party is obliged in conscience prudently to strive for the conversion of the non-Catholic party'. He warned that 'these guarantees are solemn pledges very gravely binding in conscience' and 'once given, they may not ever be disregarded or set aside'.[98]

The potency of these conditions was underlined even more when Mr Justice Gavan Duffy made a ruling in the High Court in 1951, in the Tilson case, that a promise given in writing by a Protestant husband (in relation to raising his children as Catholics) was enforceable in law, despite his subsequent wish to revoke the promise.[99] The ruling was subsequently upheld by the Supreme Court. Its relevance here lies in the fact that Mr Justice Duffy, in giving his ruling, invoked the provisions of Articles 41, 42 and 44 of the constitution, on the family, education and religion, going on to point out that:

> An order of the Court designed to secure the fulfilment of an agreement, peremptorily required before a 'mixed marriage' by the Church whose special position in Ireland is officially recognised as the guardian of the faith of the Catholic spouse, cannot be withheld on any ground of public policy by the very State which pays that homage to that Church.[100]

The Tilson case serves to illustrate the all-pervasiveness of the Catholic ethos at that time and the extent to which it was taken for granted. The decision was unquestioned, apart from a series of angry letters in *The Irish Times.*[101] It also serves to underline the potency of the 'special position' clause in the constitution to bolster the Catholic ethos, if called upon to do so.

2

A LAND OF FAITH: Impressions of Irish Catholicism in the 1950s

It is important to bear in mind that the kind of loyalty towards, and legitimisation of, Catholicism by politicians in the post-independence era was totally in keeping with the thinking and lifestyle of the vast majority of the Catholic population of the Republic of Ireland in the 1950s. This may be assessed from the extraordinary level of their religious practice, as evidenced by contemporary observers' accounts. What is lacking in empirically based research is made up for by the remarkable consistency of these accounts of Catholic life. Writing in 1964, C.K. Ward pointed out that there was:

> ... no published empirically-based estimate of proportions of Sunday church-goers and paschal communicants. These categories are generally said to contain about ninety-five percent of urban Catholics and an even higher percentage of rural Catholics.[1]

In the early 1950s, the categories would, if anything, have been higher.

A good barometer as to the state of Irish Catholic culture in the early 1950s is the summary of a report to the Congress of the Lay Apostolate, made in Rome, on 10 October 1951, by Very Rev. M. O'Halloran, administrator of City Quay parish, Dublin. Referring to the state of Irish Catholicism, he pointed out that 'we are living in an atmosphere steeped in the Faith'. He went on to express satisfaction with the fact that the Church in Ireland had almost complete control of the systems of education, explaining that this was one of the reasons why the Irish parliament was almost 100 per cent Catholic in thought and action. This, according to O'Halloran, was also the reason why trade unions were not becoming Communistic or anti-clerical, why there existed close relations between people and clergy, and why there were so many vocations for the Church. He pointed out that the numbers who attended daily Mass and Holy Communion and weekly confession were 'remarkably high and can hardly be repeated anywhere in the world', and he added that 'a priest or nun is more than welcome in any and every house, rich or poor, at any hour'. All in all, he opined, 'it would seem we are in a very happy position'.[2]

Archbishop D'Alton, Archbishop of Armagh and Primate of all Ireland, was happy to conclude in 1950:

> Where their religion is concerned, the heart of our people is essentially sound. Irish Catholics, even amidst the temptations of modern life, are deeply attached to their Faith, and loyal in the practice of it.[3]

The obligations of Catholics in terms of religious worship were laid down in the *Code of Canon Law,* which was promulgated in 1917 and passed on by the bishops and priests to members of the faithful.[4] Catholics were obliged to attend the Holy Sacrifice of the Mass every Sunday and on Holy Days of Obligation, under pain of mortal sin. Canon 859 laid down that the faithful should receive Communion at least once a year, during Easter time. Canon 906 stipulated that they should confess their sins carefully at least once a year. Added to this were what might be termed penitential obligations of fasting from meat on Fridays, and the Lenten regulations of fast and abstinence. Those between 21 and 60 years of age were bound by the laws of fast and abstinence. Every day during Lent, except Sundays and St Patrick's Day, was deemed a fast day. Only one full meal was permitted, and a 'light repast' each morning and evening. The quantity and type of food allowed in these repasts was regulated by the approved custom of each diocese. The law of abstinence forbade the use of flesh-meat or soup made from meat or meat extracts. Ash Wednesday and all the Fridays of Lent were days of both fast and abstinence.

As well as the Mass, what was noteworthy at the time was the wide variety of other devotional forms engaged in by the laity. Among them were confraternities, sodalities, parish missions, pilgrimages, processions, cults of devotion to saints, benediction, the Forty Hours Novena, Marian devotions, the rosary, devotions to the Sacred Heart, devotions to the Miraculous Medal, the Stations of the Cross and the Nine First Fridays. The fidelity of Irish Catholics to these devotional activities has been borne out by Francis Kelly in a recent study of St Mary's Parish, Granard, Co. Longford, in the period 1933–68.[5]

Ambrose Crofts OP, writing in *Doctrine and Life* in 1954, noted that:

> On Sundays and Holy Days, especially in the cities, there may be as many as ten or twelve Masses to cope with the crowds. The missing of Mass is comparatively rare. Even on week days large attendances show how much the Holy Sacrifice means to the average Irish Catholic.[6]

Such praise for Irish Catholics in relation to the practice of their religion was echoed time and again in the 1950s by priests, rural and urban, regular and secular. Fr Seamas McLoughlin, a priest in Roscommon, observed that the 'precept of attendance at Holy Mass is well observed in Ireland'.[7] Likewise, a writer in the September issue of the *Furrow* of the same year, who was worried about the so-called 'leakage' of the faith among Irish Catholics who emigrated to Britain, asserted that the 'average of Mass attendance in Ireland on Sundays and Holy Days is a record in the Catholic world today'.[8]

Jean Blanchard conducted research in Ireland in the mid-1950s. Notwithstanding his apology for the 'uneven' nature of the study, his accounts provide invaluable documentary evidence for that time.[9] He describes a parish of around 22,000 persons in a north-west Dublin suburb. Blanchard explains that 'practically the whole of the Catholic population frequent the church. The entire congregation — with a few exceptions — attend Mass every Sunday'.[10] In order to facilitate them, Blanchard writes:

> There are six Masses every Sunday: at 7.30, 8, 9, 10, 11.30 and 12.15. There is a great number of Communions. There are 5,000 for Christmas. During Lent large numbers receive Holy Communion at the 7.30 and 10 o'clock Masses.[11]

The fact that Blanchard refers to the number of communicants specifically at Christmas and during Lent is significant. Communion in those days meant recent confession — probably the previous day. The two were then linked, unlike what came to pertain in later years. The whole question of worthiness to receive the sacrament was an urgent one, and the fear of approaching the altar rails in a sinful state was a very real fear indeed. One is reminded of Frank O'Connor's short story, 'The First Confession', where the young boy is afraid of making a bad first confession and 'of burning all over in roasting hot furnaces for all eternity'.[12] The story gives an accurate portrayal of the magnitude of the guilt that people felt if they were not in a 'state of grace'. This sense of guilt was a very real phenomenon in the 1950s.[13]

On Saturday nights, there were long queues for confession throughout the length and breadth of the country. Sins had to be confessed in detail, as well as the number of times they had been committed. There was a very real fear of dying in a state of mortal sin and thus losing eternal salvation. Graphic images of hell-fire and damnation were etched into people's consciousness, in particular by the Redemptorist preachers at parish missions every few years. This inculcation of fear began in school. The spirit of catechesis in those days is captured in O'Connor's story. The teacher's approach in preparing impressionable young children for first confession was to talk 'of hell. She may have mentioned the other place as well, but that could only have been by accident, for hell had the first place in her heart'.[14]

So, Communion was by no means automatic on attendance at Mass — instead, there was a hesitancy to approach the altar rails. Kelly, in his detailed analysis of church-attendance statistics for the year 1939, found that numbers receiving Communion were relatively small.[15] Part of the *raison d'être* of sodalities was to encourage the habit of frequent Communion. Also, very strict fasting rules were still in operation until the late 1950s. Those wishing to receive Communion had to fast from liquid as well as solid food from midnight the previous night. Having due regard for the demanding nature of the fasting laws, Holy Communion was distributed only at the early Masses, on the basis that people could not sustain the fast until the late Masses. Likewise, the sermon was usually reserved for the last Mass. Blanchard noted that 'in some parishes Communion is not given during Mass, but before or afterwards', because distribution during Mass would prolong the service.[16] For the same reason, priests often distributed Holy Communion right through the Mass. There was some slight relaxation of the fasting rule in 1953, as a result of a decree promulgated by the Holy Office on 6 January of that year.[17] That said, for the generality of the priests and the faithful, the only significant change in the law was that 'natural water (that is without the addition of any element) no longer breaks the Eucharistic fast'.[18]

The external signs of a vibrant Catholic culture were everywhere to be seen at that time. In Dublin, there was a huge population expansion from the early 1950s. In the twenty-five-year period between 1940 and 1965 the population of the archdiocese grew from 709,342 people to 791,379, and the Catholic population increased from 630,000 to 725,058 people.[19] Accordingly, John Charles McQuaid, who became Archbishop of Dublin on 27 December 1940, set himself the task after the war was over and building materials became available again, of planning for the needs of the expanding city. In 1965, reviewing Dr McQuaid's twenty-five years as an archbishop, Fr Roland Burke Savage SJ, editor of *Studies,* noted that thirty-four churches had been built in the archdiocese and twenty-six new parishes founded since McQuaid's accession to the Dublin see.[20] What is particularly striking is the sheer size of these churches.

It is of interest to select a random few in the short period between April 1952 and December 1953. On 4 April 1952, Archbishop McQuaid blessed and laid the foundation stone of a new church in Ballyfermot, designed to accommodate 2,000 people.[21] Later that month, on 30 April, he blessed and laid the foundation stone of a new church in Merrion Road, with seating accommodation for 1,800.[22] This was followed by a church in Mount Merrion on 28 June 1953 with accommodation for 1,600,[23] and one in West Cabra, on 6 December 1953, to accommodate 2,000.[24] Given the number of Masses on Sundays which serviced the needs of worshippers, as has been noted, the size of these churches gives some idea of the volume of need at the time.

Another feature of Catholic life through the 1950s was people's willingness to undertake pilgrimages. This was at a time when few people owned motor cars and the arduousness, to say nothing of the expense, of travel was not to be underestimated. Pilgrimage destinations varied from Rome or Lourdes to Knock, the shrine of Blessed Oliver Plunkett in Drogheda, or Lough Derg or

Croagh Patrick. On 28 April 1950, the first national pilgrimage to Rome, in honour of the Holy Year, was led by the Archbishop of Armagh and Primate of all Ireland, Most Rev. Dr D'Alton; it numbered 1,000 people.[25] Similar numbers were recorded at the second national pilgrimage to Rome, led by Archbishop McQuaid on 16 October.[26] A further pilgrimage to Rome on 1 October had recorded over 2,000 pilgrims.[27] A figure of almost 8,000 people from all over Ireland was recorded as having taken part in a pilgrimage to Knock on 6 August 1950.[28]

Croagh Patrick and Lough Derg are Patrician shrines. Tradition has it that St Patrick, the national apostle, prayed and fasted forty days and forty nights at each. The former, popularly known as 'The Reek', is 2,510 feet high and is climbed by some pilgrims on bare feet or on their bare knees. The pilgrimage may be undertaken at any time of the year but the most popular time is on the last Sunday of July, traditionally known as 'Reek Sunday'. The *Mayo News* reported that an estimated 100,000 took part in the Holy Year Pilgrimage to Croagh Patrick on Sunday, 30 July 1950. On 29 July 1951, an estimated 75,000 people took part; in 1953, 70,000; and in 1961, 75,000.[29] Lough Derg is a three-day pilgrimage which takes place throughout the summer months. In 1950, 30,963 pilgrims visited Lough Derg during the pilgrimage season; in 1955, 31,824; in 1960, 25,878; and in 1965, 20,842.[30] (See a full statement of the yearly number of visitors to Lough Derg for the years 1945–1986 in Appendix C, and for the years 1987–2001 in Appendix L.)

A feature of Irish Catholicism in the 1950s and 1960s was the cult of indulgences. As defined in the catechism, an indulgence 'is a remission by the Church of the temporal punishment due to sin already forgiven'.[31] The teaching at that time was that the sacrament of Penance remitted 'the eternal punishment due to mortal sin', but that it did not 'always remit the temporal punishment', which God required as satisfaction for sins.[32] The catechism teaching was that 'the penance imposed by the confessor' did not 'always satisfy in full for the temporal punishment' either, but that the deficit could be 'supplied by our other good works and by indulgences'.[33] There were two types of indulgence — a plenary indulgence, which remitted 'all the temporal punishment' due to sin, and 'a partial indulgence', which remitted 'a portion of such punishment'.[34] An indulgence could be gained for oneself or for the souls in Purgatory.

A detailed list of indulgences and the conditions laid down for obtaining them was contained in *The Raccolta or Collection of Indulgenced prayers and good works.*[35] Generally speaking, the conditions for the gaining of a plenary indulgence were that the person should go to confession and to Communion, visit a public church or chapel, and pray for the intentions of the Pope.[36] The prayers prescribed were an 'Our Father', a 'Hail Mary' and a 'Glory be to the Father'. Among the many indulgences available were those for making the Stations of the Cross, or the Holy Hour, or saying the rosary or certain aspirations or prayers. Others applied to particular feast days. There were special indulgences attached to the wearing of the brown, green and blue scapulars. The Pope could also institute special indulgences, as Pope Pius XII did, for instance, for the Holy Year, 1950, and the Marian Year, 1954. Special indulgences were also available during the Lenten season and in November, particularly on All Souls Day.

The devotional cult known as the Child of Mary was a popular one in the 1950s and into the 1960s. The Child of Mary members' prayer book, published in 1948 and then in its thirty-seventh edition, gives details of devotional activities, prayers and aspirations, and the indulgences attaching to them, which could be gained by members.[37] 'Sweet Heart of Mary, be my salvation' was just one of the many examples listed under the heading of 'Indulgenced Aspirations to Our Lady', for which 300 days' indulgence was available every time it was recited.[38] There were special morning prayers for Child of Mary members, and by making the Sign of the Cross before the prayers stipulated, one could gain a 50-day indulgence, and, a footnote pointed out, 'if with Holy Water, 100 days each time'.[39] Both of these indulgences were instituted by Pope Pius IX. By saying a special prayer to St Joseph during the month of October, members could gain a three-year indulgence. If the prayer was said after reciting the rosary, a seven-year indulgence could be gained, and a 'plenary, on usual conditions, for daily recitation during [the] whole month'.[40]

Understandably, there was considerable zeal among many of the faithful in pursuit of indulgences. November was traditionally regarded as the month of the Holy Souls, and the cult of devotion to the Holy Souls in Purgatory was particularly strong in Ireland in the 1950s. There was a very strong tradition of giving up drink for Lent and in November, during which month this abstinence was 'offered up' as penance for the Holy Souls in Purgatory. A plenary indulgence could be gained for the souls in Purgatory by visiting a church and praying for the Pope's intentions between twelve noon on the feast of All Saints' Day and twelve midnight on the feast of All Souls' Day. In order to fulfil the conditions, and also gain as many plenary indulgences as possible, it was a common custom for people to leave the church and re-enter it many times. Each re-entry was then regarded as a separate visit.

Another public manifestation of Ireland's Catholic ethos was the number of crosses erected during the Holy Year, 1950. A few out of the many examples will serve to illustrate this. On 26 March 1950, 'a white four-armed cross, forty feet in height, which was illuminated at night' and could be seen ten miles out to sea, was erected by Drogheda Corporation on the south bank of the river Boyne.[41] Another twenty-foot-high cross was erected on the summit of Carrantuohill, Co. Kerry. Mass was celebrated on the summit, 'attended by 1,500 people who came from all parts of Kerry'.[42]

The encyclical, *Fulgens Corona* (1953), proclaimed 1954 the Marian Year, and the Irish bishops issued a statement on this at their October 1953 meeting in Maynooth, in which they urged the Irish people to profess their regard for the Blessed Virgin by erecting statues in her honour.[43] Their suggestion was enthusiastically taken up and acted upon. In parishes throughout the length and breadth of the country, grottoes and statues were erected to celebrate the Marian Year, 1954. One of the more impressive of these grottoes was built by the people of Valentia Island in Co. Kerry, on the site of a disused slate quarry.

Historically, Irish Catholics had great commitment to the rosary. Brady and Corish, in their account of the Irish Catholic Church during penal times, have pointed out that, 'after the Mass, the most marked devotion among Irish penal-day Catholics was to Our Lady',[44] and that, 'of all the Marian devotions, the rosary had pride of place with both clergy and laity'.[45] The late John Healy, growing up in Ireland in the 1940s, has described this devotion to the rosary as follows:

> There was no need for words now. The clock would strike ten. Grandma would put her sewing aside. From a nail on the wall she'd take the big Rosary beads ... we got up from our seats, knelt down with our backs to the fire and one another, leaned our elbows on the seat ... and made the responses. It was so in my mother's day and it would be so in my childhood days.[46]

The above descriptions would find echo in the experiences of many Irish Catholics who grew up during or before the 1950s.

This commitment was reinforced when the Family Rosary crusade was launched by Archbishop Walsh on 25 April 1954, in Tuam. The *ICD* described the event as follows:

> Thousands of people thronged the G.A.A. stadium ... From all over the archdiocese people were arriving all day and hundreds of motor cars lined the roads approaching the town. In Tuam ... hundreds of men, women and children ... walked in procession ... reciting the Rosary.[47]

Fr Peyton, the Irish-American 'Rosary Priest' had come to Ireland to appeal for greater devotion to the rosary. Enormous rallies were held all over the country right through the month of May, a traditional month for Marian devotions. Estimates of people attending these rallies were as follows: Galway, 30,000 people; Knock, 18,000; and Sligo, 20,000.[48] A figure 'close on 25,000' was reported as having participated in the pilgrimage to Knock on 15 August, the feast of the Assumption, in the Marian year, 1954.[49]

Another noteworthy feature of the public expression of Irish Catholicism at the time was the procession. Processions were held all over the country on Corpus Christi, and also in May. These processions normally took a route through the town or village in the country, or a route near the vicinity of the church in a city parish. They were followed by Benediction, either in the open air or in the church, depending on seasonal conditions. It was customary for householders along the processional route to decorate their houses with flags and bunting and, for the May procession, to erect altars to Our Lady (either outside their houses or in the windows), or to have a picture of the Sacred Heart displayed if it was the Corpus Christi procession.

Children who had made their First Holy Communion took part in the latter procession, dressed in their white Communion attire, and they strewed flowers in the path of the Blessed Sacrament. Here is how John McGahern describes the Corpus Christi procession in the rural village where he grew up:

> Colourful streamers and banners were strung across the roads from poles. Altars with flowers and a cross on white linen were erected at Gilligans, the post office.... The Host was taken from the tabernacle and carried beneath a gold canopy all the way around the village, pausing for ceremonies at each wayside altar. Benediction was always at the post office. The congregation followed behind, some bearing the banners of their sodalities, and girls in white veils and dresses scattered rose petals from white boxes on the path before the Host.[50]

The Marian Year procession through Dublin was particularly impressive. Tens of thousands thronged the streets of the city centre to watch the procession in which over 25,000 people were estimated to have taken part. It was described in the *ICD* as follows:

> An outstanding feature was the huge turn-out of trade union organisations. The procession which started from the Pro-Cathedral, passed through O'Connell Street, where all traffic was suspended for more than two hours as crowds twenty-deep packed the processional route ... As His Grace gave the benediction, army trumpeters sounded a royal salute which was carried over the public address system. A hush fell over the streets and the great throng knelt on the roadways. The heart of the city for that brief moment was silent in prayer.[51]

The fact that traffic and business were suspended on many such occasions in Ireland in the 1950s, and that the organisers had the co-operation and support of the civic authorities, spoke volumes about the shared meanings and level of social solidarity that existed at that time.

Recalling Pope Pius IX's observation about the Church's loss of the working classes in continental Europe, Jean Blanchard wrote that his impression of Ireland in the 1950s was that this certainly had not been the case. As a Frenchman, he was particularly interested in this aspect of Irish Catholicism. His own country at this time was referred to as *pays de mission* because of the alienation from the Church of large numbers of the working classes and the agricultural community. In 1950, describing what traditionally was a Catholic country, Fr P.J. Brophy of St Patrick's Diocesan College, Carlow, pointed out that: 'today France has a population of some forty millions, but less than a tenth of that number go to Mass regularly or perform their Easter Duties'.[52] The work of Abbé Godin and the worker priest movement in France, to try to re-Christianise the masses, was publicised through his book, *France pagan? The Mission of Abbé Godin* (1949), translated by Maisie Ward.[53]

An aspect of French culture and indeed Western European culture in general in the post-war era was the growth of communism, socialism and the social democratic movement and various strains thereof. There was no parallel development in Ireland, partly because of its isolated geographical position and neutrality during the Second World War. Blanchard observed:

> The family life of Irish Catholic workers and employees, with few exceptions, is steeped in Catholicism.... The majority of them support the national parties, rather than the Labour Party.... International Marxism has very little influence on the workers.[54]

In 1954, Paul Blanshard, who was unabashedly anti-Catholic, was constrained to admit that 'the Catholic Church is the Church of the Irish masses, and its hold upon those masses appears at this moment to be beyond challenge'.[55] Speaking of the Labour Party of the time, he observed that it was 'just as pro-clerical as any party in the government'.[56] It is not difficult to understand how both of these contemporary writers, Jean Blanchard and Paul Blanshard, despite coming from perspectives which could be fairly described as polar opposites, should have drawn similar conclusions when trade-union organisations and factory workers were prominently represented in the devotional activities described above. The following examples serve to illustrate this.

On 29 October 1950, a delegation representing the Workers Union of Ireland went on the Holy Year pilgrimage to Rome.[57] There were many 'industrial tributes' to Our Lady leading up to and during the Marian Year. Many factory workers erected shrines in her honour. One such was a statue of Our Lady Queen of Peace erected by CIE employees at the Broadstone station in Dublin.[58]

Several other 'industrial tributes' were recorded at the time, among them that of the workers of Sunbeam Wolsey Ltd, of Cork, numbering over 2,000 workers.[59] The factory of General Textiles Ltd, Athlone, of more than 700 workers, held a tribute on 10 May 1954.[60] Another was held in the foundry of Tonge and Taggart at Windmill Lane, Dublin, on 13 May,[61] and the employees of Foxford Woollen Mills were reported in the *Irish Independent* of 12 May 1954 as being *en fête*, when the newspaper recorded their tribute to Our Lady and the holding of solemn benediction at the mill chapel. Each of these Masses was celebrated by the local bishop.

The staff of the *Irish Independent* newspaper erected a wooden statue of Our Lady (called Our Lady of Dublin) in honour of the Marian year. The statue had a prominent position in the window of the library. It was customary for night staff to say the rosary in front of the statue at midnight. The statue was on a rotating base, so it could be turned inwards while the rosary was being recited. In the course of more recent renovations, a new bay window was built, from which position the statue now looks out over the newspaper offices.

It was not uncommon for gifts to be sent from Ireland to be presented to the Holy Father. In the *ICD*'s diary of ecclesiastical events for 1 May 1951, the following entry occurs:

> The warm gratitude of the Holy Father for the gift of chalice and ciborium has been conveyed in a letter from the Vatican Secretariat of State to Mr C. Noonan, National Treasurer, Irish Bakers, Confectioners and Allied Workers Amalgamated Union.[62]

On 10 April 1951, it was recorded that a letter was received by the Secretary of the Congress of Irish Unions, from Monsignor Montini, Substitute Papal Secretary of State and future Pope Paul VI, acknowledging the address of homage and chasuble presented to Pope Pius XII during the Holy Year, in the name of the workers of Ireland. The letter read as follows:

> At a time when so many of the workers of various countries have fallen prey to false theories and ideologies that are in direct contrast to the Christian religion, it was a source of particular gratification to His Holiness to receive this further proof of the devoted attachment of the workers of Ireland to the Vicar of Christ, and to their fidelity to the Catholic Faith, which is their nation's most precious heritage.[63]

This was the impression of Ireland held in Rome in the early 1950s — of a country which had preserved a purity of faith in the face of persecution and famine, a country loyal to Rome, in which the combined might of the apparatus of Church and state was exercised in keeping at bay the kind of modern influences that were perceived as undermining the Christian heritage. Irish prelates felt that they were indeed lucky and had good reason to be proud, and they were the envy of their European counterparts.

The fact that much of continental Europe was seen as having succumbed to the false prophets of materialism, secularism and communism made Ireland all the more attractive. Monsignor Montini was here portraying the mood of Catholicism as felt at its headquarters. The Church felt under siege by the forces of modernity which were all around it. He was re-echoing the kind of fears which were being voiced time and again by Pope Pius XII in his encyclicals and many pronouncements during his pontificate (1939–58). The Irish bishops in their pastoral letters of the time were preoccupied with the same concerns, as will be seen later. Ireland was an oasis of the faith which had to be preserved at all costs from corrupt influences. It is unlikely that many would have questioned Dr James Devane's opinion when he described Ireland as: 'the most Catholic country in the world. Perhaps the Republic of Ireland, as it is constituted today, is the only integral Catholic state in the world; a Catholic culture as it existed in the Middle Ages.'[64]

Ireland's spiritual heritage and her far-flung spiritual empire as a result of her missionary activity across the world were images constantly evoked by prelates to reassure themselves and to inspire the laity. Fr Edward Long, assessing Irish piety in 1950, observed that the 'faith and piety of our people are unquestioned'. Two good pointers to the state of the religious health of Ireland were, in his estimation, vocations to the religious life and the missionary effort. Of the latter, he was happy that 'their sound has gone forth to the ends of the earth'.[65]

But lest one be over-hasty in coming to the conclusion that these prelates may have been complacent, it is well to remember that these impressions were confirmed and, of course, reinforced in their minds by outside observers. The impressions of an Austrian priest who had visited Ireland in the autumn of 1947 were recorded in the *Furrow* in 1950, by Fr Seán O'Riordan CSsR. He was very impressed by the priests' closeness to the people. He had been to Croke Park where he 'saw priests every where ... mixing and talking with the crowd'. Like Blanchard, he too commented on the bishop throwing in the ball. Writing for his Austrian readers in *Die Furche*, he observed that 'it is still the glory of every Irish family to have a son ordained to the priesthood.[66] By comparison, he added, he 'could not help feeling rather sorry for "Catholic Austria"'.

In the same year, Archbishop P.J.B. McKeefrey of New Zealand recorded his impressions of Ireland. He saw it as 'a land of faith ... a faith that permeates every phase of personal, social and national life. It could be seen every moment of the day, be it in Church, on a street car....' He was struck with the salutations he and 'countless other priests' received continually on O'Connell Street, how eager people were to pay their respects to the priesthood and he regarded himself as 'privileged to live for a short time in an atmosphere impregnated with the faith'.[67]

Despite the glowing reports of the high level of religious practice, and the mixture of complacency and triumphalism it engendered in the Irish Church, there was, however, a growing feeling in some quarters, even in the 1950s, that Irish Catholicism left something to be desired. A Catholic clerical intelligentsia was beginning to emerge which was casting a somewhat critical eye on Irish piety and the model of church such as it existed at that time. Two new journals provided mouthpieces for the new, more critical, thinking that was emerging in the Irish Church. The *Furrow* began publication monthly from 1950, and *Doctrine and Life* was published from 1951. The thinking which served as a reference point and set the tone for these two journals did not, on the whole, harmonise with the adulatory mood of the accounts of Irish Catholicism, as recorded above.

The *Furrow* was founded in 1950 by Dr J.G. McGarry, professor of Sacred Eloquence and Pastoral Theology at St Patrick's College, Maynooth. The role of the *Furrow*, its influence and the circumstances of its foundation will be elaborated on further in Chapter 6. *Doctrine and Life*, a Dominican publication, started life as part of the *Irish Rosary* in September 1946, and was first published as a separate review in February 1951. Fr Anselm Moynihan was the founding editor. He was succeeded by Fr Austin Flannery in 1957. It was published every two months until January 1961, when it became a monthly publication.

In the first issue of *Doctrine and Life*, the then provincial of the Dominicans, Very Rev. Thomas E. Garde, saw the aim of the journal as being that of initiating people into a deeper understanding of their faith and its implications.[68] He recognised the fact that many people might query the need for such a magazine 'given the obvious faith of the Irish people'.[69] But he was not so complacent in regard to this, and he expressed concern that many people were losing the faith because they had 'never really grasped it. They never fully understood its implications. It never became for them a deep personal conviction'.[70] The ideal behind the journal was to cultivate a more doctrinally based spirituality. McGarry echoed Garde's sentiments, when he was reviewing the first edition of *Doctrine and Life.* He referred to 'our prevailing spiritual climate' and its 'lack of sound foundation and substance, evidenced — to name but one sign — in the popular rating of devotional publications'. He went on to point out the 'general need for a spiritual life founded more securely on doctrine', drawing attention to Pope Benedict's cautionary advice against a 'soft and empty kind of piety'.[71]

In order to understand the critical comments made by Garde and McGarry in the context of the time in which they were made, it is necessary to reflect briefly on the kind of religious publications that were available at that time. The Catholic Truth Society of Ireland was founded in 1899, as a propaganda outlet to promote Catholic truth, by means of small pamphlets on devotional and all manner of related subjects. There is no better way of capturing the mood of Irish Catholicism during the 1950s and 1960s than by perusing a selection of titles of CTSI publications, included in Appendix F of this book. For the most part, the pamphlets were concerned with giving information and advice about moral issues, and defending the faith, and they were written in a simple, direct style, geared to a readership whose understanding of their faith was simple and unsophisticated.

Such titles as *What to Do on a Date* and *What Not to Do on a Date* and *Temptations: Having Them and Being Them*, by Daniel Lord SJ, one of the most well-known and prolific of writers of religious books at the time, conjure up an era which was innocent and much less complicated — an era when the whole area of sexuality was viewed with great caution, not to say suspicion. They give an insight into the kind of concerns and the type of piety that typified Irish Catholicism in the 1950s and the early 1960s.

Lewis, who carried out research based on a sample group of Irish Catholics in 1961–2, has evidenced the fact that the most popular religious magazines among this group were the missionary magazines, the *Far East*, *Africa* and *African Missions.* Apart from specifically missionary magazines, he found that the most popular publication was the *Irish Messenger of the Sacred Heart*, founded by Fr James Cullen SJ, in 1888.[72] Lewis found that, whereas the missionary magazines tended to be bought to help the missions, and because children brought them home from school, the *Messenger* was 'more read than the other books'.[73] The *Messenger* was strongly associated with devotion to the Sacred

Heart, which was very popular in Ireland.[74] Hartigan, in his study of the religious life of the Catholic laity of Dublin in the period from 1920 to 1940, has pointed to the strength of this devotion during that period, and this was no different in the 1950s.[75]

The Jesuits promoted this devotion through the Apostleship of Prayer which they encouraged in the magazine. The Apostleship of Prayer to the Sacred Heart for special intentions was begun in 1844, at Vals in France, by Father Gautrelet SJ. By 1863, it had arrived in Ireland and, with the publication of the *Messenger* from 1888, it spread rapidly. Also associated with devotion to the Sacred Heart was the cult of the Nine First Fridays. Devotees of this cult were encouraged to go to confession and Holy Communion on the first Friday of nine consecutive months.

The *Messenger*, as in the case of the CTSI publications, gives a unique insight into the popular piety of the day. Apart from the devotional material of the magazine, the sections of most interest in this regard are those which contained readers' letters of thanksgiving for favours received, and another section called 'Question Box', in which very specific queries relating to issues of religious belief, practice and morality were answered.

The following entry appeared in the January 1951 issue of the *Messenger*:

> Please publish in your *Messenger* my grateful thanks to the Sacred Heart for a very special favour obtained whereby a child baptised in the Catholic faith was saved from being placed in non-Catholic hands. I frequently repeated the ejaculation, 'Sacred Heart of Jesus, I place all my trust in thee' and promised publication if my request was granted. One who trusts in the Sacred Heart.[76]

In the same issue, a further 283 favours were acknowledged. Among them were the following: 'Brother takes pledge. Religious vocation. Grace of a good confession after three years ... Conversion of husband to the faith ... Son ordained to the priesthood ... Resignation to loss of child ... Brother-in-law becomes Catholic on death-bed ... Happy deaths for 9 persons.'[77]

The following are some of the questions addressed to the 'Question Box' in some of the issues of the magazine in the 1950s:

> Is it wrong to go on a long journey on Sunday?
> [Answer] No, certainly not, so long as it does not interfere with the proper observance of the Sunday, particularly the hearing of Mass.[78]

> Is the wearing of a head-scarf proper in the church?
> [Answer] St Paul, in the early days of the Church, insisted that women should be covered in church, and this has always been the law of the Church. There does not seem to be any reason why the modern head-scarf should not suffice ...[79]

Is it right to say the Rosary in bed?
[Answer] It cannot honestly be recommended as a practice, except for invalids ... For people in the enjoyment of full health, it is hardly reverent, and they are very liable to fall asleep in the middle of it.[80]

Further examples of questions sent in to the *Messenger* in the 1950s included 'Can a person hear Mass properly without seeing the Altar?'[81] 'Is it a sin to omit one's morning prayers?'[82] 'I think the priest did not quite understand me in my last confession and I am worried, should I repeat this confession?'[83] 'I took a relic out of its case in order to touch it to an afflicted part of my body, did I commit a sin?'[84] These random examples of both thanksgiving letters and queries reflect the mood and spirit of popular piety at that time. What is important is that they reflect a religious mentality. They also beg the question — to what extent was this type of religious attitude encouraged and reinforced by the official Church?

This question is readily answered by an examination of the *Irish Ecclesiastical Record.* First published in 1864, the *Record* was under episcopal sanction and, as such, was an official organ of the Irish Church. A scholarly journal, published monthly, its articles in the main dealt with esoteric themes in ecclesiastical history. Until the arrival of the *Furrow* and *Doctrine and Life,* the *IER* held pride of place among intellectual Catholic publications. This place, of course, was shared by *Studies,* a quarterly, founded by the Jesuits in 1912. *Studies* was well established by the 1950s, publishing articles on philosophical, artistic, literary, political and sociological themes. It was highly regarded and influential in more educated circles, for its incisive and sometimes provocative critique of political and sociocultural issues. While religious topics and perspectives were also aired, they did not provide the main focus of the periodical. In the context of an examination of Catholic culture, what is of most interest in the *IER* is the 'Notes and Queries' section. It could be seen as the clerical equivalent to the 'Question Box' section of the *Messenger.* In this section, queries were sent in by priests, under pseudonyms, to experts in the areas of canon law, liturgy and moral theology. The latter examined the question in the light of the precepts of canon law, promulgated in 1917, and the local Maynooth statutes, drafted by the plenary Council of Maynooth in 1956.

Known as casuistry, this was a practice whereby experts applied general ethical principles to particular cases of conduct or conscience. Whereas the *ICD* and newspapers of the day provide examples of reportage of the events and rituals of Catholic life, a perusal of the 'Notes and Queries' section of the *IER* provides the cultural historian with a deeper insight into some of those rituals, their influence on people's lives and, more importantly, an insight into the mind and thinking of the official Church at that time. In almost every edition of the *IER* in the 1950s, there were queries in relation to indulgences. Because there was such a multiplicity of indulgences available, there was often some confusion as to the conditions attaching to them. This was particularly the case when more than one indulgence could be gained, for instance on a feast day, thereby causing an overlap in the conditions. A query was addressed to Fr J. McCarthy in the 1953 edition of the *IER*, by a priest calling himself '*Clericus*':

> Rev. Dear Sir, A plenary indulgence under the usual conditions may be gained once a month by the carrying out of a great many daily exercises, ejaculations etc. According to the *Raccolta* the phrase 'under the usual conditions' implies Confession and Holy Communion, a visit to a church ... and praying for the intentions of the Holy Father.... Assuming that one is entitled, by reason of performing a number of these daily exercises, to receive many of these Plenary indulgences once a month, is one required to make a separate Confession, a separate Holy Communion, a separate visit to a church and a separate Pater, Ave and Gloria for each Plenary indulgence?[85]

Fr McCarthy answered in considerable detail, taking each of the '*suetae conditiones*' in turn. Broadly speaking, his reply was that, provided confession was made within the octave before or after the day to which the indulgence was attached, it was not necessary to repeat it. A separate reception of Communion might be necessary unless 'all the pious exercises and the other necessary conditions were fulfilled on the same day'.[86] But he pointed out that there was no exception to the rule in regard to the other customary conditions: 'The visit to a church ... must be repeated separately for each indulgence'. The practice already pointed out above, whereby people left the church and re-entered it in order to comply with the rules, may be better understood in the context of his explanation:

> This does not mean that a separate journey must be made to the church. Several visits can be made on one and the same occasion by leaving the church and re-entering it.[87]

He pointed out that, likewise, the prayers for the Pope's intentions also had to be repeated separately for the gaining of each indulgence. The importance of such a question and the answer given has to do with the insight it gives into an aspect of Irish Catholicism which had become a way of life at that time. The concern to qualify so precisely the ritual to be performed bordered on the obsessional. There was a sense in which everything was measured out and quantified, and that if one knew the rules and fulfilled the exact conditions, all was well. But if one defaulted on any of the rules or conditions, all was perceived as lost, and this led to scrupulosity and obsessive fears. The anxiety on the part of clerics and laity to fulfil the letter of the law may be better understood on perusal of the general conditions required for all indulgences in the *Raccolta*, where, under the heading of accuracy, it was pointed out that 'too much stress cannot be laid on the importance of *carefully noting* and *exactly fulfilling* all that may be required for gaining a particular Indulgence'[88] (original emphasis).

The teaching on indulgences gave rise to a mentality whereby some people felt that they could, as it were, 'collect' spiritual favours. Of course, it is important to bear in mind that this was universal Roman Catholic Church teaching at that time, and not just Irish Church teaching. Dolan has pointed to the growing popularity of devotional Catholicism in America in the thirty years after the First World War. The features he has identified as typifying the Catholic ethos are identical to those which have been pointed out here, as, for instance, Marian and Eucharistic processions, the cult of indulgences, Marian devotions, sodalities, novenas, benediction, parish missions and pilgrimages.[89]

Because many devotional practices involved the repetition of prayers, or activities for a quantified period of time, or number of times, many people got caught up in fulfilling these obligations and missed out on the spirit of the devotion. For many, the carrying out of these activities took on the nature of magical formulae and became somewhat compulsive. Many popular devotional cults such as the Nine First Fridays, the Five First Saturdays, the Thirty Days Prayer and the Forty Hours devotion left themselves open to misunderstanding. The same applied to novenas which involved Mass, or prayers, or both, for a specified number of times, or over a specified period of time. Reflecting on similar aspects of the American Catholic experience, Dolan has pointed to the fact that the 'ritualised nature of the novena, which included the repetition of a set formula of prayers over a prescribed period of time, not only reinforced the sense of ritual, but it also gave it a very magical quality'.[90]

An example of this approach to spirituality was the tradition that existed in Dublin of visiting the Altar of Repose in seven churches on Holy Thursday. How seriously this custom was adhered to is, perhaps, nowhere as tellingly evoked as in Austin Clarke's book, *Twice Round the Black Church,* in which he recounts some of his early memories of Dublin.[91] The author recalls his excitement on Holy Thursday when his sister was 'taking [him] with her to visit seven churches according to the pious custom which was peculiar to Dublin...' and how they 'would have to be home at seven to give their mother an opportunity of visiting as many churches in the neighbourhood as she could'.[92]

The same type of mentality manifested itself in a concern among many as to how far one could go before something was sinful. For instance, in the event of being late for Mass on Sunday or a holy day of obligation, a point often discussed was at what point of lateness one was deemed not to have fulfilled one's obligation, thus committing sin. This type of concern is evidenced by a query sent in by a teacher to the liturgist in the *IER* as late as 1962. A visiting priest had told children in school that 'they were bound, under pain of mortal sin, to be present, on Sundays and Holy days of Obligation, at the Offertory, Consecration and Communion of the same Mass',[93] and the teacher sought clarification as to the correctness of this. Fr Aegidus Doolan OP replied that 'according to nearly all theologians, there is a grave obligation to assist at the double Consecration and at the Communion of the same Mass'.[94] But, he went on to explain:

> If one does this, it is sufficient, to fulfil one's obligation, to assist at another Mass for the part that was missed. If, for instance, a person came very late to Mass but was present for the beginning of the Canon and waited on to the end of Mass, it would be sufficient for him, to fulfil his obligation under sin, to be present at another Mass as far as the 'Sanctus'.[95]

According to the first commandment of the Church, people are bound to attend Mass on Sunday and Holy Days of Obligation, under pain of mortal sin. The question then arose as to what the position was in the event of being late. At a time when the fear of committing mortal sin was so great, the position had to be strictly clarified, and this led, as in the above case, to the stipulation of the minimum requirements necessary to fulfil one's obligation. Because there was little emphasis on the Liturgy of the Word in the pre-conciliar era, the teaching at that time was that if one was in before the Offertory, while technically late, one was deemed to have fulfilled one's obligation. This shifted the focus of attention on to the Canon of the Mass, in particular the Consecration. A practice which grew out of this was that many people left the church before, during, or after Communion, before the Last Gospel. It led, for many people, to what might be termed a minimalist, and thereby impoverished, understanding of the experience of the Mass.

The law in relation to fast and abstinence at this time was very strictly interpreted and enforced. Again, the same kind of thinking and concern with exactitude is revealed in a query in 1951, regarding the permissibility of using dripping made from suet, as opposed to lard, as a condiment during Lent. The writer of the letter pointed out that there was 'great confusion among priests as to whether dripping of all kinds is allowed as a condiment on a day of abstinence'.[96] While many of these queries, both in the *IER* and in the *Messenger*, might seem trivial to the present-day mind, they represented very serious concerns to the priests and people of the time, because the emphasis on keeping rules was so great, and the fear of the consequences of not doing so was even greater.

This legalistic approach was also applied to general moral issues. The moral question was judged and pronounced upon in the minutest details, divorced from its human context, giving rise to the impression that there were specific hard and fast rules, which could be applied whatever the moral dilemma one was confronted with, be it grave or trivial. It bespoke an attitude to morality which was more concerned with the letter than the spirit of the law. Morality was reduced to rule-following. Because the rules were so many and so detailed, they engendered scrupulosity in many. People sought reassurance on how far exactly they could go without committing sin. At a time when people had an inordinate fear of committing sin and being damned for all eternity, this led them to hand over responsibility for their moral decisions to the professionals — the clergy — and they, in turn, in particularly difficult cases consulted the experts. This allowed little scope for the development in people of an informed conscience or moral maturity.

Given that there were so many laws, human nature being what it is, people could not help breaking them. Rather than questioning a law that might be outdated or consistently broken, and perhaps abandoning it, what moral theologians in this tradition did was to devise clever ways of accommodating the miscreants, so that they could, in fact, on a technicality, get around the law and not commit a sin. The law was paramount — it had to stay in place. The kind of situation that this led to can best be illustrated by way of example.

In 1950 a query was addressed to Fr William Conway (later Cardinal Archbishop of Armagh and Primate of all Ireland), the canon law expert in the *IER*, by a priest calling himself '*Per Alium*'. It related to the Maynooth Statute 46:1 which inflicted '*ipso facto* suspension on priests who place a bet ... with a bookmaker — either *per se* or *per alium*', meaning that a priest could neither place a bet nor have somebody else place it for him.[97] To evade this regulation, the priest would place the bet with a friend (not a bookmaker) who would give him the odds. The friend would then 'lay off' the bet with a bookmaker, so that he would not incur the loss. While this may have been the implicit understanding, it was not made explicit, and thus the priest was infringing neither the *per se* nor the *per alium* rule.[98]

The priest writing in to Fr Conway wanted to know whether, in this kind of case, a priest would incur suspension if 'he gives money to a friend for a bet, knowing that the friend will save himself by putting it on with a bookmaker'.[99] Fr Conway replied that the censure is incurred only when the second party is acting for the priest. It is not incurred, 'if a priest makes a betting contract with a friend and if the friend subsequently makes a separate and distinct betting contract with the bookmaker'. He goes on to explain that 'this remains true even though the priest is aware that the subsequent contract will take place; mere knowledge of this kind will not of itself link the two contracts together'.[100]

Theologians in this tradition in effect made a fine art out of identifying the loopholes in the law, which would let people 'off the hook', so to speak. There is no evidence in the *IER* to indicate that the casuistic approach, with its emphasis on law and rules of behaviour (and the minimal requirements of these laws for avoiding sin), was being increasingly questioned by continental theologians at this time. This questioning led to a radically different approach to theology in the 1960s, but there was little in the *IER* in the 1950s, and indeed into the 1960s, which prepared Irish people for the change. In general, the journal could be said to typify a legalistic model of church which still reigned supreme among Irish Catholics.

3

SOCIAL CHANGE: The Influence of the Communications Media and Emigration

The Irish Catholic ethos, as described thus far, had experienced very little change in the first half of the twentieth century. The fact that Ireland was neutral during the Second World War meant that Irish society did not participate in the sweeping changes which influenced post-war Britain and continental Europe. Moreover, the rigid censorship policy which had been in force since the 1920s ensured that Irish society would be further insulated from such changes, in terms of both new ideas and social and economic developments. Favoured by Catholic Church authorities and politicians alike, it was expressly designed to protect Irish Catholics from secularist or corrupting influences emanating from abroad. Notwithstanding this, change was taking place gradually. Ironically, the growing popularity of the cinema in the 1940s and 1950s[1] was one of the factors which played a significant role in bringing about change in Irish society, and thus in Catholic culture. In 1934, there were 190 cinemas in the Republic, and 18,250,000 admissions; by 1954, when cinema's popularity peaked, annual admissions totalled 54,100,000.[2]

The Censorship of Films Act of 1923 gave a film censor the power to cut or refuse a licence to films which, in his opinion, were subversive of public morality. The film censor had considerable power, as no film could be shown without a certificate from the censor. More often than not, the method of censorship employed was the rather crude one of cutting out passages seen as objectionable, with little sensitivity towards the artistic integrity of the film.

In 1929, the Censorship of Publications Act provided for a censorship board of five people with power to prohibit the sale and distribution of any book or periodical that it considered to be indecent in its general tendency. In practice, the way that it worked was that anybody who considered a book in any way objectionable could send it, with the offending passage indicated, to the board, for consideration. As in the case of films, the offensive material was, more often than not, focused on, to the neglect of the literary and artistic merit of the book as a whole. As a result, some of the most celebrated figures of modern literature featured on the list of banned authors — Steinbeck, Greene, Gide, Hemingway, Sartre, to name but a few, and, of course, many Irish writers also, among them Frank O'Connor, Kate O'Brien and Sean O'Faolain.

Despite the far-reaching scope of the censorship laws, neither bishops nor many of the clergy were satisfied as to their effectiveness. The bishops were particularly wary of the growth of the communications media and their vast potential to influence Irish Catholics. In their pastoral letters, there were numerous references to the dangers of 'evil literature', the foreign press and films, and the necessity that people be shielded from their corrupting influences. Reference to a number of pastoral letters in the 1950s serves to illustrate the point.

Bishop Dignan of Clonfert, in his pastoral letter of 1950, lamented the sale year after year 'of millions of immoral magazines, books and novels imported from countries that have lost the faith'.[3] In 1955, Bishop Roche of Cloyne lamented the fact:

> that the cinema which could be a wonderful source of instruction and amusement is so much used as a mere means of commercial gain with an appeal only to the lower instincts of human nature.[4]

Bishop Rodgers of Killaloe observed that 'modern literature is often wholly pagan', and that 'modern cinema shows and drama often openly flout the most sacred laws of Catholic life'.[5] Bishop O'Neill of Limerick spoke of 'the philosophy of Materialism or Naturalism which permeated most of what was presented on the cinema-screen or through the newer medium of television'. He went on to speak of a 'class of writers' at home who 'seemed to deny or disregard the fact and the effects of original sin' and 'who thought that the literary gifts they possessed entitled them to pose as philosophers', and who 'seized every opportunity to sneer at the doctrines and practices of the Church'.[6]

While the concerns of the bishops were reiterated in their pastoral letters, the fears of many of the general clergy were echoed in the pages of the *Furrow* in the 1950s. They provide a unique insight into the simplicity of life in Ireland, on the one hand, but, on the other, the fact that what some regarded as undesirable influences were beginning to percolate through, by means of foreign newspapers, radio, cinema and BBC television, which was available along much of the east coast. In 1950, Fr Christopher Walsh of Cork expressed concern about 'the demand among our people for foreign publications'.[7] Publications like the *News of the World*, though 'officially banned', were finding their way to the remotest corners of the country,[8] and he was concerned as to their influence on 'religious and moral life', and the 'serious danger' they constituted 'to members of the flock'.[9]

While Radio Éireann was, generally speaking, reflective of the Catholic ethos in the 1950s,[10] some priests were concerned about the corrupting influence of some of the songs being played on the airwaves. Fr Thomas Halton of Kilnaleck, Co. Cavan, writing in 1952, turned his attention to the dangers of contemporary song, which was 'alarmingly preoccupied with the sensuous delights of love'. While 'the crudity of physical description' that marred so much 'present-day writing' was absent, nonetheless he was worried about the 'unmistakable suggestiveness' of some songs.[11] Reassured, on the one hand, that much of this was often lost on the people of Ireland, 'because of the comparative simplicity of [the] way of life', nevertheless he went on to express concern that there were some examples of 'blatant vulgarity' which created problems for the moralist. He cited, by way of example, hit songs like 'A Penny a Kiss, a Penny a Hug' and 'My Resistance is Low' — songs that were liable to be sung on the way home from the dance.[12] The latter song was problematic because, in the struggle between virtue and vice, the latter won out. Fr Halton saw:

> a danger that song-writers are engaged on a deliberate process of breaking down the barriers of reticence, and that enemies of the church are using contemporary song as an instrument for the propagation of immorality.[13]

While he felt that the process was slow, he also felt that they were undoubtedly 'making some progress'.[14]

Two years later, similar sentiments were echoed by Fr Edward Flynn of St Finian's College, Mullingar, who spoke of the 'downright demoralising' music being broadcast by Radio Éireann, particularly on sponsored programmes.[15] Many of the songs, Fr Flynn pointed out, were suggestively erotic, and much of the music emanated from Harlem, Hollywood or Tin Pan Alley. For this reason, he was anxious that some control be imposed on the kind of entertainment that advertisers were presenting for public consumption.[16]

A particular concern in the 1950s was the growing popularity of Radio Luxembourg, a popular music channel broadcasting in English. A survey published in the *Standard* of 22 January 1954 had revealed that Radio Luxembourg commanded a larger evening audience in Ireland than did either Radio Éireann or the BBC. The report stated that 'about one in three of the population over sixteen tune in to Luxembourg at some time during the evening'.[17] Commenting on this in the *Furrow* in 1954, Fr Edward Flynn lamented the resulting lowering of 'the cultural and artistic standards of the people'.[18]

The cultural impact of Radio Luxembourg, which began broadcasting in 1933, was enormous. It gave the young generation growing up in the 1950s in Ireland access to the 'rock and roll' culture of America. It was to lay the foundations of an alternative youth culture, which would, in time, find expression in new terms like the 'generation gap' and 'teenagers'. While the fears that these writers were expressing may sound quaint to the contemporary mind, the writers were, in their own way, discerning that music would, in the not-too-distant future, become a potent force in the making of culture. Given how ubiquitous 'pop' music increasingly became, music did, in fact, play a significant role in challenging attitudes and breaking down taboos which often had a religious base.

Fr Gerard Herbert, writing in the *Furrow* in 1950, observed that the glamour world of Hollywood was impressed on the mind of the 'country-lad' equally by films and the Sunday newspaper. Noting that 'the cinema is the continuation school for most of our young Irish workers', he advised that priests should be aware of 'the work done by films in Ireland in the cause of cultural imperialism'.[19] Writing on films, in the *Furrow* in 1954, Fr J.K. Dempsey of Skerries, Co. Dublin, gave the statistics for cinema attendance in the Republic. It was estimated that 965,000 people in the twenty-six counties attended the cinema each week.[20] On that basis, he pointed to the importance of taking cognisance of the cinema, as 'a profoundly potent force in moulding the minds and the lives of our people'. In general, these writers were highlighting the fact that Ireland, despite its rigid censorship, had become much more open to outside influences, which the Church viewed as undesirable.

Another factor which influenced Irish Catholic culture from the early 1950s was the fact that people in Dublin and along much of the east coast were able to receive BBC television programmes. Referring to the controversy which surrounded two documentaries relayed on BBC — one on prostitution and the other on homosexuality — Eithne Conway, the *Furrow* television critic, writing in 1958, was concerned about 'the repercussions of B.B.C. transmissions on moral and religious issues'.[21] She referred to 'the menace of television' and the distressing effect on young minds of the 'immodest dress' worn by some lady panel members and the 'embarrassing close-ups in the love scenes of many of the plays'. She remarked that while such things were commonplace in films shown in cinemas throughout the country, the problem became more acute when it was introduced into 'the last refuge and stronghold of Christian principles, the hearths and homes of the nation'.[22]

Her remarks are interesting in view of the fact that less than ten years later, very frank discussion on all manner of hitherto taboo, or delicate, topics was taking place on the native Irish television station (as will be considered in Chapter 9). In 1958, Conway looked forward to the evangelical role that an Irish television station could play, if it was capable of reaching the English public.[23] Sentiments of this kind were often expressed at that time by bishops and clergy, in particular in relation to the kind of witness to the faith that emigrants could be in 'pagan England'. Conway felt that such a television channel could 'yet prove the most powerful influence in a new age of missionary endeavour in the "*pays de mission*" which lies so close to our shores'.[24]

The thinking of bishops, priests and writers on such issues must be placed in the context of universal Catholic teaching as enunciated in papal encyclicals, addresses and statements. The Catholic Church had been concerned throughout the ages to protect its followers from material which was considered hazardous to faith and morals. The above-mentioned writers were doing no more than echoing that concern. Pius XI in his encyclical, *Vigilanti Cura*, addressed to the bishops of the US in 1936, pointed out that 'there does not exist today a means more potent than the cinema for influencing the masses'.[25] As the cinema industry began to expand and become more sophisticated, Pope Pius XII made it the subject of numerous addresses throughout the 1950s. In a speech he made to a group from the International Congress of Catholic Publishers, quoted in the *Furrow* in 1951, the Pope was concerned that '[the cinema] carries with it such a danger of intellectual decadence that already one begins to consider it a danger for all people'.[26]

Anticipating the growth of the new medium and the impact it would have, Archbishop McQuaid of Dublin established the National Film Institute in Dublin in 1943. The role of the Institute was to educate and guide Irish Catholics in their response to the film medium. The idea was to help people to enjoy films and, at the same time, to counter the more adverse effects of the medium.[27]

Both Pius XI and Pius XII were aware that cinema, of its very nature, would have far more universal appeal than either literature or radio, and that because of the immediacy of its images, it could exert a powerful influence on the minds and hearts of the young. The dilemma for the Church was that such an influential medium very often projected a philosophy of life which ran counter to Catholic beliefs. Speaking to representatives of the cinematographic industry in Italy in 1955, Pope Pius XII spoke of the film's ability 'to uplift or degrade men' and 'to produce good or spread evil',[28] which meant, in his view, that it was 'most certainly right for public authority to exercise a due intervention to hinder or check the most dangerous influences'.[29]

A problem to which he continually returned was that of presenting evil on the screen. While he allowed that the 'ideal film can also represent evil, sin and corruption', he cautioned that, in doing so, it:

> should flee from any form of apology, much less of glorification, of evil, and should show its condemnation through the entire course of the film and not merely at the end.[30]

Pope Pius XII was filled with alarm at the potentially destructive impact that the screen could have, not only on the Catholic way of life, but presumably on human life in general. One of the last encyclicals he issued was on motion pictures, radio and television — *Miranda Prorsus* on 8 September 1957.[31] He was also concerned with what he referred to in 1956, addressing an audience of book critics, as the 'overflowing tide of useless literature' and its corrupting influence.[32] So, when the Irish bishops and priests were expressing concern in relation to the evil or corrupting influence of cinema or television, they were doing no more than echoing fears that were being expressed by the popes over the years — in fact, the very idiom they used resembled closely that of Pius XII. Nor were such fears confined to Ireland and the Irish bishops.

On 1 October 1955, the bishops of Germany issued a pastoral letter on 'Contemporary Catholic literature'. They referred to the fact that modern writers tended to be chiefly concerned with the negative side of life.[33] Echoing the Pope, they were anxious that 'the depiction of man in his struggle with evil' should 'not displace nor obscure the standards of the God-given moral laws'. They went on to point out that 'the impression may not be permitted in the reader that man is irretrievably and hopelessly at the mercy of those dark instincts which he must fight'.[34] So, the idea that people must be protected and, as it were, saved from themselves was not unique to the Irish bishops. A common theme running through the discourse of all of these writers, from Fr Thomas Halton to Pope Pius XII, from the Irish bishops to the German bishops, was that people had to be protected from ideas and images that could corrupt.

In an era of mass communications, newspapers, radio, cinema and television provided ready access to a wide variety of ideas, and people could pick and choose freely what they would give allegiance to. Church authorities in general were worried because many of these ideas were at variance with Christian teaching. It was becoming increasingly difficult to shield people from ideas that the Church saw as detrimental to the common good. The bishops had little faith in people's judgement or their ability to discern things for themselves. Their approach was paternalistic, and they issued to their followers very precise rules of conduct. Given the new influences coming to bear on Irish Catholics, the bishops were concerned that they might be less influenced by traditional values and the teaching of the Church when making decisions about the conduct of their lives.

Another factor which was bringing about considerable sociocultural change in Ireland in the 1940s and 1950s was the increasing volume of emigration and migration from rural areas to Dublin. The shift in the balance of population from country to town, which was considerable by 1951, accelerated during the 1950s. A review of the statistical data and the analysis and conclusions arising from the Censuses of 1946, 1951 and 1956 presents a very clear view of this trend.[35] (See Appendices D, E, F and G.) The lessening hold of traditional values, observed by sociologists in more urbanised societies, was at its very beginning. This was borne out by Fr Alexander Humphreys SJ, a sociologist doing field work in Dublin in 1949–51. Fr Humphreys was conducting his research among 'new Dubliners', whose parents had been born and raised in rural Ireland. Among his sample of twenty-nine artisan families, he found evidence of some contrast in attitudes between the older and younger generation. He found that the younger generation, who had been born and raised in the city, were less submissive and were more ready to criticise the clergy than were their immigrant parents.[36]

Even in rural Ireland at that time, there was evidence to suggest that people's attitudes were changing. In the early 1940s O'Faolain referred to a 'new jostling spirit' in 'the wholesale exodus from the countryside'. He observed that 'men are leaving home who were content enough to stay hitherto'.[37] In his estimation, even then, Ireland was 'feeling the full force of the cold blast of social change'.[38] He saw it as having to do with a 'physical dissatisfaction' likely to have been inspired by 'the movies, which have now penetrated to the smallest villages'. But he also saw in it 'the seed of ambition', which 'is dynamite'. The results of this, he forecast, 'will show themselves slowly enough, but the comparison with other countries suggests that they will ultimately, if not altogether in our time, alter the whole appearance and conditions of Irish society'.[39] O'Faolain's words were to prove prophetic.

In 1948, when the problem of emigration was seen to have reached crisis proportions, the government appointed a commission, having as its remit to examine emigration and other population problems.[40] The commission's report, published in 1956, revealed that country people now viewed emigration in a different way. Whereas formerly, people had, paradoxically, been prepared to emigrate to protect the rural plot, so that one family member could carry on a viable unit, the report implied that the conditions of country life were now quite unacceptable to many people. The report stated:

> Through the cinema, the radio, and above all by direct experience, either personal or through relatives, people ... are ... becoming aware of the contrast between their way of life and that in other countries, especially in urban centres.... They are gradually becoming less willing to accept the relatively frugal standards of previous generations.[41]

The ready availability of work in Britain's war economy gave Irish emigrants an opportunity to earn money, which gave them an independence that hitherto, in the depressed economic conditions of Ireland, they could only have dreamed of. John Healy, in *Death of an Irish Town,* pointed to the disruptive influence these emigrants had on the social fabric of a rural community, when they returned on leave and 'hammered the last remaining defences in the rigid social and economic system'.[42]

While emigration, on the one hand, provided a safety valve which could be said to have delayed change in a society that was rigidly stratified and formerly cushioned from outside influences, the returned emigrants, on the other hand, also posed a challenge to traditional values and ways of thinking. As Healy puts it, 'now they could drink in The Hotel [sic] with the best.... Their money and their earning power was as great, if not greater, than the social hierarchy of the town.'[43] And whether, in these circumstances, local people succumbed to the temptation to emigrate, or whether they chose to remain at home, the emigrants' influence was profound. It was an aspect of changing culture which neither bishops nor priests could afford to ignore.

When the bishops addressed themselves to the problem of emigration, as they very often did in their pastoral letters, the approach of many was to lament the 'leakage' of the faith that often resulted from emigration. They warned of dangers to faith and morals of a pagan, materialistic society, the dangers of contracting 'mixed marriages', and the importance of not getting involved in the socialist Connolly clubs. The real purpose of these clubs was 'the dissemination of Communist doctrine', Cardinal D'Alton cautioned intending emigrants in his 1956 Lenten pastoral letter.[44]

Bishop Staunton of Ferns, in his Lenten pastoral of 1955, spoke of the dangers to the moral lives of emigrants in a country where the conversation, the outlook, the general atmosphere in places of work and amusement, in pictures and press, was indifferent to religion and often opposed to Christian morals.[45] The same year, Bishop Moynihan of Kerry spoke also of the 'dangers to faith and morals that awaited the young emigrants to England'. Expressing the view that 'much of the emigration was unnecessary', he went on to say that many were not compelled to go, but that they were attracted by the 'high wages and easy conditions of employment' and by 'the gaiety of city life and freedom from parents' supervision'.[46]

This is not, however, the impression one gets of the motivation of an emigrant on reading Donall Mac Amhlaigh's *Dialann Deoraí,* translated as *An Irish Navvy: The Diary of an Exile.* Leaving Ireland in 1951, he recorded that he would never have left home if he could 'have found anything to do'.[47] His book records his trips back and forth to England through the 1950s, and his constant wish to remain at home if only things were better.[48] Neither is it Healy's impression of emigration, when he reflected on it in his own home town. He paints a rather more dreary picture of what he witnessed each morning when he went to the collect the newspapers at the railway station before school. There 'morning after morning in the 1940s they went, in droves, like cattle' on the emigrant train to Dublin.[49]

> You could not avoid the dejected young girls in the windows of each carriage, some quietly crying, others just sitting there ... handkerchief, clenched and wet in a hand which had tired of wiping a face which no longer cared.[50]

Theirs was not the eager expectation of the traveller anticipating the gaiety and bright lights of foreign parts.

Yet, many bishops continued to berate the young for their flight from the land and the resultant rural decline. Many of these, like Bishop Fergus of Achonry, were concerned about the 'decline in the number of families' on the land. He lamented the number of homesteads, where there were only one or two or three people, all unmarried, and suggested that, with thrift and industry, much larger numbers of people could work out a comfortable existence on the land.[51] In his pastoral letter of 1952, Bishop McNamee of Ardagh and Clonmacnoise saw that:

> The craze for emigration in Ireland derives ultimately not from economic or political conditions, but from a false sense of values, from a growing restlessness of spirit, a mood of discontent with the old and the familiar; a craving for something new and strange; a materialistic outlook on life....[52]

He pointed out that, 'along with the highest emigration rate in the world, we have the lowest marriage rate', the combined effect of which, if not checked, could 'only lead to near extinction of the Irish race in Ireland'.[53]

These bishops were reflecting in their pastorals the kind of attitudes that were developing among people when they opted to reject the land and either to emigrate or to migrate to the city. But they did not seem to grasp that this was a symptom of a malaise that went deep — what the Commission on Emigration referred to as 'a psychological and economic malaise'[54] — and that the supposedly comfortable existence which could be eked out on the land, with a combination of industry and thrift, no longer constituted the height of their ambitions. The bishops were trying to arrest a process that was inevitable.

The widespread rejection of the conditions of rural life which had been characteristic of most western European countries since the turn of the century[55] was now happening in Ireland. In a sense, the bishops did not appear to be in touch with the realities of life for people, their changing ideas and aspirations, and, to the extent that they were in touch with them, their response was to reject them. While, on the one hand, McNamee grasped the prevailing 'restlessness of spirit' and 'mood of discontent', his subsequent remark that the level of emigration was particularly regrettable, when 'this motherland of ours was never so prosperous in her long history as she is today',[56] was particularly unrealistic, in view of the economic climate after the balance of payments crisis in 1951. The bishops, in short, were measuring what should constitute contentment by the yardstick of the past, whereas the younger generation had moved on.

The bishop who concerned himself most with the social problems arising from the flight from the land and the resulting rural disintegration was Bishop Cornelius Lucey of Cork. He had sat on the Commission on Emigration and brought out one of its minority reports. He was critical of the over-centralisation of bureaucracy in Dublin. This resulted in the over-growth of Dublin, while the rest of the country was left to languish. His remedy was 'to take away some of the state departments from Dublin and locate them in the provinces'.[57] He pointed out that, as it was, because the planners lived in Dublin, 'Dublin's needs are seen — and seen to — first'.[58]

Very often, he aired his views on this subject at Confirmation ceremonies, and, as a sociologist, he presented plenty of statistics to substantiate his arguments. At a Confirmation ceremony in Baltimore, Co. Cork, in 1954, he was forthright in his criticism of government policy: 'The decay has continued and these parts have not got the measure of prosperity which came to other parts of the country since the advent of native government'.[59] He continued that it was not a lack of money, given that the government could afford to pay £76,000 a mile on roads in Dublin, £150,000 on a new embassy in Paris, and £4 million on new offices in Dublin Castle.[60] Surely then it could 'afford a few thousand that would mean the difference between decay and development in these parts'.[61]

Bishop Lucey had the same idealised view of the life of the peasant on the small farm that de Valera had. This vision was embedded in Irish Catholic consciousness. Lucey stated, in his minority report, that: 'the rural home always has been, and is still, the best place in which to bring up a family'.[62] This ideal echoed Article 45.5 of the constitution, which expressed the hope 'that there may be established on the land in economic security as many families as in the circumstances shall be practicable'.[63]

Nevertheless, times were changing in rural Ireland. Rural electrification had progressed rapidly after the Second World War and was well advanced by the 1950s. Mechanisation was beginning to have its impact. Small farms of under thirty acres were perceived as less viable and less acceptable. Subsistence farming was going out of fashion. The trend was towards bigger farms, which would allow the farmer to invest in new machinery, and thus become more productive. Many small farmers preferred to sell out and emigrate in these conditions. The impact of labour-saving devices was devastating for farm labourers. They likewise were left with little option but to emigrate.

Lucey was very critical of these trends towards mechanisation. At a Confirmation ceremony in 1955, he expressed his views as follows: 'I often wonder if farmers are not being talked too much into buying labour saving machinery by advertisements and salesmen'.[64] He pointed out that for the price of a machine costing £200, which they could use for only a few days, 'they could have a man the whole year around' and that for the price of a combine harvester 'they could have two men the year round for four years'.[65] He persisted in the view that 'the small farm is more productive, acre for acre, than the large farm'.[66] His view was based on the fact that 'the smaller the farm the more farms' and thus 'the more farm owners there can be'. Consequently, he suggested that from both 'the social and the economic viewpoints, the case for more small holdings and small holders is overwhelming'.[67]

This was despite the fact that expert opinion, recorded at the time, stated otherwise. Joseph Johnston, professor of Applied Economics at Trinity College, and president of the Social and Statistical Inquiry Society of Ireland, conducted a number of field studies of Irish agriculture in the 1940s. Johnston was a member of the Post-Emergency Committee on Agricultural Policy, 1942–45, and as such had an opportunity to observe at close quarters the factors influencing agriculture in Ireland. The results of his investigations were published in his book, *Irish Agriculture in Transition*, in 1951. His opinions, based on empirical research (a rarity at the time) and expert knowledge, are worthy of note.

He pointed out that 'present economic conditions and recent economic experience favour the large farms and handicap the isolated small holder',[68] saying that 'modern conditions of mechanised husbandry have outmoded the small thirty acre farm as an economic unit'.[69] Because of the absolute necessity of 'access to mechanised power implements' to improve agricultural output, the larger farmer was automatically at an advantage over the small holder, he wrote.[70] He saw mechanisation as a means to 'more employment per 100 acres of crops and pasture' and, because it would make possible 'the maintenance of a large area under tillage', it would lead to 'the payment of greatly enhanced agricultural wages'.[71] The details of his analysis need not concern us here, except for his main contention that Irish agriculture was changing and that this change in its nature was going to involve upheaval in people's lives.

As in the case of the other bishops, Lucey saw a process that had been in train since the 1940s, and he was attempting, as were they, to arrest it. But the process held deeper implications of a fundamental change in people's outlook on life. Given that Irish society was primarily made up of rural small-holders, any change that would in due course bring about a shift in the balance of population was bound to affect Irish Catholicism. For this reason, the changes taking place required a more thought-out, in-depth response by Lucey and the other bishops, as opposed to the repeated insistence that people should remain on the land and count their blessings.

The practice of late marriages and non-marriage, prevalent in rural areas, which had its origin in the bleak economic conditions of post-famine Ireland, was much deplored by many of the rural bishops, and especially by Lucey. He regarded the preference for 'late marriage' as undesirable, 'particularly if so late as to entail a small family or none at all'.[72] He detected in this symptoms of the materialistic outlook much criticised by many of the bishops. People with this kind of outlook had 'little appreciation of the higher, more intangible values that raising a family offers', and thus were not prepared to make the 'sacrifice' entailed in a large family.[73] In this context, the outlook he envisaged for Ireland was bleak:

> The rural population is vanishing, and with it is vanishing the Irish race itself. For the rural families are the well springs from which the towns and cities replenish themselves, and if they are drying up, then inevitably we are doomed to wither away as a nation.[74]

'Rural Ireland', he concluded, 'is stricken and dying and the will to marry on the land is almost gone'.[75] His conclusions were to provide the inspiration for a book entitled *The Vanishing Irish* (1954), edited by Mgr J.A. O'Brien, an Irish-American priest, in which a number of writers attempted to analyse the problem. Many of them attributed it to excessive sermonising on the evils of 'company-keeping', the term by which churchmen at the time referred to relationships between members of the opposite sex. Overemphasis on sin and the tendency to exalt the celibate state were seen by some of these writers as aspects of Irish Catholic consciousness, which caused many people to look on sexuality with something of a jaundiced eye.

Long before this, the problem had been addressed by Patrick Kavanagh in an angry outburst in his poem 'The Great Hunger' (1942). Kavanagh's poem was direct and uncompromising in its harrowing account of the bleakness of rural life and the heavy price that the land exacted from those who committed themselves to it. It was a stark indictment of the harsh reality of the rural life Kavanagh saw around him growing up in Inniskeen, Co. Monaghan. He captured at first hand the sense of desperation and hopelessness which was driving young people out. Patrick Maguire's was a bitter legacy as

> He [stood] in the doorway of his house
> A ragged sculpture of the wind
> October creaks the rotted mattress,
> The bed posts fall. No hope. No lust.
> The hungry fiend
> Screams the apocalypse of clay
> In every corner of this land.[76]

The poem captures the bleak mood of the time, which changed people's consciousness and forced them into making very hard decisions about their future. Such a bitter fate, some had decided, for better or worse, was not going to be theirs.

In 1958, Muintir na Tíre sponsored the *Limerick Rural Survey*. Muintir na Tíre was founded in 1931 by Fr John Hayes of the diocese of Cashel.[77] While it started out as an economic organisation, as it evolved, it broadened its scope to concern itself with the general social improvement of the Irish countryside. The *Limerick Rural Survey* was the first sociological study undertaken in rural Ireland since that of Arensberg and Kimball in the 1930s, which was entitled *Family and Community in Ireland.* It was edited by Mgr Jeremiah Newman, professor of Catholic Sociology and Catholic Action at St Patrick's College, Maynooth, and published in 1964. The survey report noted:

> There is a continuous drift of population away from the open countryside and the very small villages ... in favour of a drift toward the city and surrounding areas and towards those places which provide possibilities of employment.[78]

The report pointed to 'a preference for life in the larger villages, due to attraction of the better amenities which they have to offer' and noted the same trend in England, Wales and Holland.[79]

Hugh Brody, writing in 1973 and reflecting on the parish in Co. Clare where he conducted his research in the 1960s, bears this out. He observed that as 'the

1950s advanced, the opportunities — social, financial and sexual — with which urban life tends to be identified were forced deeper and deeper into the consciousness of the community'.[80] He wrote: 'this emigration was new. For the first time in Irish history it did reflect a definite preference for another way of life. The peasants' determination to stay on the land seemed to have been broken'.[81]

Brody identified the same reasons for this process of change in people's consciousness as had the *Limerick Rural Survey* report. He pointed to the fact that girls, in particular, had higher expectations of marriage, inspired by their contact with urban culture. They were no longer prepared to settle for life in the countryside. They had more romantic ideas of marriage, drawn indirectly 'from films, magazines and newspapers'.[82] Maisie Ward in *France pagan?* (1949) echoed similar developments in France when she reflected on 'the new things — the radio, the cinema, the newspapers — coming from the great cities and bringing a pagan spirit that is slowly eating away the soul of France'.[83]

Brody also pointed to evidence of a more individualistic pursuit of personal fulfilment and opportunity, and more of a tendency to ignore the demands of what had been seen in the past as duty, when these demands conflicted with self-interest.[84] The spirit of sacrifice which destined Patrick Maguire to a lonely bachelor existence on the land was in retreat. The new generation was not disposed to be 'faithful to death',[85] either to the rural homestead or to an aged parent, as he had been. The revolution in consciousness had begun around the time that Patrick Kavanagh was writing his poem in 1942, and was well and truly advanced at the time of Brody's research in the mid-1960s.

Deep in Catholic consciousness was the emphasis on the necessity for sacrifice and self-denial. Bishops in their pastorals repeatedly reminded the faithful of the importance of the spirit of mortification. Also central to the thinking of Catholicism was the idea that while one's life situation might not be quite what one would have wished for, it was not right to be resentful. This had to be seen as the will of God, and accepted. The way to deal with it was to 'offer it up' and wait for a reward in the next life, because it was only then that true happiness could be attained. The fact that many people were getting discontented with their situation and were seeking to improve it, rather than simply putting up with it, had profound implications for Irish Catholicism.

~

In reflecting their disquiet about the dangers of cinema and evil literature, the threats to family life, the onset of more materialistic values and emigration, what the bishops were doing, in fact, was sketching the symptoms of a new phenomenon of deep-down social change. These were, however, merely the surface indications of new habits of mind, which would require far more sophisticated approaches than simply warnings. It is doubtful that the bishops realised this. These changes were already far advanced in the rest of Western

Europe — they happened more slowly in Ireland. Fr Alexander Humphreys SJ, whose field research was done in Dublin from 1949 to 1951, bears this out. At that time he observed that urbanisation, while it had produced very important effects upon Irish Catholic attitudes and practices, did not bring about the radical transformations that had been associated with urban life elsewhere.[86]

In the late 1940s and 1950s Western Europe was in a state of flux. The old order and fixed certainties were being questioned after the experiences of the Second World War. Totalitarian regimes had been revealed at their worst. Authority figures would never be looked at in quite the same way again. Authoritarianism and the right of some people to dictate to others were in question, and the development of psychology would hasten their demise. A new era was on the horizon, when people would be more individualistic, more independent-minded, more open to all manner of influences, less passive and conformist in their thinking. This was an era when people would travel more, become more materialistic and more concerned to find happiness in this life, rather than simply being content to make sacrifices, put up with their lot and wait for eternal happiness in Heaven. In this new era, where seemingly endless opportunities for self-fulfilment presented themselves, people would come to see a lot of ideas inspired by Church teaching as old-fashioned and not in keeping with the more 'progressive' spirit of the times.

Cardinal Suhard, the Cardinal Archbishop of Paris, under whose auspices the *Mission de Paris* was set up in order to counter the growth of the secularist culture in France, pointed out in his pastoral letter entitled *Rise or Decline of the Church*, that it was not only France that was affected. He saw Christianity, and the Catholic Church in particular, as undergoing a 'grave crisis' all over the continent. He saw the post-war era as one of transition towards a completely new civilisation, characterised by its complete universality and by the ascendancy of the world scientific over the world of ideas.[87] The question that he posed in relation to this was one which often exercised the mind of Pope Pius XII. He was concerned with the question of whether Christianity could provide the inspiration for a totally new worldwide civilisation, which would be so technical in character — a civilisation that would be universal and common to all.

This was the thinking of a Church figure who was confronted in the 1950s, head on, with the kind of secular materialistic culture that the Irish bishops only read about, or heard of in their encounters with their foreign counterparts. The key insight here though is that this new culture would become universal — that it could not be forestalled. It was here to stay. At that remove, the Irish bishops could hardly have foreseen the complexity of the age that was about to emerge, but what they certainly did have was what might be termed a vague generalised fear that change on an unprecedented scale was on the way. They sensed that foreign newspapers and books, the radio, the cinema and, in due course, television were/would be the harbingers of change and a new culture over which they would have little or no control, and which they could only warn people about.

Archbishop D'Alton gave voice to this at his launch in 1950 of the *Furrow*, the journal which would be so influential in reflecting, anticipating and stimulating change in Ireland, when he said:

> We have to face the fact that with the rise of the new inventions such as the cinema and the radio, we no longer enjoy [sic] our former comparative isolation. Our people are constantly being brought into contact with a civilization for the most part alien and materialistic in outlook.[88]

It was in this context that he took heart from the fact that the Irish were 'deeply attached to their faith and loyal in their practice of it, despite the dangers of modern life'.[89] This was typical of the mixture of fear and complacency that Church figures recorded at that time.

On the face of it, the hierarchy had little to fear. However, even in the 1950s, some reservations were being expressed as to the quality of people's religious practice, as seen in Chapter 2, and these reservations will be investigated in later chapters. Quite apart, however, from the reservations expressed, the loyalty of Irish Catholics to their religious duties might have aroused feelings other than complacency. The changes that were happening in Europe, arising out of many new and different thought patterns, were precisely the changes that the universal Church did have to face up to some years later. They were brewing now, but the Church would not come to grips with them until the Second Vatican Council. Because they happened much more slowly in Ireland, the Irish bishops had the opportunity to strengthen and deepen people's religious sense and spiritual life, so that the tide of secularisation would not sweep all before it in quite so dramatic a way as it did in other countries. In the next chapter, we turn to examine how the bishops did, in fact, respond to demands being made in the 1950s for social change and a more liberal society.

4

Demands for a More Liberal Society and the Bishops' Response

Despite politicians' dedication to upholding the Catholic ethos, and despite the obvious devotional fervour of the Catholic laity, the abiding impression gained on reviewing the bishops' Lenten pastorals in the 1950s is of their inordinate fear of threats to the Catholic social order, as it has been described. They are a unique testament to how the bishops viewed social developments at that time. The main thrust of most of these pastorals is that the Catholic way of life is in danger of being undermined, and that alien influences are attacking it from all sides. They are, in the main, warnings to the faithful of imminent dangers. Given the influence of Catholicism on the Irish way of life at that time, the urgency of these warnings is somewhat surprising, as too is their nature.

The bishops repeatedly warned about the dangers of the modern world — dangers arising from dancing, 'evil literature', modern song, drinking and so-called 'company-keeping'. In the minds of the bishops, these seemed to constitute the concrete symptoms of the advancing tide of materialistic and secularist attitudes which had already engulfed neighbouring countries, and which they were determined to resist at all costs. What the bishops referred to as the 'endless quest for pleasure', in their view epitomised a worldly outlook, which was losing sight of spiritual values.

Bishop O'Neill of Limerick, in his Lenten pastoral of 1952, was critical of what he saw as 'too much concern with amusement', which was an indication that many young people were 'yielding to the materialistic spirit of the age'.[1] In his Lenten pastoral of 1950, Bishop Roche of Cloyne lamented the 'over-indulgence in the modern craze for amusement'.[2] He was speaking in the context of warning people of 'evil modern tendencies', which, he conceded, had not 'reached the same proportions' in Ireland as they had in other countries. Having said that, families could not be complacent, he warned, but needed to safeguard themselves against 'the dangers of the modern world'. The following year, late-night dancing was condemned by Bishop O'Callaghan of Clogher, who appealed to people 'to curtail their amusements and to close all halls by midnight'.[3] In the same year, Bishop Quinn of Kilmore saw the 'craze for dancing which has gripped our young people' as a 'disquieting feature of Irish life'.[4]

The commercial dancehall was in its heyday in Ireland in the 1940s and 1950s. It had replaced the informal dances of the 1920s and 1930s, the demise of which was largely the result of clerical opposition. Bryan MacMahon explained that these halls were often built by returned exiles, who 'appreciated that the meeting of boys and girls will go on as long as the world lasts'.[5] They were really 'tin sheds glorified by the name of dance-halls'.[6] A writer in the *Furrow* in 1953 explains how parish halls were built by the clergy in response to this, to ensure 'the provision of safe, legitimate and healthy recreation' for young people.[7] Another writer on the same topic saw the parish hall as important in ensuring that the young people would have 'supervision' in 'a good Catholic atmosphere'.[8]

However, supervision was possible only up to a point, and bishops and clergy were intensely worried about what happened after the dance, on the way home. The dangers attendant on 'company-keeping' were continually emphasised in this regard. In 1954, MacMahon wrote: 'Time and again in my youth I have heard it thundered from country pulpits "It is a mortal sin to be in a lonely place with a girl"'.[9] Looking back over twenty or thirty years, he wrote: 'It would appear as if the whole artillery of our Irish church had been brought to bear on that mysterious subversive force — the "company-keepers"'.[10]

The emphasis on subduing the passions, and thus conquering the world, the flesh and the devil, was an integral part of the ideal Catholic way of life, as presented by the bishops in their pastorals. The baser instincts had to be conquered. The sexual instinct was viewed in a particularly fearful and suspicious light. In this context, the bishops saw dancing, 'company-keeping' and the consumption of alcoholic liquor as 'occasions of sin' which tempted people away from the true path to salvation. The whole thrust of their message to their followers, in this regard, was one of warning.

It is of interest to note that there were critical voices raised against these particular episcopal preoccupations in the 1950s. Referring to the 'suggestion that some Irish priests have thundered too long and too violently against "company-keeping"', turning 'this perfectly respectable term for a perfectly legitimate activity, into a euphemism for something dark and hideous', John D. Sheridan feared that 'the trouble about sermons of this kind is that they apply to the few and unsettle the many'.[11] He felt that references to the dark road and lonely place were overdone, and concluded that, in order to have marriages, 'we must have company-keeping'.[12]

These writers were reacting to what a writer in the *Furrow* in 1953 referred to as 'the grim censorious attitude in rural Ireland to girls and boys walking out together', which he saw, as did they, as being a contributory factor in the low and late marriage statistics in rural Ireland.[13] The latter issue was of considerable concern to many bishops during the 1950s. Referring to the endless chain of sermons on 'company-keeping', the same writer in the *Furrow* posed a very pertinent question at the time, when he asked:

> Are we unsure of the effectiveness, or thoroughness, of our religious instruction, dwelling more on the weakness of human nature than on its ability to steer a straight course if given a good compass?[14]

It appeared that the bishops had little faith in human nature. Their approach was to warn people constantly in their pastoral letters, to issue very peremptory statements on other occasions, and, in some cases, to prohibit, under pain of mortal sin. They made very specific rules, as for instance in the case of what time dancehalls should close,[15] as opposed to giving people positive advice or broad guidelines on how they might live their lives according to the tenets of Christianity.

MacMahon also pointed to the huge consciousness of sin that was everywhere. In an article in the *Furrow* in 1958, he pleaded: 'If company-keeping can possibly be a source of grace, why not say so?'[16] Such comments from the 1950s show that there was an awareness among some people that the Christian message, as delivered by bishops and priests, was, as far as they were concerned, somehow out of focus — that its thrust was too negative. There was a sense that, perhaps, there was an overemphasis on sin and what were known as 'occasions of sin'. This gave rise to guilt and scrupulosity in some people who were of a more anxious temperament, and Sheridan in his remarks touched on that.

Another problem associated with dancing, which concerned the bishops, was the immoderate use of intoxicating drink. Bishop Quinn of Kilmore, in his pastoral letter of 1952, warned of anxious times for parents, and the need for them to be vigilant in view of 'the dangerous allurements that lie in the path of youth'.[17] The bishops were constantly warning of the dangers to family life. Drink repeatedly came up, as did the danger of 'evil literature'. Bishop Roche of Cloyne in 1955 told parents that they had a duty to warn children 'against the harmful tendencies of these modern times'. Central among these were: 'evil literature', 'the craze for dancing', and the cinema.[18] Bishop Dignan of Clonfert in 1951 worried that there was 'a spirit of worldliness' about, which had not been there a few years before, and he wondered why it was that the young people were 'so impatient of discipline ... so restless, so given to pleasure and gaiety and dancing'.[19] Despite the level of commitment to Catholicism, as shown by people's loyalty to their religious duties, the hierarchy sensed, and were giving voice to, what they saw as a more worldly spirit influencing Irish Catholics. Whether the bishops were justified in their fears or otherwise, there were some developments in Irish society from the late 1940s which suggested that some Irish Catholics were becoming more independent in their thinking in relation to certain issues, and more prepared to assert themselves accordingly.

A feature of the political landscape from that time was the emergence of pressure groups, which were anxious to challenge the status quo in certain areas. One such group, which the inter-party government had to deal with soon after coming to power in 1948, was the rural publicans who wanted a change in the licensing laws. Though the agitation began in 1948, it was over ten years before the situation was resolved. The reason why it was so protracted was that the bishops saw this development as a threat to the Catholic social ethos, and reacted vehemently to it. The manner in which they dealt with the case, and argument put forward by the Licensed Grocers' and Vintners' Association, gives us an insight into the mind of the bishops and the position of influence they held in Irish society at that time.

The agitation was concerned with the Sunday opening of public houses. The details of this agitation have been closely examined by Whyte,[20] so it will be sufficient here to sketch the broad outline of events. Two different codes operated at the time — one for the county boroughs of Cork, Dublin, Limerick and Waterford, and one for the rest of the country. In the county boroughs, public houses could open on Sundays between 1 p.m. and 3 p.m. (1.30 p.m. in Dublin) and 5 p.m. and 7 p.m. In the rest of the country, they could open from 1 p.m. to 7 p.m., but they could serve only bona fide travellers, meaning people who came from more than three miles away. The rule was not without its funny side as told by a writer involved in the trade:

> The traveller has to perform certain antics, suggestive of membership of a secret society, to get in. He must knock but not with loud determination, on the door, then be looked on by the searching eye of the doorkeeper. He must then repeat the password 'traveller' and be prepared to answer, if asked, where he spent the night before.[21]

Abuse was widespread, and it was a well-known fact that the law was more honoured in the breach than the observance. The same writer pointed out: 'common sense holds the law to be an ass, and while the stranger performs the prescribed rites at the front door, the local inhabitant slips in by the back'.[22] He went on to explain that people felt no guilt about this, despite the fact that they were breaking a law, because the idea that a local man could not drink in his own local pub on a Sunday, but could drink in a pub three miles away, was seen as ridiculous.[23]

When a deputation met the Minister and stated their case, it seemed reasonable in the circumstances that the law as it applied in the urban areas might be made applicable throughout the country. The new Minister for Justice, General Seán MacEoin, was amenable to this, and a private members' bill was about to be introduced in the Dáil with a view to permitting the general opening of public houses between certain hours on Sunday. Before anything further could be done, however, the bishops, at their June 1948 meeting, issued a statement on the matter:

> We desire to express our grave concern at the proposal to have legislation enacted for the removal of restrictions on the sale of intoxicating drink on Sundays. We view any legislation on such lines as a most lamentable and retrograde step calculated to lead to a grave increase in intemperance and to other moral evils which follow in its train. We protest most emphatically against the violation of the precept of Sunday observance.[24]

The hierarchy in this case had the backing of two very powerful groups—the Pioneer Total Abstinence Association and the Fr Mathew Union of Total Abstaining Priests. The Pioneer Total Abstinence Association was a very powerful association in Catholic Ireland. It had been founded in the church of St Francis Xavier, Gardiner Street, Dublin, in 1898, by Fr James Cullen SJ (who had founded the *Messenger* ten years earlier). Pioneer centres were subsequently set up all over Ireland. The primary aim of the Association was, and still is, the promotion of sobriety and temperance, by means of prayer and self-sacrifice. The Association grew in strength and, in the post-war years, with the large-scale emigration from Ireland, pioneer centres were set up in Britain, the US, and as far away as Australia.[25] The Association claimed 360,000 members in July 1948,[26] and by 1957 membership was estimated to be over half a million. The first issue of the *Pioneer* magazine appeared in 1948.[27]

When joining the Pioneer Total Abstinence Association, a member made a promise to abstain from alcoholic drink for life. There was an accompanying prayer, which said that this was for the greater glory and honour of God. The custom was that every child at confirmation took the pledge, which was administered by the bishop. The pioneer pin could be seen as one of the symbols of Catholic culture in Ireland at that time. The decline in membership of the Association from the 1970s is perhaps nowhere as starkly seen as in a perusal of the ordination class-pieces of seminarians at Maynooth and elsewhere. The prominence of the pioneer pin in the photographs of the 1950s and 1960s, and its (virtual) absence later, speaks for itself.

The Pioneer Association held huge annual rallies, and its political clout was considerable, in view of the fact that it had a network of organisations spanning the whole country. This was used to effect when members lobbied their local TDs to protest against the proposed Bill. After a conference arranged by the Fr Mathew Union to sort out the issue, it was reported that the trade representatives 'accepted the position that, as Catholics, they must recognise their obligations to fulfil the wishes of the bishops in a matter which concerned the morals of the people',[28] and they subsequently agreed to withdraw their proposals for general Sunday opening.

What was important here was that the bishops were intent on bolstering morality by legislation — and this even in a situation where the law was, to a great extent, being ignored. This particular pressure group's demand for change was symptomatic of deeper social change taking place at that time. The bishops did not entertain the possibility that people might be beginning to make judgements for themselves and beginning to see that a law is a means to an end, and not an end in itself. They showed themselves more concerned with the letter of the law, than with its spirit. In this instance, as in many others, as shall be seen, the bishops' response was to bring their considerable clout to bear on the stirrings, and, in so doing, end them for the time being.

When the issue re-emerged in 1950, the chairman of the publicans' trade association was most conciliatory when he announced that 'a formula can be found which would meet the reasonable needs of the trade, while not conflicting with the wishes of the hierarchy'.[29] But before any such formula could be proposed, the bishops responded in a statement which was even more emphatic in tone and content than their 1948 statement. Having 'protested strongly' at that time, they asserted:

> Largely in deference to our wishes the Bill was decisively rejected, and we were under the impression that our guidance in this matter, so intimately connected with ... public morals, was accepted, and we expected that no further attempt would be made to modify the existing civil law forbidding the sale of intoxicating drink on the Lord's Day.[30]

The tone of the statement in this case was even more dogmatic than that of the 1948 statement. Again, the thinking was that prohibition was the best way to get people to be temperate and act morally in relation to alcohol. It bespoke an attitude that had little faith in human nature — an attitude which barely concealed its disdain for people who would dare to go against the wishes of the hierarchy.

Given that the bishops had already pointed out in 1948 that a change in legislation would lead to 'a grave increase in intemperance and to other moral evils', they were now decidedly impatient that, 'it has, therefore, become necessary for us to set forth our views on this matter once more.' On this occasion, they drew attention to Canon 1248 of the *Code of Canon Law*, which prohibited public trading on the Lord's Day, and stated that the proposed legislation, 'would be a serious violation of this ecclesiastical law'. Once again, they had recourse to law — this time Church law. But this time they went even further to emphasise the point, stating that 'it would be sinful' for people to proceed any further in this agitation.[31]

The way in which the bishops handled this issue gives a very clear indication of how they viewed themselves and their role in Irish society at that time. They regarded themselves as experts on what was best for people. As such, they expected and, in fact, presumed on people's submission, and took a very poor view of it if this was not forthcoming. In this particular case, they were vexed that their opinions were even being questioned. Within this frame of reference, there was no scope, or indeed need, for discussion of alternative views. As they saw it, they occupied the high moral ground, and it automatically followed that they had a right to be listened to and obeyed. If warnings did not prevail, they had recourse to sanctions. They could maintain that something was sinful; they could bar people from the sacraments; or they could ultimately threaten people with excommunication. Their approach was paternalistic and authoritarian. In time, the power of the bishops would be more open to question. But in 1950 there was no doubting either the power they wielded or its effectiveness. The agitation came to an abrupt close, and several years passed before courage was mustered to re-open 'negotiations'.

One of the principal concerns of the bishops, in relation to the proposal to liberalise the law relating to drinking, was that it would interfere with the observance of the Lord's Day. The precept of the Sunday observance was emphasised more as the 1950s wore on, as people became more lax in their attitudes towards it. Archbishop McQuaid of Dublin usually devoted a section of his Lenten regulations to the Sunday observance. In 1950, he stated that the 'Church commands us to sanctify the Lord's Day by hearing Mass and by abstaining from servile work'.[32] This commandment, he stated, 'is grave'. He added that as a result of the recent war crisis, 'a certain regrettable laxity in abstaining from servile work has been gradually introduced'.[33] Concessions that had been made in relation to turf-cutting and harvesting during the 'Emergency' were now being taken for granted.

Fr Seamas McLoughlin, a curate in Boyle, Co. Roscommon, writing in the *Furrow* in 1950, echoed the Archbishop, when he explained: 'war conditions and relaxations made certain things inevitable and when emergencies pass, it is often hard to get back to former observance, to get rid of a lax outlook that has come into being'.[34] Wartime conditions apart, McLoughlin saw the lax outlook as being caused by 'the spirit of secularism', which he saw as 'the root evil in the Christian world today'. It had 'conquered six days of the Christian week and is well on the way to overcoming the last citadel of the Christian Sabbath'.[35] His suggestions for combating the abuse are interesting, because they give an insight into the paternalistic approach towards the laity, which was typical of the time. He suggested mission sermons and instructions to explain the nature of the obligation. Significantly, he suggested: 'there is no need to create a new mentality, it is a matter of reviving an old'.[36] Therein lies the key to the bishops' response to change. The tendency was to try to freeze things the way they were or, in a case where things had slipped, to try to get them back to where they had previously been.

McLoughlin made a further important point, which also provides an insight into the approach of the institutional church at that time:

> Since we are dealing with a growing laxity, it may be expedient and often necessary to lean to the stricter interpretation of law and avoid the express condoning of breaches which, by a stretch, may be regarded as justifiable.[37]

Put simply, the psychology of human nature being expressed here was — do not give people an inch because, if you do, they will take a mile; if given leeway in small things, they will tend to be more relaxed in their attitudes to bigger transgressions. A broader moral outlook was not cultivated.

The law was something that people could understand and by which they could be kept in line. And even where a breach might be minor, McLoughlin felt that a benevolent attitude towards the transgressor, on the basis that 'he might be at worse', was not at all wise, because another very important issue entered in, which was that this might give scandal 'to the God-fearing Catholics who observe the Lord's Day', and they too had to be protected.[38] So, the river had to be dammed very far back. The law was interpreted strictly. The concept of an informed conscience, whereby one might see the law as the ideal and then come to a mature decision in relation to it, within one's own particular set of circumstances, did not arise at that time. It was very straightforward: the rules were there; the bishops and priests were to enforce them; it was a sin to transgress. If the sin was mortal, there was a very strong awareness that if one did not have the opportunity of confessing and was unfortunate enough to die in 'a state of mortal sin', the result would be damnation and hell fire for all eternity.

Benediction and evening devotions were seen as ways of diverting people from the tendency to secularise the Sunday. However, McLoughlin was somewhat doubtful as to their effectiveness, because he saw that times were changing, and the 'craze for amusement which dominates modern youth' seemed to be working to the detriment of the Sunday observance. People, he observed, were now moving beyond their parish for their recreation — journeying to 'the metropolis and bigger towns by train and car'.[39] Again, he is reflecting another social change, which would make more inroads into hallowed customs as the 1950s wore on.

From 1955, agitation began again for the reform of the licensing law relating to the general Sunday opening of public houses. Increasingly in the 1950s, district justices had granted exemption orders, which allowed publicans to serve local customers as well as the bona fide traveller, so the law made even less sense than hitherto.[40] On 4 July 1956, a commission was set up by James Everett, Minister for Justice in the second inter-party government, to examine the subject. The commission reported in July 1957.[41] The submissions received by the commission were heavily weighted in favour of a change. It was noted that the gardaí were finding it extremely difficult to enforce the law. On the basis of the evidence presented, the report found that there was 'a conflict between the will of the community and these provisions of the law', and thus concluded that there was 'a necessity for change'.[42]

The bishops were unimpressed, however, and, after their June meeting in 1959, issued a statement in which they attacked the proposals of the commission that there should be a liberalisation of the law. The bishops made the point that a relaxation of the law would lead to more alcoholism, endanger the youth and make road travel more dangerous. They suggested that Sunday opening of public houses, 'especially the proposal to permit opening immediately after Mass, strikes at what is most sacred in the life of our people', adding: 'the rightful observance of the Lord's Day has been one of the most powerful factors in preserving intact the Catholic life of Ireland'.[43]

The tenor of the statement was more restrained than that of the former statements. The bishops were commanding somewhat less, and there is a sense that they were appealing more. While their concern was primarily moral and religious, they pointed out that they were, 'acutely aware of the economic ills that must result from extended facilities'. In fact, they repeated this, saying that the recommendations will be 'deeply hurtful to our economic life'. This was a new departure for the hierarchy. Concern in relation to the economy did not figure prominently in their pastoral letters of the 1950s, nor did they mention it in their statements of 1948 and 1950, when the economic situation was considerably less promising.

There is a sense in which the very tentative beginnings of a changed attitude may be detected. There seems to be some recognition that it might be necessary, in changing times, to lead by consent of the governed; this can be inferred from the sentence: 'the bishops cannot believe that the vast and very reasonable majority of our decent people has shown any desire whatever for a relaxation of the law'. They are appealing to people's better judgement, an appeal which, nevertheless, is off-set by a very patronising and paternalistic tone. Finally, there seems to be a sense of resignation to the inevitable, when the statement concludes:

> The Irish hierarchy confidently hopes that legislation, when it is introduced, will not weaken the moral fibre of our nation, and will respect the deep-seated convictions of our Catholic people.[44]

On this occasion, there was no mention of sin or violations of ecclesiastical law. Nevertheless, the bishops were still opposed to change, and ultimately this is what counts when assessing the bishops' role and influence on Catholic culture.

However, despite the fact that the bishops might be determined in their stance, they did not have the final say on this occasion. The Intoxicating Liquor Bill was introduced in late 1959. The then Taoiseach, Seán Lemass, acknowledged that the hierarchy had a right to speak out, but he disagreed with their arguments.[45] In the event, the Bill became law.[46] Because it was the first time in the history of the state that a government had actually defied the recommendations of the hierarchy, it marked a watershed in Church-state relations, and thereby in Irish Catholic culture.

Irish Catholicism was also being challenged from another perspective in the 1950s. A number of clerics began to voice fears that Irish Catholicism was underdeveloped intellectually, precisely because it was too closed off and over-protected from what were seen to be corrupting influences. Fr Peter Connolly, professor of English at St Patrick's College, Maynooth, and a member of the jury of the Cork Film Festival in the 1950s, was particularly influential. From the mid-1950s, he wrote critical reviews of films for the *Furrow*, as well as contributing several articles on pertinent questions having to do with the censorship issue. Another key contributor to the debate and to a changing mood was Fr John C. Kelly SJ, who replaced Connolly as film critic of the *Furrow* in the 1960s.

Irish writers had become increasingly disaffected as a result of the workings of the censorship board, and throughout the 1940s, Sean O'Faolain, as editor of the *Bell*, had launched trenchant attacks on the censorship process. The Irish Association of Civil Liberties was founded in 1948. It had two main aims: firstly, 'to hold a watching brief for the ordinary citizen in all matters which concern his individual rights', and secondly, 'to cultivate a wider public understanding and appreciation of civil liberties'.[47] This was yet another pressure group working for change in Irish society. The Association kept a watchful eye on the operations of the censorship board. In 1956, against the background of 600 book bannings a year in the 1950–55 period,[48] it organised a public petition to the Taoiseach, John A. Costello, asking him to set up a commission of enquiry into the workings of the board.[49] While this demand was unsuccessful, it did lead to the reconstruction of the board,[50] and after this there were fewer complaints that works of genuine literary merit were banned.[51] That said, the censors still did not have powers to remove a ban imposed by their predecessors.

While writers like Connolly and Kelly focused particularly on the censorship issue, their concern was also to examine the wider Catholic censorial mentality which was wary and fearful of open communication, inclined towards secrecy and keen to enforce morality by rule of law. In this, they shared the overall vision of the founding editor of the *Furrow*, Dr J.G. McGarry. Many of the more critical Catholic thinkers emerging in the 1950s believed that reliance on legislation and an authoritarian approach of laying down very specific rules was no longer adequate to the tenor of the times. Neither, they thought, did the answer lie, as the bishops appeared to think, in erecting bulwarks to defend the prevailing Catholic ethos and protect people from what were seen as alien patterns of thought. This had resulted, they felt, in Irish Catholics having an immature approach to their religion.

In the April 1957 issue of the *Furrow*, Fr Denis Meehan, professor of Divinity and Classics at Maynooth, in an article entitled, 'An Essay in Self-Criticism', grappled with the issue head-on when he posed the question, 'Has the Irish influence in the English-speaking Church been anti-intellectual, or at best unintellectual?'[52] In 1959, Fr John C. Kelly SJ, writing in *Doctrine and Life*, addressed the matter more bluntly:

> Too many people in Ireland today are trying to make do with a peasant religion when they are no longer peasants any more. We are a growing and developing middle-class nation, acquiring a middle-class culture, and we must have a religion to fit our needs.[53]

These commentators were concerned as to whether the traditional unintellectual faith of the Irish would be able to withstand exposure to the more secularist ideas and culture of continental Europe.

In the late 1950s, there was considerable cross-fertilisation of ideas taking place at all levels and among different groups in Irish society, in the context of a growing desire for change. In 1959, Connolly delivered a lecture to an audience of the Dublin branch of Tuairim on the subject of censorship. Tuairim was a ginger-group which was actively involved in the raising of consciousness in Irish society on a variety of issues. In what turned out to be a seminal paper, published in *Christus Rex* in July of the same year, he clarified his position, as that of 'one with a special interest in literature second only to a professional interest in morals'.[54] Whereas the attitude of many of the bishops was simply to condemn what they called 'evil literature' or the bad film, and the attitude of writers like O'Faolain was one of embitterment, and the attitude of many clergy was one of fearfulness for the spiritual health of their flock, Connolly was concerned with all the ramifications of the debate. He raised it above the level of polemics and, in so doing, educated public opinion.

His approach was two-fold. He wrote on the philosophical level, examining the concept of censorship. He also bridged theory and practice, by writing on how films should be judged, and the moral classification of films, and by publishing critical essays on films (banned or otherwise), taking them seriously as works of art. He kept in mind several levels of the debate. Firstly, he made constant reference to papal pronouncements on pertinent issues. Secondly, he was concerned with the question of artistic freedom of expression, but balanced it against the necessity to protect the more vulnerable in society. In this context, he examined the extent to which the state should legislate for morality — a question which surfaced during the 1950s with the controversy over the licensing laws, and was to become an ongoing one to the present day. Finally, he was concerned with the Irish censorship process and its implications for Irish Catholics. On the basis of statements he made, it was undoubtedly the latter consideration that made him enter into the debate.

The bishops, in a statement on 31 January 1958, had registered their concern that, 'our country is being flooded with enormous quantities of books and magazines which are detrimental to public and private morality'.[55] As in the case of the 20 June 1950 statement on the agitation for change in the licensing laws, the bishops still had recourse to sanctions (in this case, ecclesiastical sanctions, given that the civil sanctions did not seem to be effective). They strictly warned newsagents and booksellers that they, 'incur grave sin if they sell books or magazines which incite to the commission of violence or unchastity', and went on to point out that, 'Catholics who persist in importing or selling such matter are not worthy to receive the Sacraments'.[56]

However, cultural protectionism was no longer a viable solution in the era of cinema and television. From now on, it was a question of facing up to the fact that the new ideas would 'seep through in any case', as Connolly put it,[57] and that the Catholic ethos would have to stand on its own merits from then on. For Connolly, the survival of Irish Catholic culture lay in developing 'an intellectual Catholic elite',[58] who would be well-versed in new currents of thought, as opposed to being protected from them.

That said, in an article highlighting the importance of a proper system of classification of films, he stressed that 'a Catholic society cannot subscribe to the liberalist rejection of all censorship and to absolute freedom of speculation and discussion'.[59] The liberal ideal, he pointed out, tended 'to presuppose a wholly adult society with a certain minimum of education, and the ability, if left to itself to choose the right thing freely'. Connolly was by no means an out-and-out liberal, nor was he under the illusion that society was perfect or incorruptible. Because the cinema was 'so much more attainable, potent, and easily understandable than the lengthy novel', he explained that the Church was all the more 'concerned to protect positively the innocent and the ignorant, the inexperienced and the emotionally unstable'.[60] But he felt sure that, 'this philosophy is being debased and etiolated when we hear only about the protective education of the personality'.[61] Connolly knew that protection was not the whole answer, and he was at pains to point out that, 'this has never constituted the whole of the Church's task'. He went on to say:

> How necessary too to train the elite and mature Catholic core towards a confident balance of freedom and responsibility, of moral theology and artistic judgment, of conscience and sensibility: a body capable of forming its own judgments, willing to apply the interior sanction, and allowed [sic] discussion to correct false emphasis.[62]

This passage illustrates the fact that Connolly was concerned with the all-round moral and intellectual development of Catholics and with the issue of censorship, in so far as its over-rigorous application in Ireland was hindering that development. He stressed that compulsion and preventive barriers did not constitute the ideal and that all-round moral education, which would lead to the free and responsible choice of the individual, should be the aim. This was at a time when moral education, such as it existed, was grounded in rote-learning of catechetical formulae, when what was sinful was very clearly defined, when there was little admission of the fact that there were grey areas in moral theology. Against this background there was little need for discussion — the concept of the informed conscience was practically non-existent, and the exterior rather than the interior sanction was the order of the day.

In order that a mature Catholic elite might develop, it was necessary, Connolly felt, that Irish Catholics be exposed to ideas that were different, and maybe sometimes even shocking to their sensibilities. A feature of Irish Catholicism at that time was that clergy were placed on a very high pedestal and seen as almost superhuman. This was reflected in an expression common at the time — 'respect for the cloth'. Against this background, in 1956, Connolly referred to a film, *Le Défroqué*, which depicted the 'fall and resurrection of a priest', and he suggested that it might 'contain drama and conflict too strong for the moral or artistic palate of the average cinema goer'.[63] He went on to observe of such a film, which presented 'human sin and weakness', that while it made good drama, it might 'not measure up to the Pope's "ideal film ... in which the dignity and nobility of man is preserved"'.[64] A few months later, he wondered why the film had not appeared in Ireland, and commented that cinema managers were probably 'chary' of it. That said, he himself admitted that he would be hesitant to show the film to a rural audience, 'believing them to be unequipped to face a priest as [a] tragic hero', but went on to recommend the film to educated audiences and seminarians.[65]

In March of the same year, reviewing the film, *The Left Hand of God,* which related the story of a layman forced by circumstances to impersonate a priest, Connolly observed that in Ireland where there was 'so much emotional devotion to the priest and perhaps little intellectual analysis of his charism and vocation, a Gallup-poll of the reaction to this film would be extremely interesting'.[66] Quite apart from film analysis, his comments are of interest both as a reflection and a critique of Irish Catholic culture at that time. The fact that Irish Catholics were so protected left them uncritical and more — rather than less — vulnerable. It is only in very recent times that the fall-out of this situation has been fully realised, given the shock-waves experienced in Irish society when confronted with the fact that churchmen can, and in some cases do, err.

For those who stopped to listen, some of Connolly's ideas were quite radical in the context of Irish Catholic culture in the late 1950s, particularly in relation to the question of the extent to which the state should bolster public morality with legislation. Citing Pope Pius XII's address to Italian jurists in 1953, when he stated that not everything which was sinful should be made illegal, Connolly stressed that, 'you can't, in fact, make men good by act of parliament',[67] and that, therefore, 'in whatever way it protects public morality civil law should define as narrowly as possible the limits placed on individual freedom'.[68] In 1959, Connolly argued:

> As the respective areas are defined today the Church ought not compromise her moral authority with the compulsions of civil law nor ought the State intrude into the private moral life unless 'public morality' or 'the public order' is being menaced. Civil law does not deal formally with sin or conscience but with misdemeanours and crimes which offend the community.[69]

He teased out the concept of indecency as defined in the Censorship Act, showing that it required a considerably more nuanced interpretation than might be imagined by the censors. It could, in fact, 'vary from one culture to the next, from country to country even within the Christian world, from one period to the next and simultaneously among the groups within any complex modern society'.[70] Here he was drawing attention to the need to recognise the rights and sensitivities of different traditions in Irish society, who might not share the predominant Catholic view of censorship. His contention that any law must try 'to balance the rival claims of various groups in the community'[71] would have registered little with bishops in the 1950s. There was little overt questioning at that time — even among the Protestant community, which was the main minority grouping — as to whether or not the law should reflect the Catholic ethos. Connolly's thinking was quite revolutionary for the late 1950s.

His voice was a prophetic one, on an issue which has been, and still is, controversial, and it is undoubtedly the case that such views, being disseminated in Catholic periodicals, were influencing many of the clergy and percolating through to the lay public, including politicians, and thus challenging prevailing assumptions. Many clergy increasingly came to subscribe to this principle, but it was not until the 1970s that the bishops issued official statements to the effect that they did not expect the civil law to uphold the Catholic moral order. This will be looked at more closely in Chapter 14.

What Connolly essentially did was to challenge what he referred to in a *Hibernia* article a number of years later, in 1964, as 'a juvenile standard of censorship',[72] which banned a book like Kate O'Brien's *Land of Spices,* 'because of two frank lines on homosexuality'.[73] He pointed out that any censorship process which looked only at the content of a book and did not try to come to terms with the general tendency of the work, or the intention of the author, led to 'intolerable absurdities'.[74] While censors might heretofore have got away with a fairly simplistic, black-and-white approach, Connolly foresaw that in the more complex pluralistic society which was even then on the horizon, their task would not be quite so easy and their decisions would be more open to question than in the past. The new era of mass communications and mass travel would demand that differences be accommodated.

Speaking in the same vein on the moral classification of films, he pointed out that even in the one country:

> ... different occupational and educated groups ... exist ... so that the application of moral principle must vary with the circumstances; and this at the level of individual conscience is the principle that what is a proximate occasion of sin for one person or group may not be so for another.[75]

On this basis, he recommended in 1957 that an X certificate be introduced like in Britain for films suitable for an over-16 audience.[76] Acknowledging that classification could, of course, vary from country to country, he observed that, 'this is a matter of scandal and surprise only to the morally naive who are not aware that there are controversial areas in moral theology which develop only through established probable opinions'.[77] In a country where Catholics had come to understand that what was right and wrong was very clearly delineated and fixed for all time, and that there was little room for controversy, questioning or conscientious choices, such thinking was different, to say the least.

Connolly was here anticipating the new, more person-centred and less legalistic theology, which had yet to be sanctioned by the universal Church in Rome. This happened at the time of the Second Vatican Council. What came to be called the 'new' theology laid more stress on the role of conscience and personal responsibility, recognising that there were areas of controversy, with which people had to grapple, and about which they had to reach their own conscientious decisions. Connolly was pressing for a more open Catholic society, which would be able to accommodate the new ideas when they made their impact. His thinking and the discourse in which he engaged were, in fact, part of a wider movement for change in the Church — a movement which sought a more updated, more open Church. Reflecting back on his influence, Patrick Hannon, a former student of Connolly's and now professor of Moral Theology at Maynooth, has observed:

> For many — most I think — the ideas which Peter Connolly stood for carried promise of a Church and country freer, less beleaguered, more hopeful. By the time my class left Arts for Theology in 1961 we had had, without knowing it, inklings of Vatican II and a new Ireland.[78]

Connolly urged that 'more contemporary standards of literature'[79] be applied in Ireland, pointing out that, 'it is unwise to lag too far behind contemporary taste'.[80] The extent to which Ireland lagged behind contemporary Catholic notions of what was acceptable, he highlighted in 1956, in relation to a film, *The Prisoner.* The film had been banned in Ireland by the censor, and had failed to pass the appeal board a few years before, while it had just been awarded the Catholic International Cinema Office's Grand Prix for 1956. His remark that this represented the verdict of the national film centres of Italy, Germany, Belgium, Spain, Luxembourg and Britain spoke volumes.[81]

The censorship issue was resolved in the 1960s by legislation, and this will be dealt with in Chapter 9. For now, we are concerned with the fact that, in the 1950s, Peter Connolly and others were raising consciousness about the issue. What is important is that the lobbying of pressure groups led to more political awareness, which, in the course of time, challenged the Church–state consensus on social and moral issues, which had prevailed thus far. We turn now to examine how the Irish political landscape was changing from the late 1940s.

5

A Changing Sociopolitical Landscape

Symptoms of social change were reflected in the Irish political landscape from the mid-1940s. One of the first signs of change was the emergence of a new political party, Clann na Poblachta, in 1946.[1] Its performance in the 1948 general election paved the way for a change of government. Fighting the election on a platform of economic and social reform, Clann na Poblachta won ten seats, thus depriving Fianna Fáil of its overall majority, which meant that the party was out of office for the first time in sixteen years. A coalition government was formed between Fine Gael, Clann na Poblachta, Clann na Talmhan, the two Labour parties and a collection of independent TDs.[2] John A. Costello of Fine Gael was appointed Taoiseach.[3]

In general, in the post-war era throughout Europe, there was a demand for greater social justice. Communists and socialists had a high profile and there was a general trend to the left in voting patterns. In this kind of climate, there were calls for economic planning and nationalisation of industry as key elements in reform programmes. The Labour Party had won a landslide victory in England after the Second World War. The *Beveridge Report,* published in England in 1942, paved the way for a wide-ranging extension of social services when the war was over. In 1946, the National Insurance Bill became law. Under this, the entire adult population was insured for sickness, unemployment and retirement benefits. In the same year, medical services were nationalised — under the National Health Service, free medical services were provided for all.

The reforms taking place in Britain and Europe involved state intervention, and the Irish bishops were ideologically opposed to this. Any kind of state intervention, welfare system or social security system was perceived by the bishops, as socialistic and a forerunner to atheistic communism. The principal dangers to the Catholic way of life at that time, as perceived by the bishops, were communism, and the associated evils of materialism and secularism. Any developments which they saw as threatening to the Catholic social order as it obtained, they were determined to fight off at all costs, as is clear from their pastorals.

Throughout the 1950s, Cardinal D'Alton, in his Lenten pastorals, called attention to these dangers. Communism was particularly feared. Every year, Archbishop McQuaid of Dublin devoted a complete section of his Lenten regulations to 'the menace of Communism'. 'Atheistic Communism' was, he said, 'a blasphemous doctrine and a perverse way of life,' which 'denied God and hated the church and attempted with every weapon of lying, treachery and persecution to wipe out the one true faith of Jesus Christ'.[4] Archbishop McQuaid always drew attention to the Holy Office Decree of 1 July 1949, warning that any of the faithful who joined communist organisations, or supported them in any way — whether by reading, writing in, or disseminating their publications — was guilty of mortal sin and could not be admitted to the sacraments. Furthermore, he insisted, those who professed 'the materialistic and anti-Christian doctrine of Communists or who defend or propagate such doctrine incur by that very fact excommunication'.[5]

In his Lenten pastoral of 1953, Bishop O'Neill of Limerick declared that 'the greatest menace to the Christian way of life, in our day, is to be found in the spirit of secularism'. He went on to speak of communism as 'the avowed enemy of God and of all religion'. While admitting that this did 'not constitute an immediate threat to our country', he went on to say that 'the secularist mentality, on the other hand, confronts us in almost all the affairs of life.'[6] Bishop McNamee of Ardagh and Clonmacnoise saw that, 'the present age has the lamentable distinction of being the first to see organised atheism set up as a cult to be followed'.[7] This was 'the most sinister threat to civilisation that has ever appeared amongst men', he warned. In many of the pastorals of 1950, the bishops were echoing the concerns of Pope Pius XII as he proclaimed the Holy Year. He had witnessed the Second World War at close quarters, together with the desolation that followed it. There was a sense that man had forgotten God, and, according to Bishop Staunton of Ferns, 'only a return to God and to the belief and practice of the Christian faith can save the shattered wreck of the world'.[8]

In his Lenten pastoral of 1950, Archbishop D'Alton of Armagh referred to the relentless persecution being meted out to the Church in countries behind the 'Iron Curtain'. He spoke of the 'arrest and imprisonment of bishops, priests and many of the laity because they dared to challenge the creed of the materialists and the claims of the state to control every department of human life'.[9] Echoing Pope Pius XII, he highlighted the importance of stemming 'the tide of materialism that threatened to engulf the Christian world'. The following year, he again criticised the 'age of materialism in which many deny the existence of God ... and bid us find all our happiness in this world', adding that the materialistic outlook views man as 'governed by economic forces alone', and having 'no higher end than the satisfaction of his physical needs'.[10]

When the bishops were articulating such fears, they were not speaking to the experience or immediate needs of the Irish people. Their fears of communism, materialism and secularism, and the state intruding into people's lives, have to be understood in the wider European context. Their response to these perceived threats was mainly influenced by Catholic social teaching, as it had developed on the Continent, in response to scientific, industrial, social and political developments in nineteenth-century Europe. The growth in scientific knowledge and the material progress that had accompanied it increasingly posed a threat to the authority of the Church and its world view.

Technological developments, industrialisation and large-scale urbanisation led to social and cultural change on an unprecedented scale. There was an increased willingness to jettison notions which hitherto had been conceived to be vital for people's very existence. Attitudes became more materialistic, where formerly they had been spiritually based. The process of secularisation was accelerated when, in 1848, Marx posed an alternative philosophy,[11] by which a material paradise was possible on this earth. The Church, with its teaching that people should accept and be happy with their lot in this life and wait for eternal happiness in the next life, began to be seen by many as a barrier to social progress.

Modern Catholic social teaching was formulated by Pope Leo XIII in his encyclical, *Rerum Novarum,* in 1891, to counter such materialistic, secularistic attitudes.[12] It was the Catholic alternative to communism. One of the most important developments in continental Catholicism at the close of the nineteenth century and in the first quarter of the twentieth century was the growth of the Catholic social movement.[13] Catholics in many countries of Western Europe had developed co-operatives, farmers' organisations, trade unions, friendly societies and such like, all of which consolidated the position of Catholics. Irish Catholicism at this time did not feel threatened in the same way, and while there were some echoes in Ireland of these developments, the Catholic social movement in Ireland was fragmented and lacked the critical dimension of its continental counterpart. *Rerum Novarum* had little impact on Ireland.

However, Ireland was to make up for lost ground from the 1930s on. The publication by Pope Pius XI, on 15 May 1931, of the encyclical, *Quadragesimo Anno,* marked the launch of the Catholic social movement in Ireland.[14] *Quadragesimo Anno* elaborated on and developed the ideas formulated in *Rerum Novarum.* The encyclical stressed the dangers of state power and the importance of diffusing power among intermediate groups. The underlying principle was one of subsidiary function: 'It is an injustice and at the same time a grave evil and disturbance of right order to assign to a greater and higher association what lesser and subordinate organisations can do.'[15] The encyclical has to be seen in the light of the tyranny of Soviet Russia, the growth of the communist movement and the rise of fascism and the totalitarian state in continental Europe at that time. Throughout the 1930s and 1940s, Catholic social teaching became a potent force in Irish Catholicism.

In the press, the *Catholic Standard* was a strong advocate of Catholic social teaching and, from the 1930s, the bishops in their pastoral letters pressed the need to implement the popes' social teaching. The Muintir na Tíre movement, founded in Tipperary in 1931 by Fr John Hayes, was the practical embodiment of ideas expressed in the encyclical. The most telling evidence of the influence of Catholic social teaching at this time was the fact that in 1939 Éamon de Valera nominated a commission, under the chairmanship of Bishop Browne of Galway, to examine the possibility of developing vocational organisation in the Irish context. When the commission reported in 1944, it was highly critical of government bureaucracy and its lack of consultation of interest groups, and it recommended that the state should act as much as possible through vocational bodies.[16] De Valera's reaction was to shelve the recommendations of the report. While he approved of vocationalism in principle, his strong views on the primacy of parliamentary democracy precluded the possibility of devolution of statutory power to vocational organisations. That said, De Valera couched his reservations whereas Seán Lemass, Minister for Industry and Commerce, argued vociferously against the report.[17]

A further development closer to the period of this research was the arrival, in 1945, of the Christus Rex movement. Approved by the bishops, its stated aim was 'the realisation in public life of the principles of the social encyclicals'.[18] A cursory glance through the articles of the society's journal in the late 1940s and early 1950s shows the major preoccupation that the writers had with what they saw as excessive state power or interference, which to them smacked of communism.[19] What was obvious at that time was that the Irish bishops and these social theorists had a very definite philosophy of what should constitute a Christian social order in Ireland, which they derived from a framework of ideas designed to suit continental European conditions. In this framework, the state's rights and obligations, the limits of its proper authority vis-à-vis society, and any indications that it might be developing monopolistic or communistic tendencies were closely screened.

The question has to be posed at this juncture — to what extent did the dangers put forward by the hierarchy pose a real threat to Irish Catholics at the time? Affluence is necessary for the development of the kind of materialistic thinking about which the bishops spoke. Ireland's economy was stagnant in the post-war era, and remained so until after the effects of the *Programme for Economic Expansion 1958* began to be felt. It was only in the 1960s, as a result of this programme, that the Irish economy showed an upturn which, in due course, gave rise to a more affluent society, in which a more materialistic outlook on life did, in fact, develop. And as regards 'the secularist mentality' that the bishops so frequently spoke of, in the context of the religious practice of the people, to say that there was no indication or sign of secularisation in the Ireland of the 1950s would be an understatement. As regards communism, the membership of the Irish Communist Party was so low that the party did not rate as a political force.[20]

Nevertheless, the threat of communism had become more urgent in the post-war era. Communists had been involved in the resistance movements in many countries during the Second World War, and their popularity increased as a result. After the War they were represented in the governments of France, Italy, Belgium and most of the German *Länder.* In due course, Stalin's expansionist policy leading to the cordoning off of eastern and central Europe and the Berlin blockade of 1948 brought an end to the uneasy marriage of convenience which had existed between the Soviet Union and the Allies. This led into the era of the Cold War and a general suspicion and fear of communism in many quarters besides the Catholic Church. But the Catholic Church authorities never had any illusions about the intentions of Communists. The persecution of Christians and the arrest, show trial and imprisonment of Archbishop Stepinac in Yugoslavia and Cardinal Mindszenty in Hungary saw to this. In the late 1940s, there was a strong awareness in Ireland of these events. The recurring references to communism by the bishops in their pastorals must be seen against this background.

Whatever about continental developments, it was inevitable that the post-war social reforms which took place in Britain would be observed closely in Ireland, if for no other reason than Ireland's close proximity to Britain. The fact that emigrants were travelling to and fro from Britain would have made people at home more aware of the inadequacy of the Irish social services. This is borne out by Donall Mac Amhlaigh, an Irish emigrant working in England in the 1950s. In the diary he kept for 1952, he contrasted the civilised nature of the English health service, where he could 'go into any doctor ... wait in a nice warm room' and, in due course, get a prescription from him, 'to take to the chemist where the best drugs and medicines are given to you with a heart and a half', with the situation that obtained 'at home', where, 'if you get a ticket to go to the doctor, you have to wait in an old ruin of a house,' surrounded by 'poverty, despair and dirt'.[21]

In post-war social and economic development, Ireland had lagged far behind Britain and mainland Europe. In 1944, Bishop Dignan of Clonfert, chairman of the National Insurance Association, published a pamphlet entitled *Social Security: Outlines of a Scheme of National Health Insurance.* He was highly critical of the medical assistance service, on which a large section of the population depended for health care, comparing it to the Poor Law system.[22] However, he did not favour direct state intervention to provide medical care, but proposed instead an insurance scheme based on voluntary contributions. Direct state assistance was in conflict with Catholic teaching on the rights of the family, in that it undermined the head of the family in his role as provider. The scheme proposed by Dignan would simply assist the head of the family in that role. On 19 October 1944, the day after the Dignan plan was published, it was rejected as impracticable by Seán MacEntee, the Minister for Local Government and Public Health.[23] Coming, as it did, in the wake of the sidelining of the Commission on Vocational Organisation report, it seemed to indicate that politicians would no longer be quite as amenable to Catholic Church teaching when it came to formulating policy. Given that two government ministers were rejecting proposals advocated by two Catholic bishops, *The Irish Times* in an editorial on 10 March 1945 argued that the notion of the Republic of Ireland as a state ruled by the Catholic bishops was hard to sustain.[24]

In fact, the mood of the government at that time *was* swinging more and more towards the need for economic planning and state intervention. Post-war economic stagnancy, the increasing volume of emigration, and the increase in the cost-of-living index were forcing civil servants to re-think drastically economic policies that had prevailed up to then. As early as 1945, Patrick Lynch, an economist in the Department of Finance, was arguing that,

> A proper direction of the Irish economy will imply increased state intervention.... What will be needed to develop a policy of full employment is controlled and planned state intervention.[25]

So, in a sense, the die was cast at this stage, which would eventually lead to a battle between the bishops and whatever government attempted a more activist role.

The first minister to tackle the need for social reform was William Norton, Minister for Social Welfare in the first inter-party government, 1948–51. In a White Paper at the end of 1949, he proposed to reform and extend the existing social insurance scheme. His proposals met with a barrage of criticisms from all manner of Catholic social theorists, including Bishop Dignan of Clonfert, author of the pamphlet on National Health Insurance.[26] Though the hierarchy as a whole did not become involved, the issue is of interest because the criticism Norton's scheme evoked, and the manner in which he dealt with it, provide key indicators to the state of Catholic culture at that time.

Replying in the Dáil to criticisms, Norton showed some impatience with the argument that his scheme was not vocational as recommended in the social encyclicals, when he pointed out, 'we are dealing with an urgent practical problem, not with one that can wait until all ancillary problems of vocationalism have been solved'.[27] He defended his proposals by appealing to religious principles, stating:

> As a Christian nation we must give practical expression to our Christianity. Surely it would not be suggested that it is a Christian attitude to allow unemployed men or women, or widows and orphans, to beg from door to door, nor would it be the Christian attitude to pay such low rates of benefit as to bear no relation to the requirements of the time.[28]

A month later, in the Dáil, he quoted a passage from Pope Pius XI's encyclical of 1937, *Divini Redemptoris,* which stated that 'social justice cannot be said to have been satisfied as long as working men ... cannot make suitable provision through public or private insurance for old age, for periods of illness and unemployment'.[29] What was important was that Norton was proposing his own idea of what he saw to be just, and also that he disagreed with the vision of the Catholic social theorists. The idea of social justice was still being developed by the Church and would really come to the fore only after the Second Vatican Council. It was a little-used concept in the discourse of the Irish Church at least until the 1960s. The inter-party government fell before Norton's measure could become law, but the matter was resolved a few years later, in 1953, by the Fianna Fáil government.

While Norton was prepared to intervene in order to improve the provision of social services, there were some areas in which state ministers were extremely reluctant to intervene at all, despite the fact that they were being subjected to considerable pressure by lobby groups. The Adoption Society was founded in 1948 to campaign that provision be made for legal adoption. In this case, because it was a delicate issue on which the Church was known to have definite views, the minister involved, the Minister for Justice, General Seán MacEoin, was reluctant to get involved in any discussion on the matter. An insight into the Minister's hesitancy in grappling with the issue is provided in a statement made by the Attorney General, Mr C.F. Casey, regarding the matter. He was defending the Minister's decision not to legislate. Speaking at the inaugural meeting of the Law students' debating society at the King's Inns, Dublin, in February 1951, the Attorney General stated that, 'we in this state are fortunate in that we are living in a country where spiritual values are still supreme and I hope will always remain so'. He continued, 'this country is predominantly a Catholic country' and while this did not mean that any creed should be penalised, he argued, 'it does mean this, that Parliament surely cannot be asked to introduce legislation contrary to that great church'.[30] While, he said, 'the Catholic church has never taught that those outside its communion cannot be saved', he went on to point out that it does teach that 'membership of the church is the best means of saving one's soul'. On this basis, he posed the question: 'How can a Catholic logically demand or permit any legislation which would endanger the soul of a single child?'[31]

The Attorney General went on to state that if adoption were legalised, in a case of illegitimacy, where a mother gave her child up for adoption, she would thereby forfeit her rights, and so be 'powerless to bring her child up in what she knows is the true faith'. His remarks have to be understood in the context of official Church teaching at the time — that outside the Church there was no salvation. A number of Protestant institutions existed at that time which catered for unmarried mothers of all denominations. The Bird's Nest was the name of one of the best known of these institutions, and was sometimes used as a generic term for all of them. They evoked considerable suspicion in Catholic quarters because they were seen as proselytising agencies, and the fear of proselytism ran deep in the Catholic psyche.[32] The Catholic Protection and Rescue Society was set up in 1913 to counteract such activities.[33] The importance of such an explicit statement of the teaching of the Catholic Church and its right to recognition in the law of the land by a high-ranking state official in 1951 cannot be overestimated. While the matter was left in abeyance because of its nature, again it shows that there were moves afoot in Ireland in the late 1940s to challenge the status quo, even on matters that might be deemed delicate, and in which the Church was known to have a vested interest.

More than all the issues dealt with so far, it was the so-called 'mother and child' controversy which provided the best insight into, and had most repercussions for, the relationship between Church and state in Ireland. The facts of the case are fully documented by Whyte,[34] so it is not necessary to recall them in detail here. However, the episode was not simply a further joust in the political battle between Church and state. In its working out, it held deeper implications in relation to more fundamental sociocultural change. As such, the present analysis is chiefly concerned to focus on some of the key episodes in the controversy, to show how they highlighted Catholic conformity, on the one hand, and the beginnings of Catholic cultural change, on the other.

A health act was enacted under the Fianna Fáil administration in 1947.[35] Certain sections of the act allowed for the provision of free health care for mothers and children up to the age of sixteen, regardless of means. This provoked objections from the hierarchy because:

> The public authority was given the right and duty to provide for the health of all children, to treat their ailments, to educate them in regard to health, to educate women in regard to motherhood and to provide all women with gynaecological care.[36]

In the provisions of the 'mother and child' scheme section of the legislation, the hierarchy saw overtones of the welfare state. As far as the bishops were concerned, the state, in claiming such rights, was going 'directly contrary to Catholic teaching on the rights of the family, the rights of the church in education, the rights of the medical profession and of voluntary institutions'. The areas of the family, health care and education were traditionally regarded by the Church as its own domain, and the bishops were determined to resist what they saw as encroachment into their area of special interest. The potential Church–state clash was averted though when the Fianna Fáil government fell. The inter-party government took office on 18 February 1948, and Dr Noël Browne was appointed Minister for Health.

The thorny issue resurfaced when the hierarchy learned of Noël Browne's proposals to provide a mother and child health scheme under the 1947 Act, when it was reported in the *Sunday Independent* on 3 September 1950. The hierarchy had already recorded its 'grave disapproval' in 1947. When the bishops met at their October meeting in 1950, in the wake of the newspaper report, they issued a statement which re-emphasised their teaching in no uncertain terms. This time the tone was more peremptory. They argued that the powers taken by the state were in direct opposition to the rights of the family and the individual, and warned that, if adopted, 'they would constitute a ready-made instrument for future totalitarian aggression'.[37] They reiterated a central tenet of Catholic teaching — that the right to provide for the family, 'belongs to parents, not to the State,' and that the state can 'intervene only in a subsidiary capacity, to supplement, not to supplant'.[38]

The proposed health scheme was also a particularly sensitive issue for the bishops because it had implications for motherhood and sexuality, on which the Church had very definite teaching. In their statement, issued after their October meeting, they stated:

> Education in regard to motherhood includes instruction in regard to sex relations, chastity and marriage. The State has no competence to give instruction in such matters. We regard with the greatest apprehension the proposal to give to local medical officers the right to tell Catholic girls and women how they should behave in regard to this sphere of conduct at once so delicate and sacred.[39]

The bishops were also aware that the British National Health Service had made family-planning facilities available to married women in 1949, and it was clear from their statement that the issue of birth control was to the forefront of their minds. 'Gynaecological care', they pointed out, 'may be, and in some other countries is, interpreted to include provision for birth limitation and abortion'. They were concerned that under the proposed services, doctors appointed as medical officers might 'give gynaecological care not in accordance with Catholic principles'.[40]

As in the case of the statement regarding the licensing laws a few months earlier, in June, the bishops had no doubt in regard to their right to be heard and obeyed. They made statements of fact, as they saw it, on which there was no argument. The idiom in which the bishops communicated their views is the key to the influence they wielded and to their perception of the God-given nature of their role. They represented far more than an interest group that wished to convey its fears and offer advice. It was not surprising, in this context, that state officials were most deferential, as we shall see from their reactions. They were dealing with a very powerful group, absolutely self-assured in relation to its role.

The hierarchy's disquiet has to be seen against all the fears they had registered over the years in their pastorals and elsewhere — fears of over-centralisation, bureaucratic models of government and state intervention. It was as if they were now all realised. Lucey, Coadjutor Bishop of Cork at that time, exclaimed: 'the welfare state is upon us. Now, under one pretext, now under another, the various Departments of state are becoming father and mother to us all'.[41] The fact was that the state was taking more responsibility for people's lives in many Catholic countries in Europe, but the possibility that there might be some positive value in this was inconceivable to the bishops.

This event marked a watershed in Irish Catholic culture which had wide and far-reaching implications. Its significance lay in the fact that it was the first head-on clash between Church and state in post-independence Ireland — the first tentative challenge to episcopal power. It had the makings of a confrontation which was not quite fully realised, because the inter-party government shrank from challenging the Church on territory deemed by the latter to be exclusively its own domain. When the hierarchy persisted with its objections to the 'mother and child' scheme, and Noël Browne was not prepared to accede to the bishops' demands, the government decided that his scheme should be abandoned and that an alternative scheme be devised to replace it, which would be in keeping with Catholic social teaching. Browne was required to tender his resignation when his negotiations with the bishops broke down. He did so on 11 April 1951.

The significance of the controversy has to do with the unique insight it gives into the power of the hierarchy at the time. It also shows how leading government spokesmen related to that power, and how each party saw the other's role and the legitimate spheres of interest of the other. The attitudes of the main politicians to the bishops' intervention may best be judged by their statements in the course of the Dáil debate which followed Noël Browne's resignation. They were more than forthcoming in proclaiming their allegiance to the hierarchy. John A. Costello in his letter to Archbishop McQuaid, informing him of the government's decision to withdraw the scheme, asserted, 'the complete willingness of the government to defer to the judgement so given by the hierarchy that the particular scheme in question is opposed to Catholic social teaching'.[42] In the course of the Dáil debate, he proclaimed, 'I as a Catholic, obey my church authorities and will continue to do so, in spite of *The Irish Times* or anything else'.[43]

Seán MacBride was no less loyal when he said, 'those of us in this House who are Catholics, and all of us in the Government who are Catholics are, as such of course, bound to give obedience to the rulings of our Church and of our hierarchy'.[44] William Norton, who had himself already fielded criticism of his proposals on social insurance by Catholic social theorists, obviously saw the hierarchy in a different light, as having to be reckoned with. He was as emphatic as the others regarding the legitimate authority of the hierarchy to pronounce and the government's obligation to conform, when he said: 'There will be no flouting of the authority of the bishops in the matter of Catholic social teaching or Catholic moral teaching'.[45]

Even Dr Browne himself in his resignation speech declared, 'I as a Catholic accept unequivocally and unreservedly the views of the hierarchy on this matter'.[46] Even if his remark was made for political reasons, it still points to the influential position of the Church. Yet his actions, premeditated or otherwise, undoubtedly had the effect of calling that influence and authority into question. Before this time, it had simply been taken for granted — accepted — as the statements made by the politicians indicate all too clearly. There was even a sense that the Church's role was somehow not a matter for public discussion. Noël Browne put paid to this by sending to the newspapers, on the day of his resignation, the text of the correspondence that had passed between himself, the hierarchy and the Taoiseach.[47] The full documentation appeared in all three papers — the *Irish Independent, The Irish Times* and the *Irish Press* — on the morning after his resignation.

Such a move was unprecedented. For the first time in the history of the independent state, the role of the Church was under public scrutiny. The fact that this was a new phenomenon and, as such, discomfiting, was revealed when the Taoiseach, John A. Costello, made the point that, 'all this matter was intended to be private and to be adjusted behind closed doors and was never intended to be the subject of public controversy.'[48] He clearly felt that the Church–state wrangle was not a subject fitting for public consumption. 'All these matters', he stated, 'could have been and ought to have been, dealt with calmly, in quiet and in council without the public becoming aware of the matter'.[49] In a sense, Costello was revealing the same kind of paternalistic approach as the Church in those days. He was protecting the Church and the people, as he saw it.

The incident marked a crossroads in Irish Catholic culture. Things would never be quite the same again. What was important was that a challenge was offered to Church authority, and the ins and outs of that challenge were made public, which meant that people were bound to get involved in the issues and take sides. This inevitably meant repercussions for the Church, but these would be felt only by degrees. It marked the widening of a sub-culture of dissent, which, generally speaking, had up to that time involved only the intelligentsia or literati. This sub-culture had its roots in the protracted debate that now began in the newspapers and various journals on the subject of Church–state relations. It is worth noting a selection of the contributions, as an indication of how irreconcilable were the differences that emerged. *The Irish Times* set the tone of the debate, when, the morning after Noël Browne's resignation, the leader writer observed that: 'the Roman Catholic church would seem to be the effective government of the country'.[50]

The question was being asked whether the bishops were overstepping their authority, and one side of the argument held, quite emphatically, that they were. One of the people who argued along these lines most vociferously was Sean O'Faolain in the *Bell.* He argued that, 'nobody has denied the right of the Catholic bishops to "comment"; or to give "advice" on proposed legislation'.[51] He even conceded the hierarchy's right to condemn a proposed piece of legislation, 'provided that, in the end, it is the parliament which freely decides.' However, he pointed out that, 'in practice the hierarchy does much more than "comment" or "advise". It "commands".'

Dr Alfred O'Rahilly, a long-time exponent of Catholic social teaching, took up the bishops' defence in several articles in the *Standard.* In one such article, he argued that the bishops' right to intervene was simply a normal liberty and, 'for a Protestant organ such as *The Irish Times* to launch an attack on this right' was 'plain totalitarianism'.[52] To some extent, the fears of the bishops could be seen as a kind of generalised concern in regard to the development of a more secular culture and the resulting lessening of the influence of religion in people's lives. Bishop O'Neill of Limerick remarked that the hierarchy was trying, 'to protect the people from dangers and evils that may arise inthe future'.[53]

In similar vein, Archbishop D'Alton, when he addressed the Catholic Truth Society of Ireland on 10 October 1951, warned that, 'never was there greater need for the strengthening of our defences and for the propagation of Catholic truth'.[54] These two statements, which placed the emphasis on protecting and defending the status quo, give an indication of how the bishops were going to come to terms with the developments which had taken place. There was little evidence from the statements in general that the bishops would be reassessing their position or their way of acting.

The bishops, for the first time, were being put in the position of defending their role as they saw it. In June 1951, Archbishop D'Alton of Armagh responded to the criticism that the bishops had intervened in 'a purely political question outside their competence', asserting that, 'from the nature of their office they have the right and the duty to intervene when religious or moral issues are involved'.[55] In his address to the CTSI in October of the same year, he made an even more emphatic statement on the Church's position, when he insisted: 'We have a right to expect that our social legislation will not be in conflict with Catholic principles'.[56] This was a crucial statement. There was no questioning this expectation up to now. It had been fact since the foundation of the state. On this basis, Catholicism had been *the* informing spirit of Irish culture. But now this principle was being questioned and, as it came more and more to be questioned, Catholicism's position as the informing spirit of Irish culture would be eroded gradually. Archbishop D'Alton's statement is also important because the Church's position, as outlined here, has been considerably refined over the period covered by this book, as will be seen.

Despite any adverse fall-out that the hierarchy might, in time, experience from the controversies of 1951, its authority was still very much deferred to. When de Valera returned to power after the general election on 30 May, consultations were arranged with the hierarchy to resolve the adoption issue. In due course, a committee of bishops laid down limits and safeguards which would have to be applied to make any prospective legislation 'consonant with Catholic teaching'.[57] Likewise, in relation to the re-introduction of the health legislation, close consultation was engaged in with the bishops, in order to arrive at proposals which were satisfactory from their point of view. Their considerable input into both pieces of legislation evidenced their authority, on the one hand, and reinforced it, on the other.

One of the most revealing statements of how one bishop saw the bishops' role was made some years later by Bishop Lucey of Cork. Speaking at a Christus Rex congress in Killarney in 1955, he observed that the Church was not just like any other group which might intervene — it was not 'a mere pressure group'. It 'had a firmer and broader basis than any of them'.[58] Citing the Health Bill controversy, he explained that, 'they intervened on the higher moral ground that the Church is the divinely appointed guardian and interpreter of the moral law', and, given that the bill was in certain respects at variance with that law, it was their duty to oppose it. The bishops were, in fact, he argued, 'the final arbiters of right and wrong even in political matters'. The state might in other areas ignore the experts but in matters of 'faith and morals it might not'.[59]

Less than five years after this statement was made, the political climate had changed radically. A new generation of politicians had emerged, among them Donogh O'Malley, George Colley, Brian Lenihan, Charles J. Haughey and others. These had not been involved in the struggle for independence, and were therefore less concerned with abstract issues like that of Irish identity, and more concerned to look to the future. De Valera had retired from active politics on 17 June 1959 and was subsequently elected President. He was replaced as Taoiseach by Seán Lemass. Lemass, though he had been involved in the Civil War, was more typical of the new breed of politicians. De Valera repeatedly expounded a vision of Irishness which upheld spiritual values and eschewed the materialistic and secularist attitudes which were developing on mainland Europe. His guiding principle had been to create an Ireland which would be culturally and economically insulated from such corrupting influences. In this he was very much in tune with the concerns of the bishops, as registered in their pastorals in the 1950s. Lemass, on the other hand, was more pragmatic and interested in people's material welfare, and thus was more at home with the new patterns of economic thinking coming from civil servants like Patrick Lynch and T.K. Whitaker in the Department of Finance.

The *Programme for Economic Expansion* (often referred to as the First Programme) was published on 12 November 1958.[60] Based on a paper by Whitaker, entitled *Economic Development,*[61] it was a watershed, in that it signalled a decisive shift in Irish economic thinking, which was to have a ripple effect right throughout Irish society. Protectionism was to be replaced by free trade; public expenditure was to be concentrated on productive industry rather than on social services; and foreign firms were to be encouraged by tax incentives to set up industry in Ireland. Economic imperatives were to guide political thinking increasingly from the late 1950s, particularly in view of the success of the First Programme when it was implemented in 1958.

It is important to point out at this remove that not all clerics in the 1950s took a dim view of state planning and intervention in the economy. As early as 1953, Dr William Philbin, professor of Dogmatic and Moral Theology in Maynooth, had taken a different line, acknowledging that there was considerable scope for state intervention to direct public policy.[62] Again in 1956, speaking as Bishop of Clonfert, at a meeting to commemorate the encyclicals, *Rerum Novarum* and *Quadragesimo Anno,* he broke new ground by asking whether there might not be 'aspects of economics, other than those dealt with magisterially in the encyclicals' for which new solutions might have to be found, other than those proposed by Catholic social teaching.[63] In particular, he drew attention to Ireland's low productivity, high emigration, and adverse balance of trade.[64] In 1957, in an article in *Studies*, he argued:

> Our greatest failure of all — the capital sin of our young Irish State — is our failure to provide for our people an acceptable alternative to emigration.[65]

It is significant that T.K. Whitaker, the secretary of the Department of Finance, in his introduction to *Economic Development* (1958), cited the bishop's words in this article as having been an 'inspiration' to him.[66] He spoke of his own study as 'a contribution in the spirit advocated by the bishop of Clonfert towards the working out of the national good in the economic sphere'.[67]

Fr Roland Burke Savage, editor of *Studies*, had challenged the political status quo in an editorial in 1955. Seeing Ireland as 'cut off almost completely from the Catholic thought of our time in Europe' and thus enjoying 'the stagnant peace of a backwater', he went on to point out the need for 'a satisfying ideal' and of 'inspiring leadership that will urge us forward towards that ideal'.[68] Many articles followed in answer to the editor's call for 'a rigorous examination of many assumptions too readily taken for granted in Ireland today'. The influence of the periodical was acknowledged by none other than Seán Lemass at a reception held in UCD in 1964, to discuss the future of *Studies*, when he expressed the view that it had provided articles which formed 'the basis of discussion which has sometimes determined the future of our country'.[69]

The realisation on the part of politicians that a more active and interventionist approach was warranted in economic and other policy areas from the late 1950s, marked a totally new departure and was in direct opposition to the thinking of many of the bishops and Catholic social theorists, who had made such alarmist forecasts in relation to the dangers of state power in Ireland, as has been seen. The Lemass decision in 1959 to ignore the bishops' statement in relation to the Intoxicating Liquor Bill was the most concrete development which ushered in a new era. Its decisiveness marked a total change from the tentative approach of past governments. The necessity to be open to foreign trade and investment, advocated by economists and politicians, did not confine itself to economic policy, but was underpinned by an attitude that was more open to foreign influences, and this gradually led to a lessening of the insular mood that characterised past Irish experience.

In 1961, Ireland joined the United Nations Educational, Scientific and Cultural Organisation (UNESCO), and, in autumn of the same year, participated in the Washington conference of the Organisation of Economic Cooperation and Development (OECD). Irish participation in this latter event was to have profound implications for Irish educational development in the years ahead, which will be elaborated on in Chapter 11. In 1961 also, Ireland applied to join the European Economic Community (EEC). The establishment of foreign-owned factories by the Industrial Development Authority (IDA), which had been established in 1949, and the development of Irish tourism by Bord Fáilte, which had been set up in 1955, meant that Irish people were increasingly influenced by different cultures and ideas. Opportunities to travel, which increased dramatically from the early 1960s, further added to these developments, all of which brought about considerable attitudinal change.

In the context of the economic optimism generated by the success of the First Programme, which effectively turned the Irish economy around, a new era of social optimism was ushered in. There is a consensus among many Irish writers of the time that Ireland as a whole underwent a profound psychological change in the late 1950s.[70] The arrival of an Irish television station in 1961, the extension of educational opportunity and the relaxation of the censorship laws from the mid-1960s served to reinforce this new mood. All of these developments had implications for the Church–state partnership that had operated and been taken for granted up to this time, and will be examined in later chapters.

Irish Catholicism, in terms of how it was presented by the bishops and how it was expressed in the devotional lives of Irish Catholics, had remained largely the same in the 1950s. But from the 1960s, it could no longer be insulated from developments at home and abroad. Radical re-thinking had been taking place among liturgists, biblical scholars and theologians in continental Europe, in order to make Catholicism more relevant and meaningful to Catholics in the post-war era. Pope Pius XII was succeeded in 1958 by Pope John XXIII. Whereas Pope Pius XII had continued the tradition of the popes of the nineteenth century, in his defensive attitude towards change, and his wariness of modern developments, Pope John XXIII was determined that the Church should come to terms with modernity. His more relaxed attitude towards modern life served to reinforce further the more open climate that was developing in Ireland socially and politically. His pontificate and his announcement of the Second Vatican Council constituted a landmark in Catholicism, which was to have repercussions in Ireland and throughout the world. It was to be the start of a new era. Before turning to examine developments in the wider Church, the question has to be posed at this juncture — did the Irish Church anticipate in any way the profound changes which were about to take place, or was it in any way prepared for them?

6

'To Drive a New Furrow'

While the bishops were concerned to preserve and defend the status quo as it obtained in the Irish Church in the 1950s, there was a growing feeling among some clergy on the ground that renewal and reform were necessary. One of the most influential of these clergymen was Dr J.G. McGarry. Born in Claremorris in 1905, McGarry received his secondary education in St Jarlath's College, Tuam, and his third-level education in philosophy and theology at St Patrick's College, Maynooth, where he was ordained in 1930. He was awarded his doctorate there in 1932. He then returned to St Jarlath's College, where he taught for a number of years, before being appointed to the staff in Maynooth in 1939 as professor of Sacred Eloquence and Pastoral Theology. He convened a meeting of Irish priests in August 1949. This event was to mark the beginning of a new, more questioning mood in Irish Catholicism. At that meeting, attended by twenty priests, Dr McGarry put forward the idea of founding a journal which would have a specifically pastoral focus and which would serve as a forum for the sharing of theological knowledge and pastoral experience.[1]

Those attending the meeting responded eagerly to McGarry's suggestion and became co-founders with him of the *Furrow.*[2] It was to be a monthly publication, and the first issue appeared in February 1950. The name of the journal was proposed by Fr Seán O'Riordan CSsR, who adapted it from the Austrian Catholic review, *Die Furche.*[3] In 1975, on the twenty-fifth anniversary of the *Furrow,* recalling that first meeting, Seán O'Riordan recalled that among this group 'there was a general recognition of the fact that the times called for a renewal and adaptation of the pastoral life of the Irish Church at all levels'.[4]

The founder members elected the editorial board of three from among themselves. Dr McGarry became chief editor and Fr Seán O'Riordan CSsR and Fr Ronan Drury became assistant editors. At that time, Fr O'Riordan taught at Cluain Mhuire, the Redemptorist seminary in Galway. Fr Ronan Drury, recently ordained, from the diocese of Meath, was then teaching English at St Mary's College, Knockbeg. Fr Michael Mooney, who taught at St Jarlath's College,

Tuam, and subsequently became president of that college, was elected treasurer. Dr McGarry resigned his post at Maynooth in 1969 and was appointed parish priest of Ballyhaunis, Co. Mayo. He continued as editor of the *Furrow* until his tragic death following a car accident in August 1977.

McGarry and his fellow contributors to the *Furrow* were aware of new developments in biblical studies, catechesis and theology, which were inspiring creative initiatives in liturgy and other areas of Catholic life in post-war Europe. They were aware that continental theologians, influenced by new currents of thought in philosophy and psychology, were grappling with the task of developing a theology which would be more relevant to the contemporary mind. While they could not have foreseen how, or when, it would happen, they instinctively knew that the universal Church was being propelled into change. And they knew that the changes in society, which were precipitating a re-examination of theological thinking on mainland Europe, would not ultimately stop at the shores of Ireland, much as the bishops might like it. They were very conscious of Ireland's insularity and the extent to which the Irish Church was unaware of, and unaffected by, these developments. Writing in retrospect about his own feelings, O'Riordan explained:

> My fear was that if our Church as a body did not open itself to participation in the new life of the Church universal in the coming years it would sooner or later be unprepared for the challenges of a new historical epoch even within its own shores.[5]

In the foreword to the first issue, the editor's opening remarks were: 'the *Furrow* is something new. It is new in the ground it opens'.[6] This was a clear signal of his intention that the journal would follow hitherto untrodden paths in pastoral theology and other disciplines. The motto '*novate vobis novale*' appeared on the cover of the journal from 1961. It was taken from Jeremiah 4:3:

> *Novate vobis novale*
> *Et nolite serere super spinas*
> Yours to drive a new furrow
> Nor sow any longer among the briers.[7]

Priests like O'Riordan and McGarry realised that the kind of legalistic authoritarian model of church that obtained in Ireland was not by any means the ideal and that it could not survive in the long run. Times were changing and even though the pace of change was not as fast in Ireland, in the new era which was on the horizon people would demand a more open, communicative church. The theology in the *Furrow* had a pastoral emphasis. McGarry was determined that it would not be theoretical knowledge divorced from its practical application.

The success of the *Furrow* was inextricably bound up with the personality of its founding editor, his vision, and the leadership he provided. One of his strengths was that he was in touch with the main body of his readership and, in this way, he was able to be sensitive to the old, as well as promoting new ways of thinking. It is important to point out that the *Furrow* in the 1950s was geared to a clerical readership, whose experience of theology in the seminaries was an extremely arid one, which was totally divorced from life in the outside world.

Recalling his seven years as a clerical student in Maynooth, from 1922 to 1929, Neil Kevin observed that, 'the daily round of prayer, study and recreation can be gone through, and in ninety-nine cases in a hundred is gone through, without reference to what is happening in the world'. He went on to point out that, 'the rule sternly forbade the reading of newspapers or other periodicals'.[8] This is the kind of seminary life that would have been experienced by priests in the 1940s, 1950s and well into the 1960s. Liam Ryan, in his survey report entitled *The Changing Direction of Irish Seminaries* (1972), observed that little had changed in the culture of the seminary between 1862 and 1962.[9] Kevin, in his book, recalled: 'the steady, undiverging orthodoxy' of theology, going on to explain that:

> the textbooks of theology might all be the work of one man. They came to us compiled, printed, and bound according to one fashion. Meandering through incredible pages of print, large and small and medium ... towards the last limitation of all that man can know.[10]

The impression given by the manuals was that knowledge was static and finite. This was the Scholastic approach to theology. Students were not encouraged to respond to, react to, or question the knowledge — they were required simply to absorb it and reproduce it at examination time. McGarry knew that such a training did not contribute to the kind of open-mindedness for which he might, at times, have wished. In this respect, his ability to keep a fruitful tension between the old and the new was of paramount importance. The articles in the *Furrow* reflected Catholic Ireland in the 1950s in terms of its ethos and attitudes, as well as anticipating and precipitating change. The style of the journal was crucial. At a time when the official Church was dogmatic and not open to question, the *Furrow* sought an exchange of views — it sought to promote enquiry and discussion. The secret of the *Furrow*'s success in steering the Irish Church towards change was that the editor was not dismissive of more conservative attitudes, and he did not expect change to come overnight — he was willing to prepare the ground slowly and carefully. Seán MacRéamoinn has perhaps captured his approach best of all, when he termed it '*brostaigh go bogh*'.[11]

An example of his approach is seen when a priest, Fr Seán Tiernan of St Nathy's College, Ballaghadereen, wrote an article, 'What Price Art?', in which he was highly critical of a book by Eric Gill, *Beauty Looks After Herself*, in which the author had 'some hard things to say about repository art and the dreadful lack of culture which makes the Catholic clergy prefer it to the real thing'.[12] Fr Tiernan, in a hard-hitting article, argued that it was a question not of preference, but of necessity. The reason, he asserted, why churches were adorned with so much repository art, was quite simply that priests could not afford to buy the original product.[13]

One of the central aims of the *Furrow*, from the outset, was to promote among the clergy an awareness of, and interest in, genuine ecclesiastical art. But McGarry did not allow his own interests to prevent him from hearing and airing other points of view. The article was published with an introductory note saying that it did 'not represent the views of the *Furrow*', but that it expressed 'the opinion of many priests', adding that, 'the editor would welcome a discussion of the points raised by Fr Tiernan'.[14] McGarry's editorial style was subtle and unobtrusive. However, he was always there in the background, leading, questioning, challenging but never imposing. In preference to writing an editorial, he chose to exercise his leadership role by means of the short introductory note, or the footnote asking a question, registering a doubt or seeking further suggestions — always attempting to promote further reflection. McGarry aimed to promote openness of communication and to renew the Irish Church. He saw these aims as inextricably interlinked, but there were also occasions when they were not necessarily in harmony.

The *Furrow* began life at a time when the Irish bishops were very authoritarian and powerful. They were determined to retain their authority and power in the secular sphere, to say nothing of their own immediate sphere of influence. Against this background, McGarry has been seen, by a commentator who knew him, as possessing the skill of an acrobat.[15] This was particularly the case in the 1950s, before the advent in the 1960s of the more liberal post-conciliar era. Given that he was highlighting many sensitive issues ahead of time, so to speak, it was important that he should not be seen as too much of a crusader. His task of leadership had to be finely balanced — indeed, had he not been able to achieve a very delicate balance, his whole enterprise might well have been put in jeopardy.

It is undoubtedly significant that the *Furrow* completely ignored the 'mother and child' controversy, the issue which most concerned the Catholic Church authorities in its very first years of publication. This may have been for shrewd political reasons of the editor's own, or because it was felt that the Church–state relationship was a matter for *Christus Rex*, which was specifically launched to deal with social and political issues. Such issues were also dealt with in *Studies*, which published a number of articles in 1951, advising readers why the scheme should be rejected on religious, medical and financial grounds.[16] Or it might well have been that the *Furrow*, in not getting involved at that time, was making the most powerful statement of all in regard to what should constitute the extent, or limitation of the Church's sphere of influence in sociopolitical questions.

The fact that McGarry was neither a radical nor perceived as such put him in a stronger position to influence his readership. Archbishop D'Alton of Armagh contributed a foreword to the first issue of the journal.[17] In McGarry's own foreword in the first issue he stated that, in pursuit of its aims,

> The *Furrow* will be guided by the mind and spirit of the Church. Obedience to the Vicar of Christ and to his bishops, whom the Holy Ghost has appointed to govern his flock, will be the corner-stone of its policy.[18]

But one senses that McGarry's was a more catholic understanding of loyalty. It was loyalty to the Church in the broadest sense, and not just to the Church in the narrow sense in which it was construed at that time — in terms of bishops, priests and a legalistic system of rules and regulations. That said, the latter model of church was the one that obtained and it had to be reckoned with.

McGarry established the Furrow Trust which was to publish the journal. The founder members then ceded their legal interest in the control of the *Furrow* to the board of trustees, of whom there were five, all priests — one from each ecclesiastical province and one other — when the trust was set up.[19] This meant that while the *Furrow* was based in Maynooth, it was independent of, and had no official link with, the college. Maynooth is in the Dublin diocese and the Archbishop of Dublin, John Charles McQuaid, was one of the most authoritarian of all the bishops at the time. Perhaps foreseeing that there could be clashes if he was to pursue his aim of renewal of the Irish Church, McGarry may have devised the trust as an effective means of getting around any difficulties that might arise in relation to what was published in the journal.

Until 1975, with the promulgation of the decree *Ecclesiae Pastorum*, 'on the vigilance of the Church's pastors regarding books',[20] a journal could be censored where it was published or where it was printed. The *Furrow* was printed by the *Leinster Leader* in Naas, in the diocese of Kildare and Leighlin. The *imprimatur* or official approval to print was granted by Bishop Thomas Keogh of Kildare and Leighlin, who appointed as censor Fr James J. Conway, parish priest of Bagenalstown, Co. Carlow. The *nihil obstat* granted by the censor and the *imprimatur* by the bishop signified that the journal did not contravene Catholic teaching on faith and morals. McGarry's decision to have the journal printed in the diocese of Kildare and Leighlin might have been arrived at for reasons of convenience, or it might have had to do with the terms he was able to negotiate with the *Leinster Leader*. But, taken in the context of the time, the decision was taken partly, if not totally, because he believed that a censor appointed in the diocese of Kildare and Leighlin would be more sympathetic to the *Furrow's* agenda.[21]

The fact that the *Furrow* was independent and approved for publication in another diocese would not, however, have prevented Archbishop McQuaid from conveying his displeasure if an item appeared that was not to his liking. As one priest interviewee has put it, on such an occasion he would simply have written to the editor, saying something along the following lines: 'I see a priest of my diocese has not served you very well'.[22] An indication that he did, in fact, have reservations about the journal is evidenced in a letter he sent to Bishop Browne of Galway on 12 March 1968, in which he pointed out that, 'the *Furrow* on its back cover for February carried a large advertisement for the Liverpool Benedictine pamphlets that are a torture to the Diocesan authorities. Confession is publicly preached down in their Church', adding, 'we are repeating every error of the early so-called Reformers.'[23] Replying to his letter two days later, Browne agreed that, 'unrest in faith is pervading here and that we should — as bishops — strike at the roots'. He continued: 'The *Furrow* in my opinion is doing harm and it should be made clear to Dr Lennon that he should not allow his diocese be an escape vent for heretics'.[24] The fact that priests had to be circumspect in what they wrote has been borne out by Fr Desmond Forristal, a priest of the diocese of Dublin, who was writing in the *Furrow* from the late 1950s. Writing in 1970, he observed what an enormous change had taken place in this respect, between the 1950s and the post-conciliar era:

> I can well remember the days before Vatican II when writing for the *Furrow* was not an exercise in prudence. It was an exercise in survival. But those days are long gone and priests can feel free to express themselves.[25]

Despite what Forristal says, however, it is fair to suggest that Bishop Browne's exchange of views with Archbishop McQuaid as late as 1968 reflected the mind-set of the majority of the Irish bishops at that time.

The norms for the granting of the *imprimatur* were revised in 1975 and, after that time, journals like the *Furrow* no longer needed an *imprimatur*. The February 1976 issue of the *Furrow* was the first to appear without the *imprimatur* and *nihil obstat*. The transition to a more open climate of Catholicism is one of the main changes in Catholic culture pointed up in this book, and the *Furrow* was in the vanguard of change in this area from the early 1950s.

From the outset, the *Furrow* opened its readers' minds to new developments and currents of thought, both in the Irish Church and beyond the shores of Ireland. In this context it published sermon notes, papal documents, Irish bishops' statements, and book, radio and film reviews. Whereas the *IER* was informative, the *Furrow* sought to be interactive as well as informative. While the *IER* did have a 'Questions and Answers' section, its approach was didactic. From the beginning, the *Furrow* included a 'Correspondence' section, and this was expanded in the 1960s as the 'News and Views' section. In the early years, in his column 'Round the Reviews', O'Riordan examined issues being raised in foreign Catholic publications, among them the question of devotion to the souls in Purgatory, the canonisation of St Maria Goretti, and the question of having the liturgy in the vernacular.[26] Articles were also published from time to time on Catholic life in various foreign countries such as France,[27] the Netherlands,[28] Denmark[29] and Germany.[30] These articles and O'Riordan's reviews gave readers of the *Furrow* an insight into Catholic life as lived on mainland Europe, and Catholic intellectual thought, at a time when Ireland was very cut off from continental European thinking.

The *Furrow* did not just publish articles at random. It became involved in issues, and sought to stimulate an awareness of them. One of these was the censorship issue. Fr Peter Connolly's articles and film reviews were very daring at a time when it would not have been considered appropriate to question the official line of thinking.[31] From time to time, a particular topic was selected as a theme, and all the articles in that issue were devoted to it. Among the issues given an airing in the pages of the *Furrow* in the 1950s were emigration,[32] Christian unity,[33] the role of the laity in the Church[34] and the Church's liturgy, and Church art and architecture. Each of these matters was sensitive in its own way at that time. The manner of their treatment was novel, to say the least, for a clerical readership, which had been schooled in a very closed, authoritarian climate. The editor's open-minded approach was crucial to his success in handling them. In so far as these issues were aired ahead of their time in Ireland, the *Furrow* exercised a prophetic role in the Irish Church.

From the first year of its publication, writers in the *Furrow* focused on the liturgy, and played a very influential role in the area of liturgical renewal. These writers were not quite as impressed by Irish Catholic devotional fervour as many of the commentators recorded above. They sensed that mere numbers at church were not in themselves an index to the spiritual health of a church. They lamented Ireland's lack of a liturgical tradition. Seeing this as a poor reflection on Irish Catholicism, the journal set as one of its aims the fostering among Irish priests of an interest in the liturgy. Writing in the *Furrow* in 1950, Fr Edward Long of Drumkeen, Co. Donegal, attributed Irish lack of interest in the liturgical movement to the fact that Ireland was far away from continental influences, and thus to the time-lag that existed before spiritual and intellectual movements made themselves felt.[35] While admitting the 'unquestioned' faith and piety of the Irish people, he bemoaned the fact that the 'approach to prayer is personal and individualistic'. 'Private needs, the worries and hopes of the individual, dominate piety,' he pointed out, 'and there is little consciousness of being a family in Christ'.[36]

Long was highlighting what was seen by many enlightened commentators as a deficiency in Irish Catholicism, as it expressed itself at the time. There was a feeling among writers like McGarry and Long that the Mass, however well attended, and the sacraments did not play the central role that they should in the lives of the people. Though they were there as a community, they did not see themselves as such. Their understanding of the Mass and sacraments was an impoverished one. They did not see them as having implications for their lives and their relationships beyond the church walls. They were passively present rather than actively involved. As silent spectators, each was absorbed in his or her own private prayers. Many people at that time 'prayed their beads' or said the rosary during Mass. Apart from the Leonine prayers (which are examined in Chapter 8) and the practice (by no means uniform) at some Masses of reading translations of the Epistle or Gospel in the vernacular after the readings themselves, at that time the entire liturgy of the Mass was in Latin. In 1950, Long pointed to the use of Latin in the prayers of the Church as a barrier to involvement, suggesting that it was time to look into the possibility of having some of the rites in the vernacular.[37]

The Irish Church in the pre-conciliar period was loath to take any initiatives, or engage in experimentation in the liturgical area. Quite simply, the bishops and priests in general saw no need. As far as they were concerned, the high level of religious practice spoke for itself. Because they had not experienced the sharp decline in religious practice that their continental counterparts had, they had little need to question the quality of people's liturgical experience. Some Irish clergy, though they were in the minority in the 1950s, did realise that the world outside Ireland was changing and that it was only a matter of time before change would also come to Ireland. They were concerned that in a more complex social context, people might no longer be satisfied to be passively present at a ritual which was not very meaningful for them. Fr Dermot McIvor of Ardee, Co. Louth, stated it thus in 1951:

> This people, that silently assists at our Masses, seems today to be entering on a crisis of the spirit, one which is likely to grow towards its climax with all the rapidity which has now become characteristic of human development.[38]

He saw that loyalty to a sacred and ancient tradition might not be able to withstand the pressures of the secular world which was beckoning the faithful, ever more compellingly, with all manner of sophisticated means at its disposal for expressing its ideas and inspiring people.[39] McGarry and the nucleus of people he drew around him, who contributed articles to the *Furrow,* were aware of the growth of the liturgical movement on the continent and the experimentation and innovation that went on from the time of Pope Pius X's pontificate (1903–14). He had repeatedly promoted the principle of the importance of active lay participation in the sacred liturgy, and of frequent Communion.

The Benedictine monks were particularly involved in the promotion of liturgical renewal on the continent. Likewise, in Ireland, the Benedictine monks of Glenstal Abbey were at the centre of the liturgical movement. The idea of a liturgical congress was proposed to the community by Fr Thomas Garde OP, when preaching their annual retreat in 1953. In 1954, the first Liturgical Congress was held in Glenstal Abbey. This was the beginning of the Irish liturgical movement. The Abbey became the venue for subsequent congresses which were held annually until 1975. McGarry was involved from the outset in the organisation of the congresses. He publicised them and promoted awareness of the progress of the liturgical movement, by publishing in the *Furrow* the papers read at the annual gatherings.

However, the liturgical movement was slow to gather pace in Ireland. An examination of pastoral letters in the 1950s shows that the matter of liturgy did not rate highly among the concerns of the bishops. And the same applied to the general run of the clergy. In the words of Fr Austin Flannery OP, who was himself involved in the movement from its earliest days in Ireland:

> Not for us, the attitude of the majority seemed to imply, that headlong rush into liturgical novelty for its own sake to which other countries had so easily succumbed. Until the Second Vatican Council, the liturgical movement remained, in the eyes of the majority, an aberration on the part of some otherwise sensible people, innocuous, however, if kept in its place.[40]

The liturgical congresses were crucial, in that they brought a wider European perspective to the discussion of the Irish pastoral situation. Over the years, the congress played host to such distinguished guest lecturers as J.A. Jungmann, Balthasar Fischer, René Laurentin and Conleth Kearns. Essentially, the continental experience was that worship became problematic. Declining numbers at church had forced continental theologians and liturgists into analysing what William Barden OP, of St Mary's Priory, Tallaght, Co. Dublin, referred to in 1954 as the 'modern problem of worship'.[41] Whereas the majority of churchmen in Ireland saw little need to scrutinise the liturgical experience that the Church offered worshippers, their continental counterparts were increasingly being led to the conclusion that the Church would have to update its liturgy, to recast it in an idiom which would speak to, and meet the needs of, the modern person in the context of a rapidly changing world. Speaking at the first liturgical congress in Glenstal, Barden explained that, 'their experience is suggesting that a new approach in worship is called for'. Significantly, he went on to point out that, 'there are indications that fresh ways, corresponding to our modern psychology and contemporary needs, are being opened up'.[42]

Pope Pius X's *Motu Proprio, Abhinc Duos Annos* of 23 October 1913 had given a decisive stimulus to the liturgical movement.[43] In due course, the Dialogue Mass was to develop out of the ideal of congregational participation proposed by Pope Pius X. In this Mass, the congregation joined in by making some of the responses in Latin. It was allowed for a particular congregation when the bishop of a diocese thought it prudent. Generally, it was used in religious communities and in homogeneous congregations like schools. A further development was the community Mass, which was sanctioned in 1943 for use in Germany, which allowed a mixture of German and Latin. Some time later, a similar form of community Mass was introduced into Austria.[44]

When Pius XII issued his encyclical, *Mediator Dei,* in 1947, it was essentially a response to the changes and experimentation that had been taking place in continental Europe. The Pope endorsed the importance of the principle of lay participation. Against this background, gradual and controlled concessions were made by the Holy See, allowing large amounts of the vernacular into the official liturgy of the Church in France in 1947, in Germany in 1950 and in America in 1954. Such concessions were made at the request of the hierarchies of many countries.[45]

Liturgical experimentation on the Continent had developed in close tandem with the architectural movement. In this way, new churches were being designed which would promote a sense of unity and facilitate active participation in the liturgy. The necessity for a more intimate community-type atmosphere was borne in mind. Irish churches built in the 1950s were of traditional design — Hiberno-Romanesque or Gothic. The imitation of past styles of architecture persisted into the 1960s, with very few exceptions.[46] There was little thought of breaking new ground or considering more contemporary styles of church-building, despite the fact that new techniques and materials were becoming available. Because Irish churchmen were not faced with the problem of shrinking congregations, they did not have to devise creative or imaginative initiatives to encourage worshippers at that time. In Dublin in the 1950s, Archbishop McQuaid simply had to accommodate the huge numbers who were flocking to church.

Archbishop D'Alton, in his foreword to the first issue of the *Furrow*, had expressed the hope that the journal would stimulate a greater interest among priests in ecclesiastical art and architecture.[47] From the outset, the editor took up this challenge and sought to promote discussion on church design, the suitability or otherwise of repository art, how churches should be furnished, and the question of building in traditional or contemporary style. As part of his programme to promote awareness of such issues, McGarry became involved in the organisation and publicisation of symposia, seminars and exhibitions, having as their subject church art and architecture.

One such symposium on 'Church architecture today' was held in Newman House, Dublin, in 1955, under the auspices of the Arts Council of Ireland. It attracted an audience of about 500 people. In June 1955, the papers read at the symposium were published in the *Furrow*. Introducing the papers, McGarry spoke of his efforts from the earliest publication of the journal, to 'make our readers aware of developments abroad in this field and of the urgent need to take stock of the situation at home'.[48] In the course of the symposium, one speaker argued the case for developing a more contemporary style in church-building, stating that, 'the liturgical movement demands of the worshippers a more active part in the divine service'. He pointed to the fact that more emphasis 'than ever before is laid on maximum visibility', and that, 'today with steel and reinforced concrete we can dispense entirely with the columns which were so necessary in earlier times'.[49]

Arising out of this symposium, the organisers established, in 1956, the Church Exhibitions Committee of the Royal Institute of Architects of Ireland. The first members of this committee were Wilfrid Cantwell, Richard Hurley, Gerald McNicholl, Brendan Ellis, Oscar Richardson and Thomas Ryan.[50] Dr McGarry and Fr Austin Flannery OP, editor of *Doctrine and Life*, were later co-opted as members. The committee organised seminars, lectures and exhibitions, and thus contributed to the education of both clergy and architects. In the course of time, a forum emerged of priests, architects and artists who were liturgically informed, and when liturgical renewal became centre stage in the 1960s, they were ready to take up the challenge it offered, and their expertise and influence were a crucial factor in smoothing the way for change.[51]

The June 1957 issue of the *Furrow* was devoted to a symposium on Sacred Art, in which a number of foreign experts in the field of sacred art contributed articles. One of these was Fr Cloud Meinberg OSB, head of the Art department of St John's University, Collegeville, Minnesota. He commented on the huge spate of church-building going on in continental Europe, largely as a result of the destruction following the War. He wrote that almost all of the new churches 'are modern in design'.[52] He observed that, 'the battle of styles is over in Europe. That was fought twenty or thirty years ago'.[53] In the new churches of the Rhineland in Germany, he noted, the altars faced the people. The driving force behind the new planning was to get people near the altar, so as to enhance their participation.

A French architectural exhibition was held in Maynooth in June 1957. Reporting on the exhibition, Fr Donal O'Sullivan expressed the wish that 'every cleric and layman in Ireland should see the exhibits, because they shocked

> the onlooker into the realisation that a whole nation, only three hours away from us today, is building and decorating churches in a contemporary style and that a church in the year 1957 need not resemble either a Roman basilica or a Greek temple.[54]

The new style of church building in Europe was a sign of cultural change. The liturgy and church buildings are public expressions of Catholic culture. Catholicism was adopting a new idiom, a new way of expressing itself in order to respond to social change.

The papers of the liturgical congresses, published in the *Furrow,* provide a unique insight into the liturgical situation, as it obtained in Ireland. An examination of these papers bears out Flannery's observation that not many clergy shared the same enthusiasm, or sense of the importance of the liturgy, as did the *Furrow* writers. When one considers the central importance accorded by the Second Vatican Council to the process of liturgical renewal, and the extent to which it was seen as a side issue, or virtually a non-issue by the bishops, seminary teachers and general run of priests in 1950s Ireland, it is a measure of how out of touch the Church in Ireland was in the pre-conciliar period with the march of ideas in the continental Church.

However, the matter of liturgy was not quite so simple in Ireland, and one could sense a certain ambivalence in attitude towards it, even in the minds of those who saw themselves as zealous liturgists. At the first Liturgical Congress in Glenstal, Fr Michael Dwyer, a priest speaking from the background of a rural parish in Tipperary, stated the dilemma thus:

> Reading enthusiastic accounts of liturgical experiments abroad, one cannot escape the feeling that the zeal and initiative displayed is, in some measure at least, provoked by the challenge of non-Catholic environment and the need of special effort to bring the faithful to church.[55]

However, he went on to point out: 'that is not at all our problem. The Irish are notably the best church-goers in the world: their devotion to the Mass and the sacraments is admirable'.[56]

The first stumbling block to progress in liturgical renewal was the attitude of many of the clergy themselves to the liturgy. There was among many, according to Placid Murray, 'a misconception of the nature of the liturgy ... considering it to be no more than rubrics or outward ceremonial'.[57] Murray, a Benedictine monk of the Glenstal community, was one of the leading figures of the liturgical movement from its beginnings. The same attitude was pointed up by Fr Michael Dwyer, when he 'regretfully' acknowledged that, 'the general body of the clergy remain uninterested' in liturgical matters. He was inclined to think that the liturgy had not 'its proper place or treatment in the curriculum of our seminaries', and he spoke of the 'considerable levity' with which he and his fellow-students had treated the subject in their seminary days.[58] He referred to the inadequate understanding that people had of the sacraments and the fact that the symbolism of the Mass 'is seldom if ever explained to them, and usually they are simply waiting passively for the ceremony to come to an end'.[59]

This was echoed by a priest speaking at the same congress, but from the perspective of an urban parish. Fr Liam Breen of Bray spoke of the attitude of 'complacency' towards the liturgy as one which was common in Ireland — an attitude that 'we should leave well enough alone'. He could see that it was hard to blame clergy, given 'the packed congregations for all the Masses on Sunday'.[60] They had no shortage of evidence to support their arguments for leaving things as they were, he observed. They could point to the impressive number of communicants at early Masses, the large number of daily communicants, the attendance at May and October devotions and the packed church for the novena devotions in honour of Our Lady. They could point to devotion to the rosary, the great number of vocations to the priesthood and the readiness of people to undertake pilgrimages to Lough Derg, Croagh Patrick and Knock. They could point to the fact that Ireland has been 'held up to the whole world, even by the Holy Father, as a great Catholic country' so often 'that we find it easy to believe'.[61] In light of all of this, it was easy to see how many clergy at the time would have felt that, as this speaker put it, 'our full churches excuse us from the suggestions made by continental writers to revive religion and fill their empty ones'.[62]

In the face of such overwhelming evidence of loyalty to religious practice and in a religious environment, which most would have seen as unchanging and unthreatened, it is easy to see that even those pushing for change and liturgical renewal might have entertained doubts. McIvor, speaking at the congress in 1955, felt, on the one hand, that, given the Irish people's 'lively sense of the spiritual', there was not 'the same urgent need for radical change'.[63] But, on the other hand, he was concerned about 'a new mood ... growing among us as a people, born perhaps of the present universal trend towards scientific exploration, and the development of life's material resources'. He saw that, 'we are no longer as content as we were with abstract themes and principles'.[64] In this, he was very much in tune with the thinking of Pius XII, who constantly in his speeches returned to the huge advances in science and the material progress to which this gave rise. His concern was that the scientific attitude would spill over into everyday life and cause the transcendent supernatural dimension of human life to be devalued.[65]

It is not difficult to understand his concern, as such an eventuality would have profound implications for the future of religious belief. The liturgy, which is the public expression of religion or the religious attitude to life, is, so to speak, at the front line of changing attitudes to religion. If people no longer choose to worship, while it cannot be taken to mean that they no longer believe in God or have a religious attitude towards life, neither can it be ignored — it is significant. On the basis of fears expressed in Rome by Pope Pius XII, and the fact that developments on the Continent were serving to confirm many of these fears, McIvor intuitively recognised that, if the Irish still had a strong sense of the spiritual, it was not to be taken for granted, 'in a world which is losing all esteem for the supernatural'.[66] McIvor and other speakers at the liturgical congresses in the 1950s sensed, and were giving voice to, the fact that life was changing and that, in a new era, people would not any longer be content to be detached silent observers at worship. They would have more expectations of their religious/liturgical experience.

These clerics were less than happy about many aspects of Irish Catholicism. Breen gave some pertinent examples of where the reality was far short of the ideal picture, as perceived and boasted of by bishops and clergy generally, and much envied, as has been seen, by their foreign counterparts. He questioned how any glory could be taken in the vast throngs in church, 'if many have no idea of why they are there other than that they are escaping mortal sin',[67] or in other cases where Mass was 'celebrated so rapidly that they could not keep up with the celebrant'. Likewise, he questioned what glory there could be in thousands receiving Holy Communion, 'if they are ignorant of its social as well as its personal implications'.[68] Given that there was no sense of 'corporate worship' at Mass, he questioned how a 'spirit of unity' could overflow from Eucharistic worship into people's 'daily lives in the spheres of the family, the factory, the economic and the political arenas'.[69]

He drew attention to the fact that many Irish people had come to see 'receiving' as more important than offering the Mass. He asked whether it was unreasonable that they should see it as something quite separate, and not an integral part of the sacrifice, given that, 'they normally receive it either before Mass begins or from a priest who distributes Holy Communion all through the Mass'.[70] He drew attention to the many worshippers who never heard a sermon or instruction, because they attended at early Mass so that they could receive Holy Communion.

Breen was drawing attention to a host of reasons why Irish Catholics had little reason to preen themselves, and he went on to sound a cautionary note, observing that, 'modern people insist on vital and progressive movement and an active share in things and we cannot feel comfortable in denying these permanently to the rising generation.' He foresaw a time when changes would no longer be optional, but would be enforced throughout the Catholic world. Breen is quite prophetic in 1954 when he makes the point that,

> we may wake up some day in the near future to find ourselves called on to do things in our churches which we will regard as extraordinary, without knowing in the least why we are to do them or what they mean.[71]

Significant changes were, in fact, being approved gradually by Pope Pius XII during the 1950s. In 1953, as already seen, he allowed some small concessions in the Eucharistic fast, and sanctioned evening Mass in certain limited circumstances, at the discretion of the local bishop.[72] However, the only place that this concession was availed of in Ireland was at Knock shrine, where evening Mass was introduced in May 1956. On 16 November 1955, a decree was issued by the Congregation of Rites, which reformed the liturgy of Holy Week.[73] Commenting on the changes in the Holy Week ceremonies, Placid Murray OSB said that, 'many of the clergy were taken by surprise at the whole idea', but that, 'all those in touch with developments abroad could have foreseen the shape of things to come'. He went on to say that 'on the whole the Irish Church had no share in the shaping of the restored rites'.[74]

In 1957, Pope Pius XII issued a decree, *Sacram Communionem*, which abolished the obligatory Eucharistic fast from midnight, and established in its place a three-hour fast from solid foods and a one-hour fast from liquids.[75] And in September 1958, a month before his death, the Sacred Congregation of Rites issued an instruction which gave general approval to the Dialogue Mass and pressed for more active participation by the faithful in the general liturgy of the Church.[76] The use of the Dialogue Mass was quite limited in Ireland. Writing in the *Furrow* in November 1959, Joseph Cunnane noted the Irish Church's lack of response to the 1958 instruction. He wrote that the efforts being made abroad to teach and encourage congregations to take a more active and intelligent part in the prayers of the Mass and other ceremonies were 'almost unknown' in Ireland.[77] He further highlighted the innate conservatism of the Irish Church, which meant waiting 'until the finished article comes to us with the stamp of the Church's approval'.[78]

However, perhaps prodded by new ideas emanating from Glenstal and the

Furrow, in 1957 the Irish hierarchy had appointed a committee, which prepared a draft *Collectio Rituum* to be submitted to Rome for approval. The committee consisted of Canon Cathal McCarthy, president of Clonliffe College; Dr Gerard Montague, professor of Liturgy in Maynooth; and Dr J.G. McGarry. It was chaired by Bishop McNamee of Ardagh.[79] The trilingual ritual, in Latin, English and Irish, was approved by Rome on 12 December 1959, and at their October meeting in 1960, the bishops issued a statement that the new ritual would come into force in Ireland on 1 February 1961.[80] Essentially, the new ritual provided for the wide usage of the vernacular in the sacraments of Baptism, Extreme Unction, the Marriage ceremony and the funeral service. In general, Latin was to be retained only in the formulae or the blessings of the sacraments.[81]

These changes were only the first waves of what was to become a veritable sea of change in Irish Catholicism in the 1960s. What is important, however, is that Irish Catholic culture was being challenged and changed from within in the 1950s. While the official Church, as represented by the hierarchy, saw little need for change, and was principally concerned with protecting and defending the status quo, some churchmen questioned the wisdom of this against the background of changes taking place in the wider European context. In order to understand the more critical stance they were adopting towards Irish Catholicism, we must examine the new theological thinking which had been developing in continental Europe, which led, in the not-too-distant future, to fundamental changes in Catholic culture worldwide.

7

THEOLOGICAL DEVELOPMENTS AND THE IRISH CHURCH

The Irish Church in the 1950s, as it has been described so far, very much reflected the outlook and mood of Pope Pius XII. From the time he was elected pope in 1939, he continued the tradition of the nineteenth-century popes in his cautious attitude towards change and his wariness of modern developments. His time as pope consolidated the autocratic, monarchical model of the papacy, and power became more and more concentrated in the curia, at the expense of the bishops. Theologically conservative, Pius XII's thinking has to be seen against the backdrop of the Church's concern since the Reformation to protect its followers from material which was considered hazardous to faith and morals.

Catholic Church theology was based on scholastic philosophy as developed in the thirteenth century by Thomas Aquinas, who integrated into Christian thought the philosophy of Aristotle. The Church's concern to defend its theological position can be charted from 1571 when Pope Paul III established the *Index of Prohibited Books,* designed as an instrument of the Counter-Reformation to suppress dissent and heresy. Another milestone along the way was the *Syllabus of Errors,* issued by Pius IX in 1864,[1] which he followed, in 1870, with the definition of Papal Infallibility.[2] The *Syllabus* took the form of the listing of eighty errors, which were issued by way of condemnation of liberal Catholics, who sought in the post-Enlightenment age to work out a reconciliation of traditional faith with the demands of modern secular culture.

The intellectual challenges to Christian doctrine became even more formidable during the pontificate of Pope Leo XIII (1878–1903). Nineteenth-century scientific advances, the development of the historical approach to the study of the Bible, the evolutionary view of man's origins, associated with Darwin, and Marxist social and economic theory all played a powerful role in influencing man's world view. A more materialistic philosophy began to take shape which was at odds with traditional Christianity.

Like Pius IX, Pope Leo XIII was conservative in his outlook towards intellectual and theological issues and, in order to counter any threats to traditional Catholic theology, in 1879, he issued an encyclical, *Aeterni Patris,*[3] which reinforced the teachings of St Thomas as the very essence of Catholic orthodoxy. But as his pontificate went on, a small but growing number of Catholic scholars began to feel that the restoration of medieval scholasticism was not the answer. In their view, the neo-Thomist synthesis was not broad enough to deal with the manifold problems raised for the Catholic faith by the developments of modern culture. They broke away from scholasticism and searched for ways of expressing their faith that would make sense to the modern mind. Known as the Modernist movement, this movement met with similar rebukes from Rome where its views were considered to be unorthodox and to pose a challenge to the central authority of the pope.[4]

In 1893, Leo issued his encyclical, *Providentissimus Deus,*[5] which ruled out any possibility of error in the Bible, and urged Catholic scholars to take as their guides the scholastic theologians and Thomas Aquinas. However, it was in the pontificate of Pius X that Modernism was finally and decisively stamped out. This happened when the decree, *Lamentabili,*[6] was issued by the Holy Office on 3 July 1907, condemning sixty-five errors, which were listed and attributed to the Modernists. This was followed by the encyclical, *Pascendi,* on 8 September 1907.[7] In order to extirpate Modernism, vigilance committees were to be set up in each diocese to detect any sign of Modernist doctrines. Each diocese was to have a body of censors who would watch over Church literature. Scholastic philosophy, in its Thomist form, was to be the basis for sacred studies in seminaries.[8]

Yet, despite his innate conservatism, Pope Pius X was to take a number of initiatives which would have profound long-term consequences for the development of Catholicism. His decree on the reform of sacred music, in 1903,[9] and his decree promoting frequent Communion, in 1905,[10] both gave momentum to the liturgical movement in the first decade of the century. And while, on the one hand, he was generally very repressive of biblical scholarship, in 1909 he founded the Biblical Institute in Rome and handed it over to the charge of the Jesuits — a move which gave a very significant impetus to Catholic biblical scholarship.

By the time Pope Pius XII became Pope in 1939, considerable development had taken place in both the biblical studies and liturgical areas. Again, though regarded as conservative, Pope Pius XII made his own distinctive contribution to both these areas. On 30 September 1943, he published the encyclical, *Divino Afflante Spiritu,*[11] approving the scholarship of Catholic exegetes. This was a most important milestone in Catholic scriptural scholarship in as much as it allowed scholars to pursue their research without having to look over their shoulder constantly at the Holy Office. Through the 1950s, as already seen, Pius XII sanctioned a number of liturgical changes, which were very significant for that time.

Pius XII's encyclical of 1943 was to have a wider application than the study of the Bible. The principles of historical criticism began to be applied also to the development of doctrine. From the 1940s in France, theologians like Congar, Chenu, De Lubac and Danielou were mapping out new directions in theology. Essentially, they were concerned with the problem of relating faith and doctrine to the changing context of cultures and civilisations. They felt that scholastic theology was excessively intellectual and tended to obscure the Christian message, instead of making it intelligible and acceptable to people in the context of modern life.

They proposed that the best way to do this was to return to the language of the Scriptures and the early Fathers of the Church. They felt that, having returned to the sources of revelation, it would be possible to set about a restatement of Church dogma, which would be more meaningful to the contemporary person. But Pope Pius XII condemned this on the basis that the magisterium or teaching authority of the Church was the guardian of the deposit of faith and had the task of formulating its contents to meet the changing needs of society. The magisterium approached this task according to the tenets of scholastic philosophy, which held that truth consists in the conformity of the human mind to reality and its immutable laws, and denied that it is possible to change the notions used in dogmatic formulae without changing their meaning. Its approach was the exact opposite to that of the theologians working on the new ideas.

One of the problems the latter saw associated with scholastic theology was that it concentrated on what was unchanging in human experience, and did not seem to take account of the flux of reality. These theologians were of the opinion that, in order to bridge the widening gap between theology and the more secularised mind, Catholic theology must be prepared to integrate more modern thought systems, which reflected the needs of, and were more meaningful to, the contemporary individual.

The new theological thinking was influenced by historicism and existentialism. The historical approach to theology was grounded in the idea that each era has to be understood in its own uniqueness, and that all systems of thought or knowledge must be assessed within the context of historical change and development. From this perspective, no one era could define knowledge or truth for all time. Existential philosophy, on the other hand, was concerned with individuals in their unique situations, in terms of their aspirations, fears, hopes, and their ultimate destiny, in the context of an ever-changing life situation.

Such ideas led to the belief that doctrines had to be made understandable to people in the context of the historical era in which they lived, and in terms of their own existential situation, as opposed to people being made to conform to doctrines and regulations, of which, perhaps, they had little understanding. This kind of thinking was condemned by Pope Pius XII as paving the way for dogmatic relativism and endangering objective truth. In his encyclical, *Humani*

Generis, promulgated on 12 August 1950,[12] he defended strongly the Church's use of scholastic philosophy and insisted that students for the priesthood must be trained according to its principles.

The Pope condemned 'false evolutionary notions with their denial of all that is absolute or fixed or abiding in human experience,' and which 'have paved the way for a new philosophy of error ... Existentialism'.[13] Its method, he argued, 'is to leave the unchanging essences of things out of sight, and concentrate all its attention on particular existences'.[14] There is too, he continued, 'a false use of the historical method, which confines its observations to the actual happenings of human life, and in doing so contrives to undermine all absolute truth, all absolute laws.'[15] He reminded Catholic theologians and philosophers of their 'grave responsibility for defending truth'.[16] Even though he did not name any particular theologians, the encyclical was considered to be aimed strongly at France's progressive theologians, and it cost several prominent writers, seminary professors and provincial superiors their positions of authority.[17]

But to what extent did the new currents of theology or the controversy surrounding them influence the Irish Church? Theological debate and questioning about fundamental issues had never been a feature of the Irish Church. The *Irish Theological Quarterly*, which began in 1906, ceased publication in 1922, and reappeared in 1951 after an absence of twenty-nine years. Walter McDonald, professor of Moral Theology at Maynooth for forty years until his death in 1920, first 'broached' the idea of a theological review to his colleagues in the theology faculty in 1905.[18] Feeling that Maynooth was 'somewhat out of touch', he 'had long felt the want ... of a journal, wholly devoted to theological science ... in which the latest questions would be discussed'.[19] Explaining that the kind of work that they 'should aim at was different from — higher than — what appeared in the *Irish Ecclesiastical Record*',[20] he continued:

> it was not ... a question of making known or popularising what had been already done by others, but of doing something which had not yet been done — of extending the bounds of theological science, partly by the discovery of truth, and in part by the exposure of untruth.[21]

While he was under no illusion that this 'would be likely to meet with opposition'[22] from the ecclesiastical authorities, and notwithstanding the fact that 'the suspicion with which [the] project was regarded manifested itself' early on,[23] he pressed ahead. Censorship was a problem from the outset, and when matters came to a head, McDonald was not prepared to seek the approval of the Trustees of the college (the bishops) for the review, because he 'felt deeply that freedom of action is as the breath of life'[24] for such a review, and, in due course, he severed his connection with the *ITQ*.[25] In 1913, he began writing his reminiscences. He died in 1920, and they were published by Jonathan Cape in 1925. In the book, entitled *Reminiscences of a Maynooth Professor*, reflecting on the *ITQ*, he referred to it as 'a colourless periodical'. He added: 'it has not, I think, done much to advance the bounds of theological science, as was our object from the beginning'.[26]

Another contemporary book which throws critical light on Maynooth, the training of priests and the ways of the clergy was the autobiographical novel, *Father Ralph*, published in 1913 and based on author Gerald O'Donovan's experiences in Maynooth and in his ministry, mainly in Loughrea, Co. Galway.[27] Born in 1871, O'Donovan entered Maynooth in 1889, some nineteen years after Walter McDonald. He got involved with Horace Plunkett in the co-operative movement and was critical of the general reluctance of the clergy to get involved. Essentially, he believed that the priest should engage with the political and economic practicalities of people's lives. Very much a maverick, he left the priesthood in 1904, during the Modernist crisis. For 'Father Ralph', it was the papal encyclical, *Pascendi* (1907), condemning Modernism, which finally drove him to leave in despair.[28]

The tendentiousness of O'Donovan's account of Maynooth and his caustic treatment of many of the clergy have been seen as detracting from the documentary value of the book, which is unfortunate in a way, because many of his observations and insights were perceptive and ring true. Of one of his lecturers in Maynooth, Ralph complained that, 'Fr Hay's lifeless abstractions and the crude legalism of moral theology left his heart cold and repelled his mind', adding that 'the Church had taken a wrong turning and used the out-of-date implements of the thirteenth century in the nineteenth'.[29] The fact that Maynooth was out of touch with the latest theological developments and that questioning of established patterns of thought was not encouraged was portrayed in the book, when Ralph recalled venturing an opinion contrary to that of the notes given by the professor of theology, Fr Dunlea, whereupon 'the professor flushed angrily, but said suavely, "What is good enough for St Thomas and me ought to satisfy you, Mr O'Brien. I'd advise you to read my notes carefully. They contain everything necessary to be known on the subject"'.[30] Ralph explained his frustrations in relation to 'the reasoning of the philosophy and theology schools with their puerile major premises assuming things as proved that bristled with difficulties' to Fr Sheldon, a thinking man. The latter's reply (when one considers that O'Donovan wrote the book between 1911 and 1913) was both pertinent and prophetic:

> 'For years I have been hoping for better things, which are slow in coming. But', his face brightened, 'they are coming. France and Italy and Germany are showing the way. Some day Ireland will move too.... Don't mind the quibbles of the schools. Try to get to the kernel inside the husk. Live your life as closely as you can on the pattern of Christ's. You'll never convert a soul from evil nor help it to heaven by a syllogism'.[31]

McDonald echoed O'Donovan's views about the narrowness of the intellectual formation of the students.[32] Allowing for the fact that both men had their own particular axe to grind, their observations provide a valuable insight into the contemporary scene. McDonald's experience with the *ITQ*, and the subsequent demise of the journal, speaks volumes about the state of theological discourse in Ireland in the first half of the twentieth century. Quite simply, Ireland was not involved in theological developments. From the time of the journal's reinstatement, however, it did provide an insight into the battle of ideas that was being played out at that time, between those theologians pressing for a 'new' theology, which would be more relevant to the contemporary person, and those who felt that any modifications of existing theology would endanger objective truth. Perhaps it is not surprising then that its attitude towards some of the new theological thinking was more wary than that of the *Furrow*, which was a more independent publication. That the *ITQ* would adopt a more apologetic stance towards the new ideas could be discerned from the tone of the foreword in 1951:

> The *Irish Theological Quarterly* is reappearing in a period as critical as any in history for the maintenance of spiritual and supernatural values. Faith has more need than ever of understanding in times when the struggle between good and evil is so largely centred in the realm of ideas and of the mind.[33]

Perhaps the best clue as to the ethos of the *ITQ* is provided by the editor's concluding remark in this foreword, describing it as 'a journal devoted to the elucidation and defence of Catholic truth'.[34] These sentiments, very similar in tone and content to the bishops' pastorals of the same time, leave one in no doubt that the theology in the journal will reflect the orthodoxy of the day. The fact that it was a Maynooth publication (like the *IER*), and that it was edited by professors of the faculty of theology at Maynooth, meant that not a lot had changed since the time of Walter McDonald. Whereas the *Furrow* might be classified as a journal of applied theology, the *ITQ* was a scientific theological journal, concerned with academic theology. It is not to suggest that the *Furrow* was less orthodox in the views it promoted, merely that because of its independent status, it could afford to be more open to, and more accepting of, new currents of thought and, even more importantly, was in a position to make them available for discussion and, in so doing, was able to influence thinking in relation to them. Indeed, it is very likely that McGarry had learned a very valuable lesson from the disappointments and frustrations which had cost McDonald so dearly.

The tone of the *ITQ* for the decade was, to a great extent, set by Pope Pius XII's encyclical, *Humani Generis*. A number of articles appeared in the *ITQ* in 1952, explaining the encyclical and summarising the Pope's stance in relation to the points raised. The writer of the first of these articles, Fr Gerard Mitchell, professor of Dogmatic Theology in Maynooth, observed that not many people in Ireland realised that 'something in the nature of a theological crisis' had been developing in recent years.[35] He went on to state, however, that 'readers of the continental periodicals were of course aware that some rather startling views were being advanced', and that, given their 'dangerous character', the encyclical, *Humani Generis,* 'came as no surprise to Catholic theologians'.[36] Basically, the article reinforced the points made in the encyclical, attacking 'the false trends in theology', and defended the pope's action in taking these theologians to task.

Fr Kevin McNamara, professor of Dogmatic Theology in Maynooth, wrote an article in the *ITQ* in 1954,[37] in which he gave an account of a book by M. Roger Aubert, professor of Theology at Louvain, published in the same year and entitled *La théologie Catholique au milieu du XXe siècle.* The book described trends in theology over the previous fifteen to twenty years. Drawing from the book, Fr McNamara explained how Existentialism, with its particular concern for individual human destiny, had 'impinged on the various departments of Catholic theology', and went on to point out that 'traditional moral theology', in particular, had 'been challenged at a number of points'.[38] He noted that Existentialists accused Catholic moral teaching 'of failing to take due account of the many external circumstances that influence human conduct in real life'.[39]

Fr McNamara wrote: 'it has been criticised too by students of modern "depth psychology", on the grounds that it does not allow sufficiently for the internal circumstances which so deeply influence conduct'.[40] He went on to explain that 'situation ethics' was 'the answer proposed by certain Catholics to the difficulties of applying general principles of moral theology to particular cases', pointing out that:

> it is intended to answer the criticism that Catholic moral theology is impersonal and legalist, concerned chiefly with ways and means for avoiding sin, rather than with developing the personalist values of freedom, sincerity and love.[41]

Whereas Catholic moral theology took as its starting point the external law, and insisted on people conforming to it, the new conception of morality being worked out started with the person in his or her concrete situation. It took the view that individuals, when confronted with a moral problem, must make their own conscientious decision in regard to it, in terms of their own circumstances and the forces impinging on them. In such a deliberation of conscience, what mattered was the person's sincerity and good will — whether the intention was to please God by the action and not whether the act was in conformity with objective rules. Too much concentration on the latter, it was felt, had led to a preoccupation with abstract impersonal casuistry.

While Fr McNamara conceded that Catholic moral theology could benefit in certain ways from the views of the proponents of 'situation ethics', he noted that Pope Pius XII in 1952 repeated the traditional Catholic teaching on morality and the importance of making moral decisions in accordance with objective moral values. Concluding his article, he stated that, 'there have been some crises in theology over the past few decades' and 'the most serious of them — that concerning the "new theology" — may not yet have been fully resolved'.[42] That said, he saw little danger that the tragedy of Modernism would be re-enacted:

> if only because the scriptural and patristic revival has shown how traditional Catholic theology can, without prejudice to the true notion of dogma, fully provide for the religious needs of the human heart. It can do so in the twentieth century equally with the first or fourth or thirteenth.[43]

The same kind of wariness of change is also obvious in an article written in 1955 by Fr William Conway, professor of Moral Theology and Canon Law in Maynooth, on 'New Trends in the Science of Moral Theology'. In the article, he explained that there was much criticism of the science of moral theology, as practised at the time. 'It is said', he wrote, that:

> it presents Christian morality as primarily a matter of conforming to rules ... the contrast between the moral teaching of Our Lord and that of text-book moral theology is felt to be very great; the one is a call to a supernatural life of heroism for the love of God and the love of one's fellow man, the other is a code of rules which constricts rather than inspires.[44]

Critics, he explained, argued that morality had become 'something external' that people conformed to, rather than something which got 'its force from within'. They believed that it should get its force 'from inner love rather than from external obligation'.[45]

This kind of thinking was, in a few short years, to form the basis for a radical reorientation of moral theology. That said, Fr Conway, one of the experts whose task it was to interpret and clarify the external rules and obligations to which people were obliged to conform, in the 'Notes and Queries' section of the *IER*, did not feel that this approach could be dispensed with. He advised that moral theology textbooks were there to help the confessor and that, while they might sometimes 'give the impression of a narrow formalism', this was 'unavoidable', because 'the drawing of a precise line in matters of human conduct must necessarily savour at times of legalism'.[46]

The articles in the *ITQ* provide an insight into the debate going on at an intellectual level, the outcome of which would perhaps be *the* most significant factor in changing Catholic culture all over the world. Equally important is the insight they provide into Irish theologians' attitudes towards the simmering changes. They stood aloof from the debate. To the extent that they did get involved, their approach was defensive, apologetic. They reflected what was happening but always from this stance. It is also important to point out that two of the aforementioned theologians subsequently became influential figures in the Irish Church — William Conway as Cardinal Archbishop of Armagh and Primate of all Ireland, and Kevin McNamara as Bishop of Kerry, and later as Archbishop of Dublin.

All in all, there was little evidence in the *ITQ* that its contributors realised that the new currents of thought were going to be as influential as they turned out to be in the course of time. This is interesting in light of the fact that, ten years later, work was well under way at the Second Vatican Council to recast Catholic theology thoroughly, precisely in order to meet the needs of people in the late twentieth century. The journal confined its theological discourse within the recognised parameters laid down by the official Church in Rome. It did not venture into territory that was 'out of bounds' or, to the extent that it did, it was to provide factual information about controversies, as seen above, and then to defend the official Church position in relation to them. It accepted and reiterated the official line of thinking, and there was no consideration of whether it should change, or be made more meaningful for Catholics of the time. This dimension of theological activity was given little or no consideration — it was seen quite simply as an academic pursuit (divorced from the practicalities of life). But if the Irish Church was dragging its heels theologically — precisely what McDonald and O'Donovan complained about — things were about to change.

When Pope Pius XII died in 1958, the fifty-one cardinals who met to elect the next pope were almost evenly divided between those who felt that there was a need for a definite break with the triumphal, centralist, monarchical model of Church which Pius XII had represented, and those who were in favour of continuing it. Angelo Roncalli, the 76-year-old Patriarch of Venice, chosen after a three-day struggle, supposedly reflected a compromise. Even though his pontificate was destined to last for only four years and seven months, it was undoubtedly one of the most important, and effectively amounted to a revolution which brought to an end the fortress mentality that had been characteristic of the Catholic Church since the Council of Trent.

His consecration as Pope John XXIII took place in Rome on 4 November 1958. On 25 January 1959, he announced his intention of calling an Ecumenical Council of the Church. The first session of the Council began on 11 October 1962. The Second Vatican Council, the twenty-first in the history of the Church, brought together the top leaders of the Catholic Church for four three-month sessions over four years, and involved them in debate on most of the vital religious issues facing mankind. The fourth and final session of the Council closed on 8 December 1965. During this time, there was a thorough-going reassessment by the pope and the Council Fathers of the Church's role in the modern world, as a result of which some sixteen documents were issued — four constitutions, nine decrees and three declarations, which, when implemented, were to produce far-reaching changes in Catholic communities worldwide.

Before the Council, bishops from all over the world were invited to make submissions to a preparatory commission. There were thirty episcopal submissions from Ireland. They came from twenty-four residential bishops, the nuncio to

Ireland, two auxiliary bishops and three retired missionary bishops. These submissions, along with five others from Maynooth College, are of interest, in as much as they provide an insight into what were seen as being the important issues of the day that the Church in council should debate. The following is a brief account of the areas of concern which were mentioned by Irish bishops as needing discussion.

The importance of a clear exposition of doctrine was highlighted. In some cases, another Marian definition was sought. Liturgical matters occupied a small part of the submissions and the main concern here had to do with codification and simplification of rubrics. That said, experience of the vernacular in the new ritual had obviously been such that a number of bishops suggested that the question of its further extension in the administration of the sacraments and to the Breviary should be discussed. Discussion on the use of the vernacular in the Mass was requested by two bishops. Bishop McNamee, in particular, who had chaired the committee on liturgy set up by the bishops in 1957, which had prepared the new trilingual ritual, desired that it should be extended further. One of the other issues raised as needing discussion was the question of Holy Days of Obligation.[47] The following were among the issues raised in the Maynooth submissions — the question of servile work, the lay apostolate, the reconciliation of 'dissenters' with the true Church of Christ, the doctrinal issue of the Church as Mystical Body and, again, the matter of clarification and rubrical simplification in the liturgical area.[48] These were the concerns of the local Irish Church as represented by the bishops and leading Church figures in the lead-up to the Council.

Even from the brief treatment that has been possible here, the general thrust of these submissions may be discerned — they were seeking to clarify and to expound the certainties of the faith. As such, they were in keeping with the spirit of the pre-conciliar Church. The Church of the Council, on the other hand, was much bigger than single issues and definitions — it epitomised a new mood, a new way of thinking. In the new context, these issues, and how they were to be resolved, the weight they were to be given, or indeed not given, could no longer be taken as a foregone conclusion. This was readily apparent from the moment that Pope John XXIII opened the Council.

The pope's opening address to the Council Fathers signalled his rejection of the state of siege mentality, which had hitherto characterised the Catholic Church in the post-Tridentine era. He stressed the importance of the Church's engaging with the modern secular world. This would require a policy of *aggiornamento* or updating of the Church's structures and teaching, in order to enable it to carry out its mission in the world more effectively. John XXIII told the assembled bishops that the Council's task was to discover the best formulae which would be meaningful for the contemporary person and he urged that they not be too hide-bound by the past in doing so. He pointed out that 'the substance of the ancient doctrine of the deposit of faith is one thing and the way in which it is presented is another'.[49]

In making this distinction, he was endorsing what had come to be called the 'new' theology, as developed by the French theologians in the 1940s, which, as seen above, had been condemned by Pius XII in his encyclical, *Humani Generis.* The 'new' theology stressed that the Church exists to serve God by serving man, and that while fundamentals do not change, they can, and must, be developed and expressed in forms more understandable and relevant to the modern-day person. When Pope John XXIII adopted a different attitude towards this debate at the time of the Vatican Council, it represented a major ground shift in Catholicism, and it is fair to say that many changes in Catholic culture are manifestations of, or can be traced to, this fundamental philosophical change of emphasis. It resulted in a thorough-going reassessment by the pope and the Council Fathers of the Church's role in the modern world.

While the old theology dwelt on what was unchangeable in the life of man and the Church, the 'new' theology dwelt more on the 'historicity' and developmental character of all life, including that of the Church. In the context of the more historical approach to theology, while the essence of the Church's worship and doctrine had to remain the same, the format, or the way it was presented, was no longer considered immutable. This had crucial implications for liturgy, which could be considered the language of religion, and for morality and the way in which Catholics lived their lives. The liturgical and theological debates which had been taking place in continental Europe were about to come to fruition.

The first debate of the Council was on the liturgy, and the question of the suitability of the use of the Latin language in the Church's worship was central to the debate. The Catholic inclination had been to see all religious practices and formulae as unchangeable. Archbishop McQuaid and Cardinal Michael Browne, an Irish Dominican and member of the Roman Curia, were among the conservative lobby at the Council. McQuaid, while he could see the point of having the sacraments in the vernacular, spoke in favour of the retention of Latin in the Mass.[50] But the mood of the Council was overwhelmingly against this kind of thinking.

The *Constitution on the Sacred Liturgy*, promulgated on 4 December 1963 at the end of the Council's second session, recognised that the Mass and sacraments had picked up over time, and in different contexts, features that were not germane to their essential nature. The fact that this had happened did not mean that such features had to be seen as sacrosanct and valid for all time. The same applied to the Church's use of the Latin language in its rituals. It proclaimed the intention of the Council 'to undertake with great care a general restoration of the liturgy'.[51] In this restoration, the 'full and active participation by all the people [was] the aim to be considered above all else'.[52]

It was noted that, 'the liturgy is made up of unchangeable elements divinely instituted and elements subject to change'.[53] Both texts and rites were to be drawn up in such a way that people would 'be able to understand them with ease and to take part in them fully, actively, and as befits a community'[54] For this reason, the use of the mother tongue in the Mass and the sacraments was to be extended. It was to apply, 'in the first place to the readings and directives, and to some of the prayers and chants'.[55] Likewise, the use of the vernacular was to be extended in administering the sacraments and sacramentals, recognising the need 'to adjust certain aspects of these rites to the requirements of our times'.[56]

These fundamental changes in Catholic Church thinking caused considerable culture shock in Ireland. Such were the currents of thought that the writers in the *Furrow* had been picking up from the Continent and that they had sought to create an awareness of, in their Irish readers. There was little evidence, in the lead-up to the Council, that the Irish bishops were aware of the new thinking. Were it not for the *Furrow* and *Doctrine and Life*, both clergy and people would have been considerably more disturbed by, and less prepared for, the profound changes instigated by the conciliar reforms. These journals were poised to take up the challenge of educating the general body of the clergy in relation to the Council. As well as devoting many articles to the Council in progress, *Doctrine and Life* became particularly involved in publishing conciliar texts and commentaries as they came out. An enlarged edition of *Doctrine and Life* in February 1964 contained the full text of the Liturgy Constitution, plus an authoritative commentary, the first in the English-speaking world. It was republished as a book reaching eight editions, growing in size as new documents were added.[57]

The Council was closely followed and reported in the *Furrow* from its historic beginning on 11 October 1962. Fr Seán O'Riordan CSsR and Fr Frederick Jones CSsR, who were teaching in the Alphonsian Redemptorist College and resident in Rome at the time, collaborated in reporting the Council from 1962 to 1965. These reports have been seen by many as popularising the Council for Irish priests, well before the Irish Church as a whole perceived the significance of an event which was to change its own life and that of the Church universal in many ways hitherto unthought-of.

The *Furrow*'s frank style in reporting the Council was almost as important as its role in educating clergy and people about the changes in Church teaching. It marked a radical departure from the kind of ceremonial coverage of Church events featured in the daily newspaper, which was the only kind of religious reporting known to most Irish people at that time. It gave Irish priests and people an insight into internal Church politics, the political manoeuvrings of the Roman Curia, disagreements between bishops, and the general cut and thrust of the Council debates. We now turn to examine the impact of conciliar thinking in the liturgical area, which began to be felt almost immediately.

8

The Impact of the Second Vatican Council

For most Catholics, the most visible and most dramatic signs of change in Catholic culture were the changes that took place in the Church's liturgy as a result of the Second Vatican Council. These changes were felt in Ireland in a particularly dramatic way because, unlike the Catholic Church in countries in continental Europe, the Irish Church in the pre-conciliar period had been loath to take initiatives or engage in experimentation in the liturgical area. With regard to the 1958 Instruction from Rome approving the Dialogue Mass, Cardinal D'Alton, in his pastoral letter of 1960, saw that it could be introduced most profitably among senior pupils in schools, and used also in parish confraternities.[1] That said, his hesitancy has to be understood in light of the fact that while people actively participated in Dialogue Mass, the quality of their participation could not be presumed upon, given that they were answering in Latin — a language which the vast majority did not understand.

Cardinal D'Alton's death in February 1963, and the accession to the Armagh see the following September of Bishop William Conway, was to initiate a new era for Irish Catholicism. Born in Belfast in 1913, William Conway studied at St Malachy's Diocesan College and Queen's University. He was ordained at St Patrick's College, Maynooth, on 20 June 1937, and took his doctorate in Divinity in 1938. From there he went to the Gregorian University in Rome where he became a Doctor of Canon Law. In 1942, he was appointed to the chair of Moral Theology and Canon Law in Maynooth. He became vice-president of Maynooth in October 1957, and was appointed as auxiliary bishop of Armagh in June 1958. When he was consecrated bishop in July of that year, he was forty-five and the youngest member of the Irish hierarchy. In his first Lenten pastoral, in 1964, he set about preparing Irish Catholics for the changes that were on the horizon, stating:

> The Council, under the Holy Father, has issued a magnificent Constitution which will, in the course of a few years, greatly simplify the ceremonies of the liturgy, bringing out more clearly their full meaning and beauty and drawing in the people to a fuller participation in them.[2]

While Bishop Conway's attitude to the changes was positive, the general tone of his pastoral was very much in keeping with the conservative style of pastoral letters as they have been described so far. His approach was cautious. He was very much at pains to reassure people that the changes were necessary, so that the Church could 'adapt her methods and her laws to the conditions of a changing world', and that while they would be 'deep', they would 'not be revolutionary'.[3] Because he recognised that the winds of change were blowing in Rome and that there was a necessity for the Irish Church to adapt itself accordingly, his leadership has been seen as vital in steering the Irish Church towards change at a critical time.

From the time of the promulgation of the *Constitution on the Sacred Liturgy*, on 4 December 1963, reform was on the way, and the first document to put this into effect was the Instruction of 26 September 1964, by which the vernacular was approved in many parts of the liturgy of the Mass, and participation by the whole congregation was facilitated and encouraged.[4] In response to this instruction, the Irish bishops issued a statement to the press from Rome on 10 November 1964, regarding 'the introduction of the vernacular, Irish and English, into certain parts of the Mass'.[5] The changes were to be introduced for the first time in Ireland, in stages, from the first Sunday of Lent, 1965. In addition to the Epistle and Gospel, it was announced, translations had also 'been approved for the prayers said at the foot of the altar at the beginning of Mass, for the *Kyrie, Gloria,* Creed, *Orate Frates, Sanctus, Pater Noster, Agnus Dei* and *Domine Non Sum Dignus*'.[6]

When the bishops were issuing their Lenten pastorals just before the changes were due to come into effect, Archbishop Conway was in Rome for his investiture as cardinal. The bishops were, in the main, concerned to reassure Irish Catholics in relation to the changes, telling them not to be afraid, and encouraging them to answer the prayers of the Mass aloud. Bishop O'Neill of Limerick wrote: 'we must accept that silent though devout attendance at Mass is now a less perfect manner of taking part in the Mass'.[7] Given that this had not been the tradition, Bishop Browne of Galway reminded people that 'this emphasis on the liturgy, therefore, must not distract us from our obligation to say our own private prayers, especially every morning and night', and he reminded people of the importance of retaining their allegiance to the rosary.[8]

There was a sense in which the bishops feared that Irish Catholics might be disturbed by the changes, and their traditional faith threatened. Bishop Quinn of Kilmore emphasised that 'changes in form should not mislead us into speaking of changes in the Mass itself'.[9] For the Irish, who had been used to seeing the Mass as unchanging, and who had had no experience of liturgical experimentation, it was easy to understand why such reassurances were necessary. Bishop Hanly of Elphin, noted that the bishops were aware that the changes 'will be the occasion of a certain amount of confusion for people who have been brought up and lived for many years with existing practices',[10] but, he continued, 'we are all called upon to make this sacrifice for the glory of God'.[11] These remarks from the bishops summed up their own attitudes and revealed their own hesitancy about changes, which, in the Irish situation, they had seen as unnecessary. They now had to convince themselves, as well as the people, of their value.

There was a further extension of the vernacular in December 1966, when a new text agreed by the bishops of England, Wales, Scotland, and Ireland was introduced. Most of the Mass was now to be in the vernacular. Also, certain changes in words and phrases, already in use in the Ordinary of the Mass, were introduced. In May 1967, the vernacular was extended to the Canon of the Mass. Revision of the liturgy of the Mass continued under the direction of the *Concilium* set up in Rome after the Vatican Council. The main textual revisions were completed in Rome and signed by Pope Paul VI on 3 April 1969, to come into effect on the first Sunday of Advent of the same year.[12] This was, in effect, the end of the Tridentine Mass. On 26 March 1970, the Sacred Congregation for Divine Worship, under the mandate of the Pope, promulgated a 'new edition of the *Roman missal* prepared in accord with the decrees of the Second Vatican Council'.[13]

Until such time as the English translation of this Latin Missal was finally approved for Irish use in 1974, still further changes were made from time to time in the form of the Mass. Because the changes were made piecemeal as texts became available, it was an uneasy period of transition for both priests and people. Priests had to use temporary leaflets until the completed missal became available. In clerical parlance, the term used was the 'paperchase', which captures the mood and awkwardness of the transitional period.

Apart from the change to the vernacular, there were other significant changes in the format of the Mass. On the basis of the new emphases of the Vatican Council, the 1964 Instruction on implementing the reforms issued guidelines for the building of churches and the layout of sanctuaries.[14] Mediaeval church architecture reflected an understanding of Church in terms of its hierarchical structure. However, in the *Dogmatic Constitution on the Church*, promulgated on 21 November 1964, the main emphasis was placed not on the hierarchical structure of the Church, but on its members, 'the people of God'.[15] Whereas formerly the priest 'said' Mass with his back to the people, and they offered the Mass 'through' him, the new understanding of the Mass was that it was a celebration by the priest and people, over which the priest 'presided'. This called for simpler and more intimate church buildings which reflected community rather than hierarchy, and humility rather than dominance; gradually, from this time, churches began to be built in a more modern idiom.[16]

The design and renovation of churches was to be monitored from then on, and liturgical, artistic and architectural opinion and expertise had to be sought by clergy intending to build or redesign churches. After the Vatican Council, in accordance with the directives of the *Constitution on the Sacred Liturgy* and of the 1964 Instruction, the Irish Episcopal Liturgical Commission was set up, which, in turn, in 1965, established an advisory Committee on Sacred Art and Architecture. This committee was chaired by Dr J.G. McGarry, and also included on it were many of the experts he had gathered around him since the 1950s, who were now, for the first time, being accorded formal recognition.

The first members of the committee were Wilfrid Cantwell, architect, who was at the time president of the Royal Institute of the Architects of Ireland; Ray Carroll, artist; A.D. Devane, architect; Austin Flannery OP; Richard Hurley, architect; Canon Cathal McCarthy PP; W.H.D. McCormick, architect; Fr Gerard Montague PP; Dr James White, director of the National Gallery of Ireland; and Fr Brendan Devlin, professor of Modern Languages in Maynooth, who was appointed secretary.[17] The changes and suggestions being made by priests, architects and artists writing in the *Furrow,* which had seemed so revolutionary in the 1950s, were now to become orthodox practice. In June 1966, the Episcopal Liturgical Commission, assisted by the Committee on Sacred Art and Architecture, issued directives on the building and reorganisation of churches. It was argued that the 'participation of the faithful can best be achieved in a church which has been properly planned or reorganised'.[18] To realise this aim of congregational participation, it was stated that the altar should be 'free-standing, to permit celebration of Mass facing the people'.[19]

Reports from liturgical commissions set up around the country showed that while the architectural design of many churches did not readily allow for this innovation, the difficulty was offset by the erection of temporary altars.[20] In this regard, the Dublin diocese was particularly slow to change, because of Archbishop McQuaid's unenthusiastic attitude towards the spirit of renewal. McQuaid's attitude to changes in the Church was best captured by his remarks addressed to the congregation when he preached at thanksgiving devotions in the Pro-Cathedral on the day he returned from the Council. Referring to the fact that in the previous four years people may 'have been disturbed at times by reports about the Council', he was at pains to lay any such anxieties to rest. He went on: 'You may have been worried by much talk of changes to come. Allow me to reassure you. No change will worry the tranquillity of your Christian lives.'[21] As the years passed, of course, it became obvious to him that profound changes were taking place in Catholicism all around him, despite his efforts to resist them. The fact that he remained unimpressed by the changed climate is revealed in a letter he wrote to Bishop Browne of Galway on 30 December 1967. The latter sought advice in relation to Holy Faith nuns who requested permission to buy a holiday home in Connemara, which was in his diocese. McQuaid was high in his praise of the sisters. Among the many compliments he paid them was that 'they are untouched by modern craze for "aggiornamento"'.[22]

However, for the most part, the bishops followed the lead given by Cardinal Conway (who had been appointed cardinal in Rome on 25 February 1965, one week before the first liturgical changes took place in the Irish Mass). Reporting for the Armagh Liturgical Commission in 1966, Francis Lenny wrote:

> A number of recently designed chapels have altars facing the people and this is the design envisaged for all new churches, two of which are at the planning stage. Temporary altars *versus populum* have been introduced in a number of churches; a number of existing sanctuaries are being re-designed for permanent altars of this kind.[23]

The *Constitution on the Sacred Liturgy* had also emphasised that 'Sacred Scripture is of paramount importance in the celebration of the liturgy', and had stressed the necessity in the restoration of promoting 'a warm and living love for Scripture'.[24] The 1964 Instruction stated that, 'there must be a homily at every public Mass on Sundays and Holy Days of Obligation'.[25] The homily was to be based on the Scripture readings or the liturgical texts of the day. From 1970, Dominican Publications began publishing *Scripture in Church* as a help to priests who needed to improve their understanding of Scripture. A quarterly, it offers commentary on the Scripture readings for Sundays and weekdays. It became very popular in English-speaking countries. The emphasis placed on the homily brought about a significant change in liturgical practice in the post-conciliar era. Irish patterns of practice in the 1950s and early 1960s varied considerably from place to place. At that time, preaching took the form of a sermon or a catechetical instruction, based on a programme of instructions on a list of subjects, such as the Creed, commandments, sacraments and prayer, which was drawn up in each diocese in accordance with decrees 248 and 249 of the Maynooth Statutes (1956). Preaching was, in some cases, omitted — in particular, at early Masses. A short catechetical instruction tended to be given at later Masses, and the longer sermon reserved for last Mass. Practice varied also as regards the timing of preaching during the Mass itself. In some cases, it took place after the Epistle and Gospel readings, while in other cases it took place after Communion and before the Last Gospel. In light of the new ruling, the programme of formal catechetical instruction was dropped.

In the post-Tridentine period, the Bible had been de-emphasised because of its association in Catholic consciousness with the Protestant tradition. In fact, people were seen as having 'fulfilled their Sunday obligation', if they were in attendance before the Offertory, which came after the biblical readings (Epistle and Gospel), as already seen. In Ireland, the tendency of the priest to rush through the Mass to get to the Consecration has also been pointed up by a contemporary commentator above. In this context, neither the readings nor, in many cases, the catechetical instructions got the attention which they merited.

In the pre-conciliar era, there was little chance that the scripture readings could make an impact on the congregation, because they were read in Latin by the priest, with his back to the people. All of the priest's activity was centred on the altar, and he read the readings at the Epistle or Gospel side of the altar, as then referred to. In the directives issued in 1966 by the Liturgy Commission, based on the 1964 Instruction from Rome, an ambo was to be placed 'within the sanctuary for the proclamation of the word of God'.[26] A chair was to be placed at the other side of the altar, from which the celebrant was to preside 'in a positive manner over the liturgical action'.[27]

The Directory stated that 'if a communion rail is to be retained it should not be allowed to be a barrier'.[28] Some changes, like that of the altar rail, took longer than others to implement, and in some churches the altar rail was not removed. But while the strict implementation of changes might have varied, the psychology or thinking behind them made immediate demands on both laity and clergy. Whereas the laity had, up to now, fulfilled their obligation by simply being present and 'hearing' Mass, and the priest by 'saying' the Mass, now the communal nature of the proceedings was underlined. The priest was more visible and there was an immediacy about the whole proceedings. The onus was on the priest to inspire unity, to create the atmosphere conducive to communal celebration, to make the occasion live for people, and to communicate its relevance to their lives.

This change was captured by Fr Thomas Carroll of St Mel's Diocesan College, Longford, when he remarked that, 'in general, the liturgical renewal seems to depend to a great degree on the earnestness of the minister'.[29] He went on to say that 'the vernacular has imposed the absolute necessity of audibility, and of the careful presentation of Word and Sacrament'. Where this is missing, he observed, the response of the people is 'weakened'. He continued:

> As president of the assembly, and leader of his people in worship, the minister can no longer shelter behind the language barrier.... Hence, the magic of the *ex opere operato* must be laid aside.[30]

Formerly, there had been a strong emphasis on this doctrine which stressed the efficacy of the sacrifice of the Mass in itself, however inaudibly said, or rushed through by the priest, or however inadequately attended to by the congregation. This had relieved the priest of the responsibility of making it meaningful. The benefits of the Mass accrued on the basis that people attended. Whether they participated actively was not at issue. The reformed liturgy placed the onus on the priest to perform better, and on the people to become involved. For the priest whose seminary training had not placed a great emphasis, other than the rubrical, on liturgy, the transition was not an easy one.

The training in communications given to the seminarian in the pre-1960s era geared him for preaching from the pulpit at a time when the majority of his listeners were less questioning, less educated and less critical. At that time, the priest was still the most visible public communicator to whom most people were exposed in an ongoing way, and the radio era did not afford people the same opportunities to develop critical faculties as did the more sophisticated television era of the 1960s. So, the centrality of the liturgy in the post-Vatican II era demanded of priests skills as liturgists and communicators, at a time when the general public came to expect more of people who sought to communicate with them and who also grew accustomed to have more choice in what they would listen to.

The new order of the Mass allowed for many more changes, which continued to be implemented through the 1970s.[31] Central concepts of the Vatican Council had been the definition of the Church as the 'people of God' and the 'priesthood of the laity', and there was a radical de-emphasisation of the hitherto vertical, authoritarian model of Church as conceived in the bishops, priests and laity model. Several other innovations were introduced from the early 1970s, which reflected this thinking and aimed to widen congregational participation. Congregational singing was to be encouraged during Mass, and greater freedom was allowed in the choice of what was to be sung. This innovation paved the way for the folk Masses that became popular in Ireland throughout the 1970s. Other changes included the introduction of the Responsorial Psalm, the Prayer of the Faithful, and the Offertory procession. It was recommended that lay people should do the readings. After the 'Our Father' and before the Eucharist, there was to be a prayer for peace, at which the priest would exchange a greeting of peace with the congregation.

Two radical changes — lay ministers of the Eucharist and the option of 'Communion in the hand' — were not envisaged in the 1969 reforms of the Mass. They were introduced in Ireland from the late 1970s, and came about as a result of separate decrees from Rome. The door to the first reform — Communion in the hand — was opened by the instruction *Memoriale Domini,* issued by the Sacred Congregation for Divine Worship on 29 May 1969.[32] It was introduced into the Dublin diocese on 15 October 1978.[33] Archbishop Dermot Ryan of Dublin, in a pastoral letter to be read at all Masses on Sunday, 8 October 1978, wrote that it was not to be seen as a 'novelty', but 'rather a return to a traditional practice', which people could avail of as a way of deepening their faith.[34] However, foreseeing that 'some people may feel that because lay people can touch the host, we now think less of the body of Christ', he pointed out that the reality was quite the opposite —rather was there a new understanding of 'the dignity and the honour of the human body'.[35]

Lay ministers of the Eucharist were first approved by Rome in the instruction, *Immensae Caritatis,* issued by the Sacred Congregation for Divine Worship, on 25 January 1973.[36] They began to be commissioned in Ireland in the late 1970s. The date of their introduction varied from place to place. As in the case of the 'Communion in the hand' option, it was appreciated that such a development would not be welcomed by all Irish people. This can be seen on perusal of the bulletin of a Dublin parish in September 1981, when lay ministers were still a novelty. The occasion was the commissioning of nine new special ministers at the 12.30 Mass.[37] The bulletin acknowledged that it was 'appreciated that some people find it strange to receive the Blessed Eucharist from the hands of a lay person', and went on to say that 'a person has every right to receive the sacraments from whom they wish'.[38]

Archbishop Dermot Ryan's comments and those of the bulletin mentioned above reflect the fact that there was a conservative element in the Irish laity, which had to be eased into the changes gently and not disturbed too much. After Vatican II, the transnational nature of the Church became more obvious. Instructions and decrees in relation to all manner of changes were issuing from Rome on a regular basis. Bishops and priests, while they may have worried about people's sensitivities, were carried along by that tide. They could do no more than try to allay their followers' fears, and then proceed with the changes. However, many have since questioned whether the clergy lost out by being more concerned to allay people's fears, as opposed to welcoming the changes enthusiastically as positive developments in the Church.

The new *Rite of Concelebration* was promulgated in Rome on 7 March 1965.[39] This made it possible, on occasions like retreats and conferences where many priests were gathered together, for them all to concelebrate Mass, as opposed to each of them celebrating privately at side altars or temporary altars. Side altars were a feature of church design in the pre-Vatican II era, but in the post-conciliar era their inclusion in the building of new churches was discouraged. The aim of concelebration was to stress the unity or the brotherhood of the priesthood, in the same way as the changes documented above were intended to emphasise for the laity the community nature of the Mass.

On 22 June 1966, the Irish bishops announced that, from the first Sunday of Advent of that year, the vernacular would be used in Confirmation, the funeral service and Holy Orders.[40] Final drafts of many of these rites were not available, however, until the early 1970s. From the first Sunday of Advent, 1974, a new version of the Breviary, the *Liturgy of the Hours*, became obligatory for all priests.[41] A revised Marriage rite was drawn up in Rome on 19 March 1969, to be put into effect on 1 July 1969.[42]

A revised *Rite of Baptism* was issued in Rome on 15 May 1969, to come into force on 8 September 1969; it came into force in Ireland on 10 January 1971.[43] This was followed by a revised *Rite for Extreme Unction* or the *Sacrament of the Sick*, as it was now called, approved by Pope Paul VI on 13 November 1972, to come into force on 1 January 1974.[44] One of the final revisions to take place was that of the *Rite of Penance*. This was promulgated by the decree of *Reconciliationem*, on 2 December 1973. The revision was completed on 7 February 1974 in Rome, and was published and came into force immediately.[45]

The new Order of Penance allowed for three forms of the Rite. Individual confession remained as Rite 1. Rite 2 was to be a communal rite with the reconciliation of many penitents, but retaining individual confession and absolution. Rite 3, which became more controversial, involved the reconciliation of many penitents, with general confession and absolution, and was to be allowed in exceptional circumstances.[46] It was decided at the June 1976 meeting of the Irish bishops that the new rite of penance or reconciliation would be compulsory in Ireland from Ash Wednesday, 1977.[47] The first two rites were approved for use in Ireland.

The changes in the ceremonies were not confined simply to externals or rubrics. They involved radically new conceptions of each sacrament, based on the changes in theology pointed up in the previous chapter, and they had profound implications for Catholic consciousness. The emphasis was decidedly more positive. This was shown clearly in the renaming of Extreme Unction as the Sacrament of the Sick. The new approach was to see the sacrament as a ministry to the seriously sick, and not just exclusively to those who were in immediate danger of death, as it had hitherto been conceived. The sacrament was now seen as a way of sustaining the sick person through illness, and as such could be administered more than once.

Likewise with Baptism, the emphasis was less on cleansing from original sin, and more on initiating the child into the Christian life. Hitherto, the emphasis had been very much on fear of what would happen in the case of neglect of Baptism. The fate of unbaptised infants who died was a question that was regularly addressed by theologians. The question of whether such infants could be saved was closely linked to another idea commonly held in the past, and certainly adhered to in the 1950s and early 1960s. This was the concept that outside the Church there was no salvation (*extra ecclesiam nulla salus*). It was generally believed that the child would be placed in Limbo, where he or she would never see the vision of God. Even though the Holy Office condemned that view in 1949, re-affirming the theory of 'baptism by desire', the idea was deeply ingrained and not to be rooted out so easily.[48]

At a time when there was a higher rate of infant mortality, it was seen as imperative that the child be baptised almost immediately after birth — so soon, in fact, that the mother was rarely present, because her period of confinement was not over. In due course, a separate ceremony was arranged for the mother. It was referred to as 'churching', and acquired the appearance of a rite of purification.[49] This ceremony, with its unfortunate connotations, was now discontinued. In the celebration of the new baptismal rite, the mother was to be present with godparents and relations. It was seen as desirable that the ceremony should take place in the presence of the community, and that a number of children be baptised together. Baptism in the past had been seen as a kind of insurance against going to Limbo. For many, it had the appearance of a kind of magical rite.

The impoverished understanding of Baptism, to which the old Latin rite had given rise, was just one aspect of a pre-conciliar Catholic mentality, which concentrated on being safe by following the rules laid down. The 'old' theology cultivated the notion that by following the rules, one had the certainty of salvation. The emphasis tended to be on avoidance of punishment, as opposed to on making a positive effort to live a Christian way of life. There was a sense in which people were so concerned to save their souls in the next life that they were inclined to lose sight of the wider dimensions of Christianity.

The 'new' theology, which was legitimated by the Vatican Council, and which translated into the sacraments, saw salvation in a more positive light. Instead of being seen as a kind of award that was won at the end of one's life by skilful manoeuvring and keeping out of trouble, it began to be seen as a developmental process, which was ongoing throughout one's life. In the new ceremony of Baptism, there was, and is, more stress on the fact that parents' responsibility does not stop simply at presenting their child for Baptism, but that they have an ongoing responsibility to nurture their child's Christian faith.

In the case of the new rite of penance, many theologians and priests had begun to question the form of the sacrament, as it had obtained up to this time. The rote-like repetition of sins in a dark confessional was seen by many as affording little opportunity for moral growth. The doctrine of *ex opere operato* had had particularly bad consequences for the sacrament of penance. While the importance of the penitent having 'a firm purpose of amendment' was always preached, by virtue of this doctrine, the emphasis had tended to be placed on the objective contribution of the sacrament — to the neglect of the subjective contribution of the penitent.

For many, the fact that their disposition in receiving the sacrament was important scarcely entered in, and confession became a rather mechanical process of confessing sins in number and kind, or if they did not have any, the sins of their past life. Such was the emphasis on 'telling' of sins, that the importance of correcting one's life was often lost sight of. There was a certain superficiality, a magic-like quality, about the experience. In 1958, Fr Daniel Duffy of Carrickmacross, Co. Monaghan, observed that confession often involved 'the wearisome recital of peccadilloes',[50] rather than presenting the opportunity for penitents 'to seek regular spiritual direction' in their lives.

In the 'new' theology, sin was conceptualised in the more biblical sense of failure to love God or one's neighbour. The emphasis was now on sin rather than, as hitherto, on sins. The new rite made far more demands on penitents. The more expansive definition of sin required them to scrutinise their lives far more closely. The social dimension of sin was given more emphasis and the importance of inner conversion and reconciliation was stressed. One of the features of Irish Catholicism criticised in the 1950s was its lack of a social sense. The old rite belonged to the paternalistic era, when the rules were very specific and left very little room for the individual conscience to make judgements. Basic to the 'new' theology was the idea of people taking responsibility for their own lives, rather than simply obeying unchanging rules. In the new approach to morality, people would no longer be able to find refuge in the old certainties.

A whole tradition of clever moral reasoning or casuistry had grown up around the old idea of sins, as has been seen. It tended to concentrate on telling people how far they could go before something would be sinful. This led to scrupulosity and moral immaturity. Many Irish Catholics in the pre-Vatican II era also tended to have what Daniel Duffy, writing in the *Furrow* in 1958, termed a 'confession complex'.[51] They had such an exaggerated idea of their own unworthiness, and fear of committing mortal sin, that they felt that they had to 'get' confession always before receiving Holy Communion — just to be on the safe side.

This kind of attitude was illustrated in Fachtna Lewis's research in rural Ireland in 1961–2.[52] Questioning a sample group of 293 Catholics, he found that 44 per cent thought that they were bound to go to confession each time before Holy Communion. While 54 per cent answered 'no' to the question, 'Are Catholics bound to go to confession each time before going to Holy Communion?', Lewis found that 'the majority of these modified their "no", with comments to the effect that they would prefer to go even though they were not bound'. He was left with 'the general impression that though they realise they are not bound to go, still they prefer to go even if they are not in mortal sin'. This mentality has to be understood against the background of the 'old' theology and its preoccupation with sin and tendency to stress the darker side of human nature with its inclination to evil.

Original sin had always been a central Church doctrine. The catechism defined original sin as the state into which people are born: 'Because of Adam's sin, we are born without sanctifying grace, our intellect is darkened, our will is weakened, and our passions incline us to evil, and we are subject to suffering and death'.[53] This gave people a very strong consciousness of evil and sin, and a sense of guilt in the event of wrong-doing. A sense of the Church's preoccupation with evil can be captured from the text of the Leonine prayer, which was said in churches after Mass. The prayer went as follows:

> St Michael, the Archangel, defend us in battle; be our defence against the wickedness and snares of the devil. May God rebuke him, we humbly pray; and do thou, O Prince of the heavenly host, by the power of God, thrust into Hell Satan and the other evil spirits who prowl about the world for the ruin of souls. Amen.[54]

The prayer was preceded by three Hail Marys and the Hail Holy Queen, and followed by the aspiration, 'Most Sacred Heart of Jesus, have mercy on us', which was said three times. Known collectively as the Leonine prayers they dated from the pontificate of Pope Leo XIII, who introduced them at a time in the late nineteenth century when the Church was perceived to be threatened by all manner of hostile forces, as represented by socialism, liberalism and Modernism. These prayers were said in the vernacular after the Last Gospel. In Ireland, they were followed by the *De Profundis*. In more recent times, they had been directed towards the conversion of Russia. The 1964 instruction implementing the *Constitution on the Sacred Liturgy* decreed that they be discontinued.[55]

The findings of psychologists emphasised the kind of neurotic guilt that can develop as a result of over-consciousness of sin and evil. The experience of confessing sins in a dark box was often seen as a contributory factor. In the post-conciliar era, there was a move away from the confession boxes to the idea of a counselling room, particularly in the newly built churches. The 'new' theology stressed the innate goodness of the person, as opposed to the darker side of human nature. All of these factors, as well as the development of penitential services, led to a more relaxed attitude towards sin and confession and, in due course, from the 1970s, to a decline in the practice of private confession.

The traditional link between reception of Holy Communion and prior attendance at confession, observed by Lewis in his sample group in the early 1960s, began to be eroded in the 1970s. Writing in the *Furrow* in 1974, Fr Patrick Baggot SJ pointed out that, 'the notable rise in Communion does indeed show that the Eucharist and penance are increasingly seen as separate sacraments not necessarily connected with each other'.[56] Archbishop Ryan of Dublin, in a pastoral letter in 1978, observed that, 'many more people receive Holy Communion with greater frequency than before'.[57] What Duffy referred to in 1958 as a hesitancy 'from a sense of unworthiness and holding back out of respect' was becoming a thing of the past.[58]

From the late 1960s, such observations were verifiable scientifically, and empirical research more often than not revealed a picture considerably more complex than surface indications suggested. The question of the quality of religious practice and experience, particularly among the younger generation, became the subject matter of surveys from the late 1960s. One of these surveys, carried out among a sample group of university students, showed that a relatively high practice rate did not necessarily presuppose an explicit awareness of religious values, or an acceptance of the Church's moral, or doctrinal teachings. In 1969, Katherine O'Doherty found that while 79 per cent of them 'were meeting all of the disciplinary obligations of the church', only 38 per cent could be 'classified as having an explicit awareness of religious values'.[59] She pointed to a lack of in-depth understanding of their beliefs on the part of many of these students.

A four-volume survey, which investigated religious practice, attitudes and beliefs among Irish Catholics in 1973–4, was published in 1975.[60] The survey was undertaken by the Council for Research and Development, one of the commissions established by the bishops in response to the recommendations of the Second Vatican Council. It was the first time that comprehensive statistics in relation to religious practice in the general population were made available, and the survey recorded a figure of 65.6 per cent who went to Communion once a month and of 46.5 per cent who went to confession once a month.[61] (See Appendix I)

It further recorded figures of 91 per cent attendance at weekly Mass; 28 per cent weekly reception of Holy Communion; and 89.8 per cent attendance at confession three times annually.[62] (See Appendices H and I) The survey was based on the situation existing in 1973–4. While the 91 per cent practising might have occasioned rejoicing, if taken as a true index of the state of Catholic faith in the country, the survey was not greeted with the kind of complacency which would have been characteristic of former times. While observing that it was 'a healthy base on which to develop', the researcher noted that:

> the gap between weekly Mass attendance 91% and weekly reception of Holy Communion 28% represents a sizeable pastoral challenge. It indicates that the increase in numbers approaching the altar rails might at best be misleading and at worst induce an atmosphere of false security.[63]

While evidence pointed to the severing of the traditional link between reception of Communion and attendance at confession, the researcher expressed regret that:

> the idea of the reception of the Body of Christ as an integral part of Eucharistic worship has not yet impressed itself on the minds of 63% of the people who crowd our churches for weekly Mass.[64]

A more general observation as to the nature of Irish Catholic belief and practice proffered by the researcher is worthy of note because it was made on the basis of scrutinising a comprehensive amount of data. On analysing the attitudes of those who practised, and their reasons for doing so, the following conclusion, similar to O'Doherty's, was drawn:

> The beliefs and practices of the majority of Catholics are insufficiently interiorised ... not personally examined and tested and then affirmed or rejected. Irish religious practice is sustained to an inadmissible extent by rule and law, social custom and a sense of duty, rather than by personal commitment of mind and heart so that such belief or faith is extremely vulnerable in a rapidly changing society.[65]

There was another respect in which the survey did not convey good news either. A problem in relation to religious practice was identified, in particular, among the young Irish population. It disclosed a sizeable and significant minority in the 18–30 age group who had abandoned the minimal regulations of their religion. Of those in the sample group who attended Mass only occasionally or rarely, 45 per cent were in the 18–30 age group. Likewise, of those respondents who never attended Mass, 24 per cent were in this age group.[66]

The data showed that of the 18- to 30-year-olds, 10.5 per cent received Communion less than yearly, and 5.7 per cent stated that they never attended. The same age group had the highest proportion of those going less than yearly to confession — 12.9 per cent; and those who never attended — 8.2 per cent.[67] Groups seen to be particularly at risk were young, single males, the urbanised and also skilled and semi-skilled workers.[68] The rates of weekly Mass attendance for single males aged 18–30 in the sample was 76.5 per cent. This was 14 per cent below the overall average of 91 per cent.[69]

A central theme of the Vatican Council had been that new symbols, new ways of communicating Christ's message, would have to be found, which would make sense in a rapidly changing world. However, a recurring theme, echoed by commentators reflecting on the Irish situation in the post-Vatican II era, was that, despite the updated liturgy, the correlation between life and liturgy, as envisaged by the Council, had not been achieved. Writing in the *Furrow* in 1979, Fr Eamonn Bredin, lecturer in Sacramental Theology at the Institute of Religious Education, Mount Oliver, Dundalk, observed that the new liturgy seemed to 'have left the inner core of people's lives untouched'.[70]

In a situation where many people were rejecting the public worship of the Church, and where many others were participating out of a sense of obligation or social custom, some priests began to question whether the liturgy, even in its updated form, could be relevant or meaningful in the context of modern-day life. Fr Desmond Keenan of Mellifont Abbey, posing the question, 'how well does liturgy go down with modern man?', faced the dilemma squarely when he opined:

> It can be safely said that the whole system of sacred seasons and feasts, penitential, festive and ordinary, such as we find in the *Calendarium Romanum*, is for him artificial and contrived. He can be persuaded to learn it and swallow it, but it is not natural to him.[71]

In 1974, Fr P.J. Brophy, president of St Patrick's Diocesan College, Carlow, echoed the same sentiments, when he stated that, 'the new liturgy seems to have little to say about tomorrow since it is presented in the categories of yesterday'.[72] For clerics like McGarry and Brophy, who had been writing in the *Furrow* since the 1950s, the Council saw their wishes come true in a way that not even 'the most optimistic enthusiast of an earlier decade had dared to hope for'.[73] What the Council could not absolutely foresee, however, was the huge impact of the consumer society, pop culture, the communications revolution, and a more individualistic age which would lead people to have far higher expectations of what was meaningful for them. The irony was that, within a decade of the close of the Council, Irish society and culture were so utterly transformed that many observers in the 1970s felt that, radical though the changes had been, and notwithstanding the traditional devoutness of Irish Catholics, the renewed liturgy did not really speak to their needs. The dilemma for the liturgy, as expressed by Bredin in 1979, was that people were now 'searching for something' in the liturgy,[74] whereas in the past they had been content to be silent observers.

Catholicism in Ireland in the 1950s had been communicating its message in a friendly environment. People were disposed to listen, whether on account of, or in spite of, the authoritarian tone of the bishops, and despite the fact that much of the liturgy went over their heads. There was little in the way of an alternative culture to deflect or distract them. As Brophy put it, speaking of his own youth, in those days 'pulpit and people talked the same language'. It was a time when 'there were very few rival spectacles', and devotions like Benediction satisfied people's 'modest longing for pageantry of some kind'. At a time when there was little in the way of diversion, 'mission time was a much discussed event'.[75] In rural Ireland, he recalled, 'the Mass house was the meeting house because there was nowhere else to go and nothing else to do'.[76]

From the 1950s, the wireless, the cinema, the dancehall, the motor car and the television — where it was available — were all helping to change this situation. They all greatly expanded people's opportunities for spending their leisure time. But it was the arrival of an Irish television station, on New Year's Day, 1962, which was to galvanise all the changes that had already taken place. Because it exposed Irish Catholics to all manner of new ideas and influences, it had a profound effect on their consciousness, inclining them to be more critical and less conformist. This, in due course, affected all aspects of their lives, not least their religious experience. We now move on to examine how television liberalised Irish society almost overnight.

Part Two

9

THE COMMUNICATIONS MEDIA AND THE IRISH CHURCH

In Ireland in the 1950s, the kind of apprehensiveness voiced by Pius XII in relation to the communications media was echoed by politicians and churchmen alike. The fact that much of the east coast was receiving BBC broadcasts from the early 1950s placed politicians under considerable pressure to set up a national television service, which could be controlled and so have a less damaging effect on the national culture.[1] The government announced on 14 March 1958 that a Television Commission was to be established by the Minister for Posts and Telegraphs, to examine all aspects of television broadcasting and to make recommendations to the government accordingly. The Church was represented on the commission by Very Rev. John Canon McCarthy, professor of Moral Theology and Canon Law at St Patrick's College, Maynooth, and Very Rev. Dr Patrick J. McLaughlin, a former vice-president of Maynooth.

The Report of the Television Commission, published in 1959, found that television was 'coming to be regarded as a prime necessity in the modern home'[2] and that if it was organised in a responsible manner, it could, in fact, be advantageous to the country. In deference to the kind of reservations expressed by Church and other interests, the report cautioned that television could have a detrimental effect on society and on children, in particular, if due steps were not taken to ensure the suitability of the material being broadcast. It emphasised the necessity of parents 'regulating the type of programmes to be viewed by their children.[3] The Commission maintained that the fact that Ireland did not have a native television service but received British programmes was 'an embarrassment', and saw it as 'imperative that Ireland should have a television service of its own, and without delay.' The alternative, it pointed out, was 'a progressively increasing number of Irish viewers taking the BBC programme', which was geared to a British audience and espousing British values.[4] The final decision to set up a native television station was taken at a cabinet meeting on 31 July 1959.[5]

In a statement issued after their October 1961 meeting at Maynooth, the Irish bishops pointed to the potential for good in the proposed national television station, but went on to emphasise that the same medium,

> can also do great harm, not merely in the diffusion of the erroneous ideas of those who are lacking in deep or accurate knowledge of religious truth, but also in the broadcasting of programmes which offend all reasonable standards of morals and decency.[6]

The same kind of apprehensiveness was echoed by President de Valera in his address at the inauguration ceremony of the national television service, on 31 December 1961, when he said:

> I must admit that sometimes when I think of T.V. and radio and their immense power, I feel somewhat afraid.... Never before was there in the hands of man an instrument so powerful to influence the thoughts and actions of the multitude.[7]

While TV and radio 'can build up the character of the whole people', he went on, it also 'can lead, through demoralisation to decadence and dissolution'.[8]

Cardinal D'Alton, welcoming the new television station the following day, echoed de Valera's sentiments, expressing the hope that the medium would not present viewers 'with a caricature of Irish life, such as we have had from our writers in recent years'.[9] In his pastoral letter the following Lent, the same anxiety towards the communications media was in evidence which had been characteristic of Church figures since the 1920s. He wrote:

> We no longer enjoy [sic] our isolation of former days. We are living in a world where many seem to have forgotten God.... In this world, through the medium of the press, the radio, and the T.V., we are subject to the impact of views wholly at variance with Catholic teaching.[10]

The kind of fears expressed by de Valera and Cardinal D'Alton had constantly preoccupied Pope Pius XII. Indeed, in either case, their sentiments might have been written by Pope Pius himself, so close were they to his thinking. The nub of the problem of the media for the Catholic Church, or indeed the other churches in Ireland, or any country, is precisely that highlighted by Cardinal D'Alton — that they could portray ideals and life-styles and value systems 'wholly at variance with Catholic' or, for that matter, any church's teaching. To some extent, these threats were still kept at bay at this time by means of censorship, but in the era of television it was no longer possible to 'protect' people in the same way from harmful ideas. The days of strict censorship were numbered.

There is no doubt that television facilitated and lent its support, as time went on, to questioning the hegemonic synthesis of Irish and Catholic, so propagated by Mr de Valera in the 1930s and 1940s, whereas Radio Éireann had, in fact, served to reinforce that identity. The kind of questioning of values and cross-fertilisation of ideas which helped this process was facilitated in a unique way by television. While the bishops might rail against the cinema, the foreign press and literature, they had little to fear from the native media until the national television network arrived on the scene in 1962 to disturb the equilibrium.

In this respect, it is important to point out that the Second Vatican Council, in terms of its attitude to communication and the media, was little different from the Irish Church in the pre-conciliar era. Given the importance of the event and how influential and far-reaching the implications of each debate were to be for the lives of Catholics all over the world, the Council did not welcome the enquiries of journalists in the early days, nor did it facilitate them, in relaying news of the proceedings of the Council at the first session. RTÉ sent Seán MacRéamoinn to report on the Council from the outset. Louis McRedmond reported on the Council for the *Irish Independent.* Writing in the *Furrow* in January 1964, after the second session of the Council, he expressed his disillusionment, that 'the journalists were refused all opportunity to compile the best evidence. They were thrown deliberately back on second and third rate sources'.[11]

Nevertheless, it was a considerable improvement on what journalists had experienced during the first session. McRedmond acknowledges this, writing that 'on the instructions of Pope Paul VI the reporters present were given many more facilities. Communiqués were fuller, press and explanatory lectures were held'.[12] So it appeared that the Council had grown in its recognition and understanding of the importance of the media's role in public relations. Indeed, it was the fact that Catholic truth had hitherto been seen as indisputable, combined with the fact that such diversity of opinion occurred between so-called 'progressive' and 'conservative' theologians,[13] in relation to what were regarded as closed questions, which actually fuelled media interest in the Church and its affairs in the post-conciliar era. And, from that time on, the Church simply had to reckon with this new situation.

Archbishop McQuaid, although generally conservative in his views, had shown himself to be ahead of his time when, in September 1959, he sent Joe Dunn and Des Forristal, priests of the Dublin diocese, to the New York Academy of Broadcasting Arts, for training in television techniques, at a time when the national television service was as yet only on the drawing board.[14] These men were to form the nucleus of religious broadcasting in time to come. In March 1965, McQuaid opened a press office and Osmond Dowling was appointed press officer for the Dublin diocese.[15]

This was followed by an announcement by the bishops, after their June meeting of 1965, that a communications centre was to be established for training clergy and laity 'in the use of mass communication, particularly radio and T.V.'[16] The facilities were to include a 'fully equipped training studio', library and offices. This development was in direct response to the Vatican Council's *Decree on the Instruments of Social Communication,* promulgated on 4 December 1963, which decreed, 'that national offices be everywhere established and thoroughly supported for affairs of the press, motion pictures, radio and T.V.'[17] The centre came into operation in 1967 under the directorship of Fr Joe Dunn.

There are some who would argue that television was the most powerful factor in changing Irish Catholic culture. What gives television its unique strength is the ability of its personnel to question, analyse and diagnose the weaknesses and strengths of a society's traditions and value systems. It can, if it chooses, play the role of self-appointed iconoclast, demolishing its sacred cows. In so doing, it can mould and revise attitudes. It follows that those with access to this medium can be very persuasive in mediating or changing culture. From the 1960s, Irish television did, in fact, play a significant role in developing an alternative, popular, consumerist culture. The impact of television, and, in particular, of the *Late Late Show,* on the national consciousness has been pointed up by several commentators. Fr Desmond Forristal, writing in 1970, saw it as having 'probably done more than any other single factor to form the national consciousness on a hundred different topics during the last ten years'.[18]

Two incidents, trivial enough in themselves, but which serve to illustrate this point, are worth mentioning. They have been adequately documented elsewhere, so there is no necessity to dwell on them at length. One was an incident which happened on the *Late Late Show* on 12 February 1966, in which a woman was asked the colour of her night attire on her wedding night, and answered to the effect that she had not worn any. The incident became a *cause célèbre* overnight, because Bishop Thomas Ryan of Clonfert sent a telegram to the producer and compere of the show, protesting at what he considered to be a 'disgraceful performance'. His secretary phoned the *Sunday Press* on the same night, objecting to the show, and saying that the Bishop intended preaching about it in his cathedral church in Loughrea the following morning and asking his people not to look at the show again.[19]

The incident got front-page coverage on both Irish Sunday newspapers the following day.[20] The television station was inundated with phone calls protesting about the show. RTÉ issued a statement apologising that part of the previous week's programme had been embarrassing to a section of their viewers.[21] *The Irish Times,* which, in its leading article the following Monday, dubbed it 'the bishop and the nightie' incident, saw it as 'an aberration', but commented that, 'a lapse of taste has been treated as if it were an outrage to morals'.[22] All the daily papers, the evening papers and many of the provincial papers and the *Irish Catholic* became involved in the furore surrounding the incident.

Its importance lies in the fact that it evoked such intense media interest and caused such a convulsion in Irish society at that time. It evidenced the kind of puritanical attitude to anything remotely connected with sexuality, referred to by writers like MacMahon, Sheridan and others in the 1950s. The fact that the incident should occasion such shock-waves is a valuable indicator of the cultural ethos existing at the time. What throws this into sharper relief is the fact that *The Irish Times*, which prided itself on being open-minded and liberal, did, in fact, consider the incident 'mildly embarrassing' and 'an aberration'.[23]

An incident following closely on this the following month, on 26 March 1966, concerned a young Trinity College student, Brian Trevaskis, who, during an appearance as a member of the panel on the *Late Late Show*, referred to Galway's new cathedral as 'a ghastly monstrosity', and called Bishop Michael Browne of Galway a moron, for his involvement in commissioning it.[24] Again, the incident received front-page coverage in the *Sunday Independent* and *Sunday Press*, and the former newspaper reported that its phone lines were jammed with protests, as were the lines in Telefís Éireann. The matter was once again taken up by the *Irish Catholic*, whose leader writer demanded to know:

> Who is responsible for wittingly or unwittingly providing those who desire to foster anti-clericalism in our midst with a gilt-edged opportunity to do so ... outraging the traditional respect of Irish people for their clergy?[25]

The issue was covered also by the *Catholic Standard* and several provincial newspapers. It also came up for discussion at county council meetings.

Eventually, the Director General of RTÉ, Kevin McCourt, issued a statement defending the *Late Late Show*, which, he said, was 'unscripted and unrehearsed' and so, he explained, of its very nature, there was a risk factor that errors of judgement, or departures from good taste could inadvertently occur at times. While he regretted 'the disparaging remarks' and also 'an unkind reference' to Archbishop McQuaid, he defended the *Late Late Show* as having 'established itself as a successful television programme with wide public acceptance'.[26] While it may be an exaggeration to say that Telefís Éireann had turned a corner at that point, the station had certainly set down its own independent criteria which it would operate, and, once it had done so, things would never be quite the same again.

What is fascinating about these two incidents is the insight they give into the immense power of television, having to do with its immediacy and the fact that, in large measure, programmes were of the spontaneous variety and therefore, of their very nature, uncensorable. The kind of mass appeal that cinema had in the 1930s and 1940s, which had caused it to be so influential, television now had, only more so, and it was still only in its infancy in Ireland. Whereas in the 1950s, the *Irish Independent* and Radio Éireann had upheld and reinforced the Catholic ethos, from the 1960s, television — a much more potent force — played a critical role, questioning social norms and values hitherto taken for granted. (We recall the fears of the television critic of the *Furrow* in the 1950s, in relation to the enormous power of a medium, which could beam itself right into the very heart of people's homes.)

Television is a commercial medium. What counted were the TAM ratings and, as the Director General so succinctly put it, the *Late Late Show*, measured by this yardstick, was highly successful. The risk of lapses of taste was the price that had to be paid for this. Television as a medium was impervious to power or position. It was undaunted in the face of tradition. It became the ultimate leveller — it could not be ignored, and any criticisms were made at the critics' peril. Whether its advances were welcome or not, it could force itself on anybody. It demystified with ease the kind of distance, aloofness and mystique which had characterised the episcopal office in the past, and its ultimate weapon was public ridicule, should anyone choose to confront it. It would, in due course, assume the role of taskmaster, and demand accountability of bishops, politicians, public servants and private persons alike.

In this respect, *The Irish Times* leader writer raised an interesting point on 29 March 1966:

> People in public life must accept the rigours of public life.... In so far as people who are not politicians take part in public life, or comment on public affairs, they must expect to suffer the same attentions — adulation and abuse — as other public men.[27]

This kind of thinking, as it gradually gained more and more currency, signalled a new era for the Irish bishops. They were no longer above reproach or beyond the reach of demands for accountability. The extent of the cultural changes set in train at that time was captured by the *Late Late Show*'s Gay Byrne, writing only seven years later. Pointing to 'how old hat and ordinary the Trevaskis outburst' would appear to people by the time he was writing, he went on:

> By 1972 we've heard all these topics discussed and expressed so much better that one has to wonder at so much notice being taken of it all in 1966, but then it was pretty original stuff to be aired in public.[28]

The Vatican Council documents, *The Dogmatic Constitution on the Church* and *The Church in the Modern World* faced up to what had, up to the time of Pope John XXIII, been unthinkable — the fusion of the ideas of Church and modernity. Until then, they had been perceived to be mutually exclusive. The television medium was the ultimate way to woo the modern person. It was likewise for the priest or bishop wishing to advance his religious message. Cardinal Conway's remarks at a talk he gave in June 1966, at ordination time in Maynooth, illustrate the change in thinking that had taken place by the mid-1960s. Speaking of communication, he reminded priests that they must take account of the kind of social changes taking place, which meant that they were 'speaking to a different kind of congregation ... more developed intellectually, more aware of what is going on in the world at large, more capable of making comparisons'. He went on to remind them that, more than ever, it was important that the priest,

> should know what his people are thinking and saying so that he can effectively communicate with them.... More than ever in a world where many voices are competing for the ears of his people he must know the art of effective communication.[29]

We have seen that the bishops were very prescriptive in their approach in the 1950s and, in many cases, out of touch with the reality of people's lives, particularly in relation to emigration. The kind of deferential treatment accorded to clergy up to this time undoubtedly meant that there was little opportunity for the latter to form a truly accurate picture of what was going on in people's minds, either in the confessional or in their personal dealings with them. Television provided the means whereby people could air all manner of views and opinions. The cross-fertilisation of ideas which developed from this stimulated further discussion and people found a new confidence in expressing their ideas. This gave Church personnel an insight into what people were thinking, in a context that was relatively informal and spontaneous.

When the communications centre was instituted in 1967, it was a concrete expression of the Irish bishops' recognition that the time had come when it was to their advantage to exploit the media, given the potency of modern television culture — as opposed to endlessly warning people of the dangers and snares that the communications media posed, as they had done in the past. Whereas formerly the Church had depended on the traditional sermon and, to some minor extent, on radio and on the printed word to present its message, from 1967, the communications centre in Booterstown played a vital role in teaching a generation of priests the skills of effective media projection.

While Catholicism in the pre-conciliar era, as portrayed in pastoral letters, tended to be preoccupied with the evil ways of the world and the perils that were lying in wait to ensnare the innocent faithful, the image of Catholicism portrayed by Cardinal Conway and a new generation of priests appearing as guests on the *Late Late Show* and other discussion programmes was altogether more optimistic about life in general. More emphasis began to be placed on the good aspects of the modern world, as opposed to continually cautioning people in relation to its dangers. The mood was persuasive rather than dogmatic. The new, more populist style was evidenced in the programme, *Outlook*, a five-minute religious programme relayed at the end of the evening's television schedule and usually devoted to a homily. Fr Austin Flannery OP presented a series of *Outlook* programmes on RTÉ in the spring of 1968.

The importance of bearing social witness to the gospel had been highlighted both by the Vatican Council and in the Pope's encyclical, *Populorum Progressio* (1967). Against this background, Flannery, editor of *Doctrine and Life* and a socially minded priest, used the programme to highlight the housing crisis. Despite the success of the *Programme for Economic Expansion 1958*, Lemass's prediction that a rising tide would lift all boats had not been realised. By the late 1960s, it was becoming very obvious that the country's new-found prosperity was unevenly spread. This was particularly evident in the area of public-housing provision. While the building industry had experienced a boom-time, this was concentrated in private housing and commercial property. The sense of grievance and anger felt by those on the housing lists led to the foundation in May 1967 of the Dublin Housing Action Committee.

In his *Outlook* programme in May 1968, Fr Flannery introduced a panel of four to discuss the housing issue. The event raised political as well as clerical eyebrows, because the panel included two members of Sinn Féin and Michael O'Riordan, the general secretary of the Irish Workers' Party — which was, in fact, the official Irish Communist party, and recognised as such, by Moscow. Father Michael Sweetman SJ was the fourth participant. The fact that the general secretary of the Irish Communist Party appeared on national television on a religious programme, at the behest of a clergyman, and on a discussion panel with another priest, underlines how much Irish society had changed in a decade. Episcopal horror of communism expressed in pastoral letters in the 1950s, throws the event into sharp relief.

Television provided priests from the 1960s with a national forum for voicing their opinions. Another priest who became a well-known national figure for his outspoken views on all manner of political and social affairs was Fr Fergal O'Connor OP, a lecturer in Ethics and Politics at UCD. He made many appearances on the *Late Late Show.* Fr Patrick Brophy, former president of St Patrick's College, Carlow, was also prominent. A natural communicator, he appeared regularly on television. On one of his *Late Late Show* appearances, he expressed the opinion that the Trinity ban was out of date and that it should be abolished.[30] (See Chapter 1, pages 15–16 above) One of the earliest contributors to the *Furrow,* Fr Brophy was never afraid to give his views openly. In the 1950s, he was one of the voices pressing for change. He and many other priests who were questioning the status quo, either by writing or by articulating their views on television, have played an influential role in changing Catholic culture.

The most successful example of a new approach to religious broadcasting in Ireland was *Radharc,* which became one of RTÉ's longest-running programmes.[31] This was a documentary-type programme produced and directed by Fr Joe Dunn. It investigated social as well as religious topics. In keeping with the tenor of the times and the post-conciliar Church, it adopted an investigative approach and did not confine itself to Ireland, but examined global issues, thus contributing to the formation of the kind of broader social consciousness that was absent in Irish Catholics in the earlier period of this research. One of the priests who worked on *Radharc* with Fr Dunn was Fr Des Forristal, who took up the role of film critic of the *Furrow* in the 1970s. In the same way as the *Furrow* had been courageous in the 1950s in the issues it tackled, so also was *Radharc* from the time of its first transmissions in 1962. Among the programmes transmitted were the following: 'The Young Offender' in 1963, depicting life in St Patrick's Institution, Mountjoy (the first time a film was shot in a jail in Ireland); 'Down and Out in Dublin' in 1964, dealing with social deprivation; 'The Boat Train to Euston' in 1965, dealing with emigration; 'Open Port' in 1968, dealing with prostitution in Cork city; and 'Black Babies are Growing Up', which examined life in a diocese in Zambia in 1973.[32]

The establishment in 1969 of the Catholic Communications Institute of Ireland further evidenced the Irish Church's recognition that a more sophisticated approach to the area of communications was called for. Its role was to advise the bishops on matters related to communications. A year later, the Institute began publication of its own pastoral and liturgical magazine, entitled *Intercom.* The Institute was formed from the merger of the communications centre with the Catholic Truth Society of Ireland.[33] This was not without cultural significance. The last CTSI pamphlets were published in the late 1960s, and the CTS stall was a familiar sight at the back of every Catholic Church in Ireland. In his Lenten Pastoral in 1962, praising the 'splendid record' of the CTSI, the first aim of which 'was to provide an antidote to the anti-Christian literature coming to our shores in increasing quantity',[34] Cardinal D'Alton went on to say: 'That aim is more urgent than ever today when besides the printed word anti-Catholic and anti-Christian views are daily finding expression amongst us through other media'. A second aim of the CTSI, he explained, was 'to awaken Ireland to a fuller consciousness of her Catholic heritage', in defence of which the 'cruellest persecution' was suffered. The society also 'used its influence', he added 'to curb the influx of evil literature'.[35]

Given that the Cardinal's words were written two months after the opening of the national television station, some seven months before the convocation of the Vatican Council, and that both film and literary censorship would be relaxed within a matter of five years, they seem to be more in tune with the past than with the mood of the early 1960s. Indeed, the CTSI catalogue of books and pamphlets for 1962 has a Janus-like quality about it, including, as it does, on the one hand, publications entitled *Marry Your Own* by Rev. Daniel J. Lord SJ and *The One True Church: Which is it?,* and, on the other hand, a pamphlet by Rev. Michael Hurley SJ, entitled *Towards Christian Unity,* and another on *The Second Vatican Council* by Dr D.C. Pochin Mould.[36] While such pamphlets, along with Irish Messenger publications, were still published into the late 1960s, increasingly they were out of touch with the mood of the times. (See Appendix J.)

After the Vatican Council, when it became more and more apparent that Catholic thought was by no means as straightforward and undisputed as the Catholic Truth Society presented it, it was clear that a more sophisticated approach was called for. Indeed, it has to be said that, even in the 1950s, Fr Peter Birch of St Kieran's College, Kilkenny, criticised the pamphlets as being 'over apologetic', though he himself was the author of a number of such pamphlets.[37] (Fr Birch was appointed professor of Education at St Patrick's College, Maynooth, in 1954, and appointed as bishop to the diocese of Ossory in 1964.)

The changes made by the Irish bishops in the area of communications were a response to conciliar thinking, but also to the radically changed sociocultural climate in Ireland in the 1960s. In the era of television, the rigid censorship policy upheld by governments and seen as crucial by Church figures for the maintenance of the Catholic ethos was no longer sustainable. Between 1964 and 1967, Brian Lenihan, the then Minister for Justice, carried through sweeping changes. Towards the end of 1964, there had been criticism in the press of the severity of film censorship.[38] Lenihan's response was to replace the appeal board with a new and more liberal team.[39] The results of the innovation were readily apparent in the film censorship statistics. Whereas only eighteen films had been appealed to the board in 1964, in 1965 exhibitors took sixty-nine films to the appeal board, and had their appeals accepted fully, or in part, in thirty-seven of the cases.[40] Interestingly, the essential change made by the new appeal board was to give certificates for limited viewing, precisely what Connolly had argued for in 1957, when he had been critical of the fact that 'very little distinction is made in fact and effectively between Universal and Adult films' in Ireland,[41] which meant that the more mature audience was being penalised because a picture which was not suitable for an under-16 audience was either banned or cut excessively.

Even though literary censorship had been less controversial since the late 1950s, because of the reconstruction of the Censorship of Publications Board in 1956–7, the Board was still active well into the 1960s. In 1965, John McGahern's second novel, *The Dark,* was banned as 'indecent or obscene'.[42] When he returned from a sabbatical year, he was dismissed from his position as a schoolteacher, on the instructions of Archbishop McQuaid.[43] Meanwhile, Professor Peter Connolly continued his work in the area of censorship, contributing to the *ITQ* in 1965 an article entitled, 'The Moralists and the Obscene'.[44] The aim of the article was to show that there are literary criteria for distinguishing between pornography and a legitimate treatment of erotic material. To illustrate his point, he used a number of examples of pornographic writing, for which he was subsequently censured by the trustees of Maynooth.[45]

In April 1966, he participated at a seminar on the writing of Edna O'Brien, organised by the cultural organisation, Tuairim, and held in Limerick.[46] By that time, all four of her novels, which presented a picture of growing up in Ireland, which many people found decidedly uncomfortable, had been banned. Connolly presented a paper in which he assessed the literary merits of the novels, and this was followed by questions addressed to O'Brien from the floor. As was his style, Connolly's approach was balanced. Drawing from the ideas and distinctions he had elaborated in his article on obscenity, he celebrated the 'cheerful, natural, ribaldry' of her portrayal of country life in her first two novels, but was uneasy about the 'quality' as opposed to the 'quantity' of the sexual imagery of her two later novels.[47] The following Monday, *The Irish Times* proclaimed in its editorial that Fr Connolly had spoken out 'boldly and learnedly on Miss O'Brien's behalf', and went on to state that, 'Father Connolly has put everyone in his debt'.[48] The relaxation of the censorship laws, which Connolly had been advocating since the 1950s, was already under way even as he spoke.

Having dealt with film censorship, Lenihan then went on to deal with the censorship of books. A major problem in this area was that the censors could not remove a ban imposed by their predecessors. In 1967, Lenihan introduced a bill in the Dáil, which provided for the removal of a ban after twenty years, provided that it had not been specifically reimposed.[49] It was the mark of a changed era that there was so little controversy about the bill in its passage through the Dáil, and that he was able to relax the measure further. The law as passed[50] allowed for the unbanning of books after twelve years,[51] and the result was the release of more than 5,000 books.[52] The relaxation of censorship, after forty years of rigorous implementation, contributed further to the opening up of Irish society.

Connolly's was a long and brave battle for someone in his position. Adams, in his standard work, *Censorship: The Irish Experience* (1968), has seen his article in 1959 as 'in many ways the best on the problem of censorship in Ireland written during the whole period from 1926',[53] and has also noted that, 'many people have seen in Fr Connolly's article the justification of the more liberal attitude of the [Censorship] Board after 1958'.[54] In 1991, Patrick Hannon, professor of Moral Theology at Maynooth, and a former student of Connolly's who later worked with him as a colleague, described him as combining a 'delight in the secular' with 'a fierce reverence for the sacred'.[55] Hannon remarked that, difficult as it might be to balance these aspects of his life, Connolly 'always spoke from the standpoint of the Church'.[56] That said, his deeper religious and literary considerations were not always appreciated by those whose interests he believed that he was serving. Unease in relation to Connolly's influence is evident in correspondence that passed between Archbishop McQuaid and Bishop Browne in 1967. They were wary of a Maynooth student magazine published from 1967 to 1969, which was inspired by Peter Connolly and called the *Agora*.[57] Writing to McQuaid in 1967, Browne was worried that 'Maynooth students have joined the university students movement'.[58] From their letters in the late 1960s, it is obvious that they were concerned about the government's plans for higher education.[59] For conservative churchmen like Browne and McQuaid, an editorial in the spring 1968 issue of the *Agora* must have seemed little short of revolutionary. It began:

> If students in the seminary and university have one thing in common at the present time it is this — they demand a voice in planning the future shape of higher education; they demand an active role in shaping the institutions of which they are a part.[60]

Demands from seminarians for 'greater consultation' and 'a share in the process of decision making'[61] did not fall easily on the ears of McQuaid and Browne. Such concepts were decidedly out of tune with their ideal of Church, despite the post-Vatican II climate. Again the following year, in March 1968, Browne expressed his reservations about 'reports of the views of young men coming out of Maynooth'.[62] Replying to his letter the following day, McQuaid wrote: 'The young priests: like master, like pupil. The bishops are afraid. Witness the outrageous views of the English Professor, who four times in my diocese gravely upset the faithful'.[63] Presumably, Connolly thought that he was helping to promote the kind of open climate to which Cardinal Conway had referred in his ordination address to seminarians, on the subject of communication, in June 1966 (referred to above). What these letters, and others already mentioned, indicate is that not all Church personnel were on the same wave length, and, indeed, that there were powerful forces in the Irish Church which were resistant to change.

As regards those bishops who entered into the censorship debate around this time, the tenor of their remarks is interesting. After the reconstruction of the film appeal board, Archbishop McQuaid of Dublin in an address to the National Film Institute, observed that 'our good ordinary people demand from the civil authority that we shall be protected from the public activities of those who neither accept nor practise the natural and the Christian moral law'.[64] But by 1964, the idiom, the paternalistic tone, the protective attitude were all somewhat out-dated. One way or another, 'the faithful' would have to cope with being 'upset' or 'disturbed' from then on. In a statement soon after the first report that literary censorship was to be reformed,[65] Bishop Lucey of Cork observed that literary censorship as it existed was too lenient. He suggested that rather than being relaxed, it should be made more stringent. He was concerned that, as the law then applied, while books could be banned, pornographers could not be penalised. He suggested that it should be made an offence to publish works that would corrupt. If there was a penalty, he argued, it would 'make authors, publishers and booksellers take a long, cool look at what they would put before the public'.[66]

Neither of these statements had any effect on government policy. In the context of the attention afforded to the variety of viewpoints being raised, the Catholic one did not take the same precedence as formerly. The voice of prohibition and sanction had become decidedly *passé* in the late 1960s. In 1966, Paul VI had abolished the *Index of Prohibited Books,* in an effort to de-emphasise the censorial image of Catholicism. Clergy mentioned in the course of this chapter, and many others also, understood the importance of communication in all its forms, and they knew that a church that attempted to deny or control it would defeat its very purpose in the long run. The style of Bishops McQuaid, Lucey and Browne was decidedly out of keeping with the more questioning and democratic era of television. Even among the Irish bishops, it had become isolated, and would become even more so. It did not reflect the philosophical change that had taken place in Catholicism as a result of the Council, and which had translated into structural changes in the Irish Church from the mid-1960s. These structural changes changed the face of Irish Catholicism, and it is to these that we now turn.

10

PHILOSOPHICAL AND STRUCTURAL CHANGE IN THE IRISH CHURCH

The extent to which Archbishop McQuaid's thinking was out of keeping with the new mood of the post-conciliar Church is captured by a remark he made when 'speaking for the last time' as Archbishop of Dublin in February 1972. He asked that the same loyalty accorded him would be also given to his newly appointed successor, Dermot Ryan, 'to rule the see of Dublin'.[1] This kind of terminology, though not typical of the general body of bishops in the early 1970s, is important to note, because it was very much in keeping with how most Irish bishops in the past had seen their role, hence the tone they had adopted in their communications to their flock. The Church was conceived predominantly in hierarchical terms before the conciliar era. Bishops were absolute rulers over their subjects. The nomenclature reflected this — they were referred to as 'princes' of the Church, they lived in 'palaces' and they 'ruled' over their dioceses.

There was, however, at the time of the Council, a radical shift of emphasis in the definition of both the role of the Church and that of the bishop. In the *Dogmatic Constitution of the Church,* promulgated by the Council on 21 November 1964, the Church, defined as 'the people of God',[2] took precedence over the section which described the hierarchical Church 'with special reference to the episcopate' as follows:

> Those ministers who are endowed with sacred power are servants of their brethren, so that all ... can work toward a common goal freely ... and arrive at salvation.[3]

In keeping with all the Council documents, this one also returned to biblical sources for its conceptualisation of authority as service in which coercion had no place — people must respond freely. The stress from then on was to be on the hierarchical Church/bishops giving leadership and, in order to do this effectively, there was a growing awareness, which found expression time and again in the Council documents, that horizontal communication and consultation was required, as opposed to the predominantly vertical communication of the past.

One of the most obvious signs of change in the Irish Church in the post-conciliar era was the structural and administrative reforms which were undertaken, in order to give concrete expression to the collaborative model of Church urged by the Council. National Episcopal Conferences were given definitive canonical status in the Church in 1965, in accordance with the conciliar *Decree on the Bishops' Pastoral Office in the Church*, 28 October 1965,[4] and the apostolic letter of Pope Paul VI, *Ecclesiae Sanctae*, 6 August 1966.[5] Formal recognition of bishops' conferences came after the Vatican Council, and the norms governing their operation were set out in the revised *Code of Canon Law*, 1983.[6]

However, the Irish bishops had been meeting in joint session at provincial level since 1749 and at national level since 1788,[7] and therefore did not recognise any break in the continuity of the conference.[8] After the Second Vatican Council, the bishops held a week-long meeting in November 1969 to review all that had happened at the Council. At that meeting, they put forward proposals to restructure the conference in accordance with the demands of the Council. These proposals were formally approved at a meeting held in March 1970. At their Mulrany meeting in 1974, they decided to redraft their statutes, which were then sent to Rome for approval. They were duly approved by Rome in 1975. In this way, the contemporary Episcopal Conference evolved.[9]

One of the most obvious signs of change was that the Archbishop of Armagh no longer automatically presided over the bishops' meetings. The president of the conference was now to be elected every five years (every three years since 1994). Nevertheless, the practice has been that the Archbishop of Armagh presides over the conference and the Archbishop of Dublin acts as vice-president. In his elected capacity, the president's role was, and is, a representative one in relation to the conference of bishops, but his jurisdiction did not, and does not at the present time, extend to dioceses outside his own.[10] Before the Second Vatican Council, the Irish bishops met twice a year in June and October to consider matters relating to Ireland as a whole. They tended to act more in isolation from one another at that time. After the Council, they began to meet in spring also and, while still autonomous in their own dioceses, they have tended to act and react collectively, by issuing joint pastorals and press releases, and holding joint press conferences.

In 1975, Bishop Edward Daly of Derry was appointed press officer to the episcopal conference and, in the same year, the Catholic Press and Information Office was established under the directorship of Jim Cantwell, to provide 'a direct link between the Church and the media'.[11] Press conferences began in the early 1970s but they became more regular and more formally structured after the setting up of the press office in 1975.[12] All of these developments were a direct result of the emphasis placed on the principles of communication, consultation and collegiality, accepted at Vatican II.

Collegiality was one of the issues which became a battleground for the 'progressive'/liberal forces at the Council versus the 'conservative'/Curialist forces. Bishops throughout the world were anxious that the nature and function of the episcopate be clarified at the Second Vatican Council, just as the universal jurisdiction of the pope had been declared by the First Vatican Council.[13] The Council did, in fact, declare for collegiality, and thus balanced the dogma of papal infallibility with that of episcopal collegiality.[14] By his announcement (at the beginning of the Council's fourth session) of the setting up of a Synod of Bishops as a permanent body to help him in governing the Church, collegiality between the pope and bishops became a structural reality, thus setting a headline for the whole Church.[15] It remained to be seen how theory and structures would be translated into practice in the course of time.

In the opinion of the Council, the collaborative concept was not confined to the episcopate. The *Decree on the Pastoral Duties of Bishops* recommended that:

> In each diocese a pastoral council be established over which the diocesan bishop himself will preside and in which specially chosen clergy, religious and lay people will participate. The function of this council will be to investigate and to weigh matters which bear on pastoral activity, and to formulate practical conclusions regarding them.[16]

The ideals expressed in this decree did not find concrete expression in Ireland as they did in the Dutch Church after the Council. Several national episcopal commissions were, however, established. By June 1965, there were eight of these, comprising commissions for liturgy, university education, post-primary education, primary education, the communications media, religious, ecumenism and emigration, and further commissions were planned.[17]

The Irish Episcopal Conference issued a press release on 9 March 1972, announcing that, 'a scheme for the re-organisation of the commissions was approved'.[18] While the membership was composed of bishops, the commissions, it was pointed out,

> are being assisted by approximately twenty advisory bodies, of priests, religious and laity, such as the Theological Commission, National Council for the Apostolate of the Laity, the Council for Social Welfare and the Irish Commission for Justice and Peace etc.[19]

The new commissions and advisory bodies were a response to the conciliar decree which stated that pastors,

> aided by the experience of the laity, can more clearly and more suitably come to decisions regarding spiritual and temporal matters.[20]

The Council was discerning 'the signs of the times'[21] the most significant features of which were the number and diversity of groups involved in complex political activity in pursuit of their vested interests in modern-day society. The Church, it realised, would have to organise and set up its own agencies, so that it too could engage in concerted, political activity to further its own ideals. To do this effectively, it was necessary to engage the best resources and expertise at its disposal. To command such expertise, it was necessary to mark off specialist areas, in which bishops and laity alike could become proficient — hence the commissions.

The commissions essentially were set up by the Irish Episcopal Conference (at the behest of Rome) to gather and disseminate information, to facilitate the exchange of views concerning various aspects of the life and activities of the Catholic Church in Ireland, and to be in a position to speak out pertinently and critically on various aspects of Irish life. While this had always taken place on an informal basis, the establishment of commissions bespoke a more systematic approach, characteristic of a modern-day, large-scale, bureaucratic organisation, operating in a complex set of social circumstances. The commissions set up to oversee the areas of ecumenism, seminaries, vocations, religious, clergy and education reflected the enormous reappraisal that became necessary in all of these aspects of Church life after the Council. Vocations declined from the 1960s, seminary life was revolutionised, and clerical and religious life underwent profound and wide-ranging change. Attitudes towards non-Catholics underwent considerable reappraisal, and there was a fundamental restructuring of education. Each of these areas will be examined later.

In order that commissions would be effective, it was vital that they had access to accurate information. As the 1960s advanced, the necessity for socio-religious research was borne home more and more on the Irish bishops, and in 1970 they established the Research and Development Unit as a branch of the Communications Institute.[22] In 1973, this became the Council for Research and Development (a commission of the Episcopal Conference), and developed as an independent unit with offices located in Veritas House, Lower Abbey Street, Dublin. Bishop James Lennon of Kildare and Leighlin was director of the unit from 1970 to 1976. When he resigned in 1976, the work of research and development was continued under Fr Joseph Dunn, who served as acting director until the appointment of Sr Ann Breslin in 1980. In April 1980, the unit moved to offices in St Patrick's College, Maynooth. From its instigation, the unit provided a steady output of data on religious practice, vocations, seminary education, parish missions, and many other aspects of Catholic life, which has provided the Episcopal Conference and the commissions with a solid basis for decision-making and future planning and development.[23]

The importance of the development of an empirical approach to the study of social life had been highlighted as far back as 1955 by Mgr Jeremiah Newman, then professor of Sociology at St Patrick's College, Maynooth, and later Bishop of Limerick. At that time, he wrote that, 'there has been practically no attention at all given to factual studies; what are called sociological studies are usually expositions of social principles'.[24] Contributors to *Christus Rex* in its early years tended to apply, uncritically, to social issues in Ireland, the principles of Catholic social teaching, instead of investigating the facts as they presented in the Irish situation, as was pointed up in Chapter 5.[25] By the late 1950s, they were beginning to adopt a more investigative approach.[26] For example, the 1956 issue of the journal was given over to a symposium on emigration, and one article in particular dealt with the 'facts and figures' of emigration in Ireland. An article in the 1958 issue explored the viability of the small farm, and in 1959 the question of juvenile delinquency was examined. While these represent a small number of the total number of articles published during these years, what is important is that they reflect the beginnings of an awareness of the necessity to substantiate theory and analysis with verifiable statistical data.

In an article published in *Social Compass*, 1964, Fr C.K. Ward, social science lecturer at UCD, emphasised the importance of research in a country 'where uniform practice must surely cloak difference in attitude and opinion'.[27] It seemed likely also, he went on to say, 'that current stereotypes of the Irish Catholic would not survive empirical investigation'.[28] He was basing his remarks on Lewis's discovery, based on his field work in 1961–2, of Irish Catholics who ranged from those who were intellectually committed and mature in their faith, to some who were alienated, some who were apathetic and others who were ill-informed.[29] Modern scientific methods of enquiry, opinion polls and market research techniques have, in fact, provided a more incisive picture of Irish Catholic life since the 1970s — a considerably more complicated picture than that which had been taken for granted in the 1950s and 1960s, as seen in Chapter 8. The recognition of the importance of research, as evidenced by the setting up of the research and development unit, was a sign of an increasing professionalisation in the Irish Church.

Changing socioeconomic conditions had financial implications for the Church authorities, which had to be dealt with from the late 1960s and early 1970s. Priests' livelihood in Ireland has traditionally depended on the financial support of the faithful, in accordance with the fifth commandment of the Church, which enjoins the laity to 'contribute to the support of your pastors'.[30] Priests received their salaries from collections at Masses and from dues offerings in their individual parishes, and these were supplemented by Mass stipends. The running and maintenance costs of parishes and capital expenditure on development projects were defrayed until the mid-1960s by different types of fundraising ventures and, from that time on, by means of planned-giving schemes organised in each parish. In the late 1960s and early 1970s, there were some modifications of these arrangements. In Dublin, in 1968, Archbishop McQuaid devised a scheme whereby there was an equalisation of income between priests. A levy was placed on wealthier parishes on the basis of the previous year's parish income (as derived from collections at Sunday Masses). These monies were sent to Archbishop's House in Drumcondra and then redistributed in parishes where insufficient income was received to support the priests.[31] This arrangement ensured that priests, irrespective of whether they ministered in poor or wealthy parishes, were on a common basic salary scheme. Nevertheless, differentials in priests' incomes still remained because Mass stipends and dues offerings are of a voluntary nature and contingent on parishioners' means.

The churches built in the 1950s and 1960s, when Catholic devotional fervour was at its highest, were built at a time when interest rates were low, as was also the cost of labour and materials. Bishop Dermot Ryan, who presided over an expanding Catholic population from the early 1970s and into the 1980s in Dublin, was not in that happy position, and church buildings had to become considerably more modest. A concomitant problem arose from the fact that in many of the urban estates, newly built to house the expanding population, there was a high rate of unemployment. In the recessionary climate of the 1970s, some parishes could not meet the cost of building and maintenance of churches and schools. In a climate of high inflation and interest rates, the Church too had to concern itself with matters of cost-effectiveness, loan negotiations and debt repayments. In order to meet the cost of building churches, houses and schools in such parishes and to support the priests ministering in them, large-scale rationalisation of resources was necessary.

When Dermot Ryan became Archbishop of Dublin in 1972, one of the first things he did was to set up a finance committee to tackle this situation. The committee comprised six priests of the diocese, as well as eight lay people with expertise in financial and relevant matters. It was chaired by Margaret Downes, a partner in the accountancy firm, Coopers and Lybrand.[32] It reflected the changing economic climate in which the Church, like any other large organisation, and perhaps even more so, needed specialist advice — lay as well as clerical — in the administrative, accounting and banking areas. Essentially, the committee's task was to raise and administer the finances which were necessary to provide and maintain schools, churches and houses in the new suburbs. In response to these demands, from 1974, a second collection was introduced at Sunday Masses. Henceforth two collections were to take place. The first collection, called the common fund collection, was to be solely for priests' salaries, and was administered as already described. The entire proceeds of the second collection, called the Share collection, were designated to provide for capital expenditure on infrastructure such as schools and churches in developing parishes.[33]

It was the *Decree on the Apostolate of the Laity,* promulgated by the Council on 18 November 1965, which paved the way for the setting up of advisory commissions of lay people to assist in the Church's pastoral work. It was recommended in the decree that 'some special secretariat ... should be established at the Holy See for the service and encouragement of the lay apostolate'.[34] By the *Motu Proprio Catholicam Christi Ecclesiam,* 6 January 1967, Pope Paul VI established the Council of the Laity in Rome.[35]

The terms of reference for an Irish Council of the Apostolate of the Laity were approved by the Irish Episcopal Conference at its Maynooth meeting on 18 June 1968.[36] The Council came into existence on 22 February 1969.[37] It comprised diocesan representatives, nominated by the bishops in the absence of diocesan councils, representatives of seventeen lay organisations, the members of the Episcopal Commission for the Apostolate of the Laity (the Archbishop of Cashel and the Bishops of Clonfert and Waterford and Lismore), and seven ecclesiastical advisors who were appointed by the Episcopal Conference for the assistance of the Council.

The theme of the laity's role was reiterated several times in the *Dogmatic Constitution of the Church,* which stated that lay people's strength lay in the fact that 'they can work for the sanctification of the world from within in the manner of leaven', because 'the very web of their existence is woven' in 'the ordinary circumstances of family and social life'.[38] Many have argued and still argue that the Irish Church has dragged its feet in the area of affording opportunities for lay involvement in the ministry of the Church. However, there is no gainsaying the fact that there has been considerable change throughout the period covered in this book. At the start of the period, Bishop Primeau's now famous ironic definition of the layman's function being to 'believe, pray, obey, pay'[39] might have been considered by many as a fitting description of lay status in the Irish Church.

The bishops' meeting in Mulrany, Co. Mayo, in 1974 stated that:

> The main thrust of the Irish Church over the next five years should be the implementation of the principle of the involvement of the laity in the spiritual mission of the Church.[40]

Commenting on the statement four years later, Monsignor Laurence Ryan at the annual general meeting of the National Conference of Priests of Ireland, considered that lay involvement at parish, diocesan and national level was too slow, in spite of the impetus given by Vatican II[41] and the bishops' stated aim in the Mulrany guidelines. And in 1981, Bishop Cahal Daly of Down and Connor, in reference to the laity, admitted that:

> It is to our embarrassment as pastors that we must confess that they are as yet a largely untapped resource. We must get to work to develop this under-developed potential.[42]

The Vatican Council had recommended that councils be established at diocesan and, as far as possible, at parochial level to assist in the apostolic work of the Church.[43] Such councils were slow to emerge in Ireland and, to the extent that they did, they tended to be concerned with aspects of parish administration, such as fund-raising and finance and liturgical programmes. However, the Council's document, *The Church in the Modern World,* 7 December

1965, envisaged that the organised Christian endeavour should reach beyond ecclesiastical affairs and attempt to answer in a more comprehensive way the pastoral needs of the community. While the Irish Church's performance may not have measured up to this by the late 1970s, what is important is that there was a recognition at the highest levels that the Church, at both diocesan and parochial level, had to be open to consultation with its non-clerical members, and that it also had to be able to harness the many lay skills at its disposal. And while progress can best be described as uneven from parish to parish and diocese to diocese, at the time of writing, such structures are either in place or there is work in progress to bring them into being. It is also important to point out that the Council was envisioning the ideal, and that local needs, circumstances and personalities dictated the extent to which blueprints were translated into reality. Bishops and clergy also point out that because the Church in the past was seen as bishops, priests and religious — and lay involvement was either non-existent or peripheral — lay people required training to enable them to participate meaningfully in the Church's apostolic mission.

The Irish Council for the Laity was restructured as the Irish Commission for the Laity, on 21 June 1978.[44] Whereas formerly the Council had served the Episcopal Commission for the Apostolate of the Laity in an advisory capacity, now the reconstituted and renamed Council, with predominantly lay membership, actually became the commission. Thus, lay people, formerly removed from the centre of influence, were now closer to the centre of power.

Priests' councils were another development in the Irish Church in the post-conciliar era. The Vatican *Decree on the Ministry and Life of Priests,* 28 October 1965, directed that councils or senates of priests should be established in dioceses, to put into effect the ideals of friendship and close association between priests and their bishop, on which their shared ministry is based.[45] The *Motu Proprio, Ecclesiae Sanctae,* 1966, made regulations as to their institution and how they should work.[46] They began to be established from about 1967. The time of their establishment and the process of their formation, whether by election or nomination (by bishop), or both, varied from diocese to diocese.[47] Regional conferences followed. The Munster conference of priests, which was set up in 1972, issued guidelines as to its structure and functioning, capturing the new democratic spirit of the times, as follows:

> The Council is a structure for consultation and partnership in which wisdom is measured by the merit of the views expressed rather than by the status of the one who propounds the views.[48]

'It may well be', the document went on, 'that custom has fused in the person of the bishop the decision-making power with the wider role of analysis and assessment', but it went on to assert that 'the latter role is meant to be shared with the Council. Every priest is a recognised source of new ideas and insights'.[49]

Priests' voices were to be heard much more frequently moulding opinions on a wide range of topics from the late 1960s, as seen in the previous chapter, and the views they expressed were no longer necessarily in keeping with the official Church's view of matters. As well as the informal media channels that priests could avail of to express their views, the establishment of the National Council of Priests of Ireland, in 1975, provided all priests with a forum at national level to discuss matters appertaining to the life and ministry of the priest in Ireland. The Council was to act as 'a forum' for discussion of pastoral problems, to represent the priests of Ireland at international meetings and on other national bodies, to liaise with the Bishops' Conference, and to present 'the viewpoint of the priests to the media'.[50]

Approved by the bishops, and thus having juridical status, the national conference was 'a representative body, elected by and from the priests, both diocesan and religious, engaged in the ministry in Ireland'.[51] All priests had the right to vote 'freely and directly for their representatives'. Diocesan priests were to be represented on the National Conference by three priests from each diocese, and religious priests were to be 'represented by six priests in the province of Dublin' and 'three priests from each of the provinces of Armagh, Cashel and Tuam, elected by their fellow-religious priests engaged in the ministry in the respective provinces'.[52]

The involvement of religious in these structural arrangements grew directly out of the *Dogmatic Constitution on the Church,* promulgated on 21 November 1964, and the *Vatican Decree on the Bishops' Pastoral Office in the Church,* promulgated on 28 October 1965, which urged that 'a well-ordered cooperation ... be encouraged between various religious communities, and between them and the diocesan clergy'.[53] Pope Paul VI led the way by appointing ten members of religious orders and congregations to the Synod of Bishops.[54] In the pre-conciliar era, there tended to be little contact between diocesan and religious clergy, and whatever contact did exist was of the informal variety, in the absence of recognised fora or channels of communication. Indeed, it may be said that not only was there a dearth of communication, but often there was considerable rivalry, not only between religious and diocesan clergy, but also between different religious congregations in their quest for vocations and in their pastoral activities, which was quite out of keeping with the vision of the Council.

Undoubtedly, the chief benefit of a professional organisation such as the priests' conference derived from its ability to engage in self-examination and critique. However, there was also the 'trade-union' dimension of the conference's role, in as much as it also concerned itself with looking after the interests of clergy. The conference ensured that priests would have an input into practical issues having to do with distribution, appointments, retirement, remuneration and their living conditions. Such matters had been dealt with unilaterally by the bishops up to then. One rather revolutionary motion, passed at the annual general meeting of the NCPI in 1978, recommended 'the establishment of conciliation and arbitration machinery to help settle disputes which may arise in the Irish Church'.[55] Such a motion essentially constituted a demand that the official Church conform to the democratic principles of secular life. Whether complied with or not is not pertinent here. What is important is that the demand was made. It reflected a mentality which would have been inconceivable ten or fifteen years previously.

The Irish Church's growing sense of the importance of research, consultation, and lobbying paralleled similar developments in other areas at national level in the 1960s. Basil Chubb has pointed to the emergence of pressure groups which sought to influence political policy from the 1960s[56] and Joe Lee has noted that the government accepted that the main economic power groups were entitled to their say in national planning.[57] While the rights of decision-making in a diocese were still the bishop's, his independence was now circumscribed by the demands of multiple interest groups. Whereas formerly he had operated in splendid isolation, by the 1970s he was experiencing the joys and headaches of the era of accountability.

The Council had emphasised the prophetic mission of the Church and the importance of discerning how the Gospel message might provide insights into the problems of the contemporary world. The emergence of priests' councils and the National Conference of Priests, the Commission for the Laity and parish councils had the effect of holding up a mirror to the institutional Church in its relations with the world. Each of these groups was involved in the raising of consciousness. Traditionally in Ireland, priests were involved in activities ranging from community work to sports. While the Council had allowed that priests, as part of their mission, had to become involved in the concrete realities of the lives of the people among whom they lived, it was also stressed that the Church's mission as such is not of a political, economic or social nature, and that the mission of the priest is principally 'to preach the Gospel, shepherd the faithful and celebrate divine worship'.[58] The statement, issued by the NCPI at its 1978 AGM, pointed out clearly that this was the essential expertise expected of the priest in his ministry — his professionalism rested on how well he performed or otherwise in this area.[59] It is interesting to juxtapose the role definition of the priest in this statement with Fr Peter Connolly's remarks in relation to how the office of priesthood was perceived in Ireland in the late 1950s. A combination of clericalism and mystique had surrounded the office of the priesthood in the past and had kept the priest a man apart.[60] In the post-conciliar era, there was a movement by priests to discard historically acquired trappings, to get away from the cult of the priesthood, and to be accepted for themselves and earn respect on the basis of their specific job performance, as in the case of any other professionals. By the 1970s in Ireland, priests and other religious were subjecting themselves to critical analysis, on the basis of the philosophy and insights contained in the Vatican documents. This was to have profound implications for many areas, not least education, an area where the Church traditionally was heavily committed, and this will be the subject of the next chapter.

11

EDUCATION: Transmitting the Catholic Cultural Heritage

In the post-war era, with the emergence of social democratic parties and their vision of a more egalitarian society in England and continental Europe, one of the strategic ways of advancing this vision was believed to be the implementation of the policy of equality of educational opportunity, which was seen as the avenue to social mobility for the less well-off sections of society. It also began to be recognised increasingly that not only did education hold the key to social progress, but that it also held the key to economic progress. It was perceived to be of the utmost importance to eliminate 'wastage of talent' in the interests of economic progress.[1]

Against this background, demand for secondary education increased. Education systems were reformed, with a view to prolonging and expanding participation rates in second-level education. In order to cater for the greater spread of intelligence and variety of aptitudes that this would introduce into the education system, there was a growing tendency to combine in one school the traditionally academic courses and the technical courses. The comprehensive school became the popular model of schooling in both Europe and America. The Cold War added another dimension to this, in as much as western powers were concerned to keep pace with the technological progress of the Soviet Union. In this context, scientific, mathematical and technical education was promoted as essential to American national survival as a superpower.

In Ireland, the Church's concentration on the humane disciplines, and its endorsement of the classical liberal education tradition had resulted in technical knowledge being undervalued. The mood of the Council of Education report on the secondary-school curriculum, in 1962, was clearly out of touch with educational thinking and developments abroad.[2] The report viewed as a 'Utopian' dream the possibility of provision of free secondary education by the state.[3] As it transpired, however, the report signalled the end of an era and had no formative influence on impending educational developments. From the late 1950s, pressure groups and individual educationalists had been lobbying for change, and gradually politicians and policy-makers became more aware of the need for changes in Irish education. At a public meeting held under the auspices of Fine Gael, in March 1956, John J. O'Meara, professor of Classical Languages at UCD, read a paper in which he criticised the 'snobbery' which meant that pupils in secondary schools were 'learning pass Irish and pass Latin and profiting from neither', when they might benefit from vocational education were it not for 'social prejudice'. His paper was subsequently published under the title *Reform in Education.*[4]

Interestingly, one of the first voices raised by way of criticism of the system's rigidity, was that of Fr Peter Birch, appointed professor of Education at Maynooth in 1954, and Bishop of Ossory in 1964. Speaking, in June 1957, to the Annual Conference of Secondary Schools, he warned:

> If the system [of education] is closed to advances by a blind devotion to tradition, it will be harmful. Any system which is not elastic will eventually strangle those who persist with its use.[5]

Pointing to the fact that 'technological and scientific advances have been so great', he went on to suggest, 'that considerable reorganisation' might be desirable in order to make the education system responsive to modern needs.[6] In so far as any reorganisation would have implications for the Church as the major interest group, Professor Birch's ideas were breaking very new ground. In an article written in the *Sunday Press* in 1959, O'Meara complained that the extensive reforms which were urgently needed in education were neglected as a result of over-caution on the part of the state, because of its respect for the Church's interest in education.[7]

Economic Development (1958)[8] and the *Programme for Economic Expansion* (1958)[9] both emphasised the crucial role that vocational education, in particular, could play in gearing the country towards the technological needs of an industrialising economy. The interplay of all these factors over a period of years impressed on politicians and policy-makers that Irish education was out of step with continental and American developments, and that increased state involvement and investment in education were necessary so that the system could be expanded and made more responsive to the needs of all the pupils and to the needs of the economy. From the early 1960s, politicians began to play a far more assertive role in education. Successive ministers of education instigated fundamental and wide-ranging reforms in the system.

At a press conference in 1963, Dr Patrick Hillery, Minister for Education in the Fianna Fáil administration, set the tone for a radical change in the state's policy vis-à-vis education. At this press conference, he explained that 'economic progress is making demands on our secondary schools [and] vocational schools', and he emphasised the 'pressing' need for a 'review of the post-primary sector'.[10] His main thrust, and one which was to be crucial in re-shaping education, was that investment in education, particularly technical education, was the key to bringing about economic progress and equality of educational opportunity. He determined to bring 'the vocational stream throughout the country to a parity of standard and evaluation with the present day secondary stream'.[11]

To further these aims, the Minister proposed to introduce 'a new principle into Irish education',[12] which was the direct provision by the state of a new type of school — the comprehensive school — in which the full range of curricular subjects, both technical and academic, would be available. The Minister also announced that the right to enter pupils for the state examinations at Intermediate and Leaving Certificate was to be extended to vocational schools, which would give parity to both types of post-primary school. This was the first move by the state to bridge the gap that existed between secondary and vocational education.

Such an initiative, which involved change in the principle of control of education and the curriculum, would have been unthinkable in so sensitive an area five, to say nothing of ten, years previously. In recognition 'of the Church's teaching authority', Hillery announced that he had 'had consultations, which [were] proceeding with the Catholic hierarchy on the management of these schools' and that he was confident that a satisfactory arrangement would be arrived at, as regards committees of management 'which would be acceptable to all the interested parties'.[13] This was the beginning of a series of radical reforms, the repercussions of which would be felt at a level far more profound than the mere structural area. The fact was that while satisfactory management arrangements were, in due course, put in place, Catholicism, as the guiding principle in secondary education, was set to be eroded at a deeper level.

Dr Hillery's policy statements were made against the background of a major analytical study of the Irish educational system, which had been initiated in 1962 by the Department of Education in co-operation with the Organisation of Economic Cooperation and Development (OECD).[14] The study was carried out by a group of economic experts, in cooperation with officials from the Department of Education and OECD education experts, under the chairmanship of Patrick Lynch, an economist. The survey team, whose brief it was to assess existing educational provision in light of overall needs for skilled manpower in the Irish economy, started their investigations in 1962 and completed their deliberations in 1965. They were published in 1966, as *Investment in Education — Report of the Survey Team,* and were anticipated by Dr Hillery when he spoke in 1963 at the press conference. The report would, he indicated, along with the report of the Commission on Higher Education (1967),[15] provide the basis for 'signposting clearly and firmly the direction of our long-term educational requirements'.[16]

Whereas the mood of the Council of Education report (1962) was complacent and saw little need for change, the mood of *Investment in Education* was in sharp contrast. The findings of the report team, based on comprehensive statistical and analytical data which had not been available in Ireland up to then, had crucial implications for future educational planning. Among the concerns raised was the lack of emphasis on science, honours mathematics and modern languages.[17] Whereas religious imperatives had been central to the Council of Education's definition of worthwhile curricular knowledge, *Investment in Education* ushered in a fundamental change in curricular emphasis. There was a movement away from the classical humanist tradition, which had always been preferred by the Church, to applied knowledge, which was economically utilisable.[18] *Investment in Education* was 'concerned to analyse the education system in the context of Irish economic development', following 'closely on the lines of the assumptions made in the *Second Programme for Economic Expansion*' (1964).[19] A key policy of the Department of Education which was to emerge from the report findings was that of aligning school curricula with the needs of an industrial economy.

The importance of such a fundamental philosophical shift in thinking on education cannot be overestimated, in terms of its impact on Irish culture. It is principally by means of the education process that society mediates its cultural heritage to the younger generation. This is precisely why the Catholic Church authorities (and those of the other denominations) had always been concerned to wield power in this area. The state's willingness to recognise and uphold the Church's interest in education ensured that Catholicism had been the guiding principle in education in Ireland.

Essentially, what happened from the late 1950s was that other interest groups began to become more conscious of the very potent force that education could be for shaping culture — something that the Church had been aware of for centuries and on which, for this reason, it had ensured that it capitalised. *Investment in Education* signalled the first incursion of economists into the education arena. The recognition by the report that 'technical education is more relevant to economic growth and development'[20] reflected the priorities of the world of business, economics and industry. At a time when the first fruits of economic growth and affluence were being experienced, and when there was real hope that 'a rising tide would lift all boats', it was not difficult to understand that such interest groups should have found it easier, as time went by, to generate consent among policy-makers for their particular educational priorities, as opposed to those of the Church.

What is noteworthy from the point of view of this research is how amenable the bishops, led by Cardinal Conway, were to the reforms. Apart from a public controversy which broke out in 1965–6 between Bishop Browne of Galway and George Colley (who had replaced Dr Hillery as Minister for Education on 21 April 1965), in relation to the Department's policy of amalgamating small country schools,[21] the bishops as a whole, in fact, welcomed the new initiatives. The tone was set by Cardinal Conway when he said, in 1966:

> The national aim of providing the best possible post-primary education is not merely welcome but has the enthusiastic support of the Church. Indeed, this has been made clear to the responsible authorities time and again since the policy was first put forward a few years ago.[22]

Archbishop McQuaid of Dublin described the plans for expanding educational facilities as 'welcome and very praiseworthy', and stressed that it was something that he had 'always advocated'.[23]

Regarding the state's willingness to play a more active, interventionist role in the field of education, and the bishops' acceptance of this, an important factor to be taken into account is the dramatic change of direction in Catholic social teaching, which was to be found in Pope John XXIII's encyclical, *Mater et Magistra,* of 1961.[24] There was a marked change of emphasis in this encyclical from Pope Pius XI's *Quadragesimo Anno* of 1931[25] — the previous papal pronouncement on social issues—which had been very influential in Ireland. Pope John XXIII allowed for much wider legitimate state power and intervention.

The first three state-run comprehensive schools opened in 1966 at Carraroe, Cootehill and Shannon. They were co-educational, open to all levels of ability, and offering a wide curriculum to match the aptitudes of their pupils. They were run by management boards comprising a Department of Education inspector, a representative of the local bishop and a representative of the local vocational educational committee. This significantly widened the base of school management. However, while successive ministers may have satisfied the fears of the bishops in relation to their proposed plans, they had not consulted teaching interests, school managers or university interests, which, in due course, led to acrimony. As the 1960s developed, there was considerable dissatisfaction among Catholic school managers that they had not been consulted about the government's educational policies. Essentially, they were fearful of the threat posed to secondary schools by the extension of the state's role in education.

Donogh O'Malley replaced George Colley as Minister for Education in July 1966. In a speech delivered to the National Union of Journalists in Dún Laoghaire on 10 September of the same year, he announced what was to be the most important policy initiative of the decade — that post-primary education would be free from September 1967.[26] This scheme, as it was proposed, was also less than satisfactory as far as Catholic managerial bodies were concerned, because they were unsure of how it would work in relation to expensive fee-paying schools in their sector, and again they were very aggrieved that they had not been consulted. On this occasion, however, O'Malley had broken very new ground because, unlike previous ministers, he had not consulted with the bishops before making his announcement.

Against this background, the education debate was becoming very heated in the late 1960s. The Autumn 1968 issue of *Studies* was devoted to a symposium on the new developments. Sean O'Connor, head of a new development unit set up in the Department of Education, contributed an article to the debate.[27] It was a highly significant article, in which O'Connor indicated in no uncertain terms that the state was, from then on, going to exercise its rightful role as power-broker in the education stakes. Anticipating the implications of the state's new policy directions, he turned his attention to 'the problem of church–state relations in respect to education'.[28] He asserted that, 'no one wants to push the religious out of education ... but I want them in it as partners, not always as masters'.[29] He, like Dr Hillery, saw the report, *Investment in Education*, as having 'signposted the direction of educational reform'.[30]

By the late 1960s, not only did many people believe that there were moves afoot to alter the education system radically, but there were also those who went so far as to suggest a conspiratorial policy on the part of the government. This is clearly evident from the responses to O'Connor's seminal article, in the same issue of *Studies,* from writers representing the various interest groups. The contributions provide a gauge which reflects how high tempers were running by this time. A submission from the executive council of the Teaching Brothers' Association described the government's reform proposals as 'nationalisation by stealth'.[31] The editor of *Studies,* Fr Peter Troddyn SJ, suspected that there was some subterfuge afoot when he noted that 'the entry of the State into the whole field of secondary education' had been 'underplayed', and that the purpose of the new developments had 'not been spelt out'.[32] He wrote in terms that hearkened back to the fears of the bishops in the 1950s, when he argued that, while a 'clerical monopoly' of education might have its dangers,

> They are no greater than those of a state monopoly and they are perhaps more easily guarded against. Neutralism has a relative value in the 'pluralistic' (usually meaning agnostic) societies of many countries. But this country has no need to import its educational norms, or forms, from industrialised America or materialistic Northern Europe.[33]

Given the hierarchy's defensive attitude in relation to education, it seems surprising that the kind of fears registered above were not, in general, expressed by the bishops. The fact that the government plans were being devised while the Vatican Council was in progress may go some way towards an explanation. The bishops were out of the country and preoccupied with Council business for considerable periods at that time. Were it not for this factor and also the spirit of conciliar thinking, they might well have reacted differently. It is possible that they might have analysed in more depth the issues involved, and detected more sinister implications, which might threaten their interests in the years ahead.

School managers' dealings with the Department had traditionally revolved around routine issues, while on matters of policy the Department had dealt directly with the hierarchy. However, from the mid-1960s, it became obvious to school managers that the changes being introduced were fundamental, and that their best interests were not being served by the kind of informal behind-the-scenes negotiations engaged in by bishops and politicians heretofore. This led to the formation of new umbrella structures, representative of managerial and episcopal interests. The Catholic Headmasters' Association (CHA) had been in existence since 1879, and the Conference of Convent Secondary Schools (CCSS) since 1929. In 1965, the Teaching Brothers' Association (TBA) was set up, and in 1966 the Conference of Major Religious Superiors (CMRS) established an Education Commission. The bishops established the Episcopal Commission on Post-primary Education in February 1966.

In May 1968, a Council of Managers — representative of the various managerial associations — was established. The Council of Managers was to be kept informed of any direct negotiations between the bishops and the Department of Education or the minister, and the Department was to be requested to consult the council on all questions pertaining to secondary education from that time. The Council facilitated the sharing of information and the co-ordination of decision-making from then on.[34] In 1972, the Catholic bishops, in agreement with the CMRS, established the Secretariat of Secondary Schools, which acted as the executive arm of the Council of Managers of Catholic Secondary Schools (CMCSS) in its negotiations with the Department of Education or the Association of Secondary Teachers of Ireland (ASTI), or in its role of serving the needs of voluntary secondary schools, as necessary. Fr John Hughes SJ, chairman of the CHA, became the first director of the secretariat. The evolution of these representative structures provided the bishops with a much firmer base for negotiating policy in relation to Catholic interests with the Department of Education from the late 1960s on. Moreover, it was a structure with a very clear line of command held by the bishops.

By this time, it was becoming increasingly clear that the kind of arrangements put in place by the Department were not going to be adequate to answer to the educational needs of the increasing number of students availing of second-level education after the introduction of free post-primary education.[35] Participation rates rose from 152,039 in 1967 to 185,574 in 1969. The following years saw continued increases in the participation rates, so that by 1972 the enrolment figure at second level had reached 219,643, and by 1975 it was 256,672.[36]

However, the solution to the Department's policy problems was on the horizon. The World Bank was prepared to finance new schools[37] which would meet certain criteria, one of which was that the proposed schools would have a community dimension. The concept of the community school was a development of the idea of the comprehensive school, taking this model a stage further. All of the unease which had been registered by religious and other interest groups in relation to developments in education finally came to a head when *The Irish Times,* on 12 November 1970, printed the text of a document in which the Department of Education proposed the setting up of a new type of school — a 'community school'.[38] This document had been sent to the Catholic hierarchy on 26 October 1970. The Department described it as a 'working document' which was not meant for publication before 13 May 1971.[39] By this time, Catholic and other interests groups were more organised and proved considerably more formidable.

The 'community schools' document, dated October 1970, outlined the Department of Education's proposals for the establishment of a nationwide, unified state system of post-primary education. The proposed new schools were to:

> be governed by a Board of Management consisting of representatives of the secondary school managers and the local Vocational Education Committee, with an independent Chairman who might be the Bishop of the diocese or other agreed chairman.[40]

The policy document caused considerable controversy by virtue of its contents and the manner in which it had been drawn up. The Catholic bishops' access to the Department of Education was much resented by other interest groups. The Irish Vocational Education Association (IVEA) did not receive a copy of the document until January 1971.[41] The document was sent to the Teacher Unions in April 1971.[42]

In May 1971, Pádraig Faulkner, Minister for Education since June 1969, clarified his proposals. He proposed that each community school should have a six-person board of management. Four members were to be nominated by the secondary school authorities involved, and two by the local Vocational Education Committee. Two of the four representatives nominated by the secondary school authorities were to be parents of children attending the school. The site and buildings were to be vested in three trustees nominated by the bishop of the diocese. One of these trustees was to be chosen from names furnished by the local Vocational Educational Committee.[43] The proposal was intended to apply initially to between fifteen and thirty schools.[44]

The Minister justified the preponderance of secondary school representatives on the grounds that many more children attended secondary schools than vocational schools.[45] It was clear that discussions with the Department had ensured that Catholic interests would dominate both the trusteeship and the boards of management in the new schools. Defending the Catholic position, Cardinal Conway argued that 'the Catholic school authorities cannot be expected to consent to arrangements which would legally de-Catholicise their schools'[46] The matter, however, was by no means settled.

The Minister's proposals produced a storm of protest. He was criticised in the Dáil for his lack of consultation with Protestant Church leaders and he was accused of denying minority groups their right to non-denominational schooling.[47] The vocational education sector was furious at what was perceived as a handover of their schools to the Church.[48] There was, at the time, much criticism of the fact that the capital finance for the community school project was being provided by the World Bank, and this was castigated as an agency hostile to traditional values.[49] An insight into the type of criticism provoked in some quarters by the proposed structural reorganisation is to be found in a booklet, entitled *Have the Snakes Come Back? Education and the Irish Child*, published (anonymously) in 1975 'by a group of Catholic parents', in which the dangers attendant on 'State control of education' were pointed out.[50] This group was particularly apprehensive about the influence of 'Deweyism' and 'progressive education', which was 'slowly penetrating into Ireland through U.N.E.S.C.O. and other sources', claiming that 'flashes of it' could be discerned in developments, such as in the recent inter-denominational Dalkey School Project's request for child-centred education.[51]

The Irish Episcopal Conference responded to the controversy in a statement issued after their meeting in Maynooth on 24 June 1971. The bishops pointed out that their primary responsibility was 'the religious and moral formation of Catholic children'.[52] They asserted that they had 'no desire' to 'take over' a single vocational school, and they recorded their resentment of 'the many other misrepresentations of our position which have appeared in recent weeks'.[53] They rejected, in particular, 'the repeated designation of Catholic schools as "sectarian"'.[54]

Quite apart from the vocational sector itself, there was a body of opinion abroad at that time which claimed that the establishment of the community schools, on the basis sought by the bishops, would weaken the vocational system and transform the proposed community schools into denominational institutions. A number of prominent clergymen from all the churches and religious groups presented a joint petition to President de Valera, seeking his support in averting the policy and stopping such a development. The petition was signed by seven Catholic priests, among them three Jesuits, two Dominicans and two diocesan priests.[55]

Such clerical dissent from official Church policy on education was yet another example of the questioning of the authority of the official Church, which became more prevalent from the late 1960s. The fact that the representations were made by clergy — and by an inter-church group at that — was also a sign of a more liberal ecumenical era. These clergy were gravely disturbed that:

> At a time when education should be a unifying factor in our community, we see these proposals as being exceptionally divisive.... these proposals, in effect, constitute a repeal of the 1930 Vocational Education Act, under which our Vocational schools have functioned so efficiently for forty years on a basis of multi-denominational co-operation and harmony.[56]

Responding to those who alleged that Catholic Church interests were primarily interested in issues of control and property rights in education, the Bishops' and Religious Commissions on Education issued a joint statement emphasising that, 'Catholic school authorities have no interest whatever in retaining managerial or property rights for their own sake'.[57] The Church's interest in education, they asserted, was 'based primarily on her duty to help parents ensure' that 'their children grow up with a deep religious faith and strong moral convictions'.[58]

At any rate, opposition to his original proposals was such that Faulkner was forced to modify them. The new arrangements that he proposed differed from the proposals of 1971 in relation to the 'instrument of management'. The composition of the six-member board was altered. It was now to consist of two representatives of the secondary school authorities, two representatives of the Vocational Education Committee (VEC) and two elected representatives of parents (which had not been allowed for initially). The trustees in whom the school property was vested were to be appointed by the Minister and not, as originally proposed, by the Catholic bishop. The new terms were circulated to interested parties as a 'draft deed of trust', in May 1974.

Two particularly contentious issues remained to be resolved, which precluded a final agreement on the deed between all parties. One was the issue of teacher representation, and the other was the issue of reserved posts for religious. The latter referred to the right sought by religious superiors, who were involved in each school, to a specified number of teaching posts for their members, provided that they were suitably qualified, and the teacher trade unions were adamant that teachers be represented on the boards of management. The power struggle to influence the character of community schools continued to be waged throughout the 1970s, involving Church interests, the Department of Education, the vocational education authorities and teacher groups. Each of these parties sought to reach agreement on a deed of trust, which would set out a governing structure for the community school, which would be in accordance with their own best interests.

In 1977, John Wilson became Minister for Education in the Fianna Fáil administration which was returned to power in that year. By this time, there were over twenty community schools functioning on an ad-hoc legal basis, and negotiations on a deed of trust had reached a stalemate. Wilson made renewed efforts to get the interested parties to agree, and agreement on the deed was eventually reached in late 1979. Under the terms of the agreement, two teachers were to be elected as voting members on the board of management, and the guarantee of reserved teaching posts to religious orders involved in community schools was conceded.[59] A clause whereby the appointment of a teacher could be vetoed on the grounds of 'faith and morals' was dropped. During the negotiations, this had caused problems for the teacher unions.

The protracted and contentious negotiations having been concluded, the first deeds of trust were signed in 1981. The new structure of management, as set out in this document, stipulated that a management board was to consist of eleven members who were to be elected or nominated. It was to consist of three representatives of the religious orders involved, three representatives of the

VEC, two elected parents of children attending the school, two elected members from the permanent teaching staff, and the principal, who would be a non-voting member of the board. The schools, at the Minister's discretion, were to be vested in trustees who were representative of the interest groups involved.[60] Deeply held convictions and fears about the merging of two educational traditions — a private denominational sector with a public non-denominational sector — had contributed to the difficulties of the negotiations. The IVEA had reservations about the management and ownership of community schools.

Following the publication, in December 1980, of the government *White Paper on Educational Development*, which appeared to favour the community school model for future development,[61] the IVEA sought a meeting with John Wilson, at which it secured an agreement that there would be no restriction on the development of the vocational sector.[62] This led to the establishment of the community college, similar in conception to the community school but with a different management structure, giving representation to vocational teachers, parents and community interests.

In any analysis of changing Catholic culture, the developments in post-primary education in the 1960s and 1970s, as described, have enormous significance. Gradually from the early 1960s, the state, as represented by successive ministers, had asserted itself in the area of education. By the 1970s, a state system of post-primary education was in place, which, in theory, was non-denominational. That state education would expand was a certainty, given the policy statements of successive ministers, and also for the more practical reason that religious orders were experiencing a decline in vocations from the late 1960s — a matter which will be elaborated on more fully in the next chapter. When one considers the very cautious statements made by politicians about education in the 1950s, their deference towards the Church's role in education, their unquestioning acceptance of the denominational nature of the educational enterprise, it becomes obvious that all of this had changed enormously by the 1970s.

However, it must also be said that the same protocol of consulting the bishops in relation to Department proposals on education was observed by Pádraig Faulkner, in 1970, as had been observed by his predecessors. The umbrella bodies that the bishops established during the 1960s ensured that they had a powerful voice in the formulation of policy. The considerable power that the bishops still wielded was evidenced by the influence they were able to exert on the character of the community schools, so that they approximated as closely as possible to the Catholic ideal of education in management, ownership and staffing. The deed of trust also made provision for the employment of a chaplain to be appointed to the community school, who would be paid by the Department of Education as a full-time member of staff, and stipulated that religious instruction 'of the order of two hours' was to be provided for the pupils of the school.[63]

However, it is important to remember that all of these developments were happening at a time when religious communities were very concerned about falling vocations and the ageing profile of their members, and the fact that these circumstances would make the financial burden of maintaining and running schools increasingly difficult. These concerns were aired very frankly in a report drawn up by a working party, which was established jointly by the Education Commissions of the Hierarchy and the Conference of Major Religious Superiors, in May 1972. The working party set out to examine 'the position of religious in education' in the 'light of trends in religious life and in society' and to review the future involvement of religious in education. Completed in February 1973, and known as the *F.I.R.E. Report*, it gives a very clear insight into the kind of concerns that were exercising the minds of the bishops and religious managers in their negotiations with the Department of Education throughout the 1970s.[64] The apprehensions of the working party were stated as follows:

> If a substantial increase in vocations does not occur, or if a significant number of religious decide to leave their congregations or orders, then the relative number of religious and lay teachers in secondary schools, will by 1978 have reached a level that will force the rapid withdrawal of religious from a large number of schools.[65]

Looking into the not too distant future, the report warned that:

> unless the right kind of practical guarantees are reached now while the religious are in a position to negotiate with the state, within a few years (three (?) at most) negotiation will no longer be possible.[66]

The concessions that were exacted during the community school débâcle ensured that the bishops and their representatives would play a central role in the new educational structures that were emerging. The fact that this role was now formalised, and that the bishops and religious corporate bodies were central to the new arrangements, was even more important for the future of the Catholic ethos in education, given the decline in the numbers and influence of religious on the ground, which was feared by the *F.I.R.E. Report.*

Notwithstanding the fact that Church interests won considerable concessions from the Department of Education, as regards staffing and representation on the boards of management, these were considerably scaled down from what they expected and, indeed, originally seemed to be achieving. The final composition of the board of management with three religious, three VEC representatives, two parents and two teachers was a much more democratic outcome in comparison to what had been envisaged in the early 1970s. In effect, it was the beginning of the democratisation of education. Many interest groups were now seeking to influence the education process. From 1970, the era was over when the Minister could simply have consultations with the bishops and assume that this was adequate.

So far, the emphasis has been on post-primary education, because the culture of the post-primary school changed radically during the 1960s. While primary schools, on the face of it, appeared to change little, there were two fundamental changes in the 1970s, both of which had implications for Catholic schooling. A new primary-school curriculum was introduced in 1971.[67] Essentially, a more child-centred approach to learning and pedagogy was introduced. The emphasis was on discovery-learning, which would stimulate children's innate interests, make them more responsive to their environment, and provoke them to adopt a more enquiring attitude towards knowledge. This approach, in essence, aimed to promote creativity and a sense of autonomy and initiative and confidence in the learner. This was the approach towards learning cautioned against in the encyclical *Divinii Illius Magistri* (1929) because it jeopardised the authority of the teacher, as seen in Chapter 1.

This approach to learning was popularised in the United States by the writings and educational experiments of John Dewey, in the 1930s, 1940s and 1950s, and castigated by the anonymous pamphleteer in the mid-1970s, as seen above. But the educational insights of Dewey, cross-fertilised, as they were, by the findings of psychology and by the insights of existentialist philosophy, received a far more enthusiastic hearing in religious/educational circles in the post-Vatican II era, because the 'new' more humanistic theology had been influenced strongly both by the findings of psychology and by existentialism, as seen. This new, more questioning, approach to knowledge and learning, which focused on the learner, placing the child at the centre of the education process, paralleled the changed theological thinking. In due course, this approach to learning also began to find its way into post-primary education.

A second significant change involved the management of the primary school. The primary or national school (as it was called), from its establishment, evolved as a de facto Catholic school under clerical management, and it has remained so. However, in 1975, the management structure was somewhat modified.[68] Richard Burke, the then Minister for Education, devised a scheme whereby the Department was willing to provide a substantial per-capita grant, covering 80 per cent of the running cost of schools where committees of management were established. On this basis, the Churches consented to committees of management composed in larger schools of six Church nominees, two teachers (one being the principal) and two parents, and in smaller schools of four Church nominees, the principal teacher and two parents.

However, this arrangement was unacceptable to the Irish National Teachers' Organisation (INTO), which sought a more even distribution of power. In 1980, the management structure was modified, giving the Churches 50 per cent representation and the teachers and elected parents 25 per cent each.[69] The managership was retained by a priest of the parish. However, the new arrangements restricted the span of his power, because he was now part of a group who shared responsibility for the school with him. State influence did not become as all-pervasive in the primary as in the secondary sector, but at the same time the change in management structure did mean a significant change in the culture of the national school.

All of the changes — structural, curricular and pedagogical — altered fundamentally the nature of Catholic schooling in the 1960s and 1970s. The very fact that lay Catholics, be they parents or teachers, were demanding a say, and that schoolchildren were encouraged to question, implied that Catholic culture had changed significantly and would change further in the years ahead. These developments heralded the end of the conformity which had typified Catholicism in the 1950s. The ethos of education had changed fundamentally in a way that no amount of structural concessions could assuage.

Those who were at the very front line of this change were the religious personnel involved in education on the ground. The kind of unease that was registered by religious in relation to the changes instigated in education can be better understood when one looks at the enormous upheaval that took place in their own lives as a result of the Council. While this brought initial confusion, within a decade it led to the development of clerics who were far more independent-minded, less deferential to ecclesiastical authority and much more questioning of their traditional roles. We now turn to look at the changes taking place in their lives in the wake of the Second Vatican Council, and how these changes influenced clerical and religious involvement in education.

12

Changes in Religious Life and their Influence on Education

The above developments in education were taking place at a time when priests and religious were undergoing reassessment and radical changes in their lives as a result of the Vatican Decree on the *Appropriate Renewal of the Religious Life*, 28 October 1965. It stressed the importance of religious relating their apostolic work 'to the changed conditions of the times', to 'the requirements of a given culture', and to 'social and economic circumstances'.[1] This decree instigated a revolution in the culture of convent, religious house and seminary life, which was destined to have a ripple effect in all spheres of activity in which religious were involved. The decree on religious life called for revision of 'constitutions, directories, custom books, books of prayer and ceremonies and similar compilations'.[2] 'This task', it was explained, 'will require the suppression of outmoded regulations'.[3]

The externals of change became obvious from the late 1960s when many nuns, now beginning to call themselves sisters, discarded their veils and shortened the length of their skirts. By degrees during the 1970s, many began to wear lay clothes, getting away from the distinctive black, navy, grey or brown colour, as the case might be. Likewise, many priests, particularly on less formal occasions, doffed the Roman collar, and gradually began to experiment with more adventurous styles and colours of dress. While these changes were external and might even sound trivial at this remove, they were symptomatic of a very profound change in thinking in relation to religious life. Religious dress symbolised the fact that the priest or nun or brother was different — a person apart from the rest of the community, whose interests and inclinations were oriented to another world beyond this. In his book, *Letters to a Nun*, published in 1947, Daniel Lord SJ, the well-known writer, captured the mood of the times. He counsels the young nun that her habit marks her 'as a person set aside for something distinctive.... You are a nurse in the army of Christ ... a citizen consecrated to special work in the kingdom of heaven.'[4]

The dress was also symbolic of the vows that a religious undertook to keep — poverty, chastity and obedience. The worst fault that somebody in religious life could be guilty of was lack of humility. Thus individualism, or what was termed 'singularity' or attention-seeking of whatever type, though it might have been unintended, was frowned upon. Uniformity was imposed. Anything even bordering on the ostentatious — for instance, colourful dress — was seen as out of keeping with the spirit of the vows of poverty. Another factor, particularly in the case of women, was that clothes which were figure-hugging, or which might enhance the wearer in any way, making her more attractive to the eye, were seen as endangering the vow of chastity. Speaking of the 'men and women who designed religious habits', Lord pointed out to the nun that the veil 'since the dawn of human experience has indicated a young virgin'. He went on:

> They bound your waist with the girdle that from the birth of human symbolism has meant chastity.... They draped you in the long folds of cloth that both symbolised and protected your modesty.[5]

The objective of the religious in all of his or her endeavours was to try to rise above human nature. Human nature was seen to be inherently flawed since the original sin of Adam and Eve in the Garden of Eden. Therefore, the religious had to be protected from the snares of the world. Sr de Lourdes Stack, whose life in the Presentation order spanned the 1930s to the 1970s, described her experience as novice:

> Visits from relations were few. Parlourising, as she called it, was frowned on by the Novice Mistress. We were protected from 'the world'. There was no radio. There were no newspapers.[6]

Special friendships, even amongst themselves, were frowned upon, because a religious life was intended to be dedicated to God, and 'special relationships' or 'particular friendships' were seen as diverting attention from their true vocation. The silver ring that nuns wore denoted that they were married to God and the Church. They were 'brides of Christ'. Docility and obedience were insisted upon, and religious who betrayed any signs of high-spiritedness in any direction were 'encouraged' to subdue their passions.

The practice of 'custody of the eyes', whereby religious were required to lower rather than raise their eyes, was designed to reinforce humility, and discourage distraction from the central focus of their lives. Human or personality development did not enter in — rather was it a question of subduing the world, the flesh and the devil and, in this way, striving to become more God-like. As Lord wrote:

> No merely human ideal will do. Any human model means that we are striving for human levels of perfection and accomplishment.... From the dawn of human history we have been striving to be godlike.[7]

While the young nun is putting before herself 'an ideal that can never be attained', because 'Christ's perfections are beyond all human reaching ... they are not beyond human aspiration,' he pointed out.[8]

The taking on of a saint's name at the time of a nun's profession reinforced all of this. The idea was to emulate the life of the saint whose name was adopted, and there was also a sense in which one suppressed or sublimated one's own personality or human nature. The regime in the convent reinforced this. Sr de Lourdes explained that 'almost every minute of the day had its own duty. We lived by the clock. We still do'.[9] The emphasis on routine was echoed by Monica Baldwin, speaking from an English perspective. She spent twenty-eight years in an enclosed order in England, until 1941. She recorded her experiences in a book entitled *I Leap over the Wall*, published in 1948. She wrote:

> Each moment of the day is provided for. One prays, reads, eats, walks in the garden, at the appointed hour; no religious is allowed to follow her own inclinations in the disposal of her time.[10]

Should the cloister bell ring 'as a signal for a change of occupation', all had to abandon whatever they were doing promptly, she explained. 'To disobey the first sound of the bell', she wrote, was 'to commit a fault'.[11]

According to Lord, the nun was 'reduced' [sic] by her habit 'to someone almost indistinguishable as an individual'. Pointing to how 'smart the founders were', Lord went on to explain that 'they were determined that only God should know [her] completely'.[12] Another interesting factor in the case of nuns was their adoption very often of male saints' names, such as Thomas Aquinas, Ambrose, Ignatius. Names having to do with events or aspects of the life of the mother of God abounded also, such as Immaculata, Annunciata, Assumpta. In keeping with the hierarchical model of Church, the superior's word was law. A nun did not disagree, or indeed look for reasons or explanations as to why she should comply with it. Baldwin explained that the 'extreme respect shown to her was based upon the idea that in the monastery she held the place of Christ'.[13] The status quo was reinforced in all sorts of what, to the modern mind, might seem trivial ways. For instance, when religious were taking a casual walk, a custom was observed whereby the senior person walked in the middle, in the event of there being three people, and the others fell in to the right or left, depending on their standing in the earthly order of things. While the examples given are from female congregations, it is important to point out that a similar regime applied to male religious and, to a great extent, also to seminarians.

The Second Vatican Council, with its emphasis on the dignity of the individual, whatever his/her earthly status, and its redefinition of the role of authority as service, heralded the death-knell of such a conceptualisation of religious life. The 'new' theology stressed the importance of human fulfilment. This thinking ran totally counter to the philosophy of self-effacement which had heretofore been the cornerstone of religious life. In the post-Vatican II era, many, particularly younger nuns, reverted to their baptismal names, which was one way of re-asserting their own human identity and personhood.

While the conciliar decree stressed the importance of obedience for religious, it was also pointed out that the 'superior should himself be docile to God's will in the exercise of his office'.[14] His authority was to be used 'in a spirit of service' for his brethren.[15] He was to govern his subjects 'as God's own sons, and with regard for their human personality', and thus to 'make it easier for them to obey gladly'.[16] He was to leave them 'appropriately free with respect to the sacrifice of penance and direction of conscience', and the responsibility was on him to exercise 'the kind of leadership' which would inspire responsible obedience in his brethren.[17] There was a pronounced emphasis on the exercise of freedom — on the religious taking responsibility for their own lives, and not simply conforming to legalistically applied rules.

Seminary and convent training in the pre-conciliar era concentrated greatly on developing discipline, docility and obedience, but it was less successful in developing a sense of initiative and personal responsibility. The system also tended to place a premium on erudition in the narrow sense, for its own sake. The student was encouraged to learn and memorise rather than to read critically and think independently. Newspapers or books, other than recommended course textbooks, were forbidden.[18] This was the Scholastic approach to knowledge and learning, and it influenced the education process from primary to secondary school to university, as well the education of clerics.

The seminary/convent protected the future priest/nun from the dangers of the world, even in a concrete physical way by the erection of high walls. In so doing, it also kept them away from any close contact with the world, its problems, dilemmas and needs. In a survey entitled *The Changing Direction of Irish Seminaries,* published in 1972, Liam Ryan noted that very little change had taken place in the culture of the seminary between 1862 and 1962. He pointed out that in the national seminary in Maynooth a sign which read, 'whoever takes a book out of this library incurs excommunication *ipso facto*' was still there in the mid-1960s.[19]

The training of seminarians and female postulants was radically and fundamentally reformed from the late 1960s, on the basis of the *Decree on Priestly Formation*[20] and the *Decree on the Appropriate Renewal of the Religious Life,*[21] both promulgated in Rome on 28 October 1965. The 'new' theology placed much more emphasis on the broader emotional, spiritual and psychological formation of seminarians and postulants. Personal development and education in human relations took on huge significance in the lives of religious in the 1970s. One has only to look at any religious journal, such as the *Furrow* or *Doctrine and Life,* to see the plethora of renewal courses available to clerical personnel, and the huge emphasis placed on personal development and relationships.[22] The attractiveness of these to religious has to be seen against the background of the training they had undergone, which had conditioned them to suppress anything that smacked of human emotion or desires, as something to be ashamed of and unworthy of their calling. Against the backdrop of the sexual revolution, a more liberal moral climate and the now ubiquitous popular music culture, which was very compelling in its argument, that 'all you need is love', it is easy to understand the heightened emphasis placed on personal fulfilment in the lives of religious.

The emphasis on personal development became even more urgent at a time when departures from the religious life and a decline in the numbers entering it were having a de-stabilising effect on clerical personnel in general. From the late 1960s, rapidly changing cultural patterns, increased affluence and the revolutionary changes in the religious ethos caused by the Council's deliberations provoked confusion and an identity crisis among many religious personnel, the resolution of which, for some, lay in withdrawal from the ministry. Between 1966 and 1970, fifteen priests were laicised. This represented 0.4 per cent of the secular priests ministering in Ireland during this period.[23] While this may seem a small number, it must be seen in the context of a time when leaving the ministry was unheard of.

What is important is that procedures were now put in place whereby clerics could be released from their vows and leave honourably. Even in the very exceptional cases when clerics did leave formerly, there was no way that they could do so without opprobrium. It was seen as defection, and the term 'spoilt priest', in the common parlance of the time, perhaps best captures the stigma associated with it. In the case of religious orders, in the period between 1965 and 1970, 104 professed brothers and 72 priests departed from the religious life. In the same period, 1965–70, 297 sisters and 169 brothers left the religious life after final profession. As in the case of secular priests, these figures, while low in percentage terms, were nonetheless significant for the same reasons.[24]

The changing cultural and economic climate was also having an adverse effect on vocations. School-leavers in the 1960s were presented with greater choice of career opportunities, and they tended to be influenced by considerations of economic rather than spiritual rewards as their counterparts had been a few short years before. Religious vocations, having peaked in 1961, declined from the mid-1960s. Overall, religious personnel peaked in 1967, and began to decline after that time.[25] A survey of Irish Catholic clergy and religious, carried out by the Research and Development Unit of the Catholic Communications Institute, and published in 1971, highlighted the 'rather steep' decline in vocations in the period 1965–70, which can be seen in Table 12.1, and which was beginning to be reflected in overall religious personnel from 1968.[26]

Table 12.1: Numbers of Vocations, 1965–70

	1965	1966	1967	1968	1969	1970
Diocesan Clergy	282	254	291	219	221	164
Religious Orders	377	390	343	325	258	261
Brothers	179	173	166	119	79	98
Sisters	537	592	509	418	283	227
Totals	1,375	1,409	1,309	1,081	841	750

Source: Irish Catholic Clergy and Religious 1970, Catholic Communications Institute of Ireland, Dublin, 1971.

Against the background of the decree on religious life, and on the basis of trends and future projections suggested by statistical data, religious were forced to re-assess radically their lives and the work in which they were involved. They had to come to terms with their shrinking resources, and decide what strategic moves this called for. Given the extensive concentration of religious personnel in schooling, one of the most important areas to be reviewed was education. Of the 591 secondary schools in the country in 1970, 517 were owned and/or managed by clergy and religious.[27]

Table 12.2 gives the percentage deployment of clerical personnel, both diocesan and religious, in teaching in 1970.[28]

Table 12.2: Deployment of Religious in Teaching as a Percentage of Total Home-based Religious Personnel in 1970

	Total Teaching	Total Number	%
Diocesan Clergy	487	3,813	13
Religious Priests/Brothers	804	2,969	27
Sisters	5,340	15,145	35
Orders of Brothers	1,328	2,198	60

Source: Irish Catholic Clergy and Religious 1970, Catholic Communications Institute of Ireland, Dublin, 1971.

Against this background, the findings of the *F.I.R.E. Report,* published in 1973, have significance far beyond the backdrop they provide to the Church–state negotiations on education, examined in the last chapter. The

F.I.R.E. Report is a highly important report in its own right, because it gives an insight into how religious communities were reassessing their role in Irish life, against the background of the Vatican Council, and in the context of the sociocultural changes taking place in Irish society. The report gives a clear indication of the issues and problems facing religious orders in the 1970s and how they proposed to respond to them. Assessing the 'distinctive' role of religious in the light of the Council decree, *Lumen Gentium*, the working party found that their response to the ideals expressed in the decree was 'adversely affected by such circumstances as diminishing personnel — due to age, lack of vocations ... and consequent overwork'.[29]

The free post-primary education scheme, introduced in 1967, and the raising of the school-leaving age from fourteen to fifteen years of age in 1972, had resulted in a huge expansion in the post-primary school population[30] and the recruitment of vast numbers of lay teachers. The report of the working party highlighted the 'considerable change in the proportion that religious have formed in the total staff in each school and in all schools.'[31] The working party presented the following figures (as shown in Table 12.3) to demonstrate the decline in the ratio of full-time registered religious teachers to full-time registered lay teachers in secondary schools between 1966 and 1972.[32]

TABLE 12.3: RELIGIOUS AS A PERCENTAGE OF ALL TEACHERS, 1966–72

Year	Percentage
1966	50
1968	45
1970	38
1972	34

Source: Report on the Future Involvement of Religious in Education by a working party of the Education Commissions of the Hierarchy and the Major Religious Superiors, Dublin, 1973.

With the decline in vocations, the report pointed out that 'one [could] anticipate a much sharper decline in the religious proportion after 1975'. The percentage figure estimated for the year 1975 was 28 per cent.[33] Department of Education figures for the academic year 1974–5, show that the percentage of religious staff in secondary and community and comprehensive schools was, in fact, 24 per cent,[34] and by 1979–80 it had further decreased to 18 per cent.[35] The following table (12.4) illustrates the further decline in vocations from 1971. Whereas the situation in regard to diocesan clergy and religious orders tended to stabilise in the 1970s, the decline has been relentless in the case of brothers and sisters, those categories with the highest involvement in teaching.[36]

TABLE 12.4: DECLINE IN VOCATIONS, 1971–79

	1971	1972	1973	1974	1975	1976	1977	1978	1979
Diocesan Clergy	179	184	157	144	154	181	206	175	175
Religious Orders	236	246	220	167	191	189	161	179	143
Brothers	81	59	40	48	55	64	66	31	27
Sisters	239	176	153	188	175	188	194	175	161
TOTALS	735	665	570	547	575	622	627	560	506

Source: Vocations in Ireland 1980, Report no. 11, Council for Research and Development, Maynooth, 1981.

Table 12.5 illustrates how the decline in vocations was reflected in the total religious population from 1965 to 1980.[37]

TABLE 12.5: TOTAL RELIGIOUS PERSONNEL, 1965–80

Year	Diocesan Clergy	Religious Orders	Brothers	Sisters	Total
1965	3,965	8,020	2,838	18,705	33,528
1970	3,944	7,946	2,540	18,662	33,092
1975	3,803	7,246	2,138	17,317	30,504
1980	3,998	6,912	1,878	16,361	29,149

Sources: A Survey of Irish Catholic Clergy and Religious 1970, Catholic Communications Institute of Ireland, Dublin, 1971; *Irish Priests and Religious 1970-1975: Survey of Catholic Clergy and Religious in Ireland,* Research and Development Commission, Dublin, 1977; *Vocations in Ireland in Ireland 1980, report no. 11,* Council for Research and Development, Maynooth, 1981.

The *F.I.R.E. Report* of 1973 recognised that:

> In the presence of a well-developed profession of lay secondary teachers and a growing involvement of the State in school financing, the nature of the demand for religious school teachers has altered considerably.[38]

In this context, and bearing in mind the thinking of the conciliar decree, the report of the working party recommended that religious concentrate their considerable resources and expertise in areas of special educational need within, but not necessarily exclusive to, the formal education process — in a word, they were recommended to diversify. Among the areas to be targeted were care of orphans and delinquent children, the handicapped, the educationally deprived, remedial education, counselling, adult education and catechesis.[39]

The assumption by the state of more responsibility for education and the new thinking of the Second Vatican Council challenged Church personnel to turn their attention to areas of greater need. Paradoxically, Vatican II also challenged them to defend the principle of Catholic schooling. They were now forced to analyse what exactly made Catholic schools distinctive, because the question was beginning to be asked — why have religious-run schools at all, unless their ethos was, indeed, distinctive and they had something that made them different? Also, given that management, ownership and staffing were Catholic, did it automatically follow that the ethos was Catholic? Such questions had seldom been raised before and, in so far as they had been, the answers could be assumed to be foregone conclusions. The answers to them from the early 1970s certainly could not be assumed — they were anything but straightforward.

In 1968, the government introduced a grant scheme to enable more students to avail of third-level education. In order to cater for the increasing numbers of students seeking to enter third level, the universities began to operate a points system as a mechanism for allocating places and also for entry to various faculties.[40] In the aftermath of the introduction of the points system, at a time when educational credentials (no longer a luxury to be attained by the privileged few) were becoming increasingly important for entry into the labour market, the dilemma posed for religious educators as precipitated by changing cultural patterns, was stated starkly in the report. It underlined the concern of people that:

> Religious orders will divert too much time away from the subjects seen by parents as necessary in a competitive world, towards less 'relevant' subjects, such as those related to religion.[41]

The working party went on to highlight 'a growing belief that the state should carry responsibility for education services', and observed:

> From about 1965 on, people have begun to question the suitability of the Church for this purpose. They feel that the religious, following their traditions, continue in their schools to put the emphasis on the humanities, while current needs call for training in technological and scientific subjects.[42]

This was the nub of the problem for religious as they faced the 1970s. The environment and context of schooling had changed utterly. Whereas education in the 1950s had evoked little interest in any section of the community outside the institutional Church, from the 1960s on, in the context of the more optimistic economic climate, increased affluence and the dramatic initiatives undertaken by politicians, it began to filter through to the general mind that a different kind of education, was, in fact, the avenue to a better way of life.

In order that the government could forward its twin aims of economic progress and equality of educational opportunity, it began to steer students towards technological education and business studies. This was achieved by a series of complementary initiatives. Following the organisational and structural changes pointed up in the last chapter, a number of new subjects of a more practical nature were introduced into the Leaving Certificate list of examination subjects for the school year 1970–71. Included in this list were Building Construction, Engineering, Business Organisation and Accounting.[43] In the same year, the third-level technological sector was expanded by the establishment of Regional Technical Colleges (RTCs). The Industrial Development Authority set about attracting the kind of businesses that would provide outlets for students with the new qualifications and also provide Ireland with the kind of industrial base, which was seen by political and commercial interests as crucial for wealth creation and economic prosperity.

The effects of these government policies were beginning to be felt at curriculum level in schools in the 1970s. There was a gradual movement away from the classical liberal curriculum to subject matter of a more applied and technical nature.[44] Perhaps the most dramatic evidence of the shift in emphasis was the extent to which the take-up rate of Latin plummeted from 67 per cent of the total number of students examined in the Leaving Certificate in 1955, to 4.9 per cent in 1979 as seen in Table 12.6 below. An influential factor here was the relaxation of the NUI ruling from 1973, whereby a pass in Latin or Greek was a mandatory matriculation requirement for entry into certain faculties.[45] A key influence here was, of course, the changed attitude towards Latin adopted by the Church authorities since the Second Vatican Council.

Table 12.6: Percentage of Leaving Certificate Students Taking Latin, 1955–89

Year	Total Examined	Number Taking Latin	% of Total
1955	6,098	4,091	67
1965	11,651	6,537	56
1969	16,986	7,461	44
1979	35,510	1,769	5
1989	58,435	609	1

Source: Department of Education Statistical Reports, 1955, 1965, 1969, 1979, 1989.

A further threat to the Catholic ethos of education, as the *F.I.R.E. Report* working party saw it, was the competitive climate ushered in by increased affluence and higher parental educational expectations for children. The main interest of religious in education, as outlined by the bishops, was their duty of passing on the faith and ensuring that the entire education process be permeated by a religious outlook on life.[46] However, in the context of a more secularised, urbanised culture influenced by consumerist values, the transmission of Catholic culture was becoming increasingly problematic.

The *F.I.R.E. Report* noted that 'a sharp contrast has emerged between the set of values placed before the child by the religious at school and by the parents in the home'.[47] 'This questioning of the Church's involvement in modern educational needs' the report saw as a manifestation of a deeper change in Catholic culture — 'partly ... the result of some general drift apart of the Church and the public'.[48] It is reflected also, the report added, 'in the private and public attitudes and behaviour towards the clergy and religious'.[49] Essentially what religious had to face up to was that their very *raison d'être* in education was being called into question and threatened in a changing sociocultural context. While Catholic interests were involved, on the one hand, in negotiating for themselves a key role in terms of the control and structuring of education, on the other hand, many religious were realising that real influence had to be wielded at a much deeper level, and that it did not automatically follow that Catholic management and control equated with a Catholic ethos.

A far deeper issue had arisen for religious — how to maintain the religious ethos in the context of the highly competitive school atmosphere, with religion seen as a low-esteem, non-examination subject. The *F.I.R.E. Report* noted 'reluctance evident in the lay teachers and even amongst religious to teach religion', which the report conceded, was 'an increasingly difficult and unpopular task'.[50] It was not unknown for religion class periods to be given over, in many cases, to what were perceived as more 'relevant' subjects, in which students needed to obtain high grades, to gain the necessary points for third-level courses.

The state was now the chief power-broker in education. While it could not afford to disregard Church interest in education, given the religious investment of resources, both financial and personal, and in terms of physical plant into the education enterprise, economic considerations had now evolved as a powerful sphere of influence. This was compounded from the mid-1970s when, in the recessionary climate, the importance of business, scientific and technological education, as articulated by the state sector in harmony with industrial and business interests, became more urgent. High unemployment, on the one hand, and greatly increased affluence, on the other, brought about what Mannheim has referred to as the dominance of the 'economic sphere', which, he asserted, 'causes great changes in the social function ... and cultural factors in our society'.[51] In the context of this changed sociocultural climate, students and parents were increasingly more influenced by utilitarian considerations when making decisions as regards what constitutes worthwhile curricular knowledge, and this was a development which the working party was only too aware constituted a grave threat to Catholic ideals in education.

In October 1974, the Conference of Major Religious Superiors (CMRS) published the findings of a follow-up report, entitled *Focus for Action.* This report was prepared by a working party, which was established to consider how religious might deploy their resources in Ireland over the following six years.[52] 'It has been widely stated', the report noted,

> that schools are far too productivity oriented. The accent — in partly misplaced response to the parents' requirements — falls heavily on examinations and scholastic achievement.[53]

The report went on to spell out the 'very special role'[54] to be fulfilled by the Catholic school within the changing context of education:

> Religious in schools should be deeply concerned with the creation of a sense of the personal value of the individual, with the student's Christian development as a whole person, his emotional development ... his growth in ability to form human relationships.[55]

The report went on to state that 'the primary concern of religious will be to foster each student's continuing religious development', at a time when 'tensions between the requirements of the working life and the spiritual will become more acute'.[56]

What is interesting about all of these recommendations is that Catholic education had always claimed to be about the education of the whole person. This was the theory of the classical humanist curriculum as outlined in the Council of Education report, but its interpretation was narrow. The Catholic school ethos had been geared towards educating the more intelligent of the school cohort towards professions in the Church, teaching, medicine, and the civil service and, as such, it had always been very competitive, selective and not equitable. While it had promoted upward social mobility based on meritocratic principles, the fact that its focus had been exclusively academic left it open to charges of elitism. It is ironic, but understandable, that religious began in earnest to scrutinise, reflect and adopt a critical stance towards what they were about, in the field of education, only when they felt under siege.

In the secondary school sector throughout the 1970s, teachers increasingly lobbied for greater promotional opportunities and the right to principalships, which resulted in tensions between religious proprietors of schools and the teachers. But while the Church, as represented by the bishops and managerial bodies, was seeking to secure its interest in education, as seen in the previous chapter, there were many religious on the ground who were beginning to question whether controlling and managing the system was as vital as it had always been perceived to be. At a time of depleted personnel, many who felt ill-suited to these appointments found themselves obliged to occupy such positions because of the Church's commitment to education. Both the *F.I.R.E. Report* and the *Focus for Action* report stressed the importance of trusting the laity — both teachers and parents — and giving them responsibility, quoting from Vatican Council documents to impress the point. The latter report stated that this dimension 'in Christian education has been far too slow in coming'.[57]

Nevertheless, there was a very pragmatic element in the thinking of religious also. The *F.I.R.E. Report* made it clear that religious schools, in order to survive the pressures to which they were being subjected, would have to 'reshape their policy'.[58] The pressures were being caused by 'underlying trends in our society, the growing shortage of religious manpower, and the policies of the Department of Education'.[59] The report anticipated that there would be increasing demand from teacher unions 'for access to the principalships in religious-owned schools'[60] and for 'representation on boards of management for schools'.[61]

It was clear to the working party that religious orders would no longer enjoy the same autonomy in the running of their schools, because teacher unions were becoming 'a force for change which it is significantly beyond the power of the secondary schools to shape'.[62] Taking these factors into consideration, one of the recommendations made by the report was that 'the management of Catholic secondary schools should be shared with Boards, appointed on a non-representational basis'.[63]

While the report team was very concerned that religious should retain power to influence the character of their own schools, the team's deliberations and recommendations represented a significant change of direction. They were undoubtedly influenced by the educational policies pursued by the state over the previous ten years, in particular the more democratic management model introduced via the comprehensive and community school. But the report also highlighted the fact that 'such a broadening of the management process ... could conceivably be the means of ensuring continuity of Catholic education in the hands of lay teachers, should religious withdraw from a school' at some future time.[64]

Some nuns and priests in the 1970s expressed the feeling that they no longer wanted to become school principals. In the past, conformity to what was seen as one's duty was a central tenet of religious life and, once someone was appointed to a task, he/she did not question it. The Conciliar decree was destined to have a considerable impact in this area. It urged a more autonomous attitude in religious towards their superiors. It encouraged them to develop their own talents and initiative. Religious 'foot-soldiers' from the 1970s began to look critically at their role in education, and some began to feel that there were other areas of the apostolate more needful of their attention.

The first appointment to the position of lay principalship of a religious secondary school was made on 9 November 1970. Liam Murphy was appointed principal of St Patrick's Classical School in Navan.[65] This appointment was particularly significant because it was to a diocesan school, and Murphy was appointed principal and manager of the school. The appointment of lay principals did not gather momentum until the late 1980s. The new modes of thinking, the seeds of which were sown at the time of the *F.I.R.E. Report*, gradually grew in influence throughout the 1970s. This led to the establishment of boards of management with lay membership, on a voluntary basis, in secondary schools from 1985.[66] The number of appointments of lay principals in religious secondary schools increased dramatically from that time.

All of these developments marked a profound change in the culture of the secondary school. They also gave religious the scope to be responsive to what many saw as more urgent contemporary needs and problems, as they had been urged by the Council. Many abandoned the cloistered life for smaller houses in estates, where they lived among lay people and became involved in different aspects of social and parish work. In this regard, the change in deployment figures for religious in Ireland from the 1970s to the 1980s is interesting to note. The percentage figure of diocesan clergy engaged in teaching remained practically the same — 12.8 per cent in 1970 to 13.2 per cent in 1981. Likewise, in the case of brothers — in 1970, 60.4 per cent of brothers were involved in teaching, and the figure for 1981 was 60.5 per cent.[67]

However, in the case of religious priests and brothers, the percentage figure for those involved in teaching declined from 27.2 per cent in 1970 to 19.4 per cent in 1981. In the case of sisters, the decline in numbers involved in teaching has been less dramatic, but significant nonetheless. Whereas 35.4 per cent of sisters were involved in teaching in 1970, the figure for 1981 had dropped to 30.7 per cent.[68] Leaving aside the figures for those who have retired from active ministry, the most dramatic changes have occurred, particularly in the case of religious order priests and brothers, because of increased involvement in social welfare and work of a pastoral nature, including counselling, visitation and general parish work.[69] Whereas in 1970, 22.1 per cent of religious order priests and brothers were involved in these categories of social welfare/pastoral work, by 1981 this figure had increased to 30.2 per cent. Similarly, the percentage figure for those involved in 'diverse works' (which included social welfare work) had risen from 9.7 per cent in 1970 to 13.3 per cent in 1981.[70]

While many religious were disappointed with the response to the *F.I.R.E. Report* at the time it was published,[71] it is nonetheless clear that considerable change had taken place even by the late 1970s. The report had sown the seeds of change, many of which would really come to fruition only in the 1980s and beyond. What is important from the perspective of the cultural historian is that from the time of the publication of the *F.I.R.E.* and *Focus for Action* reports, many religious were beginning to ask more fundamental questions about their involvement in education — questions that went beyond the issue of control and maintenance of the status quo. They were beginning to question the quality of the educational experience and the contribution that they should make to it. This questioning gathered momentum in the late 1970s and through the 1980s, against the background of a growing body of research, which suggested that the much vaunted goal of 'equality of educational opportunity' had not been realised and that the real beneficiaries of the introduction of free post-primary education in 1967 were the middle classes.[72] This development reflected the increasing concern with issues of justice, shown by the Irish Church from the 1970s, which is documented in Chapter 15.

The impact of the revised theology of religious life contained in the conciliar documents was, of course, central to all of these developments. Fr Donal Dorr SPS captured the implications of the new theological thinking in 1974, as follows:

> The change in the theory and practice of obedience over the past few years is likely to call in question the concept of the cleric.... The social utility of clerics from the viewpoint of the institutional church is that they form a tightly organised and highly disciplined corps of officials.[73]

The 'seminary training-programme and the whole life style of both secular and religious priests contributed to this,' he believed.[74] However, and this was an entirely new phenomenon for religious superiors, he went on:

> With the new attitude to authority the situation has changed radically almost overnight. Bishops and superiors are finding that they have to deal with highly educated and very articulate individuals who may differ from them on many points of discipline or of the interpretation of Christian teaching.[75]

It is undoubtedly the case that the changes in the lives of religious and their questioning and reassessment of their role in education, as outlined, could be seen as another dramatic change in Catholic culture in the period of this research. We turn now to examine another area in which considerable reappraisal of modes of thinking and ways of acting was taking place from the 1960s, namely the area of Catholic–Protestant relations.

13

THE IRISH CHURCH AND ECUMENISM

When the announcement of the convocation of the Ecumenical Council was made by Pope John XXIII on 25 January 1959, the closing day of Church Unity Octave, he stated that the proposed council was 'not only for the spiritual good of Christian people, but also to invite the separated communities to seek again that unity for which so many souls are longing in these days throughout the whole earth'.[1] From the very beginning of his pontificate, he expressed his desire for Christian unity and gave the lead in this area. However, inter-church relations in Ireland had an uneasy historical legacy to contend with, and attitudes, customs and traditions moulded over centuries were not to be dispelled overnight, notwithstanding the openness and optimism of John XXIII. The fact that there was mixed reaction to Pope John XXIII's desire for Christian unity and that it did not strike quite as deep a chord as he might have wished with all of the Irish bishops is readily discernible on examination of some of their pastoral letters.

In his 1959 pastoral, responding to the new pope's unity initiatives, Cardinal D'Alton wrote at length on the history of Christianity and how it came to be divided by Luther's revolt. While his approach to the subject was factual, his attitude was very much the traditional one — that the only viable path to unity was 'a return of separated brethren to the flock...' — to 'the one true church'.[2] Bishop Rodgers of Killaloe, in his Lenten pastoral of the same year, attacked the argument sometimes heard that 'one religion is as good as another' as 'religious indifferentism'. He went on to point out that 'some Catholics, animated no doubt, by a mistaken zeal for the conversion of our separated brethren tend to minimise the necessity of belonging to the Catholic Church'.[3] In his 1962 pastoral letter, Archbishop Walsh of Tuam pointed to the importance of praying that 'all men may be one' and the importance of living 'a truly Christian life in order to bring our separated brethren to the unity of the faith'.[4]

Lest it be thought that the Irish bishops were totally out of step with universal Catholic theological developments, it is important to point out that the first time Pope Pius XII had allowed Catholic observers at the World Council of Churches meeting had been in 1952.[5] The World Council of Churches had been founded on 23 August 1948 in Amsterdam. Representatives of 147 independent Christian Churches from 44 different countries, among them members of the Church of Ireland, and Irish Presbyterian and Methodist communities were present.[6] The Roman Catholic Church was conspicuous by its absence. Against this background it was understandable that the Irish bishops should have some difficulty in commending what to them was a novel and hitherto unexpected development, for which nothing in their experience had prepared them.

However, it would be wrong to conclude that the spirit of papal thinking found no echo in Ireland. The pamphlet *Towards Christian Unity,* written by Michael Hurley SJ and published by the CTSI in 1960, was a significant development in this area.[7] It was particularly forward-thinking for its time in the Irish context. From that time, Hurley's name became increasingly associated with inter-church activity in Ireland. In the mid-1950s, the *Furrow* had highlighted and attempted to raise consciousness in relation to the question of Christian unity.[8]

Encouraged further by the prominence given by Pope John XXIII to the importance of Christian unity, the January 1963 issue of the *Furrow* was given over to the subject of Christian unity, in order to highlight the Church Unity Octave which took place from 18 to 25 January. The octave of prayer for church unity was first instituted by members of the Anglican communion in 1908. The group which began the octave, known as the Society of the Atonement, was formally received into the Catholic Church on 30 October 1909, and in 1910 the octave was observed for the first time under Catholic auspices.[9]

Reflecting on ecumenical progress abroad and the presence of observers from other Christian churches at the Second Vatican Council, Fr McGarry of the *Furrow* expressed disappointment that, 'we have been slow to perceive in these ecumenical trends any relevance to the position in Ireland, where theological differences have been sharpened by political, historical and social circumstances', and highlighted the necessity of acknowledging our 'ecumenical responsibilities'.[10] Writing in the same issue in January 1963, Fr Denis Faul, teacher at St Patrick's Academy, Dungannon, Co. Tyrone, and secretary of the Christus Rex society, pointed out that 'before the accession of Pope John XXIII on 28 October 1958, any individuals or groups of Catholic religious or laity engaged on [sic] ecumenical work were regarded by many of us here in Ireland as good-natured eccentrics'.[11]

Another contributor, Fr Joseph Dowdall OSB, Abbot of Glenstal and chairman of the Conference of Major Religious Superiors, observed that the idea of praying for unity was 'novel', and cited the example of the refusal by the editor of a popular Irish newspaper of an article on church unity on the basis that he feared 'that many simple folk would be a little troubled by the very idea of unity'. 'For them', he said, 'it is the "one true church"', and he considered that publication would be 'unwise in a popular mass circulation paper'.[12] All of these comments by observers in the early 1960s illustrate the intractable nature of the ecumenical question in Ireland. Clerics like Hurley, McGarry, Faul and Dowdall were, to a great extent, preaching to the already converted. They had already acknowledged their 'ecumenical responsibilities'. It was obvious from McGarry's remarks in January 1963 that he hoped for a lead from the bishops, which would help bring about more normal inter-church relations among people on the ground.

Bishops Lucey and McQuaid were the most intransigent of the bishops on this issue. Their wariness of Protestantism is revealed in correspondence that passed between them in the early 1950s. In a letter to McQuaid on 12 November 1953, Lucey sought advice on what to do about Catholic girl guides who 'camp and fraternise' with Protestant Baden-Powell girl guides in his diocese. McQuaid had no doubts about his position. In his reply of 15 November, he wrote that he had never given the Baden-Powell guides 'any support', and added: 'I regard it as invariably dangerous for our young Catholics, boys or girls, to fraternise with Protestant groups, because, no matter what safeguards provided [sic], the Catholics take on the colour of the Protestant mentality and morals. Explain it as one may, the result is inevitable'.[13] Neither of them had changed in their attitude ten years later.

Speaking very much in the traditional mould, during Church Unity Octave in 1964, McQuaid viewed the octave as an occasion,

> to pray for the intentions of the Holy Father that Christians separated in doctrine and discipline from the Holy See may, at length, by the grace of God rejoin the true Church of Christ.[14]

Posing the question as to what the ecumenical approach demanded of people in Ireland in his Lenten pastoral of the same year, Lucey's reply to his own rhetorical question is worth quoting at length, as an indication of the extent to which he did not reflect the ecumenical climate developing in Rome in the conciliar era. He observed:

> Certainly not as much as some people seem to think. Our separated brethren are far more separated from us than if they were of the Orthodox faith.... Ecumenism does not mean that we Catholics are going back one jot on our claim to be the true Church of Christ: it does not mean that we may regard any form of the Protestant religion as being just as good as our own religion: it doesn't mean that we are to drop the demands of our religion that we know Protestants don't like, such as that for separate schooling or special guarantees in the case of mixed marriages; nor does it mean that we may attend their services or adopt their attitude towards things like divorce and birth control.[15]

The Catholic position on issues such as education, mixed marriages, divorce and birth control did, in fact, become more open to question in the not-too-distant future, and this situation arose partly as a result of the more ecumenical climate promoted by the Second Vatican Council.

The remarks made by McQuaid and Lucey could not, however, be said to reflect the general mood of the Irish Church in 1964. Cardinal D'Alton's death in February 1963, and the accession to the Armagh see the following September of William Conway, had initiated a new era for Irish Catholicism, not least in inter-church relations. The new archbishop's first Lenten pastoral in 1964, was in sharp contrast to the line taken by McQuaid and Lucey. Archbishop Conway pointed to the Vatican Council's promotion of 'the unity of all Christians' and the resultant change in 'the climate of the relations between Catholics and other Christians', which had 'grown markedly warmer'.[16] He reminded his flock of the words of Pope Paul VI during Church Unity Octave a month earlier, when he had stated that, 'Christians separated from us possess much that is true, good, Christian and holy'.[17] The archbishop's optimism was echoed by Bishop McNamee of Ardagh and Clonmacnoise, in his Lenten pastoral of 1964, when he pointed to the 'new climate' fostered by Pope John XXIII, which enabled all Christians to meet together 'as brothers'.[18] It would be a mistaken idea, however, to think that the viewpoint expressed by Lucey and McQuaid found no echo in Conway's thinking. The fact that it did is indicated by his drawing attention to the words of Pope Paul VI, when he said that Christian unity could 'not be obtained at the expense of the truths of the faith'.[19]

The fact that the bishops in general had not been proactive in giving a lead to Irish Catholics in the ecumenical area up to this time was obvious from the confusion that existed in the minds of Irish Catholics, regarding what was permissible in their relations with non-Catholics. This was evidenced in remarks made by Fr Michael Hurley SJ, writing in the *Furrow* as late as 1965:

> It is, e.g. not uncommonly thought that to be present at a Protestant wedding or funeral as an act of courtesy or civic duty though not as an act of worship is always and in all circumstances illicit, a sin and, in places a reserved sin.[20]

Despite the fact that Church legislation in this regard had changed in the *Code of Canon Law* promulgated in 1917, and that the Maynooth statutes (1956) had been revised accordingly, and also that more enlightened thinking was beginning to prevail in many quarters, this change had not found its way into the lives of Irish Catholics.

This situation is interesting on a number of levels. Firstly, it illustrates the fact that attitudes and traditions are deeply embedded in lived culture, and die hard. Secondly, until the time of the Vatican Council, there was little in the way of transparency in the thinking of the Church. Church documentation in Latin was not readily accessible to lay Catholics. In order that changes in rules or regulations could be translated into people's lives, it was necessary that bishops and priests actively promote new ways of thinking. But in the case of bishops and priests, attitudes and traditions are as deeply rooted as in lay people and, in many cases, it is probably fair to say that the former were content to let matters rest as they were. But in the post-conciliar era this situation changed. Translations of the conciliar documents were readily available, and the era of television and the press conference gave lay Catholics direct access to the most radical changes in the Church's teaching.

The changed attitude of the Catholic Church towards Christian unity was spelt out formally in the *Decree on Ecumenism*, which was promulgated on 21 November 1964. This decree declared 'the restoration of unity among all Christians' to be 'one of the chief concerns' of the Council.[21] This document set the stage for a radically new climate in inter-church relations. On the basis of this decree, the Episcopal Commission on Ecumenism was set up in Ireland in 1965.

Regular unofficial contacts between Catholic and Protestant clergy and laity began in Ireland with the Glenstal and Greenhills conferences. The first Ecumenical congress took place in Glenstal Abbey in Co. Limerick in June 1964, and became an annual event after that time. The Greenhills Ecumenical Conference was an initiative of McGarry's. It was organised by an inter-denominational committee including D. Mac Iomhair PP, Kilcurry, Dundalk, Kevin McNamara of Maynooth and Michael Hurley SJ, under the patronage of Cardinal Conway, and took place at the Presentation Convent, Greenhills, Drogheda, in January 1966; it was held annually from that time. Its location made it easy of access from both north and south.

All in all, considering the situation at the Douglas Hyde funeral (recounted in Chapter 1) as typifying Catholic–Protestant relations as they obtained until the mid-1960s, no small amount of progress was made in a few short years, directly as a result of the Second Vatican Council and the *Decree on Ecumenism*. The unofficial initiatives that had been taken by people like Hurley and McGarry were now coming to fruition. As in the case of the liturgists in the pre-Vatican II era, they had laid the foundations, and their efforts were now given a new impetus by being officially sanctioned. But initiatives which on the face of it purported to facilitate dialogue and advance understanding and co-operation also tended to mask some of the thornier problems which continued to frustrate meaningful inter-church dialogue.

The vexed problem of mixed marriages, or inter-church marriages as they came to be called in the post-conciliar era, was particularly acute in the Republic of Ireland, where the Protestant population had experienced considerable decline in numbers since independence (see Appendix A). An insight into this situation is afforded in an interview given by Archbishop Simms, the Church of Ireland Archbishop of Dublin, in the December 1964 issue of the *Word*, a monthly published by the Divine Word Missionaries. The fact that the interview took place was, in itself, an indication of the more ecumenical climate beginning to prevail.

Archbishop Simms was asked whether he felt that Protestants were being fairly treated as a religious minority. He answered, 'Yes, I do think so ... we have a feeling, that there is fair play for us'.[22] On the question of mixed marriages, he answered somewhat tentatively:

> Many of our people are concerned about the marriage regulations.... We would like to see if there was any way in which something positive could be said, not just to bring a relaxation, but perhaps to bring more understanding into this matter.[23]

In the same interview, when he was questioned about the effect on the Protestant population of the fact that there was no provision in Ireland for divorce and that contraceptives were banned, he appeared not to consider it a serious grievance. Asked whether he thought that 'many Protestants in the twenty-six counties would be in favour of divorce and birth-control', he replied, 'I don't think they would.'[24]

However, there was some evidence around this time which suggested that not all Protestants concurred quite so readily with Dr Simms' views. In March 1965, in *The Irish Times,* Michael Viney wrote a series of investigative articles, entitled 'The five per cent', on the Protestant population in the Republic of Ireland. In one of these articles, Viney quoted an officer of the General Synod of the Church of Ireland, Dr Kenneth Milne, as objecting to *Ne Temere,* because it struck 'at the very root of family life'. Milne went on, 'I would almost go so far as to suggest that it is contrary to the spirit, if not the letter, of the basic human rights'.[25] In another of Viney's articles, one of his respondents, a Methodist student, resented the imposition on Protestants of legislation enshrining Catholic beliefs. He remarked: 'It's none of my business if the Catholics forbid their people contraceptives. But I object on principle to restriction on my freedom of choice'.[26] The concerns expressed here reflected the more liberal climate of the 1960s, in the context of which traditional attitudes and laws would increasingly be challenged and changed.

The question of mixed-marriage legislation was brought up at the Second Vatican Council. The Council Fathers were divided on the issue and at a special discussion on matrimony, on 20 November 1964, it was decided by a vote of 1,592 to 427 that the matter would be deferred for the Pope's consideration.[27] Archbishop Conway of Armagh was one of the speakers at the debate on matrimony.[28] He argued that the Church should concentrate on forbidding mixed marriages rather than appearing to favour them in any way.[29] The Pope handed the matter over to a commission of cardinals. Meanwhile, the consensus of opinion emerging from the Council chamber was more liberal than that of Archbishop Conway, and this was reflected in two documents, which were to have significant implications for the Church's legislation on mixed marriages.

The *Decree on Ecumenism* (21 November 1964) and the *Declaration on Religious Freedom* (7 December 1965) were very positive in their attitude towards other Christians, and they brought a new understanding of the rights and responsibilities of all parents in the religious upbringing of their children. Regarding the status of non-Catholics and their churches, the *Decree on Ecumenism* in its deliberations was far removed from the spirit of the *Code of Canon Law* as hitherto applied, in as much as it recognised that other churches could also provide 'access to the community of salvation'.[30] The *Declaration on Religious Freedom* opened up a new perspective based on the dignity of the human person. It stated:

> In all his activity a man is bound to follow his conscience faithfully.... It follows that he is not to be forced to act in a manner contrary to his conscience.... Parents, moreover, have the right to determine, in accordance with their own religious beliefs, the kind of religious education that their children are to receive.[31]

Whereas Catholic legislation hitherto had recognised only the Catholic claims to a say in the religious upbringing of children, this declaration insisted that the rights of all parents must be respected, and their conscience not coerced.

In keeping with the spirit of the *Decree on Ecumenism* and the *Declaration on Religious Freedom*, Catholic marriage legislation was somewhat modified by an instruction entitled *Matrimonii Sacramentum*, issued in March 1966.[32] Whereas formerly each party had given a guarantee that all children born of the marriage would be brought up as Catholics, from then on, the Catholic party was instructed on his/her obligation to have the children so baptised and brought up, and made a promise to that effect. The Protestant party was informed of the obligation incumbent on the Catholic and was invited to promise sincerely not to place any obstacles in the way of its fulfilment. Should the Protestant party feel that it would be impossible to do this, without violation of conscience, the matter was to be referred to Rome. As regards the promises, the principal change in the law was that they no longer needed to be made in writing, if the bishop so permitted. The Apostolic Letter, *Pastorali Munis*, of 30 November 1963, had delegated to the local bishop a lot more authority in the matter of dispensations for mixed marriages, which had formerly resided in Rome.[33]

Most importantly, there was no longer any question of the Catholic party being bound to endeavour to convert the Protestant. The omission in the new instruction of all reference to this obligation constituted the formal recognition and application of the principle recognised by the Second Vatican Council that ecumenism is not concerned with conversion. It represented a major change in the Catholic ethos from what had obtained heretofore.[34] In the past, Irish Catholics had constantly been reminded of their responsibility to convert Protestants both in the Republic and in Northern Ireland, and Catholic Church authorities had impressed on intending emigrants their duty to sow the seeds of conversion in 'pagan England'.

The Irish bishops issued a statement after their meeting in Maynooth on 22 June 1966, making certain provisions, 'regarding the relations between Catholics and our separated Christian brethren'.[35] 'For consideration of friendship', they allowed that Catholics 'may attend baptisms, marriages and funerals of non-Catholics'. In the case of marriage, they were permitted 'to act as best man/bridesmaid'.[36] The bishops stated also that 'public representatives and civic officials may be present at non-Catholic services on official occasions'.[37] Mixed marriages could now 'take place in a Catholic Church, before the altar with the usual rites and blessings', and Mass was now permitted.[38] This put an end to the indignity of so-called 'sacristy weddings'. Responding to the new instruction, on 25 March, the editor of the *Church of Ireland Gazette* emphasised forcibly that it did not remove what other Christians considered to be a major obstacle to the development of contact, conversation and co-operation, in so far as it still insisted on the Catholic education of all the children.[39] Undoubtedly, the High Court ruling by Mr Justice Gavan Duffy in 1951 in the Tilson case, and the bitterness engendered by the Fethard-on-Sea boycott in 1957,[40] had lingered in Protestant folk memory.

The fact that the editor of the *Church of Ireland Gazette* was less than elated at some of the changes can, perhaps, be better understood against the background of an event which happened during Church Unity Octave week in January 1966. To mark the occasion, non-Catholic church leaders were invited to a public lecture organised by Fr Roland Burke Savage SJ, editor of *Studies* and Director of the Centre for Religious Studies and Information of which Archbishop McQuaid was founder and patron. The meeting was intended as the highlight of the week. The venue was the Mansion House, Dublin, on 18 January 1966. The historic nature of the occasion captured the public mind as witnessed by the numbers attending, and the media coverage it received. The lecture was delivered by the Belfast theologian, Monsignor Arthur Ryan, and the substance of his address was the subject of an hour-long television broadcast transmitted on Telifís Éireann. It was the first time that McQuaid and Simms had attended together at such an event, and photographs of the two archbishops shaking hands were displayed prominently in the newspapers the following day.

Reporting on the meeting in the February issue of the *Furrow,* Alice Curtayne captured something of the excitement, enthusiasm and sense of expectation generated by the event. She related that 'the Gardaí had to assemble in some strength to regulate the phenomenal crowds seeking admission', and that 'many hundreds had to be turned away', because the Round Room could not contain the numbers who tried to gain admission — such were the confident expectations that 'a great gesture was about to be made, all the more impressive in a country whose history has polarised men's minds against the unity of Christians'.[41] 'Yet', she continued, 'the unanimous reaction was a sense of disappointment'.[42] A closer look at the events of the evening helps to explain why.

Monsignor Ryan in his address paid tribute to the Republic of Ireland's 'record of tolerance' since independence, pointing out that successive heads of Christian churches and non-Christian religions in the Republic had spoken of the 'scrupulous justice manifested towards all sections of the population'.[43] He spoke of the great progress made by the Vatican Council and of the desire that 'was manifest on all sides' to 'forget the bitterness of the past'. He highlighted the importance of a change of heart, while at the same time going on to say that the Council 'could not make revolutionary changes in essentials' — that it had to 'protect what had been handed down by Christ and the Apostles'.[44] How such matters were to be reconciled, he added, was not for him to say; rather was it 'the responsibility of the local episcopal authority'.[45] The tone of the speech could best be described as 'safe' — it could not be termed inspirational. Many of those present had expected a more ecumenical sort of lecture addressed to the other Christians who attended, rather than one directed chiefly at Christians of the Catholic persuasion. But it was not just the speaker's words which fell short of expectations.

At the lecture, Archbishop Simms sat in the front row. Archbishop McQuaid, the Papal Nuncio, Fr Burke Savage and Monsignor Arthur Ryan, the lecturer, sat on the platform beside an empty chair, which the press interpreted as meaning that the Protestant archbishop was excluded from the platform. Thus Curtayne reported in the *Furrow*:

> When the meeting in question opened, it was obvious that there had been no change of mood, or attitude, to indicate a change of heart. Visually the ecclesiastical set-up followed the long familiar pattern.[46]

Curtayne lamented that 'about the whole proceedings, there was not a hint of dialogue, or open communication'. She added, that 'only the minimum courtesy was extended to the leaders of other Christian groups, who remained not merely unheard, but unseen too by the majority of the audience'.[47] The same sentiments were echoed by John Horgan, writing in *The Irish Times* the following day. He observed that the evening was 'marred' by the 'ambiguous and confused way in which the Archbishop of Dublin, Dr Simms, was referred to in the course of the evening' and reported 'that there were many who felt that the ecumenical aspect of the meeting would have been better emphasised if he had been on the platform'.[48]

A photograph of the offending platform appeared in *The Irish Times* the following day.[49] There was much criticism over the next few days of the way that the event had been handled; the many critical letters to *The Irish Times* prompted the leader writer on the following Saturday to caution that, 'it would be a great pity if the good of last Tuesday's meeting were dissipated in continuing outbursts of dismay on the one hand and even withdrawal on the other'.[50] There was criticism too in the *Church of Ireland Gazette*: 'We can only hope that ecumenism in Dublin and further afield in Ireland has not suffered too severe a set-back'.[51] The editorial in *The Irish Times* perhaps best summed up the situation when it suggested that expectations had been too high and that the laity were perhaps ahead of the clergy in embracing the ecumenical spirit of the Council, concluding soberly that:

> One can, however, regret that an opportunity for a gesture of warmth and grace beyond the call of obvious ecclesiastical duty was missed.[52]

Nevertheless, the Catholic Church's official ecumenical policy direction was, by this time, well established, and had been given concrete expression in documentation and structures; while individuals might cause embarrassment and temporarily frustrate the working out of its overall vision, this could only cause a temporary setback in the context of long-term policy. The *Decree on Ecumenism* paved the way in due course for the promulgation by the Vatican of the *Directory on Ecumenism* in 1967.[53] This directory provided the guidelines for Catholic relations with other Christians. On the basis of these guidelines, Episcopal Conferences in each country were to draw up directories which would govern the details of ecumenical dialogue and legislation in their local jurisdictions. In 1969, the *Irish National Directory on Ecumenism* was published.[54]

The importance of Catholic education, at all levels from primary to secondary schooling to third level, was a dearly held principle as far as the bishops were concerned. Attitudes appeared, if anything, to be hardening at the time of the Maynooth Synod in 1956.[55] Little in the way of the more positive attitude towards Christian unity being promoted by the Second Vatican Council was evident in McQuaid's Lenten regulations. Far from promoting the ecumenical climate, he sought to ensure that people would not become lax or careless in their attitudes. In 1964, he inserted a new clause into his customary regulations, making it quite clear that:

> Nothing in the attitude or prescriptions of the Holy See concerning the very desirable movement of Christian Unity has altered the very grave obligations of Catholic parents to preserve for their children in every phase of education, our most precious heritage of the Faith.[56]

However, a significant development relating to Trinity College took place in the late 1960s. In April 1967, Mr Donogh O'Malley, the then Minister for Education, announced a plan for merging Trinity College and UCD, primarily for reasons of cost-effectiveness and as part of the radical overall restructuring of education taking place from the early 1960s.[57] He was not unaware either of the proposed merger's other implications. Announcing the plan, he observed that it would end 'a most insidious form of partition on our own doorstep'.[58]

Going on past performance, the Irish hierarchy might have been expected to reject this proposal out of hand. When a similar suggestion had been made in 1958 by Professor J.J. O'Meara of UCD,[59] it had been roundly condemned by Cardinal D'Alton, on the basis that it would be a union of incompatibles.[60] Just weeks prior to O'Malley's announcement, both McQuaid[61] and Philbin,[62] on separate occasions, had reiterated the traditional position. But such was not to be the case on this occasion.

Cardinal Conway gave the first public reaction, saying that 'the plan contained a number of good ideas', and that 'it could mark a positive step towards a rationalisation of the situation in all its aspects'.[63] The first communiqué issued by the combined hierarchy after the announcement was non-committal, but expressed no objection in principle to the merger. Welcoming 'the efforts being made towards a satisfactory solution of this question', the bishops' statement went on to stipulate that 'any sound system of university education in Ireland must be one which respected the fundamental religious and moral principles of our people'.[64]

By June 1970, the bishops' attitude to Trinity had undergone a significant change. At the conclusion of their June 1970 meeting in Maynooth, they issued a statement to the effect that they had 'decided to seek approval from the Holy See for the repeal of Statute 287 of the Plenary Synod, by which synodal decree for 'over one hundred years the Irish Hierarchy has felt obliged to restrict ... the entry of Catholics into Trinity College, Dublin'.[65] The bishops went on to state:

> Some hope of a change that would make this institution acceptable to the Catholic conscience was provided by the announcement of a proposed merger — as it was called — of Trinity College and U.C.D. This announcement enabled the bishops to reconsider the attitude that might be adopted towards a new Trinity College.[66]

That the Vatican Council had provided the impetus for a review of the synodal decree was acknowledged by the statement, and, at the press conference the following day, announcing the decision, Cardinal Conway explained that it was 'the conclusion of a process of re-thinking which had been going on among the bishops since 1965'.[67] It must also be noted, however, that in the more liberal climate of the late 1960s, the ban was increasingly being ignored, so the hierarchy were also reacting to a situation in which their followers were far more liable to question ecclesiastical prescripts and also the right of ecclesiastical figures to impose sanctions for non-conformity to such prescripts.

Further concessions with regard to mixed marriages were given in the *Motu Proprio, Matrimonia Mixta* of 31 March 1970, which was to take effect from 1 October of that year.[68] By virtue of this legislation, no promise whether written or verbal was to be asked of the Protestant partner. Catholics partners were simply asked to recognise and acknowledge that, as Catholics, they had a grave obligation from God to do all in their power to have all their children baptised and brought up as Catholics. A promise in relation to this was required only of the Catholic party. Whether it was to be made in writing, or before witnesses, or by word of mouth alone, was not determined by the

Apostolic Letter. The non-Catholic partner was simply to be informed of the promise made by the Catholic.[69] In a statement issued from their October meeting in Maynooth 1970, the Irish bishops explained that the new regulations reflected the thinking of the Synod of Bishops in 1967 and that, in relation to the Catholic upbringing of the children, it 'was a principle of divine law' which 'neither pope nor bishops can change'.[70]

At the very end of the decade, a most important ecumenical initiative took place. This was the formal inauguration of the Irish School of Ecumenics, on 9 November 1970, by the general secretary of the World Council of Churches, Rev. Eugene Carson Blake. Three Catholic bishops, members of the Episcopal Commission on Ecumenism, were present. Michael Hurley SJ became the school's first director. He has said that 'the Catholic archbishop of Dublin in 1970 was not at all known for his ecumenism, *au contraire*', and has referred to the importance of 'the Jesuit connection and in particular the personal gifts of Cecil McGarry', the then provincial, in securing McQuaid's 'acquiescence', without which 'it would have been impossible to go ahead'.[71] The Irish School of Ecumenics invited applications for courses for the following academic year 1970–71. Courses on ecumenical theology in the school were to be conducted by a team of teachers of the main Christian traditions.[72]

The eruption of the 'Troubles' in Northern Ireland had lent a new urgency to ecumenical initiatives from the late 1960s. On New Year's Day in 1969, the People's Democracy, a left-wing nationalist group which sought civil rights for Catholics in Northern Ireland, began a march from Belfast to Derry. The last day of that eventful journey was marked by a bloody encounter between the marchers and a Protestant loyalist group at Burntollet Bridge, about five miles from Derry. This event led to the establishment of a semi-official ad-hoc committee comprising members of the Irish Council of Churches (ICC) and Catholic clergy. The ICC, an all-Ireland body, represented the main Protestant Churches. It was founded originally in January 1923 as the United Council of Christian Churches and Religious Communions in Ireland.[73]

In all, there were six clerics on this committee: Fr Patrick Walsh, then chaplain at Queen's University; Fr Denis Faul of Dungannon, nominated by Cardinal Conway; and the Reverends Harold Allen, Canon Eric Elliott, Eric Gallagher and John Radcliffe, representing the Irish Council of Churches.[74] The committee's brief was to study the developing situation in Northern Ireland and its underlying causes. This initiative led directly to the setting up of a 'Joint Group' in 1970, and this was, in fact, the first joint action taken officially by the member Churches of the ICC and the Irish Catholic Church. This led to a considerable transformation in the following decade in the ecclesiastical scene. The range and scope of ecumenical activity increased in terms of inter-church meetings, joint statements and structures being put in place to facilitate dialogue.

In the summer of 1972, Cardinal Conway issued an invitation to the member Churches of the ICC to take part in a conference at which the whole field of ecumenism in Ireland was to be surveyed.[75] The result was what the daily papers referred to at the time as 'summit conferences', held annually from that time, at Ballymascanlon Hotel near Dundalk. The first historic meeting was held on 26 September 1973, against a background of intense media interest and a protest by the Ulster Free Presbyterians, led by Dr Ian Paisley. The eighty-three delegates, lay and clerical, met under the co-chairmanship of Cardinal Conway and Archbishop Simms, in his capacity as chairman of the ICC. The conference set up a number of working parties to report on pertinent issues. These reports were discussed in further sessions in 1974 and 1975. The reports coming from the group dealing with mixed marriages drew particular attention, understandably given the Irish Protestant Churches' long-standing sense of grievance over mixed marriages.

However, as the 1970s progressed, the Catholic bishops' reluctance to be drawn into debate on certain issues, particularly those having to do with aspects of family planning and mixed marriages, served to temper the initial enthusiasm associated with the meetings and, as time went by, contributed to a mood of growing disenchantment with Ballymascanlon. The Catholic bishops issued a new *Directory on Ecumenism in Ireland* in 1976, which superseded the *Directory* of 1969. It was a lengthy document of seventy-six paragraphs with an appendix concerning the 1975 Ballymascanlon meeting.

In this document, the bishops emphasised God's will that 'all Christians should come together in one flock'.[76] They went on to stress the unique nature of the Catholic Church, while recognising the fact that other Christian Churches are endowed with many elements of sanctification and truth. Paragraph eleven revealed the bishops' fears in relation to controversial issues, and also made clear the conditions on which Catholics could participate in ecumenical dialogue:

> It would not be a correct understanding of the principles of ecumenism if Catholics, with the aim of drawing closer to other Christians, were to neglect any part of the true and integral tradition of Catholic life and worship.... Neither should they let themselves be persuaded to underestimate the beneficial effects on social and community life of the Catholic witness to certain fundamental human and Christian values e.g. the sacredness of unborn life, the indissolubility of marriage, the essential unity of the interpersonal and procreative ends of married love.[77]

In relation to the area of mixed marriages, the document had little of substance to add to *Matrimonia Mixta.* In part six of the directory, on the pastoral care of mixed marriages, the bishops simply elaborated and clarified their position. The Catholic parties to a marriage were again required to do all in their power to ensure that the children born of the marriage be baptised and brought up in the Catholic Church. The declaration was to be explained to the other party to the marriage by the priest, or by the Catholic party. The point was further made that where 'one party cannot in conscience respect the conscientious obligations of the other party, efforts should be made to convince the parties that the proposed marriage should not take place'. [78] The bishops pointed out that they saw 'no easy way in which to resolve the basic problems of mixed marriages' and that much depended 'upon the spirit and the degree of sensitivity in which traditions and directives [were] interpreted and applied'. [79] These statements captured the ecumenical dilemma from the Catholic point of view, in that they made quite clear that certain key issues were non-negotiable, and lent some credence to a remark made by Barry Deane, a well-known Church of Ireland layman, at the spring meeting of the ICC in 1976, when he spoke of 'soft words at Ballymascanlon and hard lines at the grass roots'. [80]

The Catholic Church's revised ecclesiology at the time of the Second Vatican Council, whereby the Church of Christ was said to 'subsist in', but was not exclusively identified with the Roman Catholic Church, opened the door for modification of the mixed-marriage legislation and a more nuanced approach. But this did not change the Catholic Church position, that it still had an obligation towards its members, based on its understanding of its own central role in the plan of salvation. [81] That said, while in essence the Catholic position may not have appeared to change as much as other Churches may have wished in relation to mixed marriages, as Brian O'Higgins wrote in the *ITQ* in 1974, a lot depended on the way the law was interpreted by the Roman Curia and the Catholic bishops. [82] A World Council of Churches' paper in 1975 observed that 'there is an increase in denominationally mixed marriages and these no longer inflame controversy'. [83]

The death of Cardinal Conway on 17 April 1977 created a vacuum in inter-church relations, and the next Ballymascanlon meeting did not take place until 6 March 1980. In November 1979, when he was handing over the directorship of the School of Ecumenics to his Presbyterian successor, Dr Robin Boyd, Hurley captured the uneven nature of ecumenical progress in Ireland. He was forced 'to admit that the country has not yet made the kind of ecumenical progress one would have liked to have seen', while, on the other hand, the school, he pointed out, had 'made quite remarkable progress in building itself up for the task of ecumenical education'. [84]

While progress which depended on changes in Church law and official attitudes may have been slow, by the late 1970s a different kind of progress was well under way at grass-roots level. The generation which came of age in the context of the mood of the 1960s was very concerned about issues of human rights, freedom of conscience and the right to make free and unhindered choices. Attitudes and laws hitherto unquestioned came under increasingly closer scrutiny from the late 1960s. This is evidenced by contrasting the attitudes pointed up by Michael Viney in 1965 with those of Archbishop Simms, interviewed in the *Word* magazine in 1964.

Whereas Archbishops Simms' restraint and acceptance of the status quo reflected the pre-conciliar era, concerns in relation to freedom of choice and human rights, recorded by Viney, heralded and epitomised a new more questioning era. They offered a foretaste of what were to become central questions in an ongoing debate among Catholics, as well as Protestants — revolving around the question of whether Catholic precepts should be enshrined in civil law, and what should constitute a proper relationship between Church and state in Ireland — a debate which has been ongoing. The central focus of this debate tended to crystallise around issues having to do with the right, or otherwise, to contraception, divorce and, more recently, abortion. In the context of events happening in Northern Ireland and outside Ireland, and an evolving more critical cultural climate at home, politicians were forced more and more to grapple with these issues.

14

Constitutional Review and Legislative Change

On 14 January 1965, a historic meeting took place between Taoiseach Seán Lemass and Prime Minister Terence O'Neill of Northern Ireland, giving rise temporarily to a new mood of co-operation and friendliness between Northern Ireland and the Republic, and even to an expectation in some quarters that the end of partition might be at hand. On foot of this meeting, Lemass, in 1966, established an all-party committee of the Dáil to review the constitution.[1] The committee's report, published in December 1967, and a number of its recommendations were to have profound implications for Irish Catholic culture.

Examining the sub-section of Article 41, which provided that 'no law shall be enacted providing for the grant of a dissolution of marriage',[2] it was critical of the fact that this,

> takes no heed of the wishes of a certain minority of the population who would wish to have divorce facilities and who are not prevented from securing divorce by the tenets of the religious denominations to which they belong.[3]

It went on to state that the prohibition was 'a source of embarrassment to those seeking to bring about better relations between North and South', since divorce existed in Northern Ireland and, most significantly, it reinforced the point by referring to 'the more liberal attitude now prevailing in Catholic circles in regard to the rites and practices of other religious denominations, particularly since the Second Vatican Council'.[4]

Regarding the clauses of Article 44, which acknowledge 'the special position of the Holy Catholic Apostolic and Roman Church', recognising certain other religious denominations by name, the report stated that 'these provisions give offence to non-Catholics and are also a useful weapon in the hands of those who are anxious to emphasise the differences between North and South.' Again, it invoked the provisions of the documents of the Second Vatican Council, referring specifically to the *Declaration on Religious Freedom,* 1965, and to the *Pastoral Constitution on the Church in the Modern World,* 1965, which showed that the Catholic Church 'does not seek any special recognition or privilege as compared with other religions', and went on to recommend that these provisions be deleted, observing that this would 'help to promote ecumenism'.[5]

The bishops' reaction to these two recommendations was instructive. There was no public reaction to the recommendation in relation to Article 44. When Jack Lynch (who had succeeded Lemass as Taoiseach in November 1966), in the course of a radio interview on the programme, *This Week,* in September 1969, suggested that it might be amended,[6] Cardinal Conway reacted by saying that he 'personally would not shed a tear if the relevant sub-sections of Article 44 were to disappear',[7] adding that it conferred 'no legal privilege whatever on the Catholic Church'.[8] A short time later, after the bishops' autumn meeting, it was stated officially that the proposed removal of Article 44 had been discussed and that 'they had agreed that a recent statement made by Cardinal Conway represented the bishops' views'.[9]

Accordingly, the Lynch government decided to propose the deletion of the two sub-sections of Article 44, referring to the 'special position' of the Catholic Church and the recognition of other denominations. It was to be decided by referendum on 7 December 1972. The campaign for the removal of the 'special position' clause was carried on against the background of sectarian violence in Northern Ireland, which had been steadily worsening since 1969, and it was presented to the electorate as the first step in the Republic's alignment with Northern Ireland, and as evidence of its good will towards, and willingness to accommodate the views of, Protestants. The amendment was carried by 84.4 per cent of those who voted, in a poll which involved only 50.7 per cent of the total electorate.

It is interesting to juxtapose the response of the hierarchy (only Bishop Lucey campaigned against the amendment) and the apathetic attitude of the electorate, as witnessed by the low poll, with de Valera's justification of the article in the Dáil in 1937. Nevertheless, the importance of the deletion of Article 44 at a symbolic level cannot be underestimated in the Irish cultural context. In contrast to the non-reaction to the proposal to delete Article 44, however, the recommendation of the 1967 report vis-à-vis divorce met with a prompt and sharp rejoinder from Cardinal Conway, who remarked that 'in most countries official commissions normally consult interested bodies before drawing up their reports', while in this case there had 'not been the slightest consultation of the Catholic hierarchy'.[10] While acknowledging the importance of respecting 'the tenets of ... fellow Christians', he was doubtful as to the extent of their demand for divorce facilities, and added that whatever inconvenience it caused had to be weighed up against the damage that would, as he saw it, 'almost inevitably' ensue from 'such a radical and far-reaching break with our national traditions'.[11]

Adverting to the proposal in his Lenten Regulations for 1968, Archbishop McQuaid of Dublin argued that, 'civil divorce, as a measure which purports to dissolve a valid marriage, is contrary to the law of God', and that in societies where it had been introduced it had invariably resulted 'in a series of greater sufferings and deeper evils'.[12] Bishop Lucey of Cork was less moderate in his tone which hearkened back to the 1950s. Referring to 'a proposal recently that we should have facilities for divorce in this country', he remarked:

> It is a proposal that I trust we have heard the last of. Where there are such facilities the wayward and the wanton are the chief beneficiaries; and always at the expense of the children of the marriage.[13]

Bishop Hanly of Elphin devoted his entire Lenten pastoral to the divorce proposal and Catholic teaching on marriage, commenting that, 'the State has no authority to dissolve any marriage, even the marriage of pagans'. He went on to observe that 'it is the solemn duty of every Catholic voter to register his vote against the provision of divorce facilities by the Oireachtas'.[14] Such very specific advice to their flock on how they should act or vote, very typical of bishops in the past, was to become less acceptable from now on. Neither were politicians as disposed to consult with the bishops, or take account of their reservations, as they had been in the past.

Two features of modern-day life which had impinged forcibly on the consciousness of the bishops during the Council were the development of the anovulant pill in 1960 and the increasing incidence of marital breakdown. While such matters were not of great concern in Ireland at that time, by the late 1960s they had become more centre stage. From that time, the issues of contraception and divorce forced themselves more and more onto the political agenda. Of the two issues, it was the former that was to dominate the 1970s, inevitably precipitating Church–state confrontation. The two pieces of legislation governing contraceptives in Ireland were the 1929 Censorship of Publications Act, prohibiting the publication, distribution and selling of literature advocating birth control, and the 1935 Criminal Law (Amendment) Act, section 17, which prohibited the importation, manufacture and sale of contraceptives. In the reformist post-Vatican II climate, there was widespread hope not only in Ireland, but throughout the Catholic world, that the Catholic attitude condemning birth control would change.

Traditional Catholic teaching on the matter was set out in Code 1013 of *The Code of Canon Law*, 1917, as follows:

> The primary end of marriage is the procreation and education of children: the secondary end is mutual help and a remedy for concupiscence.[15]

In his encyclical on Christian Marriage, *Casti Connubii,* 31 December 1930, Pope Pius XI stated:

> Since ... the conjugal act is destined primarily by nature for the begetting of children, those who in exercising it deliberately frustrate its natural power and purpose sin against nature and commit a deed which is shameful and intrinsically vicious.[16]

This reasoning is based on the concept of natural law, and it argues that certain practices — contraception being one such — contradict the laws of man's nature. On the basis of natural law morality, St Thomas Aquinas taught that 'right reason' enables us to discern what natural law commands.[17] In the Scholastic frame of reference, based on the unchanging essence of things, the birth-control directive was seen as immutable.

However, by the 1960s, unprecedented scientific and technological advances and findings in the fields of psychology, philosophy and sociology variously combined to alter human life almost beyond recognition, and to yield up new insights into the essence of man's changing nature. Against this background, some significant developments in the theology of marriage had taken place over a number of decades, from an emphasis on procreation to an emphasis on relationship. The new approach won approval at the Vatican Council when, in December 1965, in the *Pastoral Constitution on the Church in the Modern World,* mention of the comparative ends of marriage was omitted, and marriage was described as the

> intimate partnership of married life and love.... Hence, by that human act whereby spouses mutually bestow and accept each other, a relationship arises which by divine will and in the eyes of society too is a lasting one.[18]

Paragraph 51 of *The Church in the Modern World* was in sharp contrast to the legalistic tone of Church teaching on marriage that had obtained up to then, realising that married people

> can find themselves in circumstances where at least temporarily the size of their families should not be increased. As a result, the faithful exercise of love and the full intimacy of their lives are hard to maintain.[19]

The publication of a book by Michael Novak, *The Experience of Marriage,* in 1964, marked a breakthrough in the understanding of Catholic marriage.[20] The book presented the experience of thirteen American Catholic couples who asserted that preoccupation with rights and duties, self-control and the purposes of marriage were far removed from the daily realities of partners who wished to build up a shared companionship of life and love. Sexuality they saw as having the occasional function of procreation and a constant function of communicating and deepening their relationship. What made the book particularly noteworthy was the fact that it presented for the first time the opinions and experience of a group of Catholic wives on marital sexuality. The dawn of an age when the laity could formally advance their views was confirmed when Pope John XXIII established a Papal Commission to advise on birth, family and population. The commission was later expanded by Pope Paul VI. Of the members, the majority were lay and included economists, demographers, doctors and married couples. Five women were included in the commission.

Regarding the dignity of conscience, *The Church in the Modern World* had stated that 'conscience is the most secret core and sanctuary of a man. There he is alone with God whose voice echoes in his depths',[21] going on to say that,

> man's dignity demands that he act according to a knowing and free choice. Such a voice is personally motivated and prompted from within. It does not result from blind internal impulse nor from mere external pressure.[22]

In the freer, more open atmosphere, tinged with not a little expectancy, there were indications that some people were becoming more confident and self-reliant in their moral decision-making, and that they were prepared to lay aside the dictates of the Church, if they seemed not in harmony with the dictates of their own conscience. The worldwide debate among Catholics on the ethics of contraception had spilled over into Ireland, and both sides of the case were being argued in the media in general. In October 1966, a programme entitled *Too Many Children* was presented by Michael Viney on RTÉ television, in which, according to a contemporary writer, Donald Connery, 'a new height in candour was reached'.[23] Viney presented tape-recorded interviews in which Dublin mothers discussed openly and frankly their problems and attitudes towards family planning. Connery's impressions capture the spirit of the times in Ireland. Watching it, he felt that he,

> was witnessing a historic breakthrough in Irish life, for if *this* could be said on such a family medium as T.V., then anything could be said from now on in Ireland.[24]

Closing the programme, Viney expressed the mood of the moment, when he referred to the expectation that 'any day now a pronouncement from the Pope may well take this whole issue a big step further'.[25]

The fact that birth-control was seen as an open question was underlined not only by the many discursive books published, but also by the protracted debate on the subject, which took place in the *Furrow,* involving many shades of opinion from theologians to priests involved in pastoral ministry, to lay men and women. Fr Denis Hickey of the Servite Order, Benburb, Co. Tyrone, opened the debate by writing an informative, discursive article on 'The 1966 Theological Problem' in the *Furrow* of February 1967,[26] explaining the natural-law stance on birth-control, and exploring the possibilities that this might, or might not, change. In an article entitled 'Natural Law Ethics: Has it a Future?' in April 1968, Fr Patrick McGrath, professor of Philosophy at St Patrick's College, Carlow, pointed out that natural-law theory, while not strictly legalistic, left itself open to the charge of legalism and thus to the possibility that persons might be 'subordinated to principles'.[27] In an article the following month, entitled 'An Approach to Morality', Fr Enda McDonagh, professor of Moral Theology at Maynooth, wrote of the importance of seeing morality in terms of relationships, and actions being moral depending on whether they facilitated or retarded the growth of individuals or societies.[28]

Against the background of intense theological reflection and popular debate, there were substantial grounds for hope of some change in Church teaching. The absolute authority of the Church was, at this time, no longer taken for granted without question. The universal Church in Council had shed its authoritarian image and, to a great extent, its mystique. It had allowed itself to become vulnerable — invited questioning and even criticism — and had challenged Catholics to think for themselves. It had admitted to not having all the answers to the deep questions of life. Prominent theologians and experts had argued over the most important matters of doctrine which ordinary Catholics had considered to be closed questions.

The questioning of Church authority has to be seen against the backdrop of a worldwide phenomenon characterised by many people's desire to break free of the shackles of authority. The gloom of the post-war era was past. Man was about to reach the moon. Economic affluence, educational opportunities, the communications revolution and increased mobility made his horizons seem limitless. It was the era of individualism, 'flower-power', 'free love' and 'hanging loose'. When some felt that their style was cramped, they experimented with drugs so that they might be enabled to push out further the frontiers of experience. Alvin Toffler has termed it the 'now generation'.[29] He quoted a teenager's comments to a reporter after the mammoth Woodstock rock music festival in 1969 — the landmark which, more than any other, captured the spirit and conjured up the good and bad of an era. She explained: 'We're more oriented to the present.... It's like do what you want to do now'.[30] It was against the background of this kind of world, that the Papal Commission was making its decision in relation to the birth-control issue. It was a world where concepts of 'continence', 'abstinence' and deferred gratification had for many people become decidedly *passé*.

On 17 July 1968, Pope Paul VI promulgated *Humanae Vitae*, his long-awaited pronouncement on 'the regulation of births', reaffirming the Church's traditional teaching on birth-control.[31] The encyclical produced a storm of debate and controversy throughout the Catholic world. Some bishops, priests and laity interpreted it as a signal that the Pope was applying the brakes after the welter of change that had been taking place in the five years since the end of the Second Vatican Council. It was seen by many as a return to the old comfortable certainty and security of an era when what was right and wrong was very rigidly laid down.

Others saw it as signifying the end of the post-conciliar era — and the Church's acceptance of such things as liberty of conscience and the optimistic outlook on life and human nature promoted by Pope John XXIII. In Ireland, the controversy was far less intense than in countries like the United States and the Netherlands, but it happened nonetheless. The encyclical represented a crisis of authority for the Church, which effectively split the Catholic world in two. While theologians had disagreed about many issues in the post-conciliar era, this was different. It went to the very core of people's lives. *Humanae Vitae* was a watershed. Things would never be quite the same after it.

In Dublin, the encyclical was introduced to a crowded press conference in Clonliffe College on 29 July 1968, by Professor P.F. Cremin, professor of Moral Theology and Canon Law at Maynooth, with Archbishop McQuaid also in attendance. Professor Cremin commended Pope Paul VI's reassertion of the traditional Catholic teaching, saying, 'I personally have never received a better piece of news'.[32] The division that the encyclical brought about in Irish Catholic thinking can hardly be captured more aptly than by juxtaposing this view of the encyclical with that of Fr James Good, a UCC-based moral theologian. He described it as 'a major tragedy', and went on to say, 'I have no doubt that the document will be rejected by the majority of Catholic theologians and by Catholic lay people'.[33] Some credence could be ascribed to the view that some lay Catholics had already rejected this teaching, on the basis of a remark made at the time by a Dublin gynaecologist, Karl Mullen, that, in his experience, 40 per cent of married couples were practising methods of contraception other than the rhythm method.[34] Fr Good was duly banned by Bishop Lucey from preaching, and, some time later, from teaching theology at University College Cork.

That a change in the nature of Church thinking was expected was expressed in 1968, by Fr Denis O'Callaghan, professor of Moral Theology at Maynooth and chairman of the Irish Theological Association, as follows:

> The discovery of new methods of birth control, the force of theological argumentation, the appointment of a papal commission, the very delay in the appearance of the long-promised judgement underlined not just the possibility but the likelihood of change.[35]

The problems surrounding the reception of the encyclical were undoubtedly compounded by the Pope's delay in making the pronouncement (giving rise to hopes of change), and by the fact that when he did make it, it was a well-known fact that he went against the majority opinion of his commission. The fact that the Pope was not speaking *ex cathedra*, and that, therefore, his pronouncement had not the status of infallibly proclaimed doctrine — thus leaving the way open for possible change in the future — did nothing to allay confusion either.

The bishops issued a statement after their meeting of 9 October 1968, in which they reiterated their confidence 'that our people will accept' the Pope's teaching and 'give it that whole-hearted assent which the Second Vatican Council requires'. They reminded people that 'the pope speaks not as one theologian among many, but as the Vicar of Christ who has the special assistance of the Holy Spirit in teaching the universal Church'.[36] Much of the debate in relation to the encyclical had centred around the role of conscience. Taking this matter up, they reminded people of 'the actual words of the Second Vatican Council', quoting from the document, *Gaudium et spes*:

> Husband and wife, in their mutual relations, may not act arbitrarily but have always to be governed by a conscience which must be conformed to the divine law, submissive to the teaching authority of the Church which authentically interprets that law in the light of the Gospel.[37]

Yet there was a sense in which the tone of the bishops' statement was more humane than statements of less than ten years previously:

> We ask our people to believe that we are deeply and painfully aware of the delicate personal problems and intellectual difficulties to which this teaching may give rise for some.[38]

They went on to express their confidence that 'priests especially in the confessional will show that understanding and sympathy which Our Divine Lord himself always displayed'.[39]

The following February, the Irish bishops issued a joint Lenten pastoral in which they defended 'the indissolubility of Christian marriage'.[40] In relation to the encyclical, *Humanae Vitae*, the bishops explained that Pope Paul had felt obliged 'to reaffirm the Church's traditional condemnation of contraception'.[41] While Paul VI had certainly done this, the fact was, that the traditional position, with its bias towards procreation, had been significantly modified since the Vatican Council. The procreative and unitive purposes of marriage were no longer classified in the Council documents and in the encyclical as the primary and secondary ends of marriage. The recognition of sexuality as unitive had, in fact, been accepted in the Church's official teaching. Paul VI had not developed the natural-law argument. Playing down the biological argument, he couched it as follows: that 'each and every marriage act must remain open to the transmission of life'.[42] Such nuances were not allowed for, however, in the Irish bishops' pastoral. Their references and quotations reflected traditional teaching, and appeared not to have evolved greatly, despite new theological thinking on marriage. They pointed to the Council's reiteration of the constant teaching of the Church, 'that by their very nature the institution of matrimony itself and conjugal love are ordained for the procreation of children and find in them their ultimate crown'.[43]

The impact of *Humanae Vitae* varied from country to country, and in some countries it occasioned more acrimony than in others, and thus the pastoral approaches demanded of hierarchies varied accordingly. The Irish bishops' approach was informative, reinforcing Church teaching. Some hierarchies went a stage further, however, recognising that people might experience a conflict of conscience. One of the most notable examples was the explicit statement of the French hierarchy a few months after *Humanae Vitae* was promulgated. In very plain language, the bishops stated:

> Contraception can never be good. It is always a disorder, but this disorder is not always culpable. It can come to pass in effect that the partners find themselves faced with a real conflict of obligations. When one is placed before a choice of duties so that whatever one decides one cannot avoid evil, traditional wisdom sees its way to determine before God which duty should prevail in the given emergency. The partners will come to a decision after reflecting together with all the concern which the nobility of their married vocation imposes on them.[44]

A key insight of the 'new' theology was that the moral norm does not stand apart in frozen isolation from the concrete life situation of the person. In effect, what the French bishops were doing was giving a pastoral interpretation of *Humanae Vitae* — they were presenting the objective criteria, which should guide the Christian conscience in the context of their own community. Unlike the Irish bishops, they did not see themselves merely as a vehicle for the transmission of rules. Undoubtedly, part of the reason for this was that French society was far more secularised and thus more liable to question and reject the teaching of the Church than was Irish society at that time. This was understandable in view of the French philosophical tradition with its emphasis on liberty and equality, tracing its roots back to the revolution and the enlightenment, which led in due course to the separation of Church and state, and indeed spawned the 'new theology'.

According to the French bishops, people had to take responsibility for their own moral decisions in the light of objective moral norms. The possibility that people might not live up to the demands of the Church's teaching was referred to only obliquely by the Irish bishops, and was seen as a failure, which they assured people would receive a sympathetic hearing from priests in their pastoral capacity. This smacked of the paternalism of years past, albeit modified in tone. The bishops did not confront the practical and intellectual considerations of Irish Catholics at that time. Their 1969 pastoral was an opportunity to do this, but, written as it was in the style of an apologia, it was inadequate in terms of the needs and questions of a more sophisticated laity. They did not tease out or attempt to explain the possible reasons why Pope Paul VI did not revoke Church teaching on artificial contraception. A possible reason may have been his belief that (the) law in itself has a symbolic value, despite the fact that many people or even a majority of people might choose to break it.

A feature of the changing cultural landscape of Ireland, however, was that while the bishops might not be prepared to debate openly the issues involved, many prominent theologians and priests in the course of their pastoral work were prepared to do so, and because there was disagreement and diversity of opinion on issues, among respected theologians at home and abroad, Catholics no longer relied totally on the bishops' leadership. They also looked elsewhere for moral guidance which was more in keeping with their own intellectual convictions.

A theologian who confronted the issues head-on in an honest and balanced manner was Fr Denis O'Callaghan. In an article published in the *Clergy Review* in November 1966, and reprinted in the *Catholic World* in March 1967, entitled 'The Birth Control Crisis', O'Callaghan gave an overview of the background to the debate, as well as the current state of theological opinion, both traditional and from the point of view of those who favoured a change in the Church's teaching.[45] As such, it was an open-minded informative article, giving an insight into both sides of the argument. There is evidence to suggest that it may indeed have been too open-minded, based on correspondence that passed between Archbishop McQuaid and Bishop Browne in March of 1968. In a letter sent by Browne to McQuaid on 14 March 1968, he explained that Bishop Lennon of Kildare and Leighlin had written to him in connection with 'an article which was turned down for the *I.E.R.*' and subsequently 'sent to him for [publication] in the *I.T.Q*'.[46] The bishop of the diocese of Kildare and Leighlin provided the imprimatur for the *ITQ*. Browne explained to McQuaid that he had agreed with Lennon's suggestion that it should be sent to the Episcopal Commission on Doctrine, and added his 'own strong opinion that the article — on birth control — was not in conformity with Papal directives'.[47] McQuaid replied to Browne's letter the following day:

> But do you know that it was I who refused to allow the O'Callaghan article to be printed? Then it went to Kildare, who asked me why I had refused. I gave the answer: denies the divine law, disregards Papal ruling and must cause increased confusion among priests and Faithful.[48]

There seems little doubt that the reference was to the same article and that it was precisely its openness that upset McQuaid. It was typical of the paternalistic approach which had predominated in the past, which was to be challenged increasingly from then on. It dictated, rather than giving people the facts, suggesting some moral guidelines and letting them take responsibility for their own moral decisions. It was significant that the *IER* ceased publication in 1968. It was no longer suited to the changing times. The last two documents published in the final July–December issue (which carried

Archbishop McQuaid's imprimatur) were *Humanae Vitae*[49] and the Irish bishops' statement on the encyclical.[50]

In his 1968 article in the *Furrow,* in an attempt to explain the highly charged emotional atmosphere surrounding the debate, O'Callaghan pointed to 'the fact that established catechetical method and confessional practice had trained people to expect simple straightforward answers to problems, particularly moral problems'.[51] He wrote that 'priest, bishop and pope are not oracles' and reminded people that 'classical theology has accepted a large degree of uncertainty as part and parcel of our knowledge of the moral law'.[52] O'Callaghan's article did not soft-pedal papal teaching in any way, but it showed that the Church had, despite what the general perception might be, refined its position since *Casti Connubii,* and he ended his article with suggestions as to why the pope might have taken this position at this time. Essentially, what he implied was that the pope's teaching might well be validated in the course of time. Because his suggestions were posed as questions, they underlined his central point, that this was uncharted territory for both pope and theologians.

Two years later, O'Callaghan addressed the Medical Union on the subject of 'Family Planning — the Doctors' Dilemma'.[53] As a member of a panel that included three gynaecologists and Senator Mary Bourke (later President Mary Robinson), he pointed to the almost universal Catholic theological stance as favouring 'the practice of the infertile period', while at the same time allowing that it did admit 'the rightness of some method of birth-control other than the infertile period in difficult cases where the welfare of the family and of the marriage relationship is at stake'. 'In these situations,' he stated, 'the individual circumstances are crucial and it is not easy to give guidance in general terms'.[54] Once again, McQuaid was less than happy and, on the following day, he directed his secretary, Fr James Ardle MacMahon, to write to O'Callaghan as follows:

> His Grace the Archbishop notes in to-day's press that yesterday in the city of Dublin you are stated to have made a statement on birth prevention, or as the newspapers call it, birth control, as lawful in certain cases.
>
> I am directed by his Grace the Archbishop to request that at your very early convenience you will be good enough to furnish to His Grace an exact and full copy of the text of the statement that you are said to have made in his Diocese.[55]

O'Callaghan replied on 16 November, enclosing a copy of the text of his address, and explaining that 'the greater part of the meeting was given over to discussion in open forum' and thus 'one has little or no control over the way in which the press reports reflect what was actually said'.[56] He requested a meeting with McQuaid to discuss the matter with him, saying that he was 'well aware of its pastoral implications', to which MacMahon replied that His Grace the Archbishop 'bids me say that he would have very much more fully appreciated your offering to discuss the matter before you had left the Archbishop to deal with an acutely grave situation provoked by your speaking in his Diocese'.[57] In his further reply, O'Callaghan, while he acknowledged 'the Archbishop's concern for the pastoral situation occasioned by differing viewpoints on the birth control question', suggested that the Archbishop overstated 'the acutely grave situation' caused by his (O'Callaghan's) contribution to the debate.[58] He continued:

> The confusion in the community conscience caused by varying interpretations of *Humanae Vitae* on the part of Hierarchies in the Catholic world and by the divergent approaches in medical and confessional practice has long been evident. In addition, widespread charges of dishonesty and face-saving have undermined people's confidence in their Church.[59]

He renewed 'his request for a meeting' with McQuaid, but it was obvious from MacMahon's one-line reply a week later that the Archbishop was not interested in an exchange of views on the matter: 'I am directed by His Grace the Archbishop to acknowledge the receipt of your further answer'.[60] The matter was closed as far as he was concerned. The correspondence that passed between McQuaid and O'Callaghan was crucial in terms of the issue concerned, which was central in the lives of Catholics. It also gives an insight into a style of Church which was becoming less and less viable, and while McQuaid was said to have been bitterly disappointed that his resignation (on reaching his seventy-fifth birthday) was accepted by Pope Paul VI, little over a year after this correspondence had taken place, in December 1971,[61] it was not surprising.

Reflecting back on *Humanae Vitae* from the stand-point of the late 1970s, and again writing in the *Furrow*, O'Callaghan suggested that the pope might have retained the traditional formulation 'not by considerations of logic but by the pastoral concern of formulating practical norms'. 'This concern', he continued, sets out to exclude questioning even 'on the far limits of the norm, anticipating that exceptions would become precedents'.[62] He pointed out, however, that even the Roman curia itself was prepared to allow of a more nuanced interpretation of the phrase in paragraph 14 of the encyclical, relating to the 'intrinsic evil' of contraception. To prove this he drew on a letter from the Congregation of the Clergy sent to Cardinal O'Boyle of Washington, which enabled the latter to reinstate priests who had dissented from the encyclical's teaching. This showed that the pope's position was by no means inflexible. The letter, according to O'Callaghan, spelled out simply 'in clear language the traditional distinction between objective wrongness and subjective culpability'. He quoted from it as follows:

> While the counsellor has the obligation to render an objective judgement on the data presented to him, he should not too quickly presume either complete innocence on the one hand or on the other a deliberate rejection

of God's loving commands in the case of a person who is honestly trying to live a good Christian life.[63]

In *Humanae Vitae,* the pope was attempting to enshrine the principle of respect for human life and sexuality in all its aspects, but because he came down in such a definitive way, the Church in a sense backed itself into a corner of its own making. Ultimately, what O'Callaghan's articles were showing over a period of time was that the Pope's position was, in fact, nuanced and did allow for exceptions, but this required careful reading of the 'small print' of the encyclical and, above all, relied heavily on the role of informed conscience — a hard concept for Catholics to grapple with, as it had been understated in the pre-Vatican II era, and the casuistic method had led many Catholics to expect ready-made solutions to moral problems, regardless of their complexity. With the benefit of hindsight, what these articles also showed was that, while there were subtle shifts in the Church's theology, by the late 1960s, the pope hesitated at giving the all-clear to Catholics in the area of contraception, thus, in effect, placing the onus on them to make their own moral decisions either in accordance, or otherwise, with the guidance of the Church.

The 1960s ushered in a different kind of world, where science would provide more possibilities which would allow for more choice, but in a context where the consequences and risks were by no means clear. In an atmosphere where uncertainty prevails, the most that moral leaders can do is to give an informed, considered opinion from their particular perspective. At a time when genetic science has developed to the point where the ethical implications of the use of embryos for research purposes and the cloning of a human being have become 'live' issues in public discourse, and abortion and euthanasia have become more acceptable in certain quarters as solutions to human problems, the pope's caution, criticised by many over the years as a failure of leadership, might be more understandable. One way or another, O'Callaghan's honest confrontation with the subtleties of the contraception issue, a significant turning point in Catholic culture, was very much in keeping with the post-Vatican II climate, as well as the political, sociocultural mood in Ireland and abroad from the late 1960s.

The political situation in the late 1960s was highly charged. The Berkeley and Paris student revolts which affected the western world in general had their parallel in Ireland. The so-called 'Quiet Revolution' took place in the spring of 1969, when students in UCD protested against the manner in which the move to the new campus at Belfield was being handled. At the annual Labour Party Conference in 1967, Brendan Corish had nailed the party's colours to the socialist mast.[64] Speaker after speaker at the conference reiterated the fact of Labour's socialism. Against the background of the new mood not only in Ireland, but worldwide, Brendan Halligan, in May 1967, remarked that 'it is almost respectable now to be a socialist'.[65] In the 1950s, such rhetoric would have constituted political suicide, bearing in mind the dire warnings about socialism and communism that emanated from the bishops' pastoral letters. The Irish cultural ethos had certainly changed when the 1969 general election campaign was fought out against the background of Labour Party slogans, which confidently proclaimed that 'the seventies will be socialist'.

The 1969 election result, though not as mould-breaking as had been anticipated by some, was important in that it catapulted two new arrivals on to the political stage, who were to make their presence felt keenly in the years to come, as champions of a more pluralistic Irish society. One of these, Dr Garret FitzGerald, returned to the Dáil as a Fine Gael TD in 1969, had, in 1964, in a *Studies* article entitled 'Towards a National Purpose',[66] published his vision of a new Ireland, which would be the product of the combined Christian, liberal and socialist traditions. The new Irish society would glory 'in our mixed inheritance, despising none of it, and elevating no part to a position of pre-eminence over the rest,' he wrote.[67] Another high-profile figure returned to the Dáil as a Labour deputy in the same election was Dr Conor Cruise O'Brien, historian, writer and former diplomat, who also took a keen interest in the evolving situation in Northern Ireland.

Inevitably, Brian Lenihan's relaxation of censorship, by his legislation of May 1967, had contributed greatly to the more liberal climate which was developing in Ireland. Despite the fact that the recent legislation did not extend to those books and periodicals which advocated 'the unnatural prevention of conception', this did not preclude many Irish newspapers and periodicals from carrying letters and articles presenting the case for and against contraception. If the law had, in fact, been strictly enforced, the likelihood was that many Irish publications could have been deemed to have broken it. The *Sunday Press*, the *Sunday Independent* and *The Irish Times* dealt frankly in their columns with the topic.[68] The new Irish magazine, *Woman's Way*, which began publication in 1963, was particularly frank about sexual and family planning matters, under the editorship of Caroline Mitchell.[69]

Another indication of the mood of the times is that, despite the fact that the 1935 Criminal Law (Amendment) Act, section 17, forbidding the importation, manufacture and sale of contraceptives, remained on the statute books, the Irish Family Planning Association was established in 1969. A non-profit-making organisation, it provided contraceptives and gave advice to patients about the planning of families.

The women's liberation movement began in Ireland about 1969 and became a very influential force for change from the early 1970s. Attitudes and values were being formed increasingly by more secular, liberal views of morality. While the pope and the Irish bishops had made their respective views clear, their pronouncements were by no means taken as the last word from the late 1960s. Ironically, it was the contraception issue and the efforts made throughout the 1970s to legalise contraception in Ireland, which forced the bishops to reassess their role, and challenged them to become a force of a somewhat different kind in the new Ireland that was taking shape.

The first attempt to change the law relating to contraception came from a group of young senators — Mary Robinson, John Horgan and Trevor West — in 1971, during Jack Lynch's period as Taoiseach. Archbishop McQuaid of Dublin responded in his Lenten pastoral, stating that 'civil divorce and contraception are evil, and there cannot be on the part of any person, a right to do what is evil'.[70] The bishops issued a joint statement after their Maynooth meeting in March 1971. 'Regarding pressures being exerted on public opinion on questions concerning the civil law on divorce, contraception and abortion', they advised that 'these questions involve issues of grave import for society as a whole, which go far beyond purely private morality or private religious belief'. They added that:

> Civil law on these matters should respect the wishes of the people who elected the legislators and the bishops confidently hope that the legislators themselves will respect this important principle.[71]

On Sunday, 28 March 1971, priests in Dublin churches read out a letter from McQuaid, warning that if legislation was passed which offended the objective moral law, it would be a 'curse upon our country', and stressing that contraception was 'a right that cannot even exist'.[72] There were protests in relation to the pastoral in a number of churches. *The Irish Times* reported the following day that two women from the women's liberation movement — Mary Kenny and Máirín Johnston — had walked out of evening Mass at Haddington Road Church. When the priest read out that 'any contraceptive act is wrong in itself', Kenny, a journalist and prominent member of the movement, was reported to have stood up and said, 'This is a wicked pastoral. It is disgraceful and contrary to *Humanae Vitae.* This is church dictatorship'.[73]

From the early 1970s much of the pressure for a relaxation of the anti-contraception laws came from a section of the women's movement. In 1971, under its auspices, a spectacular publicity stunt was staged to challenge the 1935 law banning the importation and sale of contraceptives. A group of women travelled on the so-called 'contraceptive train' to Belfast on 22 May 1971, where they purchased a complement of contraceptives.[74] On their return to Connolly Station, it was up to customs officials to confiscate the offending merchandise in order to enforce the law. However, the women were allowed to walk freely through the customs barrier with their purchases intact. They had proven their point — the law had been flouted and it was seen publicly to be obsolete. While it captured the imagination of many, and despite the fact that the Lynch government had agreed in principle that it would change the law in relation to contraceptives, the government appeared to lose its resolve, and the 1971 bill was denied a first reading (perhaps in fear of the political consequences of the inevitable episcopal displeasure that it would evoke).

A second attempt to change the law relating to contraception was made by Senator Mary Robinson in 1973. Though only two years after the first attempt, a number of significant developments in the intervening two years held out possibilities for change. Firstly, the government-appointed Commission on the Status of Women reported in 1972 that parents had a right to 'regulate the number and spacing of their family' and that the methods that they chose 'must remain a matter for their mutual selection and be influenced by their moral conscience'. The report went on to recommend that 'information and expert advice on family planning should be available ... to families throughout the country'.[75]

Secondly, Archbishop McQuaid had retired in January 1972. He was succeeded by Dermot Ryan as Archbishop of Dublin, on 14 February 1972. Ryan had been a member of the Dublin Diocesan Council of Priests; it was generally expected that he would be less conservative than McQuaid. Thirdly, in February 1973, a general election had brought an end to a sixteen-year period of Fianna Fáil rule. Jack Lynch's government was replaced by a coalition under Liam Cosgrave of Fine Gael, and Brendan Corish, leader of the Labour Party. The latter had campaigned on a platform of economic expansion and social reform. The issue of contraception was looming in the background and, very soon, this government was to become deeply embroiled in it.

It did not require much perspicacity to realise that the new government would be challenged to live up to its election promise of social reform and that, after sixteen years in opposition, the coalition parties had to make their political mark. Realising that the issue of contraception was on the horizon, the *Irish Catholic* newspaper, in the lead up to the election, had urged its readers to make it their business 'to find out what those who are seeking your vote intend to do, if elected, about proposed permissive legislation'.[76] Introducing the second bill in the Seanad in early November, Mary Robinson proposed that the Minister for Health should license the sale of contraceptives via chemist shops and in hospitals, while some should be made available on prescription only.[77] It was a more moderate bill in terms of its provisions than the first had been.

On Sunday, 26 November 1973, the bishops published a major statement on the principles which should, in their view, govern Church–state relations.[78] The statement was an advance on their March 1971 statement, and its tone was in sharp contrast to that of Archbishop McQuaid's pastoral letter of 28 March 1971. They pointed out that, 'the question at issue is not whether artificial contraception is morally right or wrong. The clear teaching of the Catholic church is that it is morally wrong'. They went on to say that 'no change in the State law can make the use of contraceptives morally right since what is wrong in itself remains wrong, regardless of what state law says'.[79] It was what followed that made this statement a watershed in the history of Church–state relations in Ireland. The bishops went on to assert:

> It does not follow, of course, that the State is bound to prohibit the importation and sale of contraceptives. There are many things which the

Catholic Church holds to be morally wrong and no one has ever suggested, least of all the Church herself that they should be prohibited by the State.[80]

The most impartial observer of Church–state relations could probably be forgiven for viewing the latter statement as somewhat disingenuous. The bishops went on to develop their argument, explaining that, 'those who insist on seeing the issue purely in terms of the State enforcing, or not enforcing, Catholic moral teaching, are therefore missing the point'. The real question facing the legislators related to the 'effect ... the increased availability of contraceptives would have on the quality of life' in the Republic. Developing a point made in their 1971 statement, they stressed that this 'is a question of public, not private, morality'.[81] They emphasised that it was 'not a matter for bishops to decide whether the law should be changed or not'.[82] It was a matter for the legislators and people to weigh up all the issues, and thereby come to a conscientious decision which would uphold the common good.

Cosgrave had little inclination to press forward with legislation in the contraception area. However, within a month of the bishops' statement, an event occurred which forced the government's hand. Mrs Mary McGee had sought to import contraceptives from England for her own personal use. When Irish customs seized her parcel, she took the matter to court with the financial help of the Irish Family Planning Association. Her action was dismissed in the High Court but upheld on appeal to the Supreme Court. Mr Justice Walsh judged that 'the private morality of the citizens does not justify intervention by the state into the activities of those citizens unless and until the common good requires it'.[83] The ruling in the McGee case, in December 1973, declared the ban on the importation of contraceptives under the 1935 Act to be unconstitutional.

In February 1974, the Minister for Justice, Patrick Cooney, announced the government's intention to publish its own bill. On 27 March 1974, the government's Control on Importation, Sale and Manufacture of Contraceptives Bill proposed that contraceptives could be imported and sold under licence by chemists to married couples. The bill was quite restrictive, with severe penalties for infringements. The Robinson bill had been defeated in the Senate the previous day by 32 votes to 10. The government's bill, however, was also defeated, by a margin of 75–61 votes, on 16 July. Cosgrave and six other Fine Gael TDs voted against their own government's bill, causing considerable consternation and dismay at the time. However, the Supreme Court ruling on the McGee case ensured that this issue would not go away and that the state would be required sooner or later to adapt to a changing society, where it was becoming more obvious that conflicting opinions were held on moral and social issues.

In 1975, the bishops issued a joint pastoral letter, entitled *Human Life is Sacred.* The pastoral letter, in four parts stressed the inseparable connection between love and life in the Christian frame of reference.[84] The bishops were critical of what they termed a 'contraceptive mentality', which was contrary to 'the Christian understanding of family life'.[85] That said, they insisted that 'the church does not lack understanding of and tolerance for human weakness'.[86] In this pastoral, they developed this point in a more positive way, stating that a confessor must always point out that contraception is wrong, but that 'in assessing the degree of moral failure' it had to be recognised 'that circumstances may sometimes diminish or even exclude subjective guilt'.[87]

The Catholic hierarchy can never be seen as totally monolithic, however, and a series of statements made by Bishop Jeremiah Newman, who had been appointed Bishop of Limerick in 1974, bore witness to this. In an address to the Catholic Young Men's society in Muine Bheag, Co. Carlow, on 30 May 1976, he stated:

> My personal position in the matter is that, in the first place, the Catholic people of our State have a right — a political right — to the provision of the kind of social framework that supports them in the living out of their moral and religious principles.[88]

Quite clearly, this went very much against the spirit of the collective statement of the bishops in 1973. When asked in a radio interview whether Protestants had this right also, he replied:

> They have. But if you have a situation where there is an incompatibility between the rights, then, as there is no fundamental human right in question, obviously the right of the majority has to be respected in a particular way.[89]

Both Conor Cruise O'Brien and Garret FitzGerald argued that Bishop Newman's position was sectarian, and a public debate on Church–state relations was conducted in the press and on radio. O'Brien had defined the secular state as one which takes into account the views of all the citizens, whether they adhere to a religion whose members are in a majority, or to religions whose members are in a minority, or those professing no religion.[90] When Bishop Newman was questioned about his attitude towards the secular state, he replied that he saw it as a 'monstrosity', a 'challenge', which the Church 'would have to fight against to the end', commenting that, 'we have got to give leadership to the people to stand up against the secular state and those who represent it'.[91] Bishop Newman's statements on moral, political and other issues were published the following year, in a book entitled *The State of Ireland.*

The Irish bishops issued a statement at the conclusion of their Maynooth meeting, which took place from 14 to 16 June 1976, in which they made it clear that the sentiments expressed by Bishop Newman of Limerick did not reflect the thinking of the hierarchy as a whole. They stated that 'it is not the view of the Catholic hierarchy, that in the law of the State, the principles peculiar to our faith should be made binding on people who do not adhere to that faith'.[92] But they went on to assert that, 'the hierarchy has every right to advise their people on these issues as part of their inherent right and duty to preach the Gospel'.[93]

The contraception issue surfaced again in the Lynch administration which replaced the Fine Gael–Labour coalition in 1977. In a further statement, in 1978, the bishops turned to the 'public and social' aspect of this matter. This time, they came to the nub of the problem, as they saw it, in relation to the proposed change in the law, when they pointed out:

> In the area of contraception, laws can affect the way people think about marriage, about the family, about fidelity. Laws can affect people's attitudes about relations between the sexes, both within marriage and outside it. The law-maker ... must weigh the good against the bad.... It may be said that conscience is a sufficient safeguard of moral standards. But conscience itself can become confused and weakened by society's attitudes. A change in the law can deceive people into thinking that morality has changed also.[94]

What the bishops, in effect, were saying was that if the law permits something, which in the eyes of the Church is morally wrong, then people's sense of its wrongness over a period of time will become blunted.

It would appear, from reflecting on past issues like Sunday opening of public houses, that the Irish bishops had always felt this way in relation to the value of the law upholding moral norms, but they had never spelt it out quite so explicitly before. As to why they had not, perhaps they themselves had not thought the implications through, because the conditions of the time, as witnessed by people's compliance and deferential adherence to specific prescripts, relieved them of this responsibility. They could, in the 1950s, afford to speak in generalities and command people in a rather paternalistic way as to what they should or should not do, without explaining why.

It was during the 1970s, in relation to the issue of contraception in particular, that the bishops were forced to work out and explain their rationale in matters of sexual morality. Each of the above statements built on and added to the one which went before, making for the development by the bishops in the course of the 1970s of a clear and consistent line on where they stood on issues relating to Church, state, morality and the law. Irish Catholics by this time had become much more confident that they could arrive at moral decisions without expert guidance. For this reason, the bishops had to think more creatively — make distinctions in relation to public and private morality — so that they could present their perspective in a convincing way.

The Church now had a far more demanding spiritual role to play. This role was more subtle — one of moral enlightenment which had to be executed by persuasion and witness, rather than by the traditional laying down of rules. It was now the age of the expert society. The bishops' expertise was in the area of conscience and morality, and the new era demanded, as in the case of all professionals, that they, as bishops, develop their expertise, be prepared to explain its implications, and present it in the market place of ideas and be questioned in relation to it. Indeed, ironically, it would appear that they had to convince many people that they had, in fact, a very important and necessary role to play as moral guides. There was no room for the paternalism of the past. Through the 1970s, by way of their statements, they clarified and defended their role and, having done so, they were obliged to let the democratic process take its course.

Against this background, Charles Haughey, Minister for Health in the Fianna Fáil government in 1979, drew up his Health Bill, which was passed in July 1979 as the Family Planning Act,[95] described by Haughey as an 'Irish solution for an Irish problem'. The new law provided for contraceptives to be made available in chemist shops on production of a medical prescription. The doctor had to be satisfied that the application for a prescription was for bona-fide family-planning purposes in a marriage context. Mr Haughey consulted with the Catholic bishops and with representatives of other churches in the course of preparing the legislation.

There was no opposition to Haughey's bill. During its passage, Bishop McNamara of Kerry made a very interesting observation in an article in *Doctrine and Life*, when he noted that it was 'not the State's duty to make better Christians, still less better Catholics'.[96] This, in fact, was what the bishops were forced to come to terms with more and more. He did not add — but undoubtedly from their self-presentation through the 1970s, he and the other bishops realised — that this was, in fact, *their* spiritual and pastoral duty and that, from that point on, they would increasingly have to perform that task without the support of state legislation, on which they had formerly been able to rely.

Lay people and politicians could now call on Roman teaching to support them in their demands for civil liberties and recognition of the equal rights of all groupings in society. When they did so, they found that the retention in civil law of prohibitions, which were specifically Catholic, could not be sustained, because they did not have a legitimate theological basis. The bishops were left, in a sense, like any other interest group. They had to convince people of the legitimacy of their views, by whatever means were open to them, and hope that their case would be a convincing one.

While the events recounted might seem to suggest that the bishops during the 1970s were solely concerned with defending their traditional role, there was during this time a growing awareness among church personnel at all levels that their spiritual role had to be conceived in broader terms than hitherto. It began to be recognised that there was much more to the building of a Christian society than the imposition of legal prohibitions. This was obvious from the Irish Church's increasing concern through the 1970s with issues of social justice.

15

SOCIAL JUSTICE AT HOME AND ABROAD

One of the most significant changes in Irish Catholic culture as represented by bishops and other church personnel in the post-Vatican II era, was an increased awareness of, and concern in relation to, issues of social justice at home and abroad. In the pre-conciliar era, there was little explicit mention of specific matters of justice. The main concerns tended to hinge on the importance of preserving the Catholic status quo and of warding off things that were seen as threatening it. To the extent that the status quo was seen as problematic, it tended to have little to do with whether it was a just one or not — this was rarely if ever questioned. In order to understand why this was so, and how and why it changed, it is necessary to look beyond Irish Catholicism.

The original formulation of modern Catholic social teaching lay in the encyclicals, *Rerum Novarum,* 1891,[1] and *Quadragesimo Anno,* 1931,[2] as already discussed. While these encyclicals were landmarks in Catholic social teaching, their capacity to be a radical critique of society and its institutions was somewhat blunted by the fact that they were preoccupied with reacting to socialism and communism. Such was the preoccupation with what was perceived as the 'menace of Communism', that the evils of capitalism as an economic system tended to be lost sight of. The Church was far more concerned to stress the rights of private property and free enterprise. It would, however, be a misrepresentation of the Church's social teaching to say that there was no awareness of the injustice that an over-zealous pursuit of these ideals can give rise to and perpetuate. Pope Leo XIII in *Rerum Novarum* spoke out against 'the greed of unchecked competition',[3] and he was echoed forty years later by Pope Pius XI in *Quadragesimo Anno,* when the latter was critical of 'the errors of individualist economic teaching'.[4] But while there was a recognition of the down-side of capitalism, and the inequities to which it gave rise, the Church, because of its over-arching fear of communism, was very wary of suggesting that the state should intervene. It was only gradually that Catholic Church leaders and theologians came to realise the full extent to which economic injustice can be institutionalised in the structures of capitalist society, and also to face the fact that the state is obliged to intervene to prevent, or rectify it.

In this respect, Pope John XXIII's encyclical, *Mater et Magistra,* 1961,[5] was a watershed in the Church's social teaching. Whereas previous popes had railed against state intervention in the economy and any development that smacked of a state welfare system, John XXIII laid much more emphasis on the practical need for the public authority to intervene 'to remedy lack of balance, whether between different sectors in the economy, or between different parts of the same country, or even between the different peoples of the world',[6] because, he explained, 'governments have the care of the common good and in these conditions it is urgently necessary for them to intervene more frequently'.[7]

By making such pronouncements, he had set the tone for a totally new era in the social thinking of the Church. The issue of social justice was very much to the fore also in his encyclical, *Pacem in Terris,* 1963,[8] and in the Vatican Council's document, *The Pastoral Constitution of the Church in the Modern World,* promulgated on 7 December 1965. In the latter document, it was stated that the Church had,

> the duty to build a better world based on truth and justice. Thus we are witnesses of the birth of a new humanism, one in which man is defined first of all by his responsibility towards his brothers and towards history.[9]

This sentence encapsulates a profound change of thinking. While the Church might always, in theory, have defined its role along these lines, the cut and thrust of the Council's debate on *The Church in the Modern World* challenged the Council Fathers to give a sharper focus to their definition of the Church in the modern age, which is what we have here.

The Church in the Modern World recognised that scientific advances and the new technologies had greatly added to man's sense of his own powers of creativity, development and independence, in all manner of ways. De Chardin's evolutionary theories in the 1950s had been rejected by the official Church, but the Council legitimated the developmental theory of history. In this sense, history is not just something that happens to man — a given; rather, he has free will — he makes his own history. This has a host of implications, not least of which is that he holds responsibility for his own destiny and that of those around him.

Whereas in the past, the tendency had been to see this life as a kind of antechamber where one awaited the next life, taking care to avoid sin, within this new framework, the onus was on the individual to build God's kingdom on this earth. But it was not enough to *avoid* evil — it was necessary to *do* good actively. In the past, people suffering oppression and injustice had been enjoined to view it as the will of God, and had been advised that it was wrong to react against it. An insight into the Church's attitude to life's hardships and suffering is revealed in Pope Leo XIII's words in *Rerum Novarum* when he advised:

> Pains and hardships of life will have no end or cessation on earth; for the consequences of sin are bitter and hard to bear, and they must accompany man so long as life lasts. To suffer and to endure, therefore, is the lot of humanity; let them strive as they may, no strength and no artifice will ever succeed in banishing from human life the ills, and troubles which beset it.[10]

However, the consciousness now began to dawn that much of human misery was not a God-given unalterable fact of life, but rather that it was humanly caused and built into the structures of society, and that the causes should be highlighted and challenged with a view to changing the situation. The Vatican Council laid the foundations for the emergence of a new spirituality, which placed emphasis on concepts such as the dignity, freedom and independence of the person, and the individual's fulfilment and development — all of which attributes could be advanced only in the context of a just society. Concepts of the human condition formerly seen as static, and interpreted in the context of an established order of things, were now to be understood in a more dynamic way. *The Church in the Modern World* stated:

> The destiny of the human community has become all of a piece, where once the various groups of men had a kind of private history of their own. Thus, the human race has passed from a rather static concept of reality to a more dynamic, evolutionary one.[11]

Catholics were now called upon to identify where there was need and to become actively involved in rectifying it, in their own locality, and also, most importantly, on a global level. The message of the Council was that Christian evangelisation, whether at home or in the wider world context, had to concern itself with the temporal as well as spiritual welfare of people. Preaching and giving witness (often artificially separated in the past) were seen as inseparable.

A significant feature of changing Catholic culture in Ireland in the aftermath of Vatican II was the appointment of bishops who had leanings in a more pastoral direction. Among these was Peter Birch who succeeded Bishop Collier as Bishop of Ossory, in January 1964. He had been outspoken on educational reform in the late 1950s. He became very involved in social issues through the 1960s and 1970s. He established the Ossory Social Services Centre in 1964, which catered to the needs of the poor and disadvantaged in his own diocese.[12] In 1970, he was appointed chairman of the Irish Bishops' Council for Social Welfare, set up in the same year to advise the bishops on matters of social policy. Michael Harty was appointed Bishop of Killaloe in 1967. He too was very involved in the social aspect of the role of a bishop and, in his capacity as chairman of the Commission on Liturgy, led the organisation of Irish liturgical reform after the Second Vatican Council. Bishop Joseph Cunnane, appointed to the diocese of Tuam in 1969, had been involved in, and forward-thinking on, the subject of liturgical reform in the 1950s.

Eamonn Casey was appointed Bishop of Kerry in 1969.[13] He had been very effective working as an emigrant chaplain in England, and was appointed largely on foot of his success in this field. Bishops in their pastoral letters in the 1950s constantly bewailed the steady exodus from the country through emigration. Much of the concern at that time had to do with the 'leakage' of the faith that resulted from Irish Catholics going to 'pagan England'. From the late 1950s, a more pro-active approach was adopted by sending Irish clergy as a kind of taskforce, to work among the emigrant population in their respective work situations in England.[14] They were sent as chaplains to Irish emigrants working on the motorways, in nuclear power stations and in hotels, and also to parishes where there was a strong concentration of Irish. Archbishop McQuaid was particularly involved in promoting the emigrant chaplaincy scheme. Chaplains became increasingly concerned with the social, as well as the spiritual, welfare of the emigrant Irish.[15] In the 1960s, Eamonn Casey became a very high-profile figure, because of his work and active campaigning in relation to the housing problems of emigrants. He was the driving force behind the Catholic Housing Aid Society, which began as a series of seventy parish-based centres to help young couples with housing problems. In 1973, Casey was instrumental, with a number of other bishops, in the founding of Trócaire, an Irish agency for the organisation of aid to the Third World.

The appointment of such bishops, with a more pastoral approach, who were active in promoting social issues, represented a profound change in Irish Catholic culture — the highlighting of social concern and awareness, which had been overshadowed in the past by issues having more to do with moral rectitude. Casey's appointment was greeted with considerable surprise. In the first place, he was one of the youngest episcopal appointments up to that time. But, even more importantly, his appointment, and also that of Cunnane as Archbishop of Tuam in the same year, signified a major departure from the long tradition of appointing academics (in particular Maynooth professors) as bishops.

The Irish bishops in the pre-Vatican II era tended to focus on specific aspects of personal/sexual morality, and issue very precise commands in relation to what they saw as infringements. While in the public consciousness throughout the 1970s, the bishops may have been perceived to be still primarily concerned with sexual morality, this was not the entire picture. Against the background of the Council's emphasis on the dignity of man's conscience, they came to see their role as informers of the 'conscience of society'.[16] In the 1950s, the bishops took as their starting point the social teaching contained in papal encyclicals, which was often more pertinent to societies in continental Europe, and applied it to the Irish situation, regardless of how appropriate it was. By the 1970s, they were looking at issues and problems that were unique to the Irish situation and, with the help of the new insights of Vatican II and papal pronouncements, they were seeking to understand them and put forward viable solutions. This kind of critical social analysis had more of a cutting edge to it. It involved the bishops and other clergy in a type of political engagement, which they had eschewed formerly because they feared that it might endanger the status quo.

What might best be termed the Irish Church's new departure is evidenced in the statements that they made and activities in which they became involved throughout the 1970s. The bishops issued a statement on the *Situation in Northern Ireland* in 1970,[17] and two further statements on Northern Ireland in 1971.[18] In 1972, they issued a statement on *Ireland and Europe,* prior to Ireland's entry into the EEC.[19] In 1973, they set up Trócaire to provide aid for developing countries. In a pastoral, entitled *Development,* they outlined the aim of the new organisation as two-fold — to give 'whatever help lies within its resources to the areas of greatest need among developing countries', and to make people at home 'more aware of the needs of these countries' and of 'our duties towards them'. These duties, they stated, were 'no longer a matter of charity but of simple justice'.[20] A very important aspect of Trócaire's work was that of educating people in relation to social and political injustice in the Third World, and making them aware of the interdependence in trade between developed and developing countries, and of the responsibility of wealthy nations, including Ireland, for the poverty of the Third World.

In pre-conciliar times there was little apparent understanding of global injustice. As far as the Church was concerned, its primary responsibility to the developing world lay in the conversion of souls. But Pope Paul VI's encyclical, *Populorum Progressio,* promulgated in 1967, made it clear that the Church's responsibility went beyond this. He stressed the importance of solidarity and brotherhood between people and nations, and that 'injustices must be challenged and overcome'.[21] In his encyclical, *Octogesima Adveniens,* 1971, he developed this theme further. In their 1973 pastoral letter, the Irish bishops emphasised that it was each individual's Christian duty to help those who were more needy and 'to demand that the political authorities representing us act always with justice and responsibility towards less fortunate countries'.[22]

Mention has already been made of the importance of the episcopal commissions set up in the post-conciliar era to enable the Church to realise its new understanding of its role. The Irish Commission for Justice and Peace (1969) and the Council for Social Welfare (1970) played an important role as advisory bodies to the Episcopal Conference. Throughout the 1970s, they issued critical commentaries on all manner of social issues, ranging from family law to human rights to unemployment. Whereas the bishops in the 1950s had often been ill-informed or somewhat removed from the problems upon which they commented, the research and expertise made available by these agencies ensured that, from the 1970s, they were taken seriously as informed commentators.

In the recessionary 1970s, unemployment and poverty were focused on repeatedly. In 1971, the Bishops' Council for Social Welfare highlighted the problem of poverty in Ireland by holding a conference in Kilkenny on the subject.[23] Arising from the proceedings of this conference, a statement on social policy was issued in November 1972,[24] and this was followed by a survey report on poverty, researched in 1973 and published in 1974.[25] This was followed, in 1976, by a document entitled *Planning for Social Development: What Needs to be Done*.[26] In this document, the Council was critical of the government Green Paper, *Economic and Social Development, 1976–1980,* which 'although containing social development in its title', confined 'its discussion almost entirely to consideration of economic problems'.[27]

In June 1976, the bishops issued a statement on the *Economic Situation,* in which they pointed out that the 'better-off should be prepared to accept the greater sacrifice' caused by the economic recession, and reminded politicians of their 'special responsibility' to give 'leadership and guidance'.[28] The most significant statement made by the bishops in the area of social policy in the 1970s was a joint pastoral, entitled *The Work of Justice,* which they issued in 1977.[29] The fact that the bishops had imbibed the spirit of conciliar thinking was very evident on this occasion, when they asserted:

> Justice does not happen; it has to be willed and worked for and built into legislation. No system, as such, will by itself guarantee justice. Only a combination of moral commitment to justice and political commitment to the legislation and the structures of justice will create a just society.[30]

Addressing those who owned 'wealth, property or means of production', they reminded them of their 'obligations towards others and towards the common good of the nation', and went on to advise that 'there is no such thing in justice and no such thing in Catholic teaching as an absolute right' to do what one likes with one's money, property or land.[31] In relation to workers, while pointing out that 'the strike weapon can, of course, be abused', they acknowledged that 'workers needed the power that trade unions and the strike weapon gave them before they could get simple justice'.[32] This kind of rhetoric and analysis was decidedly left-of-centre for Irish churchmen, and it goes without saying that it would have been inconceivable in the pre-Vatican II climate. It set the tone for a new era of social critique for the Irish Church.

The same movement to the left by the Spanish Church in the 1970s has been documented by Frances Lannon in her study of Spanish Catholicism.[33] Referring to the fact that in the last decade of Franco's military dictatorship, 'the Spanish church became as much its critic and opponent as its faithful supporter', she went on to observe that 'the terminology of human rights and civil liberties was appropriated by bishops and priests brought up to hold both in deep suspicion'.[34] From the late 1960s, she noted that pastoral letters analysing social, economic and political issues, which had been 'very rare' in the 1950s, became 'almost commonplace'.[35] In his study of French Catholicism, Norman Ravitch has identified a similar movement to the left in the post-conciliar era.[36] He points to the fact that the French Church became receptive to the use of Marxist tools of social analysis, and instances an example of the French bishops' use of the concept of 'class struggle' in one of their statements at Lourdes in 1972 — something that would formerly have been anathema to them.[37]

In 1979, the Irish bishops made a further statement on the *Present Social and Industrial Situation,* in which they were critical of 'the state of tension' that existed between social groups, and the apparent 'lack of concern about the rights of weaker groups'.[38] In all of these pronouncements, they no longer prescribed dogmatically, but were more concerned to enunciate broad principles of justice and freedom. The National Conference of Priests of Ireland (NCPI) issued a statement at its annual general meeting in 1978, which asserted that the consumerist culture, characterised by greed and envy, had created an environment hostile to real religion in Ireland. The statement went on:

> It is clear from what is happening in the areas of justice, labour relations and violence that we have failed to form a Christian community.[39]

The bishops, the statement continued, had provided 'prophetic leadership', speaking out 'boldly on the famine of justice in [our] country', and the Conference urged its members to 'activate their communities to right the wrongs' that afflicted the country.[40]

The Second Vatican Council had emphasised the prophetic mission of the Church and how the Gospel message might provide insights into the problems of the contemporary world. Against this background, bishops, priests and religious have set about discerning the 'signs of the times', raising people's consciousness in relation to society's institutionalised inequities, and showing how these inequities cause problems like unemployment at home and poverty in Third World countries. A significant development from the 1970s was that many Church personnel on the ground moved beyond reflection and analysis (forsaking traditional roles in areas such as education) and became directly involved in social issues.

Priests like Peter McVerry SJ and Seán Healy SMA have become actively involved in issues of justice, poverty, deprivation and unemployment. In 1982, the Conference of Major Religious Superiors established a Justice office, and Fr Bill McKenna SJ and Sister Brigid Reynolds SM were appointed co-directors. Fr Seán Healy SMA joined the staff in 1983. A significant element of the work of the staff of this office from 1986 has been their pre-budget submissions, circulated annually to TDs, senators and policy-makers, and their critique of the budget on the day after it has been presented by the Minister for Finance in the Dáil.[41] Behind all of these developments was the emergence not just of a 'new' theology, but the beginnings of diverse theologies, in response to local problems, be they related to the unemployment situation, poverty or emigration.

Whereas Scholastic theology tended to apply theory, without too much regard for the complexities of life, theologising in the new mode took its starting point from people's life experience, reflected upon it, and only then brought the insights of the Gospel to bear on it.

Irish theology had considerable ground to make up given the dearth of theological reflection that had marked the first half of the twentieth century, as already discussed. With the establishment of the Maynooth Union Summer School of theological studies which began in 1958, progress began to be made. Experts from Ireland and abroad lectured each year on a range of theological topics, and the papers delivered were published by M.H. Gill and Son in association with the Furrow Trust, Maynooth. The Summer School project was spearheaded by four Maynooth theologians — Fr Kevin McNamara, professor of Dogmatic Theology, Frs Denis O'Callaghan and Enda McDonagh, professors of Moral Theology, and Fr Donal Flanagan, professor of Dogmatic Theology.[42] The Irish Theological Association was set up in 1966 in response to the Vatican Council. Whereas the Summer School was episodic, the ITA was in more continuous sesssion and built up communications between those interested in theology and other disciplines. Increasingly, there was a recognition that theology could not confine itself within the boundaries of its own academic discourse. There was a sense that, of all disciplines, its applied nature had to be understood and communicated more — theology had to bridge the gap between God and the ordinary everyday circumstances of people's lives; otherwise, it was defeating its very purpose. Cross-fertilisation with other disciplines was increasingly seen as a *sine qua non* for this, and the situation (of historical origin) whereby the legislation that had established the NUI (1908) had prevented the university from teaching theology as a regular subject began to be seen as more and more of an incongruity.[43]

In this regard, a sense of the tension between churchmen of the old school and those of the new school, as represented by the ITA, is to be gleaned in a letter from McQuaid to Cardinal Conway on 17 February 1970, in which he expresses himself as follows: 'I am ... very pleased that you should think as you do about the I.T.A. This group would tell us what to think and do. They are very definite about theology in the University: a very troublesome venture where a Hierarchy is concerned, not to mention the Archbishop in whose city the new university — whatever its form — is to be physically sited'.[44] Essentially what McQuaid feared was that the 'opening up' of theology would threaten orthodoxy, and the responsibility for holding the line and defending Church teaching against possible heresy would fall to those in authority like himself.[45] Writing in 1979 of the importance of the influence of the ITA, McDonagh explained that 'despite some Episcopal hesitations and attempts at restriction in its first years', the association 'helped to break the isolation experienced by individual theology teachers, especially in seminary conditions' and 'to develop an *esprit de corps* which was notably absent in earlier times'. He also pointed to 'the active participation of theologians from Maynooth' in the Irish Federation of University Teachers, founded in 1964, as having had 'an important impact on Irish theological life'. The ITA produced two reports, in 1972 and 1977, on the subject of theology in the university, thus making an important contribution to the self-understanding of theology in Ireland.[46]

By the late 1960s, theologians no longer had a monopoly on theological reflection; Vatican II had stressed how worthwhile, unique and indispensable was every person's reading, understanding and discovering the 'signs of the times'. 'Paperback theology' made theology accessible at a popular level.[47] Efforts were made, in due course, by Irish theologians like Enda McDonagh, to develop an indigenous Irish theology, which would enable people to understand the meaning of their lives, within a theological frame of reference.[48] Theology from the 1970s, as expounded by bishops, religious, priests and lay people, became more humane, dynamic, critical and radical — indeed, some would say, left-of-centre — in its critique of society. It was a long way from the abstruse theological argumentation that took place and was recorded in the *ITQ* in the 1950s, and which really had meaning or relevance only for academic theologians.

At the time of the Second Vatican Council, the Third World bishops seized the opportunity that a world forum of bishops afforded them to highlight the plight of the underdeveloped countries, raising such issues as poverty, famine, injustice and oppression. The insights of the Council paved the way for theologians in Latin American countries to develop their own indigenous theology of liberation, which drew attention to the fact that the oppression, injustice and lack of human rights that many suffered were the result of local corruption and so-called First World political and economic policies. Any account of theological development, or what might be termed the 'humanisation' of theology in the post-conciliar era, must take account of the influence of liberation theology as it evolved in the Latin American context. Whereas the Church hitherto had associated and identified with the establishment, and had, in fact, been invaluable in propping up many regimes of doubtful character, at the historic Medellin conference in 1968, the Latin American bishops announced their 'option for the poor', and this was ratified by Pope Paul VI himself who was in attendance.

By this time, the Church had come to recognise that the 'common good' was a concept of considerably more complexity than had been appreciated hitherto and that its realisation could be achieved only by engaging with the state and its institutions. All aspects of life began to be seen as having their political dimension. Pope Paul VI, in his encyclical, *Octogesima Adveniens,* in 1971, saw the necessity for Christians to become involved in political activity in order to build a better society.[49]

A book by Gustavo Guttierez, a Latin American theologian, published in Spanish in 1971, was the seminal work of the new genre in theology.[50] Liberation theology sought to enable people to interpret the circumstances of their lives; it encouraged them to question the status quo, which, more often than not, had, for centuries, been upheld, fostered and reinforced by Church authorities in poorer countries. Those who espoused liberation theology went beyond theory and analysis — they actively involved themselves in the plight of the poor and oppressed. This very often meant political involvement and confrontation. This was very far removed from traditional theology, which was apolitical. In 1973, Guttierez's book was translated into English and had widespread influence over the Catholic world, not least in Ireland, given the Irish Church's expansive missionary activity. Such a radical theology profoundly altered the nature of missionary work.

In the pre-Vatican II era, in so far as the bishops displayed an awareness of developments outside Ireland, they were fearful of them. As regards the underdeveloped world, because the principle of *extra ecclesiam nulla salus* was accepted and stressed, the Church's main preoccupation was with the conversion and baptism of pagans — with 'saving souls', taking little account of the native culture of peoples. Because there was little appreciation of how worthwhile were the traditions and customs of non-white, non-westernised peoples, little effort was made to integrate Christianity into their native culture. The approach to missionary work, it must be emphasised, was a universal Christian phenomenon and not a specifically Irish Catholic phenomenon. Missionary endeavour was still in its infancy in Ireland in the early twentieth century, in comparison to the continental missionary movement. The development of the latter was historically bound up with the colonisation movement, and Irish missionaries were absorbed into the prevailing culture.

Missionaries saw themselves as bringing not only salvation to pagans, but civilisation to primitive peoples. Perhaps it might have been expected that Irish missionaries, given their own historical experience of colonisation and British inculturation, would have had a more critical understanding of the missionary context. Edmund Hogan has written that while 'humanitarian considerations were always a factor, health care and education were undertaken primarily as a means of spreading Church influence'.[51] He has argued that action for justice formed part of the history of the Irish missionary movement, but that there was 'no formal development philosophy' underpinning missionary activity. This did not come to pass until the post-conciliar era.[52] This resulted partly from the fact that critical social analysis, as far as the Church was concerned, smacked of Marxist revolutionary theory and was, for this reason, suspect in itself. If people became aware of their situation and identified unjust structures that oppressed, in all likelihood they would act to alleviate their predicament and, in so doing, disturb the status quo. The Church always feared the consequences of such an eventuality and was philosophically opposed to precipitating it.

Papal teaching in the 1960s and the Vatican Council emphasised the importance of inculturation, and in the post-conciliar era, the approach to missionary work was more anthropological. A new, more expansive missionary consciousness found its earliest inspirational roots in Pope John XXIII's encyclicals,

Mater et Magistra, 1961, and *Pacem in Terris,* 1963. In these encyclicals, he addressed himself to the world community. The encyclicals emphasised the brotherhood of man, the solidarity that should exist between all peoples, and the importance of respecting the dignity and human rights of all persons. These two encyclicals form the basis for the thinking which emerged from the Vatican Council, as expressed in the *Decree on the Church's Missionary Activity,* 1965, which saw missionary work as promoting 'dignity and brotherly union, teaching those religious and moral truths which Christ illumined with His light'.[53] Following on from these pronouncements, Paul VI's encyclicals, *Populorum Progressio,* in 1967, and *Octogesima Adveniens,* in 1971, were milestones in the evolution of a new theology of missionary activity.

Concrete expression of the new conceptualisation of mission was evidenced in Ireland by the establishment of the Episcopal Commission for Missions, on 23 April 1968. The Irish Missionary Union (IMU) was set up in 1970.[54] Sanctioned by the bishops, it acted as an umbrella body representing missionaries working on the ground. The IMU, of its very essence, represented a radical shift in consciousness. In the pre-Vatican II era, missionary orders tended to act in discrete units, isolated from their fellow missionaries in other orders. The idea was that missionary orders would henceforth co-ordinate their ideas and resources, in the interests of the people they were going to serve, whereas formerly considerable rivalry had existed between different orders in their quest for vocations and converts.

The National Mission Council was set up by the bishops in 1977, in response to the directives of the encyclical, *Ecclesiae Sanctae,* of Paul VI.[55] This council served to co-ordinate Ireland's missionary policy on a national scale, under the authority of the Episcopal Conference. The function of the council was to liaise between the IMU, which represented the missionary societies, and the Episcopal Commission for the Missions. Sharing the resources and secretariat of the IMU, the council proceeded to co-ordinate the activities of all the missionary bodies, rationalising their resources in order to make them more effective in their tasks, and also acted as a forum for discussion on matters relating to national mission policy.

A chair of Mission Studies was established in Maynooth in 1974, and Fr Bede McGregor OP was appointed to fill it. Throughout the 1970s, courses were organised in different venues, providing mission studies, languages and cultural studies for intending missionaries, and in-service courses for priests, sisters and brothers home on leave. A national mission congress was held in Knock in April 1979. Around this time, the idea of a national mission centre was developing, and this was officially opened in Dartry, Dublin, on 12 December 1980. All of these developments bespoke a more holistic approach to missionary work, from the 1970s on.

A central concern of the new structures established was to enrich missionaries' understanding of what they were about. They also aimed to replace the somewhat impoverished notion of the missions and missionary work, which existed in the minds of Irish people, with a more realistic appreciation of what was involved. Their work was complemented by educational programmes run by Trócaire and the *Radharc* television documentary series. Despite the fact that bishops and clergy in general were very proud and constantly reminded people of Ireland's missionary record, which they saw as reflecting the healthy state of the Irish Church, people's understanding of missionary work tended to be limited. Until this time, it was symbolised in the minds of many by the ubiquitous 'Black Babies' collection boxes (in schools, shops and public houses) and subscriptions to the *Far East* and the *Divine Word* magazines. Also, there were the visits of missionary priests to schools to relate their experiences (sometimes with the aid of slides), in an effort to cultivate vocations and raise funds for their respective missionary orders. Such images are a potent reminder of the mood of Catholic culture in Ireland in the 1950s and 1960s.

Inequities were more pronounced, and their causes more sharply definable in Third World countries, and many church personnel saw their role in these countries as one of active intervention, in what were often corrupt political systems, so that people could be emancipated from oppression. In the Irish situation, however, injustices were not as readily identifiable, and the causes were more complex and thus more elusive and less amenable to analysis, but they existed nonetheless. Since the 1970s, the Irish bishops, through their pronouncements and those of their commissions, have carved out a radically new role in Irish society — that of social critic. Their elaboration of their role from that time has been in keeping with the mind of the Second Vatican Council, which emphasised the importance of Church leaders and priests developing their role as spiritual and prophetic leaders of society, both local and global. In a sense, it is only since the 1970s that they could be said to have attained the high moral ground which the Church leaders of the 1950s assumed that they occupied.

16

CONCLUSION

This book set out to examine how Catholic culture in Ireland was changing between 1950 and the late 1970s. Irish Catholicism has been explored in the context of developments in the Catholic Church at home and worldwide. The book has also explored Irish culture, seeing Catholicism as one of its most characteristic features.

During this period, Irish Catholicism changed radically in its thinking, the way it conveyed its message and its approach to people and morality. The first part of this concluding chapter sets out to summarise some of the main changes that have taken place in the expression, presentation and mood of Irish Catholicism. The influence of Catholicism on Irish culture has also changed considerably over this thirty-year period. The second part of the chapter provides a summary analysis of the many forces which have influenced the changes that have taken place.

Catholic piety in the 1950s was typified by such devotional activities as the Holy Hour, Benediction, the Forty Hours, confraternities, sodalities, novenas, processions, missions, the cult of indulgences, Lenten fast and abstinence and exercises of mortification, First Friday devotions, confession and the rosary. Clearly such features had become less popular or were de-emphasised by the 1970s. There was some concern in the pre-conciliar era that they tended to usurp the centrality of the Mass.

Many other integral features of Catholic life changed radically in the 1960s, arising out of the deliberations of the Second Vatican Council. In 1957, the Eucharistic Fast, which was obligatory from midnight, was changed to three hours; it was changed to one hour in 1965.[1] The laws in relation to fast and abstinence, an integral feature of Catholicism in the 1950s and 1960s, were considerably relaxed from Lent 1966.[2] And the law of abstinence was further relaxed in 1970.[3] The parish mission as experienced in the past, exemplified by the Redemptorist preachers thundering fire and brimstone sermons from the pulpit, on topics such as hell fire, damnation and 'sins of the flesh', became a dim and distant memory. That said, such was their influence that graphic images of their sermons are readily conjured up in folk memory. In a survey commissioned by the Redemptorist Fathers, and published as *Parish Missions, Parish Retreats and Priests' Retreats* in 1972, the Redemptorist manifesto for 'the mission for modern times', while allowing that preaching was still 'the high point of every Redemptorist mission', stressed the importance of the missioner relating to people in all aspects of their daily lives.[4]

The cult of indulgences was de-emphasised from 1967,[5] and thus something that had been a quintessential feature of Catholic life in the 1950s and into the 1960s was scarcely heard of from the 1970s. Likewise, processions, by the 1970s were, for the most part, a thing of the past. They were out of keeping with the mentality of an era which saw itself as more sophisticated. The kind of processions that had been held in the 1950s became far less viable, if only for reasons of the traffic congestion that they would precipitate. It goes without saying that many other features very typical of Irish Catholic culture in the 1950s — like tributes to the pope, and the erection of holy crosses and grottoes — had all but disappeared by the 1970s.

The Mass occupied the central place in Catholic worship, after the Second Vatican Council, and para-liturgical devotional activity declined greatly. The fact that the Council did not issue a separate decree on the Blessed Virgin, choosing instead to devote a section of *The Dogmatic Constitution on the Church*, 1964, to her 'role ... in the mystery of Christ and the Church',[6] has been seen by Mariologists as an attempt to discourage excessive tendencies in Marian devotion, not least for ecumenical reasons. Marian and other devotional activities listed above were de-emphasised in the post-conciliar era. When discussing such developments, however, it is necessary to be mindful of the sociocultural factors influencing change. Evening devotions of all sorts were adversely affected from as early as the 1950s by the increasing popularity of cinema, the availability of BBC television in the eastern part of the country, and increased mobility — all of which extended people's choices as regards how they would spend their time.

Interestingly, some examples of popular devotional activity retained a considerable following. The figures for those undertaking pilgrimages remained impressive throughout the 1970s. The estimated number of pilgrims who climbed Croagh Patrick in 1976 was between 25,000 and 30,000; in 1979, between 35,000 and 40,000; and in 1980, between 45,000 and 50,000.[7] In 1979, 18,884 pilgrims participated in the three-day pilgrimage to Lough Derg, and it is clear from the figures as shown in Appendix C that Lough Derg remained a popular pilgrimage centre in the intervening years.[8] Knock Shrine was also popular in the 1970s. On 3 April 1976, the *Mayo News* reported that Bord Fáilte was to study the needs of Knock as a tourist centre, because in the previous year an estimated 750,000 people had visited the Marian shrine.[9] The building of a new basilica with a seating capacity for 5,000 people was completed in 1976. In 1979, the centenary year of the apparitions of the Virgin, an estimated 400,000 were in attendance at Knock on the occasion of the visit to the shrine of Pope John Paul II.[10] After that time, the shrine became increasingly popular. The papal visit and the dynamism of Mgr James Horan, who was parish priest of Knock from 1963 until his death in 1986, were two very significant factors which contributed to the growing popularity of Knock as a pilgrimage centre.

Catholicism in the pre-Vatican II era placed a very heavy emphasis on duty, self-sacrifice and mortification, and fearfulness in relation to threats to sexual morality was ever-present. God was portrayed as a stern task-master, and concepts like fear of God and His wrath in the event of wrong-doing were predominant. In the post-Vatican II era, Catholicism developed a more human face. God was portrayed as a loving, understanding God, who was not out to catch people if they made a mistake. He was seen as somebody who understood people's situation and the fact that if they sinned, there might have been extenuating circumstances. Sin was defined as failure to love God, and something which disrupted one's relationship with Him. The kind of dread that filled people's minds at the idea that they might have committed a mortal sin — and not be in a 'state of grace' — no longer had the same urgency. People's sense of sin was, to say the least of it, blunted.

Many Irish people's experience of Catholicism in the pre-Vatican II era was pervaded by such concepts as 'occasions of sin' and 'impure thoughts' and their accompanying scrupulosity and guilt, and the sense that one was meant to strive continuously for an ideal which, in fact, was unattainable. Needless to mention, the sea-change in attitudes which took place after the Council provoked no small amount of confusion in the minds of Catholics. This was addressed by Seán Fagan, a Marist theologian, in a book appropriately entitled *Has Sin Changed?* (1979).

Catholicism, as presented in school religion-teaching and textbooks and Church preaching, had changed enormously by the 1970s. The new primary-school curriculum and the 'new' theology of Vatican II combined to influence a new approach to the teaching of catechetics. The new emphasis was in stark contrast to the old catechism approach. Whereas the old approach had placed the emphasis on rote-learning for catechetical examinations, the new approach, in keeping with the new emphasis in educational pedagogy, adopted a more questioning, discursive attitude towards religious knowledge. The emphasis was on the story of salvation history and getting to know God as a person — cultivating a relationship with Him. The dominant theme of the new school programmes was the love of God and one's neighbour. There was a very strong emphasis on relationships.

Sheehan's *Apologetics and Catholic Doctrine* had been the staple catechetical text in secondary schools up to and including the 1960s.[11] Its whole emphasis, as the title suggests, was on defending the truths of the faith and, as such, it was more suitable as a compendium of theology for seminarians than as a text for adolescent school students. Essentially it approached its subject with a highly intellectual, apologetic thrust. In the pre-conciliar era, rules were transmitted and imposed against the background of sanctions and fear of the

Lord. In a more free-thinking atmosphere from the 1970s, the importance of acting positively, with love of God as the motivating force in one's life, was stressed. The influence of developmental psychology, which emphasised the importance of taking cognisance of the stages of moral growth of each individual, and the fact that moral values have to be discovered and personally chosen out of conviction, was of crucial importance in the development of the new catechetical programmes. The titles of the new textbooks, both at primary and secondary level, reflected the new mood of catechesis.[12]

What is important to remember here, however, is that the core teaching in relation to faith and morals did not change. What changed was the way Catholicism was presented. In modern-day parlance, it was packaged in a more user-friendly way. Its thrust was more positive. It projected a compassionate image, where in the past it had been grim and censorious. It concentrated on what one *did* in order to live a Christian life in this world, where in the past the concentration tended rather to be on what one avoided, so as not to be damned to hell for all eternity. The optimism of a new era was remarkably captured in the growth of the Charismatic Renewal movement in Ireland from the early 1970s. An offshoot of American Catholic Pentecostalism which developed from the late 1960s, the movement radiated confidence and joy.[13]

Pre-conciliar Catholicism was legalistic, authoritarian and highly defensive. This was the legacy of the Council of Trent, 1545–63. That council had been convened in response to the Protestant Reformation, so that the Catholic Church could set out very precisely and authoritatively its doctrines on faith and morals. Post-Tridentine Catholicism was very concerned to defend and consolidate its position. This led over time to a fortress mentality. Any views which diverged from the certainties laid down at Trent were seen in an extremely fearful light and fought off at all costs. The preservation of orthodoxy was seen as crucial to the Church's very survival. Certainty was the key to this, and this was one of the foremost features of Catholicism until the time of the Second Vatican Council.

One of the ways in which this manifested itself was that Catholics were constantly reminded by their bishops and priests of their grave responsibility of converting non-Catholics. Catholics saw themselves as possessing the truth, and were frequently reminded of their duty to convert those who were less fortunate. This explains the fears for those emigrating to 'pagan' England, regrets about the 'leakage' of the faith, and the reminders to emigrants of their duty to convert the English. Similarly, it explains the wary attitude towards 'non-Catholics', and how rigorously the conditions in relation to 'mixed marriages' were upheld. It also explains the crusading zeal felt by missionaries. No greater glory was conceivable in the 1950s than that of winning souls for the glory of God. Catholics were, in a sense, involved in a battle for the hearts and minds of those who might otherwise lose their immortal souls. But Vatican II indicated that there were paths to salvation other than the Catholic one, and, from the late 1960s, the sense of urgency in relation to this evaporated.

Catholicism changed from being dogmatic to being more dialogical. It was less concerned with the imposition of rules and regulations than it was with what should be the spirit of Catholicism. Its tone became one of a pilgrim church seeking the truth, rather than an institution which had a monopoly on it, to the exclusion of all similar institutions. Perhaps the greatest change in Catholic culture through the period of this research is that Catholicism became more open to many varying opinions on the definition of the truth, and Catholics began to decide according to mature conscience the lifestyle they wished to follow. They began to see themselves as having much more leeway and freedom to interpret the truth. They no longer 'enjoyed' the security of certainty.

This fundamental ground shift in Catholic thinking came at a time when Catholics and people in general all over the western world were changing and acquiring new habits of mind. Affluence had provided people with more opportunities for fulfilment and leisure activities of all types, and this led automatically to a more positive outlook on life. In this context, people felt more independent and were less ready to accept restrictions on their independence; the authoritarian approach that the Irish Church had previously adopted was no longer acceptable. Catholics became more 'protestant' in their approach to the demands of their religion. They inclined towards following their conscience. Michael Hornsby-Smith has pointed to a similar development in English Catholicism:

> The strong emphasis on 'making up their own minds' about aspects of Catholic teaching ... suggests a strong element of private decision-making which is one mark of protestantism.[14]

The fact that Irish Catholics had developed a new mentality was clearly shown by the findings of the 1974 survey on religious belief and practice. The survey showed that while 91 per cent of those surveyed professed themselves to be practising Catholics and as being influenced by the value system of Catholicism, they did not always adhere to Church rules, particularly in the area of sexual morality.[15] The fact that such a contradiction could exist has to be understood in the light of the profoundly changed sociocultural context, where religious attitudes were no longer as obvious or as all-pervasive in the Irish way of life. Irish Catholics were by then picking and choosing which aspects of Catholicism (as preached by the official Church) they would give allegiance to and live out; and which they saw as irrelevant, and simply discarded. This was a profound transformation when compared with the 1950s. The term *à la carte* Catholicism, coined to describe American Catholicism, was now being employed in some quarters to capture what was a very new phenomenon in Irish Catholic culture.

One of the most significant changes in Catholic culture in Ireland had to do with the bishops, their concerns and their general style of leadership when addressing those issues that appertained to Catholics. Pope John XXIII's influence was profound. He was the personification of a sea-change in attitudes in the Catholic Church. His presence contrasted starkly with the austere intellectualism and aristocratic seriousness of Pope Pius XII. He set a new tone for bishops and priests in the 1960s. Cardinal Conway adapted his own style to the new mood and set a headline for the Irish bishops and priests. His way was in sharp contrast to that of his predecessor, Cardinal D'Alton, and to that of many of the older bishops like Archbishop McQuaid and Bishops Lucey and Browne.

In the pre-conciliar era, the Irish bishops were very preoccupied with warning people about dangers to faith and morality. Their fears very much centred around sexual morality and, in so far as they looked beyond Ireland, they feared the threats to Irish Catholic culture emanating from the more secular cultures of mainland Europe. Their approach was, in the main, reactive. In the post-conciliar era, their understanding of morality broadened. Its thrust was more positive. The most obvious example of this was their concern to promote justice, both locally and globally, from the early 1970s. In this area, they became pro-active. State intervention was the *bête noire* of the bishops and the Catholic social movement in the 1950s, and was the issue which caused the first Church–state confrontation since independence. However, in the 1960s, the bishops were receptive to politicians' plans to play a far more active role in education, and in their statements throughout the 1970s they continually reminded governments of their moral responsibility to actively intervene and plan for a just society. This was directly influenced by the changed social teaching of the Church from the time of Pope John XXIII.

Whereas in the past, the bishops had adopted a very prescriptive tone in their relations with people, this was considerably modified in the post-Vatican II era. In the 1950s, they resisted changes in the drinking laws which, they asserted, would damage the moral fibre of Irish society. In the 1970s, they were resisting demands for changes in legislation in the area of sexual morality. Essentially their stance had not changed. But whereas the tenor of their statements in the 1950s was tendentious in the extreme, their argumentation through the 1970s was more nuanced, and the idiom in which they spoke had altered considerably. They were forced to be more conciliatory in their approach, because they were now being challenged by many who believed that they had no right to interfere in the domain of private morality. Formerly they had commanded with not a little arrogance and disdain. They had demanded and expected conformity. They now had to interact with a far more critically aware and educated laity: people who were changing fundamentally in all sorts of ways — economically and in terms of their life experiences, opportunities and perceptions of themselves. In the new cultural context, the bishops could no longer issue directives. Their position in Irish society had changed radically.

On the basis of the evidence presented, Catholicism was *the* predominant factor influencing Irish culture in the earlier period covered in this book. This had changed by the late 1970s. However, any study of culture must be sensitive to inconsistencies and contradictions. One such contradiction is in evidence at the very end of the period of this research, when one juxtaposes the family-planning legislation passed by the Dáil in 1979, with the record attendances of Irish Catholics at the various venues visited by Pope John Paul II on the occasion of his Irish visit in 1979.[16] This was the most public display of Irish Catholicism since the Eucharistic Congress in 1932. In order to understand the nature of change and the contradictions inherent in it, we need to reflect on the forces of change operating in Irish society and outside Ireland, and also in Catholicism in Ireland and in the wider world.

Change in Irish Catholic culture cannot be divorced from the changes that emerged in post-war industrial Europe. By virtue of historical circumstances and its geographical position, Ireland was insulated from social, educational and economic developments which took place in continental Europe in the aftermath of the Second World War. Such developments did not take place in Ireland until the late 1950s. From the perspective of the Irish bishops, the 'isolation' which was 'enjoyed' by Ireland was something for which to be grateful. They did not perceive that Ireland was cut off from the long-established intellectual and cultural tradition of Catholic Europe and that this might have left Irish Catholicism somewhat impoverished. They simply concentrated on the negative aspects of that culture, and both bishops and politicians had an exalted, somewhat superior idea of the uniqueness of Irish Catholicism.

Given the then strong position of Catholicism in Irish life, it is not surprising that the bishops could afford to be dogmatic and authoritarian in their approach to the laity. They saw themselves as occupying the high moral ground and were recognised as such by leading statesmen and politicians. However, even though the 1950s appeared to be a static time, there was, in fact, considerable cultural change taking place, which in due course threatened the influence wielded by the bishops. Factors influencing changing cultural patterns in the 1950s included the widespread rejection of the land, leading to a decisive population shift from country to town and emigration overseas. Other significant factors were people's increased mobility, access to BBC television along the eastern seaboard, and the influence of cinema, which was becoming increasingly popular.

Pressure groups also began to emerge and press for a more liberal society from the 1950s. During the 'mother and child' saga, the Irish Medical Association (IMA) happened to be on the side of the bishops, but the Irish Association of Civil Liberties, the Irish Adoption Society and the Licensed Grocers' and Vintners' Union were lobbying for changes that were opposed to the thinking of the bishops. What is important is that, from the 1950s, the bishops were in the position of having to react to the claims of such vested-interest groups.

The government's decision to enter on a programme of economic planning and renewal, from the late 1950s, added a further important dimension to socio-cultural change. The optimism and hope generated by the successful launch of this programme provided the catalyst which changed the psychological mood of the country. Economic success inevitably led to change in people's perceptions of themselves, their lifestyles, morale, confidence and sense of independence. Against this background, politicians who had been deferential in their attitude to the bishops began to assert themselves tentatively from the late 1950s. Through the 1960s and the 1970s, they became increasingly more pro-active and confident in furthering their aims, particularly in the area of education. The insights in Pope John XXIII's encyclical, *Mater et Magistra*, 1961, and the conciliar decrees predisposed the bishops to be more amenable to changes in the organisation and restructuring of education, and strengthened the hand of the politicians in other areas also. All of this points to what is perhaps one of the most important findings of this research — that Irish Catholic cultural change was being influenced by a combination of forces interacting with each other over time. They included political, economic and social changes and a radical re-orientation of Catholic theology.

In the Irish Church itself, forces of change were operating from the 1950s. The emergence of a Catholic clerical intelligentsia, pressing for renewal in the Irish Catholic ethos, was a significant factor. These men were concerned as to the extent that the faith of Irish Catholics was based on conformity to external prescripts and rules, and, on being shielded from influences which might threaten, what they saw, as being based on rather shaky foundations. Such thinkers began to express their views in journals like the *Furrow* from the early 1950s. The dissemination of their ideas was a crucial factor in changing Catholic culture. They anticipated and prepared the ground for changes instigated by the conciliar decrees. The Catholic clerical forces for change operated against a backdrop of economic, political and sociocultural changes that were happening in Ireland from the late 1950s. Economic prosperity, educational change, television, travel opportunities, foreign industry, tourism — all provided the catalysts which allowed Ireland to 'catch up' with her European counterparts. All of these forces coalesced in the 1960s and made for a much more sophisticated, educated, critical, Catholic laity, which had not existed in Ireland up to that time.

In continental Europe, churchmen from the turn of the century had to relate to a more critical and secularised laity. The Second Vatican Council changed the philosophical thrust of Catholicism in order to make it more responsive to how Europeans in a new sociocultural era were thinking and living. Cultural change was delayed in Ireland. It was gathering momentum precisely at the time when the Council was making its deliberations. In this, the Irish bishops were very fortunate, in that the conciliar decrees presented Irish Catholics with a philosophy which was responsive to the mood and challenges of the late twentieth century. Because of its questioning and revision of many aspects of Catholicism seen as immutable, and its openness to, and legitimisation of, new ideas, it greatly facilitated changes that were already under way in Ireland.

The Second Vatican Council was the catalyst which forged the link between the ideas that clerics like J.G. McGarry were advocating from the 1950s, and the new kind of society that was developing as a result of changes in the secular culture. When this new kind of society did evolve in Ireland, Catholics demanded that the bishops change their approach, and insisted on a lessening of the all-encompassing, influence of Catholicism on Irish culture. At the same time, they 'modified' their Catholicism to suit their changing cultural context.

Vatican II essentially gave its approval to the theologians who were attempting to develop a theology which would take cognisance of the fact that rapid socioeconomic and cultural changes since the turn of the century had caused confusion, alienation and estrangement in many people and, at the very minimum, new kinds of problems for Catholics. Change takes place at the nexus of the world of ideas and lived culture. Theology was influenced over a period of time by new ideas, which were attempting to understand people in the circumstances of their lives and the historical era in which they lived. In this regard, developments in philosophical thought, in particular, existentialism, Marxist theory, historicism, findings in psychology and advances in scientific knowledge, all had a profound impact on theological thought.

To a great extent, the pre-Vatican II Church had been primarily concerned with the salvation of man's soul in the next life. Relative to this, his condition in this life was seen as being of minor importance. It was seen as a given. A person simply accepted it as God's will. In this frame of reference, there was no great onus on theology to be responsive to the person, his situation or the era in which he was living, and dogmatic truths were defined for all time. From the perspective of Scholastic theology, they were independent of, and in a sense superior to, the person. It was not his place to question. Rather was the onus on him to conform. He had no autonomy.

At the time of the Council, Pope John XXIII endorsed the concept of historicity — the idea that theology cannot be separated from history. Essentially this meant that Church doctrinal formulae could not be seen as immutable in themselves, but rather had to be seen as historically conditioned answers given by the Church in a particular era to questions raised by the thought currents of that specific time. The corollary of this was that theology could not be static, but had to respond to the needs of people and their environment. This bespoke a profound change in Catholic thinking on the individual. The 'new' theology, to which the Vatican Council gave a form and unity by means of its debates and decrees, was the cornerstone of a new brand of Catholicism. It represented a fundamental philosophical shift in Catholic theology, which had profound implications for all aspects of Catholic culture and also for secular society.

From that time, the emphasis was on man as the subject rather than the object of his own history. He could influence the course of his own and others' history and, indeed, had a responsibility to do so, in an effort to bring about a more just social order. There was a new emphasis on personal autonomy and fulfilment in this life. The result was a more humanistic theology which made more allowances for human nature, in terms both of its strengths and of its frailties. This explains the more positive thrust of Catholicism in the post-Vatican II era, and also the fact that Catholics were far less inclined to conform without question to Church dogma.

The 'new' theology sought to redress the imbalance between the spiritual and temporal that had been at the core of the 'old' theology. The Council documents and papal encyclicals from the time of Pope John XXIII were, in fact, the Magna Carta of a new Catholicism worldwide. They facilitated the radicalisation of the Church. They provided the stimulus to Irish bishops and Church personnel to become considerably more interested and involved in issues having to do with social justice. The kind of critique of the status quo and involvement with social issues which Church personnel have engaged in since the 1970s would, in the 1950s, have been construed by the Church personnel of the time as subversive. All of these developments — the more person-centred thrust of theology, the fact that Church personnel became increasingly involved in people's temporal welfare, and the sociocultural changes which have been documented — have led, some would say, to a lessening of the sense of the transcendental.

The importance of the media cannot be overestimated in any consideration of cultural change. The influence of the newly established Irish television station from 1962 was of particular significance. Whereas the Irish media in the main could be described as Church-friendly in the 1950s, television took the lead from the 1960s in steering the media in general into a more critical stance, and this new development gathered momentum in the 1970s. Television was less predictable than radio or the print media, more spontaneous, and therefore more threatening. The kind of rigorous censorship of cinema and the printed word, which had operated in Ireland in the 1950s, was rendered ineffective in the television age. Television very quickly pushed back the frontiers of what had hitherto been considered taboo. The essence of the potency of TV arose from the fact that it could, and did, give a platform to *all* manner of critical views. As such, it became a very powerful medium, which gradually, as time went by, cast itself in the role of self-appointed task master, demanding accountability from any institution, regardless of its traditional standing.

The kind of coverage given to the Vatican Council in religious journals and the popular media was a crucial factor in changing Catholic culture. Whereas in the pre-conciliar era the Irish media were content to present bland reportage of ecclesiastical affairs, from the second session of the Council, the communications media were given access to accurate first-hand information via press conferences, which allowed reporters to give their readers an authentic insight into the workings and debates of the Council. This ensured that conciliar affairs did not remain the preserve of a specialist audience.

Popular media coverage gave the Council an immediacy and relevance in the general mind, which it would not otherwise have had. The window provided by journalists on the disagreements that cropped up in the Council debates was a new experience for Irish Catholics, which undoubtedly changed the way they perceived the kind of dogmatic statements that had emanated from their bishops up to that time. It also went some of the way to demystifying the mystique which had surrounded the Irish bishops. In this sense, for the Irish Catholic, the manner in which the Council was reported could almost be said to have had as crucial an impact as the actual deliberations of the Council itself.

Television as a medium thrives on open-ended discussion, argument and controversy and, arguably, nothing could have provided more controversial subject matter in the Irish context in the 1960s than religion-related affairs. The Council had urged a more open, collaborative concept of church, in which all the 'people of God' had the responsibility to air their respective views. Thus the way was clear for both clergy and laity to give voice publicly to opinions they held, which were not necessarily in keeping with the official Church line on matters. Indeed, if such opinions were sincerely held, it could well be interpreted that they had a duty to air them. Against this background, one of the changing features of Catholic culture in Ireland has been that what might formerly have been seen as a breach of solidarity giving rise to scandal, over time, came to be seen by many as their duty in conscience, to help build up the Church. Television, in particular, provided an opportunity for cross-fertilisation between the world of ideas and that of lived culture, and the very novelty of the medium in Ireland in the 1960s added to its potency. As such, it could be argued that it was *the* most significant catalyst in changing Catholic culture.

The late 1960s was a time when authority structures all over the western world were being questioned, and television everywhere facilitated this. Undoubtedly, Pope Paul VI's vacillation in making a decision on the birth-control issue and his failure to provide timely leadership added to the confusion that many people were feeling, and served to exacerbate further the crisis of authority experienced by the Church in the wake of the Council. Catholics were less convinced that any real certainties could be upheld anymore (particularly in the moral area), after the disputes of theologians in the Council debates and, in particular, the controversy which preceded and succeeded the promulgation of *Humanae Vitae.*

A very real dilemma for Catholics, not only in Ireland but worldwide, in the post-Vatican II, post-*Humanae Vitae* era was that authority figures, including the pope himself, were no longer recognised as having an unquestioned right to inform or make pronouncements on social and moral issues in particular. The Council had underlined the primacy of conscience. The fact that so many experts, professional theologians, priests and informed and respected lay Catholics were openly and publicly challenging the views of the magisterium meant that the obligation of informing one's conscience demanded that one listen to differing points of view. In this context, many Irish Catholics appear to have decided that while the bishops might pronounce on issues of private morality, they — the laity — were entitled to make up their own minds.

Whereas in the pre-conciliar era the bishops had acted autonomously, having little consultation with either priests or people, they were now more answerable to both. Their change of attitude was directly influenced by some of the key insights underlined by the Council. Whereas the Church had been conceived in the past in hierarchical terms, the Council defined it as the 'people of God', emphasising the importance of the bishop and his ministry, but also stressing the key role that the laity could play in furthering the mission of the whole Church. The bishops' authority was conceptualised as service, and the importance of consultation at all levels of the Church was stressed, because each sector (bishops, priests and laity) was seen to have its own unique charisms to offer, and dialogue and collaboration were seen to provide the key to reading and interpreting the 'signs of the times' in a meaningful way. In this context, the bishops could no longer regard themselves as having a monopoly on wisdom.

At the outset of this research the title 'the transformation of Catholic culture in Ireland' was set aside, in favour of 'changing Catholic culture', because it was felt that the former might be too strong a term, and might pre-empt the findings. At this remove, it is fair to say that Catholic culture in Ireland was, in fact, truly transformed over three decades — the evidence summarised above forces one to that conclusion. So, while in statistical terms there might not have been a significant decline in the numbers of those who professed themselves to be practising Catholics, the essence of Catholicism in terms of its outlook, how it influenced its adherents, how it influenced the Irish cultural landscape, how it was presented, and, perhaps most importantly of all, how it was interpreted and translated into the way of life of Irish Catholics in the thirty-year period from 1950 to 1979 has been utterly transformed. The rate of change since 1979 has accelerated, and the nature of that change has been even more dramatic.

EPILOGUE

On Monday, 16 October 1978, Cardinal Felici appeared on the balcony of St Peter's Basilica in Rome to make the traditional announcement, '*habemus papam*', followed by the name of the new pope, Karol Wojtyla. The election of the Polish Cardinal Archbishop of Krakow, the first non-Italian pope in 455 years, was an extraordinary turn of events, and Pope John Paul II's influence, both politically and on Catholic culture worldwide since that time has been profound.[1] By the time he succeeded to the papacy, a much more liberal Catholic climate prevailed, and Catholics were more inclined to follow their own conscience in matters concerning sexual morality, priestly celibacy, laicisation and inter-church relations.

Any consideration of how Catholicism evolved after 1979 must take cognisance of the very 'hands-on' influence of Pope John Paul II. Whereas Paul VI may have been wary of many aspects of the 'new Catholicism', and his response hesitant and indecisive, John Paul II showed no such hesitancy. From the outset, he resisted the more democratic Catholicism which had evolved from the time of John XXIII's papacy and put in place what Seán O'Riordan CSsR has termed a 'decisional model of church'. Writing in 1991, O'Riordan emphasised the importance of recognising the impact of the 'phenomenon of the universal Church, newly centralised in Rome, and not merely of the Irish Church'.[2]

The enormous crowds that turned out to greet the Pope on the occasion of his three-day visit to Ireland in September 1979 appeared to echo the Catholic fervour and devotion of the 1950s, and, at the same time, John Paul II seemed to be the very epitome of a more 'relaxed' Catholicism. But in neither case did the image reflect the reality. Irish Catholicism had changed fundamentally by 1979. And Pope John Paul II was, it was felt by many commentators, applying the brakes to the more liberal Catholicism which had developed in the post-conciliar era, and was also attempting to re-assert papal authority in the aftermath of *Humanae Vitae*. To this end, he became a travelling pope. In the period that elapsed between his election as pope on 16 October 1978 and his arrival in Ireland on 29 September 1979, he had already become a highly visible figure on the world stage. He had been to Mexico, Santo Domingo, the Bahamas and his native Poland. From Ireland, he travelled to the United States where he addressed the general assembly of the United Nations.

In his homily in the Phoenix Park, Dublin, on 29 September, he warned that Irish society was now being confronted with 'values and trends' that had formerly been 'alien' to it, and that whereas sacred principles had provided the guidelines for human behaviour in the past, in modern-day society materialistic values and consumerism were endangering 'freedom, the sacredness of life, the indissolubility of marriage [and] the true sense of human sexuality'.[3] In his homily at the Mass for the youth, in Galway, on 30 September 1979, he cautioned young people. 'Do not close your eyes to the moral sickness that stalks your society today'.[4] In Limerick, at his Mass on 1 October, he challenged his audience: 'Irish people have to choose today their way forward', whether that be the path of materialism or of 'the things of the spirit'.[5] Again, he returned to the theme of 'the sanctity and the indissolubility of the marriage bond' and the destabilising effect of divorce on the institution of marriage, and went on to emphasise that 'marriage must include openness to the gift of children' and also the importance of having 'an absolute and holy respect for the sacredness of human life from the first moment of its conception'.[6]

In all of his speeches he addressed and challenged the more liberal influences which had come to prevail in Irish society in the late 1960s and particularly in the 1970s. Ironically, Pope John Paul II used all the trappings of the modern consumer society, which he so decried, to convey his message. In stark contrast to the Church's former sceptical attitude towards the modern communications media, John Paul II, a consummate communicator, was totally at home in the world of the media. In many ways, he resembled a modern-day superstar, complete with giant stage and specially designed 'popemobile'. Using the acting experience of his younger days to maximum effect, he displayed an extraordinary ability to win over the crowds by every word and gesture, as witnessed by the emotional response he evoked from his young audience in Galway, when he finished his homily with the highly charged, never-to-be-forgotten sentence, 'Young people of Ireland, I love you!'[7] All of this illustrates the extent to which changing cultural patterns have impacted on the lives of Catholics, and even on the institution of the papacy.

In an era characterised by the image-maker, the public relations expert and the spin-doctor, ironically what perhaps matters most of all when assessing the impact of John Paul II on Catholic culture worldwide is that his own personal charm and charisma have guaranteed him a wide audience, despite the traditional, conservative tone of his message, but the extent to which Catholics have been willing to apply his teaching to their everyday lives is a moot point. His message has not halted the further progress of more liberal developments in Irish society in the 1980s and 1990s. Essentially, from the early 1970s, Ireland was already on course to evolve into the kind of society warned against by John Paul II, and this fundamentally changed society is now influencing Irish Catholicism, whereas formerly the position was reversed — Catholicism was influencing Irish society.

The 1980s was a troubled decade for both Church and state, and for Church–state relations in Ireland. The economic situation had been deteriorating in the late 1970s. In 1979, the unemployment figure was 90,000.[8] The national debt was £6,540 million. In 1980, this had increased to £7,896 million, and it further increased to £10,196 million in 1981.[9] As in the 1950s, emigration was once again becoming the safety valve for a failed economy. Between 1981 and April 1986, in the region of 72,000 people emigrated and, by the end of the decade, the emigration figures had reached the heights recorded in the 1950s. By the early 1990s, the unemployment figure had exceeded 300,000.[10] Jack Lynch resigned as Taoiseach and leader of Fianna Fáil on 5 December 1979 and was replaced by Charles Haughey. On 9 January 1980, Haughey made his now infamous television broadcast on the economic state of the nation, declaring that 'as a community we are living away beyond our means ... at a rate which is simply not justified by the amount of goods and services we are producing'.[11] He emphasised the need for fiscal rectitude. The country was still suffering the effects of the second oil crisis; the agricultural sector was under pressure; the PAYE sector took to the streets of Dublin demanding reform of the taxation system; and the situation in Northern Ireland was rapidly deteriorating.

Against this background, the bishops' interest in issues of justice — socio-economic and political — which was a key feature of changing Catholicism in the 1970s, continued into the 1980s and 1990s. Cardinal Tomás Ó Fiaich, who had succeeded Conway as Archbishop of Armagh, visited the Maze Prison in Belfast in August 1980, where the prisoners in the H Blocks of the prison were engaged in the 'dirty protest', and later in a series of hunger strikes in pursuit of 'special category' political prisoner status. He argued for concessions before it was too late. On 13 October 1980, the Irish Commission for Justice and Peace issued a statement on the H Block protest.[12] There were further interventions by Cardinal Ó Fiaich, and Pope John Paul II sent his secretary, John Magee (now Bishop of Cloyne), to Northern Ireland, but it was not until 3 October 1981 that the protest was called off and, by that time, ten prisoners had died. Church leaders and groups also made several statements in relation to the deteriorating economic situation in the Republic.[13] However, the 1980s are also particularly remembered for the constitutional referenda held in 1983 (abortion) and 1986 (divorce), and the controversies surrounding their outcomes held considerable implications for Catholic cultural change.

One of the most obvious features of Irish Catholic culture — politicians' willingness to support the Catholic moral code by means of legislation — which was changing slowly but surely from the late 1950s to the late 1970s, has changed dramatically since then. Politicians since that time have pursued an increasingly independent line in social legislation and are influenced far more by the pressing demands of their electorate than by any consideration of the advice or warnings of the bishops. This is, of course, because the electorate that they serve is no longer as disposed to listen to the advice of bishops as in the past. Two very significant catalysts for change have been the ongoing sectarian tensions in Northern Ireland and the growing political importance of the women's movement.

The Haughey government was replaced in June 1981 by a Fine Gael–Labour coalition, led by Garret FitzGerald. FitzGerald very quickly sought to press again for constitutional reform, as he had done when he was Minister for Foreign Affairs in the 1970s. Speaking on radio on 27 September 1981, he stated, 'If I were a Northern Protestant today, I cannot see how I could be attracted to getting involved with a state that is itself sectarian.' While he allowed that the Republic was not 'acutely sectarian in the way that Northern Ireland was', he went on to say that 'our laws and our constitution, our practices, our attitudes reflect those of a majority ethos and are not acceptable to Protestants in Northern Ireland'.[14] The Fine Gael–Labour coalition collapsed in a matter of months, but FitzGerald's constitutional reform agenda did, in fact, set the tone for the 1980s. Garret FitzGerald once again returned to power in November 1982.

In April 1981, an anti-abortion lay pressure group was formed, calling itself the Pro-Life Amendment Campaign.[15] Known as PLAC, it was campaigning for the insertion into the Constitution of an amendment specifically outlawing abortion and was formed against the background of the increasing availability of abortion in western societies, and also a growing awareness of the number of Irish women travelling to England every year for abortion. Because of the instability of the political situation — there were three elections in the space of eighteen months — the pressure group was able to exact promises from political leaders.[16] Despite reservations, Garret FitzGerald accepted the wording of a proposed amendment to the constitution, which had been prepared by the Fianna Fáil government before leaving power, and this was put to the electorate on 7 September 1983. The eighth amendment to the constitution was passed by 66.45 per cent in favour to 32.87 per cent against, in an electoral turnout of 53.67 per cent, after a particularly acrimonious and divisive campaign.[17] While the campaign was led (in the main) by lay Catholics, a statement from the Episcopal Conference, published on 12 August 1983, recognised the right of each person to vote according to conscience but added that the bishops were 'convinced that a clear majority in favour of the amendment will greatly contribute to the continued protection of unborn human life in the laws of our country'.[18]

To some commentators at the time, the result represented a reaction and a victory by conservative Catholics against the liberalisation which had taken place in Irish society since the late 1960s. It is also likely that the visit of Pope John Paul II, and his warnings about the dangers of the permissive society, were the catalysts which encouraged the consolidation of conservative lay Catholic groups who, from that time, increasingly resisted liberalising tendencies. The bishops, however, kept to the formula they had worked out through the 1970s — namely that, in matters of personal/sexual morality, Catholics should follow their conscience — but they reserved the right to voice their opinion on issues of morality, where legislation or constitutional reform had implications for the good of society, as they saw it. As in the 1970s, there were dissenting voices among the bishops and indeed clergy speaking from the pulpit. In particular, Archbishop Ryan of Dublin and Bishop McNamara of Kerry departed from the agreed official statement and, in individual pastoral letters, urged support for the amendment.[19] While the result in some quarters was seen as a victory by the more conservative lobby for the Catholicism of pre-conciliar times, the result also reflected a new and deep urban/rural divide in Irish society, with predominantly rural constituencies overwhelmingly voting yes while urban, largely middle-class areas provided the strongest resistance to the amendment. In Dublin where the result was 51.6 per cent Yes, and 48.3 per cent No, five constituencies opposed the amendment. The seamless Catholic culture of the past was well and truly gone.

The Pro-Life Amendment Campaign to a great extent overshadowed a very important event which began in Dublin Castle on 30 May 1983 under the chairmanship of Colm Ó hEocha. This was the New Ireland Forum, an idea conceived by John Hume and Garret FitzGerald.[20] Since the Anglo-Irish Summit, which had taken place in Dublin Castle between Taoiseach Charles Haughey and Prime Minister Margaret Thatcher, on 8 December 1980, there had been a recognition that any possibility of peace and stability in Northern Ireland necessitated 'the further development of the unique relationship between the two countries'.[21] But the hunger strikes in which ten Republicans had died before they were called off on 3 October 1981 had further polarised the two communities in Northern Ireland. The idea of the Forum was to explore the nature of Irish society, with a view to bringing about the kind of social and cultural changes which would allow all traditions on the island to live in peace and harmony. All constitutional parties were invited to attend the Forum, which held twenty-eight private sessions and thirteen public sessions and received 317 written submissions from both Ireland and abroad.

The hierarchy's submission consisted of five papers in all, dealing with pluralism, the family, ecumenism, alienation of Catholics in Northern Ireland, and the Catholic school system in Northern Ireland. On the subject of pluralism, their written submission to the Forum, January 1984, provides a clear insight into the thinking of the bishops:

> To require in the name of pluralism that public policy tolerate or even facilitate forms of public morality of which the majority of the citizens could not approve may sometimes be reasonable in the interests of the common good, of harmony between all citizens; but where the offence to the moral principles of the majority of the citizens would be disproportionately serious, it is not unreasonable to require sacrifice of minorities in the interests of the common good.[22]

This was a significant statement from the hierarchy regarding its position on the debate on a more pluralist Ireland, which had been ongoing since the 1970s. While it was considerably more nuanced than the views expressed by

Bishop Newman in his interchange with Conor Cruise O'Brien in the 1970s, there was no essential difference.

The Church's position on matters of public morality was further elaborated by the Catholic Church delegation made up of bishops, senior clergy and lay people,[23] when the bishops appeared at a public session of the Forum on 9 February 1984. Leading the delegation, Bishop Cahal Daly of Down and Connor (Archbishop of Armagh from 1990) asserted:

> The Catholic Church in Ireland totally rejects the concept of a confessional state. We have not sought and we do not seek a Catholic state for a Catholic people. We believe that the alliance of Church and State is harmful for the Church and harmful for the State.[24]

He continued:

> So far as the Catholic Church and questions of public morality are concerned the position of the Church over recent decades has been clear and consistent. We have repeatedly declared that we in no way seek to have the moral teaching of the Catholic Church become the criterion of constitutional change or to have the principles of Catholic faith enshrined in civil law.[25]

While the availability of contraception was the issue that dominated the 1970s, the question of divorce, rejected out of hand by Cardinal Conway and Archbishop McQuaid when it was raised in the early 1970s, still remained to be resolved. This had first been raised arising out of the recommendations of the Commission on the Constitution set up in 1967, and the increasing instances of marriage breakdown and the deteriorating situation in Northern Ireland ensured that it remained a live and intensely emotive issue in the Republic.

The Forum provided the opportunity for politicians to 'test the waters' in this area. When John Kelly of Fine Gael asked whether the bishops would give an assurance that, in a referendum, they would not use their influence against the removal of the constitutional prohibition on divorce, Bishop Daly reiterated the official line, which was that it was the responsibility of the legislators to draft the proposal and that if there were adverse consequences for the moral life of society, the bishops would state their views accordingly, while at the same time respecting the consciences of the legislators.[26] The thrust of the other bishops' contributions was that divorce was not in the best interests of society and that its introduction would, in fact, exacerbate the problem of marital breakdown.[27]

Nevertheless, the proceedings of the New Ireland Forum undoubtedly gave Garret FitzGerald some confidence to pursue his 'crusade' for constitutional reform, which he had announced in a radio interview on 27 September 1981. On 7 February 1985, Barry Desmond, Minister for Health in the Fine

Gael–Labour coalition government, published the Health (Family Planning) (Amendment) Bill, which proposed to amend the 1979 Family Planning Act, to make non-medical contraceptives available without a medical prescription to persons of age 18 and over. Bishop Joseph Cassidy of Clonfert, speaking for the bishops, reiterated the 1973 guidelines,[28] and said that the Episcopal Conference had not changed its position since the New Ireland Forum. Bishops McNamara[29] and Newman,[30] in particular, were more trenchant in their arguments, and departed from the official line.

While the bishops' official position was to stand back from the controversy, the considerable political turmoil that it caused bore testament to the fact that legislation for public morality was going to be problematic from then on, regardless of the stance of the Catholic bishops. Three Fine Gael deputies voted against the Bill — Alice Glenn, Tom O'Donnell and Oliver J. Flanagan — as did one Labour Deputy, Seán Treacy. Desmond O'Malley made a speech in the Dáil defending the Family Planning Amendment Bill, warning that if it was defeated, the two elements who would be best pleased, ironically, would be the Unionists in Northern Ireland and the extremist Catholic wing in the Republic. It was to cause his expulsion from the Fianna Fáil party.[31]

The Dáil passed the Family Planning Amendment Bill by a narrow margin on 21 February 1985.[32] It was seen by some as a victory for the government in the second round of the battle between Church and state for the soul of Ireland. Referring to the confrontational atmosphere surrounding the proposal and passage of the bill, John Whyte wrote the following:

> If all the bishops had spoken in the same terms as Dr Cassidy and Dr Comiskey, there would have been no opportunity to describe Mr Desmond's Act of 1985 as a defeat for the Church — any more than Mr Haughey's Act of 1979 could be described in such terms. It was the statements of Dr McNamara and Dr Newman which turned the episode into a confrontation, in which one side or the other was bound to appear as a victor. Since they lost, the Church appeared to have suffered its most clear-cut defeat since the establishment of the State.[33]

However, there was another factor more in evidence than in the late 1970s, which made the atmosphere more emotionally charged, and that was the lay-led conservative Catholic right-wing group comprising SPUC (the Society for the Protection of the Unborn Child), the Pro-Life Amendment Campaign, the Irish Catholic Doctors' Guild, the Council of Social Concern and many others[34] who felt very threatened by, and were fiercely opposed to, Garret FitzGerald's professed campaign to reform the confessional aspects of the constitution.[35]

Probably the most dramatic evidence that there were groups throughout the country who were totally out of step with such thinking was, ironically, to make headline news in the week when the bill was passed. This was the reported sighting of a 'moving' statue in Asdee, Co. Kerry.[36] The claim by a group of children to have seen a statue of the Madonna and child, in the local church, open its eyes and move its hands resulted in the church becoming a place of pilgrimage for some months. This was only the first of several such sightings and claims throughout the country in the summer of 1985, the best-known being at the grotto of Ballinspittle in west Cork, where seven local people claimed to have seen the statue of the Virgin Mary move on 22 July. Almost a half a million people reportedly visited the shrine in 1985.[37] There was a resurgence of Marian devotion, directed at shrines throughout the country, in the 1980s. This and the claims of some devotees that they had seen some statues move may not have been entirely unrelated to the euphoria surrounding the pope's visit in 1979.

As in the case of the Pro-Life campaigners, these were (predominantly) lay Catholics, and the bishops and Church personnel distanced themselves from the incidents. Bishop Michael Murphy of Cork and Ross issued a statement through his press officer, on 30 July, stating that 'direct supernatural intervention is a very rare happening in life, so common sense would demand that we approach the claims made concerning the grotto at Ballinspittle with prudence and caution'.[38] Writing in the *Sunday Independent*, Fr Gabriel Daly OSA referred to the scene at Ballinspittle 'as a replica of old style evening devotions that not so long ago could be seen up and down the country', adding that, 'the prayers, the hymns, the manner of recitation ... were the same'. But he saw the phenomenon as a failure on the part of the pastors and teachers in presenting the Good News, 'when people have to turn to moving statues in order to satisfy their spiritual needs'.[39]

The fact that irrespective or otherwise of the influence of the Catholic Church authorities, a wholly different kind of Catholic Ireland existed was probably as little understood by Garret FitzGerald, when he announced details of the coalition government's proposal to hold a referendum on 26 June 1986 to remove the constitutional ban on divorce. The bishops, in response, issued a fifteen-page pastoral letter, entitled *Marriage, the Family and Divorce*, an abridged version of their 1985 pastoral letter *Love is for Life*.[40] Two weeks before the referendum, they announced that they were 'convinced that the proposed amendment would weaken rather than strengthen marriage and the family'. The statement continued:

> The questions raised in this debate are not simply political. They are also moral. Each legislator and each voter is faced with a moral decision. Changes in civil law can influence moral attitudes and affect the whole moral atmosphere of society.[41]

At the press conference, when the statement was issued, the hierarchy's official spokesman, Bishop Cassidy, insisted that Catholic people were not being told 'how to vote on this matter', and that 'conscience [was] the ultimate arbiter', implying that a Catholic could vote in favour of the removal of the constitutional ban on divorce without incurring guilt.[42] This was a new departure for the bishops. It was a new interpretation of informed conscience, which allowed Catholics to have conscientious objections to the Church's teaching and to vote accordingly. However, not all of the bishops kept to the tenor of the collective statement. Once again, Newman did not go along with the official line,[43] nor did McNamara of Dublin, who was adamant that the idea that the introduction of divorce could be morally good for society 'finds no basis in Catholic social and moral doctrine'.[44]

The fact that the hierarchy as a body had gone further in its statement on this occasion may be attributed to several factors. Firstly, the kind of acrimony surrounding these issues had been likened to the divisions and bitterness experienced at the time of the Civil War. Secondly, the kind of monolithic Church of the 1950s, which had been changing from the 1960s, was well and truly a feature of the past by the 1980s. Thirdly, FitzGerald at all times presented the proposed change in the context of his crusade for a more pluralist society in the Republic, which would improve relations with Northern Ireland and between the Unionists and nationalists north of the border. In the Dáil, he highlighted the link between the divorce referendum and his Northern Ireland policy, on 16 May[45] (just six weeks prior to the referendum), still basking in the successful signing of the Anglo–Irish Agreement and buoyed up by opinion polls which, until the week before the vote, recorded a steady increase in the number of people who supported the introduction of divorce.[46]

However, the actual results on the day reflected the resilience of traditional Catholic values — 63 per cent of those who voted rejected the government's proposal. The result was a repeat of the 1983 abortion referendum, except that on this occasion, the turnout was considerably higher, at 63 per cent of the electorate.[47] Again, Dublin constituencies voted (narrowly) in favour of divorce, whereas the majority of rural constituencies voted overwhelmingly against the amendment.[48] In an article in the *Furrow,* Laurence Ryan, Coadjutor Bishop of Kildare and Leighlin (who succeeded in 1987), captured some of the intolerance and resentment generated during the campaign and in the aftermath of the vote: 'It is doubtful if a democratic decision by the electorate ever before met with such resentment ... a resentment which amounted to a rejection of the people's right to make the decision they made'. He added:

> We still have some distance to go as a society in acknowledging clearly the respective roles of the Church and civil society in matters which concern them both and to resist the temptation to present issues as Church and State confrontations for polemic purposes.[49]

He added that 'spokespeople for the Church should set a standard here by not overstepping their own role as Ministers of the Good News and by showing tolerance in regard to excesses by others'[50] — an oblique reference, perhaps, to some of the more hysterical, injudicious contributions to the debate on both sides. To the extent that these issues were seen as a battle of strength between Church and state for the hearts and minds of Irish people, in the 1980s, despite setbacks, the Church was seen by many as having won out! However, in all of these social/moral issues on which the Church held strong views, the situation had changed totally by the mid-1990s.

Following the controversial X case in 1992, when a 14-year-old alleged rape victim became pregnant and was prevented by court injunction from travelling to Britain for an abortion, the Supreme Court ruled on 5 March 1992 that abortion was legal in limited cases, where there was a real danger that the pregnant woman was liable to commit suicide.[51] The Episcopal Conference issued a statement in the same month, recording the bishops' 'dismay at the recent Supreme Court judgement which envisages legal abortion in the Republic of Ireland'. In their statement, the bishops asserted that 'no court judgement, no act of legislation can make it morally right'.[52] They pointed out that, as bishops, they had a duty to make their 'contribution to building a society which reflects the dignity of human beings in the light of the Gospel'. Having placed their view of the situation on record, they stated that it was now up to the legislators to 'exercise their responsibility to protect the lives of unborn children'.[53] In a referendum held on 25 November 1992, the electorate voted in favour of the right to travel and the right to information on abortion services, but rejected the wording of the substantive issue relating to the circumstances under which abortion is permissible.[54]

In 1992 also, a further liberalisation of the law in relation to family planning meant that contraceptive devices became freely available throughout the country.[55] The Episcopal Conference issued a statement on the Health (Family Planning) (Amendment) Bill 1992, on 17 July 1992. The tone was matter of fact:

> The Health/Family Planning Amendment Bill has been passed through the Oireachtas and is now law. It has serious implications for moral behaviour. As pastors, we feel obliged to recall the moral law for those entrusted by God to our pastoral care.[56]

Addressing the strong arguments for widespread availability of condoms in the fight against Aids and other sexually transmitted diseases, the bishops held that 'the only sure protection against contracting Aids sexually is to abstain from sexual intercourse outside a permanent relationship with the same partner who has also been faithful'.[57] The fact that legislators well and truly ignored the advice of the hierarchy was further underlined when, in the following year, the Health Promotion Unit of the Department of Health released a series of very explicit adverts on both television and radio, which promoted safe sex through the use of condoms.[58]

In the following year, 1993, legislation was passed which legalised homosexual practices which, in Catholic Church teaching, are seen as morally wrong.

The legislation came about as a result of a directive from the European Court of Human Rights, which called for the decriminalisation of homosexual acts between consenting adults.[59] The bill as passed by the Oireachtas defined adults as people aged 17 and over.[60] A statement issued by the hierarchy was identical in thrust and tenor to all those issued since 1973. The formula was the same; only the issues changed. 'This teaching of the Church is independent of State law. No change in State law can change the moral law'.[61] When one compares the objective clinical tone of these statements to the peremptory tone of the bishops in their statement on the intoxicating liquor law in 1950, the sea-change in approach may be appreciated. In a sense, the only clue as to the bishops' strong disapproval of the legislation was their reference to 'acts which are sinful', and even then they stressed: 'the Church does not expect that acts which are sinful should, by that very fact, be made criminal offences'.[62] The expression 'sinful' attributed to those who were seeking change in the drink laws in 1950 was, in the 1990s, reserved for what the Church saw as very 'grave matter' (the term used in the old catechism when defining mortal sin). In all of these recent statements, the bishops make very clear the distinction between Church teaching on morality and state law.

The legislation legalising homosexual acts is interesting on a number of levels. In 1983, the Supreme Court had rejected (in a three to two majority ruling) an appeal by David Norris, an executive member of the National Gay Federation, against a decision of the High Court, which dismissed an action in which he sought a declaration that two Acts (inherited from the period of British rule), which made homosexual acts and conduct illegal, were unconstitutional.[63] In its judgement delivered on 22 April 1983, the Chief Justice, Mr Justice O'Higgins, explained that a key element in the deliberations that led to his rejection, and two of his fellow judges' rejection, of the plaintiff's case was the preamble to the constitution, which 'proudly asserts the existence of God in the most Holy Trinity', and points to the people of Ireland as 'humbly acknowledging their obligation to Our Divine Lord Jesus Christ'. Against the background of such a preamble, they could not see their way to declaring these laws unconstitutional, given that they 'had existed for hundreds of years prohibiting unnatural sexual conduct which Christ's teaching held to be sinful'.[64] While this refers to Christian, and not simply to Catholic, teaching, it is none the less significant.

As well as the European Court of Human Rights, Irish citizens in more recent times also have access to the European Court of Justice (usually referred to as the European Court) if they consider that their rights have been infringed.[65] From 1973, the time of Ireland's accession to the EEC, the legal framework within which the Irish government operated was no longer confined to domestic law. The European Court has also to be reckoned with when framing legislation. Community institutions have become increasingly active in the areas of social welfare and human rights. So, in the area of social legislation, by the 1980s and 1990s, not only were the bishops less able to influence politicians, but politicians themselves did not have the last word as to legislation, nor did the national courts have absolute discretion as to its interpretation.

The divorce referendum held in 1995 was the next milestone. As in the case of the previous referenda, much of the lobbying in favour of a no vote, in relation to the removal of the constitutional ban on divorce, was by members of the Catholic laity organised into various anti-divorce groups. The Episcopal Conference issued a statement[66] and individual bishops went beyond this — in particular, Archbishop Connell of Dublin[67] and Bishop Flynn of Achonry[68] (the hierarchy's spokesman). Bishop Flynn's response to journalists' questions, that Catholics who divorced and remarried 'may not receive the sacraments while living as husband and wife in a second union', became particularly contentious, to such an extent that Bishops Ryan of Kildare and Leighlin and Duffy of Clogher subsequently entered the fray in an effort to tone down his remarks.[69]

The Taoiseach John Bruton, and his coalition partners, Dick Spring, the Labour Party leader, and Proinsias De Rossa, leader of Democratic Left, all campaigned for a yes vote, as did Bertie Ahern, Fianna Fáil leader, and Mary Harney, leader of the Progressive Democrats. Clerical opposition to the official Church position had become more vocal by this time. Preaching in Drogheda two weeks before the referendum, the Augustinian theologian, Fr Gabriel Daly, reminded Catholics that the Second Vatican Council had taught that they must 'recognise the legitimacy of different and even conflicting views'. When questioned about Bishop Flynn's comments in relation to the sacraments, he explained that the bishop would have felt 'obliged to restate what traditional Church law says', but said that he would have expected the bishop to add 'some pastorally sensitive qualifications'. He expressed his surprise that,

> the position should be stated with such clinical bluntness, without any recognition that there are many priests, in Ireland and abroad, who would take a much more positive and pastoral view of concrete circumstances.[70]

It is noteworthy that President Robinson, speaking in Dublin Castle two days before the referendum, pointed to the importance of tolerance and quoted extensively from an address by Gabriel Daly, in which he expressed the view that the Christian Church of the future 'will play its part in society without seeking to have its moral convictions embodied in civil law'.[71] A factor which must be considered when analysing Catholic cultural change is the increased willingness of theologians such as Daly and other prominent Church personnel to voice their opinions candidly, even when their views do not coincide with official Church teaching. This has undoubtedly contributed to the development of a more intellectual Catholic elite, which Peter Connolly aspired to in the 1950s (Chapter 4, ref. 58). Two obvious examples would be Mary Robinson and Garret FitzGerald, both of whom have influenced significant constitutional/ legislative change.[72]

The referendum proposal was carried but by a very narrow margin, less than 1 per cent — 50.28 per cent of the electorate voted in favour and 49.72 per cent voted against the proposal.[73] Again, the urban–rural divide was reflected in the voting pattern, with rural constituencies voting along traditional lines. Just over six years later, following the publication of a Green Paper and a report by an all-party Oireachtas committee, the Fianna Fáil-Progressive Democrat coalition government, led by Taoiseach Bertie Ahern, announced that a further referendum on the issue of abortion was to be held.[74] Voters would be asked to vote Yes or No to the terms of the Protection of Human Life in Pregnancy Bill, 2002. If approved in the referendum and subsequently enacted by the Oireachtas, this would outlaw suicide as a ground for abortion, found to be constitutional by the Supreme Court in 1992.[75] The bishops welcomed the proposal, which they stated 'would appear to set aside deficient aspects of the X case judgement, including the acceptance of the risk of suicide as a legitimate ground for justifying abortion'.[76] While they shared 'the concern of many groups and individuals that the new proposal strengthens legal protection for the unborn only after implantation in the womb' and as such appeared to be 'a limited or imperfect measure', they believed that 'Catholic voters should feel free in conscience to support this measure, even if it is viewed as less than might have been desired'.[77] When the date of the referendum was set for 6 March 2002, they reiterated their support for the proposal 'as a significant improvement in the current unsatisfactory situation', describing it as an opportunity that should 'not be lost'.[78] On the weekend before the referendum, twenty-four pastoral letters were issued by bishops of dioceses wholly or partly in the Republic of Ireland.[79] The pastorals were along similar lines, urging support for the proposed change in the constitution.

However, this was not to be. In a result, which was a virtual replica of that of the divorce referendum of 1995, the electorate rejected the referendum proposal by a margin of less than 1 per cent — 50.42 per cent voted No, while 49.58 per cent voted Yes.[80] The urban–rural divide was once again decisively confirmed with the large cities of Dublin, Cork, Galway and Limerick voting No, while predominantly rural constituencies all voted Yes. While a note of caution must be struck regarding too hasty an interpretation of the outcome, given that the most extreme wing of the pro-life movement urged a No vote, considering that the amendment did not go far enough in protecting the unborn from the moment of conception, at the same time it is difficult to take issue with those commentators who have seen this as the final definitive rebuff to the influence of the Catholic Church in Ireland. *The Irish Times* in its editorial the following day proclaimed that the 'grand alignment of Fianna Fáil, the Catholic church and the official Pro-Life campaign has, for the first time, failed to produce a majority on a sensitive moral issue in middle Ireland after a lengthy and co-ordinated campaign'.[81] Be that as it may, the Bishops' Conference spokesperson, Fr Martin Clarke, when asked for his reaction on the RTÉ news on the evening that the result was confirmed, while expressing disappointment, responded that we must 'accept with serenity the people's will'.[82] Roles have surely been reversed — whereas many journalists cannot resist the temptation to be triumphant, some Church personnel have become humble. When one considers the reaction of the bishops, as recorded, in the late 1960s and early 1970s, to issues of contraception and divorce, to say nothing of abortion, it is clear that all these developments represent a watershed in Catholic culture. It begs the question, why such a profound change in a thirty-year period?

Having documented change, one way of trying to understand the background is to examine statistical data and survey material of which there has been no shortage since the 1970s. In the 1991 census, 91.6 per cent of the population professed themselves as Catholic, a slight drop on the 1981 figure of 93.1 per cent.[83] While surveys in the 1970s and 1980s showed a decline in weekly Mass attendance, from 91 per cent in 1974 to 87 per cent in 1984 to 82 per cent in 1988/89, this was still very high relative to Catholic practice in other European countries.[84] In the *European Values Study* conducted between 1981 and 1990, in which the Republic of Ireland was compared to other European countries, the weekly Mass attendance in 1981 was 87 per cent, and in 1990 it was found to be 85 per cent, compared to a European average of 42 per cent.[85] In his 1988/89 survey, Mac Gréil found that 'the majority of the sample had a positive and optimistic vision of the "world" and of "human nature"'.[86] Surveys have shown a decline in attendance at confession and an increase in weekly reception of Holy Communion[87] (see Appendices B and I). More relaxed attitudes, it would appear, have dulled the sense of sin which was a feature of Irish Catholicism in the past, making people very fearful of approaching the Communion rail unless they had first attended confession.

Another interesting finding (already recorded in 1974) is that, despite the high level of practice, one third of the respondents in the *European Values Study* reported that religious principles seldom if ever influenced their behaviour, and this figure increased to 55 per cent for city-born and 61.6 per cent for the under-30 age group. Whereas a high proportion of the respondents — 92 per cent — accepted the Church's teaching on the Assumption, and 94 per cent its teaching on the Trinity, when it came to moral teaching which had a bearing on how they lived their lives, such as the prohibition of divorce and contraception, only a minority accepted the teaching of the Church.[88] Almost all of the surveys recorded a decline in practice among young people, city-reared, males, those living in urban areas — in particular Dublin — skilled and semi-skilled workers and the unemployed.[89]

In the 1988/89 survey, the urban–rural divide was the most significant factor having a bearing on sacramental practice and, in particular, on Mass attendance. Pointing to this trend, Nic Ghiolla Phádraig noted the rapid urbanisation of the past twenty-five years as having 'contributed to an overall change in culture which is less conducive to traditional religion'.[90] That said, while evidence is uneven, there are indications that popular piety is holding its own. While down on previous decades, the number of pilgrims who climbed Croagh Patrick in 1999 was 25,000 and in the millennium year 30,000.[91] There has been a significant decline in those undertaking the three-day pilgrimage to Lough Derg since 1993. In 1992, the figure recorded was 22,122. This dropped to 18,615 in 1993, and had dropped to 11,079 in 2001 (Appendix L). Any temptation, however, to deduce from these figures that popular piety is on the wane would be to fly in the face of events of the very recent past in Ireland when, on the one hand, there is general acceptance that an estimated three million people turned out to venerate the relics of St Thérèse of Lisieux at venues in every diocese in the country from Easter Sunday to 1 July 2001,[92] and, on the other hand, the *Glenstal Book of Prayer* was at number four on the bestseller list within a fortnight of its launch on 22 June 2001.[93] It remained on the bestsellers list for the rest of the year, mostly at number one, apart from brief periods when it was out of print.

In their analysis of the results of the *European Values Study* in 1994, Whelan and Hornsby-Smith essentially echoed observations made by Ryan in 1983 and Mac Gréil in his 1988/89 survey, as regards the more optimistic outlook of Irish Catholics.[94] They concluded that, 'what is striking about Ireland is not secularisation [but] the emergence of the "new" Catholic'.[95] These 'new Catholics' had 'a liberal attitude to sexual matters' and 'an optimistic interpretation of religion, one's standing before God and the world', and an outlook that questioned the Church's right to speak with absolute authority on matters of personal morality. For this 'new Catholic', 'Hell, the Devil, sin, doom and gloom, fears of damnation [had] all taken a bad beating'.[96] More independent-minded Catholics who tailored their Catholicism to social and cultural influences other than orthodox Catholic teaching were emerging from the late 1960s, and most certainly from the 1970s. By the 1990s, the days were over of following rules laid down by a very authoritarian Church, for fear of damnation in the next life. Most probably, what hammered the final nail in the coffin of this kind of Catholicism was the series of scandals which beset the Church from the early 1990s.

Catholic Ireland may have become vastly more liberal and more independent-minded by the 1990s, but no amount of liberalisation could prepare Irish Catholics for the news that broke in May 1992 on the RTÉ news programme, *Morning Ireland* — that Bishop Eamonn Casey of Galway had had an affair with an American divorcée during the time that he was Bishop of Kerry (1969–76), that they had a son, that he had denied the mother and child, and the impression was given, rightly or wrongly, that he had used diocesan funds to pay off the mother's claims lest the secret be found out.[97]

Just at a time when it appeared that things could get no worse for the Church, case after case of sex charges against Catholic clergy became commonplace in the daily newspapers. Then in 1994, the story of Brendan Smyth, a priest of the Norbertine order, made headline news. He was arrested in Northern Ireland in 1991 on charges of paedophilia, and released on bail. He returned to his monastery in Ballyjamesduff in the Republic, and refused to return to Northern Ireland. When it emerged in October 1994 that warrants issued by the RUC for his extradition in April 1993 had not been acted upon in the Republic, questions were asked in the Dáil, and the Labour Party withdrew its support from government; and the Fianna Fáil–Labour coalition, led by Albert Reynolds, fell.[98]

Yet another clerical scandal hit the headlines in 1995. Fr Michael Cleary was a very well-known Dublin priest who had been a member of the All Priests Shows in the 1970s. He was one of the generation of priests who made maximum use of television from the 1960s, and he had his own nightly radio programme until the time of his death in December 1993. Both he and Bishop Casey had acted as masters of ceremony at the Youth Mass on the occasion of Pope John Paul II's visit to Galway in 1979. In 1995, Phyllis Hamilton released her story to the *Sunday World*, in which she claimed that she and Michael Cleary had been living as man and wife and that they had had two children, one of whom had been adopted.[99] With the publication of her story, *My Secret Life as a Priest's Wife for Twenty-Seven Years*, the Church seemed to reach a new low. In the years from 1992 to 1995, when issues having to do with abortion (the X case), the further liberalisation of contraception legislation, the law in relation to homosexual acts and divorce were central to political and social discourse, the teaching Church needed all the moral authority that it could muster to influence Irish Catholics. Revelations such as these were, to say the least, disastrous.

There is no doubting the enormous damage done to the prestige of the Catholic Church by these scandals.[100] But ironically it was precisely because of its enormous prestige and the high moral ground on which the Church had stood, that Irish Catholics were so shocked, disappointed and appalled. What sharpened the irony was that, of all aspects of morality, the Church was perceived as being particularly concerned to promote sexual morality, and these scandals flew in the face of the strict code of sexual morality so emphasised in the preaching of the Church — these were 'sins of the flesh', which many felt that the Church was obsessed with to the point of promoting prudishness. Many theologians are now critical of the narrow legalism of pre-Vatican II moral theology and have pointed to the particularly unfortunate consequences this had for sexual morality. Moral theology as contained in the handbooks, was preoccupied with defining certain acts as intrinsically evil, taking little or no account of personal, developmental considerations.[101] An over-preoccupation with sexual sins led to many people having an impoverished understanding of human sexuality, or to over-scrupulosity.[102] The cynicism which was palpable, particularly in some media reporting, was understandable. The Church had set such high standards for people that it was inconceivable to some that not all clerics were practising what they preached. Bishop Willie Walsh of Killaloe has seen much of the 'anger' as coming 'from past hurts inflicted by church personnel at a time when it wasn't easy to question the conduct of priest or religious'.[103] The fact that for many Irish Catholics in the past little humanity was in evidence, meant that, for many, there was a sense of *Schadenfreude*, now that the Church was brought to its knees.[104] For the generation who remembered the 1940s and 1950s, and who had struggled with the encyclical *Humanae Vitae*, for those in whose ears the Church's teaching in relation to scandal still rang, that 'he that shall scandalise one of these little ones that believe in me it were better for him that a millstone should be hanged about his neck and that he be drowned in the depth of the sea',[105] the latest turn of events was not easily assimilated.

Opinion polls in the wake of these scandals have attempted to measure the fall-out for the Church in terms of its moral authority and the religious practice of its followers. In an opinion poll carried out by Lansdowne Market Research for RTÉ's *Would you Believe?* programme in 1995, 65 per cent thought that the Bishop Casey affair and 59 per cent that the Brendan Smyth affair had undermined the position of parents in giving advice to their children on moral and social attitudes. The poll found that 42 per cent of Catholics had lost some respect for the Church on account of the revelations, and that 45 per cent of priests considered that the Church's teachings on moral matters had been undermined.[106] A poll commissioned by the *Sunday Independent* and the RTÉ *Late Late Show,* and carried out by Irish Marketing Surveys (IMS) in 1995, put weekly Mass attendance at 64 per cent,[107] and in a further poll commissioned by *The Irish Times* in 1996, and carried out by the Market Research Bureau of Ireland (MRBI), 66 per cent of those polled said that they attended Mass once a week.[108] In the latter poll, when questioned as to whether they followed their own conscience or the teaching authority of the Church when making serious moral decisions, 78 per cent answered that they followed their own conscience.[109] In 1997, a survey carried out by IMS on behalf of the bishops' Council for Research and Development showed that 66 per cent of those polled attended weekly Mass,[110] while an MRBI survey commissioned by RTÉ's *Prime Time* programme in 1998, less than a year later, showed that this figure had decreased to 60 per cent.[111] In the IMS survey, 11 per cent of those sampled attended confession once a month, in comparison to 47 per cent in the 1974 survey. In the MRBI survey the following year, 40 per cent claimed that they rarely or never participated in the sacrament.[112] Essentially what these polls show is that trends already observed in (the more comprehensive) surveys of the 1970s and 1980s have accelerated. As in previous surveys, this applies, in particular, to the young, those living in urban centres, and the socially deprived.[113] Whether the sharper decline in religious practice in the 1990s is related to scandals in the Church, or continuing sociocultural change, or both, is a moot point, and not something that can be answered definitively despite the best efforts of sociologists of religion.

The Church's inability to deal publicly with these crises has exacerbated its situation. In Bishop Casey's case, he fled the country and his fellow bishops were left to 'pick up the pieces', which they did very awkwardly. In the television age, the media dictated the appropriate style in which public figures should express sorrow for their sins — this was by means of public confession; public exposure was the penance exacted to earn compassion and forgiveness, as illustrated in the examples of the businessman, Ben Dunne, and the Labour Party politician, Emmet Stagg, when they were the subjects of scandalous reports. An interesting sociocultural development of the 1980s and 1990s is the increasing desire on people's part to air their problems publicly and seek advice over the airwaves. Leaving aside public personalities, for many of the general public, the priest-confessor's role of the past has been filled by the chat-show host. Problems are phoned in, and the latter counsels and adjudicates on the basis of audience reaction and advice. The forum is entirely democratic, and conclusions are drawn and decisions reached in a consensual manner — unlike the past where penance was handed down in a unilateral manner on the basis of clearly defined Church teaching.

Neither were religious sisters and brothers untouched by what was beginning to be seen by many as the darker side of the triumphal Irish Catholicism portrayed in the earlier chapters of this book. A series of scandals relating to the abuse of children in industrial schools, reformatories and orphanages began to emerge also from the early 1990s. Allegations of negligence, sexual abuse and brutality were levelled against a number of institutions. Several of the most controversial cases were the subject of television documentaries. 'Dear Daughter', shown on RTÉ in February 1996, portrayed life in a Dublin orphanage, run by the Sisters of Mercy in Goldenbridge in the 1950s and 1960s, as brutal and uncaring.[114] This was followed, on 20 June 1996, by an RTÉ *Prime Time* documentary, 'The Secret Baby Trail',[115] which related how Church and state had colluded in the 1950s and 1960s in arranging foreign adoptions for Irish (mainly illegitimate) children. The overriding fear of Catholic Church authorities at that time was that a Catholic child might end up in Protestant care, as already seen. A more recent RTÉ documentary, 'States of Fear', broadcast in three parts in April and May 1999,[116] recounted the experiences of people who had spent their childhood years in state industrial schools run by religious orders. All of these documentaries provoked intense controversy and criticism of the institutional Church.

The wheel had turned full circle from the deference afforded the Church in the 1950s by politicians, the laity and the media. The close relationship between Church and state, which had made it very convenient for the state to hand over responsibility for the disadvantaged in Irish society, now came under scrutiny. Whereas the ultimate responsibility for the care of inmates of these institutions was a matter for the state, many religious pointed out that the state had abdicated its responsibility. These documentaries were very one-sided and extremely negative towards the institutional Church, and tended to generate more heat than light. Roles were reversed in the 1990s — the media were now demanding accountability. They were the new taskmasters; in the 1970s they had begun to be more critical of the institutional Church. By the 1990s, many felt that they were on a witch-hunt. The dangers inherent in a climate of self-righteous condemnation were nowhere as starkly underlined as in the case of Nora Wall, a former Mercy nun, found guilty in June 1997 of the rape of a 10-year-old girl at St Michael's Child Care Centre in Cappoquin, Co. Waterford, in the late 1980s.[117] She and her co-accused, Paul McCabe, subsequently had their convictions quashed on appeal, when the Director of Public Prosecutions admitted the non-disclosure of relevant information to the defence.[118] Apart from the personal trauma involved in the case, its implications were tragic in any consideration of Irish Catholicism, in as much as it had reached a stage where there was almost a presumption of guilt when allegations were levelled at religious in charge of people in care in institutions.

Nevertheless, very sensitive and emotive issues had been raised over a number of years and were now in the public domain, and demands were being made for accountability and compensation. Repeated allegations and controversies led to the setting up, on 23 May 2000, of a government commission, headed by Judge Mary Laffoy, to inquire into child abuse. The commission sought and has received and heard submissions from those who experienced abuse in their childhood while in an institution or foster care. Such institutions include industrial schools, reformatories, orphanages, hospitals, children's homes and primary and post-primary schools.[119] The commission published an interim report in May 2001.[120] A further interim report was published on 30 November 2001, and the commission sought a three-year extension because of the numbers of people seeking to give evidence.[121] Meanwhile, civil cases have also been taken, and a number of garda enquiries are in progress, examining allegations made against members of religious orders who ran various institutions.

On 30 January 2002, after fourteen months of negotiations between the Government and CORI, the latter announced that religious orders were to make contributions to the value of €128 million to the redress scheme set up by the State for people who had suffered abuse while in residential care.[122] On the basis of the agreement reached, the Government agreed to indemnify the religious orders directly concerned against all present and future claims arising from past child abuse, which are covered by the Residential Institutions Redress Bill, 2001. Victims will be able to get compensation from the Residential Institutions Redress Commission, but they will be unable to sue the religious orders separately later.[123] However, brothers and nuns who were found guilty of abuse will still be liable to criminal actions as the agreement does not grant criminal indemnity. Given that the expert group set up by the Minister for Education and Science, Michael Woods, reported that the cost of compensating an estimated 3,500 victims could reach €500 million,[124] organisations representing individuals who were abused in institutions in the past have been critical of what they see as the religious orders' success in evading their full financial responsibility, and some see it as an example of the influence still wielded by the Catholic Church in Irish society.[125]. That said, the minister, when introducing the Residential Institutions Redress Bill in the Dáil, pointed out that the primary responsibility for what happened rested with the State.[126]

Passed by the Dáil on 20 February 2002, the bill does not cover victims of abuse by Catholic priests who are under the jurisdiction of the bishops.[127] On Easter Monday, 1 April 2002, Bishop Brendan Comiskey announced at a press conference that he had tendered his resignation as Bishop of Ferns, to Pope John Paul II, on the previous Thursday.[128] His resignation came at the end of two weeks of bitter controversy relating to his handling of sex-abuse complaints in his diocese. In a BBC *Correspondent* documentary, entitled 'Suing the Pope', screened on 19 March 2002, four victims, now in their thirties, outlined their experiences of abuse, as teenagers, by Fr Seán Fortune, a priest of the diocese of Ferns. The programme rekindled memories of other complaints of abuse made against priests in Ferns over the years — complaints which were not followed up on. Archbishop Brady of Armagh and Cardinal Connell of Dublin, as president and vice-president respectively of the Episcopal Conference, issued a joint statement, calling the sexual abuse of children by priests 'an especially grave and repugnant evil'. They said that 'trust in the Catholic church [has] been damaged' and also 'the faith of the people and the morale of clergy'.[129] They both came under fire in the media for their failure to comment further, notwithstanding their insistence that they had no jurisdiction in a fellow bishop's diocese.

The results of an opinion poll published by the local *Wexford Echo* put further pressure on Bishop Comiskey — 62 per cent of those polled thought that he should resign as against 22 per cent who thought that he should remain as bishop; 77 per cent declared that they had no confidence in the bishop, while 92 per cent considered that he did not do enough to remove Fr Fortune from his position; and 96 per cent believed that the diocese should pay compensation to Fortune's victims.[130] The cover story in the 1 April issue of *Time* magazine, entitled 'Can the Catholic Church save itself?' recounted allegations of clerical sex abuse, and official attempts to cover up, which have made headline news in many countries from the US to Poland in recent months, and included events in Ferns diocese.[131] The gravity of such matters and the fact that they go far beyond the local was confirmed, if confirmation were needed, when, in his Holy Thursday address to priests, Pope John Paul II referred to the 'sins of some of our brothers who have betrayed the grace of Ordination in succumbing even to the most grievous forms of the *mysterium iniquitatis* at work in the world'.[132]

Pressure on Bishop Comiskey mounted and he announced his resignation on the day before RTÉ was scheduled to repeat the BBC documentary. On RTÉ it was preceded by a *Prime Time* discussion of the issues raised. The panel included Bishop Colm O'Reilly of Ardagh and Clonmacnoise; David Quinn, editor of the *Irish Catholic*; and two victims of alleged abuse — Colm O'Gorman, who had been involved in the BBC documentary, and Marie Collins, who had complained to Cardinal Connell of being abused by a hospital chaplain as a teenager in 1960 in Our Lady's Hospital for Sick Children in Crumlin, Dublin.[133] Once again, the Church was 'outed' by the media and found to be wanting. In separate statements, both Bishop Comiskey[134] and

Cardinal Connell[135] acknowledged that abuse had taken place and that their response to complaints had been less than satisfactory, and they apologised to the victims. There were calls for Cardinal Connell to resign also.

What was most damning from the Church's point of view was that instances of abuse had been ongoing and had been brought to the attention of the relevant Church authorities repeatedly, and the latter were deemed to have been less than forthcoming in dealing with them. Thus a picture of a Church less than honest, less than caring, whose main priority was its own institutional self-preservation, whatever the cost, has emerged in the mind of many. Legal advice would appear to have prevailed over pastoral considerations. While it would be naïve for any serious commentator to deny that legal and financial considerations can be totally overlooked by any institution wishing to influence modern society, the Church's position is more vulnerable than that of any other institution, as its authority is in the moral sphere. This begs the question as to whether sinful actions by some of its ministers compromise the ability of the Church as an institution to proclaim the Gospel, and the answer would appear to be most definitely yes, and this is particularly so if those in authority fail to act or attempt to side-step or cover up, if and when they are informed of wrong-doing. The irony of ironies for the Church has been that — such has been its preoccupation with avoiding scandal — it has left itself open to accusations of the most grievous scandal of all — the failure to practise what it preaches, what it stands for. Indeed, recent victims of alleged abuse have professed themselves to be equally, if not more, hurt by what they saw as the insensitive attitude and response of those in authority when they reported their experiences, than they were by the actual abuse itself, and these sentiments have been echoed in public debate on the issue.

On 4 April, Minister for Health Mícheál Martin appointed Senior Counsel George Birmingham to draw up a report to advise the Government on how best to proceed in what is uncharted territory for both Church and state.[136] In a statement on 6 April, the Vatican confirmed that Bishop Comiskey had been asked to resign because he was unsuitable for office and that his resignation had been accepted by the Pope and that Bishop Eamonn Walsh, auxiliary bishop in Dublin, chairperson of the bishops' Child Protection Committee (established in 2001) and a trained barrister, had been appointed as Apostolic Administrator of the diocese of Ferns.[137]

In the wake of these events, the bishops held two extraordinary general meetings in Maynooth. While bishops' meetings are normally sombre occasions, the full impact of how extraordinary these meetings were was borne home on the Irish public when the evening news programme relayed pictures of bishops and the Papal Nuncio, Dr Giuseppe Lazzarotto, being waylaid and confronted by former victims of abuse.[138] There was little evidence of the kind of deference shown towards bishops in the past, and the fact that these scenes took place in Maynooth College, the national seminary and 'headquarters' of Catholic Ireland, threw the events into even sharper relief. Arising out of the first meeting, the bishops issued a statement indicating their willingness to co-operate fully with the government investigation and also their decision to undertake an independent audit of how each diocese has dealt with abuse allegations. They stated that their 'supreme concerns' were 'the safety of children, the welfare of victims and the common good' and that these would be 'the sole determining factors in carrying out this audit, so that the truth can be established'.[139] They also announced that a recently retired judge, Ms Gillian Hussey, was to succeed Bishop Eamonn Walsh as chairperson of the bishops' Child Protection Committee.[140]

The second of the bishops' meetings was held against the background of thirteen US bishops journeying to Rome for a two-day meeting to get the Vatican's advice on policy guidelines for handling future complaints in this area.[141] A directive from Rome to bishops in May 2001,[142] that all such complaints be forwarded to the Vatican, has placed local bishops in a difficult situation. It has also raised questions about bishops' obligations as citizens under civil law, as opposed to their obligations to the Church under canon law, and how these can be reconciled in certain situations.

The Church has maintained its influence, albeit reduced, in the areas of education, health and social welfare, through the 1980s and 1990s. The state has taken on more responsibility in all of these areas since the 1960s. A government White Paper on education, published in 1995, set out the constitutional and legal framework within which education in Ireland was to be placed on a statutory basis. The White Paper referred to Articles 40, 42 and 44 of the constitution, and the preamble, as having implications, which sometimes were in conflict given the denominational nature of schools.[143] It recognised that this could be discriminatory against parents in their choice of school, or against teachers or pupils in staffing or admissions. There was a case in Wexford in 1985 of a teacher, Eileen Flynn, who lost her position in a convent secondary school because the school authorities held that because she was co-habiting, she was undermining the ethos of the school.[144] Such an eventuality would seem unlikely to recur in the Ireland of today.

That said, when the president referred the Employment Equality Bill, 1995, to the Supreme Court to test its constitutionality, the judgement, delivered on 15 May 1997, was that the bill prohibiting denominational schools from discriminating against teachers on the grounds of their religion was not constitutional.[145] The following year, on 25 March 1998, the Supreme Court found against the Campaign for the Separation of Church and State (CSCS) in its case which challenged the constitutionality of the payment by the state of the salaries of community-school chaplains.[146] A secularist lobby group, launched in 1987, the CSCS focused in particular on Church influence on education issues. They had argued that the payments made annually to chaplains in such schools were in breach of Article 44.2.2 of the constitution, which guarantees that the state does not endow any religion.[147]

Both of these cases underlined the strong constitutional position of Catholic (and other denominational education) in Ireland, and the Education Act, 1998, served to place it on an even firmer footing.[148] However, this is no longer adequate to protect the ethos of Catholic education. The problems facing Catholic education, first identified in the *F.I.R.E. Report* in 1973, have intensified in more recent times. At a conference organised by the Education Commission of the Conference of Major Religious Superiors (CMRS, now Conference of Religious of Ireland — CORI) in 1991, it was said that the tension experienced by Catholic school managers in contemporary society arises because 'the school, as an agent of the State's educational provision, is required to legitimate and reinforce an excessively competitive and individualistic ethos'.[149] The reversal in the balance of power is here captured succinctly — the state now dictates the ethos of schooling. When one considers the power struggles of the 1970s, it is not without irony that an issue raised at the conference concerned 'the fact that virtually all primary and a majority of post-primary schools are Catholic [made] it difficult for such schools to assert their identity', and the point was further made that 'a defence of the principle of denominational schooling may require an effort to promote the growth of other types of schools including non-denominational schools'.[150] Further tension arose from the 'efforts to deliver Catholic education in a changing pluralist society'. The fact that, 'an increasing number of the children attending Catholic schools come from families which do not have a faith commitment', and that, 'many teachers in these schools also do not have a faith commitment' exacerbated the situation, was also pointed out.[151]

Whereas formerly the importance of religion, not only as a subject, but also as something permeating the whole school ethos, was taken for granted, from the 1970s, religion as a subject has been increasingly marginalised by the competitive examination culture. The introduction of the Stay Safe programme in primary schools from 1989[152] and the introduction of the Relationships and Sexuality Programme (RSE) in secondary schools from 1998[153] were significant curricular initiatives introduced by the Departments of Education and Health in an area formerly seen by the Church as its own exclusive domain. The RSE programme for post-primary schools includes advice/information on matters pertaining to sexual relations outside marriage, contraception and homosexuality in a non-confessional environment.[154] More recently, the Department of Education has drawn up a new syllabus for religion as an optional subject in post-primary schools, which, in due course, will be examined at Junior and Leaving Certificate level.[155] These are all significant developments which, in the not too distant future, will undoubtedly have implications for religious education as it is currently understood in schools, and indeed for Catholic cultural change in the broader sense.

Undoubtedly, however, the main problem facing the Church in maintaining its influence on all aspects of Irish life, including education, is the continuing decline in vocations to the religious life.[156] Nuns, priests and brothers have been the mainstay of Catholic education in Ireland over the past two centuries. The percentage ratio of full-time registered religious teachers to full-time registered lay teachers in secondary, community and comprehensive schools in 1984–85 was 13.8 per cent; in 1989–90, 10.3 per cent; in 1994–95, 6.2 per cent; and in 1997–98, it was 4.7 per cent.[157] Again, this is not without irony, when one considers the guarantee of reserved places for their members which religious managers fought for and secured in the protracted negotiations which preceded the signing of the deed of trust of community schools. The problem of the decline in vocations, however, does not stop at Catholic schooling, nor is it a problem simply of numbers. In the past, when the religious life was seen as a prestigious career option, the educational standard of entrants was high. The changed economic and cultural context has meant that school-leavers since the 1970s enjoy more career choice. This has led inadvertently to a drop in the educational attainment of those who enter religious life. At a time when the educational standard of the general public has improved greatly, and people are more inclined to be critical of would-be leaders in society, this also has inevitable implications for Catholic cultural change, which will make themselves felt in time. The notion of sacrifice so idealised in the Catholicism of the past has lost its appeal in a more individualistic age. This has been borne out by Tony Flannery CSsR in his book, *The Death of Religious Life?* (1997). He has pointed to the espousal of concepts of personal freedom and self-development which replaced the values of self-denial and compliance, the bedrocks of community life in the past, as having played a major part in the disintegration that began to take place in religious life from the late 1960s.[158]

As in education, the Church's influence on the area of health and social welfare arose because of the religious authorities' ownership and control of many hospitals, nursing homes and hospices.[159] This influence has also lessened because of the decline in the numbers of religious personnel and the state's increased involvement. Ability to influence policy-making, training for doctors and nurses, and staffing requires representation at Board of Management level. This has meant that medical procedures which would have been unthinkable in the 1960s, such as sterilisation, tubal ligation in the case of women, and vasectomy (contrary to Catholic Church teaching) have been available since the 1980s.[160]

While the Church's role as carer has been under critical scrutiny, conversely it is precisely in the area of social welfare and justice issues that the voice of the Church is heard most frequently in recent times. Gregory Baum has seen the 1971 Synod of Bishops' declaration, *Justice in the World*, as the turning point in Catholic social teaching,[161] and Irish theologians like Donal Dorr and Dermot Lane have contributed to the development of a more socially-minded theology.[162] It is ironic that while the Church at all levels has increasingly identified with the marginalised since the 1970s, this section of Irish society has become more alienated from the Church, as evidenced in the results of surveys. Key issues in relation to the economy have been addressed by the bishops through the 1980s and 1990s. In their statement, *Christian Faith in a Time of Economic*

Depression, in 1983, the bishops warned of 'the moral and social responsibilities of property, wealth and power', reminding all sections of the community of their responsibility to society at large.[163] In 1992, the bishops issued a pastoral, *Work is the Key: Towards an Economy that Needs Everyone*, which was a well-researched critical analysis of socioeconomic policy.[164] In 1999, the bishops' pastoral letter, *Prosperity with a Purpose*, addressed the moral challenges posed for Catholics in a period of rapid economic growth.[165] As well as its direct involvement in the areas of social welfare, health and education, what has been most significant since the 1970s is the Church's continuing commitment to research and policy formation by means of various agencies established since that time. All of these have been active in monitoring, raising awareness and influencing policy-making in relation to key areas of public concern, such as poverty, unemployment, emigration, social welfare, health services, children's rights, childcare services and penal policy.[166]

In the case of the Commission for Justice and Peace, its involvement has been in the area of human rights and social justice in Ireland and abroad.[167] The education office of the CMRS (now CORI), since it was set up in 1987/88, has been involved in raising public awareness in relation to poverty and educational disadvantage. It has monitored all the major issues relating to education, and has published several policy papers[168] highlighting the inequities institutionalised in the educational system, the effects of the more competitive ethos on pupils — in particular, the weaker more vulnerable, educationally disadvantaged child — and the fact that the education system can, in fact, perpetuate advantage for some and disadvantage for others. The Justice office of CORI has been actively involved with other agencies (Society of St Vincent de Paul, the government's Combat Poverty Agency, and trade unions) throughout the 1980s and 1990s in seeking justice for disadvantaged groups; government legislation in April 2000, introducing a basic minimum wage for all workers, has undoubtedly been influenced by its lobbying and that of other groups.[169] It has continued to press for a basic income (free of tax) for everybody. Solidarity with the marginalised and what has been termed the 'ministry of influence' with regard to public policy has become an increasingly important area for religious in relation to a growing number of national and international issues.[170] Indeed, a recent commentator has seen CORI as subversive, having 'a left-wing politico-economic agenda' and accused it of 'monopolising the Church's social justice teaching'.[171]

While the above-mentioned agencies facilitate a more open, horizontal model of Church as envisaged by Vatican II, there has also been much evidence on the ground which suggests that the authoritarian, vertical model is the one which actually, as opposed to theoretically, obtains. The extent to which this is a local church problem, or whether it has to do with the vision of Church proposed in Rome is a moot point. The concepts of collegiality of bishops and the priesthood of the laity were given structural form after Vatican II. They were a radical development for the Church. The bishops were to share in the decision-making role of the pope,[172] and the importance of the laity's contribution to interpreting the 'signs of the times' was also emphasised. There has been much disquiet registered by clerical commentators in recent years who feel that Pope John Paul II has neutralised, if not negated, these conciliar aims by his dogmatic approach to certain controversial matters of conscience, and also in his appointment of bishops. Concern has been voiced that the influence of the Papal Nuncio has been to the forefront in many cases in the appointment of bishops, excluding the views of the local clergy, and that an overemphasis on loyalty to Rome and orthodoxy of views precludes the appointment of bishops who might exercise the more prophetical leadership needed at a time when the Catholic viewpoint on moral, social and political issues is no longer guaranteed a hearing, as it was formerly. It is interesting to recall that many of the bishops were less than enthusiastic when W.T. Cosgrave established diplomatic relations with the Vatican in 1929.[173]

Fr Joe Dunn's book, *No Lions in the Hierarchy,* provided a valuable insight into the politicking which takes place in relation to the making of bishops, and the manner of appointments to the episcopal sees. As director of the Catholic Communications Institute of Ireland (CCII), he was directly responsible to the hierarchy's representative for communications, Archbishop Tom Morris of Cashel. Having worked closely with the bishops for fourteen years, he got to know the 'culture'. In his experience, 'laity and priests have no say ... everything is decided for them between Rome and (sometimes) the local hierarchy in total secrecy'.[174] He cites a number of examples of where, in his view, unsuitable candidates were 'forced' on local hierarchies. The fact that the bishops themselves have little knowledge of what takes place was borne out in an interview that the present writer conducted recently with a bishop. In Dunn's estimation, 'Rome places too much emphasis on loyalty to the Holy See to the detriment of other important leadership qualities', and the system is 'too open to manipulation'.[175] This has been borne out by Fr Thomas Reese in his book, *Inside the Vatican.* Writing in general on the appointment of bishops, he maintains:

> Questions on orthodoxy and church discipline are crucial. A priest supporting the ordination of women, optional priestly celibacy or birth control will not be made a bishop.[176]

Referring to the undue influence of the Nuncio in the selection of bishops, some observers have been more caustic in their comments. Writing in the *Furrow* in October 1993, Seán Freyne, professor of Theology at Trinity College, formerly a priest of the Archdiocese of Tuam and professor of New Testament at Maynooth, saw the Irish Episcopal Conference, as at present constituted, 'as having a serious image problem, perceived more as a collective of Vatican civil servants than as pastors with a genuinely independent concern for the real needs of their flocks'.[177] A survey by the Dublin Diocesan Council of Priests, of the attitudes of 323 Dublin priests, in April 1996, found 'general church leadership' to be their single greatest source of stress.[178] Independent-mindedness was the hallmark of the Irish bishops of the nineteenth century who had to balance the demands of Rome, London and their own constituency, both religious and lay. While London is no longer part of the equation, at the start of the twenty-first century, the bishops have to perform a far more delicate balancing act between two ideas of Catholicism — one dogmatic and hierarchical, the other more open and democratic — at a time when divergent views and demands are the order of the day, both in clerical and lay circles. The fact that they must do so in a highly visible environment, unlike in the past, makes their task still more demanding.

At the level of the institutional Church, demands for openness, transparency and accountability are not easily reconcilable with the distance and aloofness enjoyed in the past. The area of communications has been seen by many as the *bête noire* of the Irish Church. An incident in which this was highlighted was the removal by the bishops of Fr Kevin Hegarty from his post as editor of *Intercom,* from January 1995.[179] Hegarty had been attempting to open up for discussion issues which were sensitive for the Irish Church, and this was seen as the reason why his contract was not renewed by the bishops.[180] A number of articles had appeared in which observations were made which were somewhat close to the bone. In a very angry article on 'Women and Priesthood' in March 1993, Mary McAleese wrote of the 'growing anger and disillusionment among women in the Church', in particular those 'committed to the Church who see work to be done, who feel called to do it and able to do it, but who are told their services are unnecessary — they are not part of God's plan'.[181] In September 1993, a rather light-hearted article was written by Fr Brendan Hoban, in which he expressed the view that 'we have too many priests in Ireland'. He went on: 'Unless the old Church dies, the new lay-driven Church can't be born and the decline in vocations could well be God's way of giving us a little push in that direction.'[182] In the December 1993/January1994 issue, Philip Mortell, a senior social worker with the Mid-Western Health Board, contributed a piece entitled 'Clerical Sexual Abuse: Twenty Questions for the Bishops'. The intention of the article was 'to open up a discussion on the agenda' for the new guidelines for handling 'allegations of child sexual abuse against clergy and members of religious orders', which was being drawn up by the bishops, and thus to 'widen the consultation process'.[183] This article and its aims have a particular resonance in light of the sad trail of events which have come to light in the Ferns diocese, as described above. In 1996, the bishops did publish guidelines for handling allegations of clerical sexual abuse,[184] but confidence in their implementation has been eroded, because in both cases which have come into the public arena in recent times, the bishops concerned have admitted that their response was less than adequate. Had the Church been more open and less defensive in its approach, more trusting and willing to engage with the laity sooner, matters might not have evolved quite so tragically. As it was, it took the media to force the issue and the Church has (now) been forced to react, whereas it might have been more pro-active all along. *Intercom* was attempting to foster a more open communicative Church in the early 1990s, but it appeared that the candid exchange of views, such as was contained in some of its articles, was a bridge too far for a magazine published by Veritas, an agency of the Bishops' Commission on Communications and primarily read by priests. In June of 1994, Fr Hegarty was told by the bishop of his diocese, Bishop Finnegan of Killala, that he was being transferred to Belmullet, Co. Mayo, as curate, and he wrote his final editorial in the December 1994/January 1995 issue of *Intercom*.[185]

Ironically, frank and open discussion was precisely what was needed, many people felt, if the Church wanted to retain its integrity as an institution. The incident represented a clash between (the) two versions of Catholicism, and the outcome showed the gulf that existed between them. The fact that a critical voice could be silenced so abruptly served to underline the fact that the old authoritarianism still obtained. On the other hand, the critical comment it elicited, from both clerical and lay observers, served to underline the fact that, in a different sociocultural context, the price to be paid for this approach is very high. At a time when rapprochement, conciliation and consensus are the order of the day in social, political and industrial relations, the Church as an institution is seen by many as 'out of step'. Such an approach can arouse disillusionment at best and, at worst, can result in its being ignored. Since its establishment in the 1950s, the *Furrow* has been as an antenna which has sensitively captured the consciousness of Irish Catholicism — even a cursory perusal of articles contributed to the journal in the 1990s bespeaks a mood of disaffection among many reflective Catholics.[186]

A particularly thorny area in the Irish context has been the issue of ecumenism and inter-church relations. The emphasis placed by the Vatican Council on the dignity of conscience and religious liberty, combined with the fact that society has become more liberal in general, has led to Catholics becoming more independent in their approach to the situation of inter-church marriage, and less concerned with the dogmatic principles of their own church. While that would appear to be the case at grass-roots level, so to speak, when it comes to doctrinal issues, the Church cannot see its way to make concessions in the interest of ecumenical dialogue. This became very clear when the bishops, after a meeting of their standing committee, issued a statement which was critical of President Mary McAleese,[187] because she had received Communion at an ecumenical service in Christ Church Cathedral, in December 1997.[188] When Archbishop Connell of Dublin, a member of the standing committee, went on to elaborate the Catholic Church's position on the reception of Communion in a Protestant church, on a radio programme the following day, describing it as 'a sham', his remarks and the controversy which ensued were seen by many in Catholic, as well as Protestant, circles as an unfortunate setback for ecumenical relations.[189]

In January 1998, the Catholic bishops' conferences of Ireland and Britain issued a joint teaching document, *One Bread, One Body*, in which the bishops stated: 'we do not judge the celebration of the Eucharist at an ecumenical gathering or event to be a situation in which sacramental sharing might be considered as appropriate in our countries.'[190] In August 1998, the Congregation for the Doctrine of the Faith (CDF) issued the decree, *Dominus Jesus*, which stated definitively that, 'there exists a single Church of Christ, which subsists in the Catholic Church, governed by the Successor of Peter and by the Bishops in communion with him'.[191] This Roman document on which Connell worked as a member of the CDF has provoked bitter controversy amongst the leaders of the other Christian Churches in Ireland. It has served to underline once again, that when it comes to certain doctrinal issues of faith and morals, the Catholic position is uncompromising.

On the eve of Desmond Connell's departure for Rome to attend at the consistory at which he was to be appointed cardinal — a promotion seen by many Church and other commentators as reward for his loyal and outspoken defence of papal policy on various controversial issues — he vigorously defended his position in relation to inter-church Communion.[192] This was not the first time that Mary McAleese, a committed Catholic and a member of the delegation representing the Episcopal Conference at the New Ireland Forum, clashed with the Church. Previously critical of the Church's policy on celibacy and women priests, she spoke on these matters again when she addressed the AGM of the National Council of Priests of Ireland (NCPI) in September 2000. On that occasion, she pointed to 'disappointment and impatience on many fronts — the mixed messages about ecumenical dialogue with sister Christian churches ... the failure to utilise the full giftedness of women, the paucity of avenues for debate, and the sense of drift rather [than] direction in the face of the collapse of vocations in the Western world'.[193] In this, she captured the major issues facing the Catholic Church in Ireland and elsewhere at the end of the twentieth century.

Women were the backbone of Catholicism, as described in the earlier part of this book — since that time, while they have grown politically, many feel that because they cannot be ordained, they are excluded from a full role in the Church, and that this is a slight on their womanhood. A survey carried out in 1992 by a sub-committee on women in the Church, under the aegis of the Irish Commission for Justice and Peace, among women who considered themselves committed Catholics, found evidence of a growing level of alienation from the institutional Church — 68 per cent of those surveyed felt angry at the Church's treatment of women; only 11 per cent felt that the Church authorities were supportive of women.[194] On the issue of the ordination of women, a communiqué signed on 28 October 1995 by Cardinal Joseph Ratzinger, Prefect of the CDF, reiterated that the Church's teaching on a male-only priesthood, as set down in the Apostolic Letter, *Ordinatio Sacerdotalis*, 1994, 'requires definitive assent', and is to be understood 'as belonging to the deposit of the faith'.[195] What is seen by many women as the Church's failure to recognise and engage women in a meaningful way has become one of the most significant emergent issues in Catholicism worldwide in the 1980s and 1990s, and the Church's capacity to grapple with this is one of its biggest challenges.

Essentially, the Second Vatican Council changed the direction of theology in the Catholic Church — the 'new' theology was more pastoral in its focus and took as its starting point the individual's concrete experience. This was a truly liberating development, and the euphoria that followed the Council and its decrees was understandable. The Church was now 'the people of God', a 'pilgrim' Church, searching for answers to the deep questions of life, by reading the 'signs of the times'. The Church was no longer perceived as having a monopoly on Truth, and people awakened to a new understanding of their human dignity and their power to discern moral issues by means of their conscience. Juan Arias's book, *The God I Don't Believe In,* captured the mood of the new era. Catholics could now 'make their own' of God, so to speak — or so it appeared![196]

However, while Church teaching might be presented in a more positive fashion, while clergy might have dissenting views of what is permissible, and while the laity might be less fearful and more optimistic as regards what constitutes or does not constitute sin, official Church teaching in relation to crucial areas such as sexuality, celibacy, women priests and inter-Communion has not changed. It would appear that certain doctrines are so deeply ingrained in Roman Catholic tradition that departure from them is deemed impossible. So, was the Second Vatican Council simply an exercise in window dressing or packaging of the Church's teaching in a more user-friendly fashion? The answer is both yes and no. When one reflects back on Pope John XXIII's opening address at the Council, it is very clear that it was the way that faith was 'presented' which was to be changed. The assembled bishops were told that the Church's task was to discover the best formulae which would be meaningful for the contemporary person, but he pointed out that 'the substance of the ancient doctrine of the deposit of faith is one thing and the way in which it is presented is another'. He explained that fundamentals do not change, but that they can and must be developed and expressed in forms more understandable and relevant to the modern person. The Council was an attempt to reconcile faith with contemporary culture. The fact that this was a matter of urgency was again underlined by Pope Paul VI in his encyclical, *Evangelii Nuntiandi,* in 1975, when he stated that 'the split between the Gospel and culture is without doubt the drama of our time'.[197] That the importance of establishing an ongoing dialogue between faith and culture is increasingly recognised both in Ireland and abroad is evidenced by the many books and articles written by Catholic theologians, in recent years, on the relationship between faith and culture.[198]

The theologian, Edward Schillebeeckx, has defined the Church as an 'interpretative community',[199] and all the evidence suggests that this is a definition that sits comfortably with present-day Irish Catholics, despite the authoritarian winds emanating from Rome. Essentially, what surveys since the 1970s show is that there has been a widening gap between official Church teaching and the religious practice and attitudes of Irish Catholics. In the 1998 MRBI survey, 19 per cent agreed with the Church's position on artificial birth-control, 21 per cent with its position on priestly celibacy, and 23 per cent with its position on the ordination of women. Of those surveyed, 30 per cent agreed either totally or somewhat with Catholic teaching on divorce.[200] Apart from Pope John Paul II, Cardinal Joseph Ratzinger, Prefect of the CDF, has probably been the most influential (curial) churchman over the past thirty years.[201] One of the influential theologians at Vatican II, he became less optimistic about contemporary culture as time went by and grew more wary of the Church's dialogue with modernity.[202] In an interview with Vittorio Messori, published as *The Ratzinger Report* in 1985, the cardinal expressed concern that 'on the part of many Catholics in recent years there has been an unrestrained and unfiltered opening to the world ... to the dominant modern mentality, which at the same time brings up for discussion the very foundations of the *depositum fidei* which for many were no longer clear'.[203] He expressed similar views in an interview, published in the *Sunday Business Post* in December 1995, when he took issue with the suggestion that the pope had in some way betrayed the 'spirit' of the Vatican Council, saying, 'if truth be told, there were two Councils in the 1960s, a Council of the bishops, and a Council of the media'. He maintained that the media 'created a certain perception of what the "spirit" of the Council was; that it was about conforming the Church to the modern world, that it was about placing the Church in the "service" of progress'. This, he insisted, was a mistaken idea, and he said that far from 'betraying' the spirit of the Council, in all his dealings with the pope, he was struck by how completely he identified with the Second Vatican Council.[204]

There are many in the Church — bishops, theologians, priests and indeed lay people — who would not agree with the cardinal's view. Whether one agrees or not, his words are important when analysing Catholic culture, because they are a clear indication that the struggle for a more relevant contemporary Catholicism has yet to be resolved. This is a human struggle of minds and ideas. The roots of the struggle lie deep in history. The tensions surfaced and were played out at the time of Vatican II. The single most important legacy of the Council was that it challenged Catholics to discern, in conscience, the 'signs of the times', and to live their lives accordingly, with all the doubt, risks and responsibility that this entailed. This was its contribution to Catholics in the modern world. The fact that they responded to the challenge was underlined in no uncertain terms by the reaction to *Humanae Vitae*, which many Church personnel, as well as lay Catholics, have seen as **the** most dramatic turning point in changing Catholic culture.

At the time of writing, the most controversial issue in Catholicism is the issue of clerical child sexual abuse. It is dominating discussion in Ireland and abroad. While there has been no shortage of newsprint forecasting the imminent demise of Catholicism, in a survey such as the author is engaged in here, it is impossible to predict what implications these latest events will have for Irish Catholicism in the long term. It is too close to events as they unfold. Even so, given how serious and emotive an issue this is, one senses that it holds within it the seeds of long-term potential damage for the Church's standing and credibility. The fact that this is understood at the highest level was underlined in the pope's Holy Thursday 2002 address to priests, when he spoke of the 'grave scandal' it has caused, resulting in 'a dark shadow of suspicion' being cast over the work of those priests who 'perform their ministry with honesty and integrity and often with heroic self-sacrifice'.[205] But many would say that the Vatican must move beyond words and give the lead in cultivating a more democratic, open climate in the Church, which would allow issues, however unsavoury, to be named and excised.

There is no doubt that the crisis represents a watershed for the Church. Like *Humanae Vitae*, this is an issue which goes to the very core of people's lives, lay and clerical. For the institutional Church it raises fundamental questions in relation to aspects of Catholic culture which have been examined in the course of the present study. These questions relate to authority in the Church, collegiality, communication, justice, celibacy, religious formation, attitudes towards the laity, sexuality and many other areas. There are also, of course, implications for the financial stability of the Church as an institution. There are those who accuse the Church of losing sight of its true mission, such has been its preoccupation with preserving its viability as an institution, and that this has been at the expense of its humanity. The most potentially corrosive charge of all that the Church has to face and deal with is that of hypocrisy — of defending the indefensible. Whether Irish Catholicism can survive the storm that now threatens will depend on the public's judgement of the Church authorities' willingness to practise the virtues of openness, transparency and accountability in their dealings with any inquiry that is set up, lessons which have been learned only too well and at great cost by many who have occupied leadership roles in secular society in recent years. If soul-searching questions are asked, answered honestly and acted upon, it may well be that the crisis could have a purgative effect on Catholicism in the long run. The Church must now put its house in order and, most importantly, it must be seen to do so. Otherwise there is no doubt that the fall-out could prove even more damaging to the Church's moral authority and credibility than what was experienced in the aftermath of *Humanae Vitae.*

Appendices

Appendix A
Religious Composition of Population of Twenty-Six Counties of Republic of Ireland, 1861–1981

Year	Population	Roman Catholic	C of I	Presb.	Meth.	Jewish	Other Religion	No Religion	No info supplied
1861	4,402,111	89.4	8.5	1.5	0.4	0.008		0.22	
1871	4,053,187	89.2	8.4	1.5	0.4	0.006		0.42	
1881	3,870,020	89.5	8.2	1.5	0.5	0.001		0.32	
1891	3,468,694	89.3	8.3	1.5	0.5	0.004		0.33	
1901	3,221,823	89.3	8.2	1.5	0.6	0.09		0.36	
1911	3,139,688	89.6	7.9	1.4	0.5	0.12		0.38	
1926	2,971,992	92.6	5.5	1.1	0.4	0.12		0.33	
1936	2,968,420	93.4	4.9	0.9	0.3	0.13		0.27	
1946	2,955,107	94.3	4.2	0.8	0.3	0.13		0.27	
1961	2,818,341	94.9	3.7	0.7	0.2	0.12	0.19	0.04	0.20
1971	2,978,248	92.4	3.3	0.5	0.2	0.09	0.21	0.26	1.57
1981	3,443,405	93.1	2.8	0.4	0.2	0.06	0.31	1.15	2.06

Source: Religious Practice and Attitudes in Ireland 1988–1989, Mícheál Mac Gréil, Survey and Research Unit, St Patrick's College, Maynooth, 1991.

APPENDIX B
PARTICIPATION BY IRISH CATHOLICS IN MASS, HOLY COMMUNION AND SACRAMENTAL CONFESSIONS, 1988–89

Frequency	Mass		Holy Communion		Sacramental Confession	
1. Daily	6.5%		5.5%		—	
2. Several times a week	8.1%	(14.6%)*	6.7%	(12.2%)	—	
3. Once a week	67.0%	(81.6%)	30.5%	(42.7%)	1.8%	
4. 1–3 times a month	5.6%	(87.2%)	20.1%	(62.8%)	16.3%	(18.2%)*
5. Several times a year	6.5%	(93.7%)	17.3%	(80.1%)	35.5%	(53.6%)
6. Less Often	3.7%	(97.4%)	14.0%	(94.1%)	35.1%	(88.7%)
7. Never	2.5%		5.7%		11.0%	
	N = 943		N = 941		N = 941	

* Cumulative percentage in brackets

Source: Religious Practice and Attitudes in Ireland 1988–1989, Micheál Mac Gréil, Survey and Research Unit, St Patrick's College, Maynooth, 1991.

Appendix C
Statement of the Yearly Number of Pilgrims who participated in the Three-day pilgrimage to Lough Derg, 1945–86

1945	21,883	1959	27,088	1973	16,421
1946	23,564	1960	25,878	1974	16,692
1947	23,105	1961	28,175	1975	20,751
1948	24,695	1962	24,337	1976	19,961
1949	25,024	1963	22,400	1977	20,431
1950	30,963	1964	22,381	1978	19,799
1951	32,554	1965	20,842	1979	18,884
1952	34,645	1966	19,921	1980	21,559
1953	33,269	1967	20,071	1981	21,457
1954	34,039	1968	19,081	1982	24,330
1955	31,824	1969	18,054	1983	26,443
1956	28,649	1970	18,048	1984	29,172
1957	30,369	1971	19,060	1985	28,004
1958	25,044	1972	17,210	1986	27,622

Source: Records held by the Prior, St Patrick's Purgatory, Lough Derg, Pettigo, Co. Donegal.

Appendix D
Population of Each Irish Province, 1926–66

Year	Leinster	Munster	Connacht	Ulster*	Total
1926	1,149,092	969,902	552,907	300,091	2,971,992
1936	1,220,411	942,272	525,468	280,269	2,968,420
1946	1,281,117	917,306	492,797	263,887	2,955,107
1951	1,336,576	898,870	471,895	253,252	2,960,593
1956	1,338,942	877,238	446,221	235,863	2,898,264
1961	1,332,149	849,203	419,465	217,524	2,818,341
1966	1,414,415	859,334	401,950	208,303	2,884,002

* Figures for Ulster are for Counties Cavan, Donegal and Monaghan.

Source: Census of Population of Ireland, 1979, Central Statistics Office, 1979, 1980.

Appendix E
Net Emigration by Province, 1946–51

Area	Total
Dublin County Borough, Dún Laoghaire Borough and remainder of Co. Dublin	+ 16,385*
Rest of Leinster	31,554
Munster	52,206
Connacht	35,715
Ulster (Cavan, Donegal, Monaghan)	18,541
Total	121,631

* Net immigration

Source: Census of Population of Ireland, 1951, Preliminary Report, Central Statistics Office, 1951.

Appendix F
Average Annual Rate of Net Emigration per 1,000 of Average Population in the Intercensal Periods 1946–51, 1951–56, 1956–61, 1961–66 and 1966–71

Province	1946–51	1951–56	1956–61	1961–66	1966–71
Leinster	2.1	11.4	13.1	1.5	2.2
Munster	11.7	12.8	14.2	6.4	3.9
Connacht	15.1	17.4	18.3	13.6	10.6
Ulster*	14.6	19.6	20.7	14.2	6.9
Total	8.2	13.4	14.8	5.7	4.2

* The figures for Ulster are for Counties Cavan, Donegal and Monaghan.

Source: *Census of Population of Ireland, 1971, Preliminary Report*, Central Statistics Office, 1971.

Appendix G
Estimated Natural Increase/Decrease in Population and Estimated Net Emigration in Each Province in Each Intercensal Period, 1926–61

(i) Leinster

	Increase/Decrease	Estimated Net Emigration
1926–36	+ 71,319	4,283
1936–46	+ 60,706	36,641
1946–51	+ 55,459	13,229
1951–56	+ 2,461	75,999
1956–61	- 6,793	87,646

(ii) Munster

	Increase/Decrease	Estimated Net Emigration
1926–36	- 27,630	78,269
1936–46	- 24,966	71,699
1946–51	- 18,436	52,021
1951–56	- 21,727	56,768
1956–61	- 28,035	61,400

(iii) Connacht

	Increase/Decrease	Estimated Net Emigration
1926–36	- 27,439	54,577
1936–46	- 32,671	52,454
1946–51	- 20,902	35,784
1951–56	- 25,674	40,031
1956–61	- 26,756	39,515

(iv) Ulster (Cavan, Donegal and Monaghan)

	Increase/Decrease	Estimated Net Emigration
1926–36	- 19,822	29,622
1936–46	- 16,382	26,317
1946–51	- 10,635	18,534
1951–56	- 17,389	23,965
1956–61	- 18,339	23,442

Source for G i, ii, iii, iv: *Census of Population of Ireland, 1961*, Central Statistics Office, 1963.

Appendix H
Mass Attendance by Irish Catholics, 1973–74

Overall Attendance	%	Cum %
Daily	5.6	5.6
More than once weekly	17.8	23.4
Weekly	67.5	90.9
1–3 times monthly	3.4	94.3
Less than once monthly	3.0	97.3
Never	2.6	(2.6)
	N = 2,499	

Appendix I
Communion and Confession Attendance by Irish Catholics, 1973–74

Frequency	Communion		Confession	
	%	Cum %	%	Cum %
Daily	3.6	3.6	—	—
More than once a week	6.1	9.7	—	—
Once weekly	18.3	28.0	0.8	0.8
2–3 times a month	16.2	44.2	5.3	6.1
Once monthly	21.4	65.6	40.4	46.5
About 6 times a year	13.5	79.2	23.3	69.8
Up to 3 times a year	12.7	91.9	20.0	89.8
Less than yearly	(5.1)	—	(6.4)	—
Never	(3.0)	—	(3.7)	—
	N = 2,495			

Source Appendices H and I: *A Survey of Religious Practice, Attitudes and Beliefs in the Republic of Ireland, 1973–1974,* Research and Development Unit, Catholic Communications Institute of Ireland, Dublin, 1975.

APPENDIX J

The following is a selection from the *Catalogue of Books, Booklets and Leaflets* of the Catholic Truth Society of Ireland (CTSI), Veritas House, Dublin, 1962. (In the case of a number of titles listed, the author's name is not published.)

Angels and Devils, Rev. D. Rumble MSC
Are Indulgences for Sale? Grover Ables
Brown Scapular of Our Lady of Mount Carmel, The, Rev. E. Elliott, O.Carm.
Catholic Answers to Questions posed by Protestants, Rev. J. Murphy CSsR
Catholic Education: Its Function and Scope, Most Rev. J.C. McQuaid DD, Archbishop of Dublin and Primate of Ireland
Catholic Truth Society of Ireland: Its Origin and Purpose, The, His Eminence John Cardinal D'Alton, Archbishop of Armagh
Catholics and Freemasonry, Rev. L. Rumble MSC
Celebration of the Holy Hour, Ven. J. Archdeacon Browne, PP
Devotion to the Holy Ghost, Benedictine Convent, Missouri
Devotions for the Holy Souls, Rev. Fr Reginald OFM Cap.
Devotions to St Mary Magdalene: Novena and Prayers, Fr Reginald OFM
Divorce is a Disease, Rev. Martin J. Scott SJ
Don't Marry a Catholic, Rev. Daniel A. Lord SJ
Don't Swear Like That, Rev. D.A. Lord SJ
Escaping Purgatory, Rev. A. Gits SJ
Fall and Original Sin, The
Fashionable Sin, Rev. D.A. Lord SJ
From One Exile to Another, T. Gavin
Have I a Vocation?
Hell, Rev. Wm. P. O'Keeffe CM
Hints on Child Character Training, A Psychologist
Holy Hour of Prayer, The, Rev. R. O'Kennedy
Holy Hours, Rev. William Moran PP
How to make an Act of Perfect Contrition, Rev. L. Dowling SJ
How to Pray the Mass, Rev. D.A. Lord SJ
'I Can Read Anything', Rev. D.A. Lord SJ
I Have a Soul to Save, Mary Foster
'I Was Going Steady', Rev. D.A. Lord SJ
Individual and the State, The, Most Rev. Dr Philbin, Lord Bishop of Clonfert.
Indulgences: What Are They? Rev. John A. O'Brien PhD
Jehovah Witnesses, The, Rev. L. Rumble MSC
Lent: Its Meaning and Observance, Dom Mark Tierney OSB
Manual of the Sacred Heart Confraternity, A
Miraculous Medal, The, Rev. W. O'Keeffe CM
Marry Your Own, Rev. D.A. Lord SJ
May I Keep Company? Rev. J. Gorey CSsR
Modesty and Modernity, M. de R. Swanton

Mortal Sin and How to Avoid it, Rev. Wm. P. O'Keeffe CM
Novena in Honour of the Little Flower, A, Rev. D.A. Lord SJ
Novena of Grace to St Joseph, Rev. Fr Reginald OFM Cap.
Novena of Holy Communion, A, Rev. Basil Rosario SJ
One True Church: Which is it? The, Rev. P. Finlay SJ
Patricians, The, Frank Duff
Priest and Protestants, A, Rev. R. Nash SJ
Pure of Heart, The, Rev. D A. Lord SJ
Purgatory
Sacred Heart Novena and Prayers, The, Fr Reginald OFM Cap.
Scruples: How to Avoid Them, Rev. W.P. O'Keeffe CM
Second Vatican Council, The, Dr D.C. Pochin Mould
Simple Method of Doing the Stations of the Cross, A
Social Teachings of the Church, The, His Eminence Cardinal D'Alton, Archbishop of Armagh and Primate of All Ireland
Thirty Days Prayer in Honour of the Sacred Heart, Rev. Edward Lazzarini SJ
Towards Christian Unity, Rev. M. Hurley SJ
Vocations for Boys and Girls, A Priest
What NOT to Do on a Date, Rev. T.J. McGloin SJ
What to Do on a Date, Rev. D.A. Lord SJ
What You Ought to Know before Marriage, Rev. Godfrey Poage CP
'Worship' of Mary, The, Rev. W.J. Lonergan SJ
Year of Plenary Indulgences, A, compiled by M.M. Heavey
Youth's Ideal: A Chaste Courtship, Rev. J. O'Brien PhD

APPENDIX K
RELIGIOUS COMPOSITION OF POPULATION OF TWENTY-SIX COUNTIES OF REPUBLIC OF IRELAND, 1991

Year	Population	RC	C of I	Pres.	Meth.	Jew	Other	No rel.	No info.
1991	3,525,719	91.6	2.5	0.4	0.14	0.04	1.1	1.9	2.4

Source: Census 91, volume 5, Religion, CSO, Dublin, November, 1995.

Appendix L

Statement of the Yearly Number of Pilgrims who participated in the Three-day pilgrimage to Lough Derg, 1987–2001

1987	28,741	1992	22,122	1997	11,771
1988	28,216	1993	18,615	1998	10,973
1989	27,661	1994	15,813	1999	10,134
1990	25,390	1995	13,779	2000	12,251
1991	24,863	1996	12,382	2001	11,079

Source: Records held by the Prior, St Patrick's Purgatory, Lough Derg, Pettigo, Co. Donegal.

Notes

Introduction and Overview (pp xii–xviii)

1. *Census of Population of Ireland, 1946, 1961, 1971, 1981*, Dublin.
   See Appendix A.
2. Mícheál Mac Gréil, *Religious Practice and Attitudes in Ireland: Report of a Survey of Religious Attitudes and Practice and Related Issues in the Republic of Ireland, 1988–1989*, published by the Survey and Research Unit Maynooth, 1991, 8, 9, 65–9.
   See also Brendan Walsh, *Religion and Demographic Behaviour in Ireland*, Economic and Social Research Institute, Paper 55, Dublin, 1970.
   See also Appendix B.
   While surveys in the 1970s and 1980s showed a decline in religious practice, it was gradual. Opinion polls in the 1990s have indicated a more rapid and significant decline in religious practice. This will be elaborated in the epilogue.
3. *Economic Development*, Dublin, 1958.
   Programme for Economic Expansion, Dublin, 1958.
4. Information conveyed to the author by Fr Ronan Drury, editor of the *Furrow*.
5. *Commission on Emigration and Other Population Problems, 1948–1954*, Dublin, 1956.
6. *Commission on Emigration and Other Population Problems: Minority Report* by Most Rev. Dr Cornelius Lucey, Dublin, 1956.
7. Alexander J. Humphreys, *New Dubliners: Urbanization and the Irish Family*, London, 1966.
8. *Limerick Rural Survey*, Tipperary, 1962.
9. *Investment in Education — Report of the Survey Team*, Dublin, 1966.
10. *Report of the Council of Education on the Curriculum of the Secondary School*, Dublin, 1962.
11. *A Survey of Religious Practice Attitudes and Beliefs in the Republic of Ireland, 1973–1974*; report no. 1, *Religious Practice*, May 1975; report no. 2, *Religious Beliefs and Values*, 1975; report no. 3, *Moral Values*, 1976; report no. 4, *Attitudes to the Institutional Church*, 1976, Research and Development Unit, Catholic Communications Institute of Ireland, Dublin, 1975, 1976. See bibliography for a detailed list of surveys and reports.

Prologue (pp xix–xxxviii)

1. Oliver MacDonagh, 'The Politicization of the Irish Catholic Bishops, 1800–1850' *Historical Journal*, 18/1 (1975), 38.
2. Patrick J. Corish, *The Irish Catholic Experience: A Historical Survey*, Dublin, 1985, 242.
3. See MacDonagh, 'The Politicization of the Irish Catholic Bishops', 38–9.
4. Ibid., 40–41. See also C.D.A. Leighton, 'Gallicanism and the Veto Controversy: Church, State and Catholic Community in Early Nineteenth Century Ireland' in R.V. Comerford, M. Cullen, J.R. Hill, C. Lennon, eds., *Religion, Conflict and Coexistence in Ireland*, Dublin, 1990, 135–58.

5. See also Tom Bartlett, *The Fall and Rise of the Irish Nation: The Catholic Question 1690–1830,* Dublin, 1992, 311. Bartlett has highlighted a number of factors which led to the increased politicisation of the Catholic peasantry in the sixty years leading up to 1826, such as the increase in opportunities to socialise offered by secret societies, fairs and markets, Protestant proselytism and the shared historical memory that grew up around the 1798 rebellion. He has argued that this development, which was essentially local and lay-inspired, had by 1826 reached a level which O'Connell could shape and mobilise to secure the political aims of Catholic Ireland.
6. Ibid., 335 8.
7. D. George Boyce, *Nineteenth-Century Ireland: The Search for Stability,* Dublin, 1990, 38–9.
8. Bartlett, *The Fall and Rise of the Irish Nation,* 339–40.
9. Boyce, *Nineteenth-Century Ireland,* 46–7.
10. Emmet Larkin, 'Church, State and Nation in Modern Ireland', *The Historical Dimensions of Irish Catholicism,* New York, 1976, 1248.
11. MacDonagh, 'The Politicization of the Irish Catholic Bishops', 42. See also Fergus O'Farrell, 'The Only Lever ...? The Catholic Priest in Irish Politics 1823–29', *Studies,* 70 (1981), 308–24.
12. D. George Boyce, *Nineteenth Century Ireland,* 53.
13. MacDonagh, 'The Politicization of the Irish Catholic Bishops', 43.
14. John Coolahan, *Irish Education: History and Structure,* Dublin, 1981, 9.
15. Ibid., 4.
16. D.H. Akenson, *The Irish Educational Experiment: The National System of Education in the Nineteenth Century,* London, 1970, 392.
17. R.V. Comerford, 'The British State and the Education of Irish Catholics, 1850–1921' in Janusz Tomiak, ed., *Comparative Studies on Governments and Non-Dominant Ethnic Groups in Europe, 1850–1940,* vol. 1, New York, 16.
18. Akenson, *The Irish Educational Experiment,* 157–61.
19. Comerford, 'The British State and the Education of Irish Catholics', 17–8.
20. Ibid., 19.
21. Corish, *The Irish Catholic Experience,* 165.
22. Coolahan, *Irish Education,* 14–6.
23. See Sean Cannon, *Irish Episcopal Meetings, 1788–1882,* Rome, 1979.
24. Ibid.
25. Donal Kerr, *Peel, Priests and Politics: Sir Robert Peel's Administration and the Roman Catholic Church in Ireland 1841–46,* Oxford, 1982, 3.
26. Ibid.
27. Archbishop Murray of Dublin (from 1823) and Bishop Doyle of Kildare and Leighlin (J.K.L.) were in favour of the national school system from the outset, while Archbishop MacHale of Tuam (from 1834) was vehemently opposed to it. Murray of Dublin served as a commissioner on the Board of Education set up to administer the system. Doyle of Kildare and Leighlin spoke with a very ecumenical voice in the context of the time. With regard to the Queen's Colleges, Archbishops Crolly of Armagh and Murray of Dublin were inclined to accept them, though with reservations, whereas MacHale of Tuam and a majority of the bishops favoured purely Catholic colleges. On this issue, Cullen was in agreement with MacHale. Archbishop Walsh, who was appointed Archbishop of Dublin in 1885, was in favour of an interdenominational solution to the university problem, which would embrace Trinity College. Cullen was vehemently opposed to the Fenians, as was Bishop Moriarty of Kerry, and he successfully got a

decree issued against them by Rome. MacHale bitterly opposed him on this issue and protected a pro-Fenian priest, Fr Lavelle of Partry, who constantly defied Cullen. Bishop O'Dwyer of Limerick was one of two bishops who went against the body of bishops, when the latter rejected the papal decree against the Plan of Campaign, 1888, while he spoke out vehemently against General Maxwell after the execution of the leaders of the 1916 Rising. These are just a few of many examples of how individualistic and independent-minded the Irish bishops were in the nineteenth century.

28. Corish, *The Irish Catholic Experience*, 166.
29. Kerr, *Peel, Priests and Politics*, 2.
30. Ibid.
31. Emmet Larkin, 'Economic Growth, Capital Investment and the Roman Catholic Church in Nineteenth Century Ireland', *The Historical Dimensions of Irish Catholicism*, New York, 1976, 853.
32. See D.W. Miller, 'Irish Catholicism and the Great Famine', *Journal of Social History*, IX/1 (1975), 81–98.
33. Corish, *The Irish Catholic Experience*, 166–7. See also Patrick J. Corish, 'The Catholic Community in the Nineteenth Century', *Archivium Hibernicum*, 39 (1983), 27. Corish disputed Miller's 1975 estimates, considering them too low. More recently, Miller has revisited his data and, with the benefit of more advanced technology, he has examined it in more detail. His conclusions may be found in David W. Miller, 'Mass Attendance in Ireland in 1834' in Stewart J. Brown and David W. Miller, eds., *Piety and Power in Ireland 1760–1960: Essays in Honour of Emmet Larkin*, Indiana, 2000, 158–79.
34. For an account of religious life and practice in a rural parish between 1800 and 1829, see Mark Tierney, *Murroe and Boher: The History of an Irish Country Parish*, Dublin, 1966, 44–52. See also John Hogan, 'Patron Days and Holy Wells in Ossory' in Kilkenny Archaelogical Society's proceedings 1872–3, *Journal of the Royal Society of Antiquaries of Ireland.* See also K. Theodore Hoppen, *Ireland since 1800: Conflict and Conformity*, London and New York, 1989, 65–6. See also Kerr, *Peel, Priests and Politics*, 48.
35. Patrick J. Corish, *Maynooth College, 1795–1995*, Dublin, 1995, 3–25.
36. Hoppen, *Ireland since 1800*, 61.
37. Ibid.
38. Cited in ibid., 62.
39. John A. Murphy, 'Priests and People in Modern Irish History', *Christus Rex* xxiii/4 (October 1969), 236.
40. Ibid. See also Kerr, *Peel, Priests and Politics*, 30.
41. See *Syllabus of the Most Principal Errors of Our Time, which are Censured in Consistorial Allocutions, Encyclicals, and Other Apostolical Letters of Our Most Holy Lord Pope Pius IX, IER*, I (February 1865), xxxiv–xliii. A central tenet of the nineteenth-century liberal movement was that Church and state should be separate and this was condemned by Pope Pius IX in error no. 55.
42. Cited in Kerr, *Peel, Priests and Politics*, 38.
43. *Catholic Directory*, Dublin, 1844, 305.
44. J.G. Kohl, *Travels in Ireland* (English translation) London, 1844, 110, 125.
45. W.M. Thackeray, *The Irish Sketch Book*, London, 1879, 39.
46. Caitriona Clear, *Nuns in Nineteenth-Century Ireland*, Dublin, Washington, 1987.
47. Emmet Larkin, 'The Devotional Revolution in Ireland', *The Historical Dimensions of Irish Catholicism*, New York, 1976, 630.
48. J. Johnston, *A Tour in Ireland, with Meditations and Reflections*, London 1844, 120.

49. See Kerr, *Peel, Priests and Politics,* 44–51.
50. See Larkin, 'The Devotional Revolution', 625–52. In this article published in 1972, Larkin put forward the thesis that Archbishop Paul Cullen championed the consolidation of a 'devotional revolution' in post-famine Ireland. More recently this theory has been much criticised. For an overview of the debate, see T.G. McGrath, 'The Tridentine Evolution of Modern Irish Catholicism, 1563–1962: A Re-examination of the "Devotional Revolution" Thesis' in Réamonn Ó Muirí, ed., *Irish Church History Today: Cumann Seanchais Ard Mhacha Seminar, 10 March 1990,* Armagh, n.d., 84–99.
51. Patrick Wallace, 'Irish Catechesis — The Heritage from James Butler II, Archbishop of Cashel 1774–91', Ph.D. thesis, Catholic University America, 1975, 105–11.
52. Maureen Wall, 'The Rise of a Catholic Middle Class in Eighteenth Century Ireland', *Irish Historical Studies,* 11 (1958), 91–115.
53. Corish, *The Irish Catholic Experience,* 172.
54. Sean Connolly, *Religion and Society in Nineteenth Century Ireland,* Dundalk, 1985, 53–4.
55. Corish, 'The Catholic Community in Nineteenth Century Ireland', p. 26.
56. Larkin, 'Church, State and Nation', 1253.
57. Larkin, 'Economic Growth, Capital Investment and the Roman Catholic Church', 862–3.
58. Connolly, *Religion and Society,* 54. See also Larkin, 'The Devotional Revolution', 627, 639.
59. Corish, *The Irish Catholic Experience,* 193–4.
60. Ibid., 195.
61. Gallicanism, though it received its name from the French Church, was not a phenomenon restricted to France, but was part of a wider European movement, which sought to restrict the power of the pope over national churches and temporal rulers.
62. Ultramontane is the term which describes those Catholics who strongly support the authority of the pope over national or diocesan authority. The term was derived from the idea that the pope, for the greater part of Europe, resides beyond the mountains — beyond the Alps.
63. Connolly, *Religion and Society,* 12.
64. Corish, *The Irish Catholic Experience,* 201.
65. Corish, *The Irish Catholic Experience,* 162.
66. Jansenists subscribed to the preaching of Cornelius Jansen (1585–1638), Bishop of Ypres in West Flanders. His doctrines were condemned by Pope Urban VIII in 1642, Pope Innocent X in 1653 and again by Pope Clement XI in the papal bull, *Unigenitus,* of 1705. Despite this, the rigorisms of Jansenism persisted particularly in France. For this reason the movement is often confused with Gallicanism and the terms are often used in an interchangeable way as though they were identical. The following writers have considered this question: Desmond Keenan, *The Catholic Church in Nineteenth Century Ireland,* Dublin, 1983, 22, 97; M. Turner, 'The French Connection with Maynooth College 1795–1855', *Studies,* LXX (1981), 81–2; John Healy, *Maynooth College: Its Centenary History,* Dublin, 1895, 274, 283; S.J. Connolly, *Priests and People in Pre-Famine Ireland 1780–1845,* Dublin, 1982, 45, 47, 113, 185; Desmond Bowen, *Paul Cardinal Cullen,* Dublin, 1983, 44–5; Emmet Larkin, 'Church, State and Nation', 1255–6; Patrick J. Corish, *Maynooth College 1795–1995,* Dublin, 1995.
67. See Tom Inglis, *Moral Monopoly: The Rise and Fall of the Catholic Church in Modern Ireland,* Dublin, 1998, for an interesting account of the Irish civilising process and the part played by nuns, priests and brothers.

68. Connolly, *Religion and Society*, 25.
69. Ibid., 26.
70. Ibid., 27.
71. Corish, *The Irish Catholic Experience*, 206.
72. Ibid., 207. The downside of this though was that it was bedevilled by lack of resources. The Intermediate Education Act of 1878, which made grants available on the basis of students' performance in a range of subjects in public examinations, went some way towards alleviating this.
73. MacDonagh, 'The Politicization of the Irish Catholic Bishops', 48.
74. J.H. Whyte, 'Political Problems 1850–60' in Patrick J. Corish, ed., *A History of Irish Catholicism*, 5/2, Dublin and Melbourne, 1967, 13.
75. Ibid., 24–5. See also J.H. Whyte, 'The Influence of the Catholic Clergy on Elections in Nineteenth Century Ireland', *English Historical Review*, 75 (April 1960), 239–59.
76. Whyte, 'Political Problems 1850–1860', 24.
77. Ibid., 26.
78. Patrick J. Corish, 'Political Problems 1860–1878' in Patrick J. Corish, ed., *A History of Irish Catholicism*, 5/3, Dublin and Melbourne, 1967, 9. The chorus of condemnations was led by Cullen and Bishop Moriarty of Kerry, who became infamous for his remark that hell was not hot enough nor eternity long enough for those who joined the organisation.
79. Larkin, 'Church, State and Nation', 1261.
80. See R.V. Comerford, *The Fenians in Context: Irish Politics and Society 1848–82*, Dublin, 1985, 1998, 111.
81. Cited in Donal McCartney, *The Dawning of Democracy: Ireland 1800–1870*, Dublin, 1987, 187–8.
82. Larkin, 'Church, State and Nation', 1261.
83. Ibid., 1260–61.
84. See R.V. Comerford, 'Churchmen, Tenants and Independent Opposition, 1850–56', in W.E. Vaughan, ed., *A New History of Ireland, vol. 5*, Oxford, 1989, 400.
85. Corish, 'Political Problems 1860–1878', 17–8.
86. See R.V. Comerford, 'Gladstone's First Irish Enterprise 1864–70' in W.E. Vaughan, ed., *A New History of Ireland, vol. 5*, Oxford, 1989, 439.
87. Ibid., 432
88. Ibid.
89. See E.R. Norman, *The Catholic Church and Irish Politics in the Eighteen Sixties*, Irish History Series, 5, Dundalk, 1969, 16–7.
90. See E.R. Norman, *The Catholic Church and Ireland in the Age of Rebellion 1859–1873*, London, 1965, 139–151.
91. See Comerford, 'Gladstone's First Irish Enterprise' in *A New History of Ireland*, 441–3.
92. Corish, 'Political Problems 1860–78', 29–30. As a result of the Tithe Commutation Act of 1837 the tax was included in the rent paid by tenants to their landlords to appease Catholics and non-conformists. However, as this was simply a cosmetic exercise, the tithe remained a source of contention.
93. Ibid., 31–2.
94. Ibid., 34–5.
95. D. George Boyce, *Nineteenth Century Ireland*, 125.
96. K. Theodore Hoppen, *Elections, Politics and Society in Ireland 1832–1885*, Oxford, 1984, 17–8.

97. Many historians have referred to this. See K.H. Connell, 'Catholicism and Marriage in the Century after the Famine' in K.H. Connell, *Irish Peasant Society: Four Historical Essays*, Oxford, 1968, 113–61. See also David Fitzpatrick, 'Marriage in Post-Famine Ireland' in Art Cosgrave, ed., *Marriage in Ireland*, Dublin, 1985, 116–31.
98. The act laid the foundation for legal protection for the tenant and compensation in the event of eviction.
99. Corish, 'Political Problems 1860–78', 44–7.
100. Ibid., 50.
101. Dom Cuthbert Butler, *The Vatican Council 1869–1870*, London, 1930, 1962, 400–17.
102. Ibid. 416.
103. Corish, 'Political Problems 1860–78', 55–7.
104. Ibid., 57
105. Larkin, 'Church, State and Nation', 1264–5.
106. Cited in ibid., 1265.
107. Patrick Murray, *Oracles of God: The Roman Catholic Church and Irish Politics, 1922–37*, Dublin, 2000, 5.
108. Larkin, 'Church, State and Nation', 1262–3.
109. Ibid., 1265–6. See also Hoppen, *Ireland since 1800*, 121.
110. D. George Boyce, *Nineteenth Century Ireland: The Search for Stability*, Dublin, 1990, 181
111. Larkin, 'Church, State and Nation', 1266–7.
112. The Wyndham Land Act, 1903, was the most successful of all the land acts. It provided £100 million to help tenants to buy out their farms. The act was an immediate success. Between 1903 and 1920, about eleven million acres of land changed hands.
113. David W. Miller, *Church, State and Nation in Ireland 1898–1921*, Dublin, 1973, 124–5.
114. Fergal McGrath, 'The University Question' in Patrick J. Corish, ed., *A History of Irish Catholicism*, 5/6, Dublin and London, 1971, 132.
115. Ibid.
116. Ibid.
117. Ibid., 133–5.
118. Larkin, 'Church, State and Nation', 1267.
119. Ibid., 1269–70. See also Hoppen, *Ireland since 1800*, 166–7.
120. Patrick Murray, *Oracles of God*, 4–7.
121. Ibid., 7.
122. Ibid., 5.
123. Larkin, 'Church, State and Nation', 1271–2.
124. See text of bishops' pastoral letter in *The Irish Times*, 11 October 1922, 5. See also Murray, *Oracles of God*, 425–30.

Chapter 1 The Legitimisation of the Catholic Ethos (pp 3–18)

1. Emmet Larkin, 'Church, State and Nation in Modern Ireland', *American Historical Review*, LXXX/5 (December 1975), 1267.
2. Ibid., 1276.
3. Raymond Williams, *The Long Revolution*, Harmondsworth, 1966, 171–2.
   See also Raymond Williams, 'Base and Superstructure in Marxist Cultural Theory' in Roger Dale, Geoff Esland and Madeleine MacDonald, eds., *Schooling and Capitalism*, London, 1976, 205.
4. *Census of Ireland, 1911*, London, 1912.

5. David W. Miller, *Church, State and Nation in Ireland 1898–1921,* Dublin, 1973, 493.
6. Ronan Fanning, *Independent Ireland,* Dublin, 1983, 54–7.
7. Cited in Ibid., 56.
8. Dermot Keogh, *The Vatican, the Bishops and Irish Politics 1919–1939,* Cambridge, 1986 138*ff.*
9. *Irish Independent,* 11 February 1932.
10. See *The Irish Times,* 20–27 June 1932 for details of ceremonies during Eucharistic Congress.
11. *Irish Press,* 2 May 1932.
12. Jan Olaf Smit, *Pope Pius XII,* adapted into English by James H. Vanderveldt, London, 1950, 218–9.
    See also Anne Fremantle, *The Papal Encyclicals in their Historical Context,* New York, 1956, 228–94.
13. Maurice Moynihan, *Speeches and Statements by de Valera 1917–1973,* Dublin, 1980, 233.
14. *Irish Press,* 18 March 1935, 2.
15. *Irish Press,* 18 March 1943, 1.
16. Fanning, *Independent Ireland,* 59.
17. J.H. Whyte, *Church and State in Modern Ireland 1923–1970,* Dublin, 1971, 50.
18. For a detailed account of the church personnel consulted in the drafting of the constitution see Dermot Keogh, *Twentieth-Century Ireland: Nation and State,* Dublin, 1994, 96–104. See also Dermot Keogh, *Ireland and the Vatican: The Politics and Diplomacy of Church–State Relations 1922–1960,* Cork, 1995, 132–40. In addition to his ongoing close consultations with Dr John Charles McQuaid, de Valera also consulted with Cardinal MacRory of Armagh, the Papal Nuncio Paschal Robinson, and Archbishop Byrne of Dublin. It is important to point out that as well as consulting Catholic Church interests, he also consulted the Church of Ireland Archbishop of Armagh, Charles Frederick D'Arcy; the Church of Ireland Archbishop of Dublin, John Allen Gregg; the Presbyterian Moderator, Dr J.A.H. Irwin; and Rev. W.H. Massey, head of the Methodist Church in Ireland. See also Seán Faughnan, 'The Jesuits and the Drafting of the Irish Constitution of 1937', *Irish Historical Studies,* 26/101 (May 1988), 85. See also Don O'Leary, *Vocationalism and Social Catholicism in Twentieth Century Ireland,* Dublin, 2000, 55–8. O'Leary discusses the influence of Fr Edward Cahill SJ and fellow Jesuits, and also submissions made by Dr Cornelius Lucey and Dr Michael Browne, all of whom were outspoken advocates of Catholic social teaching as enunciated in the papal encyclicals *Rerum Novarum,* 1891, and *Quadragesimo Anno,* 1931.
19. *Bunreacht na hÉireann,* Dublin, n.d. 136.
20. Ibid., 138–40.
21. Ibid., 144, 146.
22. Ibid., 144.
23. Ibid.
24. *Dáil Debates,* 67, col. 1890 (4 June 1937).
25. Ibid., col. 1891. Cardinal MacRory and Dr J.C. McQuaid were anxious that the Catholic Church be recognised in Article 44 as the one true church. In order to avert a Church–state crisis, Joseph Walshe, secretary of the Department of External Affairs, was sent to Rome where he sought the advice of the cardinal secretary of state Eugenio Pacelli, who was later to become Pope Pius XII. While the Vatican would have liked a more exclusive recognition to be accorded the Catholic Church, diplomacy prevailed and it was decided to remain neutral, which left the way open for de Valera to use the

term churches in recognition of the other Christian bodies. See Keogh, *Twentieth Century Ireland*, 100–1. See also Keogh, *Ireland and the Vatican*, 132–40.
26. The Earl of Longford and Thomas O'Neill, *Eamon de Valera*, London, 1970, 298, 300.
27. *Irish Press*, 24 June 1937.
28. *Irish Catechetical Directory (ICD), 1949* (24 February 1948), 705.
29. *Irish Independent*, 26–28 December 1949.
30. *ICD, 1951* (11 January, 26 April 1950), 725, 737.
31. *Irish Weekly Independent*, 4 November 1950.
32. Whyte, *Church and State*, 158.
33. Ibid., 158–9.
34. See Whyte, *Church and State*, 167–71
35. Ibid., 163–5. For a detailed account of the influence of the Maria Duce movement see Enda Gerard Delaney, 'Fr Denis Fahy C.S.Sp. and Maria Duce 1945–1954', M.A. thesis, St Patrick's College Maynooth, 1993.
36. Evelyn Bolster, *The Knights of St Columbanus*, Dublin, 1979.
37. *ICD, 1951* (11 January 1950), 725.
38. Ibid., 739.
39. Ibid., 737.
40. Ibid., 733.
41. John McGahern, *Irish Independent*, 31 July 1993, in 'Weekender', 1.
42. *ICD, 1954* (28 January 1953), 702.
43. Mary Ryan, 'The American Parade' in Lynn Hunt, ed., *The New Cultural History* California, 1989, 131–53.
44. Anthony Giddens, *Capitalism and Modern Social Theory: An Analysis of the Writings of Marx, Durkheim and Max Weber*, Cambridge 1971, 105–18.
See also Ian Thompson, *Religion*, New York, 1991, 4–7.
45. John Skorupski, *Symbol and Theory: A Philosophical Study of Theories of Religion in Social Anthropology*, Cambridge, 1976, 84.
46. See Thomas R. Bates, 'Gramsci and the Theory of Hegemony', *Journal of the History of Ideas*, 36 (1975), 360.
See also Rosamund Billington, Sheelagh Strawbridge, *Culture and Society*, London, 1991, 26–8.
47. Emmet Larkin, 'The Devotional Revolution in Ireland 1850–1875', *American Historical Review*, LXXVII/3 (June 1972), 644–5.
48. See Séamas Ó Buachalla, *Educational Policy in Twentieth Century Ireland*, Dublin, 1988, 50.
49. Ibid., 255.
50. *Dáil Debates*, 159, Col. 1494 (19 July 1956).
51. Cited in John Mescal, *Religion in the Irish System of Education*, Dublin, 1957, 136–7.
52. *Report of the Council of Education on (1) The Function of the Primary School, (2) The Curriculum to be Pursued in the Primary School*, Dublin, 1954. (Hereafter referred to as *Council of Education Report on the Primary School*.)
53. *Report of the Council of Education on the Curriculum of the Secondary School*, Dublin, 1962. (Hereafter referred to as *Council of Education Report on the Secondary School*.)
54. See *Council of Education Report on the Primary School*, paras. 195, 196, 130, 132.
55. Ibid., 132.
56. See *Council of Education Report on the Secondary School*, paras. 150, 164, 80, 88.
57. Ibid., 90.

58. Ibid., 144.
59. Ibid., 184, 190.
60. See Pope Pius XII, 'Technological Concept of Life', *Irish Ecclesiastical Record,* 83 (January–June, 1955), 297–306.
    Pope Pius XII, Extract from the papal message to the world on 'The Technological Spirit', 24 December 1953, in P.J. McLaughlin, *The Church and Modern Science,* Dublin, 1957, 208–15.
    See also Papal Allocution to the Plenary Assembly of the Pontifical Academy of Science, 24 April, *Furrow,* 7/5 (May 1956), 261–8.
    See also many addresses and messages similar in theme delivered by Pope Pius XII throughout the 1950s as published in *The Pope Speaks,* Washington, 1954–7.
61. *Divinii illius magistri, Encyclical Letter of His Holiness Pope Pius XI on Christian Education of Youth, 1929,* London, 1942.
62. Ibid.
63. Ibid.
64. Raymond Williams, 'Base and Superstructure in Marxist Cultural Theory' in Roger Dale, Geoff Esland and Madeleine MacDonald, eds., *Schooling and Capitalism,* London, 1976, 205.
65. Max Weber, *The Protestant Ethic and the Spirit of Capitalism,* London, 1991.
66. Horace Plunkett, *Ireland in the New Century,* London, 1904, 101–2.
67. Michael O'Riordan, *Catholicity and Progress in Ireland,* London, 1906.
68. See Frank A. Biletz, 'The Irish Peasant and the Conflict between Irish-Ireland and the Catholic Bishops, 1903–10' in Brown and Miller, eds., *Piety and Power in Ireland,* 108–29.
69. Patrick Kenny, *Economics for Irishmen,* Dublin, 1907.
70. Patrick Kenny, *The Sorrows of Ireland,* Dublin, 1907.
71. W.P. Ryan, *The Pope's Green Island,* London, 1912.
72. See letter from J.M. O'Sullivan TD, Minister for Education, to Bishop Keane of Limerick on the 1930 Vocational Education Act, 31 October 1930, published in Ó Buachalla, *Educational Policy,* 399–403.
73. Ibid., 401.
74. Ibid.
75. *Dáil Debates,* 77, col. 1565 (1940).
76. *ICD, 1951* (15 August 1950), 753.
77. See *Furrow* 5/10 (October 1954), 665. See also *Furrow,* 6/12 (December 1955), 793.
78. See for example *Irish Independent,* 5 February 1951, 4, 6. See also *Irish Independent,* 1 March 1954, 8, 10. See also *Irish Independent,* 13 February 1956, 8–11.
79. These circulation figures were given in reply to a parliamentary question in the Dáil in 1947. See *Dáil Debates,* 106, col. 1523 (11 June 1947).
80. See John A. Coleman SJ, *The Evolution of Dutch Catholicism, 1958–1974,* Berkeley, 1978, 63, 74.
81. Ibid., 87.
82. Ibid., 60.
83. Whyte, *Church and State,* 44–7, 169–71, 322–5.
84. *Irish Independent,* 20 February 1950, 8. *Irish Independent,* 25 February 1963, 6.
85. Ibid. This regulation in fact varied little between 1950 and 1964. See also C.H. Holland, ed., *Trinity College Dublin and the Idea of a University,* Dublin, 1991, 29–53.
86. *Acta et Decreta, Concilii plenarii episcoporum Hiberniae: quod habitum est apud Maynutiam die 2 Augusti et diebus sequentibus usque ad diem 15 Augusti 1927,* Dublin, 1929.

87. *Acta et Decreta, Concilii plenarii episcoporum Hiberniae: quod habitum est apud Maynutiam die 7 Augusti et diebus sequentibus usque ad diem 15 Augusti 1956,* Dublin, 1960, Statute 287, 100–01.
88. See Michael Hurley SJ, 'Chronicle', 'Ecumenism: Joint Worship', *Furrow,* 16/4 (April 1965), 235–7.
89. *Codex Iuris Canonici Pii X Pontificis Maximi Iussu Digestus,* Rome, 1917.
90. *Acta et Decreta, Concilii plenarii episcoporum Hiberniae: quod habitum est apud Maynutiam die 2 Augusti et diebus sequentibus usque ad diem 15 Augusti 1927,* Dublin, 1929. *Acta et Decreta, Concilii plenarii episcoporum Hiberniae: quod habitum est apud Maynutiam die 7 Augusti et diebus sequentibus usque ad diem 15 Augusti 1956,* Dublin, 1960, Statute 287, 100–01.
91. Austin Clarke, 'Burial of an Irish President' in Maurice Harmon, *Austin Clarke: A Critical Introduction,* Dublin, 1989, 191–3. See *Irish Independent,* 15 July 1949, 1, 4.
92. *Ne Temere, Decree Concerning the Juridical Form of Marriage, Pope Pius X, 2 August, 1907,* to take effect from Easter Sunday, 19 April 1908, *Acta Sanctae Sedis,* XL (Rome, 1907), 525–30.
93. *Codex Iuris Canonici Pii X Pontificis Maximi Iussu Digestus,* Rome, 1917.
94. *Acta et Decreta, 1956.*
95. For an account of Catholic treatment of inter-church marriage under Canon Law see Alasdair Heron, *Two Churches — One Love,* Dublin, 1977, 38–45. See also Brian O'Higgins, 'Mixed Marriages: The 'Cautiones'', *Irish Theological Quarterly,* 41 (1974), 218–21. For further background information, see ref. 23, Chapter 13 of this book.
96. *Irish Independent,* 25 February 1963, 6.
97. Ibid.
98. Ibid.
99. For a full account of this case see J.H. Whyte, *Church and State,* 169–71.
100. Ibid., 169–70.
101. Ibid., 171.

Chapter 2 A Land of Faith (pp 19–36)

1. Conor K. Ward, 'Socio-Religious Research in Ireland', *Social Compass,* XI/3, 4 (March–April 1960), 26.
2. *ICD, 1952* (10 October 1951), 710–11.
3. Archbishop D'Alton, 'The Furrow and its Programme', *Furrow,* 1/1 (February 1950), 6.
4. *Codex Iuris Canonici Pii X Pontificis Maximi Iussu Digestus,* Rome, 1917.
   This Code was revised and a new *Code of Canon Law* was promulgated on 25 January 1983.
5. See Francis Kelly, *Window on a Catholic Parish, St Mary's, Granard, Co. Longford, 1933–1968,* Dublin, 1996, 32–43, 46–7.
6. Ambrose Crofts, 'The Irish Way', *Doctrine and Life,* 4 (June–July 1954), 258.
7. Seamas McLoughlin, 'The Encroachment of the Sunday', *Furrow,* 1/5 (June 1950), 240.
8. Robert Culhane, 'Irish Catholics in Britain', *Furrow,* 1/8 (September 1950), 389.
9. Jean Blanchard, *The Church in Contemporary Ireland,* Dublin, 1963.
10. Ibid., 27
11. Ibid.
12. Frank O'Connor, 'First Confession' in Augustine Martin, ed., *Exploring English: An Anthology of Short Stories,* Dublin, 1969, 65–73, 66.

13. See sermon notes of Fr Donal O'Lehane, curate in Granard, for a Holy Hour, which he conducted in April 1951, reproduced in Kelly, *Window on a Catholic Parish*, 58–9. The sermon was on the subject of sin.
14. See Martin, ed., *Exploring English*, 66.
15. See Francis Kelly, *Window on a Catholic Parish*, 35, 49–55.
16. Jean Blanchard, *The Church in Contemporary Ireland*, Dublin, 1963, 31.
17. *Apostolic Constitution, Christus Dominus, 6 January 1953*, translated in *Furrow*, 4/7 (July 1953), 400–13.
18. Ibid., 408.
19. Roland Burke Savage, 'The Church in Dublin: 1940–1965', *Studies*, LIV/216 (Winter 1965), 306.
20. Ibid.
21. *ICD, 1953* (4 April 1952), 639.
22. Ibid., 640.
23. *ICD, 1954* (28 June 1953), 721.
24. *ICD, 1955* (6 December 1953), 619.
25. *ICD, 1951* (28 April 1950), 737.
26. Ibid., 764.
27. Ibid., 758.
28. Ibid., 751.
29. See *Mayo News*, 5 August 1950, 1; ibid., 4 August 1951, 1; ibid., 1 August 1953, 1; ibid., 5 August 1961, 1.
30. Information communicated to the author by the Prior, St Patrick's Purgatory, Lough Derg, Pettigo, Co. Donegal.
31. See *A Catechism of Catholic Doctrine*, Dublin, 1951, question 409, 95.
32. Ibid., question 405, 94.
33. Ibid., question 407, 95.
34. Ibid., question 410, 95.
35. *The Raccolta or Collection of Indulgenced Prayers and Good Works*, trans. Fr Ambrose St John, 11th ed., London, 1930.
36. See ibid., xiii–xvi.
37. See *The Child of Mary*, compiled by Francis Daly SJ, Irish Messenger Publication, Dublin, 1948.
38. Ibid., 146.
39. Ibid., 8.
40. Ibid., 184–5.
41. *ICD, 1951* (26 March 1950), 734.
42. Ibid., 740.
43. Irish Bishops' Statement on the Proclamation of 1954 as Marian Year, *Furrow*, 4/11 (November 1953), 666–8.
44. John Brady and Patrick J. Corish, 'The Church under the Penal Code' in Patrick J. Corish, ed., *A History of Irish Catholicism*, 4, Dublin, 1971, 72.
45. Ibid., 73.
46. John Healy, *Nineteen Acres*, Galway, 1978, p. 9.
47. *ICD, 1955* (25 April 1954), 627.
48. Ibid., 629, 630, 633.
49. Ibid. (15 August 1954), 641.
50. John McGahern, *Irish Independent*, 31 July 1993, in Weekender, 2, 4.

51. *ICD, 1955* (16 May 1954), 632.
    See also *Irish Independent*, 17 May 1954, 5.
52. P.J. Brophy, 'France Today', *Furrow*, 1/9 (October 1950), 459.
53. Maisie Ward, *France pagan? The Mission of Abbé Godin*, London, 1949.
54. Jean Blanchard, *The Church in Contemporary Ireland*, 30.
55. Paul Blanshard, *The Irish and Catholic Power*, London, 1954, 55.
56. Ibid., 57.
57. *ICD, 1951* (29 October 1950), 765.
58. *Irish Independent*, 4 May 1953, 2.
59. *Irish Independent*, 10 May 1954, 11.
60. *Irish Independent*, 11 May 1954, 5.
61. *Irish Independent*, 14 May 1954, 6.
62. *ICD, 1952* (1 May 1951), 659.
63. Ibid., 652–3.
64. James Devane, *Irish Rosary*, December 1952.
65. Edward Long, 'Irish Piety', *Furrow*, 1/2 (March 1950), 12. For a comprehensive survey of the Irish missionary movement, see Edmund M. Hogan, *The Irish Missionary Movement: A Historical Survey, 1830–1980*, Dublin, 1992.
66. Seán O'Riordan, 'Current Opinion', *Furrow*, 1/1 (February 1950), 49.
67. Archbishop P.J.B. McKeefrey, 'Farewell to Shannon', *Furrow*, 1/2 (March 1950), 5–8.
68. See Thomas E. Garde, 'Foreword', *Doctrine and Life*, 1/1 (February 1951), 2–3.
69. Ibid., 2.
70. Ibid., 3.
71. J.G. McGarry reviewing *Doctrine and Life*, 1/1, *Furrow*, 2/3 (March 1951), 189.
72. Fachtna Lewis OFM, 'The Motives for Attending Holy Mass: A Case Study of a Selected Group of 293 Irish Rural People', Ph.D. thesis, Universitas S. Thomae de Urbe, Rome, 1963, 56–61.
73. Ibid., 60.
74. For a history of this devotion, see Chris de Buitléir, *Message and Messenger: History of Devotion to the Sacred Heart in Ireland*, Dublin, 1987.
    See also Gerry O'Hanlon SJ, *A Renewed Devotion to the Sacred Heart*, Dublin, 1992.
75. See Maurice Hartigan, 'The Religious Life of the Catholic Laity of Dublin 1920–1940', Ph.D. thesis, St Patrick's College, Maynooth, 1990.
76. See *Irish Messenger of the Sacred Heart*, LXIV/1 (January 1951), 19.
77. Ibid., 20.
78. Ibid., 23.
79. Ibid., LXIV/2 (February 1951), 47.
80. Ibid.
81. Ibid., LXIV/3 (March 1951), 71.
82. Ibid., LXIV/4 (April 1951), 95.
83. Ibid., LXVII/1 (January 1954), 22.
84. Ibid., LXVIII/5 (May 1955), 134.
85. See 'Notes and Queries', *IER*, LXXIX, 1953, 381.
86. Ibid., 381–3.
87. Ibid., 383.
88. See *The Raccolta*, xiv.
89. Jay P. Dolan, *The American Catholic Experience: A History from Colonial Times to the Present*, New York, 1987, 384–7.

90. Ibid., 387.
91. Austin Clarke, *Twice Round the Black Church: Early Memories of Ireland and England*, London, 1962, Dublin, 1990.
92. Ibid., 43–51.
93. See 'Notes and Queries', *IER*, XCVII, 1962, 402.
94. Ibid., 403.
95. Ibid.
96. See 'Notes and Queries', *IER*, LXXV, 1951, 460.
97. See 'Notes and Queries', *IER*, LXXIII, 1950, 448.
98. The present writer has been reliably informed in regard to this by a priest who is a racing enthusiast and who was placing bets in this way through the 1950s, though he could not attend race meetings.
99. See 'Notes and Queries', *IER*, LXXIII, 1950, 448.
100. Ibid.

Chapter 3 Social Change (pp 37–51)

1. See Lance Pettitt, *Screening Ireland: Film and Television Representation,* Manchester, 2000, 33.
2. See H. Byrne, 'Going to the Pictures' in M.J. Kelly and B. O'Connor, eds., *Media Audiences in Ireland,* Dublin, 1997, 88–106.
3. *Irish Independent,* 20 February 1950, 8.
4. *Irish Independent,* 21 February 1955, 4.
5. Ibid.
6. Ibid.
7. Fr Christopher Walsh, 'What Do We Read?', *Furrow* 1/2 (March 1950), 35.
8. Ibid., 34.
9. Ibid., 35.
10. See Maurice Gorham, *Twenty Years of Irish Broadcasting,* Dublin, 1967.
11. Fr Thomas Halton, 'Contemporary Song', *Furrow,* 3/1 (January 1952), 87.
12. Ibid., 87–8.
13. Ibid., 87–8.
14. Ibid., 88.
15. Fr Edward Flynn, 'Chronicle', *Furrow,* 5/2 (February 1954), 111.
16. Ibid., 111–2.
17. *The Standard,* 22 January 1954.
18. Fr Edward Flynn, 'Chronicle', *Furrow,* 5/3 (March 1954), 169.
19. Gerard Herbert, 'About the Film', *Furrow,* 1/7 (August 1950), 383.
20. Fr J.K. Dempsey, 'Chronicle', *Furrow,* 5/1 (January 1954), 36.
21. Ethna Conway, 'Ireland and Television', *Furrow,* 9/1 (January 1958), 33.
22. Ibid., 34.
23. Ibid., 37.
24. Ibid., 38.
25. *Vigilanti Cura, Encyclical Letter of Pope Pius XI on Motion Pictures Addressed to the Bishops of The United States, 29 June 1936,* in Claudia Carlen, *The Papal Encyclicals 1909–1939,* Raleigh, 1990.
26. See Note in *Furrow,* 2/4 (April 1951), 222.
27. This was the precursor of the present-day Film Institute of Ireland. The Institute also promoted the use of audio-visual media in schools and colleges and was involved in

the production and distribution of films and in the training of teachers in the use of film. The Institute also published a newsletter in which it gave advice in relation to films and their suitability for viewing. My informant on the establishment and background of the National Film Institute was Sunniva O'Flynn, the curator of the archives of the Film Institute of Ireland.

28. See *Address of the Holy Father, Pope Pius XII, to the Representatives of the Cinematograph Industry of Italy, 21 June 1955, Furrow,* 6/11 (November 1955), 707.
29. Ibid., 708.
30. See *Address of the Holy Father to Representatives of the Cinema Industry, Furrow,* 7/8 (August 1956), 497.
31. *Encyclical Miranda Prorsus, Encyclical of Pope Pius XII on the Communications Field: Motion Pictures, Radio, Television, 8 September 1957,* in Claudia Carlen, *The Papal Encyclicals 1939–1958,* Raleigh, 1990, 347–64.
32. See address delivered to an audience of book critics by Pope Pius XII on 13 February 1956 and published in *Furrow,* 7/7 (July 1956), 432.
33. See the text of the pastoral letter dealing with 'Contemporary Catholic Literature' issued by the Bishops of Germany, 1 October, 1955 published in *Furrow,* 7/2 (February 1956), 115.
34. Ibid., 116.
35. *Census of Population of Ireland, 1946,* Preliminary Report, in particular, 2, 7–12, 16.
    See also *Census of Ireland, 1951,* Preliminary Report, in particular, 7–18.
    See also *Census of Ireland, 1956,* Preliminary Report, vii–xii, 2.
    See Appendices D, E, F, G.
36. Alexander J. Humphreys SJ, *New Dubliners: Urbanization and the Irish Family,* London, 1966, 158.
37. Quoted in Terence Brown, *Ireland: A Social and Cultural History, 1922–1985,* Dublin, 1985, 199.
38. Ibid.
39. Ibid.
40. *Commission on Emigration and Other Population Problems 1948–1954,* 1954, folio typescript, held at St Patrick's College, Maynooth.
41. Ibid., para. 438, 172.
42. John Healy, *No One Shouted Stop: Death of an Irish Town,* Achill, 1988, 20.
43. Ibid.
44. *Irish Independent,* 13 February 1956, 10.
45. *Irish Independent,* 21 February 1955, 4.
46. Ibid.
47. Donall Mac Amhlaigh, *An Irish Navvy: The Diary of an Exile,* trans. Valentin Iremonger, London, 1964, 3.
48. Ibid., 180–82.
49. Healy, *No One Shouted Stop,* 38.
50. Ibid.
51. *Irish Independent,* 21 February 1955, 4.
52. *Irish Independent,* 25 February 1952, 6.
53. Ibid.
54. *Commission on Emigration,* para. 463, 180.
55. See Michael D. Biddis, *The Age of the Masses: Ideas and Society in Europe since 1870,* London, 1977, 29–45.

See Reference 35 above for population trends in Ireland in the late 1940s and 1950s. See Appendices D, E, F, G.

56. *Irish Independent*, 25 February 1952, 6.
57. *Commission on Emigration and Other Population Problems: Minority Report* by Most Rev. Dr C. Lucey, 1.
58. Ibid., para. 27, 3.
59. *Cork Examiner*, 28 May 1954.
60. Ibid.
61. Ibid.
62. *Commission on Emigration: Minority Report*, para. 467, 25.
63. *Bunreacht na hÉireann 1937*, Article 45: v, Dublin, 150.
64. *Cork Examiner*, 23 May 1955.
65. Ibid.
66. *Commission on Emigration Report: Minority Report*, para. 426, 17.
67. Ibid.
68. Joseph Johnston, *Irish Agriculture in Transition*, Dublin, 1951, 160.
69. Ibid., 165.
70. Ibid., 160.
71. Ibid., 161.
72. *Cork Examiner*, 4 March 1955.
73. *Commission on Emigration: Minority Report*, para. 211, 7.
74. Cited in John A. O'Brien, 'The Vanishing Irish', John A. O'Brien, ed., *The Vanishing Irish*, London, 1954, 41.
75. Ibid.
76. Patrick Kavanagh, *Selected Poems*, London, 1996, 44.
77. Muintir na Tíre was founded one week before the publication of the papal encyclical, *Quadragesimo Anno*, 1931, which was published on the fortieth anniversary of *Rerum Novarum*, 1891. Both of these encyclicals were the foundation documents of Catholic social teaching. Fr Hayes adopted the principles set out in *Quadragesimo Anno* as the inspiration for Muintir na Tíre. This will be further elaborated on in Chapter 5.
78. *Limerick Rural Survey*, Tipperary, 1964, 254.
79. Ibid., 251–2.
80. Hugh Brody, *Inishkillane: Change and Decline in the West of Ireland*, London, 1973, 99.
81. Brody, *Inishkillane*, 71.
82. Ibid., 128.
83. Maisie Ward, *France pagan? The Mission of Abbé Godin*, London, 1949, 67.
84. Brody, *Inishkillane*, 165–6.
85. Kavanagh, *Selected Poems*, 22.
86. Humphreys, *New Dubliners*, 5.
87. See review of Cardinal Suhard's pastoral letter, *Rise or Decline of the Church*, by Michael I. Mooney, *Furrow*, 1/2 (March 1950), 50–53, 51.
88. Archbishop D'Alton, 'The Furrow and its Programme', *Furrow*, 1/1 (February 1950), 6.
89. Ibid.

Chapter 4 Demands for a More Liberal Society (pp 52–66)

1. *Irish Independent*, 25 February 1952, 6.
2. *Irish Independent*, 20 February 1950, 8.
3. *Irish Independent*, 5 February 1951, 4.

4. Ibid.
5. Bryan MacMahon, 'Getting on the High Road Again' in John A. O'Brien, ed., *The Vanishing Irish,* London, 1954, 213.
6. Ibid.
7. Fr Michael I. Mooney, 'The Parish Hall', *Furrow,* 4/1 (January 1953), 6.
8. Fr Maurice Browne, 'The Parish Hall', *Furrow,* 4/1 (January 1953), 11.
9. Bryan MacMahon in *The Vanishing Irish,* 211.
10. Ibid.
11. John D. Sheridan, 'We're Not Dead Yet' in *The Vanishing Irish,* 188.
12. Ibid.
13. Charles E. Kelly, 'May We Laugh Please?', *Furrow,* 4/12 (December 1953), 700.
14. Ibid.
15. See Lenten Pastorals of Bishops of Clogher and Kilmore, *Irish Independent,* 5 February 1951, 4.
    See also Lenten Pastorals of Bishops of Clogher and Waterford, *Irish Independent,* 21 February 1955, 4.
    See also Lenten Regulations of the diocese of Achonry 'in regard to public dancing', *Mayo News,* 21 February 1953, 1.
16. Bryan MacMahon, 'The Priest in His Parish', *Furrow,* 9/12 (December 1958), 807.
17. *Irish Independent,* 25 February 1952, 6.
18. *Irish Independent,* 21 February 1955, 4.
19. *Irish Independent,* 5 February 1951, 4.
20. See Whyte, *Church and State,* 174–8, 325–30.
21. Quoted in ibid., 174.
22. Ibid., 174–5.
23. Ibid., 175.
24. *ICD, 1949* (22 June 1948), 721.
25. See *Pioneering for Eighty Years: Historical Aspects of the Pioneer Association* presented at the International Pioneer Seminar in Clongowes Wood College, Co. Kildare, in July 1978, 4–9.
    See also leaflet *What it Means to be a Pioneer,* published by Pioneer Association, 27 Sherrard St, Dublin 1.
26. *Pioneer,* 1/7 (July 1948), 1.
27. See *Pioneering for Eighty Years,* 9.
28. Rev. S. McCarron SJ, 'Sunday Opening', *Pioneer,* 3/6 (June 1950), 6.
29. Quoted in Whyte, *Church and State,* 177.
30. Statement of the Archbishops and Bishops of Ireland, 20 June 1950, published in *Furrow,* 1/7 (August 1950), 363–6.
31. Ibid, 363–4.
32. *Irish Independent,* 20 February 1950, 8.
33. Ibid.
34. Seamas McLoughlin, 'The Encroachment of the Sunday', *Furrow,* 1/5 (June 1950), 241.
35. Ibid., 240.
36. Ibid., 242.
37. Ibid.
38. Ibid.
39. Ibid., 243.
40. See Whyte, *Church and State,* 325.

41. *Reports of the Commission of Inquiry into the Operation of the Laws Relating to the Sale and Supply of Intoxicating Liquor,* Dublin, 1957, 3–10.
42. Ibid., 6, 23–7.
43. *Statement of the Irish bishops on the intoxicating liquor laws, June 1959, Furrow,* 10/8 (August 1959), 553–4.
44. Ibid.
45. *Dáil Debates,* 178, cols. 391–2 (25 November 1959).
46. Intoxicating Liquor Act, 1960, No. 18, in public statutes of the Oireachtas, 1960.
47. See *Thom's Directory of Ireland,* 1960, 2: 445.
48. Michael Adams, *Censorship: The Irish Experience,* Alabama, 1968, 119.
49. Ibid., 148.
50. Ibid., 120–21.
51. Ibid., 122–4.
52. Fr Denis Meehan, 'An Essay in Self-Criticism', *Furrow,* 8/4 (April 1957), 209–14.
53. Fr John C. Kelly SJ, 'Solid Virtue in Ireland', *Doctrine and Life,* 9/5 (October–November 1959), 120.
54. Fr Peter Connolly, 'Censorship', *Christus Rex,* XIII/3 (July 1959), 151.
55. See *Statement from the Bishops of Ireland issued to the press on 31 January 1958, in relation to 'Indecent Publications', Furrow,* 9/3 (March 1958), 193–4.
56. Ibid., 194.
57. Fr Peter Connolly, 'Censorship', *Christus Rex,* 170.
58. Ibid.
59. Fr Peter Connolly, 'Censorship and Moral Classification of Films', *Furrow,* 8/2 (February 1957), 113.
60. Ibid., 114.
61. Fr Peter Connolly, 'Censorship', *Christus Rex,* 153.
62. Fr Peter Connolly, 'Censorship and Moral Classification of Films', *Furrow,* 114.
63. Fr Peter Connolly, 'Films', *Furrow,* 7/2 (February 1956), 111.
64. Ibid.
65. Fr Peter Connolly, 'Chronicle', 'Religious Films', *Furrow,* 7/10 (October 1956) 621.
66. Fr Peter Connolly, 'Films', *Furrow,* 7/3 (March 1956), 160–61.
67. Fr Peter Connolly, 'Censorship', *Christus Rex,* 156.
68. Ibid.
69. Ibid., 155.
70. Ibid., 159.
71. Ibid., 156.
72. Fr Peter Connolly, 'Turbulent Priests', *Hibernia,* 28/2 (February 1964), 9.
73. Fr Peter Connolly, 'Censorship', *Christus Rex,* 165.
74. Ibid., 164–8.
75. Fr Peter Connolly, 'Censorship and the Moral Classification of Films', *Furrow,* 114.
76. Ibid., 110–11.
77. Ibid., 111.
78. See Patrick Hannon, 'Heart in Pilgrimage' in James H. Murphy, ed., *No Bland Facility: Selected Writings on Literature, Religion and Censorship, Peter Connolly,* Gerrards Cross, 1991, 47.
79. Fr Peter Connolly, 'Censorship', *Christus Rex,* 169.
80. Ibid., 170.
81. Fr Peter Connolly, 'Films', *Furrow,* 7/10 (October 1956), 620–21.

Chapter 5 A Changing Sociopolitical Landscape (pp 67–81)

1. Clann na Poblachta was formed at a meeting held in Barry's Hotel, Dublin, on 6 July 1946. For a historical account of the origins and development of the party, see Eithne MacDermott, *Clann na Poblachta*, Cork, 1998.
2. Ibid., 64–82.
3. For an account of the formation of the inter-party government and the appointment of John A. Costello as Taoiseach, see ibid., 64–77.
4. *Irish Independent*, 20 February 1950, 8.
5. Ibid.
6. *Irish Independent*, 16 February 1953, 8.
7. *Irish Independent*, 20 February 1950, 8.
8. Ibid.
9. Ibid.
10. *Irish Independent*, 5 February 1951, 4.
11. See Karl Marx and Friedrich Engels, *The Communist Manifesto*, Harmondsworth, 1967.
12. *Rerum Novarum, Encyclical of Pope Leo XIII on the Condition of the Working Classes, 15 May 1891* in Anne Fremantle, *The Papal Encyclicals in their Historical Context*, New York 1956, 1963, 166–95.
13. See Whyte, *Church and State*, 62.
14. *Quadragesimo Anno, Encyclical of Pope Pius XI on Reconstruction of the Social Order, 15 May 1931* in Claudia Carlen, *The Papal Encyclicals 1909–1939*, Raleigh, 1990, 415–41.
15. Ibid., para. 79, 428.
16. *Report of the Commission on Vocational Organisation*, Dublin, 1944.
17. Don O'Leary, *Vocationalism and Social Catholicism in Twentieth-Century Ireland*, Dublin, 2000, 185–8, 130–37.
18. See notice on the cover of each issue of *Christus Rex* from 1949.
19. See for instance Very Rev. Aegidus Doolan OP, 'The Service State in the Light of Catholic Social Principles', *Christus Rex*, 1 (October 1947), 3–13; Rev. Patrick J. Conway, 'The State in Economic Life in ibid., 2 (June 1948), 3–16; James McPolin MD, 'The Medical Profession and the State' in ibid., 2 (September 1948), 13–30; Rev. James Bastible, 'Modern Trade Unionism in the Light of Catholic Principles' in ibid., 3 (1949), 3–18; Rev. E.J. Hegarty, 'The Principles Against State Welfare Schemes' in ibid., 4 (1950), 315–33.
20. Information conveyed to the author by Michael O'Riordan, General Secretary of the Communist Party of Ireland.
21. Donall Mac Amhlaigh, *An Irish Navvy: The Diary of an Exile*, London, 1964, 65.
22. Most Rev. J. Dignan, *Social Security. Outlines of a Scheme of National Health Insurance*, Sligo, 1945, 12.
    See also Adrian Kelly, 'Social Security in Independent Ireland, 1922–52', Ph.D. thesis, St Patrick's College, Maynooth, 1995.
23. O'Leary, *Vocationalism and Social Catholicism*, 109–11.
24. Ibid., 135.
25. Quoted in Ronan Fanning, *The Irish Department of Finance 1922–1958*, Dublin, 1978, 384–6.
26. See Whyte, *Church and State*, 179–80.
27. Quoted in ibid., 182.
28. Ibid.
29. Ibid.

30. See text of Mr C.F. Casey SC, Attorney General's address at the inaugural meeting of the Law Students' Debating Society at King's Inns, Dublin, 13 February 1951, in Adoption of Children, General File, S10815A, Part 1, Department of the Taoiseach, in the National Archives, Bishop St, Dublin, 2.
31. Ibid., 3.
32. See Whyte, *Church and State,* 190–91.
33. Ibid., 191.
34. Ibid., 196–302.
35. Health Act, 1947, No. 28 in public statutes of the Oireachtas, 1947.
36. See Whyte, *Church and State,* 426.
37. Ibid., 404.
38. Ibid.
39. Ibid.
40. Ibid., 404–5.
41. *ICD, 1952* (12 November 1951), 715.
42. *Dáil Debates,* 125, col. 781 (12 April 1951).
43. Ibid., col. 784.
44. Ibid., col. 789.
45. Ibid., col. 952 (17 April 1951).
46. Ibid., col. 668 (12 April 1951).
47. See Noël Browne, *Against the Tide,* Dublin, 1986, 185–6. See also John Horgan, *Noël Browne: Passionate Outsider,* Dublin, 2000.
48. *Dáil Debates,* col. 739 (12 April 1951).
49. Ibid., col. 784.
50. *The Irish Times,* 12 April 1951.
51. Sean O'Faolain, 'The Dáil and the Bishops', *Bell,* XVII/3 (June 1951), 6.
52. *Standard,* 20 April 1951.
53. *ICD, 1952* (22 April 1951), 655.
54. *ICD, 1952* (10 October 1951), 708.
55. *ICD, 1952* (18 June 1951), 681.
56. *ICD, 1952* (10 October 1951), 709.
57. *Statement of Episcopal Committee on Adoption, 8 January 1952, Furrow,* 3/2 (February 1952), 98–9.
58. *The Irish Times,* 13 April 1955.
59. Ibid.
60. *Programme for Economic Expansion,* Dublin, 1958.
61. *Economic Development,* Dublin, 1958.
62. Very Rev. W.J. Philbin, 'The Individual and the State', *IER,* 79 (January 1953), 3–19.
63. Quoted in Whyte, *Church and State,* 314.
64. Cited in ibid.
65. Most Rev. W.J. Philbin, 'A City on a Hill', *Studies,* XLVI/46 (1957), 259–70.
66. *Economic Development,* Dublin, 1958, Chapter 1, Introduction, para. 21, 9.
67. Ibid.
68. Roland Burke Savage SJ, 'Ireland Tomorrow', *Studies,* XLIV/44 (1955), 3.
69. Quoted in Brian P. Kennedy, 'Seventy-Five Years of Studies', in Brian Lennon SJ, ed., *Towards a New Irish Identity, Studies, The 300th Issue, 1912–1986',* Dublin, 1986, 361.
70. See Timothy Patrick Coogan, *Ireland Since the Rising,* London, 1966, 105–8; Tony Gray, *The Irish Answer: An Anatomy of Modern Ireland,* London, 1966, 118–20; Oliver MacDonagh,

Ireland, New Jersey, 1968, 132–3; Alan Bestic, *The Importance of Being Irish*, London, 1969, 2–3; Donald S. Connery, *The Irish*, New York, 1968, 29–30; Charles McCarthy, *The Distasteful Challenge*, Dublin, 1968, 112; Garret FitzGerald, *Planning in Ireland*, Dublin, 1968, 41.

Chapter 6 'To Drive a New Furrow' (pp 82–96)

1. Interview in March 1992 with Fr Seán O'Riordan CSsR, who was among the priests who attended the August 1949 meeting, and was subsequently elected assistant editor. See also Seán O'Riordan, 'Towards a Prophetic Church', *Furrow*, 26/3 (March 1975), 139–40.
2. Ibid., 140.
3. Interview with Fr Ronan Drury on 16 March 1994. Fr Drury was managing editor of the *Furrow* from the beginning, and general editor from 1977.
4. Much of the background information on the *Furrow* was gleaned from the above interviews.
5. Seán O'Riordan, 'Towards a Prophetic Church', *Furrow*, 26/3 (March 1975), 140.
6. See 'Foreword', *Furrow*, 1/1 (February 1950), 5.
7. See 'News and Views' , *Furrow*, 14/4 (April 1963), 250.
8. Don Boyne (Neil Kevin), *I Remember Maynooth*, London, 1945, 95.
9. See Liam Ryan, *The Changing Direction of Irish Seminaries, A Survey Report*, Research and Development Unit, CCII, 1972, 7. See also reference 19, Chapter 12 of this book.
10. Boyne, *I Remember Maynooth*, 26, 28.
11. Interview with Seán Mac Réamoinn on 15 February 1994.
    See also Seán Mac Réamoinn, *Vatacáin II agus an Réabhlóid Chultúrtha*, Baile Átha Cliath, 1987, 26.
12. Seán Tiernan, 'What Price Art?', *Furrow*, 3/5 (May 1952), 190.
13. Ibid., 192–3.
14. Ibid., 190.
15. Louis McRedmond, 'A Silver Jubilee', *Furrow*, 26/2 (February 1975), 70.
16. See Edward J. Coyne SJ, 'Mother and Child Service', *Studies*, XL/40 (1951), 129–49; see also in ibid., John F. Cunningham, 'The Medical Problem', 150–53; Alexis FitzGerald, 'The Problem of Finance', 154–7.
17. See Archbishop D'Alton of Armagh, 'The Furrow and its Programme' *Furrow*, 1,/1 (February 1950), 6–9.
18. See 'Foreword', *Furrow*, 1/1 (February 1950), 5.
19. Information about the Furrow Trust was conveyed to the author in the course of an interview with Fr Ronan Drury on 16 March 1994.
20. See *Ecclesiae pastorum vigilantia circa libros*, Congregation for the Doctrine of the Faith, 19 March 1975, in AAS, 67 (Rome, 1975), 67–281. The requirement remained in place for official biblical and liturgical texts and their translations; catechisms and prayer books; scholastic textbooks dealing with doctrinal and moral matters; and literature sold or given away in churches. See Michael Glazier and Monika Hellwig, eds., *The Modern Catholic Encyclopaedia*, Dublin, 1994, 420.
21. This was explained to the author in the course of interviews with Fathers Seán O'Riordan CSsR and Austin Flannery OP.
22. This was explained to the author in the course of an interview with Fr Austin Flannery OP.
23. I am grateful to Mr Tom May, archivist, Galway Diocesan Archives, for providing me with a copy of Archbishop McQuaid's letter to Bishop Browne of Galway of 12 March 1968 from Bishop Browne's papers.

24. See letter from Browne to McQuaid, 14 March 1968, in Dublin Diocesan Archives, AB8/B/XV. Bishop Lennon succeeded Thomas Keogh as Bishop of Kildare and Leighlin on 25 September 1967. Browne was replying to a letter from McQuaid (12 March) in which he expressed his reservations about the *Furrow* and Browne agreed in his reply of 14th March. The context of his reply is interesting, in that an article turned down for the *IER* was sent to Dr Keogh for the *ITQ*. The bishop of the diocese of Kildare and Leighlin granted the *imprimatur* for the *ITQ* as well as for the *Furrow*. The latter was concerned as to its orthodoxy and sent it to Browne, suggesting that it might be sent to the Episcopal Commission on Doctrine.
25. Desmond Forristal, *Furrow*, 20/9 (September 1970), 588.
26. See, for instance, *Furrow*, 2/1 (January 1951), 28–32. In his column 'Round the Reviews' Seán O'Riordan examined the treatment of a number of issues pertinent to Catholic life in some of the foreign periodicals of the day. The question of devotion to the souls in purgatory came up for discussion in the November issue of the American *Homiletic and Pastoral Review* (November 1950); the French review, *L'Ami du Clerge* (21 September 1950), discussed the canonisation of St Maria Goretti; the question of having the liturgy in English was examined by Mgr R.A. Knox in the *Clergy Review* (November 1950).
27. See P.J. Brophy, 'New Trends in France', *Furrow,* 1/4 (May 1950), 179–86. See also P.J. Brophy, 'France Today', *Furrow,* 1/9 (October 1950), 459–62. See also J.P. Donnelly, 'A Priest Worker' in ibid., 67–71. See also C.B. Daly, 'The New French Revolution', *Furrow,* 3/5 (May 1952), 177–89. See also Frederick M. Jones, 'The Church in 1957', *Furrow,* 9/1 (January 1958), 14–27.
28. See Henry Boelaars CSsR, 'Catholic Life in Holland', *Furrow,* 3/2 (February 1952), 59–68. See Henry Boelaars CSsR, 'Catholic Life in Holland II', *Furrow,* 3/3 (March 1952), 126–33.
29. See F.R. McCluskey, 'The Church in Denmark', *Furrow,* 4/9 (September 1953), 487–94.
30. See Seán O'Riordan CSsR, 'In Germany Today', *Furrow,* 4/3 (March 1953), 119–31. See also Joseph Huijgen, 'The Church in Peril', *Furrow,* 2/4 (April 1951), 246–54.
31. Fr Connolly's name crops up in correspondence that passed between McQuaid and Browne in 1967. This is in connection with the Maynooth student magazine, *Agora,* articles written by students in the magazine, and the fact that Connolly was the inspiration behind them. Again in a letter of 14 March 1968 (already cited in reference 24 above), Browne expresses disquiet about 'the views of young men coming out of Maynooth in the last few days', and in his reply of 15 March 1968, McQuaid refers to 'the young priests: like master, like pupil', adding 'the Bishops are afraid — witness the outrageous views of the English Professor, who four times in my diocese upset the faithful'. Again I am grateful to Mr Tom May, archivist, Galway Diocesan Archives, for providing me with copies of Archbishop McQuaid's letters (8 February 1967, 15 March 1968) from Bishop Browne's papers.
32. 'Irish Catholics in Britain' was the subject of the first special issue published by the *Furrow* in September 1950. Five priests with first-hand experience of the problems associated with Irish Catholics emigrating to Britain contributed articles. In April 1954, the *Furrow* held a further symposium on the subject of 'The Irish in Britain'. The April 1958 issue of the journal was on the theme of 'The Church and the Emigrant'. The articles in these special issues, and many others also devoted to this subject in the 1950s, and the letters that were written in response to them, give a keen insight into

the way Church personnel viewed emigration at that time.

33. See John M. Todd, 'Christian Unity', *Furrow*, 6/1 (January 1955), 25–33. See also Patrick J. Devine, 'The Ecumenical Movement', *Furrow*, 7/1 (January 1956), 22–30. See also Enda McDonagh, 'One Fold', *Furrow*, 9/10 (October 1958), 646–53.
34. See His Eminence Valerian Cardinal Gracias, 'The Doctrinal Foundations of Lay Apostolate', *Furrow*, 4/10 (October 1953), 551–68. See also Lancelot C. Sheppard, 'Independence of the Laity', *Furrow*, 4/10 (October 1953), 569–75. See also G. Michonneau, 'Laymen: Associates in the Apostolate', *Furrow*, 4/10 (October1953), 585 6. Scc also Scamas Grace, 'The Layman in the University', *Furrow*, 4/10 (October 1953), 587–94. See also Laurence Forristal, 'Intellectuals and the Lay Apostolate', *Furrow*, 5/10 (October 1954), 618–26.
35. Edward Long, 'Irish Piety', *Furrow*, 1/2 (March 1950), 12, 14.
36. Ibid., 14.
37. Edward Long, 'Irish Piety'. *Furrow*, 1/2, (March 1950), 15.
38. Dermot McIvor, 'The Mass and the People', *Furrow*, 2/7 (July 1951), 464–5.
39. Ibid., 465.
40. See Introduction by Austin Flannery to *Contemporary Irish Church Architecture*, Richard Hurley and Wilfrid Cantwell, eds., Dublin, 1985, 12.
41. William Barden OP, 'Phases of the Liturgical Movement', a paper read at the Liturgical Congress, Glenstal, in April 1955, and published in *Furrow*, 5/11 (November 1954), 668.
42. Ibid.
43. *Abhinc duos Annos, 23 October 1913, Motu proprio de officiis divinis novo aliqua ex parte modo ordinandis Pius pp. X, AAS,* 5 (Rome, 1913), 449–51. See Address of His Holiness, Pope Pius XII, to the International Congress on Pastoral Liturgy, held in Assisi, 22 September 1956, and published in *Furrow*, 7/10 (October 1956), 646.
44. See Edward Long, 'The Background to *Mediator Dei*', *Furrow*, 1/9 (October 1950), 450–51.
45. John P. O'Connell, 'The new American Ritual', *Furrow*, 6/7 (July 1955), 426–7.
46. See Hurley and Cantwell, *Contemporary Irish Church Architecture*, Introduction by Austin Flannery, 18, 25. For an account of the few churches built in a modern idiom during the 1950s and 1960s, see ibid., 35–68.
47. Archbishop D'Alton, 'The Furrow and its Programme', *Furrow*, 1/1 (February 1950), 6.
48. J.G. McGarry, 'Foreword', *Furrow*, 6/6 (June 1955), 338.
49. W.H.D. McCormick, 'The Case for the Contemporary', *Furrow*, 6/6 (June 1955), 356.
50. See Richard Hurley and Wilfrid Cantwell, eds., *Contemporary Irish Church Architecture*, Dublin, 1985, 25.
51. J.G. McGarry, 'Foreword', *Furrow*, 6/6 (June 1955), 338. For further background information on these developments and the people involved in them, see Introduction by Austin Flannery OP, in Richard Hurley and Wilfrid Cantwell, eds., *Contemporary Irish Church Architecture*, Dublin, 1985.
52. Cloud Meinberg, 'The New Churches of Europe', *Furrow*, 8/6 (June 1957), 364.
53. Ibid., 365.
54. Donal O'Sullivan, 'Chronicle', *Furrow*, 8/7 (July 1957), 465.
55. Michael O'Dwyer, 'The Liturgy in a Rural Parish', *Furrow*, 5/11 (November 1954), 685.
56. Ibid., 685–6.
57. Placid Murray OSB, 'Liturgical Piety', *Furrow*, 5/11 (November 1954), 677.

58. Michael Dwyer, 'The Liturgy in a Rural Parish', *Furrow,* 5/11 (November 1954), 685.
59. Ibid., 689.
60. Liam Breen, 'The Liturgy in a City Parish', *Furrow,* 5/11 (November 1954), 692.
61. Ibid.
62. Ibid., 693.
63. Dermot McIvor, 'Sunday Mass and the Faithful', *Furrow,* 6/10 (October 1955), 606.
64. Ibid., 603.
65. See reference 60, Chapter 1.
66. Dermot McIvor, 'Sunday Mass and the Faithful', *Furrow,* 6/10 (October 1955), 603.
67. Liam Breen, 'The Liturgy in a City Parish', *Furrow,* 5/11 (November 1954), 694–5.
68. Ibid., 695.
69. Ibid., 693–4.
70. Ibid., 695.
71. Ibid., 691–2.
72. See *Instruction of the Holy Office 'Christus Dominus', 6 January 1953,* translated in *Furrow,* 4/7 (July 1953), 400–13.
73. See *Maxima Redemptoris* translated from the Latin text in *L'Osservatore Romano,* 27 November 1955, and published in *Furrow,* 7/1 (January 1956), 43–53.
74. Placid Murray OSB, 'Third Liturgical Congress', *Furrow,* 7/4 (April 1956), 242.
75. See *Motu proprio, Indulta a constitutione Apostolica 'Christus Dominus' extenduntur Sacram Communionem,* as taken from *L'Osservatore Romano,* 23 March 1957, *Furrow,* 8/4 (April 1957), 272–3.
76. See 'Instruction from the Sacred Congregation of Rites', *Furrow,* 10/1 (January 1959), 43–67.
77. Joseph Cunnane, 'The Layman's Part at Mass', *Furrow,* 10/11 (November 1959), 687–99.
78. Ibid., 699.
79. Most Rev. James Joseph McNamee, The Bishop of Ardagh, 'The Latin-vernacular ritual', *IER,* 94 (July–December 1960), 337–41.
80. See 'The New Ritual' resolution adopted by the bishops of Ireland at their general meeting, 11 October 1960, *Furrow,* 11/11 (November 1960), 765.
81. See J.G. McGarry, 'The New Ritual for Ireland', *Furrow,* 11/12 (December 1960), 798–803.

Chapter 7 Theological Developments and the Irish Church (pp 97–108)

1. See 'The Syllabus of Pius IX' in Anne Fremantle, *The Papal Encyclicals in their Historical Context,* New York 1956, 1963, 143–52.
2. Ibid., 152.
3. *Aeterni Patris, Encyclical of Pope Leo XIII on the Restoration of Christian Philosophy, 4 August 1879* in Claudia Carlen, *The Papal Encyclicals 1878–1903,* Raleigh, 1990, 17–27.
4. See Darrell H. Jodock, ed., *Catholicism Contending with Modernity: Roman Catholic Modernism and Anti-Modernism in Historical Context,* Cambridge, 2000.
5. *Providentissimus Deus, Encyclical of Pope Leo XIII on the Study of Holy Scripture, 18 November 1893,* in ibid., 325–38.
6. *Lamentabili Sane, 3 July 1907, Syllabus Condemning the Errors of the Modernists* in Fremantle, *The Papal Encyclicals in their Historical Context,* 202–7.
7. *Pascendi Dominici Gregis, Encyclical of Pope Pius X on the Doctrines of the Modernists, 8 September 1907* in Claudia Carlen, *The Papal Encyclicals 1903–1939,* Raleigh, 1990, 71–97.

8. See Thomas Bokenkotter, *A Concise History of the Catholic Church*, New York, 1990, 317.
9. See *Motu proprio Tra le sollecitudini on the Restoration of Sacred Music, 22 November 1903* and *Il desiderio, Letter to Pietro Cardinal Respighi, Vicar General of Rome on the Restoration of Sacred Music, 8 December 1903, IER*, 15 (January–December 1904), 161–70, 170–75.
10. See *Decree of the Sacred Congregation of the Council Regarding Daily Communion 20 December 1905, IER*, 19 (January–December 1906), 376–80. See also *Decree Granting Indulgences for Daily Communion without the onus of weekly Confession 16 February 1906*, ibid., 469–70.
11. *Divino Afflante Spiritu, Encyclical of Pope Pius XII on Promoting Biblical Studies, 30 September 1943* in Claudia Carlen, *The Papal Encyclicals 1939–1958*, Raleigh, 1990, 65–78.
12. *Humani Generis, Encyclical of Pope Pius XII Concerning Certain False Opinions, 12 August 1950* in Anne Fremantle, *The Papal Encyclicals in their Historical Context*, New York 1956, 1963, 294–8.
13. Ibid., 295.
14. Ibid.
15. Ibid.
16. Ibid., 296.
17. See John Deedy, *The Catholic Fact Book*, Cork, 1992, 176–7.
18. Walter McDonald, *Reminiscences of a Maynooth Professor*, Denis Gwynn, ed., Cork, 1967, 194.
19. Ibid.
20. Ibid., 197.
21. Ibid., 198.
22. Ibid.
23. Ibid.
24. Ibid., 204.
25. Ibid., 209.
26. Ibid.
27. Gerald O'Donovan, *Father Ralph*, Dingle, 1993.
28. See Catherine Candy, *Priestly Fictions: Popular Irish Novelists of the Early Twentieth Century*, Dublin, 1995, 54–61.
29. O'Donovan, *Father Ralph*, 203.
30. Ibid., 205.
31. Ibid., 203–4.
32. McDonald, *Reminiscences*, 54–86.
33. See 'Foreword', *ITQ*, XIIX (1951), iii.
34. Ibid.
35. Gerard Mitchell, 'Humani Generis and Theology', *ITQ*, XIX (1952), 1.
36. Ibid., 1, 3.
37. Kevin McNamara, 'Catholic Theology Today: A Recent Survey', *ITQ*, XXI/3 (1954), 243–58.
38. Ibid., 250–51.
39. Ibid.
40. Ibid., 251.
41. Ibid.
42. Ibid., 258.
43. Ibid.
44. William Conway, 'The Science of Moral Theology: New Trends', *ITQ*, XXII (1955), 155.
45. Ibid.

46. Ibid., 158.
47. For a detailed description of the Irish bishops' submissions, see *Acta et Documenta Concilio Oecumenico Vaticano II Apparando,* series I, ii, (Vatican, 1960), 63–109.
48. For a detailed account of the submissions from Maynooth, see ibid., series I, iv (Vatican, 1961), 419–47.
49. See Pope John XXIII's opening speech to the Council, 11 October 1962, in Walter M. Abbott SJ, ed., *The Documents of Vatican II,* London, Dublin, 1966, 715 (hereafter referred to as Abbott, *Vatican II Documents*). For a detailed description of the Irish bishops' submissions, see *Acta et Documenta Concilio Oecumenico Vaticano II Apparando,* series 1, 2 (Vatican, 1960), 63–109.
50. Xavier Rynne, *Letters from Vatican City,* London, 1963, 108, 117.
51. *Constitution on the Sacred Liturgy, promulgated 4 December 1963* in Abbott, *Vatican II Documents,* 146.
52. Ibid., 144.
53. Ibid., 146.
54. Ibid.
55. Ibid., 150.
56. Ibid., 159.
57. Austin Flannery OP, ed., *Vatican II: The Liturgy Constitution,* Dublin, 1964.

Chapter 8 The Impact of the Second Vatican Council (pp 109–123)

1. Cardinal D'Alton, Lenten Pastoral, 'Participation in the Mass', *Irish Independent,* 29 February 1960, 9–10.
2. Ibid., 10 February 1964, 6.
3. Ibid.
4. See *Instruction of the Sacred Congregation of Rites on the Proper Implementing of the Liturgy 26 September 1964* in Austin Flannery, ed., *Vatican II: The Liturgy Constitution,* Dublin, 1964, 116–41.
5. See statement issued to the press by the Irish Bishops from Rome on 'The Use of the Vernacular', 10 November 1964, *Furrow,* 15/12 (December 1964), 785–6.
6. Ibid.
7. *Irish Independent,* 1 March 1965, 7.
8. Ibid., 6.
9. Ibid., 7.
10. Ibid., 6.
11. Ibid.
12. See *Missale Romanum,* Apostolic Constitution of Pope Paul VI promulgating the Roman Missal revised by Decree of the Second Vatican Council, 3 April 1969, in *The Roman Missal,* official English text, Dublin, 1974, ix–xii.
13. See *Decree of the Sacred Congregation for Divine Worship promulgating the New Edition of the Roman Missal, 26 March 1970,* in *The Roman Missal,* official English text, Dublin, 1974, x.
14. See *Instruction by the Sacred Congregation of Rites on the Proper Implementing of the Liturgy Constitution* in Austin Flannery, ed., *Vatican II: The Liturgy Constitution,* Dublin, 1964, 116–41.
15. *Dogmatic Constitution on the Church* in Abbott, *Vatican II Documents,* 24–37.
16. See Hurley and Cantwell, eds., *Contemporary Irish Church Architecture,* 26–9. See also 46–137 for examples of churches built in the modern idiom from 1964.
17. Ibid., 27.

18. See Episcopal Liturgical Commission of Ireland, Pastoral Directory on the Building and Reorganisation of Churches, June 1966, *Furrow*, 17/7 (July 1966), 471, 471–7.
19. Ibid., 473.
20. See reports of the secretaries of diocesan liturgical commissions in 'Liturgy Renewal in Ireland', *Furrow*, 17/5 (May 1966), 297–312.
21. *The Irish Times*, 10 December 1965, 11.
22. McQuaid very often recorded his reply on the page above the letter. See Browne's letter to McQuaid, dated 29 December 1967, and McQuaid's reply, dated 30 December 1967, in the manner explained in D.D.A., AB8/B/XV.
23. Francis Lenny reporting from Armagh on 'Liturgy Renewal in Ireland', *Furrow*, 17/5 (May 1966), 300–01.
24. *Constitution on the Sacred Liturgy* in Abbott, *Vatican II Documents*, 147.
25. See *Instruction on Implementing the Liturgy Constitution* in Austin Flannery, ed., *Vatican II: The Liturgy Constitution*, 130.
26. See Episcopal Liturgical Commission, 'Pastoral Directory', *Furrow*, 17/7, (July, 1966), 476.
27. Ibid., 477.
28. Ibid., 473.
29. See Thomas Carroll reporting from the Diocese of Ardagh and Clonmacnoise on 'Liturgy Renewal in Ireland', *Furrow*, 17/5 (May 1966), 300.
30. Ibid.
31. For a summary and explanation of the changes in the new order of the Mass, see Peter Coughlan, 'The New Order of the Mass', *Furrow*, 20/5 (May 1969), 294–301.
    See also Patrick McGoldrick, 'Aspects of the Order of the Mass', *Furrow*, 20/12 (December 1969), 657–64.
32. See *Memoriale Domini, Instruction on the Manner of Distributing Holy Communion*, issued by the Sacred Congregation for Divine Worship on 29 May 1969, in Austin Flannery, ed., *Vatican II: The Conciliar and Post-Conciliar Documents*, Dublin, 1975, 148–53.
33. See pastoral letter from His Grace the Archbishop concerning the option of 'receiving Holy Communion in the hand', 29 September 1978, Archbishop's House, Dublin.
34. Ibid., 1.
35. Ibid., 2.
36. See *Immensae Caritatis, Instruction on Facilitating Sacramental Eucharistic Communion in Particular Circumstances* issued by the Sacred Congregation for Divine Worship on 25 January 1973, in Austin Flannery, ed., *Vatican II: The Conciliar and Post-Conciliar Documents*, Dublin, 1975, 225–32.
37. *Bulletin, Sutton Parish, Dublin on 'Building up the Body of Christ'*, September 1981.
38. Ibid.
39. See *Ecclesiae Semper, Decree on Concelebration and Communion under Both Species*, issued by the Sacred Congregation of Rites, 7 March 1965, in Austin Flannery, ed., *Vatican II: The Conciliar and Post-Conciliar Documents*, Dublin, 1975, 57–60.
    See 'The New Concelebration Rite', *Furrow*, 16/8 (August 1965), 353–7.
40. See Statement on 'Liturgy' issued by the Irish hierarchy, 22 June 1966, *Furrow*, 17/7 (July 1966), 478.
41. See Statement of the Irish Episcopal Conference, September 1974, *Furrow*, 25/11 (November 1974), 632.
42. See *Decree of the Sacred Congregation of Rites 19 March 1969* in *The Celebration of Marriage*, Dublin, 1980, vii.

43. See *Decree of the Sacred Congregation for Divine Worship on the Rite of Baptism, 15 May 1969* in *Rite of Baptism for Children*, Dublin, 1970, 5.
    See 'The New Rite of Baptism', *Furrow*, 21/11 (November 1970), 698–703.
    See also J.G. McGarry, 'The New Rite of Baptism', *Furrow*, 20/10 (October 1969), 562.
44. See *Apostolic Constitution on the Sacrament of the Anointing of the Sick, 13 November 1972, Furrow*, 24/3 (March 1973), 184–7.
45. See *Decree of the Sacred Congregation for Divine Worship promulgating the New Rite of Penance, 2 December 1973* in *Rite of Penance*, Dublin, 1976, 2.
    See also *Reconciliationem, Decree promulgating the New Order of Penance, 2 December 1973* in Austin Flannery, ed., *Vatican Council II: More Post-Conciliar Documents*, Dublin, 1982, 20–21.
46. See *Rite of Penance Approved for Use in the Dioceses of Ireland*, Dublin, 1976.
47. See *Furrow*, 27/11 (November 1976), 640–41.
48. Michael Ledwith, 'Theology Forum', *Furrow*, 26/6 (June 1975), 334–5.
    For an insight into this debate and the different positions adopted in relation to the 'fate of unbaptised infants' in the 1950s, see questions addressed to Rev. J. McCarthy in the 'Notes and Queries' section of *IER*, 74 (July–December 1950), 436–43; ibid., 75 (January–June 1951), 61–3, 453–7; ibid., 76 (July–December 1951), 319–25.
49. See *The Catholic Encyclopaedia*, Vol. III, New York 1908, 761.
50. Daniel Duffy, 'Eucharistic Piety in Irish Practice', *Furrow*, 9/6 (June, 1958), 368.
51. Ibid., 358.
52. Fachtna Lewis, 'The Motives for attending Holy Mass: A Case Study of a selected group of 293 Irish rural people', Ph.D. thesis, Universitas S. Thomae de Urbe, Rome, 1963, 102–5.
53. *A Catechism of Catholic Doctrine*, Dublin, 1951, Question 56, 22.
54. *Prayer to St Michael composed by Pope Leo XIII*, Tan Books and Publishers, Inc., PO Box 424, Rockford, Illinois 61105.
55. See *Instruction by the Sacred Congregation of Rites on the Proper Implementing of the Liturgy, 26 September 1964* in Austin Flannery, ed., *Vatican II: The Liturgy Constitution*, Dublin, 1964, 128.
56. Patrick A. Baggot, 'The Sacrament of Forgiveness', *Furrow*, 25/8 (August 1974), 412.
57. Pastoral letter from His Grace, the Archbishop of Dublin, concerning the option of 'receiving Holy Communion in the hand', Archbishop's House, 29 September 1978, 2.
58. Daniel Duffy, 'Eucharistic Piety in Irish Practice', *Furrow*, 9/6 (June 1958), 359.
59. Katherine O'Doherty, 'Where Have All the Faithful Gone?', *Furrow*, 20/10 (October 1969), 582–91, 583, 588.
60. *A Survey of Religious Practice, Attitudes and Beliefs in the Republic of Ireland 1973–4*, report no.1 on *Religious Practice* (hereafter referred to as *Religious Practice*, report no.1, 1974) Research and Development Unit, CCII, Dublin, 1975, 71.
61. Ibid., 51.
62. Ibid., 71.
63. Ibid.
64. Ibid.
65. Quoted in Peter R. Connolly, 'The Church in Ireland since Vatican II', *Furrow*, 30/12 (December 1979), 755–66.
66. *Religious Practice*, report no. 1, 1974, 13.
67. Ibid., 37.
68. Ibid., 4, 37.

See also Máire Nic Ghiolla Phádraig, 'Religious Practice and Belief in Ireland' in *Ten Years of Research and Development 1971–1981,* Council for Research and Development, Maynooth, 1981, 34, 51.

69. *Religious Practice,* report no. 1, 1974, 4.
70. Eamonn Bredin, 'The Liturgy: Problems and Prospects', *Furrow,* 30/1 (January 1979), 45.
71. Desmond Keenan, 'News and Views', *Furrow,* 21/1 (January 1970), 66.
72. P.J. Brophy, 'Whatever Happened to Our Liturgical Dreams?', *Furrow,* 25/4 (April 1974), 214.
73. Ibid.
74. Eamonn Bredin, 'The Liturgy: Problems and Prospects', *Furrow,* 30/1 (January 1979), 53.
75. P.J. Brophy, 'Whatever Happened to Our Liturgical Dreams?', *Furrow,* 25/4 (April 1974), 215.
76. Ibid., 218.

Chapter 9 The Communications Media and the Irish Church (pp 127–138)

1. See *Dáil Debates,* 129, cols. 217–8 (31 January 1952).
2. *Report of the Television Commission,* Dublin, 1959, para. 9, 11.
3. Ibid., paras. 13, 14, p. 12; para. 65, p. 24.
4. Ibid., paras. 19, 20, 21, pp. 13–4.
5. See Robert J. Savage, *Irish Television: The Political and Social Origins,* Cork, 1996, 208. The background to all of the events leading up to the setting up of the native television service is elaborated on in this book.
6. Statement of Irish hierarchy on forthcoming Irish TV network, Maynooth, October 1961, *Furrow,* 12/11 (November 1961), 695–7.
7. President de Valera's address at the launch of Telefís Éireann, 31 December 1961, in Martin McLoone and John MacMahon, eds., *Television and Irish Society: Twenty-One Years of Irish T.V.,* Dublin, 1984, Appendix 1, 149.
8. Ibid.
9. *The Irish Times,* 1 January 1962, 3.
10. *Irish Independent,* 5 March 1962, 14.
11. Louis McRedmond, 'Dialogue in the Church: The Journalist', *Furrow,* 15/1, (January 1964), 6.
12. Ibid., 7.
13. See E.H. Schillebeeckz OP, 'Vatican II — A Struggle of Minds' and 'Misunderstandings at the Council' in *Vatican II: A Struggle of Minds and Other Essays,* Dublin, 1963, 1964.
14. See Joseph Dunn, *No Tigers in Africa,* Dublin, 1986, 9.
15. *The Irish Times,* 16 March 1965, 1.
16. Statement issued to the press by the Irish hierarchy after their 22–23 June meeting, 1965, *Furrow,* 16/8 (August 1965), 514.
17. See *Decree on the Instruments of Social Communication, 4 December 1963* in Abbott, *Vatican II Documents,* para. 21, 329.
18. Desmond Forristal, 'The Late Late Show', *Furrow,* 23/10 (October 1970), 655.
19. Incident recalled by Gay Byrne in *To Whom it Concerns,* Dublin, 1972, 71–4.
20. *Sunday Press,* 13 February 1966, 1.
    Sunday Independent, 13 February 1966, 1.
21. Byrne, *To Whom it Concerns,* 76–7.

22. *The Irish Times*, 14 February 1966, 9.
23. Ibid.
24. Byrne, *To Whom it Concerns*, 86–91.
25. *Irish Catholic*, 31 March 1966, 1.
    Ibid., 7 April 1966, 1, 2, 3.
    Catholic Standard, 1 April 1966.
26. Byrne, *To Whom it Concerns*, 94–5.
27. *The Irish Times*, 29 March 1966, 9.
28. Byrne, *To Whom it Concerns*, 89
29. Cardinal Conway speaking at Maynooth, 19 June 1966, quoted in *Furrow*, 17/7 (July 1966), 470.
30. As recorded by Gay Byrne in *To Whom it Concerns*, Dublin, 1972, 109.
31. See Joseph Dunn, *No Tigers in Africa*, Dublin, 1986, vii.
32. Ibid., 143–66.
33. The Institute also had a marketing and commercial aspect to it. The CTSI had acquired premises in Abbey St, Dublin, in 1924 and, in 1928, Veritas company was formed, which managed the commercial aspect of CTSI. From 1969, Veritas company, Veritas publications and Veritas video productions were all subsumed under the umbrella structure of the Catholic Communications Institute. Veritas company has retail outlets in Dublin, Cork, Sligo, Ennis and Letterkenny and serves as a repository and marketing outlet for selling all manner of religious items and books. In effect, Veritas replaced the CTSI. The background events leading to the transition are explained by Joseph Dunn in his book, *No Vipers in the Vatican: A Second Anthology of Sorts*, Dublin, 1996, 290–91.
34. *Irish Independent*, 5 March 1962, 14.
35. Ibid.
36. See *Catalogue of Books and Booklets of the Catholic Truth Society of Ireland, 1962.*
37. See letter written by Fr Peter Birch and published in *Furrow*, 2/3 (March 1951), 202.
38. *The Irish Times*, 21 November 1964.
    Sunday Independent, 22 November 1964, 6, 24. *Sunday Independent*, 29 November 1964, 1.
39. *Sunday Independent*, 29 November 1964, 1.
40. Fergus Linehan, 'Films', *The Irish Times*, 14 February 1966.
41. See also Fr Peter Connolly, 'Censorship and the Moral Classification of Films', *Furrow*, 8/2 (February 1957), 110–11.
    Des Hickey, *Sunday Independent*, 22 November 1964, 24.
42. See Dympna Glendenning, *Education and the Law*, Dublin, 1999, 372.
43. Ibid.
44. See Peter R. Connolly, 'The Moralists and the Obscene', *ITQ*, xxxii/2 (1961), 116–28.
45. See Patrick Hannon, 'Heart in Pilgrimage' in James H. Murphy, ed., *No Bland Facility: Selected Writings on Literature, Religion and Censorship, Peter Connolly*, Gerrards Cross, 1991, 49.
46. See Murphy, *No Bland Facility*, 10–13.
47. See *The Irish Times*, 23 April 1966, 7. The novels in question were *The Country Girls* (1960); *Girls with Green Eyes* — originally *The Lonely Girl* (1962); *Girls in their Married Bliss* (1964); *August is a Wicked Month* (1965).
48. See *The Irish Times*, 25 April 1966, 9.
49. *Dáil Debates*, 228, col. 680 (10 May 1967).
50. Censorship of Publications (Amendment) Act 1967, No. 15 in public statutes of the Oireachtas, 1967.

51. *Dáil Debates*, 228, col. 1445 (24 May 1967).
52. Michael Adams, *Censorship: The Irish Experience*, Alabama, 1968, 199.
53. Ibid., 157.
54. Ibid., 158.
55. See Hannon, 'Heart in Pilgrimage', in Murphy, ed., *No Bland Facility*, 44.
56. Ibid., 49.
57. Letter from Archbishop McQuaid to Bishop Browne on 8 February 1967. I am grateful to Mr Tom May, archivist, Galway Diocesan Archives, for providing me with a copy of Archbishop McQuaid's letter from Bishop Browne's papers.
58. See letter from Bishop Browne, 17 March 1967, replying to Archbishop McQuaid's letter above, in Dublin Diocesan Archives, AB8/B/XV.
59. Letter from Archbishop McQuaid to Bishop Browne, 12 March 1968; Browne's reply on 14 March 1968, Dublin Diocesan Archives, AB8/B/XV; McQuaid's reply to Browne on 15 March 1968. Again, I am grateful to Mr Tom May, archivist, Galway Diocesan Archives, for providing me with copies of McQuaid's letters.
60. See *Agora*, 2/1 (Spring 1968), 3–4.
61. Ibid., 3.
62. Letter from Browne to McQuaid, 14 March 1968, in Dublin Diocesan Archives, AB8/B/XV.
63. Letter from McQuaid, 15 March 1968, replying to above letter from Browne. Again, I am grateful to Mr Tom May, archivist, Galway Diocesan Archives, for providing me with a copy of Archbishop McQuaid's letter from Bishop Browne's papers.
64. *The Irish Times*, 18 February 1965, 1.
65. *Sunday Independent*, 8 May 1966, 1.
66. *The Irish Times*, 16 May 1966.

Chapter 10 Philosophical and Structural Change in the Irish Church (pp 139–148)

1. *Irish Independent*, 14 February 1972, 6.
2. *Dogmatic Constitution on the Church, 21 November 1964* in Abbott, *Vatican II Documents*, 14–96.
3. Ibid., Chapter 3, para.18, 37.
4. Decree on the *Bishops' Pastoral Office in the Church, 28 October 1965* in Abbott, *Vatican II Documents*, paras. 37–8, 424–6.
5. *Ecclesiae Sanctae, Apostolic Letter of Pope Paul VI on Norms for carrying out Certain of the Conciliar Decrees, 6 August 1966, AAS*, 58 (Rome, 1966), 773–4, para. 41, 1–4.
6. See *The Code of Canon Law*, London, 1983, cans. 447–59, 80–82. The announcement that the 1917 *Code of Canon Law* was to be revised was made by Pope John XXIII at the same time as his proclamation of the Second Vatican Council. It is worth noting that there is no reference to bishops' conferences in the 1917 *Code of Canon Law.*
7. See Sean Cannon CSsR, 'Irish Episcopal Meetings, 1788–1882: A Juridico-Historical Study', D.C.L. thesis, Universitas S. Thomae de Urbe, Rome, 1979, 41–62, 111–16. For historico-political reasons to do with Ireland's colonial status, the Irish bishops throughout the nineteenth century were aware of the importance of presenting a united front in matters where they wished to represent the interests of the Irish Church to Rome.
8. This has been explained to the author by Bishop Michael Smith of Meath, secretary to the episcopal conference from 1985 to 1998.
9. These stages in the restructuring of the Irish bishops' conference after the Second Vatican Council have been conveyed to the author by Bishop Michael Smith of Meath.

10. This information in relation to the episcopal conference has been conveyed to the author by Jim Cantwell, director of the Catholic Press and Information Office from 1975 to 2000.
11. See *Irish Catholic Directory and Diary 1997*, 17.
12. Information in relation to bishops' press conferences was conveyed to the author by Jim Cantwell, director of the Catholic Press and Information Office from 1975 to 2000.
13. Frederick M. Jones, 'The Early Days of the Second Session', *Furrow*, 14/11 (November 1963), 678–81.
14. Seán O'Riordan, 'The Second Vatican Council: The Pope, the Curia and the Bishops', *Furrow*, 14/12 (December 1963), 736–9.
15. Pope Paul VI established the Synod of Bishops with the *Motu Proprio*, '*Apostolica Sollicitudo*', 15 September 1965. See Seán O'Riordan, 'The Fourth Session', *Furrow*, 16/11 (November 1965), 682–3. See also Peter Hebblethwaite, *Understanding the Synod*, Dublin, 1968.
16. *Decree on Bishops' Office in the Church, 28 October 1965*, in Abbott, *Vatican II Documents*, para. 27, 416.
17. Statement issued by the Irish hierarchy after Maynooth meeting, 22–23 June 1965, *Furrow*, 16/8 (August 1965), 514–5.
18. Statement issued by the Irish Episcopal Conference, 9 March 1972, *Furrow*, 23/4, (April 1972), 259–60.
19. Ibid., 259.
20. The *Dogmatic Constitution on the Church, 21 November 1964* in Abbott, *Vatican II Documents*, para. 37, 65.
21. See *Apostolic Constitution, Humanae Salutis, 25 December 1961*, in which John XXIII convoked the Second Vatican Council, in Abbott, *Vatican II Documents*, 704.
22. See Council for Research and Development, *Ten Years of Research and Development 1971–1980*, Maynooth, 1981, vi–vii.
23. Ibid.
24. Rev. Jeremiah Newman, 'Towards a Catholic Sociology' *University Review*, 1/4 (Spring 1955), 9.
25. See reference 15, Chapter 5.
26. A perusal of issues of *Christus Rex* in the late 1950s and early 1960s shows a much greater emphasis on empirical research. See, for instance, Rev. P. McConville, 'Emigration from Ireland: Facts and Figures' 10 (1956), 335–44; Cornelius Murphy, 'Should the Small Farm Survive?' in ibid., 12 (1958), 278–92; Rev. E.J. Hegarty, 'Statistics: Juvenile Delinquency' in ibid., 13 (1959), 297–302. In 1959, the journal began a feature on statistics.
27. C.K. Ward, *Social Compass*, XI/3, 4, 1964, 28.
28. Ibid.
29. Fachtna Lewis OFM, 'The Motives for attending Holy Mass: A Case-Study of a selected group of 293 Irish rural people', Ph.D. thesis, Universitas S. Thomae de Urbe, Rome, 1963.
30. Rev. James Abbott, *Catechism Key for Primary and Continuation Schools and for Converts*, Dublin, 1960, 44.
31. Information in relation to the reorganisation of priests' incomes by Archbishop McQuaid in 1968 was conveyed to the author by Mgr John Wilson, Financial Administrator, Finance Secretariat, Dublin archdiocese, Archbishop's House, Drumcondra, Dublin 9.

32. This information about the setting up of the finance committee in Dublin diocese in 1972 was conveyed to the author by Mgr John Wilson as in the previous reference.
33. This information relating to the introduction of the Share collection in 1974 was given to the author by Mgr John Wilson as above.
34. *Decree on the Apostolate of the Laity, 18 November 1965*, in Abbott, *Vatican II Documents*, para. 26, 515.
35. *Catholicam Christi Ecclesiam, 6 January 1967, AAS*, 59 (Rome, 1967), 25–8.
36. See Irish Council for the Apostolate of the Laity: terms of reference approved by the Irish Episcopal Conference, Maynooth, 18 June 1968, *Furrow*, 19/11 (November 1968), 662–3.
37. See W.M. Cashman, 'The Laity Council's First Year', *Furrow*, 21/4 (April 1970), 248–55. The first meeting was in St Patrick's College, Drumcondra, Dublin. Vincent Grogan, the representative of the Knights of St Columbanus, was elected chairman, and Dr Cornelius O'Leary, Queen's University, Belfast, and the representative of the diocese of Down and Connor, was elected vice-chairman. A solemn inaugural ceremony took place the following day, on 23 February, at St Patrick's College, Maynooth, beginning with a concelebrated Mass at which Cardinal Conway delivered the homily.
38. *Dogmatic Constitution on the Church, 21 November 1964* in Abbott, *Vatican II Documents*, para. 31, 57–8.
39. Xavier Rynne, *The Second Session: The Debates and Decrees of Vatican Council II*, from 29 September to 4 December 1963, London, 1963, 1964, 111–2.
40. See *Mulrany Guidelines: Report of Special Meeting of Irish Bishops*, 1974, para.1.1.3, 1.
41. Michael V. Daly reporting on the National Conference of Priests of Ireland AGM, 1–3 May 1978, *Furrow*, 29/6 (June 1978), 370–71.
42. Quoted in Maura Hyland, 'Epilogue: What People of God?' in Alan Falconer, Enda McDonagh, Seán Mac Réamoinn, eds., *Freedom to Hope?*, Dublin, 1985, 96.
43. *Decree on the Apostolate of the Laity, 18 November 1965* in Abbott, *Vatican II Documents*, para. 26, 515.
44. Walter Forde, 'European Congress of National Laity Councils', *Furrow*, 29/12 (December 1978), 779–81, 780.
45. *Decree on the Ministry and Life of Priests, 7 December 1965* in Abbott, *Vatican II Documents*, para. 7, 548–9.
46. *Ecclesiae Sanctae, Apostolic Letter of Pope Paul VI on Norms for carrying out certain of the Conciliar Decrees, 6 August 1966, AAS*, 58 (Rome, 1966), 757–87.
47. See report on Councils of Priests in Irish Dioceses, *Furrow*, 18/5 (May 1967), 257–62. See also second report on same, *Furrow*, 20/12 (December 1969), 636–52. (The reader's attention is drawn to the fact that there is a misprint in this issue of the *Furrow*. It is entitled November, volume 20, no. 11 in error.)
48. See Guidelines on the Structure and Functioning of Priests' Councils, issued by the Munster Conference of Bishops, published in *Furrow*, 23/2 (February 1972), 120.
49. Ibid.
50. Constitution of the National Conference of Priests, *Furrow*, 26/7 (July 1975), 444–6.
51. Ibid., 444.
52. Ibid.
53. *Decree on the Bishops' Pastoral Office in the Church, 28 October 1965* in Abbott, *Vatican II Documents*, para. 35.5, 423.
54. See Seán O'Riordan, 'The Fourth Session', *Furrow*, 16/11 (November 1965), 682.

55. Michael V. Daly, reporting on third AGM of the NCPI in Galway, 1–3 May 1978, *Furrow*, 29/6 (June 1978), 373.
56. Basil Chubb, *The Government and Politics of Ireland*, London, 1982, 118–41, 138.
57. J.J. Lee, 'Seán Lemass in Ireland 1945–1970' in J.J. Lee, ed., *Ireland 1945–70*, RTÉ Thomas Davis Lectures series, Dublin, 1979, 20.
58. The *Dogmatic Constitution on the Church, 21 November 1964* in Abbott, *Vatican II Documents*, para. 28, 53.
59. See statement of the NCPI, *Furrow* 29/6 (June 1978), 382–3.
60. See Peter R. Connolly, 'The Priest in Modern Irish Fiction', *Furrow*, 9/12 (December 1958), 782–97.

Chapter 11 Education (pp 149–162)

1. See Burton Clark, *Educating the Expert Society*, San Francisco, 1962, 3.
2. *Report of the Council of Education on the Curriculum of the Secondary School Curriculum*, Dublin, 1962.
3. Ibid., 252.
4. See John J. O'Meara, *Reform in Education*, Dublin, 1958, 16.
5. Peter Birch, 'The Secondary Programme and Modern Needs', published in the *Report of the Conference of Convent Secondary Schools*, 1957.
6. Ibid.
7. *Sunday Press*, 4 October 1959.
8. *Economic Development*, Dublin, 1958.
9. *Programme for Economic Expansion*, Dublin, 1958.
10. See statement by Dr P.J. Hillery TD, Minister for Education, regarding post-primary education, at press conference, 20 May 1963 (hereafter referred to as Hillery Press Conference, 1963) published in Eileen Randles, *Post-Primary Education in Ireland 1957–1970*, Dublin, 1975, 328–37, 328.
11. Ibid., 337.
12. Ibid., 332.
13. Ibid., 334.
14. *Investment in Education — Report of the Survey Team*, Dublin, 1966.
    Investment in Education — Annexes and Appendices, Dublin, 1966.
15. Commission on Higher Education 1960–67, *Presentation and Summary of Report*, I, II, III, Dublin, 1967.
16. Hillery Press Conference, 1963, in Randles, *Post-Primary Education in Ireland 1957–70*, 328.
17. Ibid., paras. 10.21–10.22, 277–9.
18. See Louise Fuller, 'An Ideological Critique of the Irish Post-Primary School Curriculum: The Economic, Socio-cultural and Political factors influencing its Development', M. Ed. thesis, St Patrick's College, Maynooth, 1990.
19. *Investment in Education*, paras. 16.4–16.5, 388.
20. *Investment in Education*, para. 10.31, 283.
21. See Sean O'Connor, *A Troubled Sky: Reflections on the Irish Educational Scene, 1957–1968*, Dublin, 1986, 124–8.
22. *The Irish Times*, 27 January 1966.
23. *The Irish Times*, 14 October 1967.
24. *Mater et Magistra, Encyclical Letter of Pope John XXIII Concerning a Re-evaluation of the Social Question in the Light of Christian Teaching, 15 May 1961*, trans. Rev. H.E. Winstone, CTS, London, 1961.

25. *Quadragesimo Anno, Encyclical of Pope Pius XI on Reconstruction of the Social Order, 15 May 1931* in Claudia Carlen, ed., *The Papal Encyclicals 1909–1939,* Raleigh, 1990, 415–43.
26. See *Sunday Independent,* 11 September 1966.
27. Sean O'Connor, 'Post-Primary Education: Now and in the Future', *Studies,* LVII, (Dublin, 1968) 233–49.
28. Ibid., 249.
29. Ibid., 233.
30. Ibid.
31. See the Executive Council of the Teaching Brothers' Association response to Sean O'Connor, *Studies,* LVII (Dublin, 1968) 281–3.
32. Ibid., 226.
33. Ibid., 227.
34. As no archival sources are available for this period, much of the background information on these developments has been conveyed to the author by Mr Liam Murphy, who, in his capacity as chairman of the CHA from 1975, chairman of the CMCSS from 1977 to 1987 and president of the AMCSS from 1990 to 1996, has had very close professional involvement in the events and developments recounted here.
35. See O'Connor, *A Troubled Sky,* 160.
    See also Mulcahy, *Curriculum and Policy in Irish Post-Primary Education,* 26–8.
36. See *Statistical Reports of the Department of Education, 1966–67, 1968–69, 1971–72* and *1974–75.*
37. Ó Buachalla, *Education Policy,* 378.
38. *The Irish Times,* 12 November 1970.
39. See Pádraig Faulkner's response to questions in the Dáil on 19 May 1971, *Dáil Debates,* 253, cols. 1964–9 (19 May 1971).
40. Ibid., 348.
41. *Dáil Debates,* 253, col. 454 (22 April 1971).
42. Ibid.
43. Ibid., cols. 1964–9 (19 May 1971).
44. *The Irish Times,* 12 May 1971, 1.
45. See interview with Mr Faulkner, *The Irish Times,* 15 May 1971, 1, 16.
46. *The Irish Times,* 12 May 1971, 1.
47. *Dáil Debates,* 253, cols. 1969–76 (19 May 1971).
48. For the reaction of the Irish Vocational Education Association, see *The Irish Times,* 11 May, 1; ibid., 12 May, 1; and ibid., 2 June 1971; for reaction from the Vocational Teachers' Association, see *The Irish Times,* 27 May 1971, 1.
49. Cited in Ó Buachalla, *Education Policy,* 378.
50. See *Have the Snakes Come Back? Education and the Irish Child,* by a Group of Catholic Parents, Dublin, 1975.
51. Ibid., 38–9.
52. See *Statement on Community Schools issued by the Irish Episcopal Conference, Maynooth, 24 June 1971, Furrow,* 22/9 (September 1971), 594.
53. Ibid., 595.
54. Ibid.
55. See Formal Petition by a group of clergymen to President de Valera on the Community School issue, published in Ó Buachalla, *Education Policy,* 398.
56. Ibid.
57. See *Joint Statement of bishops and religious on education, Furrow,* 23/8 (August 1972), 506.

58. Ibid.
59. See *Model Lease for Community Schools,* Dublin, 1996.
60. Ibid.
61. *White Paper on Educational Development,* Dublin, 1980, paras. 9.4–9.10, pp 66–8.
62. See Louis O'Flaherty, *Management and Control in Irish Education: The Post-Primary Experience,* Dublin, 1992, 82.
63. See Association of Community and Comprehensive Schools, *Model Lease for Community Schools,* Dublin, 1996.
64. See *F.I.R.E. Report by the Working Party Established by the Education Commissions of the Hierarchy and the Conference of Major Religious Superiors to Examine the Future Involvement of Religious in Education,* Dublin, 1973 (hereafter referred to as *F.I.R.E. Report),* 24.
65. Ibid., 23.
66. Ibid., 24.
67. See Department of Education, *Curaclam na Bunscoile — Primary School Curriculum, Teacher's Handbook,* Parts 1, 2, Dublin, 1971.
68. Department of Education, *Scheme of Capitation Grants,* Dublin, 1974.
69. *The Irish Times,* 8 October 1980, 1.

Chapter 12 Changes in Religious Life and their Influence on Education (pp 163–177)

1. See *Decree on the Appropriate Renewal of the Religious Life, 28 October 1965* in Abbott, *Vatican II Documents,* 468–9 (hereafter referred to as *Decree on Religious Life*).
2. Ibid., 469.
3. Ibid.
4. Daniel Lord SJ, *Letters to a Nun,* Missouri, 1947, 133
5. Ibid.
6. See Sr De Lourdes Stack, *As We Lived It,* Tralee, 1981, 100.
7. Lord, *Letters to a Nun,* 110.
8. Ibid.
9. Stack, *As We Lived It,* 100.
10. Monica Baldwin, *I Leap Over the Wall: A Return to the World after Twenty-Eight Years in a Convent,* London, 1948, 83.
11. Ibid., 83–4.
12. Lord, *Letters to a Nun,* 134.
13. Baldwin, *I Leap Over the Wall,* 90.
14. See *Decree on Religious Life,* 476.
15. Ibid.
16. Ibid., 477.
17. Ibid.
18. See references 8, 9, Chapter 6.
19. Liam Ryan, ed., *The Changing Direction of Irish Seminaries,* Research and Development Unit, CCII, Dublin, 1972, 7.
20. *Decree on Priestly Formation, 28 October 1965* in Abbott, *Vatican II Documents,* 437–57.
21. *Decree on Religious Life,* 466–82.
22. See advertisements for courses and training programmes in human relations, development studies, counselling and group work in *Furrow,* 27/4 (April 1976), 246; ibid., 252; ibid., 30/2 (February 1979), 133; ibid., 30/5 (May 1979), 320.
    See similar advertisements in *Doctrine and Life,* 26/2 (February 1976) 146; ibid., 26/11 (November 1976), 831–3; ibid., 30/8, (August 1978), 503; see also special issue of

Doctrine and Life, (March–April 1977), 160–61.

23. See *Survey of Catholic Clergy and Religious in Ireland 1970*, carried out by the Research and Development Unit of the CCII (hereafter referred to as *Catholic Clergy and Religious 1970*), Dublin, 1971, 27.
24. Ibid., 43, 76, 103.
    Some of the statistics for religious priests, nuns and brothers include those who left while novices, after first profession and after final profession, and do not correlate well with the survey figures for secular priests. For this reason, the latter have not been included. This report contains a detailed breakdown and analysis of each category, and merits closer study on the part of the reader.
25. See *Vocations Survey 1971*, report no. 2, Research and Development Unit of the CCII, Dublin, 1971, 6.
26. *Catholic Clergy and Religious 1970*, 4.
27. *F.I.R.E. Report*, 1973, Appendix 10 (M), 73.
28. See *Catholic Clergy and Religious 1970*, 17, 18, 47, 48, 79, 80, 106, 107.
29. *F.I.R.E. Report*, 11.
30. See *F.I.R.E. Report*, 23.
31. Ibid.
32. Ibid, 46, 50a, 51, 72.
33. Ibid., 46, 51.
34. See *Statistical Report of the Department of Education, 1974–75.*
35. See *Statistical Report of the Department of Education, 1979–80.*
36. See *Vocations in Ireland 1980*, report no. 11, Council for Research and Development, Maynooth, 1981, 5, 10, 18, 23.
37. See *Catholic Clergy and Religious 1970*, 3.
    See also *Irish Priests and Religious 1970–1975: Survey of Catholic Clergy and Religious in Ireland*, Research and Development Commission, Dublin, 1977, ix.
    See also *Vocations in Ireland 1980*, report no 11, 2.
38. *F.I.R.E. Report*, 15.
39. Ibid., 38–40.
40. The points system began in UCD in 1970, when it was introduced by the university in order to regulate entry to the medical faculty, and it developed from there.
41. *F.I.R.E. Report*, 22.
42. Ibid.
43. See *Rules and Programme for Secondary Schools, 1969–70*, Dublin, 1969. See also *Rules and Programme for Secondary Schools, 1970–71*, Dublin, 1970.
44. See Louise Fuller, 'An Ideological Critique of the Irish Post-Primary School Curriculum: The Economic, Socio-cultural and Political factors influencing its Development', M.Ed. thesis, St Patrick's College, Maynooth, 1990.
45. See *The National University of Ireland Calendar 1972*, 210–11; see also *The National University of Ireland Calendar 1973*, 195.
46. See references 52 and 58, Chapter 11 of this book.
47. *F.I.R.E. Report*, 24.
48. Ibid., 22.
49. Ibid.
50. Ibid., 38, 29.
51. See Karl Mannheim, *Essays on the Sociology of Knowledge*, Paul Kecskemeti, ed., London, 1952, 244.

52. See *Focus for Action,* Report by the working party set up by the Conference of Major Religious Superiors to consider appropriate action by religious in Ireland in the next six years (hereafter referred to as *Focus for Action*), Dublin, 1974.
53. Ibid., 16.
54. Ibid., 14.
55. Ibid.
56. Ibid.
57. Ibid., 17.
58. *F.I.R.E. Report,* 27.
59. Ibid.
60. Ibid., 23.
61. Ibid., 19.
62. Ibid., 31.
63. Ibid., 28.
64. Ibid., 19.
65. Liam Murphy was interviewed by the author in August 1997. See reference 34 in Chapter 11.
66. See *A Manual for Boards of Management of Catholic Secondary Schools* by the Council of Managers of Catholic Secondary Schools, Dublin, 1985. In the articles of management which were drawn up, a clear distinction was made between control over capital expenditure and decision-making in relation to policy and ethos, and other powers which were at the discretion of the management boards. In this way, religious communities reserved the right to influence the philosophy and ethos of their schools.
67. See *Irish Catholic Clergy and Religious 1970–1981,* report no. 17, Council for Research and Development, Maynooth, 1983, 24, 131.
68. Ibid., 54, 94, 95.
69. Ibid., 54.
70. Ibid.
71. See article by Fr Paul Andrews SJ (Chairman of the *F.I.R.E. Report* working party), 'Irish Education Transformed', *Studies,* 86/342 (Summer 1997).
72. See Patrick Clancy, *Participation in Higher Education,* Dublin, 1982.
    See also David B. Rottman, Damian F. Hannan, Niamh Hardiman and Miriam M. Wiley, *The Distribution of Income in the Republic of Ireland: A Study in Social Class and Family-cycle Inequalities,* ESRI paper no. 109, Dublin, 1982.
    Frank Litton, ed., *Unequal Achievement: The Irish Experience,* Institute of Public Administration, Dublin, 1982.
    Vincent Greaney and Thomas Kellaghan, *Equality of Opportunity in Irish Schools: A longitudinal study of 500 students,* Dublin, 1984.
    Richard Breen, *Education and the Labour Market: Work and Unemployment among recent cohorts of Irish school-leavers,* ESRI paper no. 119, Dublin, 1984.
73. Donal J. Dorr, 'Priest or Cleric?', *Furrow,* 25/8 (August 1974), 427.
74. Ibid.
75. Ibid.

Chapter 13 The Irish Church and Ecumenism (pp 178–192)

1. Michael Hurley SJ, *Towards Christian Unity: An Introduction to the Ecumenical Movements,* Dublin, 1960, 24–5.
2. *Irish Independent,* 9 February 1959, 10.

3. Ibid., 11.
4. *Irish Independent,* 5 March 1962, 14.
5. See John J. McDonnell, *The World Council of Churches and the Catholic Church,* Toronto, 1985, 244.
6. Hurley, *Towards Christian Unity,* 3–5.
7. Hurley, *Towards Christian Unity,* Dublin, 1960.
8. See articles contributed to symposium on Christian unity in *Furrow,* 6/1 (January 1955), 3–33. See also Patrick J. Devine, 'The Ecumenical Movement', *Furrow,* 7/1 (January 1956), 22–30.
9. Hurley, *Towards Christian Unity,* 16–20.
10. J.G. McGarry, 'The Unity Octave', *Furrow,* 14/1 (January 1963), 3.
11. Denis Faul, 'Catholic Ecumenical Activity', *Furrow,* 14/1 (January 1963), 17.
12. Joseph Dowdall, 'Offering the Mass for Unity', in ibid., 5.
13. See Lucey's letter to McQuaid, dated 12 November 1953, and McQuaid's reply, dated 15 November 1953 in DDA, AB8/B/XV.
14. Cited in Fergal Tobin, *The Best of Decades: Ireland in the 1960s,* Dublin, 1984, 79.
15. *Irish Independent,* 10 February 1964, 6.
16. Ibid.
17. Ibid.
18. Ibid.
19. Ibid.
20. See Michael Hurley SJ, 'Chronicle', 'Ecumenism: Joint Worship', *Furrow,* 16/4 (April 1965), 237–8.
21. See *Decree on Ecumenism, 21 November 1964* in Abbott, *Vatican II Documents,* 341.
22. *Word,* December 1964.
23. Ibid.

    For an account of Catholic treatment of inter-church marriage under Canon Law see Alasdair Heron, *Two Churches — One Love: Inter-church marriage between Protestants and Roman Catholics,* Dublin, 1977, 38–45.

    See also Michael Hurley, ed., *Beyond Tolerance: The Challenge of Mixed Marriage, A Record of the International Consultation held in Dublin, 1974,* London, 1975.

    See also Patrick Devine, 'Mixed Marriages and the Report from the Roman Catholic Church, the Lutheran World Federation and the World Alliance of Reformed Churches Dialogue' *ITQ,* 45 (1978), 47–72.

    See Brian O'Higgins, 'Mixed Marriages: The "Cautiones"', *ITQ,* 41 (1974), 218–21.

    See also Brian O'Higgins, 'Mixed Marriages: The "Cautiones" II', *ITQ,* 41 (1974), 274–88.
24. *Word,* December 1964.
25. Michael Viney, *The Irish Times,* 25 March 1965, 10.
26. Ibid, 24 March, 10.
27. See Xavier Rynne, *The Third Session: The Debates and Decrees of Vatican Council II, September 14 to November 21 1964,* London, 1964, 1965, 284–5.
28. Ibid., 284.
29. See William Sullivan, *Mixed Marriages: An Honest Appraisal,* Indiana, 1965, 42.
30. See *Decree on Ecumenism,* in Abbott, *Vatican II Documents,* para. 3, 346
31. See *Declaration on Religious Freedom, 7 December 1965* in Abbott, *Vatican II Documents,* paras. 3, 5, pp 681, 683.
32. See *Instruction de Matrimoniis Mixtis, Matrimonii Sacramentum, 18 March 1966, Sacra Congregatio Pro Doctrina Fidei, AAS,* 58 (Rome, 1966), 235–9.

For an account of the history of the Catholic Church's theological position in relation to mixed marriage and how its legislation regarding same changed after Vatican II and how this was applied, see Brian O'Higgins, 'Mixed Marriages: The "Cautiones"', *ITQ*, 41 (1974), 205–21, 274–88.
See also Heron, *Two Churches — One Love*, 46–62.
See also Michael Hurley, 'Mixed Marriages', *Furrow*, 17/5 (May 1966), 279–87.

33. See *Apostolic Letter Pastorale Munus, 30 November 1963, AAS*, 56, (Rome, 1964), 5–12.
34. See Michael Hurley, 'Ecumenism: Non-Sectarianism or Christian Co-operation', *Furrow*, 16/12 (December 1965), 770–72.
See also Michael Hurley, 'Ecumenism and Conversion', *ITQ*, XXXI (1964), 132–49.
35. See *Statement issued by the Irish Hierarchy, Maynooth, 22 June 1966, Furrow*, 17/7 (July 1966), 477.
36. Ibid.
37. Ibid.
38. Ibid.
39. *Church of Ireland Gazette*, 3/20 (25 March 1966), 2.
40. See Whyte, *Church and State in Modern Ireland*, 322–5 for an account of the circumstances surrounding the boycott by Catholics of their Protestant neighbours in Fethard-on-Sea, Co. Wexford, in 1957. It arose because the Protestant partner in a mixed marriage wished to revoke her promise that the children would be brought up as Catholics.
41. See Alice Curtayne, 'Ecumenism in Dublin', *Furrow*, 17/2 (February 1966), 116.
42. Ibid., 117.
43. *The Irish Times*, 19 January 1966, 9.
44. Ibid.
45. Ibid.
46. Alice Curtayne, 'Ecumenism in Dublin', *Furrow*, 17/2 (February 1966), 117.
47. Ibid.
48. *The Irish Times*, 19 January 1966, 1.
49. Ibid., 5.
See also *Irish Independent*, 19 January 1966, 5.
50. *The Irish Times*, 22 January 1966, 9.
51. *Church of Ireland Gazette*, 3/11 (21 January 1966), 1.
52. *The Irish Times*, 22 January 1966, 9.
53. *Directory concerning Ecumenical Matters*, issued by the Secretariat for promoting Christian Unity, 14 May 1967, *Furrow*, 18/8 (August 1967), 463–79.
54. See *Irish Directory on Ecumenism*, issued by the Episcopal Commission for Ecumenism, 15 January, *Furrow*, 20/2 (February 1969), 104–09.
55. *Acta et Decreta, Concilii Plenarii Episcoporum Hiberniae*, Dublin, 1960, Statute 287, 100–01.
56. *Irish Independent*, 10 February 1964, 6.
57. *The Irish Times*, 19 April 1967, 1.
58. Ibid.
59. See *Irish Weekly Independent*, 3 April 1958, 8.
60. Ibid., 26 June 1958, 7.
61. See *Sunday Independent*, 12 February 1967, 8.
62. See Bishop Philbin's contribution in *Commission on Higher Education, 1960–1967, 1: Presentation and Summary of Report*, Dublin, 1967, 49–50.
See *The Irish Times*, 22 March 1967, 1, 12.
63. *The Irish Times*, 22 April 1967, 1.

64. Ibid., 21 June 1967, 1.
65. See Statement by the Irish Episcopal Conference, 25 June 1970, 'Maynooth 11' regarding Trinity College, *Furrow*, 21/8 (August 1970), 532–3.
66. Ibid.
67. See *The Irish Times*, 26 June 1970, 1. Rome's approval for the lifting of the statute was announced a few months later. See ibid., 7 September 1970, 1. It was reported that Cardinal Conway had announced the previous Saturday that the Holy See had ratified the hierarchy's decision to repeal its ban on attendance by Catholics at Trinity College.
68. *Motu Proprio Matrimonia Mixta*, issued by Pope Paul VI, Rome, 31 March 1970, *Furrow*, 21/6 (June 1970), 388–94.
69. C.B. Daly, 'Inter-Church Marriages', *Furrow*, 25/1 (January 1974), 30.
70. See *Statement of the Irish Hierarchy, Maynooth, 1970, issued by Pope Paul VI, Rome, 31 March 1970, Furrow*, 21/11 (November 1970), 732–3.
71. I am indebted to Fr Michael Hurley for his own personal account of the ISE which was to be published in the *Jesuit Yearbook, 1997.*
72. See *Furrow*, 21/7 (July 1970), 432.
    See also Eric Gallagher and Stanley Worrall, eds., *Christians in Ulster 1968–1980*, Oxford, 1982, 141–2.
73. Michael Hurley SJ, *Irish Anglicanism 1869–1969*, Dublin, 1970, 70–71.
74. See Gallagher and Worrall, eds., *Christians in Ulster*, 132–3.
75. Ibid., 137–8.
76. *Directory on Ecumenism in Ireland*, in *Doctrine and Life*, 26/7 (July 1976), 495–518. See para. 4, 496.
77. Ibid., para. 11, 498.
78. Ibid., para. 61, 514.
79. Ibid., paras. 8, 10, p. 518.
80. Quoted in Gallagher and Worrall, eds., *Christians in Ulster*, 138.
81. For an understanding of the Catholic Church's ecclesiological position, see Patrick Devine, 'Mixed Marriages and the Report from the Roman Catholic Church, the Lutheran World Federation and the World Alliance of Reformed Churches Dialogue', *ITQ*, 45 (1978), 47–72.
    See also Brian O'Higgins, 'Mixed Marriages: The "Cautiones II"', *ITQ*, 41 (1974), 274–88.
82. See Brian O'Higgins, 'Mixed Marriages: The "Cautiones"', *ITQ*, 41 (1974), 218–21.
83. Cited by Patrick Devine, quoting from a World Council of Churches paper entitled 'How can Unity be achieved?' 1975, *ITQ*, 45 (1978), 62.
84. Quoted in Gallagher and Worrall, eds., *Christians in Ulster*, 142.

Chapter 14 Constitutional Review and Legislative Change (pp 193–212)

1. *The Irish Times*, 4 April 1966, 11. See also ibid., 3 September 1966, 1.
2. *Report of the Committee on the Constitution*, Dublin, 1967, 43.
3. Ibid.
4. Ibid.
5. Ibid., 47–8.
6. *The Irish Times*, 22 September 1969, 1, 11.
7. Ibid., 23 September 1969, 1.
8. Ibid.
9. Ibid., 10 October 1969.
10. *The Irish Times*, 15 December 1967.

11. Ibid.
12. *Irish Independent,* 26 February 1968, 7.
13. *Irish Independent,* 26 February 1968, 6.
14. Ibid., 7.
15. *Codex Iuris Canonici Pii X Pontificis Maximi Iussu Digestus,* Rome, 1917.
16. *Casti Connubii, Encyclical of Pope Pius XI on Christian Marriage, 31 December 1930* in Claudia Carlen, *The Papal Encyclicals 1903–1939,* Raleigh, 1990, para. 54, 399.
17. See Fr Denis Hickey, 'The 1966 Theological Problem', *Furrow,* 18/2 (February 1967), 92–5.
18. *Pastoral Constitution on the Church* in *the Modern World, 7 December 1965,* in Abbott, *Vatican II Documents,* para. 48, 250. (Hereafter referred to as *The Church in the Modern World.*)
19. Ibid., para. 51, 255.
20. Michael Novak, ed., *The Experience of Marriage: The Testimony of Laymen,* London, 1964. See also William Birmingham, ed., *What Modern Catholics think about Birth Control,* New York, 1964.
21. See *The Church in the Modern World* in Abbott, para.16, 213.
22. Ibid., para. 17, 214.
23. Donald S. Connery, *The Irish,* New York, 1968, 203.
24. Ibid.
25. Quoted in Ibid., 205.
26. Fr Denis Hickey, 'The 1966 Theological Problem', *Furrow,* 18/2 (February1967), 91–9.
27. See Fr Patrick McGrath, 'Natural Law Ethics: Has it a Future?', *Furrow,* 19/3 (April 1968), 200–11.
28. See Fr Enda McDonagh, 'An Approach to Morality', *Furrow,* 19/6 (June 1968), 307–17.
29. Alvin Toffler, *Future Shock,* London, 1971, 407.
30. Ibid.
31. *Encyclical Letter of His Holiness Pope Paul VI, Humanae Vitae: On the Regulation of Births, 21 July 1968* (hereafter referred to as *Humanae Vitae*), *Furrow,* 19/9 (September 1968), 542–56.
32. See *The Irish Times,* 30 July 1968, 1.
33. Ibid.
34. Quoted in ibid., 1 August 1968, 6.
35. Fr Denis O'Callaghan, 'After the Encyclical', *Furrow,* 19/11 (November 1968), 635.
36. Statement issued by the Irish hierarchy on the encyclical, *Humanae Vitae,* Maynooth, 9 October 1968, *Furrow,* 19/11 (November 1968), 661–2.
37. Ibid., 661.
38. Ibid.
39. Ibid., 661–2.
40. See Pastoral letter of the Irish hierarchy on Christian marriage, 16 February 1969, in *Justice, Love and Peace: Pastoral Letters of the Irish Bishops, 1969–1979,* Dublin, 1979, 11–33. See also *Irish Independent,* 17 February 1969, 14–5.
41. *Irish Independent,* Ibid., 15.
42. See *Humanae Vitae, Furrow* (September 1968), para. 11, 547.
43. *Irish Independent,* 17 February 1969, 15.
44. Cited by Fr Denis O'Callaghan in 'Theology Forum: *Humanae Vitae* in Context', *Furrow,* 28/4 (April 1977), 232–3.

45. Denis O'Callaghan, 'The Birth-Control Crisis', *Catholic World* (March 1967), 326–34. I am grateful to Mgr O'Callaghan for providing me with a copy of the article.
46. See letter sent by Bishop Browne of Galway to Archbishop McQuaid on 14 March 1968 in DDA, AB8/B/XV.
47. Ibid.
48. I am grateful to Mr Tom May, archivist, Galway Diocesan Archives, for providing me with a copy of Archbishop McQuaid's letter to Bishop Browne of 15 March 1968.
49. See *Humanae Vitae*, 25 July 1968, *IER*, 110 (July–December 1968), 100–15.
50. See Statement of the Irish hierarchy on the encyclical, *Humanae Vitae*, 9 October 1968, in ibid., 183–4.
51. O'Callaghan, 'After the Encyclical', *Furrow*, 19/10 (October 1968), 634.
52. Ibid.
53. Copy of letter, 3 November 1970, confirming date and time of panel discussion (13 November 1970), organised by the Medical Union to take place in the Shelbourne Hotel, given to the author by Mgr Denis O'Callaghan.
54. Copy of Fr Denis O'Callaghan's address to the Medical Union, 13 November 1970, given to the author by Mgr Denis O'Callaghan.
55. The author is grateful to Mgr Denis O'Callaghan for providing her with copies of the correspondence which passed between him and Fr James Ardle MacMahon, Archbishop McQuaid's secretary. Letter from Fr MacMahon to Rev. Prof. Denis O'Callaghan dated 14 November 1970.
56. O'Callaghan's reply to above letter on 16 November 1970.
57. MacMahon's further reply on 17 November 1970.
58. O'Callaghan's further reply on 18 November 1970.
59. Ibid.
60. MacMahon's reply to above letter one week later on 25 November 1970.
61. John Cooney, *John Charles McQuaid: Ruler of Catholic Ireland*, Dublin, 1999, 416–7, 426–9.
62. Fr Denis O'Callaghan, 'News and Views', *Furrow*, 28/4 (April 1977), 244.
63. Denis O'Callaghan, 'Theology Forum: *Humanae Vitae* in context', *Furrow*, 28/4 (April 1977), 231–2. See also Canon F.H. Drinkwater, 'News and Views', *Furrow*, 24/2 (February 1973), 116–7.
64. Fergal Tobin, *The Best of Decades: Ireland in the 1960s*, Dublin, 1984, 213.
65. Cited in ibid.
66. Garret FitzGerald, 'Towards a National Purpose', *Studies*, 53 (Winter 1964), 337–51.
67. Ibid., 350.
68. Cited in Whyte, *Church and State*, 346.
69. Cited in Connery, *The Irish*, 40, 202–3, 208–9.
70. *Irish Independent*, 22 February 1971, 6.
71. Statement issued to the press by the Irish Episcopal Conference, Maynooth, 11 March 1971, *Furrow*, 22/4 (April 1971), 244. See also *The Irish Times*, 12 March 1971, 1.
72. See *The Irish Times*, 29 March 1971, 11.
73. Ibid., 1.
74. See *The Irish Times*, 24 May 1971, 1, 13.
75. *Report of the Commission on the Status of Women*, Dublin, 1972, 223–5, 225.
76. See *Irish Catholic*, 15 February 1973, 1, 3. See ibid., 22 February 1973, 1, 3.
77. See *Catholic Standard*, 6/48 (23 November 1973), 1.
78. Statement of the Irish Episcopal Conference, 25 November 1973, published in *The Irish Times*, 26 November 1973, 1–16.

79. Ibid., 1.
80. Ibid.
81. Ibid.
82. Ibid.
83. See *The Irish Times*, 20 December 1973, 1, 13, 15.
84. *Human Life is Sacred*, Pastoral letter of the archbishops and bishops of Ireland to the clergy, religious and faithful, Dublin, 1975.
85. Ibid., Part Four, para. 112, 5.
86. Ibid., Part Four, para. 123, 10.
87. Ibid., para. 124, 11.
88. See *The Irish Times*, 1 June 1976.
89. Radio interview with Kevin O'Kelly, RTÉ, 30 May 1976.
90. For an insight into this debate and the issues raised, see *The Irish Times*, 29 March 1976, 1; ibid., 31 March 1976, 1; ibid., 1 April 1976, 1; ibid., 29 April 1976, 1; ibid., 1 June 1976, 6; ibid., 2 June 1976, 1, 4. Refer also to radio interview with Olivia O'Leary, RTÉ, 30 May 1976.
91. Radio interview with Kevin O'Kelly, RTÉ, 30 May 1976. See also Jeremiah Newman, *The State of Ireland*, Dublin, 1977.
92. *Statement issued by the Irish Catholic Bishops' Conference after their meeting in Maynooth, 14–16 June 1976*, *Furrow*, 27/7 (July 1976), 444.
93. Ibid.
94. *Statement by the Irish Bishops' Conference on proposed legislation dealing with family planning and contraception, 4 April 1978*, *Furrow*, 29/8 (August 1978), 525.
95. *Health (Family Planning) Act 1979*, No. 20 in public statutes of the Oireachtas, 1979.
96. Kevin McNamara, 'Church and State', *Doctrine and Life*, 30/3, 4 (March–April 1979), 141.

Chapter 15 Social Justice at Home and Abroad (pp 213–224)

1. *Rerum Novarum, Encyclical of Pope Leo XIII on the Condition of the Working Classes, 15 May 1891* in Anne Fremantle, ed., *The Papal Encyclicals in their Historical Context*, New York, 1956, 166–95.
2. *Quadragesimo Anno, Encyclical of Pope Pius XI on Reconstruction of the Social Order, 15 May 1931* in Claudia Carlen, ed., *The Papal Encyclicals 1909–1939*, Raleigh, 1990, 415–43.
3. *Rerum Novarum*, in Fremantle, *The Papal Encyclicals*, 167.
4. *Quadragesimo Anno*, in ibid., 233.
5. *Mater et magistra, Encyclical of His Holiness, Pope John XXIII, 15 May 1961*, trans. Rev. H.E. Winstone, London, 1961, para. 54, 19.
6. Ibid., 19.
7. Ibid.
8. *Pacem in Terris, Encyclical Letter of Pope John XXIII on Establishing Universal Peace in Truth, Justice, Charity and Liberty, 11 April 1963* in Carlen, *The Papal Encyclicals 1958–1981*, 107–27.
9. See *The Church in The Modern World, 7 December 1965* in Abbott, *Vatican II Documents*, 199–308.
10. *Rerum Novarum*, in Fremantle, *The Papal Encyclicals*, 173–4.
11. See *The Church in The Modern World, 7 December 1965* in Abbott, *Vatican II Documents*, 203–4.
12. See Michael Ryan, ed., *The Church and the Nation: The Vision of Peter Birch, Bishop of Ossory 1964–1981*, Dublin, 1993.

13. See *ICD*, 1970 (21 July 1969), 756.
14. Information in relation to the emigrant chaplaincy scheme in Britain was conveyed to the author by Fr Paul Byrne OMI, executive secretary since 1995 of the Irish Episcopal Commission for Emigrants (set up by the bishops in 1971).
15. The history of the Irish emigrant chaplaincy is documented by Fr Kieran O'Shea in *The Irish Emigrant Chaplaincy Scheme in Britain 1957–1982*, Naas, 1985.
16. Liam Ryan, 'Church and Politics: The Last Twenty-five Years', *Furrow*, 30/1 (January 1979), 3–18.
17. See *Justice, Love and Peace, Pastoral Letters of the Irish Bishops, 1969–1979*, Dublin, 1979, 37–9. (Hereafter referred to as *Justice, Love and Peace.)*
    See also *Statement of the Irish Episcopal Conference, 29 September 1971, Furrow*, 22/11 (November 1971), 722–4.
18. See *Justice, Love and Peace*, 39–42.
19. See *Furrow*, 23/2 (February 1972), 123–4.
20. See *Justice, Love and Peace*, 69–73, 72–3.
21. *Populorum Progressio, Encyclical Letter of Pope Paul VI on the Development of Peoples, 26 March 1967* in Carlen, *The Papal Encyclicals 1958–1981*, 183–200, para. 32, 189.
22. See *Justice, Love and Peace*, 71.
23. The papers delivered at this conference were published in *Social Studies*, 1/4 (August 1972).
24. See *A Statement on Social Policy*, published by the Council for Social Welfare, a Committee of the Catholic Bishops' Conference, November 1972.
25. See *The Meaning of Poverty*, published by the Council for Social Welfare, a committee of the Catholic Bishops' Conference, Dublin, 1974.
26. See *Planning for Social Development: What Needs to Be Done*, published by the Bishops' Council for Social Welfare, Dublin, 1976.
27. Ibid., 1.
28. See *Justice, Love and Peace*, 194–5.
29. See *The Work of Justice*, pastoral letter of the Irish bishops, September 1977, Dublin, 1977.
30. Ibid., 15.
31. Ibid., 6–7.
32. Ibid., 7.
33. See Frances Lannon, *Privilege, Persecution, and Prophecy: The Catholic Church in Spain 1875–1975*, New York, 1987.
34. Ibid., 224–5
35. Ibid., p. 251.
36. See Norman Ravitch, *The Catholic Church and the French Nation 1589–1989*, London, 1990, 151–61.
37. See excerpt from the statement of the assembled bishops of France at Lourdes 1972 in ibid., 151–2. See also 153.
38. See *Justice, Love and Peace*, 195–6, 195.
39. See statement issued by the NCPI at its AGM, 1–3 May 1978, *Furrow*, 29/6 (June 1978), 382.
40. See statement issued by the NCPI on 'Justice: What Can the Church Do?' *Furrow*, 30/9 (August 1979), 536.
41. Information in relation to the work of the Justice Office of the CMRS, now called CORI, was conveyed to the author by Sr Brigid Reynolds SM, co-director of the Justice Office since it was set up in 1982. The other co-director is Seán Healy SMA.

42. Information about the Summer School was conveyed to the author by Mgr Denis O'Callaghan.
43. For an insight into the situation and the historical background, see Pádraig Corkery and Fiachra Long, eds., *Theology in the University: The Irish Context*, Dublin, 1997.
44. See McQuaid's letter to Conway, dated 17 February 1970, in DDA, AB8/B/XV. The reference to the new university refers to the move by UCD to the Belfield campus.
45. The tension between conservative and more liberal schools of theology is also evident in McQuaid's reply on 15 March 1968 to Browne of Galway's letter of 14 March 1968 (referred to above in reference 24, Chapter 6), when he explained that it was he who had 'refused to allow the O'Callaghan article to be printed' in the *IER* because, he wrote, it 'denies the divine law, disregards Papal ruling and must cause increased unease among priests and faithful'. The article already referred to in Browne's letter was on birth control and was written by Fr Denis O'Callaghan, professor of Moral Theology, Maynooth and chairman of the ITA in 1968.
46. See Enda McDonagh, *Doing the Truth*, Dublin, 1979, 196–202, 216–7.
47. See Charles Davis, *The Study of Theology*, London, 1962; E.H. Schillebeeckx, *Vatican II — A Struggle of Minds*, Dublin, 1963; Hans Küng, *That the World May Believe*, trans. Cecily Hastings, London, 1963; Bernard Häring, *The Johannine Council: Witness to Unity*, Dublin, 1963; Hans Küng, Yves Congar and Daniel O'Hanlon, eds., *Council Speeches of Vatican II*, London, 1964; Hans Küng, *The Changing Church: Reflections on the Progress of the Second Vatican Council*, trans. Cecily Hastings, William Glen-Doepel and H.R. Bronk, New York, 1965; Hans Küng, *The Church and Freedom*, trans. Cecily Hastings, London, 1965; Hans Küng, *The Church*, trans. Ray and Rosaleen Ockenden, London, 1971; Hans Küng, *Why Priests?*, trans. John Gumming, London, 1972; Hans Küng, *Infallible? An Enquiry*, trans. Eric Mosbacher, London, 1977.
48. See Enda McDonagh, ed., *Irish Challenges to Theology, Papers of the Irish Theological Conference 1984*, Dublin, 1986.
    See also Enda McDonagh, ed., *Faith and the Hungry Grass: A Mayo Book of Theology*, Dublin, 1990.
49. *Octogesima Adveniens, Apostolic Letter of Pope Paul VI to Maurice Cardinal Roy, President of the Council of the Laity and the Pontifical Commission Justice and Peace on the 80th Anniversary of the Encyclical Rerum Novarum, 14 May 1971, Tablet*, 225 (22 May 1971) 506–14.
50. See Gustavo Gutierrez, *A Theology of Liberation: History, Politics and Salvation* originally published as *Teologia de la liberacion, Perspectivas*, Lima, 1971, trans. and ed. by Sister Caridad Inda and John Eagleson, New York, 1973.
51. See Edmund M. Hogan, *The Irish Missionary Movement: A Historical Survey, 1830–1980*, Dublin, 1992, 137.
52. Ibid., 137–8.
53. See *Decree on the Missionary Activity of the Church, 7 December 1965*, in Abbott, *Vatican II Documents*, 584–630, 599.
54. See *Irish Missionary Union Interim Committee Report 1970–83.*
55. *Ecclesiae Sanctae, Apostolic Letter of Pope Paul VI on Norms for carrying out certain of the Conciliar Decrees, 6 August 1966, AAS*, 58 (Rome, 1966), 757–87

Chapter 16 Conclusion (pp 225–236)

1. See announcement in relation to change in *IER*, 103 (January–June 1965), 66.
2. See *Apostolic Constitution, Paenitemini on Christian Penance as a Means of Perfection, 17 February 1966* in *The Pope Speaks*, Vol. XI, Washington, 1966, 213.

3. See Statement issued by the Irish Episcopal Conference on 3 July 1970 in relation to the law of abstinence, *Furrow*, 21/8 (August 1970), 533–4.
4. Cited in *Parish Missions, Parish Retreats and Priests' Retreats: A Report on the Survey of Attitudes of Irish Diocesan Clergy 1971*, Research and Development Unit, CCII, Dublin, 1972, 1.1–1.3.
5. See *Apostolic Constitution, Sacrarum Indulgentiarium Recognitio promulgatur Paulus Episcopus, 1 January 1967, AAS*, 59 (Rome, 1967), 5–24. (The reforms came into force on 30 April 1967.) See 'New Norms on Indulgences' dealing with the reform of indulgences in the Church in 'Notes and Queries' section of *IER*, 108 (July–December 1967), 273–5, 344–6, 418–21.
6. See *Dogmatic Constitution on the Church, 21 November 1964* in Abbott, *Vatican II Documents*, 85–96.
7. See *Mayo News*, 31 July 1976, 1; ibid., 4 August 1979, 1; ibid., 30 July 1980, 1.
8. See Appendix C.
9. See *Mayo News*, 3 April 1976, 4.
10. See *Irish Independent*, 1 October 1979, 8.
11. See The Most Rev. M. Sheehan DD, *Apologetics and Catholic Doctrine: A Course of Religious Instruction for Schools and Colleges*, Dublin, 1953.
12. See Daniel Lowery CSsR, *Life and Love: The Commandments for Teenagers*, New York, 1964. See Irish Catechetical Programme commissioned by the Irish Hierarchy's Episcopal Commission on Catechetics, and prepared by the Commission on Post-Primary Catechetics, Part I, *Christ with Us*, Dublin, 1972; Part 2, *Saved in Christ*, Dublin, 1973; Part 3, *United in Christ*, Dublin, 1974. See also Sister Maria de la Cruz, and Sister Mary Richard, *On Our Way* series (8 vols.), Dublin, 1964–6, including the following titles: *Christ's Life in Us, Christ Leads the Way, God Our Father, With Christ to the Father*. See also *Children of God* series for primary schools commissioned by the Irish Episcopal Commission on Catechetics prepared by Seán McEntee, Kathleen Glennon, William Murphy, Dublin, 1976, including the following titles: *The Father Loves You* (infant), *Come and See* (first class), *My Friends* (second class), *Remember Me Together* (third class), *A Time to Grow* (fourth class), *Your Kingdom Come* (fifth class), *Called to Serve* (sixth class).
13. See Thomas Flynn, *The Charismatic Renewal and the Irish Experience*, London, 1974; Edward D. O'Connor CSC, *The Pentecostal Movement in the Catholic Church*, Indiana, 1971.
14. See Michael P. Hornsby-Smith, *Roman Catholics in England: Studies in Social Structure since the Second World War*, Cambridge 1987, 216.
15. See *A Survey of Religious Practice, Attitudes and Beliefs in the Republic of Ireland 1973–1974*, Research and Development Unit, CCII, report no. 1, *Religious Practice*, Dublin, 1975, 2, 17.

    See also report no. 2, *Religious Beliefs and Values*, Dublin, 1975, and report no. 3, *Moral Values*, Dublin, 1976, 16.
16. See *Irish Independent*, 1 October 1979.

Epilogue (pp 237–268)

1. Jonathan Kwitny, *Man of the Century: The Life and Times of Pope John Paul II*, New York, 1997. See also George Weigel, *Witness to Hope: The Biography of Pope John Paul II*, New York, 1999.
2. See Seán O'Riordan, 'Priests in a Divided Church', *Furrow*, 43/9 (September 1992), 490. See also Seán O'Riordan, 'Towards a Decisional Model of Church', *Furrow*, 42/11 (November 1991), 607–15.
3. See *The Pope in Ireland: Addresses and Homilies*, Dublin, 1979, 10.
4. Ibid., 47.

5. Ibid., 77.
6. Ibid., 79–80.
7. Ibid., 49.
8. J.J. Lee, *Ireland 1912–1985: Politics and Society*, Cambridge 1989, 489.
9. Dermot Keogh, *Twentieth Century Ireland: Nation and State*, Dublin, 1994, 328.
10. Ibid., 354.
11. Haughey speech in Martin Mansergh, ed., *The Spirit of the Nation: The Speeches and Statements of Charles J. Haughey (1957–1986)*, Cork and Dublin, 1986, 324.
12. See 'The H-Block protest in the Maze prison, Northern Ireland', Statement issued by the Irish Commission for Justice and Peace, 13 October 1980.
13. See *Christian Faith in a Time of Economic Depression*, pastoral letter of the archbishops and bishops of Ireland, Dublin, 1983; see also *Emigration*, a pastoral letter from the western bishops, 15 March 1987.
14. Garret FitzGerald, *All in a Life: An Autobiography*, Dublin, 1992, 378.
15. See Michael Solomons, *Pro Life? The Irish Question*, Dublin, 1992, 54. The Pro-Life Amendment Campaign (PLAC) was launched in April 1981. See also Richard Sinnott, *Irish Voters Decide — Voting Behaviour in Elections and Referendums since 1918*, Manchester, 1995, 227.
16. There were elections in June 1981, February 1982 and November 1982. See Sinnott, *Irish Voters Decide*, 226–8.
17. *The Irish Times*, 9 September 1983, 1. See also Tom Hesketh, *The Second Partitioning of Ireland: The Abortion Referendum of 1983*, Dublin, 1990, 364.
18. *Statement issued by Irish Episcopal Conference, 22 August 1983, The Irish Times*, 23 August 1983, 5.
19. See *The Irish Times*, 8 September 1983, 6.
20. Keogh, *Twentieth Century Ireland*, 368.
21. Mansergh, ed., *The Spirit of the Nation*, 406.
22. *Submission to the New Ireland Forum from the Irish Episcopal Conference, January 1984*, Dublin, 1984, 18.
23. The other members of the delegation representing the Irish Episcopal Conference were as follows: Bishop Joseph Cassidy of Clonfert, media spokesman for the Bishops' Conference; Bishop Edward Daly of Derry; Dr Dermot O'Mahony, Auxiliary Bishop of Dublin and president of the Irish Commission for Justice and Peace; Fr Michael Ledwith, secretary of the Bishops' Commission for Ecumenism; Mr Matthew Salter, lecturer in Education at Queen's University, Belfast; and Mrs Mary McAleese, Reid Professor of Criminal Law, Criminology and Penology at Trinity College, Dublin.
24. *New Ireland Forum Report*, No.12, Public Session, Thursday, 9 February 1984, Dublin Castle, Dublin, 1984, 2.
25. Ibid.
26. Ibid., 40–47.
27. Ibid., 1–47.
28. See report by Joseph Power, religious affairs correspondent with *Irish Independent*, of an RTÉ interview with Bishop Cassidy, *Irish Independent*, 14 February 1985, 1–2.
29. See *The Irish Times,* 8 February, 1985, 9. See also *The Irish Times,* 11 February 1985.
30. *The Irish Times,* 11 February 1985. See also *The Irish Times,* 12 February 1985.
31. See *Dáil Debates,* 356, cols. 272–85 (20 February 1985). Desmond O'Malley had already lost the party whip because he diverged from his party leader, Charles Haughey's view that the only resolution of the Northern Ireland problem was the united Ireland option.

Less than a year later, he launched a new political party, the Progressive Democrats.

32. Health (Family Planning) (Amendment) Act, 1985, No. 4 in public statutes of the Oireachtas, 1985.
33. J.H. Whyte, 'Recent Developments in Church State relations', *Journal of the Department of the Public Services*, 6/3, 1985.
34. See Hesketh, *The Second Partitioning of Ireland*, 8, 384.
35. Richard Sinnott, *Irish Voters Decide*, 226–7.
36. Tim Ryan and Jurek Kirakowski, *Ballinspittle: Moving Statues and Faith*, Cork, Dublin, 1985, 41.
37. Ibid.
38. *Cork Examiner*, 31 July 1985, 1.
39. *Sunday Independent*, 22 September 1985, 6.
40. *Love is for Life*, Lenten pastoral letter issued on behalf of the Irish hierarchy, Dublin, 1985.
41. *The Irish Times*, 12 June 1986, 7.
42. Ibid., 1.
43. See *The Irish Times*, 23 June 1986, 8.
44. Ibid. See also *The Irish Times*, 20 June 1986, 8.
45. *Dáil Debates*, 366, cols. 1391, 1392 (16 May 1986).
46. See *The Irish Times*, 25 June 1986, 1, 9, for results of MRBI poll conducted 19, 20 June (one week before referendum, 26 June) compared with results of poll published in *The Irish Times*, 5 May 1986, 9.
47. See *The Irish Times*, 28 June 1986, 1.
48. Ibid.
49. Laurence Ryan, 'Some Post-Referendum Reflections', *Furrow*, 37/8 (August 1986), 492.
50. Ibid.
51. *The Irish Times*, 6 March 1992.
52. 'The Sacredness of Human Life', a statement of the Irish Episcopal Conference, *Furrow*, 43/4 (April 1992), 251.
53. Ibid., 251–2.
54. *The Irish Times*, 26 November 1992. See also Ailbhe Smyth, ed., *The Abortion Papers*, Dublin, 1992.
55. Health (Family Planning) (Amendment), Act, 1992, No. 20 in public statutes of the Oireachtas, 1992.
56. Statement issued by the four archbishops in the name of the Irish Episcopal Conference, on the Health (Family Planning) (Amendment) Bill, 1992, 17 July 1992, *Furrow*, 43/9 (September 1992), 514–5.
57. Ibid.
58. See Tom Inglis, *Moral Monopoly: The Rise and Fall of the Catholic Church in Modern Ireland*, Dublin, 1998, 226–7.
59. See European Court of Human Rights, *Case of Norris v. Ireland, Judgement of 26 October 1988 (Series A no. 142)*, Effects of Judgements or Cases, 1959–98.
60. Criminal Law (Sexual Offences) Act, 1993, No. 20 in public statutes of the Oireachtas, 1993.
61. Irish Bishops' Conference statement on government proposals to change the law on homosexuality, *The Irish Times*, 23 June 1993, 19.
62. Ibid.
63. *The Irish Times*, 23 April 1983, 1, 8.

64. Ibid.
65. See Basil Chubb, *The Government and Politics of Ireland*, London, New York, 1997, 305–8.
66. *Irish Catholic*, 9 November 1995.
67. *The Irish Times,* 10 November 1995, 1.
68. *The Irish Times,* 11 November 1995. See also *The Irish Times,* 13 November 1995.
69. *The Irish Times,* 13 November 1995, 1, 5.
70. Quoted by Andy Pollak, religious affairs correspondent, *The Irish Times*, 13 November 1995, 5.
71. Quoted by Andy Pollak, *The Irish Times,* 23 November 1995, 9.
72. It is not easy to gauge this influence, but when the author questioned Fr Daly on this point, while he agreed that influence of that nature is not easy to measure, he said that he has received many letters over the years from people who have thanked him for speaking out, because it reassured them that the fact that they held certain views not in keeping with official church thinking did not preclude them from considering themselves as 'good' Catholics.
73. *The Irish Times*, 27 November 1995, 1.
74. See *The Irish Times*, 2 October 2001.
75. See *Use your vote, Twenty-fifth Amendment of the Constitution (Protection of Human Life in Pregnancy) Bill, 2001*, an explanatory booklet published by the Referendum Commission (Dublin, 2002). See also *Statement for the Information of Voters on the Twenty-fifth Amendment of the Constitution (Protection of Human Life in Pregnancy) Bill, 2001.*
76. See *Statement of the Irish Episcopal Conference on the proposed abortion referendum,* Press Release issued by the Catholic Communications Office, 12 December 2001.
77. Ibid.
78. See Press Release, *Catholic Bishops welcome announcement of date for abortion referendum,* issued by the Catholic Communications Office, 7 February 2002.
79. See Press Release regarding the *Texts of Bishops' Pastoral Letters on Abortion Referendum,* issued by the Catholic Communications Office, 3 March 2002.
80. See *The Irish Times*, 8 March 2002, 1.
81. Ibid., 15. See also p. 14.
82. Reaction by Fr Martin Clarke, spokesperson for the bishops, when questioned by Charlie Bird, chief news correspondent, RTÉ, on 6.01 news, RTÉ, 7 March 2002.
83. *Census 91, vol. 5, Religion,* CSO, Dublin, 1995.
84. See *Religious Practice,* Report no. 1, 1974. See also *Religious Beliefs, Practice and Moral Attitudes: A Comparison of Two Irish Surveys 1974–1984,* Report no. 21, Council for Research and Development, Maynooth, 1985. See also Mícheál Mac Gréil, *Religious Practice and Attitudes in Ireland: Report of a Survey of Religious Attitudes and Practice and Related Issues in the Republic of Ireland 1988–1989,* Maynooth, 1991.
85. See Michael P. Hornsby-Smith and Christopher T. Whelan, 'Religious and Moral Values' in Christopher T. Whelan, ed., *Values and Social Change in Ireland,* Dublin, 1994, 21–2. See also *European Values Study 1981–90, Summary Report* [Aberdeen], Gordon Cook Foundation, 1992.
86. Mícheál Mac Gréil, *Religious Practice and Attitudes, 1988–9,* 67.
87. Máire Nic Ghiolla Phádraig, 'Trends in Religious Practice in Ireland', *Doctrine and Life,* 42/1 (1992), 5.
88. Liam Ryan, 'Faith under Survey', *Furrow,* 34/1 (January 1983) 6. See report by Michael Fogarty, *Irish Values and Attitudes: Irish Report of the European Values Study Group,* Dublin, 1984.

89. Ibid., 11–15. See also Mac Gréil, *Religious Practice and Attitudes 1988–89,* 65, 66, 68. See also Nic Ghiolla Phádraig, 'Trends in Religious Practice', 6-9. See also John A. Weafer, 'A Church in Recession — Three National Surveys, 1974–1992, *Furrow,* 44/4 (April 1993), 219–25.
90. Nic Ghiolla Phádraig, 'Trends in Religious Practice', 7–8.
91. Figures from *RTÉ News,* 25 July 1999, and *The Irish Times,* 31 July 2000.
92. See Audrey Healy and Eugene McCaffrey OCD, *St Thérèse in Ireland: Official Diary of the Irish Visit, April–July 2001,* Dublin, 2001. See article by Bishop Brendan Comiskey, *The Irish Times,* 17 July 2001, 12.
93. *Glenstal Book of Prayer,* Dublin, 2001. By mid-October 2001, in the region of 80,000 copies of the book had been sold in Ireland and the book went in to its fourth print of 30,000 copies for the Irish market. Within two weeks of its launch on 22 June 2000, the book was number 4 on the Irish bestseller list. It remained on the bestseller list (apart from periods when it was out of print) at number 1 for fourteen weeks and in December 2001 it was at number 2. Information supplied to the author by Brian Lynch, marketing department, Columba Press, publishers.
94. See Liam Ryan, 'Faith under Survey', 9–10; Mac Gréil, *Religious Practice and Attitudes, 1988–9,* 67. Hornsby-Smith and Whelan, *Values and Social Change in Ireland,* 44.
95. Hornsby-Smith and Whelan, *Values and Social Change in Ireland,* 44.
96. Ibid.
97. *The Irish Times,* 7 May 1992, 1. See Joe Broderick, *Fall from Grace,* Dingle, 1992.
98. *The Irish Times,* 14, 18 November 1994. See also Chris Moore, *Betrayal of Trust: The Father Brendan Smyth Affair and the Catholic Church,* Dublin, 1995.
99. *Sunday World,* 25 June 1995; *The Irish Times,* 26 June 1995. See also Phyllis Hamilton with Paul Williams, *Secret Love: My Life with Father Michael Cleary,* Dublin, 1995.
100. Church personnel interviewed were all in agreement on this.
101. In the course of interviews with the author, many theologians and other church personnel, who received their theological training in the pre-Vatican II Church, have attested to the damage caused on a human level, not least to themselves.
102. See Donal Dorr, 'Sexual Abuse and Spiritual Abuse', *Furrow,* 51/10 (October 2000), 523–31. See also Denis O'Callaghan, 'News and Views', *Furrow,* 51/12 (December 2000), 693–4.
103. See Bishop Willie Walsh, 'The Church in the new Millennium' in Denis Carroll, ed., *Religion in Ireland: Past, Present and Future,* Dublin, 1999, 167. Bishop Walsh expressed similar sentiments in the course of an interview with the author.
104. Church personnel interviewed agreed with this viewpoint, and Mary Kenny, in her book, *Goodbye to Catholic Ireland,* made a similar observation.
105. *New Testament,* Matt. 18: 6.
106. *The Irish Times,* 2 March 1995, 2.
107. See *Sunday Independent,* 5 November 1995, 1, 2, 3, 9.
108. See *The Irish Times,* 16 December 1996, 1, 5.
109. Ibid.
110. See Oliver V. Brennan, *Cultures Apart? The Catholic Church and Contemporary Irish Youth,* Dublin, 2001, 75–9.
111. Ibid., 79–81.
112. Ibid., 83–4.
113. Ibid., 76–81.
114. 'Dear Daughter', RTÉ documentary broadcast February 1996.

115. 'The Secret Baby Trail', RTÉ documentary broadcast on *Prime Time*, 20 June 1996. See also book based on interviews undertaken for documentary, Mike Milotte, *Banished Babies: The Secret History of Ireland's Baby Export Business*, Dublin, 1997.
116. *States of Fear* — a three-part documentary broadcast by RTÉ in April–May 1999. See Mary Raftery and Eoin O'Sullivan, *Suffer the Little Children: The Inside Story of Ireland's Industrial Schools*, Dublin, 1999.
117. See *The Irish Times*, 11 June 1999, 1.
118. See *The Irish Times*, 24 July 1999; ibid., 27 July 1999, 4; ibid., 28 July 1999, 1, 4; ibid., 29 July 1999, 6; ibid., 2 November 1999, 4; ibid., 3 November 1999, 5.
119. See advertisement by Commission to Inquire into Child Abuse, inviting persons to give evidence, *The Irish Times*, 3 July 2000, 5.
120. See *Commission to Inquire into Child Abuse, Interim Report*, Dublin, 2001.
121. *RTÉ News*, 30 November 2001.
122. See Statement from Conference of Religious of Ireland, *The Irish Times*, 31 January 2002, 7.
123. Ibid., 1.
124. See *The Irish Times*, 31 January 2002, 1.
125. Ibid., 7. See also *The Irish Times*, 1 February 2002, 7, 14, 15.
126. See *The Irish Times*, 31 January 2002, 1.
127. *Residential Institutions Redress Act, 2002*, No. 13 in public statutes of the Oireachtas, 2002. See *The Irish Times*, 1 February 2002, 7.
128. See *The Irish Times*, 2 April 2002.
129. See *Joint statement issued by Archbishop Sean Brady and Cardinal Desmond Connell, President and Vice President respectively of the Irish Episcopal Conference* on 1 April 2002, *The Irish Times*, 2 April 2002, 7.
130. Cited by Ronan Fanning, *Sunday Independent*, 31 March 2002, 17.
131. *Time*, 159/13 (1 April 2002), 60–73.
132. See *Letter of the Holy Father Pope John Paul II to Priests for Holy Thursday, 2002*, issued on 17 March 2002.
133. See *The Irish Times*, 4 April 2002, 9.
134. See transcript of Bishop Comiskey's resignation statement, *The Irish Times*, 2 April 2002, 7.
135. See full text of Cardinal Connell's statement relating to Marie Collins, *The Irish Times*, 15 April 2002, 5.
136. See *The Irish Times*, 5 April 2002.
137. RTÉ *News at One*, 6 April 2002.
138. RTÉ 6.01 news, 8 April 2002. See also *The Irish Times*, 9 April 2002, 1, 3.
139. See *The Irish Times*, 9 April 2002, 1.
140. Ibid.
141. See *The Irish Times*, 23 April 2002.
142. See *Epistula a Congregatione pro Doctrina Fidei missa ad totius Catholicae Ecclesiae Episcopos aliosque Ordinarios et Hierarchas interesse habentes: De Delictis Gravioribus eidem Congregationi pro Doctrina Fidei reservatis, Rome, 18 May 2001, AAS*, 93 (Rome, 2001), 785–8. All of the events recounted here were happening very recently and were closely detailed in the daily and weekly newspapers.
143. See *Charting our Education Future*, White Paper on Education, Department of Education, Dublin, 1995, 216.
144. Eileen Flynn, a teacher in a voluntary secondary school in New Ross, Co. Wexford, was

living in the town with a married man and had become pregnant by him. She was subsequently dismissed by her employer, the Holy Faith religious order, and this was upheld by the Employment Appeals Tribunal. When the matter was appealed to the High Court, the appellant argued that her private life was a matter for herself. Judge Costello ruled that the plaintiff was not dismissed for reasons arising from her pregnancy, but rather because her lifestyle did not accord with the ethos of the school and the norms of behaviour that the school existed to promote, and thus his judgement was that the plaintiff was fairly dismissed. For a more detailed account of the circumstances surrounding the case and the subsequent judgement, see Dympna Glendenning, *Education and the Law*, Dublin, 1999, 430.

145. *The Irish Times*, 16 May 1997, 4.
146. *The Irish Times*, 26 March 1998, 5.
147. The Campaign for Separation of Church and State was founded at a public meeting in Buswells Hotel, Dublin, in 1987. See David Alvey, *Irish Education — The Case for Secular Reform*, Dublin, Belfast, 1991. The author is grateful to David Alvey, secretary of the CSCS for furnishing her with information about the campaign.
148. Education Act, 1998, No. 51 in public statutes of the Oireachtas, 1998.
149. Conference of Religious of Ireland, *The Catholic School in Contemporary Society*, Dublin, 1991, 127. For an overview of the main themes and issues which emerged from the conference, see pp 122–31.
150. Ibid., 128.
151. Ibid., 127–8.
152. See *Report of the Expert Advisory Group on Relationships and Sexuality Education*, Dublin: Government Publications, 1995. See also *Relationships and Sexuality Education: Going Forward Together, An Introduction to Relationships and Sexuality Education for Parents*, Dublin: Government Publications, 1997. See also *Relationships and Sexuality Education: An Aspect of Social, Personal and Health Education*, interim curriculum and guidelines for primary schools, National Council for Curriculum and Assessment (NCCA), Dublin, 1996.
153. See *Relationships and Sexuality Education: An Aspect of Social, Personal and Health Education*, interim curriculum and guidelines for post-primary schools, NCCA, Dublin, 1996.
154. Ibid.
155. See Junior Certificate Religious Education Syllabus, NCCA, Dublin, 2000. See also *Guidelines for the Faith Formation and Development of Catholic Students, Junior Certificate Religious Education Syllabus*, The Irish Catholic Bishops' Conference, Dublin, 1999.
156. See *Vocations in Ireland, 1989*, Council for Research and Development, Maynooth, 1989. See also *Trends in Irish Church Personnel 1990–1994*, Council for Research and Development, Maynooth, 1995. See also Tony Flannery CSsR, *The Death of Religious Life?*, Dublin, 1997.
157. See Statistical Reports of the Department of Education 1984–5, 1989–90, 1994–5, 1997–8. See also *Irish Priests and Religious 1970–1975: A Survey of Catholic Clergy and Religious in Ireland*, Research and Development Commission, Dublin, 1977.
     See also *Vocations Returns 1996*, Council for Research and Development, Maynooth, 1996.
158. See also Tony Flannery CSsR, *The Death of Religious Life?*, Dublin, 1997.
159. See Ruth Barrington, *Health, Medicine and Politics in Ireland 1900–1970*, Dublin, 1987.
160. For an insight into the controversy surrounding the provision of a vasectomy clinic in Letterkenny General Hospital, see Inglis, *Moral Monopoly*, 226.

161. Gregory Baum, *Theology and Society*, New York, 1987.
162. See Donal Dorr, *Option for the Poor: A Hundred Years of Vatican Social Teaching*, New York 1983, 1992; Donal Dorr, *The Social Justice Agenda: Justice, Ecology, Power and the Church*, Dublin, 1991; Dermot A. Lane, *Foundations for a Social Theology: Praxis, Process and Salvation*, New York, 1984.
163. *Christian Faith in a Time of Economic Depression*, pastoral letter of the archbishops and bishops of Ireland, Dublin, 1983.
164. *Work is the Key: Towards an Economy that Needs Everyone*, pastoral letter of the archbishops and bishops of Ireland, Dublin, 1992.
165. *Prosperity with a Purpose: Christian Faith and Values in a Time of Rapid Economic Growth*, Dublin, 1999.
166. See *Conference on Poverty 1981: Papers of the Kilkenny conference, 6–8 November 1981*, Dublin, 1982. *The Prison System — A Study of the System in the Republic*, and a discussion on some of the moral issues raised for Christians by the use of imprisonment, Dublin, 1983. *Future Directions in Health Policy*, papers of a conference, Malahide, Co. Dublin, 6–7 April 1984, Dublin, 1984. *Comments on the Report of the Commission on Social Welfare*, a statement of support for the central recommendations of the Commission and a discussion of some aspects of the social welfare system which merit further examination, Dublin, 1986. *Submission to the Commission on Health Funding*, a proposal for a set of principles to inform health-care provision and an examination of various options for health funding in the light of these, Dublin, 1987. *Taxation and Poverty: A Survey of Public Attitudes*, results of an opinion poll, commissioned from IMS, testing public perceptions of poverty and attitudes to maintaining or increasing taxation to deal with it, Dublin, 1989. *Unemployment, Jobs and the 1990s*, Dublin, 1989. *Response to the Report of Commission on Health Funding*, and a statement of support for the Commission's emphasis on equity as a key principle in health-care provision, and for its recommendation that health care should be primarily publicly funded and regulated, Dublin, 1990. *The Rights of the Child: Irish Perspectives on the U.N. Convention*, Dublin, 1991. *Emerging Trends in the Social Welfare System?*, an exploration of the implications of the principal changes introduced in the 1992 Social Welfare Act and of other changes signalled, Dublin, 1992. *Submission on the Green Paper 'Education for a Changing World'*, an examination of some of the Green Paper's proposals from the perspective of Ireland's obligations under the United Nations Convention on the Rights of the Child, Dublin, 1993.
167. See *Human Rights, Justice, Equity and Peace*, an Irish Commission for Justice and Peace submission on the Green Paper on Education, Dublin, 1993. *Human Rights in Prison*, Comments on the Draft Prison Rules contained in *The Management of Offenders: A Five Year Plan*, Department of Justice, June 1994. *Women in the Church in Ireland: Work in Progress*, Dublin, 1995.
168. *Inequality in Schooling in Ireland*, Dublin, 1988. See also *Inequality in Schooling in Ireland: The Role of Selective Entry and Placement*, Dublin, 1989. *Towards an Agenda for the Debate on an Education Act*, Dublin, 1991. *Study Guide to the Green Paper on Education: Education for a Changing World*, Dublin, 1992. *Education and Poverty: Eliminating Disadvantage in the Primary School Years — Discussion Paper*, Dublin, 1992. *Considered Responses to the Green Paper on Education: Education for a Changing World*, Dublin, 1993. *Presentation to the National Education Convention*, Dublin, 1993. *Education Bill 1997: An Analysis*, Dublin, 1997. *The Points System: An Analysis and Review of Some Alternatives*, Dublin, 1998. *Inequality in Education: The Role of Assessment and Certification*, Dublin, 1998. *Social Transformation and Lifelong Learning: Towards Policy on Adult and Community Education, Dublin*, 1999.

169. See CORI Justice Commission, *Budget Response 2000: Critique and Analysis of Budget 2000,* Dublin, 2000. *Social Policy in Ireland: Principles, Practice and Problems,* Dublin, 1998.
170. See Michael J. Breen, ed., *A Fire in the Forest: Religious Life in Ireland* (including survey by John A. Weafer), Dublin, 2001, 116.
171. See David Quinn, 'Is the Conference of Religious in Ireland going too far with its teachings on Social Justice?', *Magill* (September 2001), 36–41.
172. For an understanding of events leading to the setting up of the Synod of Bishops and for an account of the proceedings and the order of business of the first synod in 1967, see Peter Hebblethwaite, *Understanding the Synod,* Dublin, 1968.
173. See Dermot Keogh, *The Vatican, The Bishops and Irish Politics 1919–39,* Cambridge 1986, 123–57, 226. See also *Ireland and the Vatican: The Politics and Diplomacy of Church–State Relations, 1922–1960,* Cork, 1995, 36–44.
174. Joseph Dunn, *No Lions in the Hierarchy: An Anthology of Sorts,* Dublin, 1994, 27, 47. See also 'A Bishop for Cork: New departure or same old story?',*Céide: A Review from the Margins,* 1/1 (September, October, 1997), 10–11.
175. Ibid., 47–8.
176. Thomas J. Reese SJ, *Inside the Vatican: The Politics and Organization of the Catholic Church,* Cambridge, London, 1996, 236. For an account of the selection process and appointment of bishops, see pp 234–42.
177. Seán Freyne, 'What Crisis? Some Thoughts on Irish Catholicism', *Furrow,* 44/10 (October 1993), 538.
178. See *Reading the Signs of the Times, A Survey of Priests in Dublin* by the Dublin Diocesan Council of Priests (Dermot A. Lane, ed.), Dublin, 1997, 19, 22, 30.
179. Interview with Fr Kevin Hegarty in which he explained to the author the sequence of events which led to his removal. In 1997 he began editing a new review called *Céide: A Review from the Margins.*
180. See Kevin Hegarty, 'Saying the Uncomfortable Thing' in Eamonn Conway and Colm Kilcoyne, eds., *Twin Pulpits: Church and Media in Modern Ireland,* Dublin, 1997, 160–66.
181. Mary McAleese, 'Women and Priesthood: A View', *Intercom* (March 1993), 20–21.
182. Brendan Hoban, 'Social Agenda', *Intercom* (September 1993), 13.
183. Philip Mortell, 'Clerical Sexual Abuse: Twenty Questions for the Bishops', *Intercom* (December 1993, January 1994), 35.
184. See *Child Sexual Abuse: Framework for a Church response, Report of the Irish Catholic Bishops' advisory committee on child sexual abuse by priests and religious,* Dublin, 1996.
185. See Kevin Hegarty, editorial, 'A First and Final Word', *Intercom* (December 1994/January 1995), 4–5.
186. See, for instance, the following articles: Seán O'Riordan, 'Towards a Decisional Model of Church', *Furrow,* 42/11 (November 1991), 607–15; Brendan Hoban, 'What Are We At?', *Furrow,* 43/9 (September 1992), 491–6; Seán Freyne, 'What Crisis? — Some Thoughts on Irish Catholicism', *Furrow,* 44/10 (October 1993), 532–42; Helena O'Donoghue, 'Is the Irish Church in Crisis?' and Pádraig Standún, 'Priestly Options in a Retrenching Church, *Furrow,* 44/2 (February 1993), 67–77, 84–7; Owen O'Sullivan, 'The Silent Schism', *Furrow,* 45/1 (January 1994), 3–10; Enda McDonagh, 'The Winter Name of Church' and Patrick O'Brien, 'A Letter to the Papal Nuncio', *Furrow,* 46/1 (January 1995) 3–22; John O'Donoghue, 'The Irish Church: Beyond the Bleak Landscape', *Furrow,* 46/3 (March 1995). See also letter by Fr Eltin Griffin O.Carm. published in 'News and Views', *Furrow,* 46/1 (January 1995), 48–9.
187. See *The Irish Times,* 16 December 1997.

188. See *The Irish Times*, 8 December 1997.
189. See *The Irish Times*, 17 December 1997.
190. *One Bread, One Body: A Teaching Document on the Eucharist in the Life of the Church, and the Establishment of General Norms on Sacramental Sharing*, issued by the Catholic Bishops' Conferences of England and Wales, Ireland and Scotland, London, Dublin, 1998.
191. *Dominus Jesus, Declaration on the unicity and salvific universality of Jesus Christ and the Church*, Congregation for the Doctrine of the Faith, 6 August 2000, *AAS*, 92 (Rome, 2000), 742–65, 758.
192. *Sunday Business Post*, 18 February 2001.
193. See President Mary McAleese, address at AGM of the NCPI in All Hallows College Dublin, 25 September 2000, *N.C.P.I. News Bulletin*, Spring 2001.
194. See *Women in the Church in Ireland*, Irish Commission for Justice and Peace, Dublin, 1993.
195. See Apostolic Letter, *Ordinatio Sacerdotalis*, of John Paul II to the bishops of the Catholic Church on reserving priestly ordination to men alone, 22 May 1994, *AAS*, 86 (Rome, 1994), 545–8.
196. Juan Arias, *The God I Don't Believe In*, trans. Paul Barrett, Cork, Dublin, 1973.
197. See Apostolic Exhortation, *Evangelii Nuntiandi of His Holiness Pope Paul VI to the episcopate, to the clergy and to all the faithful of the entire world on evangelization in the modern world*, 8 December 1975, *AAS*, 68 (Rome, 1976), 5–76.
198. See Dermot A. Lane, ed., *Religion and Culture in Dialogue*, Dublin, 1993; Hervé Carrier SJ, *Evangelizing the Culture of Modernity*, New York 1993; Donal Murray, 'Faith and Culture: A Complex Relationship' in Eoin G. Cassidy, ed., *Faith and Culture in the Irish Context*, Dublin, 1996; Michael Paul Gallagher SJ, *Clashing Symbols: An Introduction to Faith-and-Culture*, London, 1997; Dermot A. Lane, ed., *New Century, New Society*, Dublin, 1999; David Tracy, 'The Uneasy Alliance reconceived: Catholic Theological Method, Modernity, and Post-Modernity', *Theological Studies*, 50/3 (September 1989), 548–70; Edward Schillebeeckx, *Church: The Human Story of God*, trans. John Bowden, London, 1990.
199. Schillebeeckx, *Church: The Human Story of God*, 44–5.
200. See Brennan, *Cultures Apart*, 84.
201. John L. Allen Jr., *Cardinal Ratzinger: The Vatican's Enforcer of the Faith*, New York, London, 2000.
202. See *The Ratzinger Report: An Exclusive Interview on the State of the Church*, Joseph Cardinal Ratzinger with Vittorio Messori, trans. Salvator Attanasio and Graham Harrison, Leominster, 1985, 27–53.
203. Ibid., 36.
204. See *Sunday Business Post*, 17 December 1995, 25–6.
205. See *Letter of Pope John Paul II to Priests for Holy Thursday, 2002*, issued on 17 March 2002.

Select Bibliography

Primary Sources

1. Church Legislative Documents
- (a) Irish Church Legislation
- (b) International Church Law, the Documents of the Second Vatican Council, and the Post-Conciliar Documents

2. Papal Encyclicals

3. Irish Bishops' Pastoral Letters and Statements
- (a) Irish Bishops' Lenten Pastorals, Statements, Directives
- (b) Catholic Bishops' Conferences of England, Wales, Ireland and Scotland

4. Interviews
- (a) Conducted by the Author
- (b) Other Recorded Interviews

5. Communications Received by the Author

6. Government Publications

7. Census Results

8. Liturgical Texts/Collections

9. Theology Manuals

10. Devotional Works

11. Catechetical Works

12. Socio-Religious Reports

13. Statements, Commentaries, Submissions Issued by Commissions of the Irish Episcopal Conference
- (a) Council for Social Welfare
- (b) The Irish Commission for Justice and Peace

14. Statements, Commentaries, Submissions Issued by Commissions of the Conference of Religious of Ireland (CORI, formerly CMRS)
- (a) Education Commission
- (b) CORI Justice Commission

15. Unpublished Reports

16. Miscellaneous Documentation

17. Journals, Newspapers and Other Serials

18. Contemporary Works
- (a) Accounts/Chronicles
- (b) Inspirational/Spiritual Guidance

19. Works of Reference

20. Directories

21. Published Reminiscences
22. Archbishop John Charles McQuaid papers, Dublin Diocesan Archives
Galway Diocesan Archives

SECONDARY SOURCES
23. General Histories
24. Special Subjects
25. Works of Fiction
26. Unpublished Theses

PRIMARY SOURCES

1. Church Legislative Documents

(a) IRISH CHURCH LEGISLATION

Acta et Decreta, Concilii Plenarii Episcoporum Hiberniae: quod habitum est apud Maynutiam die 2 Augusti et diebus sequentibus usque ad diem 15 Augusti 1927, Dublin, 1929.

Acta et Decreta, Concilii Plenarii Episcoporum Hiberniae: quod habitum est apud Maynutiam die 7 Augusti et diebus sequentibus usque ad diem 15 Augusti 1956, Dublin, 1960.

(b) INTERNATIONAL CHURCH LAW, THE DOCUMENTS OF THE SECOND VATICAN COUNCIL, AND THE POST-CONCILIAR DOCUMENTS

Abbott, Walter M SJ, ed., *The Documents of Vatican II,* Dublin, 1966.

Acta Apostolicae Sedis, Rome, 1907–2000.

Codex Iuris Canonici Pii X Pontificis Maximi Iussu Digestus, Rome, 1917.

Directory on the Ministry and Life of Priests, Congregation for the Clergy, Dublin, 1994.

Documents from the Fifth Synod of Bishops (concerning catechesis), Rome, Dublin, 1977.

Dominus Jesus, Declaration on the Unicity and Salvific Universality of Jesus Christ and the Church, Congregation for the Doctrine of the Faith, 2000.

Flannery, Austin, ed., *Vatican Council II: The Conciliar and Post-Conciliar Documents,* Dublin, 1975.

Flannery, Austin, ed., *Vatican Council II: More Post-Conciliar Documents,* Dublin, 1982.

Veuillot, Mgr Pierre, *The Catholic Priesthood according to the Teaching of the Church, Papal Documents from Pius X to Pius XII,* Dublin, 1957.

The Code of Canon Law 1983, London, 1983.

2. Papal Encyclicals

Aeterni Patris, Encyclical Letter of Pope Leo XIII on the Restoration of Christian Philosophy 1879.

Casti Connubii, Encyclical Letter of Pope Pius XI on Christian Marriage, 1930.

Divinii Illius Magistri, Encyclical Letter of Pope Pius XI on Christian Education of Youth, 1929.

Divino Afflante Spiritu, Encyclical Letter of Pope Pius XII on Promoting Biblical Studies, 1943.

Evangelii Nuntiandi, Apostolic Exhortation of His Holiness Pope Paul VI to the Episcopate, to the Clergy and to All the Faithful of the entire world on Evangelization in the Modern World, 1975.

Fides et Ratio, Encyclical Letter of Pope John Paul II to the Bishops of the Catholic Church on the Relationship between Faith and Reason, 1998.

Humanae Vitae, Encyclical Letter of Pope Paul VI on the Regulation of Births, 1968.

Humani Generis, Encyclical Letter of Pope Pius XII concerning Certain False Opinions, 1950.

Laborem Exercens, Encyclical Letter of Pope John Paul II on Human Work and the place of Labour Unions as an indispensable element of Modern Industrial Society and a vehicle for the struggle for Social Justice, 1981.

Lamentabili Sane 1907, Syllabus Condemning the Errors of the Modernists.

Mater et Magistra, Encyclical Letter of Pope John XXIII concerning a re-evaluation of the Social Question in the light of Christian teaching, 1961.

Mediator Dei, Encyclical Letter of Pope Pius XII on the Sacred Liturgy, 1947.

Miranda Prorsus, Encyclical Letter of Pope Pius XII on the Communications field: Motion Pictures, Radio, Television, 1957.

Mystici Corporis Christi, Encyclical Letter of Pope Pius XII on the Mystical Body of Jesus Christ and our Union with Christ therein, 1943.

Octogesima Adveniens, Apostolic Letter of Pope Paul VI to Maurice Cardinal Roy, President of the Council of the Laity and the Pontifical Commission Justice and Peace on the 80th Anniversary of the Encyclical Rerum Novarum, 1971.

Pacem in Terris, Encyclical Letter of Pope John XXIII on establishing Universal Peace in Truth, Justice, Charity and Liberty, 1963.

Pascendi Dominici Gregis, Encyclical Letter of Pius X on the Doctrines of the Modernists, 1907.

Populorum Progressio, Encyclical Letter of Pope Paul VI on the Development of Peoples, 1967.

Providentissimus Deus, Encyclical Letter of Pope Leo XIII on the Study of Holy Scripture, 1893.

Quadragesimo Anno, Encyclical Letter of Pope Pius XI on Reconstruction of the Social Order, 1931.

Rerum Novarum, Encyclical Letter of Pope Leo XIII on the Condition of the Working Classes, 1891.

Veritatis Splendor, Encyclical Letter of Pope John Paul II to all the Bishops of the Catholic Church regarding Certain Fundamental Questions of the Church's Moral Teaching, 1993.

Vigilanti Cura, Encyclical Letter of Pope Pius XI on Motion Pictures addressed to the Bishops of the United States, 1936.

3. **Irish Bishops' Pastoral Letters and Statements** (chronological order)

(a) IRISH BISHOPS' LENTEN PASTORALS, STATEMENTS, DIRECTIVES

The Bishops' Lenten Pastorals have been acquired by means of a comprehensive search of the *Irish Independent* for the period of the 1950s–1960s. From the 1970s, joint pastorals became more common and some pastorals were published. Bishops' statements and directives have been examined in the *Furrow, The Irish Times* and the *Irish Independent.*

McQuaid, The Most Rev. John C., Archbishop of Dublin and Primate of Ireland, *Wellsprings of the Faith* (a compilation of pastoral letters and addresses of Archbishop McQuaid), Dublin, 1956.

McQuaid, His Grace the Most Rev. John Charles DD, *Higher Education for Catholics* (Irish Messenger Publications), Dublin, 1961.

Conway, Cardinal William, *Catholic Schools,* 8 December 1970, Dublin, 1970.

Human Life is Sacred, Pastoral Letter of the Archbishops and Bishops of Ireland to the Clergy, Religious and Faithful, Dublin, 1975.

Marriage and Pastoral Care, issued by the Archbishop of Dublin to his Priests, August 1975, Dublin, 1975.

Statement by Archbishop Dermot Ryan and Bishop Cahal B. Daly on the Synod of Bishops held in Rome, 1977.

Justice, Love and Peace, Pastoral Letters of the Irish Bishops 1969–1979, Dublin, 1979. This compilation of some of the most significant of the bishops' joint pastorals for the period 1969–1979 contained pastoral letters and statements on the following areas:

Christian Marriage, 16 February 1969
Northern Ireland, 21 May 1970
Northern Ireland, 12 September 1971
Northern Ireland, 21 November 1971
Change in the Church, 14 September 1972
Development, 2 February 1973
Prayer in the Home, 2 December 1973
Human Life is Sacred, 1 May 1975
The Economy, June 1976
The Work of Justice, 11 September 1977
The Present Social and Industrial Situation, June 1979
Ireland awaits Pope John Paul II, 2 September 1979

Ireland, Christianity and Europe: in Pursuit of an Ideal, pastoral letter of the Archbishops of Ireland, 1 March 1979, Dublin, 1979.

Christian Faith in a Time of Economic Depression, pastoral letter of the Archbishops and Bishops of Ireland, Dublin, 1983.

Submission to the New Ireland Forum from the Irish Episcopal Conference, January 1984, Dublin, 1984.

Love is for Life, pastoral letter issued on behalf of the Irish hierarchy, Lent, 1985, Dublin, 1985.

Marriage, the Family and Divorce, a Statement by the Irish Bishops, Dublin, 1986.

Work is the Key: Towards an Economy that Needs Everyone, pastoral letter of the Archbishops and Bishops of Ireland, Dublin 1992.

Prosperity with a Purpose: Christian Faith and Values in a time of rapid economic growth, Dublin, 1999.

(b) CATHOLIC BISHOPS' CONFERENCES OF ENGLAND, WALES, IRELAND AND SCOTLAND

One Bread, One Body: A Teaching Document on the Eucharist in the Life of the Church, and the establishment of general norms on sacramental sharing, issued by the Catholic Bishops' Conferences of England, Wales, Ireland and Scotland, London, Dublin, 1998.

4. Interviews

(a) CONDUCTED BY THE AUTHOR

Fr P.J. Brophy, contributor to the *Furrow* from the 1950s (15 February 1993).

Fr Martin Clarke, director of the Catholic Communications Office and chief spokesperson for the Irish Episcopal Conference (13 September 2001).

Fr Gabriel Daly OSA, theologian (2 July 2001).

Mgr Patrick Devine PP, former secretary of the Bishops' Advisory Committee on Ecumenism (22 August 1997).

Fr Ronan Drury, founder member of the *Furrow* and present editor (16 March 1994).

Fr Austin Flannery OP, former editor of *Doctrine and Life* (22 February 1994, 7 September 2001).

Sr Maria Goretti Griffin, Sister of Mercy, Tralee, Co. Kerry (28 December 1993).
Fr Patrick Hannon, professor of Moral Theology, St Patrick's College, Maynooth (3 December 2001).
Fr Kevin Hegarty CC, former editor of *Intercom* (8 August 2002).
Mr Seán Mac Réamoinn, journalist, broadcaster (15 February 1994).
Fr Patrick McGoldrick, professor of Liturgy, St Patrick's College, Maynooth (4 March, 11 May 1994).
Bishop Bill Murphy of Kerry (20 August 2001).
Mr Liam Murphy, former chairman of the Catholic Headmasters' Association (20 August 1997).
Rev. Placid Murray OSB, Glenstal Abbey (29 July 2002)
Mgr Denis O'Callaghan PP, Mallow, Co. Cork, and formerly professor of Moral Theology, St Patrick's College, Maynooth (14 April 2001).
Fr Dan O'Riordan PP, Tralee, Co. Kerry (21 August 2001).
Fr Seán O'Riordan CSsR, founder member of the *Furrow* (1 September, 20 October 1994; 23 March, 18 August 1995; 8 December 1997).
Mr Joe Power, religious affairs correspondent of the *Irish Independent* (24 September 1994).
Bishop Laurence Ryan of Kildare and Leighlin, formerly president of the NCPI and of the ITA (28 June 2001).
Bishop William Walshe of Killaloe (11 April 2001).

(b) OTHER RECORDED INTERVIEWS

Interview of Bishop Newman of Limerick by Kevin O'Kelly Radio Éireann, 30 May 1976, RTÉ Sound Library.
Interview of Conor Cruise O'Brien by Olivia O'Leary, Radio Éireann, 30 May 1976, RTÉ Sound Library.

5. Communications Received by the Author

Communications (including unpublished reports) received from following sources:

Association of Community and Comprehensive Schools
Association of Managers of Catholic Secondary Schools
Campaign to Separate Church and State
Catholic Communications Institute of Ireland
Catholic Press and Information Office
Conference of Religious of Ireland (Education Office)
Conference of Religious of Ireland (Justice Office)
Council for Research and Development, Maynooth
Council for Social Welfare
Department of Education, Statistics Section
Film Institute of Ireland
Gaelic Athletic Association
Irish Commission for Justice and Peace
Irish Episcopal Commission for Emigrants
Irish Messenger of the Sacred Heart Office
Irish Missionary Union
Knock Shrine manager, Mr Pat Lavelle
National Centre for Liturgy, Maynooth
Pioneer Total Abstinence Association
Prior of Lough Derg, Co. Donegal

6. Government Publications (chronological order)

Census of Population of Ireland, 1911, London, 1912.

Dáil Éireann Debates.

Bunreacht na h-Éireann 1937, Dublin, n.d.

Report of the Commission on Vocational Organisation, Dublin, 1944.

Report of the Council of Education on (1) The Function of the Primary School, (2) The Curriculum to be pursued in the Primary School, Dublin, 1954.

Report of the Department of Education, 1954–55.

Commission on Emigration and Other Population Problems, 1948–1954, Dublin, 1956.

Commission on Emigration and Other Population Problems: Minority Report by Most Rev. Dr. Cornelius Lucey, Dublin, 1956.

Reports of the Commission of Inquiry into the Operation of the Laws relating to the Sale and Supply of Intoxicating Liquor, Dublin, 1957.

Economic Development, Dublin, 1958.

Programme for Economic Expansion, Dublin, 1958.

Report of the Television Commission, Dublin, 1959.

Report of the Council of Education on the Curriculum of the Secondary School, Dublin, 1962.

Statistical Report of the Department of Education, 1964–65.

Rules for National Schools under the Department of Education, Dublin, 1965.

Investment in Education — Report of the Survey Team, Dublin, 1966.

Investment in Education — Annexes and Appendices, Dublin, 1966.

Statistical Report of the Department of Education, 1966-67.

Commission on Higher Education 1960–67, I *Presentation and Summary of Report*, Dublin, 1967.

Commission on Higher Education 1960–67, II *Report*, vol. I, chapters 1–19, Dublin, 1967.

Commission on Higher Education 1960–67, II *Report*, vol. 2, chapters 20–32, Dublin, 1967.

Report of the Committee on the Constitution, Dublin, 1967.

Statistical Report of the Department of Education, 1968–69.

Department of Education Rules and Programmes for Secondary Schools 1969–70, Dublin, 1969.

Department of Education Rules and Programmes for Secondary Schools 1970–71, Dublin, 1970.

Department of Education Curaclam na Bunscoile — Primary School Curriculum, Teacher's Handbook Parts 1, 2, Dublin, 1971.

Statistical Report of the Department of Education, 1971–72.

Commission on the Status of Women Report to the Minister for Finance, Dublin, December 1972.

Department of Education Scheme of Capitation Grants, Dublin, 1974.

Statistical Report of the Department of Education, 1974–75.

Statistical Report of the Department of Education, 1978–79.

Statistical Report of the Department of Education, 1979–80.

White Paper on Educational Development, Dublin, 1980.

New Ireland Forum Report, no. 12, Public Session, 9 February 1984, Dublin, 1984.

Boards of Management of National Schools: Constitution of Boards and Rules of Procedure, The Stationery Office, Dublin, n.d.

Statistical Report of the Department of Education, 1984–85.

Statistical Report of the Department of Education, 1988–89.
Statistical Report of the Department of Education, 1989–90.
Statistical Report of the Department of Education, 1994–95.
Statistical Report of the Department of Education, 1997–98.
Education for a Changing World, Green Paper on Education, Dublin, 1992.
National Education Convention Report, Dublin, 1994.
Charting our Education Future, White Paper on Education, Department of Education, Dublin, 1995.
Report of the Advisory Group on Relationships and Sexuality Education, Dublin, 1995.
Relationships and Sexuality Education: an aspect of social, personal and health education, interim curriculum and guidelines for primary schools, NCCA, Dublin, 1996.
Relationships and Sexuality Education: an aspect of social, personal and health education, interim curriculum and guidelines for post-primary schools, NCCA, Dublin, 1996.
Relationships and Sexuality Education: going forward together, an introduction to Relationships and Sexuality Education for Parents, Dublin, 1997.
Statistical Report of the Department of Education 1997–98.
Junior Certificate Religious Education Syllabus, NCCA, Dublin, 2000.
Interim Report, Commission to Inquire into Child Abuse, Dublin, 2001.

7. **Census Results** (chronological order)
Census of Ireland, Preliminary Report, 1946, Dublin, 1946.
Census of Ireland, Preliminary Report, 1951, Dublin, 1951.
Census of Ireland, 1946, vol. 3, Dublin, 1952.
Census of Ireland, 1956, Dublin, 1956.
Statistical Abstract of Ireland, 1959, Dublin, 1959.
Census of Ireland, 1961, vol. 1, Dublin, 1963.
Statistical Abstract of Ireland, 1964, Dublin, 1964.
Statistical Abstract of Ireland, 1965, Dublin, 1965.
Statistical Abstract of Ireland, 1966, Dublin, 1966.
Census of Ireland, Preliminary Report, 1971, Dublin, 1971.
Census of Ireland, Preliminary Report, 1979, Dublin, 1979.
Census of Ireland 1979, vol. 1, Dublin, 1980.
Census of Ireland, Preliminary Report, 1981, Dublin, 1981.
Statistical Abstract of Ireland, 1988, Dublin, 1988.
Census 91, vol. 5, Religion, Dublin, 1995.
That was then, This is now: Change in Ireland, 1949–1999, A publication to mark the 50th anniversary of the Central Statistics Office, Dublin, 2000.

8. **Liturgical Texts/Collections** (chronological order)
The Celebration of the Mass: A Study of the Rubrics of the Roman Missal (vol. 1 The General Rubrics of the Missal) by Rev. J. O'Connell, London, 1949.
The New Liturgy of the Holy Week, compiled in accordance with the Decree of the SCR of 16 November 1955, by Dom Gaspar Lefebvre OSB, Bruges, Belgium, 1956.
The Masses of Holy Week and the Easter Vigil, arranged for use in parishes by Godfrey L. Diekmann OSB, London, 1957.
Collectium Rituum, Dublin, 1960.
Ordo Divini Officii Recitandi, Missaeque Celebrandae in annum MCMLXV, a Singulis Episcopis Hibernicis Approbatus, Dublin, 1965.

The Complete Sunday Lectionary and Mass Book, London, 1970.

The Rite of Baptism for Children, Dublin, 1970.

Holy Week: People's Book, approved for use in the churches of England, Wales, Ireland and Scotland, London, Dublin, 1971.

The Roman Missal, Dublin, 1974.

The Sunday Missal, Texts approved for use in England and Wales, Scotland, Ireland and Africa, Harold Winstone, ed., London, 1975.

The Veritas Mass Book for Sundays and Solemnities with the official liturgical texts approved for use in Ireland and selected personal prayers, Dublin, 1975.

Daily Mass Book: The Prayers of the Roman Missal in English translation as revised by Decree of the Second Vatican Council and published by authority of Pope Paul VI, Sydney, Dublin, 1975.

Rite of Penance approved for use in the dioceses of Ireland, Dublin, 1976.

Celebrations during the Visit of His Holiness Pope John Paul II to Ireland, 29 September–1 October 1979, Dublin, 1979.

The Celebration of Marriage, Dublin, 1980.

Sunday and Holy Day Liturgies, Cycle C: Good News for the Poor, by Flor McCarthy SDB, Dublin, 1985.

Sunday and Holy Day Liturgies, Year A: Good News for the Poor, revised ed. by Flor McCarthy SDB, Dublin, 1986.

St Paul Sunday Missal 1993, Texts approved for use in Ireland, England and Wales and Scotland, Athlone, 1992.

9. Theology Manuals (chronological order)

Summarium Theologiae Moralis ad recentem codicem iuris canonici accommodatum by Antonius M. Arregui SI, Bilbao, 1919.

The Spiritual Life: A Treatise on Ascetical and Mystical Theology, by Very Rev. Adolphe Tanquerey SS, DD, Tournai, Belgium.

Handbook of Moral Theology, by Dominic M. Prummer OP, Rev. Gerald W. Shelton, trans., Cork, 1956.

Fundamentals of Catholic Dogma, by James Canon Bastible, English ed., Patrick Lynch, trans., Cork, 1958.

10. Devotional Works (chronological order)

The Raccolta or Collection of Indulgenced Prayers and Good Works, Fr Ambrose St. John, trans., (11th ed.), London, 1930.

Prayers of an Irish Mother, compiled by Mary T. Dolan, Dublin, 1934.

The New Revised 'Triple' Novena Manual of Jesus, Mary and Joseph, by Fr Stedman, director of the Confraternity of the Precious Blood, New York, 1943.

With Jesus to the Priesthood: Meditations for Seminarians and Priests, by Jules Grimal, Gerald Shaughnessy, Bishop of Seattle, trans., Philadelphia, 1946.

The Child of Mary, compiled by Francis Daly SJ, Irish Messenger Publication, Dublin, 1948.

The Drama of the Rosary: some informal thoughts on the fifteen mysteries, by Isidore O'Brien OFM, Paterson, New Jersey, 1952.

Legio Mariae, The Official Handbook of the Legion of Mary, Dublin, 1953.

The Treasury of the Sacred Heart: with Epistles and Gospels for the Sundays and Festivals of the Year, Belgium, 1954.

Mary, My Hope, by Rev. Lawrence G. Lovasik SVD, New York, 1954.
God and I: A Prayer Book, compiled by Rt Rev. Mgr H. Finnegan, Dublin, 1956.
The Key of Heaven: A Manual of Prayers and Instructions for Catholics, Mohill, n.d.
Holy Week: A Commentary, by Dom Mark Tierney OSB, Dublin, 1958.
Alone with Thee: Readings for the Holy Hour, by Rev. B.J. Murdoch, Milwaukee, 1963 (first ed. 1934).
Communion, The New Rite of Mass, by Seán Swayne, Dublin, 1974.
Prayers and Devotions from Pope John Paul II, ed. with an introduction by Bishop Peter Canisius Johannes van Lierde OSA, Harmondsworth, 1994.
Glenstal Book of Prayer, Dublin, 2001.

11. Catechetical Works (chronological order)

A Catechism of Catholic Doctrine, Dublin, 1951.
Cronin, Rev. Kevin CM, *Teaching the Religion Lesson*, London, 1952.
Sheehan, Most Rev. M., *Apologetics and Catholic Doctrine: A Course of Religious Instruction for Schools and Colleges*, Dublin, 1953.
Jungmann, Josef Andreas, *Handing on the Faith: A Manual of Catechetics*, Freiburg, London, 1959.
Abbott, Rev. James, *Catechism Key for Primary and Continuation Schools and for Converts*, Dublin, 1960.
Catalogue of Books and Booklets of the Catholic Truth Society of Ireland, 1962.
de la Cruz, Sr Maria and Richard, Sr Mary, *On Our Way* series (8 vols.) including the titles *Christ's Life in Us, Christ Leads the Way, God our Father, With Christ to the Father*, Dublin, 1964–6.
Lowery, Daniel L. CSsR, *Life and Love: The Commandments for Teenagers*, New York, 1964–6.
A New Catechism: Catholic Faith for Adults, London, New York, 1967.
Irish Catechetical Programme textbooks (1) *Christ with Us*, (2) *Saved in Christ*, (3) *United in Christ*, commissioned by the Irish Hierarchy's Episcopal Commission on Catechetics, Dublin, 1972.
Children of God series including the titles *The Father Loves You, Remember Me Together, A Time to Grow, Your Kingdom Come, Called to Serve*, commissioned by the Irish Episcopal Commission on Catechetics, Dublin, 1976.
Forristal, Desmond, *The Christian Heritage*, part of the senior cycle of the Irish Catechetical Programme, commissioned by the Irish Episcopal Commission for Catechetics prepared by Sr Nano Brennan, Br John Heneghan and Fr Desmond Forristal, Dublin, 1976.
Brennan, Nano, Forristal, Desmond, Heneghan, John and Murray, Donal, *The Moral Life*, Dublin, 1977.
Tynan, Mgr Michael, *Catechism for Catholics: A guide to living the faith in our time*, Dublin, 1983.
Catechism of the Catholic Church, Dublin, 1994.
Guidelines for the Faith Formation and Development of Catholic Students, Junior Certificate Religious Education syllabus, the Irish Catholic Bishop's Conference, Dublin, 1999.

12. Socioreligious Reports (chronological order)

Dignan, Most Rev. J., *Social Security: Outlines of a Scheme of National Health Insurance*, Sligo, 1945.
Ward, C.K. *Priests and People*, Liverpool, 1961.

Limerick Rural Survey, Jeremiah Newman, ed., Tipperary, 1962.

Humphreys, Alexander J., *New Dubliners: Urbanization and the Irish Family*, London, 1966.

Arensberg, Conrad M., Kimball, Solon T., *Family and Community in Ireland*, Cambridge, Mass., 1968.

King, J.D. OSA, *Religious Education in Ireland: A Survey of Catechetics in the Primary and Secondary Schools, and in the Training Colleges and Catechetical Centres of Ireland*, Dublin, 1970.

Walsh, Brendan, *Religion and Demographic Behaviour in Ireland*, ESRI paper 55, Dublin, 1970.

Survey of Catholic Clergy and Religious in Ireland 1970, Research and Development Unit, Catholic Communications Institute of Ireland, Dublin, 1971.

Survey 1971, Report no. 2, Research and Development Unit, CCII, Dublin, 1971. (All surveys on vocations in Ireland between 1971 and 1996 have been examined.)

Ryan, Liam, *The Changing Direction of Irish Seminaries, a Survey Report*, Research and Development Unit, Maynooth, 1972.

Parish Missions, Parish Retreats and Priests Retreats: A Report on the Survey of Attitudes of Irish Diocesan Clergy 1971, Research and Development Unit CCII, Dublin, 1972.

F.I.R.E. Report by the working party established by the Education Commissions of the Hierarchy and the Conference of Major Religious Superiors to examine the Future Involvement of Religious in Education, Dublin, 1973.

Focus for Action, Report by the working party set up by the Conference of Major Religious Superiors to consider appropriate action by Religious in Ireland in the next six years, Dublin, 1974.

Mulrany Guidelines: Report of special meeting of Irish Bishops, 1974.

A Survey of Religious Practice, Attitudes and Beliefs in the Republic of Ireland 1973–4, Report no. 1, *Religious Practice*, 1975; Report no. 2, *Religious Beliefs and Values*, 1975; Report no. 3, *Moral Values*, 1976; Report no. 4, *Attitudes to the Institutional Church*, 1976, Research and Development Unit, CCII, Dublin, 1975, 1976.

Rumpf, E., Hepburn, A.C., *Nationalism and Socialism in Ireland*, Liverpool, 1977.

Irish Priests and Religious 1970–1975: Survey of Catholic Clergy and Religious in Ireland, Research and Development Commission, Dublin, 1977.

Vocations in Ireland 1980, Report no. 2, Council for Research and Development, Maynooth, 1981.

Vocations in 1980: A Profile of the Entrants, Report no. 13, Council for Research and Development, Maynooth, 1981.

Ten Years of Research and Development 1971–1981, Council for Research and Development, Maynooth, 1981.

Clancy, Patrick, *Participation in Higher Education*, Dublin, 1982.

Rotman, David B., Hardiman, Niamh, Wiley, Miriam M., *The Distribution of Income in the Republic of Ireland: A Study in Social Class and Family-cycle Inequalities*, ESRI paper no. 109, Dublin, 1982.

Irish Catholic Clergy and Religious 1970–1981, Report no. 17, Council for Research and Development, Maynooth, 1983.

Breen, Richard, *Education and the Labour Market: Work and Unemployment among Recent Cohorts of Irish School-leavers*, ESRI paper no. 119, Dublin, 1984.

Fogarty, Michael, *Irish Values and Attitudes: Irish Report of the European Values Study Group*, Dublin, 1984.

Greaney, Vincent and Kellaghan, Thomas, *Equality of Opportunity in Irish Schools: A longitudinal study of 500 students*, Dublin, 1984.

Religious Beliefs, Practice and Moral Attitudes: A Comparison of Two Irish Surveys 1974–1984, Report no. 21, Council for Research and Development, Maynooth, 1985.

Vocations in Ireland, 1989, Council for Research and Development, Maynooth, 1989.

Mac Gréil, Mícheál, *Religious Practice and Attitudes in Ireland: Report of a Survey of Religious Attitudes and Practice and Related Issues in the Republic of Ireland 1988–1989*, Maynooth, 1991.

The European Values Study 1981–1990, Summary Report, [Aberdeen], Gordon Cook Foundation, 1992.

Trends in Irish Church Personnel, 1990–1994, Council for Research and Development, Maynooth, 1995.

Vocation Returns 1996, Council for Research and Development, Maynooth, 1996.

Kelly, Francis, *Window on a Catholic Parish, St Mary's, Granard, Co. Longford, 1933–1968*, Dublin, 1996.

Child Sexual Abuse: Framework for a Church Response, Report of the Irish Catholic Bishops' advisory committee on child sexual abuse by priests and religious, Dublin, 1996.

Reading the Signs of the Times: A Survey of Priests in Dublin undertaken by the Dublin Diocesan Council of Priests, Dermot A. Lane, ed., Dublin, 1997.

Fulton, John, Abela, Anthony M., Borowik, Irena, Dowling, Teresa, Long Marler, Penny and Tomasi, Luigi, *Young Catholics at the New Millennium: The Religion and Morality of Young Adults in Western Countries*, Dublin, 2000.

Breen, Michael J. (ed.), *A Fire in the Forest* (including survey by John Weafer), Dublin, 2001.

13. Statements, Commentaries, Submissions Issued by Commissions of the Irish Episcopal Conference (chronological order)

(a) Council for Social Welfare

A Statement on Social Policy, published by the Council for Social Welfare, a committee of the Catholic Bishops' Conference, Dublin, 1972.

The Meaning of Poverty, published by the Council for Social Welfare, a committee of the Catholic Bishops' Conference, Dublin, 1974.

Planning for Social Development: What Needs to be Done, published by the Council for Social Welfare, a committee of the Catholic Bishops' Conference, Dublin, 1976.

Submission to the Commission on Taxation, Dublin, 1980.

Conference on Poverty 1981: Papers of the Kilkenny Conference, 6–8 November, 1981, Dublin, 1982.

The Prison System, a study of the system in the Republic, and a discussion on some of the moral issues raised for Christians by the use of imprisonment, Dublin, 1983.

Future Directions in Health Policy, Papers of a conference, Malahide, Co. Dublin, 6–7 April 1984, Dublin, 1984.

Comments on the Status of Children Bill, 1986, Dublin, 1986.

Comments on the Report of the Commission on Social Welfare, a statement of support for the central recommendations of the Commission and a discussion of some aspects of the social welfare system which merit further examination, Dublin, 1986.

Submission to the Commission on Health Funding, a proposal for a set of principles to inform health-care provision and an examination of various options for health funding in the light of these, Dublin, 1987.

Taxation and Poverty: A Survey of Public Attitudes, results of an opinion poll, commissioned from IMS, testing public perceptions of poverty and attitudes to maintaining or increasing taxation to deal with it, Dublin, 1989.

Unemployment, Jobs and the 1990s, Dublin, 1989.

Response to the Report of Commission on Health Funding, an examination of the report's main proposals, and a statement of support for the Commission's emphasis on equity as a key principle in health-care provision, and for its recommendation that health care should be primarily publicly-funded and regulated, Dublin, 1990.

The Rights of the Child: Irish Perspectives on the U. N. Convention, Dublin, 1991.

Emerging Trends in the Social Welfare System?, an exploration of the implications of the principal changes introduced in the 1992 Social Welfare Act and of other changes signalled, Dublin, 1992.

Submission on the Green Paper 'Education for a Changing World', an examination of some of the Green Paper's proposals from the perspective of Ireland's obligations under the United Nations Convention on the Rights of the Child, Dublin, 1993.

The Dole Truth: Voices of the Unemployed, Dublin, 1996.

(b) THE IRISH COMMISSION FOR JUSTICE AND PEACE

The H-Block Protest in the Maze Prison, Northern Ireland, Statement by the Irish Commission for Justice and Peace, 13 October 1980.

Human Rights, Justice, Equity and Peace, an Irish Commission for Justice and Peace submission on the Green Paper on Education, Dublin, 1993.

Women in the Church in Ireland, proceedings of a study day held on 23 October 1993 in Clonliffe College, Dublin, 1993.

Human Rights in Prison, comments on the Draft Prison Rules contained in *The Management of Offenders: A Five Year Plan*, Department of Justice, June 1994.

Women in the Church in Ireland: Work in Progress, proceedings of a study day held on 14 October 1995 and a follow-up meeting on 25 November 1995, Dublin, 1996.

14. Statements, Commentaries, Submissions Issued by Commissions of the Conference of Religious of Ireland (CORI, formerly CMRS)

(a) EDUCATION COMMISSION

Inequality in Schooling in Ireland, Dublin, 1988.

Inequality in Schooling in Ireland: The Role of Selective Entry and Placement, Dublin, 1989.

The Catholic School in Contemporary Society, CORI, Dublin, 1991.

Towards an Agenda for the Debate on an Education Act, Dublin, 1991.

Study Guide to the Green Paper on Education: Education for a Changing World, Dublin, 1992.

Education and Poverty: Eliminating Disadvantage in the Primary School Years — Discussion Paper, Dublin, 1992.

Considered Response to the Green Paper on Education: Education for a Changing World, Dublin, 1993.

Presentation to the National Education Convention, Dublin, 1993.

Response to Position Paper on the Governance of Schools, presented at Dublin Castle, 12 September 1994, Dublin, 1994.
Education Bill 1997: An Analysis, Dublin, 1997.
Religious Congregations in Irish Education: A Role for the Future? A Reflection Paper, CORI, Dublin, 1997.
The Points System: An Analysis and Review of Some Alternatives and Certification, Dublin, 1998.
Inequality in Education: The Role of Assessment and Certification, Dublin, 1998.
Social Transformation and Lifelong Learning: Towards Policy on Adult and Community Education, Dublin, 1999.

(b) CORI JUSTICE COMMISSION
Healy, Seán J. SMA and Reynolds, Brigid SM, *Health and the Future of Healthcare,* CMRS, Dublin, n.d.
Social Policy in Ireland: Principles, Practice and Problems, Dublin, 1998.
Prosperity and Exclusion: Towards a New Social Contract, Dublin, 2000.
Budget Response 2000: Critique and Analysis of Budget 2000, Dublin, 2000.
Budget 2001, Analysis and Critique, Dublin, 2001.
The PPF, Budget 2001 and Social Welfare, Briefing Document, January 2001, Dublin, 2001.
Pre-Budget Briefing 2002, November 2001, Dublin, 2001.

15. Unpublished Reports
'Irish Missionary Union, Interim committee report 1970–83'.
Report of the Conference of Convent Secondary Schools, 1957.

16. Miscellaneous Documentation
Address of Pope John Paul II to the Irish Bishops, 26 June 1999, when they paid their 'ad limina apostolorum' visit to Rome from 17 to 26 June 1999.
Association of Community and Comprehensive Schools, Constitution, April 1989, Dublin 1989.
Bulletin, Sutton Parish on 'Building up the Body of Christ', September 1981.
Catalogue of Books, Booklets and Leaflets of the Catholic Truth Society of Ireland 1962, Dublin, 1962.
Effects of Judgements on Cases in the European Court of Human Rights 1959–1998, documentation acquired from the Human Rights Unit, Department of Foreign Affairs, Dublin.
Formation of Priests in Circumstances of the Present Day, a summary document prepared by the Catholic Press and Information Office from the *Lineamenta* of the World Synod of Bishops secretariat, Dublin, 1989.
Group of Catholic Parents, *Have the Snakes come back? Education and the Irish Child,* Dublin, 1975.
Homiletical Programme for the Sundays and Holy Days of the Three-Year Liturgical Cycle, prepared for the archdiocese of Dublin by a sub-committee of the Diocesan Liturgical Commission, Dublin, 1980.
Management Board Members' Handbook produced by the Catholic Primary School Managers' Association, Dublin, 1982.
Manual for Boards of Management of Catholic Secondary Schools published by the Council of Managers of Catholic Secondary Schools, Dublin, 1985.
Manual for Boards of Management of Catholic Secondary Schools published by the Council of Managers of Catholic Secondary Schools, Revised edition, Dublin, 1991.

Model Lease for Community Schools, Dublin, 1996.
Parish Councils, compiled by the Irish Council for the Apostolate of the Laity, Dublin, n.d.
Pastoral Letter from Archbishop Dermot Ryan concerning the option of receiving Holy Communion in the hand, Dublin, 19 September 1978.
Pioneering for Eighty Years: Historical Aspects of the Pioneer Association presented at the international Pioneer seminar in Clongowes Wood College, Co. Kildare in July 1978.
Prayer to St Michael composed by Pope Leo XIII in leaflet form published by Tan Books and Publishers, Inc., PO Box 424, Rockford, Illinois 61105.
Report of a Study into a Possible Framework for Intermediate Structures in Education in Ireland, AMCSS discussion document, Dublin, 1993.
Study Book for Special Ministers of Holy Communion, London, 1980.
The Catholic Church in Ireland: Information and Documentation, issued by the Catholic Press and Information Office, Dublin,1984.
What it means to be a Pioneer, published by the Pioneer Association, Dublin.

17. Journals, Newspapers and Other serials

The principal basis for material in this book was a detailed reading of the *Furrow* from 1950 to 1979, and other publications listed below have been investigated to a greater or lesser extent for the period in question.

Agora
American Historical Review
Archivium Hibernicum
Bell
Catholic Standard
Céide
Christus Rex
Church of Ireland Gazette
Cork Examiner
Doctrine and Life
English Historical Review
Hibernia
Historical Journal
History Ireland
Intercom
Irish Catechist
Irish Catholic
Irish Ecclesiastical Record (IER)
Irish Historical Studies
Irish Independent
Irish Messenger of the Sacred Heart
Irish Press
Irish Rosary
Irish Theological Quarterly (ITQ)
Irish Times, The
Irish Weekly Independent
Journal of the Department of the Public Services
Journal of the History of Ideas

Journal of the Royal Society of Antiquaries of Ireland
Journal of Social History
Kerryman
Licensed Vintner and Grocer
Limerick Leader
Mayo News
Pioneer
The Pope Speaks
Scripture in Church
Social Compass
Social Studies
Standard
Studies
Sunday Business Post
Sunday Independent
Sunday Press
Tablet
Theological Studies
University Review
Word

18. Contemporary Works

(a) ACCOUNTS/CHRONICLES (chronological order)

Ryan, John A., D.D., L.L.D. and Miller, Moorhouse F.X. SJ, *The State and the Church* written and edited for the Department of Social Action of the National Catholic Welfare Council, New York, 1922.

Concannon, Mrs Thomas, *The Queen of Ireland: An Historical Account of Ireland's Devotion to the Blessed Virgin*, Dublin, 1938.

Rynne, Xavier, *Letters from Vatican City: Vatican Council II (first session) Background and Debates*, London, 1963.

Pope John XXIII, *Journal of a Soul*, London, 1964.

Rynne, Xavier, *The Second Session: The Debates and Decrees of Vatican Council II, September 29 to December 4, 1963*, London, 1964.

Rynne, Xavier, *The Third Session: The Debates and Decrees of Vatican II September 14 to November 21, 1964*, London, 1965.

Contraception and Holiness: The Catholic Predicament, a symposium introduced by Archbishop Thomas D. Roberts, London, 1965.

Outlook, Talks from the RTÉ series (speaker Fr Gabriel Daly, OSA), Dublin, 1971.

Natural Family Planning, The Billings Method, Cork, 1976.

The Pope in Ireland: Addresses and Homilies, Dublin, 1979.

Young People of Ireland, Homily of Pope John Paul II at the Mass for the Youth of Ireland, Galway, 30 September 1979, Dublin, 1979.

Building Trust in Ireland: Studies commissioned by the Forum for Peace and Reconciliation, Dublin, 1996.

Healy, Audrey and McCaffrey, Eugene, OCD, *St Thérèse in Ireland: Official diary of the Irish Visit, April–July 2001*, Dublin, 2001.

(b) INSPIRATIONAL/SPIRITUAL GUIDANCE (alphabetical order)

Boylan, Eustace SJ, *What is Chastity: How to Give the Instructions*, Dublin, 1954.

Buckley, Joseph, SM, *Purity, Modesty, Marriage: A Christian Design for Sex*, Notre Dame, 1960.

Daughters of St Paul compilation, *Religious Life in the Light of Vatican II*, Boston, 1967.

Drinkwater, F.H., *Talks to Teenagers: An Aid Book with Catholic School-Leavers*, London, 1965.

Elenjimittam, Anthony, *Saints for Young Men of Today*, Athlone, 1956, 1960.

Eymard, S.M. PBVM, *This Girl is You*, Dublin, 1964.

Father Canice, OFM Cap., *Mary: A study of the Mother of God*, Dublin, 1954.

Gebhardt, Dr., *The Catholic Teenager*, trans. Stephen Deacon, Cork, 1966.

Keenan, Alan OFM, Ryan, John, M.B., *Marriage: A Medical and Sacramental Study*, London, 1955.

Kelly, Very Rev. Mgr George A., *The Catholic Youth's Guide to Life and Love: Advice on Courtship, Sex, Marriage and Religion* (foreword by Cardinal Spellman), London, 1962.

Kelly, Gerald SJ, *Modern Youth and Chastity*, St Louis, 1941.

Kelly, Gerald SJ, *Guidance for Religious*, London, 1956.

Kelly, John R. SJ, *The Right Answers to Teen-age Boys' Sex Questions*, St Louis, 1963 (sixth printing, first ed., 1956).

Lavaud, Benoit, OP, *The Meaning of the Religious Life*, trans. Walter Mitchell, London, 1955.

Lord, Daniel SJ, *Letters to a Nun*, Missouri, 1947.

Martindale, C.C. SJ, *The Difficult Commandment: Notes on Self-Control especially for Young Men*, London, 1950.

Nash, Robert SJ, *Is Life Worthwhile?*, Dublin, 1949.

Sellmair, Josef, *The Priest in the World*, London, 1959.

Sheed, F.J., *Communism and Man*, London, New York, 1951.

Sheed, F.J., *Theology and Sanity*, London, New York, 1951.

Sheed, F.J., *Society and Sanity*, London, New York, 1954.

Sheed, F.J., *Marriage and the Family*, London, New York, 1960.

Sheen, Bishop Fulton J., *Peace of Soul*, London, 1953.

Sheen, Bishop Fulton J., *Go to Heaven*, New York, 1960 (first ed. 1949).

Sister Mary Laurence OP, *One Nun to Another*, London, 1959.

St Clair, Miriam T., *The Vice of Today*, (no place of publication) printed in Limerick in early 1940s, n.d.

Suenens, Cardinal Leon Joseph, *Christian Life Day by Day: Talks to the Family*, London, 1963.

Von Gagern, Baron Frederick, M.D., *The Problem of Onanism*, trans. Meyrick Booth, Cork, 1959 (second reprint in English).

Windham, Joan, *Sixty Saints for Boys*, London, 1948.

Windham, Joan, *Saints Specially for Girls*, London, 1970.

Windham, Joan, *Saints Specially for Boys*, London, 1970.

19. Works of Reference

Bouscaren, T. Lincoln SJ, Ellis, Adam Charles SJ, *Canon Law: A Text and Commentary*, Milwaukee, 1948.

Carlen, Claudia, ed., *The Papal Encyclicals 1740–1878, The Papal Encyclicals 1878–1903, The Papal Encyclicals 1903–1939, The Papal Encyclicals 1939–1958, The Papal Encyclicals 1958–1981*, Raleigh, 1990.

Catholic Encyclopedia, New York, 1908.
De Breffny, Brian, ed., *Ireland: A Cultural Encyclopaedia*, London, 1983.
Deedy, John, *The Catholic Fact Book*, Dublin, 1992.
Ekstrom, Reynolds R., *The New Concise Catholic Dictionary*, Dublin, 1995.
Fremantle, Anne, *The Papal Encyclicals in their Historical Context*, New York, 1956.
Glazier, Michael, Helwig, Monika K., eds., *The Modern Catholic Encyclopedia*, Dublin, 1994.
Hepburn, A.C., *Ireland, 1905–1925, vol. 2: Documents and Analysis*, Newtownards, 1998.
Hyland, Áine, Milne, Kenneth, ed., *Irish Educational Documents, vol. I*, a selection of extracts from documents relating to the history of Irish education from the earliest times to 1922, Dublin, 1987.
Lee, Joseph, ed., *Irish Historiography, 1970–1979*, Cork, 1981.
New Catholic Encyclopedia, Washington, 1979.
O'Day, Alan, Stephenson, John, *Irish Historical Documents since 1800*, Dublin, 1992.
Rahner, Karl, ed., *Encyclopedia of Theology*, London, 1975.
Rahner, Karl, Vorgrimler, Herbert, *Concise Theological Dictionary*, trans. Richard Strachan, London, 1965.
Sheehy, Gerard, Brown, Ralph, Kelly, Donal, McGrath, Aidan OFM, eds., *The Canon Law, Letter and Spirit: A Practical Guide to the Code of Canon Law*, Dublin, 1995.
Stravinskas, Peter M.J., ed., *Our Sunday Visitor Catholic Encyclopedia*, Huntingdon, 1991.

20. Directories

Dublin Diocesan Guidebook
Directory of Irish Archives, Seamus Helferty and Raymond Refausse, eds., Dublin, 1999.
Irish Catholic Directory
The National University of Ireland Calendars 1970–1974.
Thom's Directory of Ireland, vol. 2, 1960.

21. Published Reminiscences

Andrews, C.S., *Dublin Made Me*, Dublin, 2001 (first ed. 1979).
Baldwin, Monica, *I Leap Over the Wall: A Return to the World After Twenty-Eight Years in a Convent*, London, 1948.
Bennett, Jackie, Forgan, Rosemary, eds., *There's Something about a Convent Girl*, London, 1992.
Boyne, Don, (Neil Kevin), *I Remember Maynooth*, London, 1945.
Browne, Noël, *Against the Tide*, Dublin, 1986.
Byrne, Gay, *To Whom it Concerns: Ten Years of the Late Late Show*, Dublin, 1972.
Carbery, Mary, *The Farm by Lough Gur: The Story of Mary Fogarty*, Cork, 1973 (first ed., 1937).
Clarke, Austin, *Twice Round the Black Church: Early Memories of Ireland and England*, London, 1962.
Clarke, Austin, *A Penny in the Clouds: More memories of Ireland and England*, Dublin, 1990.
Crosbie, Paddy, *Your Dinner's Poured Out! Memoirs of a Dublin that has disappeared*, Dublin, 1991.
Cross, Eric, *The Tailor and Ansty*, Cork, Dublin, 1999 (first ed., 1942).
Donoghue, Denis, *Warrenpoint*, London, 1991.
Doyle, Paddy, *The God Squad*, London, 1989.
Flannery, Tony CSsR, *The Death of Religious Life?*, Dublin, 1997.

Gaughan, J. Anthony, *At the Coalface: Recollections of a city and country priest 1950–2000*, Dublin, 2000.
Hyde, Douglas, *I Believed: The Autobiography of a former British Communist*, London, 1952.
Jeffares, A, Norman, Kamm, Antony, eds., *Irish Childhoods: An Anthology*, Dublin, 1992.
Kerrigan, Gene, *Another Country: Growing up in 50s Ireland*, Dublin, 1998.
Kiely, Benedict, *Drink to the Bird: A Memoir*, London, 1991.
Leonard, Hugh, *Home before Night*, Harmondsworth, 1981.
Leonard, Hugh, *Out after Dark*, Harmondsworth, 1990.
Mac Amhlaigh, Donall, *An Irish Navvy: The Diary of an Exile*, trans. Valentin Iremonger, London, 1964.
MacMahon, Bryan, *The Master*, Dublin, 1999.
McDonald, Walter, *Reminiscences of a Maynooth Professor*, Denis Gwynn, ed., Cork, 1967.
Meehan, Denis, *Window on Maynooth*, Dublin, 1949.
O'Brien, Edna, *Mother Ireland*, Harmondsworth, 1978.
O'Faolain, Sean, *Vive moi! An Autobiography*, London, 1993 (first ed. 1963).
O'Sullivan, Patrick, *I Heard the Wild Birds Sing: A Kerry Childhood*, Dublin, 1993.
Ryan, John, *Remembering How We Stood: Bohemian Dublin at the Mid-Century*, Dublin, 1975.
Stack, Sr De Lourdes, *As We Lived It*, Tralee, 1981.
Taylor, Alice, *To School Through the Fields: An Irish Country Childhood*, Dingle, 1988.
Thomson, David, *Woodbrook*, London, 1991.
Touher, Patrick, *Fear of the Collar: My Terrifying Childhood in Artane*, Dublin, 1994.
Ussher, Arland, *The Face and Mind of Ireland*, London, 1949.
Walsh, John, *The Falling Angels: An Irish Romance*, London, 2000.

22. Archbishop John Charles McQuaid papers, Dublin Diocesan Archives
Correspondence between Archbishop McQuaid and his fellow Bishops, in particular Bishops Browne, Lucey and Cardinal Conway.
Galway Diocesan Archives
Mr Thomas M. May, Galway Diocesan archivist, kindly made available copies of a number of letters from correspondence between Archbishop McQuaid and Bishop Browne of Galway, from Bishop Browne's papers.

SECONDARY SOURCES
23. General Histories
Beckett, J.C., *The Making of Modern Ireland, 1603–1923*, London, 1981.
Bokenkotter, Thomas, *A Concise History of the Catholic Church*, New York, 1990.
Boyce, D. George, *Nineteenth-Century Ireland: The Search for Stability*, Dublin, 1990.
Brown, Terence, *Ireland: A Social and Cultural History, 1922–1985*, London, 1985.
Coogan, Timothy Patrick, *Ireland since the Rising*, London, 1966.
Fanning Ronan, *Independent Ireland*, Dublin, 1983.
Foster, R.F., *Modern Ireland, 1600–1972*, London, 1988.
Hoppen, K. T., *Ireland since 1800: Conflict and Conformity*, London, 1989.
Keogh, Dermot, *Ireland and Europe 1919–1989: A Diplomatic and Political History*, Cork, Dublin, 1990.
Keogh, Dermot, *Twentieth-Century Ireland: Nation and State*, Dublin, 1994.
Laqueur, Walter, *Europe in Our Time: A History 1945–1992*, Harmondsworth, 1993.
Lee, J.J., *Ireland, 1912–1985: Politics and Society*, Cambridge, 1989.
Lyons, F.S.L., *Ireland since the Famine*, London, 1971.

Murphy, John A., *Ireland in the Twentieth Century*, Dublin, 1975.
Vadney, T.E., *The World since 1945*, London, 1987.
Vaughan, W.E., ed., *A New History of Ireland, vol. 5*, Oxford, 1989.

24. Special Subjects

Adams, Michael, *Censorship: The Irish Experience*, Alabama, 1968.
Akenson, D.H., *The Irish Educational Experiment: The National System of Education in the Nineteenth Century*, London, 1970.
Alexander, Yonah and O'Day, Alan, eds., *Terrorism in Ireland*, London, 1984.
Algisi, Leone, *John XXIII*, trans. Peter Ryde, London, 1966.
Allen, John L., Jr., *Cardinal Ratzinger: The Vatican's Enforcer of the Faith*, New York, London, 2000.
Alvey, David, *Irish Education — The Case for Secular Reform*, Dublin, Belfast, 1991.
Anciaux, Paul, *The Episcopate in the Church*, trans. Thomas F. Murray, New York, 1965.
Arbuckle, Gerald A. SM, *Strategies for Growth in Religious Life*, New York, 1986.
Ardagh, John, *Ireland and the Irish: Portrait of a Changing Society*, London, 1994.
Arias, Juan, *The God I Don't Believe In*, trans. Paul Barrett OFM Cap., Cork, Dublin, 1973.
Arnold, Matthew, *Culture and Anarchy*, J. Dover Wilson, ed., Cambridge, 1988 (first ed., 1932).
Augusteijn, Joost, ed., *Ireland in the 1930s: New Perspectives*, Dublin, 1999.
Barrington, Ruth, *Health, Medicine and Politics in Ireland 1900–1970*, Dublin, 1987.
Bartlett, *The Fall and Rise of the Irish Nation: The Catholic Question 1690–1830*, Dublin, 1992.
Baum, Gregory, *Theology and Society*, New York, 1987.
Beale, Jenny, *Women in Ireland: Voices of Change*, Dublin, 1986.
Bence-Jones, Mark, *Twilight of the Ascendancy*, London, 1998.
Berger, Peter L., *A Rumour of Angels: Modern Society and the Rediscovery of the Supernatural*, Harmondsworth, 1969.
Berger, Peter and Luckman, Thomas, *The Social Construction of Reality: A Treatise in the Sociology of Knowledge*, London, 1984.
Berlin, Isaiah, *The Age of Enlightenment*, Oxford, 1979.
Bestic, Alan, *The Importance of Being Irish*, London, 1969.
Biddis, Michael D., *The Age of the Masses: Ideas and Society in Europe since 1870*, London, 1977.
Billington, Rosamund and Strawbridge, Sheelagh, *Culture and Society*, London, 1991.
Birmingham, William, ed., *What Modern Catholics Think About Birth Control*, New York, 1964.
Blanchard, Jean, *The Church in Contemporary Ireland*, Dublin, 1963.
Blanshard, Paul, *The Irish and Catholic Power*, London, 1954.
Blazynski, George, *Pope John Paul II: A Man from Krakow*, London, 1979.
Bolster, Evelyn, *The Knights of St Columbanus*, Dublin, 1979.
Bowen, Desmond, *Paul Cardinal Cullen*, Dublin, 1983.
Brady, Raymond, ed., *Towards the Church of 2001: Proceeds of Mount Oliver International Summer School, Maynooth 1981*, Dublin, 1982.
Brassloff, Audrey, *Religion and Politics in Spain: The Spanish Church in Transition 1962–96*, Basingstoke, London, 1998.
Breen, Richard, Hannan, Damian F., Rottman, David B. and Whelan, Christopher T., *Understanding Contemporary Ireland: State, Class and Development in the Republic of Ireland*, London, 1990.

Brennan, Oliver V., *Cultures Apart? The Catholic Church and Contemporary Irish Youth*, Dublin, 2001.

Briggs, Asa, *Victorian People*, Harmondsworth, 1967.

Brinton, Crane, *Ideas and Men: The Story of Western Thought*, London, 1951.

Broderick, Joe, *Fall from Grace*, Dingle, 1992.

Brody, Hugh, *Inishkillane: Change and Decline in the West of Ireland*, Harmondsworth, 1973.

Brooke, John Hedley, *Science and Religion: Some Historical Perspectives*, Cambridge, 1991.

Brown, Stewart J. and Miller, David W., *Piety and Power in Ireland 1760–1960: Essays in Honour of Emmet Larkin*, Indiana, 2000.

Buckley, Fr Pat, *A Thorn in the Side*, Dublin, 1994.

Butler, Dom Cuthbert, *The Vatican Council 1869–1870*, London, 1962.

Candy, Catherine, *Priestly Fictions: Popular Irish Novelists of the Early 20th Century*, Dublin, 1995.

Carlson, Julia, ed., *Banned in Ireland: Censorship and the Irish Writer*, London, 1990.

Carrier, Hervé SJ, *Evangelizing the Culture of Modernity*, Maryknoll, New York, 1993.

Carroll, Denis, ed., *Religion in Ireland: Past, Present and Future*, Dublin, 1999.

Carty, Francis Xavier, *Why I Said No to God*, Dublin, 1986.

Cassidy, Eoin G., ed., *Faith and Culture in the Irish Context*, Dublin, 1996.

Chadwick, Owen, *The Secularization of the European Mind in the Nineteenth Century*, Cambridge, 1975.

Chubb, Basil, *The Government and Politics of Ireland*, London, New York, 1982, 1997.

Clancy, Patrick, Drudy, Sheelagh, Lynch, Kathleen and O'Dowd, Liam, *Ireland: A Sociological Profile*, Dublin, 1986.

Clancy, Patrick, Drudy, Sheelagh, Lynch, Kathleen and O'Dowd, Liam, *Irish Society: Sociological Perspectives*, Dublin, 1995.

Clark, Burton, *Educating the Expert Society*, San Francisco, 1962.

Clarke, Desmond M., *Morality and the Law*, Dublin, Cork, 1982.

Clarke, Desmond M., *Church and State: Essays in Political Philosophy*, Cork, 1985.

Clear, Caitriona, *Nuns in Nineteenth-Century Ireland*, Dublin, Washington, 1987.

Coleman, John A., *The Evolution of Dutch Catholicism 1958–1974*, London, 1978.

Collins, Stephen, *The Power Game: Fianna Fáil since Lemass*, Dublin, 2000.

Comerford, R.V., *The Fenians in Context: Irish Politics and Society 1848–82*, Dublin, 1985, 1998.

Comerford, R.V., *The British State and the Education of Irish Catholics, 1850–1921*, Dartmouth, n.d.

Comerford, R.V., Cullen, M., Hill, J.R. and Lennon, C., eds., *Religion, Conflict and Co-existence in Ireland*, Dublin, 1990.

Comiskey, Bishop Brendan, *It Could Happen to a Bishop*, Galway, 1991.

Condron, Patricia, Ní Bhrolcháin, Muireann, Nyland, Dominic, eds., *Cannonballs and Croziers: A History of Maynooth*, Maynooth, 1994.

Connell, K.H., *Irish Peasant Society: Four Historical Essays*, Oxford, 1968.

Connery, Donald S., *The Irish*, New York, 1968.

Connolly, Peter, *Literature and the Changing Ireland*, Gerrards Cross, 1982.

Connolly, Seán, *Priests and People in pre-Famine Ireland 1780–1845*, Dublin, 1982.

Connolly, Seán, *Religion and Society in Nineteenth-Century Ireland*, Dundalk, 1985.

Convey, Martin A., *Keeping the Faith in a Changing Society: Religious Practice and Belief in Ireland in the light of Vatican II*, Dublin, 1994.

Conway, Eamonn and Kilcoyne, Colm, eds., *Twin Pulpits: Church and Media in Modern Ireland*, Dublin, 1997.

Conway, Eamonn, Duffy, Eugene and Shields, Attracta, *The Church and Child Sexual Abuse: Towards a Pastoral Response*, Dublin, 1999.

Coogan, Timothy Patrick, *Ireland since the Rising*, London, 1966.

Coolahan, John, *Irish Education: History and Structure*, Dublin, 1981.

Cooney, John, *No News is Bad News: Communications policy in the Catholic Church*, Dublin, 1974.

Cooney, John, *The Crozier and the Dáil: Church and State in Ireland 1922–1986*, Dublin, Cork, 1986.

Cooney, John, *John Charles McQuaid: Ruler of Catholic Ireland*, Dublin, 1999.

Corish, Patrick J., ed., *A History of Irish Catholicism, vols. 1-6*, Dublin, 1967–1971.

Corish, Patrick J., *The Catholic Community in the Seventeenth and Eighteenth Centuries*, Dublin, 1981.

Corish, Patrick J., *The Irish Catholic Experience*, Dublin, 1985.

Corish, Patrick J., *Maynooth College, 1795–1995*, Dublin, 1995.

Corkery, Daniel, *The Hidden Ireland: A Study of Gaelic Munster in the Eighteenth Century*, Dublin, 1989 (first ed., 1924).

Corkery, Pádraig and Long, Fiachra, eds., *Theology in the University: The Irish Context*, Dublin, 1997.

Cornwell, John, *Breaking Faith: The Pope, the People and the Fate of Catholicism*, London, 2001.

Cosgrove, Art, ed., *Marriage in Ireland*, Dublin, 1985.

Cox, Harvey, *The Secular City: Secularization and Urbanization in Theological Perspective*, Harmondsworth, 1968.

Craig, Mary, *Man from a Far Country: A Portrait of Pope John Paul II*, London, 1979.

Craig, Patricia, ed., *The Oxford Book of Ireland*, Oxford, New York, 1998.

Dale, Roger, Esland, Geoff and MacDonald, Madeleine, eds., *Schooling and Capitalism*, London, Henley, 1976.

Danaher, Kevin, *The Year in Ireland: Irish Calendar Custom*, Cork, Dublin, 1972.

Davis, Charles, *The Study of Theology*, London, 1962.

Deedy, John, ed., *The Catholic Church in the Twentieth Century*, Minnesota, 2000.

De la Bedoyere, Michael, ed., *Objections to Roman Catholicism*, London, 1964.

De la Bedoyere, Michael, ed., *The Future of Catholic Christianity*, Harmondsworth, 1968.

De Breffny, Brian and Mott, George, *The Churches and Abbeys of Ireland*, London, 1976.

De Buitléir, Chris, *Message and Messenger: History of Devotion to the Sacred Heart in Ireland*, Dublin, 1987.

De Rosa, Peter, *Vicars of Christ: The Dark Side of the Papacy*, London, 1989.

Devitt, Patrick M., *Willingly to School: Religious Education as an Examination Subject*, Dublin, 2000.

Dolan, Jay P., *The American Catholic Experience: A History from Colonial Times to the Present*, New York, 1987.

Donoghue, Denis, *We Irish: Essays on Irish Literature and Society*, London, 1986.

Donoghue, Quentin and Shapiro, Linda, *Bless Me, Father, For I Have Sinned: Catholics Speak Out about Confession*, Toronto, 1985.

Dorr, Donal, *Option for the Poor*, New York, 1983, 1992.

Dorr, Donal, *The Social Justice Agenda: Justice, Ecology, Power and the Church*, Dublin, 1991.

Duff, Frank, *The Spirit of the Legion of Mary*, Glasgow, n.d.

Duggan, G.H. SM, *Hans Kung and Re-union*, Cork, 1964.
Dunn, Joseph, *No Tigers in Africa, Recollections and Reflections on 25 years of Radharc*, Dublin, 1986.
Dunn, Joseph, *No Lions in the Hierarchy, An Anthology of Sorts*, Dublin, 1994.
Dunn, Joseph, *No Vipers in the Vatican: A Second Anthology of Sorts*, Dublin, 1996.
Dunne, Seán, *The Road to Silence: An Irish Spiritual Odyssey*, Dublin, 1994.
Elliott, Marianne, *The Catholics of Ulster: A History*, London, 2000.
Evans, E. Estyn, *Irish Folk Ways*, London, 1976.
Fagan, Seán SM, *Has Sin Changed?*, Dublin, 1978.
Falconer, Alan, McDonagh, Enda and Mac Réamoinn, Seán, eds., *Freedom to Hope?*, Dublin, 1985.
Fallon, Brian, *An Age of Innocence: Irish Culture 1930–1960*, Dublin, 1998.
Fanning, Ronan, *The Irish Department of Finance 1922–1958*, Dublin, 1978.
Farmar, Tony, *Ordinary Lives: Three Generations of Irish Middle Class Experience, 1907, 1932, 1963*, Dublin, 1995.
Farrell, Brian, ed., *Communications and Community in Ireland (The Thomas Davis Lecture Series)*, Dublin, Cork, 1984.
Farren, Sean, *The Politics of Irish Education 1920–65*, Belfast, 1995.
Feeney, John, *John Charles McQuaid: The Man and the Mask*, Dublin, 1974.
Fennell, Desmond, ed., *The Changing Face of Catholic Ireland*, London, 1968.
Fennell, Desmond, *The State of the Nation: Ireland since the Sixties*, Dublin, 1983.
Finnegan, Frances, *Do Penance or Perish: A Study of Magdalen Asylums in Ireland*, Piltown, 2001.
Fisher, Desmond, *The Church in Transition*, London, 1967.
Fisher, James Terence, *The Catholic Counterculture in America, 1932–1962*, North Carolina, 1989.
FitzGerald, Garret, *Planning in Ireland*, Dublin, 1968.
FitzGerald, Garret, *Towards a New Ireland*, Dublin, 1972.
FitzGerald, Garret, *All in a Life: An Autobiography*, Dublin, 1992.
Flanagan, Donal, McDonagh, Enda, McNamara, Kevin and O'Callaghan, Denis, *Truth and Life: An Outline of Modern Theology*, Dublin, 1968.
Flannery, Tony, *From the Inside: A Priest's View of the Catholic Church*, Cork, 1999.
Fleetwood, John F., *The History of Medicine in Ireland*, Dublin, 1951, 1983.
Flynn, Thomas, *The Charismatic Renewal and the Irish Experience*, London, 1974.
Foley, J. Anthony and Lalor, Stephen, eds., *Gill & Macmillan Annotated Constitution of Ireland 1937–1994 with Commentary*, Dublin 1995.
Fremantle, Anne, *The Age of Belief*, New York, 1957.
Gallagher, Eric and Worrall, Stanley, eds., *Christians in Ulster*, Oxford, 1982.
Gallagher, Michael Paul SJ, *Clashing Symbols: An Introduction to Faith and Culture*, London, 1997.
Giansanti, Gianni, *John Paul II: Portrait of a Pontiff*, Shrewsbury, 1996.
Giddens, Anthony, *Capitalism and Modern Social Theory: An Analysis of the Writings of Marx, Durkheim and Max Weber*, Cambridge, 1971.
Glendenning, Dympna, *Education and the Law*, Dublin, 1999.
Goldthorpe, J.H. and Whelan, C.T., eds., *The Development of Industrial Society in Ireland*, Oxford, 1992.
Gorham, Maurice, *Forty Years of Irish Broadcasting*, Dublin, 1967.
Goudsblom, Johan, *Dutch Society*, New York, 1968.

Gough, H., *Europe 1763–1970*, Dublin, 1974.

Gray, Tony, *The Irish Answer: An Anatomy of Modern Ireland*, London, 1966.

Gray, Tony, *Ireland this Century*, London, 1996.

Gutierrez, Gustavo, *A Theology of Liberation: History, Politics and Salvation* (originally published as *Teologia de la liberacion, Perspectivas*, Lima, 1971) trans. and ed. Sr Caridad Inda and John Eagleson, New York, 1973.

Hall, Mr and Mrs Samuel Carter, *Ireland: Its Scenery and Character*, first published in three vols. London, 1841; condensed edition published as *Hall's Ireland: Mr and Mrs Hall's Tour of Ireland*, Michael Scott, ed., London, 1984.

Hamilton, Phyllis with Paul Williams, *Secret Love: My Life with Father Michael Cleary*, Dublin, 1995.

Hampshire, Stuart, *The Age of Reason*, New York, 1956.

Hannon, Patrick, *Church, State, Morality and Law*, Dublin, 1992.

Hanratty, Gerald, ed., *Light from Paris: Cardinal Lustiger on Faith and Contemporary Culture*, Dublin, 1995.

Häring, Bernard, *The Johannine Council: Witness to Unity*, Dublin, 1963.

Häring, Bernard CSsR, *Christian Renewal in a Changing World*, New York, 1964.

Häring, Bernard, *Sin in the Secular Age*, Slough, 1974.

Harmon, Maurice, *Austin Clarke: A Critical Introduction*, Dublin, 1989.

Harris, Peter, Hastings, Adrian, Horgan, John, Keane, Lionel and Nowell, Robert, *On Human Life: An Examination of 'Humanae Vitae'*, London, 1968.

Hastings, Adrian, ed., *Modern Catholicism: Vatican II and After*, London, 1991.

Healy, John, *Nineteen Acres*, Galway, 1978.

Healy, John, *Maynooth College: Its Centenary History*, Dublin, 1985.

Healy, John, *No One Shouted Stop: Death of an Irish Town*, Achill, 1988.

Healy, Seán J. SMA and Reynolds, Brigid SM, *Ireland Today: Reflecting in the Light of the Gospel*, Dublin, 1985.

Hebblethwaite, Peter, *Understanding the Synod*, Dublin, 1968.

Hebblethwaite, Peter, *The Runaway Church*, London, 1975, 1978.

Hebblethwaite, Peter, *Introducing John Paul II*, London, 1982.

Hebblethwaite, Peter, *In the Vatican*, London, 1986.

Hederman, Miriam, *The Road to Europe: Irish Attitudes 1948–61*, Dublin, 1983.

Hellwig, Monika, *What are the Theologians Saying?*, Dayton, 1970.

Hennessy, James SJ, *American Catholics: A History of the Roman Catholic Community in the United States*, New York, Oxford, 1981.

Heron, Alisdair, *Two Churches — One Love*, Dublin, 1977.

Hesketh, Tom, *The Second Partitioning of Ireland: The Abortion Referendum of 1983*, Dublin, 1990.

Hitchcock, James, *The Decline and Fall of Radical Catholicism*, New York, 1972.

Hogan, Edmund M., *The Irish Missionary Movement: A Historical Survey 1830–1980*, Dublin, 1990.

Holland, C.H., ed., *Trinity College Dublin and the Idea of a University*, Dublin, 1991.

Hoppen, K. Theodore, *Elections, Politics and Society in Ireland 1832–1885*, Oxford, 1984.

Horgan, John, *Mary Robinson: An Independent Voice*, Dublin, 1997.

Horgan, John, *Noël Browne: Passionate Outsider*, Dublin, 2000.

Horgan, John, *Irish Media: A Critical History since 1922*, London, 2001.

Hornsby-Smith, Michael P., *Roman Catholics in England: Studies in Social Structure since the Second World War*, Cambridge, 1987.

Hornsby-Smith, Michael P. and Whelan, Christopher T., eds., *Values and Social Change in Ireland*, Dublin, 1994.
Hulme, Kathryn, *The Nun's Story*, London, 1962.
Hunt, Lynn, ed., *The New Cultural History*, California, 1989.
Hurley, Michael, ed., *Beyond Tolerance: The Challenge of Mixed Marriage, A Record of the International Consultation held in Dublin, 1974*, London, 1975.
Hurley, Michael SJ, *Towards Christian Unity: An Introduction to the Ecumenical Movement*, Dublin, 1960.
Hurley, Michael SJ, *Irish Anglicanism 1869–1969*, Dublin, 1970.
Hurley, Richard, and Cantwell, Wilfrid, eds., *Contemporary Irish Church Architecture*, Dublin, 1985.
Inglis, Brian, *West Briton*, London, 1962.
Inglis, Tom, *Moral Monopoly: The Catholic Church in Modern Irish Society*, Dublin, 1987, 1998.
Inglis, Tom, Mach, Zdzislaw and Mazanek, Rafal, eds., *Religion and Politics: East–West Contrasts from Contemporary Europe*, Dublin, 2000.
Jodock, Darrell H., ed., *Catholicism Contending with Modernity: Roman Catholic Modernism and Anti-Modernism in Historical Context*, Cambridge, 2000.
Johnson, James, *A Tour in Ireland, with Meditations and Reflections*, London, 1844.
Johnson, Paul, *Pope John XXIII*, London, 1975.
Johnston, Joseph, *Irish Agriculture in Transition*, Dublin, 1951.
Jones, Jack, *In Your Opinion: Political and Social Trends in Ireland through the Eyes of the Electorate*, Dublin, 2001.
Joyce, Jerry, PP, *The Laity, Help or Hindrance?*, Cork, Dublin, 1994.
Kaiser, Robert, *Inside the Council: The Story of Vatican II*, New York, London, 1963.
Kavanagh, Patrick, *Collected Poems*, London, 1968.
Kavanagh, Patrick, *Selected Poems*, London, 1996.
Keane, Molly and Phipps, Sally, eds., *Molly Keane's Ireland: An Anthology*, London, 1994.
Kearney, Richard, ed., *Across the Frontiers: Ireland in the 1990s*, Dublin, 1998.
Kecskemeti, Paul, ed., *Karl Mannheim: Essays on the Sociology of Knowledge*, London, 1952.
Keenan, Desmond, *The Catholic Church in Nineteenth Century Ireland*, Dublin, 1983.
Kelly, M.J. and O'Connor, B., eds., *Media Audiences in Ireland*, Dublin, 1997.
Kennedy, Brian P., *Dreams and Responsibilities: The State and the Arts in Independent Ireland*, Arts Council, n.d.
Kennedy, Eugene C. MM, *The People are the Church*, New York, 1969.
Kennedy, Kieran A., ed., *Ireland in Transition: Economic and Social Change since 1960*, Cork, Dublin, 1986.
Kennedy, Robert E., *The Irish: Emigration, Marriage and Fertility*, Berkeley, 1973.
Kennedy, Sr Stanislaus RSC, ed., *One Million Poor: The Challenge of Irish Inequality*, Dublin, 1981.
Kenny, Mary, *Goodbye to Catholic Ireland*, London, 1997, 2000.
Kenny, Patrick D., *The Sorrows of Ireland*, London, 1907.
Kenny, Patrick D. (Pat), *Economics for Irishmen*, Dublin, 1907.
Keogh, Dermot, *The Vatican, the Bishops and Irish Politics 1919–1939*, Cambridge, 1986.
Keogh, Dermot, *Ireland and the Vatican: The Politics and Diplomacy of Church–State Relations 1922–1960*, Cork, 1995.
Kerr, Donal, *Peel, Priests and Politics: Sir Robert Peel's Administration and the Roman Catholic Church in Ireland 1841–46*, Oxford, 1982.

Kiely, Benedict, *Modern Irish Fiction: A Critique*, Dublin, 1950.
Kirby, Peadar, *Is Irish Catholicism Dying?*, Dublin, 1984.
Kohl, J.G., *Travels in Ireland*, translated from the German, London, 1844.
Kosnik, Anthony, Carroll, William, Cunningham, Agnes, Modras, Ronald and Shulte, James, *Human Sexuality: New Directions in Catholic Thought*, a study commissioned by the Catholic Theological Society of America, London, 1977.
Küng, Hans, *That the World May Believe*, trans. Cecily Hastings, London, 1963.
Küng, Hans, *The Council and Reunion*, London, New York, 1964.
Küng, Hans, Congar, Yves and O'Hanlon, Daniel, eds., *Council Speeches of Vatican II*, London, 1964.
Küng, Hans, *The Changing Church: Reflections on the Progress of the Second Vatican Council*, trans. Cecily Hastings, William Glen-Doepel and H.R. Bronk, New York, 1965.
Küng, Hans, *The Church and Freedom*, trans. Cecily Hastings, London, 1965.
Küng, Hans, *The Church*, trans. Ray and Rosaleen Ockenden, London, 1971.
Küng, Hans, *Why Priests?* trans. John Gumming, London, 1972.
Küng, Hans, *Infallible? An Enquiry*, trans. Eric Mosbacher, London, 1977.
Küng, Hans, *Church and Change: The Irish Experience*, Dublin, 1986.
Küng, Hans, *The Catholic Church: A Short History*, trans. John Bowden, London, 2001.
Kwitny, Jonathan, *Man of the Century: The Life and Times of Pope John Paul II*, New York, 1997.
Lane, Dermot A., ed., *Liberation Theology: An Irish Dialogue*, Dublin, 1977.
Lane, Dermot, *Foundations for a Social Theology*, New York, 1984.
Lane, Dermot A., ed., *Religious Education and the Future*, Dublin, 1986.
Lane, Dermot A., ed., *Religion, Education and the Constitution*, Dublin, 1992.
Lane, Dermot A., ed., *Religion and Culture in Dialogue: A Challenge for the Next Millennium*, Dublin, 1993.
Lane, Dermot A., ed., *New Century, New Society: Christian Perspectives*, Dublin, 1999.
Lannon, Frances, *Privilege, Persecution and Prophecy: The Catholic Church in Spain 1875–1975*, Oxford, 1987.
Larkin, Emmet, *The Roman Catholic Church and the Creation of the Modern Irish State 1878–1886*, Dublin, 1975.
Larkin, Emmet, *The Historical Dimensions of Irish Catholicism*, New York, 1976.
Larkin, Emmet, *The Roman Catholic Church and the Plan of Campaign, 1886–1888*, Cork, 1978.
Larkin, Emmet, *The Roman Catholic Church and the Fall of Parnell, 1888–1891*, Chapel Hill, North Carolina, 1979.
Larkin, Emmet, *The Making of the Roman Catholic Church in Ireland 1850–1860*, Chapel Hill, North Carolina, 1980.
Lazzarini, Andrea, *Pope John XXIII: A Life of the New Pope*, New York, Edinburgh, London, 1959.
Lee, Joseph, *The Modernisation of Irish Society 1848–1918*, Dublin, 1973.
Lee, J.J., ed., *Ireland 1945–1970, RTÉ Thomas Davis Lecture Series*, Dublin, 1979.
Lee, Joseph, ed., *Ireland: Towards a Sense of Place*, Cork, 1985.
Lee, Joseph and Ó Tuathaigh, Gearóid, *The Age of de Valera*, Dublin, 1982.
Lennon, Brian SJ, ed., *Towards a New Irish Identity, Studies the 300th Issue 1912–1986*, Dublin, 1986.
Litton, Frank, ed., *Unequal Achievement: The Irish Experience*, Dublin, 1982.
Logan, Patrick, *The Holy Wells of Ireland*, Gerrards Cross, 1980.

Longenecker, Dwight, *The Path to Rome: Modern Journeys to the Catholic Church,* Leominster, 1999.

Longford, Earl of, and O' Neill, Thomas, *Eamon de Valera,* London, 1970.

Luddy, Maria and Murphy, Cliona, *Women Surviving: Studies in Irish Women's History in the 19th and 20th Centuries,* Dublin, 1989.

Macardle, Dorothy, *The Irish Republic,* London, 1937.

McCaffrey, Laurence J., *The Irish Catholic Diaspora in America,* Washington, 1997.

McCarthy, Charles, *The Distasteful Challenge,* Dublin, 1968.

McCarthy, Conor, *Modernisation: Crisis and Culture in Ireland, 1969–1992,* Dublin, 2000.

McCarthy, Justine, *Mary McAleese: The Outsider,* Dublin, 1999.

McCartney, Donal, *The Dawning of Democracy: Ireland 1800–1870,* Dublin, 1987.

MacCurtain, Margaret and Ó Corráin, Donncha, eds., *Women in Irish Society: The Historical Dimension,* Dublin, 1978.

McDermott, Eithne, *Clann na Poblachta,* Cork, 1998.

McDonagh, Enda, ed., *Moral Theology Renewed, Papers of the Maynooth Union Summer School 1964,* Dublin, 1965.

McDonagh, Enda, *Doing the Truth: The Quest for Moral Theology,* Dublin, 1979.

McDonagh, Enda, ed., *Irish Challenges to Theology, Papers of the Irish Theological Association Conference, 1984,* Dublin, 1986.

McDonagh, Enda, ed., *Faith and the Hungry Grass: A Mayo Book of Theology,* Dublin, 1990.

McDonagh, Enda, *Faith in Fragments,* Dublin, 1997.

MacDonagh, Oliver, *Ireland,* New Jersey, 1968.

McDonnell, John J. CM, *The World Council of Churches and the Catholic Church,* Toronto, 1985.

McGarry, Rev. J.G., *Sermon Notes on the Sunday Gospels,* Dublin, 1960.

McGarry, Patsy, ed., *Christianity,* Dublin, 2001.

MacGregor-Hastie, Roy, *Pope Paul VI,* London, 1966.

Machin, G.I.T., *Churches and Social Issues in Twentieth-Century Britain,* Oxford, 1998.

McLaughlin, P.J., *The Church and Modern Science,* Dublin, 1957.

McLeod, Hugh, *Religion and the People of Western Europe 1789–1970,* Oxford, 1981.

McLoone, Martin and MacMahon, John, eds., *Television and Irish Society: 21 Years of Irish Television,* Dublin, 1984.

McQuaid, His Grace the Most Rev. John Charles DD, *The Gift of Faith* (Irish Messenger Publications), Dublin, n.d.

Mac Réamoinn, Seán, ed., *Pobal: The Laity in Ireland,* Dublin, 1986.

Mac Réamoinn, Seán, *Vatacáin II agus an Réabhlóid Chultúrtha,* Baile Átha Cliath, 1987.

Mac Réamoinn, Seán, ed., *Authority in the Church,* Dublin, 1995.

Mac Réamoinn, Seán, ed., *The Church in a New Ireland,* Dublin, 1996.

Mac Réamoinn, Seán, ed., *Crime, Society and Conscience,* Dublin, 1997.

McRedmond, Louis, *The Council Reconsidered,* Dublin, 1966.

McRedmond, Louis, *Thrown Among Strangers: John Henry Newman in Ireland,* Dublin, 1990.

McSweeney, Bill, *Roman Catholicism: The Search for Relevance,* Oxford, 1980.

McVeigh, Joseph, *A Wounded Church: Religion, Politics and Justice in Ireland,* Cork, Dublin, 1989.

McVeigh, Joseph, *Renewing the Irish Church: Towards an Irish Liberation Theology,* Cork, Dublin, 1993.

Mansergh, Martin, ed., *The Spirit of the Nation: The Speeches of Charles J. Haughey (1957–1986),* Cork, Dublin, 1986.

Marx, Karl and Engels, Friedrich, *The Communist Manifesto*, Harmondsworth, 1967.
Marx, Karl and Engels, Friedrich, *Ireland and the Irish Question*, New York, 1972.
Mescal, John, *Religion in the Irish System of Education*, Dublin, 1957.
Miller, David, *Church, State and Nation in Ireland 1898–1921*, Dublin, 1973.
Milotte, Mike, *Banished Babies: The Secret History of Ireland's Baby Export Business*, Dublin, 1997.
Moore, Chris, *Betrayal of Trust: The Father Brendan Smyth Affair and the Catholic Church*, Dublin, 1995.
Mosse, George L., *The Culture of Western Europe: The Nineteenth and Twentieth Centuries*, London, 1963.
Moynihan, Maurice, *Speeches and Statements by Eamon de Valera 1917–1973*, Dublin, 1980.
Mulcahy, D.G., *Curriculum and Policy in Irish Post-Primary Education*, Dublin, 1981.
Murphy, James H., ed., *No Bland Facility: Selected Writings on Literature, Religion and Censorship, Peter Connolly*, Gerrards Cross, 1991.
Murphy O'Connor, Jerome OP, *What is Religious Life: A Critical Reappraisal*, Dublin, n.d.
Murray, Patrick, *Oracles of God: The Roman Catholic Church and Irish Politics 1922–37*, Dublin, 2000.
Newman, Jeremiah, Bishop of Limerick, *The State of Ireland*, Dublin, 1977.
Newman, Jeremiah, Bishop of Limerick, *The Postmodern Church*, Dublin, 1990.
Nichols, Peter, *The Pope's Divisions: The Roman Catholic Church Today*, London, Boston, 1981.
Norman, E.R., *The Catholic Church and Ireland in the Age of Rebellion 1859–1873*, London, 1965.
Norman, E.R., *The Catholic Church and Irish Politics in the Eighteen Sixties 1859–1873*, Irish History series, no. 5, Dundalk, 1969.
Novak, Michael, *The Experience of Marriage: The Testimony of Laymen*, London, 1964.
Novak, Michael, *The Open Church: Vatican II, Act II*, London, 1964.
Nowlan, Kevin B. and Williams, T. Desmond, eds., *Ireland in the War Years and After*, Dublin, 1969.
O'Brien, Conor Cruise, *States of Ireland*, St Albans, 1974.
O'Brien, John A., ed., *The Vanishing Irish*, London, 1954.
O'Brien, John B., *The Catholic Middle Classes in Pre-Famine Cork*, O'Donnell lecture delivered in UCC, 29 March 1979.
Ó Buachalla, Séamas, *Education Policy in Twentieth Century Ireland*, Dublin, 1988.
O'Callaghan, Denis, ed., *Sacraments: Papers of the Maynooth Union Summer School, 1963*, Dublin, 1964.
O'Connell, Michael, *Changed Utterly: Ireland and the New Irish Psyche*, Dublin, 2001.
O'Connor, Edward D. CSC, *The Pentecostal Movement in the Catholic Church*, Indiana, 1971.
O'Connor, Fionnuala, *In Search of a State: Catholics in Northern Ireland*, Belfast, 1993.
O'Connor, Sean, *A Troubled Sky: Reflections on the Irish Educational Scene 1957–1968*, Dublin, 1986.
O'Connor, Ulick, *Celtic Dawn: A Portrait of the Irish Literary Renaissance*, Dublin, 1999.
O'Dwyer, Peter, O.Carm, *Mary: A History of Devotion in Ireland*, Dublin, 1988.
O'Faolain, Sean, *The Irish*, Harmondsworth, 1947.
O'Farrell, Padraic, *The Burning of Brinsley MacNamara*, Dublin, 1990.
O'Ferrall, Fergus, *Catholic Emancipation: Daniel O'Connell and the Birth of Irish Democracy, 1820–30*, Dublin, 1985.

O'Flaherty, Louis, *Management and Control in Irish Education: The Post-Primary Experience*, Dublin, 1992.
Ó Gráda, Cormac, *The Great Irish Famine*, Dublin, 1989.
O'Hanlon, Gerry, *A Renewed Devotion to the Sacred Heart*, Dublin, 1992.
O'Leary, Daniel J., *Lost Soul? The Catholic Church Today*, Dublin, 1999.
O'Leary, Don, *Vocationalism and Social Catholicism in Twentieth-Century Ireland*, Dublin, 2000.
O'Mahony, T.P., *The Politics of Dishonour: Ireland 1916–1977*, Dublin, 1977.
O'Meara, John J., *Reform in Education*, Dublin, 1958.
Ó Muirí, Réamonn, ed., *Irish Church History Today: Cumann Seanchais Árd Mhacha seminar 10 March 1990*, Armagh, n.d.
ó Ríordáin, John J., CSsR, *Irish Catholics: Tradition and Transition*, Dublin, 1980.
O'Riordan, Michael, *Catholicity and Progress in Ireland*, London, 1906.
Orlandis, Jose, *A Short History of the Catholic Church*, trans. Michael Adams, Dublin, 1985.
O'Shea, James, *Priests, Politics and Society in Post-Famine Ireland: A Study of County Tipperary, 1850–1891*, Dublin, 1983.
O'Shea, Kieran, *The Irish Emigrant Chaplaincy Scheme in Britain 1957–1982*, Naas, 1985.
O'Toole, Fintan, *A Mass for Jesse James: A Journey through 1980's Ireland*, Dublin, 1990.
O'Toole, Fintan, *The Ex-Isle of Erin: Images of a Global Ireland*, Dublin, 1998.
Paul-Dubois, Louis, *Contemporary Ireland*, Dublin, 1908.
Perman, David, *Change and the Churches: An Anatomy of Religion in Britain*, London, 1977.
Pettitt, Lance, *Screening Ireland: Film and Television Representation*, Manchester, New York, 2000.
Plunkett, Horace, *Ireland in the New Century*, London, 1904.
Power, John SMA, *Mission Theology Today*, Dublin, 1970.
Princess Grace Irish Library, ed., *Irishness in a Changing Society*, Gerrards Cross, 1988.
Puirséal, Pádraig, *The G.A.A. in its Time*, Dublin, 1984.
Quigley, Carol IHM, ed., *Turning Points in Religious Life*, Wilmington, 1987.
Quinn, Richard, *The Missionary Factor in Irish Aid Overseas*, Dublin, 1980.
Rafferty, Oliver P., *Catholicism in Ulster 1603–1983: An Interpretative History*, Dublin, 1994.
Rafroidi, Patrick and Joannon, Pierre, eds., *Ireland at the Crossroads: The Acts of the Lille Symposium, June–July, 1978*, Lille, 1978, 1979.
Raftery, Mary and O'Sullivan, Eoin, *Suffer the Little Children: The Inside Story of Ireland's Industrial Schools*, Dublin, 1999.
Randles, Sr Eileen, IBVM, *Post-Primary Education in Ireland 1957–1970*, Dublin, 1975.
Ravitch, Norman, *The Catholic Church and the French Nation 1589–1989*, London, 1990.
Reese, Thomas J., *Inside the Vatican: The Politics and Organization of the Catholic Church*, Cambridge, London, 1996.
Rice, David, *Shattered Vows: Priests who Leave*, New York, 1990.
Riordan, Patrick SJ, *A Politics of the Common Good*, Dublin, 1996.
Robertson, Roland, ed., *Sociology of Religion: Selected Readings*, Harmondsworth, 1969.
Ryan, Michael, ed., *The Church and the Nation: The Vision of Peter Birch, Bishop of Ossory 1964–1981*, Dublin,1993.
Ryan, Tim and Kirakowski Jurek, *Ballinspittle: Moving Statues and Faith*, Cork, Dublin, 1985.

Ryan, W.P., *The Pope's Green Island*, London, 1912.
Savage, Robert J. Jr., *Irish Television: The Political and Social Origins*, Cork, 1996.
Schillebeeckx, E.H. OP, *Vatican II — A Struggle of Minds and Other Essays*, Dublin, 1963.
Schillebeeckx, E.H., *Church: The Human Story of God*, trans. John Bowden, London, 1990.
Schneiders, Sandra M. IHM, *New Wineskins: Re-imagining Religious Life Today*, New York, 1986.
Sheehy, Michael, *Is Ireland Dying? Culture and the Church in Modern Ireland*, London, 1968.
Sinnott, Richard, *Irish Voters Decide: Voting Behaviour in Elections and Referendums since 1918*, Manchester, New York, 1995.
Skorupski, John, *Symbol and Theory: A Philosophical Study of Theories of Religion in Social Anthropology*, Cambridge, 1976.
Smit, Most Rev. Jan Olaf, *Pope Pius XII*, adapted and trans. James H. Vanderveldt, London, 1950.
Smith, Raymond, *Father O'Flynn — The Well of Love*, Dublin, 1964.
Smyth, Ailbhe, ed., *The Abortion Papers Ireland*, Dublin, 1992.
Smyth, Ailbhe, ed., *Irish Women's Studies Reader*, Dublin, 1993.
Solomons, Michael, *Pro Life? The Irish Question*, Dublin, 1992.
Somerville-Large, Peter, *Irish Voices: An Informal History 1916–1966*, London, 2000.
Strange, Roderick, *The Catholic Faith*, Oxford, 1989.
Suenens, Mgr Leon-Joseph, *Edel Quinn*, Dublin, 1954.
Sullivan, William, *Mixed Marriages: An Honest Appraisal*, Indiana, 1965.
Tanner, Marcus, *Ireland's Holy Wars: The Struggle for a Nation's Soul, 1500–2000*, New Haven, London, 2001.
Taylor, Lawrence J., *Occasions of Faith: An Anthropology of Irish Catholics*, Dublin, 1997.
Thackeray, W.M., *The Irish Sketch Book 1842*, Belfast, 1985 (first ed. 1843).
Thompson, Ian, *Religion*, London, New York, 1991.
Tierney, Mark OSB, *Modern Ireland 1850–1950*, Dublin, London, 1972.
Tillard, J.M.R. OP, *Dilemmas of Modern Religious Life: Work for Justice an Integral part of the Apostolate*, Dublin, 1986.
Tobin, Fergal, *The Best of Decades: Ireland in the Nineteen Sixties*, Dublin, 1984.
Toffler, Alvin, *Future Shock*, London, Sydney, 1971.
Tóibín, Colm, *The Sign of the Cross: Travels in Catholic Europe*, London, 1994.
Treacy, Bernard, OP and Whyte, Gerry, *Religion, Morality and Public Policy*, a *Doctrine and Life* special, Dublin, 1995.
Van Der Plas, Michel and Suèr, Henk, eds., *Those Dutch Catholics*, London, Dublin, Melbourne, 1967.
Vitz, Paul C., *Psychology as Religion: The Cult of Self-Worship*, Tring, Herts, 1979.
Wall, Maureen, *The Penal Laws, 1691–1760*, Irish History series, no. 1, Dundalk, 1967.
Walshe, John, *A New Partnership in Education: From Consultation to Legislation in the Nineties*, Dublin, 1999.
Ward, Maisie, *France pagan? The Mission of Abbé Godin*, London, 1949.
Waters, John, *Jiving at the Crossroads*, Belfast, 1991.
Weber, Max, *The Protestant Ethic and the Spirit of Capitalism*, first published as a two-part article in 1904-5, this edition, London, 1976.
Weigel, George, *Witness to Hope: The Biography of Pope John Paul II*, New York, 1999.
Welch, Robert, ed., *Irish Writers and Religion*, Savage, 1992.

Whiteside, Lesley, *George Otto Simms*, Buckinghamshire, 1990.
Whyte, J.H., *The Tenant League and Irish Politics in the Eighteen-Fifties*, Irish History series, no. 4, Dundalk, 1966.
Whyte, J.H., *Church and State in Modern Ireland 1923–1970*, Dublin, 1971.
Whyte, J.H., *Church and State in Modern Ireland 1923–1979*, Dublin, 1980.
Whyte, John H., *Catholics in Western Democracies*, Dublin, 1981.
Wicker, Brian, *Culture and Liturgy*, London, New York, 1963.
Willey, David, *God's Politician: John Paul at the Vatican*, London, 1992.
Williams, Desmond, ed., *The Irish Struggle 1916–1926*, London, 1968.
Williams, George Huntston, *The Mind of John Paul II: Origins of his Thought and Action*, New York, 1981.
Williams, Raymond, *Culture and Society 1780–1950*, Harmondsworth, 1963 (first ed., 1958).
Williams, Raymond, *The Long Revolution*, Harmondsworth, 1966.
Williams, Raymond, *Culture*, London, 1981.
Wilson, Brian, *Christianity*, London, 1999.
Wilson, Bryan R., *Religion in Secular Society*, Harmondsworth, 1969.
Wojtyla, Karol, Pope John Paul II, *Love and Responsibility*, trans. H.T. Willetts, London, 1982.
Wojtyla, Karol, Pope John Paul II, *Crossing the Threshold of Hope*, Vittorio Messori, ed., London, 1994.
Woodard, Rev. David, *Our Separated Brethren*, London, 1968.
Yallop, David, *In God's Name: An Investigation into the Murder of Pope John Paul I*, London, 1985.
Young, Filson, *Ireland at the Crossroads: An Essay in Explanation*, London, 1907.
Yuhaus, Cassian CP, ed., *The Catholic Church and American Culture: Reciprocity and Challenge*, New Jersey, 1990.

25. Works of Fiction

Boylan, Clare, *Holy Pictures*, Harmondsworth, 1984.
Broderick, John, *The Pilgrimage*, London, 1975 (first ed., 1961).
Cleeve, Brian, *Cry of Morning*, London, 1972.
Joyce, James, *A Portrait of the Artist as a Young Man*, Harmondsworth, 1960 (first ed., 1916).
Kavanagh, *The Green Fool*, Harmondworth, 1975 (first ed., 1938).
Kavanagh, Patrick, *Tarry Flynn*, Harmondsworth, 1978 (first ed., 1948).
Kilroy, Thomas, *The Big Chapel*, Dublin, 1987 (first ed., 1971).
McGahern, John, *The Barracks*, London, 1963.
McGahern, John, *The Dark*, London, 1965.
MacManus, Francis, *The Greatest of These*, Cork, 1975 (first ed., 1943).
MacNamara, Brinsley, *The Valley of the Squinting Windows*, Dublin, 1965 (first ed., 1918).
Moore, Brian, *Catholics*, Harmondsworth, 1977.
O'Brien, Edna, *The Country Girls*, Harmondsworth, 1966 (first ed., 1960).
O'Brien, Edna, *Girl with Green Eyes*, Harmondsworth, 1966 (first published as *The Lonely Girl*, 1962).
O'Brien, Edna, *Girls in their Married Bliss*, London, 1964.
O'Brien, Kate, *The Land of Spices*, London, 1941.
O'Connor, Frank, *My Oedipus Complex and Other Stories*, Harmondsworth, 1963.

O'Donovan, Gerald, *Father Ralph*, Dingle, 1993 (first ed., 1913).
Plunkett, James, *Strumpet City*, London, 1969.
Sheehan, Canon P.A., *My New Curate: A Story Gathered from the Stray Leaves of an Old Diary*, Dublin, 1958 (first American ed., 1899; first Irish ed., 1928).
Sheridan, John D., *God Made Little Apples*, London, 1963.
Trevor, William, ed., *The Oxford Book of Irish Short Stories*, Oxford, 1991.

26. Unpublished Theses

Cannon, Sean, CSsR, 'Irish Episcopal Meetings 1788–1882: A Juridico-Historical Study', D.C.L. thesis, Universitas S. Thomae de Urbe, Rome, 1979.
Delaney, Enda Gerard, 'Fr Denis Fahy CSSp and Maria Duce 1945–1954', M.A. thesis, St Patrick's College, Maynooth, 1993.
Fuller, Louise, 'An Ideological Critique of the Irish Post-Primary School Curriculum: The Economic, Socio-Cultural and Political factors influencing its Development', M.Ed. thesis, St Patrick's College, Maynooth, 1990.
Hartigan, Maurice, 'The Catholic Laity of Dublin 1920–1940', Ph.D. thesis, St Patrick's College, Maynooth, 1992.
Kelly, Adrian, 'Social Security in Independent Ireland, 1922–1952, Ph.D. thesis, St Patrick's College, Maynooth, 1995.
Lewis, Fachtna OFM, 'The Motives for Attending Holy Mass: A Case Study of a selected group of 293 Irish rural people', Ph.D. thesis, Universitas S. Thomae de Urbe, Rome, 1963.
Rogan, Edward, 'Irish Catechesis: A Juridico-Historical Study of the Five Plenary Synods, 1850–1956', Ph.D. thesis, Pontificae Universitatis Gregorianae, Rome, 1987.
Wallace, Patrick, 'Irish Catechesis — the Heritage from James Butler II, Archbishop of Cashel 1774-91', Ph.D. thesis, Catholic University of America, 1975.

Index